Nicolai Hartmann
Aesthetics

M000250959

Nicolai Hartmann
Aesthetics

Translated with an Introduction by Eugene Kelly

DE GRUYTER

ISBN 978-3-11-055443-4
e-ISBN (PDF) 978-3-11-027601-5
e-ISBN (EPUB) 978-3-11-038134-4

Library of Congress Cataloging-in-Publication Data
A CIP catalog record for this book has been applied for at the Library of Congress.

Bibliographic information published by the Deutsche Nationalbibliothek
The Deutsche Nationalbibliothek lists this publication in the Deutsche Nationalbibliografie;
detailed bibliographic data are available on the Internet at http://dnb.dnb.de.

© 2017 Walter de Gruyter GmbH, Berlin/Boston
This volume is text- and page-identical with the hardback published in 2014.
Typesetting: jürgen ullrich typosatz, Nördlingen
Printing: CPI books GmbH, Leck
♾ Printed on acid-free paper
Printed in Germany

www.degruyter.com

Table of Contents

Part Two: **The Bestowal of Form and Stratification**

Part Three: **Values and Genera of the Beautiful**

First Section: The Aesthetic Values

Second Section: The Sublime and the Charming

Translator's Introduction: Hartmann on the Mystery and Value of Art

Imagine a book taking on the question of what beauty is. Imagine further that the question is pursued in all its generality: beauty in nature, beauty in the human frame, and beauty in all the various human creations that we call art: painting (portrait, history, landscape, still life, abstraction), literature (drama, poetry, the novel and short story), music (pure and program), architecture (monuments, houses of worship, palaces and homes), and ornamentation. Imagine then raising the question of the structure of human receptivity to beauty and creativity in art and nature, specifically how the subjective act of aesthetic beholding "reveals" strata in the ontic entity said to be beautiful in a process of give-and-take between the structured object and its beholder. Imagine the book then turning to the analysis of key aesthetic values: sublimity, grace, and the comic, considering and emending earlier analyses of them and discovering new questions about their value that lie upon their periphery. And, finally, imagine a writer who brings to this tripartite phenomenological schema of act, object, and the transaction between them a lifetime of research heavily weighted with ontology and a willingness to take on questions of the metaphysical horizons of aesthetics, yet only up to the point that current research allows – and you would have the present work, *Aesthetics* (*Ästhetik*), by Nicolai Hartmann.

The work leaves many striking questions in aesthetics still unsettled – Hartmann uses the word "mystery" many times, identifying only a few mysteries as genuine aporia of aesthetical reason and thus at least apparently unresolvable given the current state of aesthetics. Indeed, the discoveries made by Hartmann's aesthetics enable the deconstruction and resolution of many aporia of aesthetics that past research had discovered and left intact. Only towards the end of the book and after palpable progress in aesthetical phenomenology and analysis, do new or formerly unclearly formulated mysteries and antinomies in aesthetics become clearer and more salient.

To be sure, *Aesthetics* was left unfinished at Hartmann's death in 1950 at age 68, not in the sense that he intended to add to it – it concludes with his own postscript – but that he did not live to complete its revisions, a process that he carried out for his other published works. The book is nonetheless highly organized, and, while it contains on every page remarkable insights into how specific cases of art and nature "work" by their physical and formal qualities to carry us to a supersensible world, an overview of its achievements is relatively easy to present.

1 Beauty and the Perception of Beauty

First, perception is the doorway to beauty: we see the sunset's colors and the spatial masses of its clouds and sky, and feel its sublimity, its worth. In all perception there is an element of sense, which gives us the physical appearance of a thing, and of feeling as a response to values carried by things or situations, whether those values are aesthetical, ethical, or non-moral. The only cognitive source we have for knowledge of value of any kind is our feeling; we know the color green by seeing it and we know the disvalue of cowardice by feeling it. The two perceptual forms are interlinked (Chap. 1a); for example, we perceive the grace of an animal in its leap.

This notion of a noetic or intentional feeling of values as a source of knowledge of their material content is prominent in phenomenology; it is present in Edmund Husserl,[1] and was raised to a principle of inquiry in ethics by Max Scheler.[2] Now a person who lacks feeling for aesthetic or moral values cannot be taught them any more than a person without sight can be taught the colors of the rainbow. Yet most of us do possess such a capacity for feeling, and that capacity can be developed. When phenomenologists turn to aesthetics, they bring with them a developed capacity for revealing, re-performing, and exhibiting the structural features of these feelings and the aesthetic response they make possible, and of their aesthetic objects, in which together the "miracle" of beauty appears.

The beholding of and responding to a value in a relation of appearance, where an object appears out of some formal structure of tones, sounds and words to a person taking an aesthetic attitude towards what appears, tracks in some measure the Husserlian concept of noematic objects and noetic acts that constitute all states of consciousness. The noematic and noetic phenomena accessible to philosophical aesthetics of beauty are, accordingly, (1) the *object,* or thing of beauty – the grace of an animal, the charm of a village landscape, the sweetness of a piece of simple music (oddly, Hartmann does not discuss here dance as an art), the tragedy of Oedipus' downfall – and (2) the *receptive act* of beholding in which such values are given, whose most general characteristic is the Kantian "disinterested enjoyment." These two can again be divided: on the side of the object, one may study either (a) the structure and the ontology of the aesthetic object, or (b) the values it bears. On the side of the reception of the object, one may study either (a) the structure of the receptive (or appreciative) act, or (b) the fashioning involved in its production, i.e.,

---

1 Cf. especially Husserl, Edmund, *Husserliana*, Vol. 28 and 37, The Hague: Kluwer 1950ff.

2 Cf. Scheler, Max, *Formalism in Ethics and Non-Formal Ethics of Values*, translated by M. Frings and R.L. Funk, Evanston: Northwestern University Press 1973 ("Der Formalismus in der Ethik und die materiale Wertethik," in: Scheler, Max, *Gesammelte Werke*, Vol. 2, ed. Maria Scheler and Manfred Frings, Bonn: Bouvier 2000).

the skill and genius of the artist (Intro., § 5). And, finally, (3) one may study the relationship between noema and noesis in aesthetic beholding.

Hartmann works with four concepts that he applies again and again to his task of pursuing these aims. They are (1) the beholding of an aesthetic value as a relationship between the act of beholding (noesis) and what appears (noema). The term *Erscheinungsverhältnis* is used to designate the relationship between the nature of an object thought to be beautiful and the appearing of the qualities carried by the object to a properly prepared mind; (2) the *stratification* (*Schichtung*) of the art work; (3) the *transparency* of a stratum such that one can see through it (*Durchschauen*) to the strata behind it; and (4) the *bestowal of form* (*Formung*) by an artist upon matter and his material (i.e., some physical substances and the themes or *sujet* of the work). These terms are utilized in the exhibition of the various genera and forms of the phenomenon of beauty, but they also (as with much phenomenology of value) have a practical side: they are intended to provide a stable platform for the evaluation of works of art, that is, the determination of the structural features that contribute to the making of some works of great art and of others less than great. It does not solve the problem of aesthetic value entirely, however, for although an artist creates his own "laws" under the constraint of these more general and abstract structures to which he is subject, the artwork he produces is a unique and individual value. In great works of art the mysterious genius of the artist creates, across the strata of his work, a synthesis of his material and the forms he chooses to express it. The beholder senses the lawful rightness of the work, even if he is unable to grasp its rightness fully.

The aesthetically prepared mind is not engaged in simple hearing or seeing and feeling, that is, in perception alone. Perception through the senses and through the visceral and mental centers of feeling (the "heart") are, no doubt, the material conditions of appearance, just as some material things – flecks of paint on a canvas, tones and words – make up the sensibly perceived objects. Aesthetic beholding sees or hears *through* the sensibly given real elements in the foreground of the artwork *to* the elements in the background – the figures on canvas, the play with color, the free play with form in music, the elements of a narrative that words reveal, and so on. The real foreground elements are the grounds of the possibility of the background becoming visible in an act of beholding them. The appearance of beauty in art is hence tied to an existing object: to the work of an artist in which he or she has "objectivated" some meanings and values, or to the work of nature.[3] Art has for Hartmann an ontological significance, for the being of

---

3 Hartmann does not mean by "objectivation" simply the making of a physical object. Rather the values beheld in the created thing are made objective and thereby become available to an

what appears is neither real nor ideal; it exists merely as a being-for-us. For the ontology of the art object lies not in its reality as a thing but in its appearance to someone as an aesthetic value. This is not to say that "beauty is in the eye of the beholder," for the beauty is in the object, not in a beholder who is thought to "project" it upon the object. Beauty is in the object, but *it exists only for the mind able to behold it*. Thus we have the peculiar ontological status of aesthetic values for Hartmann. Even the beauties in nature appear as beautiful only to a mind that is capable of penetrating the construction of their immediate physical foreground to the depth of values concealed in their background – not mysteriously concealed in them, but opening themselves easily to a mind that takes up an aesthetic standpoint upon them. Stars may be only points of light and be perceived as such, but to Kant's beholding eyes, they possessed or expressed a noumenal quality; to most humans they have a sublime beauty.[4]

2 The Stratification of Beholding and the Object Beheld as Beautiful

The achievement of this aesthetic "beholding" is what Hartmann calls *Durchschauen* – a seeing-through the real physical foreground given to the senses into an "unreal" background of objects and ideas that appear through and by means of the foreground. (393) A thing becomes beautiful when the real foreground becomes transparent. Both the perceptual seeing of a foreground and the aesthetic beholding of a background are *stratified*, a term that, for Hartmann, is essential in ontology, ethics, and aesthetics, though it functions differently in each. For aesthetics, Hartmann adopted three kinds of stratification. We first encountered this phenomenon in the act of beholding; sensible perception and feelings are two cognitions, the latter lying upon the former. In perception we grasp the matter of the artwork; in feeling we grasp cognitively the material content of the values carried "upon the back" of the colors, sounds, and tones we perceive. Second, intentional acts of feeling are also stratified, in that we experience higher and lower (deeper and more shallow) emotions, whose relative height is measured by their distance from each other with respect to matters of our greater or lesser concern and the depth to which they penetrate us and affect our

---

intentional act of feeling by the beholder. The Mona Lisa is a physical object, no doubt, but it makes objective the value and character of an individual woman, her mood, her animation, etc. Its de-actualization separates its value from the physical realm and establishes it in an ideal aesthetical realm.

4 For Hartmann on beauty in nature, cf. *Aesthetics*, Chap. 9b.

hearts – deep emotions that intend the welfare of families or of humankind, say, in contrast to our more shallow emotions that intend the prettiness of a village or a simple ballad.

Third, values and disvalues themselves are stratified along the spectrum of their worth relative to each other. Max Scheler had identified five such strata that he considered phenomenologically evident: On the lowest level, the physical values of pleasure and pain; then the use-values of utility and disutility; then vital values, such as health and sickness, and nobility and vulgarity; then spiritual values, such as beauty and ugliness, truth and falsity, goodness and wickedness; then, finally, values of the sacred: holiness and the profane. Hartmann disputed some features of this ladder of values – he held, for example, that the class of objects that are sacred or profane is most likely empty and therefore the values lack instances – and he treated the virtues and vices differently than Scheler. He claimed that Scheler had not understood properly the nature of the vital values. However, he did not dispute Scheler's idea of a stratified realm of "pure" values, i.e., values as material qualities divorced from individual instantiations of them. Indeed, Hartmann achieved a phenomenological description of several strata of aesthetic values in the concluding chapters of the present book. The sublime and the beautiful are the highest aesthetic values, while the charming, the graceful, and the comic are lower values. The difference in relative rank may be traced to the moral values that they carry, for the former suggest matters of highest concern – death, majesty, and the presence of powers we sense to be superior to our own – and the latter tend to appear on the more external strata of a work of art.

But Hartmann's greatest achievement lies in his discovery and analysis of strata in the aesthetic work itself. A complex work of art possesses a series of organized strata, and on each stratum the artist gives form to its contents. This stratification takes different forms in different art media. As a product of human creativity, art is vaguely analogous to the creativity of blind nature, or to human technology; it is a meaningful organization of matter. But artistic creation is not primarily a realization of a physical object – though it requires, as we have seen, material objects to do its work. Art creates (as in a painting) something invisible and indeed unreal, and the de-actualization or *Entwirklichung* of the painting (e.g., by putting it in a frame) so that it cannot be confused with what is real, places its content in a stratified transparent realm where the invisible and the unreal may then appear to the mind. These invisible and unreal aesthetic values, which appear only in art, are different from moral values, which exist as ideal being. The latter place us before moral necessity. The men Aristotle and Homer may have possessed real moral qualities worthy of admiration for themselves and for what was achieved through them, but Rembrandt's "Aristotle Contemplating a Bust of Homer" in the Metropolitan Museum of Art has merely aesthetic value. It suggests moral excellence, and makes that excellence beautiful (in part through the visible admiration of the younger man for the genius of the older), but the work does not bear it; we recognize those values through the deeper strata of the work. The strata found in a work of art vary with the kind of matter upon which the artists bestow form. They make aesthetic value objective by forming the "matter" of words, paint, or stone to give them aesthetic value and new meaning.[5]

Hartmann's concept of form is quite nuanced; he denies, for example, that "form" and "matter" are opposed concepts, for every work of art must possess both. But the bestowal of form is not simply upon "matter," that is, upon the substances out of which it is made (colors, stone, tones, words). The process of bestowing form takes place across the entire series of strata that constitutes the work. He writes,

> What is here of primary importance is that the giving of form on a single stratum, seen as isolated and taken in itself, is not at all aesthetical form. The aesthetics of form has always misunderstood that. It thought to take to itself a definite kind of formal element, i.e., that of some one stratum, for example, the stratum in which literary material is treated, and to investigate just as such its intrinsic "laws." That may be possible, but it fails to achieve its purpose, for in this way one does not arrive at aesthetical form at all. For that begins only with the succession of forms of different kinds. (257)

For the work of art consists of formed strata arranged so that the beholder may see *through* the formal arrangements in each stratum *into* the full meaning and value of the structured work. For example, in representational art, six strata receptive of form can be distinguished. Their analysis will be abbreviated for the sake of this presentation. We will assume a reference to a painting with human figures, although the same sort of analysis (one that might refer to fewer, additional, or different strata) would apply, *mutatis mutandis* to a literary work or a sculpture. Naturally, the painting does not possess these strata as physical components of it; the painting simply is as it appears. In a way, these strata are questions that the critical viewer of a painting or sculpture can ask of it: what does it let appear, and on what discernable intellectual levels can we place these appearances as part of our analysis of the painting? As such, the strata are very useful not in interpreting a work, but in engaging in an internal dialogue with the work as it is viewed, and in understanding how the painting works its magic upon us, how it provokes the disinterested pleasure that Kant thought to be the appropriate aesthetical response.

---

5 Hartmann uses the word "*Formung.*" The grammatical cognate "forming" does not work in English, and in this translation the phrase "bestowal" (or "bestowing") of form is used.

The first stratum is the foreground, the ontic stuff: say, visible specks of paint or carved marble, spoken or written words. Behind the colors and shapes, the second stratum is the three-dimensional spatiality embracing things that are visible in the "light within the picture": the scene that the colors and shapes "represent." In the third stratum, motion appears, made intuitively visible by the depiction of a phase of movement or by a pose. From behind this motion, on a deeper level, appears the living quality of the figures; this is the fourth stratum. Then, on the fifth stratum, we have the human psychic realm: the inner life of persons, their passions and their dispositions, as they appear through their apparent motion and the living quality in a phase of a situation. On the sixth stratum, in works of unusual depth, something of the individual Idea of the persons depicted may appear – what here and in the *Ethics* Hartmann calls the "intelligible idea" of a person. Thus we behold a human being "whole," as it were. And finally, on the seventh stratum various kinds of universal ideas appear: the idea of childhood or old age, the destiny of a family or of humanity, and the like. These ideas may emerge from the theme of the work, as in religious scenes, but the artist also may camouflage them. Knowledge of the meaning of the scene, or of the "legend" behind it, gives depth to our response to it, but it plays an extra-aesthetical role (206).

The character of our appreciation depends on a distinctive feature of a stratified work of art, namely the *transparency* of the strata, i.e. the ability of a stratum to transmit the content of strata behind it and thus allow them to affect us appropriately, i.e. according to the creator's intentions. This transparency de-pends entirely upon the skill of the artist, and it takes different form depending on the stratum. For example, the transparency of the state of old age that we see in the self-portrait of Rembrandt as an old man that is cited by Hartmann (183) opens the viewer to the next-deeper stratum, upon which we are given the intelligible Idea of a man who has fought his way through long conflicts with his métier and with life itself. The transparency of that figure opens to us in turn the final stratum: the idea of old age itself as an essential state of men and women who have fought their way to it, a state the viewer, too, will perhaps one day reach.

In a non-representational art such as music, the phenomenology of strata is simpler. Only three background or "inner" strata exist in music. The foreground is constituted by the sounds to which the listener responds with a kind of resonance. This begins in the beat of dance music, but it belongs to all music. The sound addresses and captures the listener. Second is the stratum in which the listener, by a deeper penetration into the composition, is gripped by it. This stratum causes psychic agitation; it reveals and proclaims. It raises what was hidden in the listener's Self out of the depths. The third is the metaphysical stratum, in the sense that Schopenhauer gives to the appearance of the "universal Will."

For great music has always the character of an encounter with dimly sensed but unknown forces of destiny. In contrast, specific human destinies can be communicated objectively by painting and drama, but pure music cannot give content to the forces of destiny it conveys to the listener. No doubt, when moved by a piece of music, we try to describe the values in the music that moved us, but only limited success is possible. We call these values, to use Hartmann's examples, "sublime" or "majestic"; we speak of its "dark depths" or its "radiance." We express our own response to the music as "ravishment, excitement," or as "being put in a mellow mood." Of course these characteristics are not utilized by the composer to represent any entity. But the indeterminateness and suggestiveness of music consists precisely in the inability of its background forms to be contained in any formal value-structure. Hartmann notes that aesthetics has not yet touched on how "the sounds and the sequences are able to make the most inward and inarticulate phenomena of the life of the soul appear" (216).

3 Hartmann's Deconstruction of Familiar Antinomies in Aesthetics

a) The listener and the critic. But this analysis makes visible a curious conflict that Hartmann attempts to overcome, as he does for many such conflicts. Music stands over against us as an object, yet the soul apprehends it reverentially and is absorbed by it; how can we be absorbed by it and yet maintain the aesthetic distance required to understand it? This might be called the antinomy of the listener and the critic. The antinomy is real, yet further study resolves it, Hartmann believes:

> The internal strata of music have the means to grip the entire person and, in this state, he becomes one with it; the external strata have the means to focus his attention and even to form the object of his attention itself. The structural elements of the tonal composition are what hold [the hearer] firmly at a distance from and in a state of contemplation of what is objectively present. (218)

We cannot, while listening, stand in disinterested contemplation and ignore the external forms of the music. The lover of music, becoming one with it, is led ever more deeply into its beauty as he remains attentive to the formal composition. The critic simply remains coolly at the doorstep of the third stratum while he analyzes the structure of the external strata.

Music is a revelation, Hartmann says; its miracle is that it awakens inner moods perhaps unfamiliar to us, and gets us to "enter a great inward vital life, to give [ourselves] over to feelings that cannot be put under categories. And in this way the miracle of a community of listeners in the emotional experience of music takes place" (216). Think of the beginning of Bergman's film *The Magic Flute*, where we observe people from all walks of life, ages, and nationalities, all floating off with the overture to the fantasy world brought to life by Mozart's music.

b) Truth in art. Although art presents content that is present only to aesthetical beholding and hence unreal, it nonetheless bears a relation to truth. The capacity of the mind to penetrate the foreground and behold a non-existent background seems at first mysterious. Children, failing to understand the aesthetic relation, may think a represented world to be real. But Hartmann writes,

> The perception of the invisible along with the visible loses much of its mystery when we realize how it plays a broad role even in relation to far simpler objects. [...] Upon each thing, we are able to see more and more of what is invisible: we "see" the hardness or elasticity of things, or even their weight and the inertia that resists efforts to move them. And similarly [...] we hear steps in an adjacent room, but "see" in the mind's eye a human form in motion as it goes about some business or other; or we hear the quiet rustle of a wicker chair but we see inwardly how the person sitting upon it is rocking in some specific way. (50)

The dark presentiment-laden tie to an unknown object hidden behind an artistic construct is thus to a large extent already present in everyday perception; the augmentation by feeling and imagination and the revelation of the object in a work of art therefore is quite natural. We get lost in it for a while, but the ties that bind us to reality are never absent; hence, our sense of mystery can be enjoyed but then be overcome.

In representational art there is an apparent conflict regarding its truth. Art as representation comes under the category of *mimesis*, the use of nature, human or otherwise, as a model to be represented. This does not mean that the representation must be a mere copy of the thing represented; at the very least the thing represented is of a different kind of material than the representation. Nor does it mean that, as in Plato's metaphysics, a physical object is a representation in the world of becoming of some eternal blueprint of its essence, or what Plato calls its Form, and the art work a representation of the formal qualities of the object. Hartmann sees these two forms of *mimesis* as correct only in part. The aesthetic object or objectified form falls under two categories of poetic truth: the true-to-life (*Lebenswahrheit*) and the essential truth (*Wesenswahrheit*) (Chap. 23d). The former has one pole in the outside world, which it represents; the latter lies in the artwork itself as "inward agreement, unity, completeness, and consistency in itself." These need not be in harmony, for, he writes, "a writer can represent a character whose forms are lifted up to a mythical dimension, and yet thereby enter an essential sphere, perhaps even where it has the sense of a certain fanatical attachment to value, although what is true-to-life – human life as it is – is not attained by him in this way" (323).

Such peculiar conflicts between essential truths and the true-to-life are instructive, and suggest how these tensions, interactions, and relationships may affect the aesthetic value of a work of art. He notes that at one extreme a poet cannot sift off a few essential characteristics of human nature and, so to speak, allow them to come onstage and do a solo (325), for art has as one of its functions the revelation of features of real life that might otherwise be hidden. Some classical operas, especially those of the late eighteenth and early nineteenth centuries (generally classified *opera seria*) present highly idealized and romanticized kings and heroes that are hardly true to life; producers today tend to "humanize" them by allowing more realistic emotions and attitudes to be presented by means of new forms of stage setting, gesture, and costume. Of course, a poetic or operatic work that was simply true to life and contained no tendency toward some ideas is hardly thinkable; yet one that is "tendentious" towards its ideas would be in danger of becoming aesthetically derailed in both ways. He writes, "The moral tone, the idea, the philosophical presuppositions can themselves be erroneous, that is, be in conflict with our experience of life, and they can be represented incorrectly – too obviously, too insistently, or even too darkly, too veiled, misleadingly, unclearly – and can then be repellent or even disappear" (313).

In sum, the representational aim of such art must walk a line between its two functions: that of letting us see the world as it is more clearly and that of bringing the beholder to a deeper understanding of what is possible in life for a person. And where the true-to-life is congruent with its deeper ideal aesthetic values, this congruence becomes identical with beauty.

c) The unity of aesthetic value. A sense of a mystery in aesthetic experience may arise from the seeming disunity of the realm of moral and aesthetic value and from the incompleteness of our knowledge of it. Aesthetic discourse then breaks down and leaves us in a state of perplexity that is akin to mystery. Is no progress in aesthetical understanding possible? Does randomness prevail here? Is there, for example, a comprehensive typology of artistic values present on the relevant strata in different media? The effort to put the experience of beauty into some kind of large pattern and to establish the structure of the whole realm of aesthetic values has failed up to now. It is not surprising that the problem of unity appears aporetical and undecidable; the natural desire of reason for unity is unsatisfied. Yet as Hartmann argues in his *Ethics*,[6] it is premature to assume that disunity is essentially impossible to resolve, that is, to assume that we can never discover an

---

6 Cf. Hartmann, Nicolai, *Ethics*, London: George Allen & Unwin 1932, Vol. 1, p. 79. On this theme cf. Kelly, Eugene, "Hartmann on the Unity of Moral Value," in: *The Philosophy of Nicolai Hartmann*, ed. Roberto Poli, Carlo Scognamiglio, Frederic Tremblay, Berlin and Boston: De Gruyter 2011.

underlying unity. A value-conflict may appear to be irresolvable only because of the undeveloped state of the inquiry in which it appears. The disunity is a problem, not a limitation, of aesthetics. Thus, we may still hope that some local mysteries may be resolved in a higher synthesis that today may not be visible.

d) Architecture and its culture. Aesthetics may determine how a practical structure can express the spirit of a culture. Questions of three kinds may arise: (1) is there tension between the practical task and the forms through which it is achieved; (2) is there tension in the harmony or disharmony of parts and whole, which may involve a conflict between the spatial and the dynamic layout; (3) is there an opposition between the practical ends pursued and the spirit and style of life expressed by the structure. However, the question of how architectural structure expresses the life of its creators is not answerable by philosophical aesthetics only because these are questions of history and even of social and political criticism, which are external to aesthetics.

No doubt we wonder how certain architectural structures give voice, in the form of style, to the life of the people who erected it and who live or lived in and around it, and the means they used to express that style. As time passes, the voice of style in a piece of architecture becomes muted, though its formal structure still may impress us. For the style belongs to the culture that put itself in the hands of an architect who made use of the forms and materials then available to make objective the functioning social and political values of a community or leadership elite. "Only where this connection [between life and architecture] is found can the life and the nature of man appear in his buildings" (232), Hartmann writes. This connection can be forgotten. When that happens, we stand befuddled before many such creations, having lost historical contact with their creators. We won-der what they could have intended to communicate by some object, and what responses they were intended to provoke in their contemporaries. We wonder, for example, what is the meaning of the empty stares of the figures on Easter Island, or why the granary of Great Zimbabwe was given the odd spiral form it has. In such cases, the mystery is not one of aesthetics, but derives from the loss of the keys to aesthetic interpretation; we cannot reconstruct adequately the function of the object, the purposes of its creators and how these purposes emerged from the larger cultural structures that nurtured their sensibilities and their beliefs. Hart-mann notes in passing that the contemporary apartment building fails to convey anything of the spiritual life of the residents; it is given form and structure only for the values of utility and parsimony; it lacks style. Thus, the actual life of the inhabitants cannot be discovered from an examination of their architecture; the spirit of that life is simply not present in them at all.

There may be mystery, too, in the incompleteness and frequent disunity of our responses to art, or to beauty more generally, but that mystery may lie in our unique nature as acculturated persons, and not in the object in question. Oddly, Hartmann does not describe this form of the problem of the give-and-take between the beholder and what he beholds, perhaps thinking it intractable. Much of our response to art, as to life as a whole, is personal, in the sense that objects resonate in each of us in an individual way. Let us assume that we are developed art critics and our sensibility has been nourished and refined by years of beholding, of listening, of reading, such that we may be able to analyze a given work adequately, to understand how it "works" throughout its various distinguishable elements. But we are not just critics; we may still be puzzled by our own response to the work, how we "feel" about the face in a portrait, how her humanity relates to our own, or even what she might "have been feeling while the artist painted her"; how she "affects" our emotions. It is hard to chart just how our mood responds to, say, Frank Gehry's Pritzker Pavilion in Chicago's Millennium Park, or to a specific performance of *Rigoletto*. Here the mystery – and it is real – does not lie in art or in beauty, but in ourselves, in the lack of transparency of the sources of our emotions.

4 Unresolvable Mysteries of Aesthetics

a) Creativity. The deepest mysteries of art lie in the creativity of the artist and in the individuality of the artwork. One of Hartmann's real merits is to have discovered, on the basis of this phenomenological procedure, mysteries that cannot be deconstructed, and limit the capacity of aesthetics to make progress in areas that are genuinely its own. Of the four avenues of aesthetical inquiry listed earlier, the fourth, that of creation in art, presents us with a special mystery. Hartmann writes,

> Nothing is darker and more mysterious than the work of the creative artist. The very pronouncements of a genius about his work fail to cast any light upon the essence of the matter. Usually they prove only that he, too, knows nothing more than other men do about the miracle that was consummated in him and through him. The act of production seems to be of a kind that excludes any accompanying consciousness of itself. Therefore, we know only its external side and can draw conclusions about its inner nature only from its achievements. (9)

Even to the genius, the mystery is palpable.

The problem of form is fundamental to the phenomenon of genius. For "we cannot follow the various features of aesthetic form through all the strata" (238). Even single forms can be described only in the most banal generalities.

Why does just this particular form – purely in itself, without any further transparency [without opening upon deeper strata] – seem beautiful, why does the slightest alteration of it destroy the impression? Aesthetics cannot hope to provide an answer. It is just in this that the imponderable mystery of art consists; it belongs in a region whose laws even the artist does not comprehend, where laws can be adhered to only out of the pure feelings of a genius. (239)

How do the forms on a lower stratum feed into strata higher than their own? How can these formal structures, each peculiar to its own stratum, still give us a sense of the wholeness and unity of the work?

If the possibility existed of analyzing "structurally" the entire phenomenon of aesthetic form purely as such, we could take a direct route here, in such a way, for example, as biology describes and analyzes organic forms or as ontology does for formal structures of being. But this possibility is not given: it would as such be equivalent to the revelation of the mystery of artistic production. This revelation is prohibited to philosophical inquiry. (248)

The appearance-relation, in which an ideal content appears to a mind, governs the transformation of content to ever-higher degrees of ideality as we pass from stratum to stratum, that is, as the mind penetrates ever more deeply into the work. Genius consists precisely in the creator's skill in bestowing form so as to allow the deeper ideal elements to appear through the less deep elements, until the foreground elements – which are entirely "matter" – are understood in terms of the ideal elements they allow to appear. We then "understand" the work as a lawfully structured individual order, but we cannot grasp how it achieved those ends.

b) Uniqueness. But there is a greater mystery that limits a philosophy that seeks to *understand* beauty and ugliness, though it does not impede the aesthetically beholding mind from responding to the work. After some reflections upon laws of great generality that govern aesthetics and can be formulated by a philosophical aesthetics, Hartmann notes,

The nature of beauty in its uniqueness, as the specific aesthetic value-content, does not lie in these general laws, but in the particular lawfulness of the unique object. This particular lawfulness is fundamentally unavailable to all philosophical analysis. It cannot be grasped by any epistemic technique. Its nature is to be hidden, and to be felt only as present and as coercive, but never capable of becoming an object of thought. (3)

Aesthetical criteria for the value of a work of art exist, and they may orient the critical patron of the arts, yet not require his assent in any given case. The laws of beauty that matter are individual ones. Thus the capacity of aesthetics to establish the relative quality of individual art works, as opposed to art criticism exercised by a particular art critic, who speaks out of his tradition and his peculiar sensibility, is limited. "Aesthetics thus cannot [...] do the same for the aesthetical beholding as logic does for thought" (3).

The beauty of each work is unique just because the world it reveals is unreal; it requires a beholder, that is, some individual reader, hearer or onlooker for whom it exists as an artwork, whose peculiar qualities he can behold and, in so doing, "complete" it. Hartmann does not use the term "interpretation" of a work of art, a term that has become so important in contemporary discourse, especially in the light of hermeneutical and deconstructive practices of artists and their public. The term suggests that the work of art becomes other than what it is in the interpretive process and Hartmann will not sanction such an idea. By "completion" he refers to the double process in which a work is responded to: the process by which the "prepared" viewer or auditor or reader grasps the way in which the artist has achieved in him the "disinterested pleasure" that is the primary response to art as art, and the process by which the subjective and personal spirit, shaped by its own milieu and art history, responds in its own way to the work as embodying (objectivating) values. In both cases, the process is both personal and objective; the unique structure of the artwork and the aesthetic values it carries are there in the work, but exist only for the viewer, who leaves the work intact. Without that act of completion, there would be no aesthetic object. We would have only the physical object, like the paintings by van Gogh that, according to the story, were used to close holes in the walls of barns; they become something alien to their nature.

Accordingly, the key mystery of art is the unanalyzable, but still lawful, nature that is present in the work of art. As with a human being, we can speak of the integrity of a work of art, or of its lack thereof; of a person's or an artwork's success or failure in "becoming what he is or it is intended to become," he or its ability to be understood in his or its uniqueness, or his or its withdrawal from our comprehension, he falling into madness and becoming an object of psychiatry, or it falling into the margins of life and becoming a recollection of art history. Analysis may capture the general features of men or of art works, but fail to touch their individuality and uniqueness, which simply "appears." To understand the forms that make the artwork beautiful would be equivalent to understanding what Scheler called the "ordo amoris" of a person, the laws of the heart that make him who he is. Neither philosophers nor psychologists can aspire to do so; like the critic before the indeterminacy of music, they stand at the doorway of personality. Only loving devotion to a person or work can enter the intimate individuality of a person, into the unobjectifiable forms of his personhood as a value or into the individuality of a great work of art. Hartmann writes, "For what is personal is unique, and requires a loving gaze to make it visible" (52).

In his *Ethics,* Hartmann spoke of personal love as he speaks in the *Aesthetics* of "devotion" to a thing of beauty. To love another person is to joyously affirm precisely the peculiar individuality and uniqueness of that person, who may or may not reciprocate; to hate another is to reject him or her as broken, morally ugly, silent. Similarly, we rejoice in and affirm great works of art; they speak to us personally and, in so doing, affirm our own individuality. Others do not touch or speak to us, for they may lack individuality, lack spirit and life, or they may lack resonance with a personality like their own. And, as with persons, our response to art may run across a spectrum of rejection, interest, and loving affirmation. Art is spirit made objective, which, like the human spirit that created it, deifies reduction to categories. As with another person to whom we are open in friendship, the artwork must be beheld intuitively in order to feel close to it – indeed, as Scheler would say, the noetic acts that found its communications must be "re-executed" (*nachvollzogen) in mente* in order to grasp at all its unique nature. Great art, like genuine personal love, gives the highest meaning and highest joy possible for a human being. Ontologically, human love and human art are built up from matter, but for Hartmann their works illuminate life from the top down.

Especially strange and mysterious is Hartmann's claim, given the parallel of the individuality of art to human individuality, that works of art on the highest level tend to converge. The senses render to us the myriad materials out of which a work of art is made, and these diverse objects condition what appears through them. One cannot create music out of stone, or human characters out of tones. But on the highest levels of art great works of all kinds reveal a similarity in their nature even in their middle strata. The universally human is revealed in these strata, and what is universally human is held in common by all. Even where, as in the representational arts, the intelligible essence of some individual appears, it does not oppose itself to the universally human, but affirms it in its opposition: *King Lear* gives both the essence of an individual as well as the universally human, to which he is both opposed in his individuality but which he nonetheless represents in his essence. So Hartmann expresses the law: "All art of slight or even of a more median value diverge immensely and are hardly comparable; but, in contrast, all truly great works of art converge and come close to an impalpable identity" (497). His examples of this purported phenomenon ("Thus the Parthenon and [J.S. Bach's] *Art of the Fugue*, the ceiling of the Sistine Chapel (perhaps in the figures of youths or of the Prophets) and Shakespeare's *Henry IV* (including the figure of Falstaff), Rembrandt's self-portrait in old age (Amsterdam) and the Apollo on the pediment [of the temple of Zeus] at Olympia, Beethoven's fifth or seventh symphony ..." (497)) are less than convincing at first sight, but he insists that we can see this convergence when our eyes penetrate to the deepest and most inward parts of these great works.

The irreducible uniqueness of the work of art arises out of the creative freedom of the artist. There the mystery – or paradox – of art grows deeper. In morals, freedom stands under necessity – I must not kill, although I can. The artist's freedom is limited by nothing, not even by some ideal – Hartmann cites Hölderlin: the artist has the "freedom to set forth wherever he will"[7] (44) – except by the logic of his unique creation. For an effective artwork, like an integrated person *has* a logic, an *ordo amoris*. But how can a logical order be unanalyzable? Why can it be only "felt"? Hartmann does not question how this utter freedom of the artist coheres with the aesthetical necessity of law-like form that must limit his freedom, any more that Scheler was able to reconcile the creative freedom of the individual – the freedom to create oneself – with the inborn law-like order of the heart that he attributes to the human person and the category of individual fate that make coherent personhood possible. As with Scheler's "models and leaders," art inspires us not by "moralizing, pedantry, or admonition" (292), nor by its logic, but by the characters, figures, and tones it presents to us. They elevate and deepen us mysteriously. Perhaps their lucid presence in our lives makes it possible for us to "become what we are."

5 The Value of Art

The notion of the function of art, seemingly resolved by contemporary analyses of its social, political, and educational values, seems at first somewhat unclear for Hartmann. In the introduction to *Aesthetics* (§5), he discusses the problem as an aporetic in the foundation of art: art may have no function at all or, perhaps, the extra-aesthetical function of elevating the human spirit to a state beyond life and quotidian entanglements; thus, l'art pour l'art. Others will argue for engaged or political art (or its contrary, "decadent" art), whose function is the fostering (or dismantling) of solidarity and the achievement (or abandonment) of political goals. If this aporetic can be resolved, it will be possible only on the basis of an analysis of the noematic correlate of the aesthetic attitude, i.e., the art object and its ties to human life, says Hartmann (Cf. 12).

Hartmann eventually answers the question of the function of art in the following way. Art has a reciprocal tie to human life. It is tied, on the one hand, to the human world, which it expresses and represents in an aesthetic space outside of the ontic world. But in so doing, it elevates the beholder into a realm of its own. The beholder does not remain there, however; he returns to his quotidian life, but

---

7 Hölderlin, Friedrich, "The Course of Life," in: *Poems of Friedrich Hölderlin. The Fire of the Gods Drives Us to Set Forth by Day and by Night*, selected and translated by James Mitchell, San Francisco: Ithuriel's Spear 2004, p. 25.

one now illuminated by what he has beheld. What is "bestowed" by aesthetic values upon man is a unique meaning and value of which we have need: the light in the darkness, the joy in the sorrow. These meanings and values are gratuitous, for unlike moral values they do not burden us with responsibility, and unlike vital value, they do not burden us with necessity. They are, as Hartmann quotes Nietzsche, like gold, "uncommon and of no use and luminous and mild in [their] lustre," and they always bestow themselves (441).[8]

But these aesthetical meanings have no metaphysical tie to physical nature. Western civilization was mistaken, Hartmann believes, to assume a teleology either theological or metaphysical, to be operative in nature. For if the world had a "meaning" to which it was tending, man would perforce be required to serve that end. But the meaningfulness of life does not require recourse to a greater whole, to the world in its origins or its ends.

> [E]very morally good act, every wise thought, every adequate response to a value, is mean-ingful and bestows additional meaning just out of itself alone. Out of itself alone: that means that it does not have meaning only for the sake of something else. Such is every act of benevolence, every participation in the spiritual and the inner life – every sympathetic understanding and every interpersonal involvement that breaks through icy loneliness precisely where a man wishes to be seen and appreciated – are meaningful just for themselves alone; yet they bestow a meaning upon other things, and a deep need of the human heart for the realization of meaning is thereby satisfied. (439)

Nietzsche's dramatic proclamations that, with the loss of God and teleology, "we are lost wanderers in an endless nothingness," and we "create art to shield us from the truth" imply that we have wandered away from a home that was once ours, and must lie to ourselves to protect us from the truth of our meaningless-ness: "Alas to him who yet has no home."[9] But, Hartmann observes, "if man [...] is capable of bestowing meaning and value, [...] the senselessness of the world as a whole obtains a meaning for him" (439). What is great about humankind is bestowed upon us not by the Forms, or by a Logos or God, but by ourselves. This fact need not make us overly proud, but rather content with what we are able to see and do. Science, art, and philosophy are themselves affirmations of the mean-ingfulness of life, not justifications of pride in ourselves. Hartmann writes,

---

8 Nietzsche, Friedrich, *Thus Spoke Zarathustra: A Book for Everyone and Nobody*, translated and edited by Graham Parkes, Oxford and New York: Oxford University Press 2005, First Part, "On the Bestowing Virtue," p. 65.
9 Friedrich Nietzsche, *Kritische Studienausgabe Werke*, 2nd edition. Edited by Giorgio Colli and Mazzino Montinari, Vol. 11, p. 329, fr. 28[64]. Berlin/New York, Munich 1999.

> The bestowal of meaning that comes into human life via aesthetic values consists funda-
> mentally in nothing other than in the convincing feeling of standing face to face before
> something of absolutely intrinsic value – before something for whose sake alone it would be
> worth living, regardless of how the conditions of one's life stand otherwise. That is so, not
> least because it is a question of no practical interest in beauty, or of the desire to use it or to
> make it one's own, but simply because of the joy taken in the object; or the pleasure we feel
> in living in a world in which such glorious things exist. (440)

Although Hartmann speaks frequently of mysteries and secrets, of aporia and
antinomies in art, most of them can be deconstructed by reducing them to other
mysteries, or resolved by continued examination of the phenomenological facts
of the case – with two exceptions, and these impede a thoroughly philosophical
aesthetics. There is the mystery of artistic creativity and mystery of the absolute
individuality of the artwork, or even the individuality of natural beauty. These
mysteries are not a function of human thought. They are founded in the mysteries
of human individuality and of human creativity. They may also be peculiar to the
attitude of reverence owed to God or to the world as such. Scheler wrote,

> Whenever we pass beyond the irreverent, that is, the typical scientific explanatory attitude,
> and attain the reverential attitude toward things, we see how something is added to things
> that they did not possess, how something in them becomes visible and palpable that they
> formerly lacked: just this 'something' is their mystery, their deep value.[10]

6 The Future of Aesthetics

Hartmann, to my knowledge, never attempted a philosophical anthropology as a
platform on which to pursue these mysteries, although, on occasion, he spec-
ulates on human nature and how art responds, via certain aesthetical categories,
to that nature. Perhaps a generation or two hence the "typical scientific explana-
tory attitude" will discover the sources of the human mind in the physiology of the
brain, such that the laws of individuality and creativity will be thoroughly understood, and all "mysteries" of art will be thoroughly understood. Whether 'tis is a
consummation devoutly to be wished, we may leave to the reader's reflections.

It may also be that modern painting, sculpture, music, and poetry – all those
forms of the arts that underwent a fundamental change during Hartmann's life –

---

10 Scheler, Max, "On the Rehabilitation of Virtue," in: *American Catholic Philosophical Quarterly*,
79, No. 1 (2005), p. 32 ("Zur Rehabilitierung der Tugend," in: Scheler, Max, *Gesammelte Werke*,
Vol. 3, ed. Maria Scheler and Manfred Frings, Bonn: Bouvier 2000).

are no longer relevant to Hartmann's aesthetics. The most recent writers mentioned by Hartmann were Knut Hamsun and Thomas Mann. Otherwise, the work of the early twentieth century seems to have passed him by. Many of its artists intend precisely to blur the strata of their works, or even to deny that such strata exist in them. The average viewer, hearer, or reader often comes to new work with the expectation, grown out of his familiarity with the achievements of works from the long past, that the work will "mean" something, that it have a formal structure on many levels, each of which is so constructed as to allow the appearance of some deeper meaning behind it. Yet much of contemporary art must be experienced differently, as a flat and inarticulable phenomenon: as colors and shapes on canvas, or musical tones that have no apparent relation to each other and with no sense of musical development, or poetry as images that tell no tale and possess no deeper coherence that might suggest a singular meaning intended by the author to which his images point. Incoherence, remoteness, randomness, and expressiveness *sui generis* seem to constitute the character of much of what characterizes art today. If this is so, Hartmann's aesthetics would seem to have little point of contact or application for the generations that created art after him. Perhaps a different articulation of strata in painting or sculpture is needed, for example the analysis of strata such as materials (base, paint types), of the geometry of the construction of figures in space, of the size of a work – all ways in which materials may work upon the sensibility of a beholder. Then, too, the final stratum of the work of painting might be reworked to account for the mystical and surreal intentions of many artists in the twentieth century. Such related categories as the "absurd" that are treated by the drama and the novel would have to receive a novel treatment upon Hartmann's platform for aesthetics. Perhaps a new account of aesthetic beholding is also required. Then, too, there is the interesting question of the extent to which, if at all, Hartmann's procedure is applicable to traditions foreign to that of European art, to which Hartmann does not refer in this work.

But it may be that Hartmann's aesthetics is precisely what modern art is running from. Some pundits have argued that such abstract and non-representational features of modern painting, atonality in music, and similar postmodern elements in avant-garde literature are liberating, for a work of art is allowed to be simply about itself. In such liberation, as in all liberation of an agent from the moral, political or even aesthetic rules and structures of his milieu, there are subtle dangers. Art would then escape all criteria for its quality, and divorce itself from its beholders, who are similarly liberated from an obligation to interact mentally and not just viscerally with the work, and who simply respond, as in social media, with a "like" or "dislike" – and that is the end of the matter! In the place of the transparency of the work or lack thereof and the appropriateness of viewers' responses to it, we have today an art establishment that possesses obscure criteria for the acceptability and monetary value (often based simply upon an artist's past successes and total sales of the works they display and vend). In all of this the concept of beauty and sublimity gets lost, and Hartmann's threefold analytical schema becomes irrelevant. The old notion, "there is no accounting for taste!" which liberates the individual from the burden of accounting for his own taste, becomes today the rule. Consumers of art are now free to take a work or leave it – or, perhaps, to enter the art establishment as a tastemaker.

This assessment of the place of art today is dismal to excess, and no doubt unfair. Yet if Hartmann is generally unread today, that may be due to the fact that he speaks out of a tradition of art that has been successfully deconstructed, and new forms of art have liberated themselves from older traditions and created our not always brave new world.

I wish to give special thanks to Thomas Pemberton of the Institute of Education, University of London, for his suggestions for improving the manuscript and for the unpleasant but necessary work of proofreading.

Introduction

1 The Aesthetical Attitude and Aesthetics as Knowledge

One writes aesthetics neither for the creator nor for the patron of the arts, but exclusively for the thinker, for whom the doings and the attitudes of both have become a puzzle. The lover of art, sunk in contemplation, can only be troubled by such thought, the artist only put in a bad mood and annoyed by it; so at least, when thought tries to comprehend what the two of them are doing and what their object is. The aesthetician tears both of them from their visionary standpoint, although to both the sense of the puzzling is familiar enough, and belongs to their perspective. To both, this perspective is precisely what is obvious; they know of an inner necessity, and in that they do not lose their way. But they accept it precisely as a gift of heaven, and this acceptance is essential to their perspective.

The philosopher begins where both men turn over the miracle of what they are experiencing to the powers of the depths and the unconsciousness. He follows up the clues left by this puzzlement; he analyzes. In the analysis, however, he brackets the perspectives of devotion and vision. Aesthetics exists only for one taking a philosophical perspective.

Viewed the other way around, the perspectives of appreciation and vision overturn the philosophical. Or, at least, they encroach upon it. Aesthetics is a kind of knowledge, indeed one with a genuine tendency to become a science. And the object of this knowledge is that attitude of appreciation and that visionary attitude. Not these alone are its objects, to be sure; it is focused, just as much as they are, upon the beautiful, but also upon them. It follows from this that aesthetical appreciation is, at its foundations, different from that of philosophical knowledge, which takes such acts of appreciative devotion as its object. The aesthetical perspective is in general not that of the aesthetician. The former is and remains the aesthetical attitude of beholding and creating; the latter is that of the philosopher.

Neither the one nor the other is obvious. The natural exclusion by one of the other, if it were total, would make, in the end, the epistemic reflections of the aesthetician impossible. He must be capable of the aesthetical perspective, for he can learn it only by his own exercise of it. In any case, some notable thinkers had the opposite conviction. Schelling[11] made aesthetical intuition the Organon of philosophy. The German Romantics dreamed of the unity of "philosophy and

---

11 [Translator's note:] Friedrich Wilhelm Joseph Ritter von Schelling (1775–1854).

poetry"; thus Friedrich Schlegel[12] and Novalis[13]. The latter conceived of the philosopher as (2)[14] the "magician" who could, following only his desires, put the "universal organ" to work and conjure up a world to his tastes. This idea is taken unmistakably from the activity of the poet. And, on the other hand, it appeared to them that only the eye of the artist could penetrate the secrets of nature and of the life of the spirit. This seemed to be so because people believed they could recognize in all things and in the whole of the world as its background the same fundamental nature that becomes conscious in the ego. With this anthropomorphic formula for the world, the identity of what in themselves are quite different ways of looking at the world stands or falls. And when the formula was consciously suspended, which began as early as Hegel[15], the enormity of the opposition between artistic and scientific thought, between appreciative beholding and the analytic work of the intellect, became apparent once again.

The separation of these acts as seen from the other side is just as little obvious. Since the beginning of aesthetics proper in the eighteenth century, the unspoken presupposition was tenaciously held that this philosophical discipline must have something essential to teach to the beholder of beauty and even to the productive artist. This idea must have seemed convincing as long as one saw a kind of knowledge in the aesthetical manner of looking, although it is a kind of knowledge different from rational knowledge. These were the days when people believed that logic, too, could teach the thinker how to think. And yet the relationships here are far more complex. Logic, at least, can show invalid reasoning the nature of its invalidity and indirectly contribute in a practical way to consistent thinking. For aesthetics, anything similar is secondary, and comes into consideration only in a very rough way. As logic determines only subsequent to thought what laws any consistent reasoning must adhere to, and only in this way may arrive at a system of logical consistency, so too – and to an even greater degree – for aesthetics, and even than only provided it is possible to speak at all of its ascertaining the laws of the beautiful.

Aesthetics presupposes things of beauty, likewise the mental acts that appreciate them, along with a peculiar way of beholding, a sense of beauty, and an inward devotedness; even more, it presupposes the much more amazing act of artistic creation, and both, let it be noted, without laying claim to distilling their lawfulness from them in the same way that logic distills laws from relations of

---

12 [Translator's note:] Friedrich Schlegel (1772–1829).
13 [Translator's note:] Georg Philipp Friedrich Freiherr von Hardenberg (1772–1801).
14 Page numbers in parentheses refer the reader to the pages in the second German edition, 1966.
15 [Translator's note:] Georg Wilhelm Friedrich Hegel (1770–1831).

ideas. Aesthetics thus cannot, for that reason alone, do the same for the aesthetical beholding as logic does for thought.

2 Laws of Beauty and Knowledge of Them

At this point, we must make a further distinction. The laws of logic are universal; they vary only slightly with their object-domains. The laws of beauty are highly specialized and are fundamentally different for each object. This means: they are individual laws. Beyond that, there are no doubt also general laws, those that refer in part to all aesthetical (3) objects, in part to entire classes of them. And, within certain limits, aesthetics can also attempt to deal with them. With what success is a quite different question and one must not become optimistic regarding its potential. But these general laws are just only preconditions, perhaps categorical in nature or otherwise somehow constitutive. The nature of beauty in its uniqueness, as the specific aesthetic value-content of an object, does not lie in these general laws, but in the particular lawfulness of the unique object.

This particular lawfulness is fundamentally unavailable to all philosophical analysis. It cannot be grasped by any epistemic technique. Its nature is to be hidden, and to be felt only as present and as coercive, but never capable of becoming an object of thought.

The creative artist also does not grasp it. He creates according to it, but does not reveal it and therefore cannot even speak of it. He also cannot speak of it because he also does not have objective knowledge of it. Even less has the beholder of beauty such knowledge. He is no doubt gripped by it, but only as by a mystery he cannot uncover; for his part, he does not grasp it. In certain circumstances he can learn the extent to which such lawfulness actually dominates the work, or how far the work has mixed with elements external to art and thus has failed as art. But even then the structural nature of the law defies his efforts to know it.

There is no genuine consciousness of the laws of beauty. It appears to lie in their nature to remain concealed from consciousness and only to form the secret of the background, while entirely hidden from sight.

That is no doubt the reason why aesthetics can say, as a matter of its principle, what beauty is and even what its kinds and levels are, along with their general preconditions, but cannot teach in the practical sense what is beautiful, or why the particular form of some construction is a beautiful one. Aesthetical reflection is in all cases *post facto*: It can take its ground after the acts of beholding aesthetically and simply indulging in the enjoyment of beauty has taken place. It need not come after them at all, but when it does, it can rarely add anything of substance to them. In that it can achieve even less than the systematic study of art, which can at least point to unnoticed aspects of an artwork, and in that way make it accessible to a consciousness that is only inadequately receptive. And aesthetics can give even less in the way of practical principles to guide the working artist. Within certain limits, it can teach us to recognize what is impossible for art as such to achieve, and protect it from losing its way. But to specify in a positive way what and how a thing should be given form is far from aesthetics' sphere of competence.

All theories that have gone in that direction, and all unacknowledged hopes of this kind, however they may attach themselves innocently to the efforts of philosophy in aesthetics, have long demonstrated their vanity. (4) If one wishes to make a serious effort to examine the problem of beauty in life and in the arts, one must from the outset and for all time abstain from all such pretensions.

Before concluding this topic, a further point should be discussed. There is a more radical prejudice that concerns the relation of art and philosophy in general. According to this prejudice, artistic understanding is only a preliminary stage of the understanding that knows and comprehends. Hegelian philosophy, with its "absolute sprit" arranged in a step-like series, articulated such a standpoint. Only upon the level of the concept does the Idea come to its complete "being-for-itself," i.e., its genuine knowledge of itself. If a person today would hardly give himself the trouble of defending this metaphysics of spirit, the idea that art is a form of understanding in which appearance to the senses is a demonstration of its inadequacy as knowledge is still widespread.

That in this way the peculiarly "aesthetical" element, that is, that which is given to the senses in artistic understanding, is fundamentally and entirely mistaken – while instead it is its clarity to the senses that demonstrates the superiority of in the arts over the concept – requires no further discussion. But the error that dooms this theory lies in the notion that aesthetical understanding (intuitive vision) is a kind of cognition, and thus of the same kind as epistemic cognition. In that way, its nature is entirely misunderstood. The older aesthetics had long enough dragged itself about with this error. In Alexander Baumgarten[16], art is still entirely a matter of a kind of *cognitio*, and even Schopenhauer[17] cannot loosen the grip of this pattern of accounting for knowledge upon his Platonizing aesthetics of ideas, even though he consciously denies its rationality.

Now of course certain elements of knowledge are contained in aesthetical beholding. Just perception through the senses, upon which the act is based, is

---

16 [Translator's note:] Alexander Gottlieb Baumgarten (1714–1762).
17 [Translator's note:] Artur Schopenhauer (1788–1860).

productive of knowledge, because perception is initially a stage upon which objects are grasped. But these elements do not constitute the peculiar nature of such beholding; they remain subordinate to it. What constitutes its peculiar nature is not even touched by those perceptual elements. That peculiar nature can be uncovered only by a detailed analysis. For here elements of the cognitive act of an entirely different kind come into play than those of cognition, elements of assessment (the so-called judgment of taste), of the capturing and retaining of the mind by its object, the devotedness to the object, and the enjoyment and rapture it causes. Intuition itself obtains here another character than it has in the domain of theory. It is far from being merely sensible looking-at. And the higher levels of beholding are no longer cognitive understanding, but present an aspect of productive creativity, which the knowledge-relationship neither knows nor can know of. Art is not a continuation of knowledge; beholding enacted by the viewer is also not such a continuation.

For its part, aesthetics is also no continuation of art. It is not a stage above it, to which art (5) must or even could rise. Aesthetics is not such a thing, any more than literature is psychology or sculpture is anatomy. Its task is in a certain sense just the opposite. Aesthetics attempts to remove the veils from the mystery that is carefully preserved by the arts. It attempts to analyze the act of beholding that enjoys its object, which can continue as long as it is not disrupted and disturbed by thinking. It makes into an object what is not an object in this act and cannot become one, the act itself. For that reason also the art object is something different for aesthetics, i.e., an object of reflection and inquiry, which it cannot be for aesthetical beholding. Here is found the reason why the attitude of the aesthetician is not an aesthetical attitude, such that it naturally follows the latter; it subordinates itself to it, but does not place itself within it, and *a fortiori* does not place itself in a position inferior to or above it.

3 Beauty as the Universal Object of Aesthetics

We may now ask: is "the beautiful" really the comprehensive object of aesthetics? Or, put another way: is beauty the universal value of all aesthetic objects – in the same way, approximately, as the good is properly the universal value of every-thing that is morally valuable? Both are usually assumed without saying so, but both have also been disputed. If one wishes to maintain them, then they must be justified.

Upon what does the objection to the central place of the beautiful in aes-thetics rest? It rests upon three kinds of considerations, in fact, upon three different objections. The first one holds that what is considered artistically successful is certainly not always beautiful; the second notes that there are classes of aesthetically valuable things that cannot be absorbed into the beautiful; and the third argues that aesthetics deals also with things that are ugly.

Of these three, we can deal most easily with the third. No doubt aesthetics has to do with the ugly, among other things. To a certain extent, it indeed belongs with all kinds of beauty. For even to beauty, limits are present everywhere, and the contrast is just as essential here as in other spheres of value. Beyond that, there are degrees of beauty, an entire scale from the perfectly beautiful to what obviously lacks beauty, but that is not a problem in itself, for it is already contained in the problem of beauty. It lies in the nature of all values that they have a counterpart in a corresponding disvalue. What must be considered is never the valuable by itself, but a value and its corresponding disvalue. The discoveries made by the analysis of value have shown us that with the character of some value the character of the corresponding disvalue is also given, and vice versa. The method of Aristotle originally rested upon that: it determined the genera of the virtues on the basis of those of "badness." And what is true in the field of ethics is valid to a great extent in aesthetics. The fundamental phenomenon, here just as there, is the entire scale, i.e., the dimension of values, in which value and disvalue are polar opposites. (6)

One problem no doubt remains as to whether, in all special dimensions of the beautiful, we find also the ugly. That is never disputed in the case of the products of men, though it has been for the products of nature. It might very well be that everything produced by nature has its beautiful aspects, even when we do not easily become conscious of them. One must keep this possibility open – in contrast with older theories, which left considerable latitude for natural deformities (e.g., Herder[18] in his *Caligone*) [*Vom Erhabenen und vom Ideal*, 1800]. But this too would change little for the problem of ugliness. It rather means only that natural constructs contain nothing ugly. That would rest upon the peculiarity of nature, e.g., upon its lawfulness or its typical forms, but not upon the nature of beauty.

But it is otherwise with the objection mentioned first: what succeeds as art is not always the beautiful. In a painting of a markedly unpretty person we distinguish as obvious and with no effort on our part the artistic qualities of the work from the appearance of the person represented by it, and, indeed, especially when the representation is unmercifully realistic. We are familiar with the same distinction in the literary representations of ineffective or repellant characters, or upon the bust of an ancient boxer with a broken and disfigured nose. And then we say

---

18 [Translator's note:] Johann Gottfried von Herder (1744–1803).

something such as this: the artistic achievement is significant, but the object is not beautiful.

An aesthetically mature person is caused no difficulties by this distinction. But one wonders on occasion: can one call the whole object "beautiful"? The represented object is surely not "made beautiful" by the representation, even one of genuine genius. And yet something of beauty is found in the work. That something of beauty lies on another level, and does not drop a veil over what is represented. It depends just upon the representation itself. It is the genuine artistically beautiful, the poetically beautiful, the beauty of drawings or paintings.

Apparently, two fundamentally different kinds of beauty and ugliness have been connected in series. And they each refer to different kinds of object. Representation in painting or literature itself has just in itself an "object," i.e., that which it represents. That is not true for all art, not for ornamental art, architecture, and music, but it is true for sculpture, painting, and the art of poetry. The object in these cases is everywhere primarily the work of the artist, the work of representation as such, as also much of what extends beyond the process of bestowing form upon it. Only subsequently does the represented object appear from behind it – not, to be sure, in the sense of temporally subsequent, but in the sense of being mediated. And the success of the work we correctly designate as its being beautiful, its failure, in its triviality or its lack of clarity (the latter is often found, for example, in literature) as being ugly. For the value or disvalue of artistic achievement lies unambiguously here and not in the qualities of what is represented. (7)

Beauty in the first and the second senses apparently vary freely against each other within a large domain. The poorly painted object of beauty seems to us, in the end, as lacking beauty, the well-painted ugly object seems to us artistically beautiful. And even in the well-painted beautiful object the two kinds of the beautiful are and remain clearly distinguishable; in the badly painted ugly object the two kinds of ugliness are distinguishable. Whoever confuses the one with the other – not only upon reflection but also in the act of beholding itself – lacks a sense of art. The skillful representation has nothing to do with embellishments; to the contrary, where such things are mixed in, they detract from beauty and even worse: the work lacks artistic beauty; it fails as art, it becomes banal, becomes kitsch.

In this sense, it is quite appropriate to retain "the beautiful" as the universal and basic value of aesthetics, and subsume under it every work of art that is well done and effective. What this state of being well done consists in remains a question of another kind. It is almost congruent with the fundamental question of the whole of aesthetics: What, precisely, is beauty? –

Of the three objections, only the second is left. It asserted: the beautiful is only one of the genera of the aesthetically worthwhile. Next to it stands the sublime, generally recognized as such in its unique independent nature. Then a series of other value-qualities enter, although their independence is not similarly conceded: the graceful, the pleasing, the touching, the charming, the comical, the tragic, and many kinds more. If one enters the individual domains of art, one will find a richness of aesthetic value-qualities of a much more specialized kind, and it is easy to find a disvalue corresponding to each of them, even when language does not always know how to call them by name.

But just because the list is so long, and because they all can claim the right to consideration in aesthetics, there must certainly also be a general value-category that encompasses them, and it must have enough space for their multiplicity. One can no doubt dispute whether it is reasonable to characterize the value-category as beauty. For "beauty" is in the end a word from everyday speech, and, as such, ambiguous. If one ignores the word-use that is found in domains external to aesthetics, then what is in dispute here is apparently always a narrower concept of beauty, one with an additional meaning. The first stands in opposition to the sublime, charming, comical, etc.; the second encompasses them all without exception – as is the case no doubt only when one understands the named designations in their purely aesthetical sense, for they all possess a non-aesthetical meaning. Such a condition may be conceded, for it is also the presupposition of the opposition to beauty in the narrow sense.

When we look upon the issue in this way, the entire dispute about meanings turns into one about words. No one can prohibit another person from understanding the concept of beauty narrowly and oppose it to those more specific concepts, but it is also true that no one (8) can command another to take the term in its broad sense, and understand it as a concept superimposed upon all aesthetic values. One must only hold tight to the meaning one has chosen, use it consistently, and not again absent-mindedly confuse it with the other.

In the following section, we will lay the foundations of the broader meaning. We will also focus on the point at which special genera force their way into the foreground. The latter will then all appear as species of the beautiful. This has the practical advantage that the most familiar aesthetical concept will be advanced as the foundational concept, and the worries about an artificially constructed and superimposed concept become nugatory.

4 Aesthetical Act and Aesthetic Object. Four-Part Analysis

The direction of our inquiry can take several routes. But they are not all equally accessible, notably not in some of the specific places where the problem occurs. All methodological procedure must be oriented toward whatever aspects of a total problem are presently accessible. In aesthetics that is of special importance, because up to now it possesses only very few useful analyses of the phenomena and the entire complex of its questions, as measured against its difficulties, has been only slightly dissected aporetically. By this observation, no criticism of the achievements of worthy researchers is implied. The situation right now simply shows how much aesthetics is still tied to its beginnings and is groping forward with carefully measured steps. For we are not lacking in daring sketches and blueprints. But they are instructive only in their errors.

Since the beautiful is essentially directed toward a beholding subject, the specific orientation of whose acts is presupposed, we are presented from the outset with two courses that might be undertaken: one could take both the object and the act whose object it is as the themes of the analysis. These could again be divided. With respect to the object, one could examine its structure and way of being, or else the character of its aesthetic value. Similarly, one could direct the analysis of the act either towards the receptive act of the observer, or towards the productive act of the creator. To what degree one could separate the directions of these courses of inquiry from each other is a question in itself, and can, for the time being, be set to one side.

In any case, four kinds of analysis result. Of those, the first three, at least, are accessible routes for the procedure, while the fourth places at the very beginning insurmountable barriers in its way. Nothing is darker and more mysterious than the work of the creative artist. Even the pronouncements of a genius about his work fail to cast any light upon its nature. Usually they prove only that he, too, knows nothing more than other men do about the miracle that was consummated in him and through him. The act of production seems to be of a kind that excludes any accompanying consciousness of itself. Therefore (9) we know only its external side, and can draw conclusions about its inner nature only from its achievements.

Conclusions of such a kind are, however, uncertain and easily slip into fantasizing. Like all inferences about metaphysical objects, they have free play; one cannot verify them, one can just as little support as refute them. In the Romantic era, attempts were made to advance in this direction; they were undertaken by poets, and were in step with the enthusiasm for the romantic joy of creativity, but they assumed a speculative picture of the world that they could not pretend to demonstrate. Even today, credulous people are seduced by such theories, but they only tend to make more mature thinkers feel skeptical.

If one is critical, and ignores all metaphysics of art, one may still take one of three remaining courses. Of them, the analysis of values is in the most difficult position, because aesthetic values, understood concretely, are highly individualized. Any classification of them according to the genera and types they bear would touch only a few of their external aspects. The systematic study of art and literature has achieved a great deal in this area. Analyses of style have been carried out; tendencies and gradations have been made visible there. We have become conscious of kinship among similar types, and important tensions among them can be properly comprehended. Yet if we look more closely, we must conclude that such characterizations concern rather the structural elements of a work of art – and similarly beauty external to art – but much less the real value-components as such.

As language no longer has any name for the latter – unless we refer to the quite superficial ones given to certain genera – so also thought has no concepts for them. Where people coin concepts for them and give them names more or less randomly, they tend not to satisfy artistic sensibility rightly. Even the concepts that are common among us today, such as the sublime, the comical, the tragic, the graceful, etc., suffer from this lack. They are highly suggestive and indispensable as structural concepts, but as value-concepts, they are silent when questions are raised that are truly germane to aesthetics. This situation corresponds to those in other areas of value, for example, the ethical. Here too the analysis can directly describe only the content, but it cannot capture value-character itself; it appeals only to the emotional sense of value – it calls it in as a witness, as it were.

There is the additional consideration that this call for a witness in aesthetics comes primarily from the beautiful itself – from the created work of the artist or even from a natural object – but the call emanating from the descriptive analysis of its structure is quite weak. Nevertheless, one must travel this road ever again, though within certain limits; it must at least be kept open. For there is no other pathway to specialized research into values. All progress along that road still remains dependent upon, and tied very tightly to, the analysis of object and act, which are not essentially related to it. (10)

This also implies that almost the entire weight of what aesthetics can achieve is borne by the two remaining means of procedure: 1) By the analysis of the structure and ontic nature of the aesthetic object and 2) By the acts of observing, beholding, and enjoying.

We will work almost entirely with these two kinds of inquiry, even where problems of value enter the discussion. It would be wrong to wish to decide matters for only one of them, for they constantly intersect each other in the aporetics of beauty. Both are fragmentary and dependent upon each other in every detail. That may cause some irregularity in the course of the inquiry; given the state of research today, that is not to be avoided. And it is the lesser evil in contrast with the terrible one-sidedness to which one necessarily falls victim when one leaps to judgment prematurely.

In a certain sense, the primary task, at least at first, belongs to the analysis of the structure of the object, just because this work is still in a primitive state, and has not kept pace with the analysis of the act, which has advanced in many branches of research.

In the nineteenth century, aesthetics was, after all, subjectively oriented, for the most part; the neo-Kantian idealism and psychologism had a large influence upon it. That led not only to errors and one-sidedness, but also to progress in the analysis of the act. In the light of its neglect, it is appropriate to develop the analysis of the object. But it would be entirely mistaken to concern ourselves only with the latter. Only with the cooperation of both can we hope to pass beyond the stagnation to which we have been maneuvered by the one-sidedness of the past.

5 Separation from and Attachment to Life

Moreover, the natural point of departure is from the object. The expression, "fine arts," which we use without thinking, is fundamentally misleading. Art itself is in no way fine, but only the work of art is. Similarly, the viewing or the enjoyment of beautiful objects is just as little to be called beautiful, regardless of whether the enjoyment was produced by art or by some feature in nature. In viewing an object, beauty exists again only in the object, despite whatever sympathy the participation of the beholding consciousness brings to it.

But from the perspective of the act, too, the object is the natural place to attack the question. It is precisely the person who views and enjoys what he sees that is attending entirely to the object he is beholding, and he may even be so lost in his appreciation that he thoroughly forgets himself. This mental act is no doubt quite different from the epistemic attitude of an aesthetician, though it has nonetheless one thing in common with him: he attends to the object in the same way. Aesthetical analysis of course does not attend to the object alone, but shifts its attention to the act, also. But it finds itself (11) primarily attending to the object – simply because it comes upon the act of viewing while attending to it.

Now in this attendance lies a problem that has concerned aesthetics from its very origins. We know it as the problem of separating the object from its connection to other objects. Very closely related to this issue is the question of the isolation of the act of beholding from the contexts of life and thought of the person. Becoming lost in an object of beauty is the same as the forgetting one's selfhood and all else in life that is present, real, important, or oppressive.

The object appears in majestic isolation away from the contexts of life; the man who submits to the impression it makes on him experiences in his own person the same isolation – from everydayness, care, life's passing trivialities, and emptiness. For him, the environing world sinks beneath the horizon, and he, along with his object, seems to make up a world apart. This phenomenon is apparently essential for the genuine enjoyment of art, and in many cases – perhaps when listening to great music – it can become so overwhelmingly powerful that, when it is over, one feels an almost painful awakening from a moment of rapture.

This state of elevation above the everyday world is a form of genuine *ek-stasis*. But since such states are experienced most strongly only by those whose nature is of a more profound sort, we have been led to the belief that it is in general the nature and task of art to create a world of rapture and elevation above life, a world that has its meaning and purpose in itself, and excludes all other interests. It would then seem possible that life serves art, but not that art serves life. For that would subordinate art to a purpose external to itself.

For us living today, such an intensification of the intrinsic value in art and in the artistic life seems rather remote. But it was not always so. Therefore, we should discuss it here. It played a great role in the "l'art pour l'art" movement, and it was not only raised to the level of theory but it also won considerable influence upon artistic sensibility and the creative process themselves.

A man of healthy sensibility sees clearly and irrefutably that an art that stands over against life with all its demands loses entirely the ground beneath its feet and is left hanging in the air. But given that this separation of life from art is erroneous, it is still not entirely transparent how art is tied to life and is empowered to resolve some problem in the spiritual situation of its contemporary world without losing its characteristic aesthetical autarchy. This aporia cannot be resolved at his point; it will be treated in other contexts. For only in an advanced stage of the analysis of the object will we find the materials needed for its resolution. Here we must merely point to the problem as such. For neither aestheticism nor an art tied to the cheap trends of the moment should have the final say. (12)

The central task is to unify the two demands correctly, that is, to unite them in a genuine synthesis. It will become apparent that there exists a much deeper tie between them; that only an art that has grown out of a lively cultural life can arrive at the creation of works that are lifted above and beyond all epochs. Similarly, only a spiritual life capable of motivating such works is in a position to bring its own current aspirations to their highest effectiveness. For spiritual creations draw their strength precisely from their ties to life, allowing them to reach the fullness of their unique nature and their genuine greatness, and it is only on the background of those ties to life that their own insular separation becomes visible; and, similarly, the opposite: only such creative works are capable of bestowing upon the life of individuals and communities an adequate consciousness of their own hidden power and depths.

6 Form and Content, Matter and Material

Nothing in aesthetics is as familiar as the concept of form. All beauty we encounter, whether in nature or in the creations of artists, presents itself as having a certain kind of form. And, as observers, we feel immediately that the slightest change in the form would necessarily destroy the work's beauty as such. The unity and wholeness of the work, its uniqueness and its self-containment depends entirely on form; and we know, without being able to prove it, that it is not a question here of the external appearance alone, is contours or borders, not even of what is visible or given to the senses, but of the inner unity and completeness of its structure, of its logical order and interconnectedness, of its being penetrated by lawfulness and necessity.

Thus, we speak of "beautiful form" as something quite familiar, and in no way problematic, but we mean very different kinds of things by it. We refer as much to the noble proportions of a sculpture as to the distribution of masses in a building, to the rhythm and succession of intervals of a melody, to the structure of an entire musical "movement" or to the artistic way scenes are arranged in a play; but no less do we refer to the play of lines about some terrain in which we stand, the heavy figure of an immense tree, the fine veins upon a leaf: and we always mean by these thing the structuring of the object from within, the form that points beyond itself, and which is essential to the whole. This has been called the "inner form" as opposed to the merely contingent external form of a thing, and in it hovers darkly the sense of the old Aristotelian "*Eidos*," which, as an active inner force, constitutes at the same time the principle of form of the outward appearance.

But what, then is "inner form"? Precisely the connection to an historically obsolete metaphysics should cause us to reflect. It would be difficult for our contemporaries to be willing to assume an ideal realm of preexisting *essentiae* for the sake of solving the problem of form in aesthetics, and to make the puzzle of how a sense of form arises in the observer with great immediacy (13) could be dependent upon such a thing. Moreover, in that way, he would come in dangerous proximity to a theoretical understanding of the problem and, with that, to the corresponding ontic structure of things. For the *Eidos* was meant as the principle of such a structure.

And even without such metaphysics, any blurring of the borderline separating the concept of form from the mere ontological relation is a threat to the aesthetical concept of it. Naturally, this concept refers to an essential relation in the structure of the thing. But that is just as valid for it as for an object of knowledge: it is valid for the organism, for the cosmos, and for the physical organization upon which it exists, for man as a character and a type, for the state, whose structures as an existing human community are completely formed from its inner depths outward. "Inner form" says too little; its content is too general and too thin.

The specifically aesthetical problem of form has therefore hardly been touched upon as yet. And how could it be otherwise? "Beautiful form" is fundamentally nothing much more than another term for beauty, thus as a definition it is almost tautological. Only when we succeed in saying in what consists the special feature of "beauty" in beautiful form can this be otherwise. Many kinds of initiatives have been taken in response. Some saw the special feature as unity, or in the harmony of the parts or members, or in the mastery of a collective multiplicity; also, more subjectively, in the pleasing quality, the immediate clarity, or even in the animation or spiritualization of what offers itself to the senses. But these efforts render only very general definitions, and all are almost empty of content if no fundamental definition with a capacity to bear these phenomena effectively stands beneath them. Some of them are not true for all cases, while others are not true for the aesthetical concept of form proper, because they attach themselves far more to all organization of things, especially the higher types.

Still more difficulties are to be found. Could it be that which bears the content of a poem, of a portrait, or of some given mood in nature is excluded from being beautiful? Or is the opinion that all so-called "content" in this sense belongs together with form? That is conceivable. But then why do people speak of form alone, while it pertains to the concept of form itself that it characterizes an opposition to all content, which is first given structure by means of form?

It is possible that these inconsistencies rest upon inconsistencies in the concept of content. Let us therefore attempt to replace it with something more determinate. The analysis of the categories gives us a starting-point for this effort. For "matter" stands complimentary to form. By this term we do not mean ontologically just anything that fills space; matter in the broadest sense is everything that is indeterminate and undifferentiated in itself, so far as it is capable of receiving form – all the way down to the bare dimensions of space and time. These two also clearly play the role of matter in the aesthetic object, as we have both spatial and temporal arts.

But in our understanding of aesthetics there is still another, more narrow, sense of matter. We mean the realm of the sensible elements over which the process of organizing ranges, in the sense that stone or clay (14) is the matter of sculpture, color is the matter of painting, tones are the matter of music. Here matter has the significance not of something ultimate or indissoluble, even less of something substantial, but only and entirely the species of the sensible elements, which, in the shaping done by the artist, receive form of a unique kind.

Now this relation is without doubt foundational for all further analyses of beauty on the side of the object. Indeed, it belongs to the very first steps of the analysis. It is thus easy to see that the entire way of bestowing form encountered in the arts depends largely on the kind of material upon which form is bestowed. The universal and the categorial "law of matter" asserts itself here; it states that on all object-domains of any kind, matter and form are together determinants, for not every kind of form is possible for any kind of material, but only certain kinds of form for specific kinds of matter. Of course, this law does not put an end to the autonomy of form in any way, but only limits it. Here the roots of the well-known phenomena of the limits of what can be represented by the individual art forms, which appeared out of the eighteenth-century dispute about the figure of Lao-coön. Sculpture cannot shape in marble all of what literature can easily represent in verbal material. These are genuine phenomena that limit and separate the domains of art, and the lawfulness of these phenomena, once discovered, cannot be in any way denied.

In its complete opposition to matter as a principle that indicates the scope of domains, the aesthetical concept of form obtains its first clear definition. And this can be easily maintained throughout all domains of the arts, for it so happens that every one of its domains has its specific matter. Indeed, one may say that the entire classification of the fine arts primarily depends upon the differences in matter. But to some extent, the principle of differentiation functioning here reaches even into the broad domain of beauty beyond that of the arts.

Nevertheless, this relation concerns only one side of the concept of form. This can be already seen in the fact that it is precisely the element of "content" in a work of art, i.e., what one inadequately designates by the term, which is not absorbed by such a concept of matter as this; indeed, it is hardly touched by it. Therefore, there must be another concept opposed to form if the concept of content is to have any clear meaning for us at all.

This second opposition is clearly present everywhere that there is a question of representation, where, in other words, the bestowal of form consists in making something visible to the senses that exists or could exist in the world this side of art. Thus, literature represents human conflicts, passions, and destinies, sculpture the forms of bodies, and painting almost everything that is visible. These domains of content are in themselves not artistic, only the bestowal of form by the arts makes them so. But they are the ones that give the "themes" for such bestowal, the "*sujet*," hence in this sense the "material" that is brought into the presence of eyes and mind by the creative artist. (15)

"Material" in this sense is not found in all the arts, not, for example, in music (at least not in pure music), not in architecture, not in ornamental art. Its concept becomes questionable only in the domain of natural beauty. But it is certainly a constitutive element for the representational arts, including literature, and that fact, despite these examples, is sufficient to secure the concept a place in aesthetics. But then it must be valid at least for these specific arts that the category of form appears in them as a double state of opposition: on one side, to the matter "in" which form is bestowed, on the other, to the material "which" they give form. Clearly, there must exist here a specifiable relation between the bestowal of form in the first and the second senses.

The problem that now becomes apparent has broad implications. Solving it with a single blow would be hard to achieve. Are there in fact two kinds of bestowal of form in one and the same construct? Must not the bestowal of form upon matter and bestowal of form upon material be one and the same thing? And yet, is the first not only distinguishable from the second, but even essentially different from it? If, on the one hand, a writer bestows form upon characters and lived destines, while on the other he gives shape to the words by giving them expression, it is clear that the former can never be identical with the latter. In the created work, however, perhaps in a well-formed and executed play, both grow together to form a unity in such wise that they appear not only as inseparable, but are given as a single bestowal of form that expresses itself on two sides.

Is that an illusion, or does such simultaneous two-sided bestowal of form exist? The latter might mean that one and the same bestowal masters two kinds of unformed or potentially formable things. It might be that precisely in this two-sided relation the mystery of beauty as such can be understood – and if we cannot succeed entirely all at once, still perhaps we can solve an essential part of it.

Now it is obvious that in this case the category of form itself might not be adequate for such a task, and in its place would come categories of the structure of the object that allow us to understand the characteristic interweaving of two apparently heterogeneous relations, and their joining forces in the unity of a manifest multiplicity – or rather in the manifest unity of two multiplicities.

7 Intuition, Enjoyment, Assessment, and Productivity

While the problem of the aesthetic object, even in the first analysis of its external features, has shown its considerable complexity and allows us to suspect the presence of background elements that can of course be felt by an observer but not be grasped by him, the second problem of the responsive act reveals itself to be no less complicated.

Just the fact alone that there is more than one name for it points to that complexity. For every name corresponds to an essential aspect of the act, but these essential aspects are no less heterogeneous than those of the object. (16) In the act there can be clearly distinguished, at a minimum, the elements of intuition, of enjoyment, and of assessment. Of these, that of enjoyment is the most peculiar, but it is also the one most distinct from acts of the same spiritual height and individuality.

This element has long been familiar. Plotinus[19] was the first to recognize it, and Kant held fast to it almost exclusively in his Analytic of Beauty. He had the expression for it: delight and pleasure. He chose both terms consciously as the contradictories of the intellectual attitude. But both were strictly oriented towards the object and were so understood that they included reference to the element of reception. Indeed, they were intended also to contain the element of assessment. For what Kant calls the "judgment of taste" is nothing other than the expression of the pleasure that we feel before things of beauty, and not a second act that goes with it.

One can, accordingly, find in Kant's aesthetics the unification of all three sides of aesthetical receptivity. But too little was done to differentiate them. Instead, a fourth element makes a powerful entrance in the background of the receptive attitude, that of autonomous engagement or of spontaneous achievement, which stands opposite to the devotional and self-forgetful attitude of enjoyment, and the receptive act seems thereby to approach the act of the productive artist. In Kant, this took the form of a reactive engagement, a "play of the powers of the mind," of the "imagination," and of the "understanding," which proceeds according to its own inner laws and has the clear character of an inward re-creation of the original creation of the artist, but re-created solely in the act of beholding.

In the nineteenth century, these Kantian doctrines were often taken up and imitated in different ways; people found many things to alter and improve in them. They did not go far beyond them. The most significant work by them was the assimilation of the act of assessment to that of enjoyment, or, as Kant expressed it, of the "judgment" to the "delight." A well-known and central doctrine of this analysis consisted in the demonstration that aesthetical satisfaction lays a claim to universal validity (for all subjects), but does not attempt to base this claim upon a "concept." This generality "without concepts" is unique in Kantian philosophy; and for that reason it has always attracted the special attention of his followers. And in fact there is present here a fundamental and essential part of the strange interweaving of acts in the aesthetically attentive consciousness.

But what is insufficient in this doctrine is the aspect of intuitive beholding, which once stood higher than all others in the intuitive aesthetics of Plato and Plotinus. The act of beholding a thing is precisely the most important part of this

---

19 [Translator's note:] Plotinus (204/5–270 CE).

interweaving of acts, or at least the element that bears it. Delight or enjoyment and the value judgment that lies within them have more the character of a reaction to the impression received in the act of beholding; they are responsive act-elements, and therefore are not the first in the entire warp and woof of acts. They can (17) appear only where what is given in the form of a picture is already there, for they are thus mediated by an act of reception. And it can hardly be doubted that this receptive act is of an intuitive kind.

To this corresponds even the well-established expression, "aesthetical." The word means nothing but "of the senses"; what is intended along with it is that the external senses, eyes and ears, are the receptive tools of beauty. But with that, its opposition to intellectual comprehension is simply characterized once more. And yet the senses are not brought in simply as mediators of something already present, as in everyday perception, but rather as the stimulus for a process of a higher order that can only begin with it. The meaning of this relationship is evident as soon as we reflect that what is intended here is the element of genuine "intuition" within the activity of the senses. This is not the same thing as receptivity, but it is indissolubly tied to it only in perception. Yet perception retains the clarity of intuition even where it is built into a larger context of acts by which receptivity is entirely swamped – as happens almost always within the structure of knowledge.

It does not lose this character of intuition even in the quite different structure possessed by acts of aesthetical observation. It is just here that it comes dominant; a large class of elements characteristic of intuition, which are concealed in the knowledge-relation by the latter's claims to ontological knowledge and purposely passed over, turn out to be essential here. Light and shadow are for knowledge only a means to recognize the shapes of things, and are hardly noticed; in the viewing of drawing and painting they take on objective independence and become the main focus. That is also valid for perspective, for colors, and for color contrasts. Similar things can be said about other areas of aesthetical receptivity and understanding. The writer also ties himself to what in life are unnoticed and imponderable features of human movement and gesture, and, if he is unable to offer them to our eyes, he lets them appear to our inner visions via a detour through words.

But even with that, we have not exhausted intuition; its role extends further. Seeing by the senses is only half of aesthetical seeing. Above the former, a viewing of a second order arises by the agency of the sense-impressions, but it is not absorbed by them, and, with respect to the act, is clearly independent of them. This other kind of viewing is not, as it may seem, a beholding of essence, not the Platonic grasping of some general principle, not intuition in the sense of some higher level of knowledge. Rather, it always attends entirely upon the individual object in its uniqueness and individuality, but it sees upon it what the senses cannot grasp directly. Upon a landscape it sees the elements of mood, upon a human being the element of his mental state, his suffering or passion; upon a scene playing out before it, it sees the element of conflict. Whether this is true of all aesthetical understanding, we may leave to one side. For art, in the narrow sense, and for the (18) clear-sighted viewing of the beauty in life and in nature, it may well be true as a whole. And we must orient ourselves toward those central domains of aesthetical phenomena.

It is important before all else that this beholding, or viewing of a second order, not be thought of simply as supplementary, a matter of an afterthought that could at times be absent. No doubt it may occasionally happen that what constitutes a work of art or an attractive human face may open itself to this beholding only gradually, but that is to a great extent true for first-order viewing also, and may not, therefore, be considered as a special character in contrast to the former. Rather, the characteristic we find is that the second order is firmly tied to the first order, beholding to viewing, and must always be there with it, at least at the start, if it is later to push itself forward and deepen. But in many cases, the relation is turned around, such that the focus moves from beholding back to viewing of the sensible details, as if those needed some special attention, a need that was first provoked by the weight and significance of the act of beholding.

Whatever the nature of this act of beholding, it is not to be discerned before the analysis of the object. That will therefore become the topic of a later inquiry. But we can draw some implications even at this point that will give an authoritative measure to all that follows: in the aesthetical receptive act two kinds of vision lie in sequence; and it is just the collaboration of both that constitute what is specific to the attitude appropriate to seeing artistically.

From this position, it is also easy to see that both kinds of looking-at form an indivisible whole, in that they interpenetrate each other in various ways, and condition each other mutually. It may, therefore, be expected that neither one nor the other will be the bearer of enjoyment (of "delight") and of judgments of taste concerning the object, but always only both together in their interpenetration.

From this position, too, some light falls for the first time on the impact of spontaneity in the structure of the receptive acts. For here there is latitude for the inward productive attitude, whose presence we darkly sense in the receptive act that is executed by the observer, but we do not know how to specify in detail. Beholding, the second-order form of looking, is apparently creative, at least secondarily. What it beholds is not given to perception, but is only occasioned by it; moreover, it is spontaneously motivated. It consists for that reason simply as a representation for intuitive consciousness – concrete and variegated as is always what we experience – yet not experienced, but rather spontaneously produced (by the "imagination" as Kant says); it is a piece of sleight-of-hand by fantasy, yet firmly tied to the sensible impression.

There is an attempt at explicating this inward relation of the twofold looking-at in the *Critique of the Power of Judgment*. A "play of the powers of the mind," Kant called it, and thereby grasped the characteristic unity (19) of the opposed powers of consciousness. But he characterized both "powers" that were in question as "imagination and understanding" and in that way reached too high along the vertical series of our "faculties." He distanced himself too far from the senses. For clearly, one member of the double looking-at has a sensible nature. The other should not be characterized as much as an intellectual capacity, as the expression "understanding" suggests. If one assumes that grasping something is a function of the understanding, then the intuitive nature of the second member would be annulled. It would therefore be better to leave the understanding to one side, and understand the interplay as one of sensible and supersensible vision, where the latter is not a mysterious sinking into the sea, but means simply spontaneous, inward, and productive beholding that adds something new to what is immediately given to the senses. For this, Kant's "imagination" is in fact the adequate expression.

However that may be, we can hold fast for the time being to the switching back and forth between the two kinds of viewing, for it is indeed foundational for the entire structure of the receptive act executed upon the aesthetical standpoint. Viewing through the senses is the first conditioning element, inward beholding the second; the latter is conditioned by the first, but then the two enter into a relation of reciprocal conditioning. Thus only with the onset of beholding is viewing through the senses lifted out and above everyday perception and receives from it a special aesthetical character. Further, both together make up the supporting act-elements called delight, pleasure, or enjoyment, as far as these three can appear only where the inward enlightenment of these senses occurs by means of a supersensible beholding. And again: provided this enlightenment and becoming enlightened in viewing are not themselves sensed as one of the elements of that act – whose relation is concealed from the beholding consciousness – but rather as a relation among elements or strata of the objet to which the act-elements are correlated, will the object viewed appear as beautiful.

The aesthetical judgment gives expression to this appearing-beautiful. Assessment as an element of the act is likewise supported by the interpretation of the twofold viewing. And that cannot be otherwise, where delight itself is also supported by precisely this interpenetration. For a judgment of taste is only the intellectual expression of that which delight makes directly present to our senses.

8 Beauty in Nature, Human Beauty, and Beauty in Art

Not a few inquiries have been made under the heading of aesthetics that are in reality only philosophy of art. That is understandable, for it is in the arts where the fundamental questions of beauty and our grasp of it appear to have the greatest promise, and are for that reason usually more readily analyzable. One who is oriented to the arts also usually brings along a prejudice in favor of artistic beauty, of a kind, perhaps, such that from the outset it seems to him to be the higher form of beauty. Usually we find even today a certain (20) exaggeration of the value of art on the part of those who understand some things about it. And, then, of course, all beauty that comes from nature will be inadvertently assigned a lower rank.

Obviously, such opinions represent an extreme. No one would deny that value-elements of a unique kind appear in the arts that are lacking in all other forms of beauty. After all, it is the skill of the artist himself that constitutes the real meaning of the word "art"; we experience this element upon the artwork as the artist's craftsmanship, and we admire it as a genuine value-quality. That does not, however, justify considering the absence of these qualities in beauty outside of art to be a deficiency in them.

Thus, we must first take our point of departure from beauty in general, regardless of when and where it appears. And to that end, natural and human beauty must take up a position of equality next to works of art.

It is no doubt common to speak in this context only of nature. But man, too, and much that is within the sphere of his life and behavior has an aesthetical aspect; man is, after all, not only a part of nature, but also the possessor of an entire spiritual world, which is superimposed upon the natural realm. And if it is true that aspects of character and morality in our actions and attitudes essentially make up human beauty, it does not follow at all that aesthetics turns into ethics, and the beautiful into the good. Human beauty can also be found in the play of the passions, even where they are uninhibited and can in no way be called good. Conflicts and struggle, suffering and defeat, produce dramatic tension and release, not only, to be sure, for the writer, who seeks them out as material in order to bestow artistic form upon them, but simply for anyone living a life who is able to bring the distance and peace required to see them in their natural drama. It is very probable that the onstage drama exists only because there is a drama in life, which can, just as such, affect us aesthetically. That is even truer of the comical in life, which likewise flourishes and has its effect upon us even without being reworked formally in literature. There are humorists without a pen, planted right in the middle of life, and not just where they manifest themselves in striking aphorisms; it depends upon an inner attitude, on a way of seeing and living, on the sense for the all-too-human. The unintended comedy in human life becomes visible by depending on a certain orientation of the observer, on his distance, his ability to stand above it, and on the pleasure he takes in it. The man taking part in or affected by the comedy of life will find it hard to meet these conditions.

The entire domain of possible aesthetic objects is thereby extended considerably. One may seriously ask whether, if that is so, there are any objects in the world at all that fail to have an aesthetical aspect. If we must assent to that, and all entities come under the rubrics of (21) "beautiful" and "ugly," then it becomes necessary once again to separate out of this multitude those things that have a right to aesthetical evaluation in a more narrow and specific sense.

To achieve that, it is not sufficient to reserve only the narrower precinct for the work of art and to skim off everything else from it. Works of art may also turn out to have little value; they can be subject to critical attack by reference to what the artist was trying to achieve, and works of nature can have high aesthetic value and be quite convincing beyond all measure. But there is more. The question arises whether the ugly or the vapid are to be sought only in the realm of art, namely in artistic failures, and whether everything in nature is beautiful. And one can question further whether all of that is not true for the domain of humanity. Perhaps the incapacity to see beauty everywhere lies only in deficiency of the observer's sense for different kinds of beauty. If Herder used the example of the "loathsome crocodile" as proof of ugliness among the forms of living things, the claim seems rather subjective to us today. The case of human faces and figures is similar: classical epochs of sculpture and painting created certain ideals of beauty that exerted a dominant influence on tastes for hundreds of years, and whatever did not meet those ideals was counted as ugly. But other tastes and epochs came along, and other ideal types became the norm. All norms of such kind have shown themselves to be historically conditioned, transient, and relative. With what right, therefore, do we living assume that just because the forms we meet with in life displease us they should therefore be thought ugly?

With questions of this kind, we straightaway reach a form of relativism in aesthetic values. And then it may appear that beauty is an inconstant and arbitrary norm that is conditioned by factors external to aesthetics, i.e., by social conditions, the dominant practical interests of a time, by what is useful for life, or also by the tendencies in our preferences that might have arisen out of our biological nature, which then attempts to give those tendencies expression in the form of certain ideals.

We must recognize the fact of fluctuation in history without reservation. One need not ignore phenomena of this kind to realize that with such fluctuations and other phenomena of that kind the essence of beauty is not affected; rather what is affected are the historical forms it takes. Thus we are left with the quite fundamental question of whether ugliness exists in the domain of nature, even if our sense of natural beauty varies considerably and appears in history relatively late.

This question too, will be treated in its proper place. Specifically, it will take the form of whether, in the diversity of our sense of nature, conditioned historically as it is, something that is held in common and basic to all such sensibility may be found that is objectively constitutive for a "sense of beauty" in general. Today we have certain means of access to such a phenomenon, but this access is such that intellectualistic and psychologistic aesthetics cannot find them. They lie (22) in the domain of recent developments in ontology and anthropology and point back to certain relationships among foundational categories. In general, on the side of content, the question of natural beauty borders on research in natural philosophy, which is today in a very painful state; similarly the problem of human beauty borders on the problem of anthropology. In this case as in the other, one must beware of blurred borders between disciplines, but one must also not allow the respect for disciplinary borders to go so far as to separate violently what is related.

To stay on the only feasible route, from which many dead ends split off, may in fact be a task of great difficulty. The old ontological ideas of perfection that the nineteenth century falsely assumed everywhere would scarcely help us here. But it is conceivable to dig out of it a useful nugget of an idea that could be salvaged by a new kind of analysis informed by phenomenology. The general place of departure for such an effort will appear as soon as it becomes clear that so-called "nature" does not consist in a system of laws, but in a hierarchy of structures whose fabric is derived from an inner unity and wholeness, regardless of whether they possess a merely dynamic or organic character.

The arrangements of such natural fabrics are variable, subject to disruption and destruction, and every disruption is something negative, something also perceptible in feeling as negative, as a palpable *modus deficiens*, both objectively upon the thing and subjectively in intuition. Here space is given for the appearance of ugliness in the realm of nature. Of course, the presupposition for this is the existence of an immediate sensible-intuitive consciousness, both of what is intact and complete, and of any disruption of these forms.

But of course, that would have to be established within certain limits, during the course of an appropriate analysis of the phenomena.

9 Idealistic Metaphysics of Beauty. Intellectualism and the Focus on Material Content

With that, the question of procedure once again appears in the foreground. Not that it is possible to sketch out a methodology in advance. Rather we must hold fast to the insight that the consciousness of method is always secondary in comparison to a live and working method that focuses only upon its object.[20] But of course there are certain preliminary questions that can be settled upon on the basis of the historical experience of a variety of attempts and efforts. Given the current retrograde state of aesthetics, these questions have not been sufficiently treated beyond what the above fourfold analysis has achieved.

So young as aesthetics is, it already incorporates a series of very different tendencies that are not exhausted by the two contrasted analyses of act and object. (23) As early as in Baumgarten and Kant[21], these two analyses were inextricably linked to each other. In Schelling, Hegel, and Schopenhauer, both are lowered almost down to the level of mere elements for the sake of some fundamental metaphysical conception. The center of concern was transferred to the arts, which then celebrated the momentous triumph of their superior status, and the beauty of nature this side of the arts sank to an affair of second rank.

That had its basis in the far more general metaphysics of idealism, and especially in the role assigned to the arts in the whole of the life of the spirit. If an "unconscious intelligence" or an "absolute reason" lies at the foundation of all existing things, then the works of nature are one-sided articulations of this reason; and yet if the life of the spirit is the self-consciousness of this same reason realizing itself in stages, then the arts, too, can be nothing but the stages of this self-consciousness: not the highest stage, to be sure, for the arts are tied to the senses, but for our limited human nature they are indispensable, and cannot be replaced by understanding. No doubt for Schelling the relation was turned around, because he assigned to intuition a higher rank than to conceptual understanding, and in the end elevated intuition to the universal instrument of all philosophy. Therewith the artist becomes not only a visionary but also the bearer of the destiny of spirit; the philosopher, for his part, becomes the model artist, as is appropriate for the ideal of romanticism. Hegel, in contrast, continued to maintain the superiority of the concept, and considered it a deficiency of art that it did not break through to the conceptual level. That makes sense only when one

---

20 Cf. for this point *Aufbau der realen Welt* [*The Construction of the Real World*], 2nd edition, 1950, Chaps. 62a, b.
21 [Translator's note:] Immanuel Kant (1724–1804).

grants the idea upon which this idealism is based, that is, the existence of the Absolute at the foundation of all reality, which, in the creation of art, comes to consciousness in the form of a clear and intuitable image.

This metaphysics of beauty is relatively indifferent to the other aspect of the presupposition of idealism: that the Absolute must be a "rational" principle. That is proved by Schopenhauer's aesthetics, which is built upon the same schema, but which places at the foundation of things a world-will bereft of reason and intelligence. Indeed, precisely at this point, the entire picture becomes transparent, because not only consciousness but intelligence, too, is the possession of man. In this theory, ancient Platonism enjoys a late rebirth: nature is a realm firmly stamped with Forms; an "idea" lies at the root of every species of organized thing, and individual cases take shape according to the idea peculiar to that species. The arts allow these ideas to appear in each individual work, and this appearance is a glimmer of beauty. Music reaches even deeper, for it does not imitate any object-like forms, but brings the original nature of things, the "world will" to direct expression. But in its entirety, this theory, too, assimilates the achievement of the arts to a consciousness of what already exists in itself entirely without the arts.

This last idea is unquestionably a remainder of the intellectualism that from ancient times infected thoughts about aesthetics; not, to be sure, an intellectualism in the narrow sense, which reduces everything to thought, concepts and (24) judgments, but surely an intellectualism in the broad sense that understands aesthetical beholding as a kind of cognition. Schelling's promotion of intuition above the conceptualization does not affect this error at all. The basic thesis is entirely indifferent to the order of rank of the kinds and levels of cognition, for the knowledge-schema remains the same in all these formulations; it is tied firmly, as it were, to the aesthetical act, even when the theory itself tries, however hard, to protect itself from that bond by means of subordinate distinctions.

More important in this matter is a second element. Theories of beauty that correctly understand the act of beholding by analogy with knowledge are by nature primarily focused upon the content of the arts, and for this reason cannot do justice to the element of form, that is, to everything that is genuinely structural and sculptural in artistic creations. This criticism does not speak for a separation of "form and content"; that will in any case have sufficient justification when new inquiries demonstrate that the specifically artistic content consists precisely in the bestowal of form. But these metaphysical theories of art are far from such an insight. Rather, they take the element of content to be the pre-given "material," just in the sense mentioned above of the theme or *sujet*. Of course then the material element is itself extended and enlarged; it is raised to the level of a metaphysical world-view.

But that does not change at all the fact that the matter of bestowing form in art – and, we may add to that, precisely by the total inward formal structure itself – comes short of the mark. At least it must be admitted that the significance of the autonomy and intrinsic value of form, as are characteristic of every artistic achievement, has not been understood. Any number of examples from the wide-reaching aesthetics of Hegel can be given for that; his interpretation of the idea of tragedy in the case of Sophocles' *Antigone* is known worldwide, where the conflict is understood as a purely moral one between the written and the unwritten law.

Giving a central role to the "thematic" element is closely connected to the widespread notion that in all art the process of creation is a function of moral and religious life. This conception is not tied to specific epochs and theories; it is as much alive today as it was 150 years ago. We must not forget that historically the greatest art has usually grown upon the soil of a highly developed religious life; indeed, it was at first developed as a direct expression of it. The implications that have been drawn from this fact, however, are doubtful, and remind us dubiously of the Hegelian metaphysics of spirit. For then it appeared as though this relation is not only a principle constitutive of all art, but is also the inward principle of artistic productivity itself. But then, of course, the problem of aesthetical form is pushed to one side, and the autonomy of aesthetic values becomes problematic. (25)

Of all this, what alone can be salvaged is that artistic production tends to grow more readily where men are moved by great ideas, and the passion for ideas demands expression – one might rather say, demands objectivation. That is true for every highly developed spiritual life, once it is awakened. Religious life, more than all others, is dependent upon art as a means of expression, precisely because its content lies beyond what can be communicated directly. The arts have the magic wand that gives shape to what cannot be grasped; they achieve what mere words and formulas – for example, dogma – cannot; they bring close to the senses what is supersensible and incapable of being seen, and thereby bestow upon the hearts of men the kind of power that only what is felt as close and present can give. Religious life, once awakened, can do not otherwise than call for art, and so it does, and fills it with its deepest impulses, its passion, its ideas.

But art, once awakened, finds other things in the world that call out to it: moral and social life with its conflicts and its sense of destiny, the depths of the human heart with its needs, its struggles, with its inexhaustible variety, found in each unique individual; and then at last the realm of nature with its incomprehensible wonders. For the spiritual nature that is man, the spiritual life has by far the greatest actuality. Its circle of themes therefore stands in first place for men; their inner urge to realize them is the strongest.

But the bestowal of form itself in the arts, which satisfies that inner urge, is and remains for that reason something quite different, and can in no way be understood simply on the basis of what may condition its material. It also cannot be understood on these terms even if in fact the spiritual impulse to bestow form must be sought in the material alone.

10 The Aesthetics of Form and of Expression

It is understandable that the reaction against these metaphysical dealings with the content of art would eventually go to the opposite extreme. Some reflected upon the independence of artistic form, and tried then to understand beauty by means of purely formal principles. In this way, people aimed, in a quite consistent manner, at the structural elements of beautiful objects, especially in works of art. The method of research is, in itself, just as much objectivistic as the material procedure, but it saw the essence of the object not in something prior that is then represented, but in the special qualities of the representation itself. But in this way, of course, we came not one significant step closer to the essence of beauty.

Nonetheless, one must immediately note that this task presents itself as infinitely more difficult than one might have imagined at the outset. For only now men stood before the real puzzle of beauty, and the means of inquiry that one had to apply were quickly seen as insufficient for the task. They merely sketched out the problem, but could not penetrate very far into its depths. One might say that only here (26) does it become apparent how, in general, very little aesthetical form is an object of possible knowledge.

Today, when we look back on these recent failures, we are tempted to cry out: "How could it be otherwise! After all, is not form given only to intuition and not to conceptual understanding?" But that was not so obvious and certain, not to say self-evident, to those who got themselves ready for this new undertaking. And so it happened that, at first, elements external to aesthetics were called upon to fill in some way the gap in understanding that had now become apparent. Yet these thinkers could not get beyond the most general characterizations: harmony, rhythm, symmetry, the order of the parts of the whole, the unity in diversity, and many designations like these. Concepts of this type are enumerated in a nearly exhaustive manner and varied in order to track down the secret of beauty from the side of the object. One cannot fail to recognize something that is correct here, but only in the direction taken. But it is easy to see that the designations are much too general, and that in the end they brush only the surface of what in the qualities of form is specifically aesthetical in nature. Unity in diversity belongs to every work of nature, as well as the order of the parts, and in many other cases symmetry, also. Harmony and rhythm, in contrast, provided that they assert something different from the first two, are borrowed from the circle of phenomena of one of the arts, music (which is of course the prototype of all pure beauty of form); they are therefore tautologous in relation to that form of art without being exhaustive of it, but they are valid for the other arts only by analogy, and for that reason they are, of course, even less exhaustive.

The enormous variety of forms in the arts, and a similar variety in the beauties of nature, have not been touched upon as yet by any of the preceding. Yet the real problem of form begins just here. This problem starts with the question: why, then, are quite specific forms in the visible world (or what can be represented by means of organized speech) beautiful while others only slightly different from them are not? For ugliness is not simply that which is without form, but that which, although intended as determinate form, misses the mark, or fails. The main element is thus lacking, despite worthy attempts, and it is questionable whether the correct way to find them is on the road heretofore taken.

It is not more promising when one defines aesthetical form as expression. For the question immediately arises, "of what" it is supposed to be the expression. The answers given are like these: expression of life, expression of the soul, expression of the human, the spiritual, the significant, even expression of meaning, of purpose, or of value. Even these are possibilities that one cannot simply discard. Clearly, they hold true for many aspects of beauty in and out of the arts. But hardly for all things beautiful. In addition, we must reflect upon three issues. First, the phenomenon of expression is also to be met with outside of aesthetics, e.g., in everyday language, in gesture and facial expression. Second, not all expression is beautiful, even when it (27) is intended as such by the artist. And thirdly, with the question of what the expressed content may be, we are again turned away from the question of form to that of material. The problem of form itself, therefore, is not done justice in this way.

It is also not helpful to say that it is a question of form in unity with the substance, something like a question of the "appropriateness of the form to the content" (Wilhelm Wundt[22]), or the "form of the idea in a real manner of appearance."[23] For one would rather be told what the "appropriateness" consists in, how it stands with the unification of the form with the content, or what in fact brings the "form of the idea" into appearance. Systematic theoretical work in the individual arts has been carried further in this direction: Hanslick[24] in music, Adolf von Hildebrand[25] in the fine arts. Certainly, from the perspective of the problem of style in the arts and in epochs of art much can be also learned concerning the

---

22 [Translator's note:] Wilhelm Wundt (1832–1920).
23 [Translator's note:] Translation E.K.
24 [Translator's note:] Eduard Hanslick (1825–1904).
25 [Translator's note:] Adolf von Hildebrand (1847–1921).

nature of form and expression. Yet the advantage here is borrowed from the disadvantage of specialization, and one increases one's distance ever more from what is foundational as one delves more concretely into specifics.

Thus here as everywhere in aesthetics we come up against the same methodological difficulties: the phenomenon is present only in the single individual case, but the universal principle cannot be grasped in the individual case, and, where the latter can be grasped, the phenomenon is torn asunder and destroyed. That is the reverse of the situation that was apparent right at the beginning: where vision is intact, there is no understanding, and where understanding begins, vision is disturbed. How may we pass beyond this negative dialectical relation? Only further inquiry can teach us.

What in fact is hidden in the principle of "expression" ought rather to be a relationship of appearance, and indeed one of a peculiar kind. But it requires the appearance neither of an "idea," nor of life, nor of a meaning. Rather, what is specific to an object we think beautiful will have to be sought in the type of appearance itself. Then, however, we will have free latitude for a different type of concept of form, one specific to aesthetical phenomena. For the question here must touch in some way the form of appearance as such. And we may expect that entirely different rules of the game will be valid for it than for other phenomena in which form is bestowed.

11 Psychological and Phenomenological Aesthetics

Running parallel to the objective and formal interpretation of beauty, but partly in opposition to it and partly united with it by surprising turns of phrase, is the development of a conception that is psychological and subjective. This belongs to the general movement called psychologism, and shares with it the tendency to reduce everything to psychic processes. Given the difficulties that the analysis of form encounters, it is quite understandable that for a time the future of aesthetics seemed to be in its hands. (28)

Naturally, it is a question here only of the analysis of the act. But that is not yet the essence of the matter; without the analysis of the act, no progress in aesthetics is possible at all. The weight lies rather on the claim that the aesthetic object and its values can be explicated from the nature of the act. Theodor Lipps[26], for example, understood the object as entirely dependent upon the observer, specifically in such a way that the object is completely penetrated by

---

26 [Translator's note:] Theodor Lipps (1851–1914).

the activity of the subject; it becomes an aesthetic object only when a person, in his own inward activity, "empathizes" with it, and thereby experiences himself in it. Beauty is accordingly the quality that the object attains for the observer by means of this empathy. The enjoyment of beauty, however, is in the end a self-enjoyment of the ego, naturally an indirect enjoyment, and one brokered by the object into which the ego enters empathetically.

Alongside of this theory of empathy one can place a long list of additional conceptualizations, which are similar in their main principle that beauty does not consist in a condition in the object, neither in its form nor in its content, but rather in an attitude, activity, or state of the subject. Of course, these formulations seem more subjectivist than they are intended to be, because according to the psychologism that was dominant in those days, the idea that the object is carried by the act was taken as self-evident. But the enormous difficulty that was created in fact by this view cannot be lessened by its apparent obviousness. That difficulty lies in how it is possible to ascribe the execution of one's intentional acts to the object as its value-quality and then enjoy that quality as its own. For what is beautiful in this entire situation is not the ego and its activities, but the object alone.

Theories of this kind tend always to become more complicated and artificial the more they reflect upon the phenomena that are actually given and then try to do justice to them. This is what happened to psychologistic aesthetics: it had to be reconstructed, improved, and reapplied, for without that, one could not progress in any meaningful way. That the theory had arrived at the dead end that its opponents predicted, became obvious to all – of course, without anyone being able to state the real reasons of this failure.

One thing will not be misunderstood today, thanks to a sufficiency of historical distance that we now enjoy: there exists as a matter of fact a certain kind of dependency of the aesthetic object upon the beholding subject, and this dependency, which even in the time of Kant was seen and disputed, was quite obscured by the theory of empathy, but at the same time it had been brought into the light and made an object of possible discussion. For this much became clear about it: beauty is not, like ontic characteristics, attributed to things independently of the manner of seeing and the perceptive powers of the subject, but is entirely determined by a very specific standpoint or inner attitude that is different for each form of art and even, to some extent, for every individual object. (29)

What one learned from this was something fundamental and permanent. It is connected only loosely to any specific psychological interpretation and does not at all stand or fall with the latter. It asserts that no beauty in itself exists, but only beauty "for someone," and that the aesthetic object itself, whether in nature or in art, is such an object not in itself, but only "for us"; and that too only provided that we bring to it a definite inward receptive orientation, whether one understands that orientation as a kind of attitude or as a kind of active doing. We do not, for this reason, have to become immediately victims of subjectivism, whether of an idealistic or a psychologistic kind, for the subjectivity of beauty is not asserted by it, but rather a certain kind of mutual conditioning by the subject. That mutuality is consistent with the objective demands of an aesthetics of form, and indeed perhaps only with such a synthesis of those two will the emergence of a uniform picture become possible.

If we look from these questions back to Kant, we find the basic conception quite precisely but inchoately sketched in his Analytic of Beauty. It lies in the "play of the powers of the mind." The object itself appears as beautiful or not provided this play takes place. One may ask oneself why this thought did not establish itself in aesthetics immediately. But there is an understandable reason for it: in Kant, the object of knowledge, i.e., the "things," without any distinctions among them, are all conditioned by the co-activity of the subject. That is the nature of "transcendental idealism." Thus according to the theory, these conditions make no distinction between the "empirically real object" and the beautiful object. And even if the contribution of the subject is essentially different in the two cases, the fundamental situation, it holds, is the same. The way of seeing typical of idealism itself was the reason the opposition in question became blurred, and the difference in the ontology of the aesthetic object was never done justice. Idealism – even one as carefully considered as transcendental idealism – is not the ground upon which one can work out in theory such ontological differences. We see precisely here that without careful distinctions of this kind (in the end differences in ontology) we cannot approach the problem of form in aesthetics.

The thought of an appropriate synthesis of subjectivist and objectivist readings was not lacking in doctrinal disputes. In a certain sense, it was found also in the aesthetics of "expression," such as that represented by Benedetto Croce[27]: the act is not expression, but rather the object; its expression does not exist in itself, but "for" a subject that understands it. So it is also with beauty: it is not the beholding that is beautiful, also not the skill involved in its production, but the object alone – yet not taken as it is for itself, but only for a beholding subject who is in a special state of devotional appreciation.

There remains something for this analysis of the act to undertake, something that only it can achieve, and that indeed, notwithstanding the special task of the analysis of the object, towards which, moreover, the former analysis must rather be appropriately accommodating. That both (30) go their own way with a certain

---

27 [Translator's note:] Benedetto Croce (1866–1952).

amount of independence, taking their point of departure from different sides of the total phenomenon, may be a priceless advantage. For in just this way all things that are compatible or even render mutual support to each other gain a justification that approaches the notion of a criterion of truth.

If we reflect upon this problematic in a relatively unprejudiced manner, that is, not from the position of one or the other theories that had worked within it, but rather by distancing ourselves from their intentions, we will not be able to conceal that, as a whole, the situation has seen some quite favorable developments. The question is now how they are to be assessed. And it must be observed that far too little has been done in this direction. The advances that have been recorded since the beginning of the century have gone off in one or another direction without recognizing either the task of synthesis or the advantage that it offers.

The most significant of these advances was initiated by phenomenology. In this manner of inquiry the methodological conditions of possible success were at least to be found. For nothing could assist us here except the tendency to approach the phenomena themselves as closely as possible, to grasp them more precisely than had been done up to then, to learn to see them in all their diversity, and only then to return once more to the more general questions. If phenomenology, during the first decades of our century when it came to blossom so astonishingly, had been able to press forward evenly from each side of the problem, a resounding success in aesthetics would not have been wanting. But the fields of work that immediately opened to it on all sides were too large, it seems, and the number of thinkers schooled under Husserl[28] too small, to be able to master them all. People believed, moreover, that they had to build new foundations in all areas of philosophy, and aesthetics did not appear to them to be the most important. Thus here too, then, the problems that had arrived at a certain state of readiness for development were not evaluated.

The analysis was begun, of course, but only on the side of the subject and the act. Even there, it must be noted, it was trapped within a certain one-sidedness, since only the element of enjoyment [*Genuss*], thus what Kant called "satisfaction" [*Wohlgefallen*] became the subject of earnest new inquiry. Moritz Geiger[29] was the one to conduct this analysis. What we owe to it is in fact something new and, in its own way, significant. But it still is too close to psychologistic aesthetics – as phenomenology arose, in general, out of psychology – to be able to attain to the fundamental problem of beauty. An analysis of the act alone could not reach beyond certain incidental phenomena that shone out from the object of

---

28 [Translator's note:] Edmund Husserl (1859–1938).
29 [Translator's note:] Moritz Geiger (1880–1937).

enjoyment; it was unable to grasp the mode of being, the structure, and the value-aspects of the aesthetic object. Yet it lies in the nature of the case that this newly created method might have been applied in a fruitful way to the problem of beauty when the fundamental (31) quality of the act, i.e., aesthetical beholding in its dual nature, had been opened for description, and where at the same time the results of the latter could have been brought into contact with those of a parallel analysis of the object.

We see here once again what has been pointed out already in the preceding: the analysis of the act is a step ahead in its development; the analysis of the object is in a relatively backward state. There results the necessity of having to rescue the latter from its backwardness. The chances of doing that today are not unfavorable. The very failure of phenomenology to take up this program of analysis can both put us on the right road and can give us at the same time the means for progress. Then there is no good reason why the essences of acts should be more capable of analysis than the essences of objects. After all, it is precisely those essences of objects that are accessible to a consciousness upon the natural attitude (*intentio recta*), while the essences of acts must be made available by artificially reflecting upon the consciousness of an object (*intentio obliqua*).

It was the prejudice of phenomenology in its early development that the reverse was true: the act was immediately given. One shared in those days some philosophical presuppositions about immanence with psychologism and neo-Kantian idealism, from which most thinkers had emerged after having first purged them of their cruder errors. But a breakthrough, demanded in all areas of inquiry, into a nearby realm of the given, that of the object-phenomena, was still wanting. For that reason the cry sent out by Husserl, "Back to the things themselves!" bore no fruit, and thus the effort to press onward from the theoretical level, to that of existing things, from ethics to a real analysis of value, from aesthetics to the essence of the beautiful, was unsuccessful.

But that, too, has changed since then. The pathway into the open air stands free. It has long been accessible to the inquiry into real being; in ethics, it has led us to new analyses of material values. Only aesthetics has not yet set upon this roadway in earnest.

12 Modes of Being and Structure of the Aesthetic Object

Just because a person turns to the senses, he thinks that the beautiful object is a thing like all other things: perceptible, cognizable, having the same reality as himself. Is that true? Why, then, is it not appreciated and enjoyed by all those who see it, but always only by the selected few for whom it is something other than a thing? This appreciation and enjoyment are obviously not achieved by perception. Two people pass through a burgeoning spring landscape; both are inwardly occupied with it. One estimates with a glance how much the field will bring in, what the value of the hewn wood may be. The other's full heart leaps joyously at the spring greenery, the odor of the soil, and the wide blue sky. The sensible impressions are the same; the things that give rise to them likewise, but the object that they convey is nonetheless entirely (32) different. What distinguishes the landscape that one man has before his eyes from the landscape that the other sees?

To speak of two kinds of object says very little. The real land along with what is cultivated upon it is the same. Thus, the case depends solely upon the manner of looking at it; that is what has always been asserted. But with that, the aesthetic object becomes entirely a function of the act, and subjectivism is right: why then is it necessary at all to walk through the real landscape, why to perceive it? Apparently the man who is enjoying aesthetically cannot simply "look," in imagination, upon a landscape whenever and wherever he will, but rather he is tied to its real presence and to perception.

But, as with all practically oriented consciousness, reflection occurs along with it and brings an objectively different domain of interconnections. So too with an aesthetically oriented consciousness, called up by the same objects, a different kind of looking and a different object of looking occur. Here one is thrown back upon the looking of the second kind, or beholding, of which we spoke above. And in it, we seem to have found, despite some uncertainty, the solution to the problem. This allows us once again to divert the problem of the object into the problem of the act.

The situation changes only when one notices that the joyful feeling had by the one who beholds and enjoys is not entirely private or individual; that rather he shares it with anyone of his spirit and sensibility, and, moreover, that even given the same psychic preconditions, there exists a certain objectivity, universal validity, and necessity here; in a similar way, it is not any landscape at all, but one of a definite type that lets itself be beheld and enjoyed in this specific way. Both the one and the other point unmistakably to an objective source of natural beauty, however much the subjective orientation and the way of seeing things may play a role in it.

What this source consists in will not yet be discussed here. It would not be to the point to apply again outworn categories to one or the other of them, for example, the form of what is perceived or its function as expression; that would bring us no further. Likewise, it would not be to the point to appeal, on the side of the subject, to empathy or to an interpretative function related to it. We will be better off by examining the phenomenon with regard to its mode of being and the structure of the object itself. That would allow us at least to say something before entering a more detailed analysis. We may then leave open for later discussion the extent to which it can be justified.

The man enjoying the spring landscape aesthetically has just as little concern for what is given as real through the senses as the one who is estimating its practical value. Both have something different before their eyes; for both of them, something that is not seen peers out from behind what is sensibly given, but that something is genuinely important to them; they both look-through upon this other thing and stay with it a bit, the one reflecting on his economic (33) calculations, the other in the state of psychic release we call devoted appreciation. In the case of the first, it is easy to see what this other thing is, but in the second case, it is harder to say. But it is there, and indeed objectively so – perhaps as the great rhythm of life in nature, which dominates powerfully both within and outside ourselves, although it is just as little visible as in the first case.

That is merely a preliminary result. Let us stick with it, for the moment, and try to observe how the whole of the aesthetical natural object is structured. Two forms of looking are arranged in series, each one after the other becoming active; the first is directed upon what is really present to the senses, the second upon this other thing, which exists only "for" us, the observers. But this other thing is not projected into the first randomly; rather it is clearly dependent upon the sensibly seen. It cannot appear to us in any given perceived object, but only in a particular one, and is thus conditioned by it. But at the same time, more than a simple conditioned state is at work here; what is looked upon is also largely determined, with respect to content, by means of the real object that is seen: "imagination" does not freely govern here, but is guided by perception. Therefore, what is inwardly beheld upon the object is also not a pure product of fantasy, but something called forth: called forth precisely by means of the sensible structure of what is seen.

Accordingly, the aesthetical natural object is structured in two strata, which apparently become active one after the other in series, like the two levels of vision. In this state, the relation of the two strata is so close that we sense directly the felt and enjoyed spirit of spring as belonging to the landscape itself, and attribute the existence of that spirit to the landscape. Thus, the aesthetic object appears to us as a unity, without gaps and seams, although we know very well that in reality the spirit of spring does not belong to the object, but to us.

This phenomenon of unity is nothing less than self-evident; it is neither exhausted nor explained at all by what has been said. It is a specifically aesthetical phenomenon, and constitutes the real essential nature of the aesthetic object. How it comes to be remains a great puzzle, namely the puzzle of natural beauty itself.

For within this phenomenon, matters are not at all what theories of empathy had thought them to be. There is no activity of the soul that we project into the object. No doubt, however, there is a familiarity with fields, meadows, and woods, which does not have to be built up by association, but which announces itself in us as a vital feeling, and which points to a connection between man and nature, out of which we all emerge, however much we may have lost our sense of it. The urge to turn towards the sun, the bursting forth and sprouting, is the same in man and in the flora beneath the sky. Man does not need to feel himself empathetically into it; he finds it within, and it awakes a mighty resonance within him. The (34) communion with all living things strikes him as a miracle – precisely him, the renegade who in his daily life has separated himself so far from the sources of being, while they, though indifferent to his forgetfulness, hold him upon the old Earth within their embrace.

With respect to this relationship of nature in us to nature outside of us, we must beware of making sentimental analogies and classifications that were once widespread in German romanticism, for the understanding of the phenomenon can only be confused by such exuberance. Those Romantic visions are, to be sure, closely related to the aesthetical beholding of nature, and may perhaps be taken into the complex of facts before us (the ones seen historically) as their limiting phenomena. But for that very reason, we may not simultaneously call upon them to explain the phenomena. For what is in fact essential here is not at all the extent to which the resonance that is felt and experienced can be explained anthropologically – or even metaphysically – but only that some second something experienced and intensely felt in second-order seeing (beholding) is given objectively just as much as the first (that which is directly perceived), and that the former appears with the latter interlocked in a fixed unity.

This indicates the schema according to which both the structure and the mode of being of any beautiful object may be understood. The beautiful thing is a double-faceted object, but united as one, as one single object. It is a real object, and is given to the senses that way, but it is not reducible to that givenness; rather it is equally a quite different, unreal kind of object that appears in the real one, or arises from behind it. What is beautiful is neither the first object nor the second alone; they exist only both in each other and with each other. More correctly expressed, it is the appearance of the one in the other.

Clearly, given such a structure, the mode of being of the aesthetic object cannot be a simple one. As it contains a twofold object, so it is also a twofold being, a real being and an unreal, merely apparent, being. And what is peculiar is that this duality of being, despite its complete heterogeneity, allows the object to appear undivided and unified. The relation between the two parts that constitute it must accordingly be quite intimate; one may say it is a functional kind. What the being-beautiful of the object most essentially depends upon is the specific role of the reality in it (that which is given through the senses) in allowing the quite alien unreal element to appear.

Here is found the reason why the mode of being of the whole must be a divided one, while in terms of structure, the object is unified and completely undivided in its effect. The unity lies in appearance. What allows something to appear must be real, and what appears must be unreal, for the latter consists only in this appearance of itself. That is the ambivalence in the mode of being of beauty: it is there and it is not there. Its existence hovers about it. (35)

In beholding and in enjoying, we feel this floating as the magic of beauty. If we understood the object itself as divided, the magic would vanish. Only provided that we encounter it as an undisturbed unity, and sense in it the opposition of existence and non-existence, are we able to experience the magic of the appearance-relation.

13 Reality and Illusion. De-actualization and Appearance

Now nineteenth-century aesthetics had much to say about appearance. But what was always meant by it is the appearance of an "idea" – whether one thought of this term metaphysically, as did Schopenhauer, or as a human thought, a work of fantasy, a dreamed-up ideal, etc. In all such cases, the relation was conceived much too narrowly. That is not so easily visible in the case of natural beauty, even less so with beauty in art. The poet lets figures appear that are entirely creations of his fancy, but they need not all be ideals (moral ones, for example); their appearance satisfies the claim to aesthetic value if it is a genuinely clear and evident (true to life) appearance. For that is by no means self-evident in the substance of speech, upon which the poet bestows form.

Now that is the first tangible idea in opposition to idealistic aesthetics. What is thought to appear need not have the quality of an idea, whether ethical or otherwise; it may be, perhaps, some segment or other drawn from life. It is a question only of the kind of appearance. That will be maintained even when what should result in practice is a certain selection from the material that is appropriate for representation. For it is a question here of "material," as we defined it above.

The second idea, however, concerns appearance itself. Since the Romantic age, fortified by Hegelian aesthetics, writers have spoken of "illusion" [*Schein*] as the mode of being of beauty. But by this was meant that the object represented is in reality not present; it has no reality, but it approaches the beholder in such manner as if it were real. We see this in the concreteness of gay colors, in the richness of detail, even just in the submersion of what is beheld in what is perceived. For one who beholds aesthetically does not separate what is seen through the senses from what he beholds in spirit, but rather sees both as one, and thus believes that he perceives what is not perceptible along with what is. If one wishes to draw an inference from this, it must be that the essence of aesthetical beholding possesses an element of deception or illusion, but the essence of the object must possess an element of something deceptively presented as content.

Now of course there is a technique in dramaturgy and perhaps a technique in the narrative arts that work with illusion as a means, and in that way achieve a realistic effect. It is, however, a question whether that is a genuine artistic effect, or whether art then approaches mere trickery or sensationalism, and appeals thereby to quite different reactions from the audience than true art does. In general, the audience knows quite accurately that the action on stage is not real; it knows (36) the "separation" [of stage and audience], distinguishes clearly the actor from the character he portrays, and just for those reasons the audience can appreciate the actors' work. If the audience believed that the triumph of the plotters, or the suffering and downfall of the hero was real, it would be morally impossible that the audience could peacefully sit there and allow itself to enjoy the proceedings. For that reason, there are limitations to realism in dramaturgy: the stylization of language by writing in verse, the stage setting framed like a picture, the apron, and much else. Analogous measures are found in the narrative and in the representational arts in general.

Just this simulation of reality is foreign to true art. All theories of illusion and deception that take this direction fail to understand an important characteristic of the nature of the artistic letting-appear. It is this: art does not simulate reality, but rather understands appearance just as appearance, it is not integrated as an element in the real course of life, but rather it is lifted out of life and stands before us, as it were, shielded from the weight of reality.

This state of being lifted out and shielded from reality reappears in all the arts that have taken something from reality, or, each in its own way, have represented something freely invented. This is most familiar in painting, where the frame creates isolation. It would not occur to any viewer to take the painted landscape as a real one, or a portrait as the person depicted. That precisely is essential to giving the appearance-relation its full effect. Its contrast with the reality that surrounds it is a conditioning factor here, even when it is quite true that the devoted onlooker forgets his immediate environment, for he is lifted out of it just as much as the object is. The forgetfulness of the environment and the consciousness of being lifted out of it do not, strangely enough, conflict with each other, although a remainder of the environing world is contained in the consciousness of the beholder. Here, too, the relationship is ambivalent; but even that is sufficient for our sense of being happily lifted up over ourselves, of falling away from everyday life and from our cares, of detachment and relaxation; we flee to this state of limbo when we wish to escape stress and psychic strain.

This error slips in only when we wish to interpret this act of running away as a flight into illusion. If it were really a question of illusion or deception, we would illusorily be exchanging one burden for another: we would be taking the appearance as real, and thereby experience a new state of restraint. For that reason, we hold the concept of appearance firmly in a state of neutrality with respect to the mode of being of what appears, and do not confuse it with illusion. For to illusion belongs the falsification of reality. But what is essential to art is precisely the opposition to being real, which we also sense as present in the object. (37)

A stratified structure and a highly peculiar suspended mode of being of the aesthetic object emerged from the above discussion. The latter depends upon the fundamentally different kind of existence of the two strata in it: reality in the foreground, which is given to the senses, appearance in the background; being in itself in the former, mere being for us in the latter. That is not disputed or even put in question, if one avoids attributing deception and illusion to the appearing background. Rather illusion would do injury to the character of pure appearance, because it would simulate reality. Its exclusion is thus precisely the condition under which the back-and-forth activation of the two modes of being can produce a stable and unified picture.

Accordingly, the two modes of being do not become mixed. They are too heterogeneous for that. And even in aesthetical beholding they do not quickly merge with each other, but remain distinguishable, although they are tied into each other and re-experienced as an indivisible unity. The whole is an entirely objective thing, and that means that it is a pure objective creation that contrasts with all of the elements in the act of beholding and enjoying, although it is co-conditioned, with regard to its more weighty constituents, i.e., to the subject and its act, and without their involvement would not come to be at all. It therefore again exists only "for" a subject who beholds it adequately. An objective element is just not the same as an existing thing that is independent of the subject. Objectivity itself, in this context, is a thing that is in part real, but in part also unreal. Only in this way is it possible that something that appears "in" some real thing could simultaneously distance itself from the sphere of the real and also not return to it, and still stand before us as a thing given in a concretely intuitable way, as otherwise only objects can be.

Such distance from real existence is de-actualization. With this phenomenon, a new fundamental characteristic of the beautiful object appears within our range of vision as a thing suspended between two heterogeneous modes of being. This element first becomes tangible in the activity of the artist, even if the puzzle of that activity is not thereby clarified. For at this point there intrudes the contrast to the practical activity of man and the burden of moral responsibility. All doing is a realizing. Purposes or aims, still unreal but posited by consciousness as an end, so far as we sense them as commanded or as ought-to-be, are made real by means of action; and the freedom with which we choose to act is the capacity to measure up to the ideal necessity of the Ought, where it still lacks real possibility. The realization of the unreal thus consists in making it possible. At first sight, it appears as if the activity of the artist was a realization, perhaps a realization of an idea, or of an ideal that hovers before his mind. But if one looks more closely, we find quite the opposite. His creativity is precisely not realization, and therefore also not a making-possible. What hovers before his mind is not translated into reality, but only represented. And that means: it is brought to appearance. (38)

The procedure of the creative artist is a distancing from the actual; it is de-actualization. He does not need to procure the conditions of possibility that are lacking, he does not need to put in motion the inert weight of the sphere of real things, but only to offer what is unreal as such to the beholding eye. He needs a real object only as a mediating element in which the former, the unreal, can appear; and only in the production of such real things can he be said to realize something. But what comes therein to appearance remains entirely unreal, and, indeed, so decisively and unmistakably unreal that even the appearing object in its sensible tangibility does not deceitfully lead us to think it real.

For that reason, the freedom of the artist is different from that of the man of action. The former is driven by no Ought, and no responsibility burdens him. In return, an unlimited realm of possibility stands open to him, one not tied to the conditions of the real. Artistic freedom is not only different from moral freedom; its domain is also much larger. It corresponds precisely to de-actualization as the mode of being of artistic activity, and it stands in the pure freedom of having nothing required of it.

14 Imitation and Creativity

Nothing in aesthetics has been as much disputed as imitation in the arts. In Plato we have the origin of the theory of "*mimesis*"; we find in Aristotle its classic formulation, and it is to be found even today in many other forms – yet most of them, though based upon the same schema, do not call themselves by that name.

At first, the term meant the imitation of things, of real persons and their hustle-bustle; later people thought of the Ideas after which, they believed, things were formed. In both cases, the artist has already set before what he is to give shape to, and only one question regarding this skill remained: to what extent is he able to measure up to the models. Such an interpretation limits considerably his creative work. That he might be able to show the world something new, something it does not yet possess, was not at all considered.

Little changes if one interprets the meaning of *mimesis* as representation. For from this concept, too, one still senses primarily and most strongly the element of imitation. Whoever listens closely to its subtext will no doubt find a different element in it: that is the one just discussed, the letting-appear – and, in fact, letting-appear in a substance of a quite different nature from what is represented: in words, in tones, in color, in stone. Now if, as was seen to be necessary, one does not transfer the essence of the beautiful object into what appears, but rather into appearance itself, then the independence of the creative achievement in the activity of the artist increases all at once to a considerable level, rises quickly and becomes the main feature of the created work. For it is easy to see that artistic representation is nothing but letting-appear itself. And then the genuine bearer of aesthetical (39) value is precisely the artistic achievement, and the specific "material" to which form is given by the work of the artist falls back to the second rank.

But this does not say enough. Are in fact the representational arts and their material referred back to some ready model, whether taken from nature or from the sphere of human life? Even in this respect, would the artist not also enjoy many kinds of freedom? Can he not reach beyond what is given and, in the very act of composing, lift his material above the domain of experience and in that way show the observer something that he does not find in life? Some idea of this kind was meant by the aesthetics of Plotinus, of Schelling, of Schopenhauer, when they spoke of the "ideas" that were brought to appearance. However, according to them, the ideas themselves were already present to and previously sketched out for the artist, so that the only productive tools left to him were a penetrating eye and the ability to draw from a model.

What happens if this presupposed metaphysics of ideas shows itself to be untenable? What if the pre-existent "primordial images" that allow themselves to be understood and brought to appearance are not really there at hand at all, and yet what if the artist has shaped projects beyond everything empirical and rises up to the level of ideas and symbols? If so, has the creative artist not also contributed to the creation of the appearing content, and been the first to lift it above and beyond what is given in life?

A simple reflection will teach us that this question must be answered affirmatively. If it is true that literature can also instruct us, that it can make palpable perspectives on values and meaning in human life, and even awaken in us the earnest desire to be worthy of them – and who could deny that? – then we may understand this truth in no other way than as a form of practical guidance. We do not need to interpret such things immediately as pedagogical efforts; on the contrary, precisely where there are no such efforts at all, influences of this kind arise most quickly. But then the writer must also be able to bring to appearance what lies beyond the given world.

The leadership of humanity by the arts is no longer a real aesthetical problem. But from that problem a light falls back upon the fundamental problems of aesthetics, at least where art has not been falsified by "pedagogical ends," which alter the proper "mood" of a viewer. For this kind of leadership has one advantage before all others: it is immediately convincing, in a way that only the living of our lives can otherwise do, and just for the same reasons: literature does not speak to us as a teacher, but in clear and concrete figures, which are enlightening as such. They awaken our feeling for values and open our vision to the profundities in the conflicts in life, and do so in a manner of which we are not capable in life itself. The inward growth and maturity fostered by such literary effects are not delusions. Everyone not badly educated who approaches great art experiences these effects in himself. How can we distinguish radically genuine art, which is always without bias, from contrived work, or even from work (40) done at a moment's notice on order? For these latter seem inartistic, and affect us accordingly; they achieve, in the end, rather the opposite of what they were after: the intended beholder turns away from them. Only what the artist has genuinely beheld and bestowed form upon in concrete figurations achieves the power to move men, a power that convinces, reveals, and shows us the way, because it unintentionally forces itself upward and out of the depths.

Here is rooted the high mission of literature and, in ordered grades, the other arts. Entire generations and epochs can be defined in terms of the creations of high art. From ancient times, men knew the secret of literature, which lies namely in its power to direct the human heart toward what is great, to elevate it, and to inspire by its very depths what a pedantic moral lecture can only soberly recommend or encourage.

Here lies also the main reason why the arts may not retire from real life, although they have their own kind of autonomy from life – at least, that is, if they do not wish to forget their own life. For it is from life, specifically from those things that move our hearts, that they draw their themes and their material, and their effects flow into that life ever again. They can be what they are in essence only in the context of an historical reality out of whose mother soil they arise, but not in order to become an aestheticizing shadow-life next to it, as the feeble epigones of creative epochs retrospectively imagine. From this soil arises the task that only the arts can handle, just because their creative activity is not intended to affect reality. It is well known how highly productive epochs have been aware of this task, and how they revered the artist as the bearer of great ideas – in such a way that they thought of the poet as a prophet (*vates*), and for hundreds of years called upon him as their witness.

But note: this task is no longer an aesthetical one. It is given to art, no doubt, for no other function in the life of the spirit can fulfill it, and it is for that reason also entirely a matter of artistic concern, but not on its aesthetical, but only on its cultural side. To separate these two would be equivalent to tearing art from its mutual relations with life, without which its diverse emotional ties to and inspiration by life could not come to pass. For so is man: only that which moves him inwardly, in living and struggling, in yearning and desiring, drives him to creative work. The whole of life, in which the artist stands, offers both fruitful soil and the land itself upon which he toils. What he produces, however, is far from being merely aesthetical in nature.

Two things also follow from these points that concern the purely aesthetical activity of the artist. The first is this: the influences of art external to aesthetics are a proof of its creative aspect, provided that they lie also in the content of great works of art; thus we have a proof of its extension beyond all imitation and of its autonomous intuitive beholding of what possesses the nature of ideas. For without such intuitive beholding, any extension beyond what is prefigured in life, beyond what we all know, is simply an impossibility. (41)

Why this creativity regarding content is so tightly interwoven with formal and sensible characteristics remains puzzling in many respects. That no other kind of creative work results in such an achievement still does not explain this fact. The achievement might be, after all, denied to men; that it is yet in principle possible for them and succeeds in lucky cases is one of the miracles of the creative spirit. Perhaps it is the bestowing of sensible form itself that, with respect to content, lifts the genius above and beyond the given. We may remain certain only of this: for great figures in the history of art there is always available a visionary sort of life, and the creative man is really torn out from and lifted above himself, laid hold of by his idea as by an inner destiny that he takes upon himself and lives out in his creative work.

What also follows from these reflections is a perspective upon genuine artistic freedom that lies in creativity itself. It rests, as we have shown, upon the fact that the artist has nothing to realize, that is, he does not make some real thing possible, but limits himself merely to letting something appear. On the level of appearance, however, he rules without limit. Here he does not come up against the hard resistance of reality; here unlimited possibilities open for what is not possible in reality. The only valid law is his own, which he promulgates and imposes as he gives form to his material. For that reason, what he intuitively beholds is not only autonomous but also self-governing – and there are no gods next to him.

This peculiar power of the creative artist is, in the highest sense, as in the phrase of Hölderlin[30], his "freedom to set forth wherever he will."[31] (42)

---

30 [Translator's note:] Johann Christian Friedrich Hölderlin (1770–1843).
31 [Translator's note:] Hölderlin, Friedrich, "The Course of Life," in: *Poems of Friedrich Hölderlin. The Fire of the Gods Drives Us to Set Forth by Day and by Night*, selected and translated by James Mitchell, San Francisco: Ithuriel's Spear 2004, p. 25.

Part One: **The Relationship of Appearance**

First Section: The Structure of the Aesthetical Act

Chapter 1: On Perception in General

a) Looking through

The word "aesthetics" tells us that the form in which the beautiful is given to us is perception. This is our point of departure. However, it becomes immediately apparent that not any concept of perception at all will be adequate to the task of aesthetics. Therefore, we must attempt to shape the concept in a way that does justice to the phenomenon – specifically with respect to the structure of the aesthetical act, whose foundation in the consciousness of the beholder is formed by perception.

Long enough have we understood perception as though it contained only the elements of the visible, the tangible, the audible, or colors, volumes, sounds, and the like, in short as though reducible to a collection of sensations. Modern psychology has shown not only that perception cannot be so reduced, but also that we know nothing of elements of sensation as such. Such elements may only become subsequently the objects of analytic psychology; but this science has had difficulty in isolating them experimentally in a way that makes them available. To do that requires artificially produced conditions that do not occur in life.

In the content of genuine perception a complex figure is always given, a pictorial whole, a joining of many details of contrasts and transitions, whether merely a single "thing" is perceived or an entire complex of things (in practice, the latter is usually the case), a state of affairs or even something more than that. Along with what is seen belongs that which is grasped in seeing, something which is no longer given directly to the senses, but which is its entirely self-evident completion. For we never see in a purely optical sense everything that is visible upon a thing, but rather we complete the thing immediately, we interconnect and unify it, and do not even notice that we are active in this way. The line between what is optically given and what we supplement it with disappears (43) in perception. For what is achieved synthetically in perception occurs quite this side of all reflection. To be sure, it occurs on the basis of experience, but not by an inference, a comparison, a combining, or similar subsequent mental acts.

That is by no means all. In everyday perception there is contained much that is not at all comprehensible by the senses. We see the tree and the insect, but we see life in the two of them as well, differentiated, of course, as living being of two distinct types. When we enter a room, we see the poverty or wealth, the slovenliness or the good taste of the inhabitants. We see a face or a form in motion, though perhaps only from the rear, and yet just from that glimpse alone we learn something about the inward life of the person, about his character and his destiny.

Now it is precisely this, viz., the genuinely non-visible, that tends to be for us the essential matter of perception, for the sake of which we turn our attention toward an object, or rest our attention for a while upon what we see. The external aspects alone of the object would not be likely to attract our attention, no less hold it. Thus we see people looking at each other's faces: perception forces its way through the visible forms towards what is fundamentally quite different, towards the inwardness, towards the soul; and that is so true that we normally have difficulty later in remembering the visible forms of the person and in visualizing them – while the non-visible aspects, which we perceived along with the visible, can remain before our minds in all their concrete distinctness. Our consciousness grasped the former immediately, while it hardly noticed the latter, merely grazed them, as it were, and dealt with them as something inessential and transparent as it passed through them.

Let us not object too soon by asking whether this is really a "seeing." The fact is that as a practical matter we do not know cases of seeing persons without this kind of seeing-through. And the latter is not given subsequent to the former, in reflection or by thinking the matter over; rather it is present with the sensible perception at just the same time as the self-evident and familiar completion of an object. The acts – if they are really two acts connected one behind the other in series – do not appear as temporally separate.

How are we to explain this? How can what is not perceptible be the essential element in perception?

The situation is not as paradoxical as it may appear, once one reflects that our consciousness is not simply perceptual, and that there is a risk in isolating perception theoretically – as if perception ever stood by itself alone. To the contrary, every perception occurs upon the background of a complex of interrelated acts and contents, which are always built up in two stages, as a momentary nexus of the mental act [*Erlebnis*] and as a nexus of experience [*Erfahrung*] that is broadly extended in time. (44)

These two stages of the nexus always form a structured unity in which the order of a manifold is already present. And in this unity everything apprehended, anything presenting itself to consciousness in any way is given order: that which has been told us, and that which we have experienced personally; one's own thoughts or fancies, as well as what one has perceived.

However, within this unity dominates, as a rule, a narrow circle of objective elements upon which the interests of the perceiver depend: persons and their qualities, situations in life, the inner moods, dispositions, and intentions of men, their benevolence, their animosity, their envy, their aversions and approbations, and much more. The remainder is arranged about these elements, in the main, and out of them the external aspect of what is perceived fills itself with the inward aspect, which was not apprehensible by the senses, but which always arises immediately, and appears to be given along with them.

Because this strange phenomenon of "looking through" [*Hindurchblicken*] the external aspects of a thing is so universal and familiar, we are hardly surprised by it, although the delusions that we often suffer at its expense should be enough to make us thoughtful. And that is the reason why, in the end, we usually experience consciously only the inner elements of perception, while we pass over the external elements, despite their being that which is given to us through the senses directly and serve to mediate the former. In this sense, we may say: I "see" anger, melancholy, or suspicion in the changing expressions on people's faces. For this reason we are usually far from being able to explain "how" all this is expressed in the play of people's features.

In the face of such phenomena, it is unimportant how we characterize them as mental acts, that is, whether we should count them as a form of perception, but this becomes nothing more than a play with words. What is important is to understand correctly the facts of the case, and even then not only for all perception, but primarily for those having to do with persons, situations, and relationships that occur in the context of practical life. In these cases, we see that with every perception there is firmly tied the integration of pre-given interconnections of lived experience and of experience in general – so firmly that without these contexts, we do not count them as perceptions; rather we have the impression of not having perceived at all. The essential matter for us is just this looking-through into what has not been grasped by the senses.

b) The perceptual field as practically selected

Although we have no intention here of bypassing discursive consciousness, it is nevertheless true that a variety of general considerations are involved here. Thus, for example there is the case of the simple elaboration of what is perceived through the senses into the representation of a thing: the pattern of the thing is already present, not, to be sure, in the form of a concept, but also not in any sense in "strict" universality, as the scientific attitude would require. Nonetheless, it is still present in a loose form and not infrequently with compelling power. (45)

This universal element is the simple precipitation of experience, and operates in our understanding of objects as an "empirical analogy," which as such need not become conscious. One could also say: it is there as a kind of familiar well-worn pathway of representations, which is no longer traced or inspected, and for that reason it is in a certain way indifferent to objective correctness or incorrectness. For if inferences from analogy are questionable, how much more so must be the analogies that we draw without noticing them! Similarly we associate, for example, based on a single past experience, certain kinds of human character (or even just with single character traits, such as kindness, reliability, frivolity, or frailty), with certain facial types; and this picture appears again immediately as a completed pattern when we again meet the same external facial characteristics. Such a phenomenon has been called "association" since the time of Hume; but this phenomenon differs from that described by Hume in that it is always already carried out in perception itself.

However much this kind of generalization may be liable to error, most of what we possess in life of shared knowledge of the inner life of other persons rests upon it. The person who has experienced much of life is one in whom such knowledge possesses a broad foundation. With this broadness of foundation, however, generalizations as such force themselves into consciousness, where they usually take the form of conceptual knowledge and can be examined and surveyed. What is taken in along with the act of perception itself is clearly different from this manifestly higher standpoint, and it is the former alone that we are considering here.

Behind the phenomenon thus described there stands, as we have already noted, an element of practical interest; we are directed towards what appears as urgent in some way. We live, of course, in need to orient ourselves continuously within the conditions of the environment. However, we cannot understand a situation without a certain amount of additional knowledge about the intentions, aspirations, and attitudes of our fellow men. For in life they are our antagonists, and it is precisely their intentions that determine the character of a situation. Understood in this manner, all practical situations are of an inward kind: what is essential about them is the play of unseen powers of the soul. And these powers are precisely the object of acts of perception that have been extended by the element of the universal in experience.

The perception of the invisible along with the visible loses much of its mystery when we realize how it plays a broad role even in relation to far simpler objects. Think, for example, of how our ability to replace the sense of touch by that of sight increases as our consciousness matures. Upon each thing, we are able to see more and more of what is invisible: we "see" the hardness or elasticity of things, or even their weight and the inertia that resists efforts to move them. And similarly *mutatis mutandis* for the sense of hearing: we hear steps in an adjacent room, (46) but "see" in the mind's eye a human form in motion, as it goes about some business or other; or we hear the quiet rustle of a wicker chair, but we see inwardly how the person sitting upon it is rocking in some specific way. In these cases also, perception is directed, without any concern for the limits of the sensibly given, toward that which is important to us because of some interest we have in it.

At this point, the insight is immediately apparent that our entire perceptual field is pre-structured by practical interest. Perception itself, and to a great extent experiential events, are both subject to a principle of selection by the prior accents that we ourselves bring into the act of perception by our states of interest. Out of all the things that may be given to us as objects of potential experience, only those that carry these accents appear in the full light of consciousness; the direction of our attention depends upon them. What appears thus as emphasized or as salient is not what is essential in itself, but only what is essential for us.

In a highly developed theoretical consciousness, naturally, what is essential in itself may be approached; but then consciousness makes a sharp distinction between what is given to the senses and what is not, and perception takes on the form of consciously focused observation. At that point, we have quite a different kind of standpoint, one that is quite far from everyday perception.

Finally, also standing behind this process of accentuation and selection in perception are clearly demonstrable value-qualities. All states of interest can be traced back precisely to value-elements, which we bring to experience and then transfer to the circuit of the perceptible. In his day, Max Scheler[32] saw this phenomenon and described it for the first time in all generality. The result may be summarized in his own words: the field of perception is subject to a principle of selection that is oriented towards values. Of course in no sense do the higher ethical values play a role here originally, or only on a secondary level; rather, the values of goods (including a variety of values relative to situations) and of vital states are primary. Most prevalent are precisely the standpoints relative to "getting one's bearings" [*Sich-Zurechtfinden*] and "asserting oneself" [*Sich-Durchsetzen*]. Such standpoints, along with the values themselves that stand behind them, are nevertheless elements that are essentially removed from perception.

Let us add here parenthetically a word about knowledge of human nature. It does not normally rest upon genuine knowledge, but rather upon a sharpened intuitive vision, and thus essentially upon a seeing of what is not visible along with what is visible. Such knowledge belongs as such precisely in the circle of perceptual phenomena that has been described here. It is similarly conditioned by thoroughly practical considerations, and is led by value perspectives. The nature of such knowledge is constituted, along with the plasticity of the experience, by apt generalizations from what has been previously experienced, thus

---

32 [Translator's note:] Max Scheler (1874–1928).

again by empirical analogies. For that reason, it possesses some of the liabilities inherent in all thinking by analogy: it limits itself frequently to generalizations; it forms models, and is sound (47) only when these models are appropriate. The eye of the man who knows the ways of men is therefore directed upon the typical, and it fails him when it is faced with authentic personal existence. For what is personal is unique, and requires a more loving gaze to make it visible.

c) Emotional components

All of this goes far beyond perception itself. And yet it belongs to perception, and is quite closely and intimately related to it, such that we are not familiar with it in any other way. The solution of this puzzle is the one given above, namely that there is no purely perceptual consciousness, not, at least, in human beings, and not at all in spiritually developed ones. All these perceptual phenomena are thus already placed within a very broad context upon which they all are arranged.

These phenomena can also be viewed from the other side, and then they appear as follows: perception "transcends" itself. This expression is to be taken literally: perception goes beyond itself; it passes beyond its own limits, which were imposed upon it by the faculties of sense. On its own, it forces itself toward something different from itself, something that is not given to it directly; it claims it nevertheless for itself, and indeed without any concern for whence it came. So it forces its way towards entities, unities, interrelationships, backgrounds – and in such an elemental and immediate way that we imagine ourselves to be experiencing such things in perception, and we accept them as having been given along with it. Thus it happens that we think we "see" the ulterior motives of a person in his face, and, in a certain sense, we really are able to see them.

This "self-transcendence" of perception thus consists in the fact that it does not remain within itself, but rather expands beyond itself. And for that very reason, the phenomena of perception do not allow themselves to be isolated psychologically. We find them only woven together with an abundance of much higher functions, and, in a strict sense, in perception we are always immediately dealing with the whole of consciousness.

This is in no sense valid only for its entirely objective and material elements; it is valid also for the emotional elements. It is valid in fact primarily and properly only to them, for here their interconnectedness is more intimate, and deeper and more fundamentally rooted.

Purely objective perception, familiar to us in observation, developed as a late product of consciousness in human culture, and even today it is usually found only in rather mature adults. The objects of perception in the consciousness of the child or the primitive man who lives close to nature are still infected with all sorts of affective accents: for example, the unknown is infected with the accents of the fearful or the terrible, and yet these emotions still possess an amazing capacity for being occasionally eclipsed by the element of attractiveness provided by curiosity. A place can take on the qualities of uncanniness or dreadfulness, or the opposite, of the familiar and welcoming – and this happens, of course, at our first glance, purely through (48) perception alone. Things like events can appear as threatening, sinister, or malicious, just as they can also be beneficent, well-meaning, kind, or affectionate. Children often take quite harmless things to be "good" or "evil"; the latter not in the sense of morally evil, but rather hostile or malevolent. The bright sunshine, a babbling brook, the dark forest, the cool of the evening, a gnarled oak tree, in short the entire perceptual world, are permeated with such emotional accents.

Much of this can be traced to the times when men were genuinely threatened by the power of nature; the case is similar to what man finds favorable to himself in the environing world. Such experiences may have remained in him in the form of instinctive visceral responses. We see reflected here also the animistic worldview of primitive cultures; although alien to our thought today, it has yet remained on the perceptual level of our consciousness – modified in different ways in different human types, but still within certain limits apprehensible sympathetically by all of us. And in fact even today man lives, on a certain level of his consciousness, within a complex of ineradicable teleological notions, which announce themselves to him, surprise him, as it were, at moments when his more sober thought is not on the alert. At such times, what is perceived is no longer indifferent to him; everything "makes demands on him," be it for good or ill, even when he is still far beyond all mythical reminiscences. Primeval elements of dread may play the main role in such events.

Emotional components of this type are not secondary to perception and merely supervene upon it; rather they are the original elements of it, and that objective perception freed itself from their control later. For that reason, they echo at times in the perceptions of minds that have long become sober and tractable. They break out from the dark depths of the subconscious, and attach themselves to perception.

In everyday contemporary human life, affective components still play a contributory role in perception. Certain elements of desire and aversion are also not absent, and they, arising out of perceptions, dominate our moods. We speak of such things as a "joyful sight" or a "disgusting impression," even when no direct involvement in the matter affects our interest. Our hand glides with obvious pleasure over the soft fur of a cat, but we hate to touch a tortoise or a spider. Vital responses lie unmistakably at the root of such phenomena. It is similar with frightening or piercing noises, with restful, rhythmical sounds, or those that make us drowsy; just the words alone express unambiguously the affective tone in each. Consider also that our sense of smell is infected even more by aversion and delight, and completely so our sense of taste.

Largely, we can say analogous things about the appearance of a person. A man, too, may seem strange when we first glance at him; he may disgust us, or he may attract us and win our confidence. Emotional responses that stand at the gateway of morality are already found here. Yet always they (49) attach themselves to perception immediately and in an entirely spontaneous fashion. Upon them rests the mystery of the phenomenon of "first impression."

In general, the line between objective and emotional perception is blurry. Originally both may have been one, and perhaps indeed the emotional aspect may have been prevalent. These phenomena also can be characterized as a kind of self-transcendence of perception. Here, however, the transcendence is entirely in the opposite direction: not toward the completion or enrichment of the object, but rather toward greater vibrancy of the impression, of the appearance as such, or, simply, it is transcendence toward its "being-for-us." From the perspective of the subject, it has the form of a transcendence that reaches back towards the original sense experience, towards the kind of emotional tonality from which objective perception had originally been won. And if one should object that these tonalities do not really belong to the object, we may reply as Democritus once did to a quite different question: even colors and sounds do not belong to the object, but exist only for us. The emotional tonalities, similar to colors and sounds, are to be attributed to the object, such that the attribution itself has the same immediacy in both cases, and is thus not truly an attribution. Rather, what we feel in perception as menacing and attractive is as immediate as redness and greenness as qualities of objects. Only a relatively later reflection teaches us to distinguish between the objective and the subjective in such cases.

The world of things appears, in perception just as in immediate experience, as subject to these tonalities of feeling that are given to us. Strangely, even when we no longer are inclined to ascribe them in earnest to things, and when their "being-for-us" has long ago been correctly understood, they still are able to resonate in our perception, and on occasion are even able to dominate it.

For that reason we must say that they are given to us in the form of properties of the object, and not in the form of subjective additions (which, considered in themselves, they may largely be); not as elements of acts, but rather entirely as elements of the content of objects.

We must not forget in this connection that they are also to a great extent – at least originally – entirely signs of objectively existing relationships, of dangers, threats, opportunities, and the like; and this is especially apparent wherever their origin out of significant vital responses can be clearly sensed sympathetically.

The relatedness of things to us, which is rooted in our dependence upon them, is hence in no wise an illusion, but concrete reality. It remains thus rooted even in those particular cases in which it is only imagined. Ontological relationships no doubt permeate the entire objective field; but a sure criterion of reality and illusion-is not given by providence to man in his cradle. (50)

Chapter 2: Aesthetic Perception

a) Return to the original attitude

What is valid for perception in general is valid even more for aesthetic perception. Here what is seen and felt through perception becomes the genuinely essential element.

In the everyday life of the contemporary adult, tonalities of feeling in perception are largely disconnected from conscious awareness, or at least repressed. The modern man is, in general, attuned objectively to his environment, and only existing things have meaning and weight for him. Within certain limits, he has learned to distinguish between what is real and what is imaginary: the former has all his interest and the latter concerns him only on occasion. His consciousness of the world is directed primarily at acquiring knowledge, and, indeed at acquiring practical knowledge of the world.

The superiority of the spiritual over the non-spiritual consciousness consists just in its taking things as they are in themselves, i.e., apart from its comprehension of them. Naturally, it does that only as far as it can, but the tendency to do so is there. And that alone is sufficient to transform radically our view of the environing world, and to give us the attitude basic to objectivity, which signifies a consciousness of the transobjectivity of all objects of knowledge.[33] And this consciousness extends itself downwards into perception.

It is quite otherwise with aesthetic perception. In it, the first and most important element is the reversal of this tendency, that is, the return to the original attitude. This is true not in every respect, but certainly with respect to the emotional tonalities that are attached to the object perceived. For those tonalities, e.g., the "coolness" of a blue-green hue or the "warmth" of red or yellow-brownish hues, become once again the essential matter. The secretive and the

---

33 On consciousness without mind, cf. *Das Problem des geistigen Seins* [*The Problem of Spiritual Being*], 2nd edition (1949), Chaps. 9a–c; for the concept of transobjectivity, cf. *Grundlegung der Ontologie* [*Foundations of Ontology*], 3rd edition (1948), Chap. 25.

eerie appearance of the dark forest, the dreadfulness of the howling wind, the loneliness and helplessness we feel when we are surrounded by broad, bare cliffs: all this impresses itself upon us once again, and becomes in certain circumstances our chief concern. The same is true of what appears in the shape of objects as menacing us or as filling us with dread, as cozy and snug, as exhilarating and oppressive, so far as perception makes visible in that shape a proud or a fearful attitude; it is true also for the sense of freedom that a view of vast heights offers, or for the oppressiveness of narrow passageways.

Aesthetic perception does not question the validity of the subjectivity or the anthropomorphism that may be contained in it; it neither questions nor reasons at all. All these phenomena may accompany it unreflectively but essentially, in the cases of both natural objects and works of art; and they lend to what is given by means of aesthetic perception an entire dimension of peculiar qualities: in the landscape, in interior design, in church (51) architecture, most forcefully, perhaps, in music (in timbre and harmony), but also in verbal form, as in works of poetry.

This does not imply a return to non-spiritual consciousness. The latter would without hesitation take to be real the qualities of feeling that are given along with perception; even more, it would relate this dread, terror, or menace to itself, and become really afraid. Aesthetic perception does no such thing: it is not a cognitive perception of the real. It is like the original form of perception only in that it is capable of perceiving such qualities at all, and in that it comes to see and feel a manifold of objects that are thoroughly permeated and richly tinged by them, but is different in that it does not confuse or mix in it even partially the real world of things. Rather, the strict and rigorous separation of the two is the rule. The return to the original attitude of perception is not a return to the primitive conception of the environing world. Once achieved, objectivity remains complete and whole; indeed, it is not even affected, to say nothing of being injured, by the fact that consciousness has discovered joy in the beautiful. Aesthetic perception coexists peacefully with the objective world. It looks in another direction, and its objects are different – even when the same objects offer themselves together, to the one and to the other.

It is not easy to understand these facts in a positive way. What is clear about them at first is only the withdrawal of cognitive awareness, especially of rational thought and its objective mode of apprehension, but also of practical consciousness with its purposive intentions. Rationality and the sober pursuit of ends are what, in the spiritual consciousness, do away so radically with the tonalities of feeling in perception. This clearing away takes place in the name of an objective orientation upon the world. But it is just this orientation that disappears in the aesthetical consciousness. Here we are directed neither upon present realities nor upon facts and matters of fact, but upon an object that has been lifted out of both of these in the act of seeing.

In aesthetical awareness, perception is also not directed upon the objective interconnections of things, but upon another kind of connectedness, one that is found only in relation to the subject and his way of seeing. But in this other interconnection what has been achieved by the spiritual consciousness by no means disappears: objectivity itself remains, and with it the distance from the object that objectivity establishes. Both become strengthened and more accentuated. For in aesthetic perception the opposition of the two, of the observer and his object, cannot be eliminated. However, the disengagement of the tonalities of feeling does disappear; the emotional aspect of perception comes into its own once again; it is in a certain sense released, and freely comes forth.

A vast realm of major and minor tones appears, and the limits of what can be said or even expressed at all (52) are shifted. How could it be otherwise? The most inward elements that an artist reveals in his creative work are of the same kind, have the same inward being, and move on the same level, as these tonalities of perception; and what resonates in perception as fullness, as vitality, as intimacy of feeling, is fed from this deepest inwardness.

On the other hand, this objectifying of the subjective in aesthetic perception is only possible because it does not aim at reality, or, more precisely, because it does not attempt to place its object into the environing real world. It rather takes the object out of the sphere of reality, isolates it, and reveals it in every detail as a world unto itself. At the same time, this other way of seeing embeds its object in a new framework. The connection with the world, reflected in all other contexts of perception, is not at all injured by this act of removal, but it is kept apart from the content of aesthetical vision, and what is seen in such perception stands against the world, neutralized and insular.

If the return of the emotional element in aesthetic perception were conceived of as laying claim to knowledge, such that it pretended to establish the reality of the thing perceived, one could at most speak of a regression to the attitude of nonspiritual consciousness. However, it makes no such claim; indeed, it lays no claim at all to a relationship with knowledge. Rather, it removes itself unambiguously and with full awareness from the arena of knowledge. For that very reason, the animation of inanimate life, or the humanization of the non-human, may reappear without reproach. Malevolence and affection are, in such cases, not attributed to real objects, but rather only to what is seen, and seen as such; the "yearning" that we attribute to the blue skies or even more forcefully to the sunset are not also ascribed to aerial perspectives or to the selective absorption of the rays of the sun. We speak in the same way of a "smiling sun" or of a "lonely meadow," although we have not forgotten that the former is not smiling and the latter is not lonely.

In these ascriptions, there is nowhere real deception in-the components of feeling in perception, nowhere illusion. And in this way, aesthetic perception is distinguished from the original or primitive kind. Similarly, it abolishes neither aesthetical distance nor objectivity as such. Rather, it establishes next to objective knowledge (and next to practical and immediate knowledge) a new, peculiarly aesthetical distance and objectivity, one unmixed with the former. The mode of being of this world of objects is that it exists only for the person who perceives aesthetically.

Within its restricted sphere, however, aesthetic perception constitutes its own domain of objects, which maintains itself alongside of reality, and indeed, with respect to its vivid fullness, stands perhaps above it. In the aesthetical experience of nature and of things human, it plays a decisive role. A primeval relation to the environing world resonates within it, and extends itself into the very midst of discursive experience of the world, but it does not distort that relation or that experience, and it remains also unaffected by them. A dark sympathetic sense of mysterious unseen regions forces itself among hard facts, but it does not flow (53) into them, it does not deform them and is not deformed by them. In this realm next to the real there is room for free play, without borders and without inhibitions.

This fact is confirmed when we examine the "playtime" of children. In play there is a kind of consciousness at work that is similar to the primeval consciousness; it is a creative consciousness to a large extent, and is closely related to aesthetical consciousness. Playthings have the tonalities of feeling of perception attached to them; they are to a great extent seen anthropomorphically, as possessing attitudes of their own, and as being "good" or "bad." For that reason a doll, however primitive in aspect, can be a person, one with a character that may be nice or not-so-nice; it possesses its own willfulness, conflicts, guilt, and culpability. In this world, a couple of lines on the floor become a house, and a few rules of the game become the rules of life. But the awareness of reality, out of which the game has been lifted, remains untouched; and even a child is able to return to reality without any confusion of the two spheres when reality calls him back.

Within certain limits, the same is the case in grown-up games, into which a man enters when he seeks to "relax" from the harshness and stress of life. He obeys, as does the child, the rules of the game, once he has learned them; he acts according to them, and thereby enters a realm created by fantasy that has been lifted out of the real world. The difference between him and the child is only that he remains aware of the game as such, and that he is not able to forget the real world around him as he plays. To him, the game remains a fiction.

b) The given-with and the process of revelation

Still more important in the aesthetical relation is the other aspect of the element of transcendence in perception: objective elements and even entire sides or levels of the object are given along with it. These elements cannot be given as such through the senses because they are not accessible to the senses (not visible, not audible, etc.). We are nonetheless sensible of them as though they had been perceived directly along with the givens of the senses (Cf. Chaps. 1a, b).

What happens without exception in everyday perception, but is rarely noticed because it fits into the context of experience and is familiar to us as a completion of it, rises in aesthetic perception to the level of the essential. For here it is precisely a question of the overlapping of two or more levels of the perceptual object, such that one can "appear" in the other.

Thus, for example, in the leap of a fleeing deer we perceive grace, lightness, the mastery of space, and, with them, though dimly, even the purposefulness of life. These things are not comprehended only subsequently in reflection; we are struck immediately by the grace of the leap, and our being so stricken is a part of aesthetical vision. But at the same time, this vision is tied so intimately to perception that we think we have perceived gracefulness itself directly. (54)

It is the same when we see a bird of prey on the wing, or even the movement of a human body. In an impulsive turn of the body, a slight inclination of the head, or a momentary contraction of the lips, we comprehend directly what is not perceivable in itself, the psychic reaction, the inward state, that which the man felt. The movement is expression, and the expression speaks convincingly to us as we look upon it. An entire inward world appears, either illuminated as if by lightning, or clad in ominous darkness; but always something that had been hidden is revealed. Perception thus transcends itself, it "reveals." And if the revelation in perception goes beyond that which is humanly knowable or other-wise accessible, and with a stroke breaks beyond the limits of understanding and takes on the character of "appearance" in an unusual sense, then we become sensible of it – not as having enriched our insight, but rather as beauty.

This concept of revelation must be placed at the center of the phenomenon of aesthetic perception.[34] This does not define the concept as yet. To do so will be our further task. The task cannot be completed by reference to the phenomenon

---

34 Whoever thinks that "revelation" [*Offenbarung*] is too high-flown a term should remember how [Friedrich Daniel Ernst] Schleiermacher [1768–1834] uses it in his moral philosophy for the capacity of men to reveal themselves wordlessly.

of perception alone; it is the main concern of the entire field of aesthetics, and will occupy us in all that follows.

What is disclosed is just as much an individual limited thing as that which is given to us directly through the senses. It is tied to the here and now of perception, and shares the uniqueness of the experiential act and the givenness of the object, a givenness that is felt as "contingent." The examples given demonstrate that very clearly, especially if we note the element of the surprising, which governs them on many levels. But there is much more present in the object disclosed, a general element, even when, in fact, the general element itself – that which is typical about the object, perhaps – does not enter consciousness. At least the consciousness of the general does not have to be clear.

This may be seen in our example. When we look upon the elastic and powerful leaping movement of an animal in the wild we somehow know directly that the grace and the sure mastery of motion are not tied to this one moment, that they belong to the animal essentially, that this is a lasting ability and perfection of the animal, and that it belongs to all members of its species. There is revealed here something of the great secret of organic nature, the purposefulness of all living things.

This realization occurs to us suddenly. It may, afterwards, occupy our thoughts considerably, but at first it is given only momentarily in perception, with a suddenness that can be frightening. We look as it were through a narrow passageway into a realm of wonders that we see only for a moment. Yet our amazement at what we see is already an amazement at what is essential in it, and thus we are stricken (55) by something larger, more wide reaching, and immeasurably meaningful. And our feelings can rise to the level of being genuinely moved, even to our standing reverentially before what we do not know and can only suspect.

But even that remains firmly tied to the pictorial content of perception. The fullness of content of the thing seen is in it and given with it, in the same way as if it had also been perceived. Even when we dwell upon it later, what has been seen remains tied to the picture. It has disappeared, of course, but is still inwardly present. The transient quality of the appearance changes nothing.

We may call this phenomenon the "mediated immediacy" in aesthetic perception.[35] The mediation occurs through the external sense impression; the immediacy is the disappearance of the mediation in the perceiving consciousness. Through it then the element mediated in this consciousness stands unmediated before us, and we become sensible of it as such.

---

35 This expression is a free adaption of a well-known concept of Hegel (*vermittelte Unmittelbarkeit*), which, however, was coined for use in a different context.

This entire relationship is obviously coincident with that of the two kinds of beholding in the act of aesthetical apprehension, about which we have spoken at the very outset (Introduction, §12). A second act of seeing clings to the first, but in such a way that both are connected in series, and yet both are there simultaneously. The second act is not separated off from the first, and the entire complex is only *one* act of seeing. What may be most important here is that even the mediated element of the general is given intuitively in complete immediacy, and not discursively or by abstraction.

In this respect, aesthetic perception is similar to everyday practical perception. But the former penetrates further, and it does not limit itself to those present realities that are dictated by interest. It is in this way quite without limits. Even the limits of the real do not exist for it. What appears to be given along with it may as well be something that is unreal, even if it appears only in intuition. This is essential for the arts – for romances, fables, and fantasy. Here is found the basis of aesthetical vision's freedom from the limitations of the merely experiential, and its escape by force into the realm of the possible.

c) Dwelling upon the "picture"

With this the question appears once again how aesthetic perception differs from everyday perception. From what we have just said, it may appear as though the difference were simply quantitative. That cannot be; there must be a fundamental difference present here. If not, whatever was an object of sober perception in everyday life would be simply "less beautiful."

We might also express our question as follows: how is the relation of aesthetical appearance constituted? We have already seen that the relation of appearance in general exists in all perception, or at least (56) is attached to it. What constitutes the peculiar nature of this relationship in intuitive aesthetical seeing?

We cannot answer this question all at once. The first thing that can be said about it is this: in aesthetic perception, the relation of appearance as such is accentuated, it is forced into consciousness and, in a certain sense, it is even grasped objectively.

We cannot say that in everyday perception appearance is only a passageway to something else or a means to an end (for it is precisely practical ends that, in life, determine perception) and that the means themselves are simply not noticed. Everyday perception is concerned with comprehending existing things. By contrast, in aesthetic perception the means are the essential thing. Our vision does not glide over and beyond the pictorial content of sense perception, but rather rests awhile with it. And while it is dwelling there, it takes what appears in it as set within a picture. It takes this appearance to be something that can only be grasped in it, and as capable of being sensibly intuited by means of it, but not as identical with it.

Intuitive vision is autonomous here. It is not there to serve, but to be the dominant authority; it is there for its own self alone. For that reason, it is close to perception and set within it, as it were; it does not cast perception off, but keeps its eye upon what is given through the senses, despite its elevation over it. For it does not advance to a conceptual level – not even from its higher standpoint – any more than to the level of insight and judgment. And where we nonetheless find an element of conceptualization in it – for after all, a concept is fundamentally also only a kind of vision – its role is rather a subordinate one, that of a mere means that vanishes when its goal is achieved.

Aesthetical vision itself comes to rest in the act of seeing. For that reason, it clings to that act. That is understandable even in the case of perception. For there does not exist a higher form of vision apart from it, but only with it and integrated in-it. Thus, when the soul is uplifted in aesthetical vision, perception is not abandoned; rather one could say that it is elevated along with it. That role is not granted to everyday perception: there it is utilized, integrated into experience, but then left behind and forgotten.

We can understand why that is so by making a contrast with the relation of knowledge. Aesthetic perception is not concerned with insight and understanding, any more than with the achievement of ends, even those of the highest kind. It does not carry here the burden of obligation, nor does it have the task of discovering truth. It proceeds freely in whatever direction it goes. Aesthetic perception is satisfied by pictorial quality, by the binding of bright fullness, by unity, wholeness, polish, and structure in the whole; and in such a way that this unity includes what is given to the senses and what is therein given along with it. In pictorial quality of this kind, the most remote and most general things, which are seen along with it, also participate in it as the proximate and immediate elements of its givenness. And much that remains incomprehensible in the indirect way of conceptualization can be given in this immediacy of the "picture." (57)

What once made up the first thesis of the "Analytic of the Beautiful" in the *Critique of the Power of Judgment* is confirmed here from a somewhat altered standpoint: the detachment of the mind from all interest in the thing at hand. A practical or theoretical desire prescribes, by leading and selecting, a certain direction to our everyday perception. Aesthetic perception aims neither at something desired nor at something real (truth); it also does not aim at knowledge of human nature, however much that may seem to be the case, simply because such knowledge is to a large extent obtained by it. The perceptual field is not in this case subject to a prior orientation towards values. Neither what is important in itself nor for us alone is decisive here. Values of this kind may well play the role of directing our attention; aesthetic perception engages itself, after all, in the very midst of life, and appropriates its object only then – just by engaging itself. Yet in aesthetic perception an orientation towards values is not decisive. It occupies itself in the selection from among what is at hand, or in summoning forth what is not at hand, and does this according to rules of its own: it floats freely about, it is playful, and loves to tear things asunder and reunite them again, to add things together and break links between them. Its connecting threads may run obliquely across those of real life, but it has at the very least a certain indifference to them.

That fact is reflected in the altered position it takes to the pictorial content of sense perception as such, of which we spoke earlier as the first distinctive characteristic of aesthetic perception.

In everyday perception, the "picture" disappears when it has succeeded in making available that which is invisible. The picture itself is unimportant; it is only a means, and is forgotten – and often forgotten in an instant – for the sake of the thing that is the object of its interest. Who remembers the precise shape of a human face at which one is gazing, even a face that fully engrosses one? Surely no one, except possibly a person who is trained and practiced in drawing. But even he no longer perceives in an "everyday" manner, but rather as a draftsman would, that is, aesthetically. What we remember otherwise about a face, what we really apperceive from the very outset, is its inner expressiveness, for example its goodness, its air of suspicion or of suppressed rage. Beyond that, what we remember is at most something of the psychophysical dynamics of the play of features, but even they belong for the most part to the level of the invisible.

On the other hand, in aesthetic perception the picture not only remains essential, but also constitutes an independent unity of form and is present to this perception for its own sake. This is not as though the invisible element that it mediates is overlooked, or not viewed for its own sake; it becomes an object of our vision precisely at this point, but not detached, not made independent. The two levels of vision remain united, and the truth is that the entire picture, in which both the first and the second act of viewing it are only parts, is viewed together. The picture as a whole, with its sensible and non-sensible contents, is present to aesthetical vision.

We see this in painting, that is, in the creation of an artist: we are not indifferent to the color technique or even to the brushstrokes; both (58) belong essentially to what is seen in the work of art, just as much as what is represented by it, viz., the landscape or human figures and the psychic states that they express. And precisely this integration of the two levels of objects seen is the genuine object of aesthetical vision. He who sees only the figures, the scene, or the emotion, does not see artistically; such a person is attuned only to the content and to the human natures represented by the picture. He is looking just as one may look at human figures passing by: his perception is basically of the everyday kind. Likewise, the person who sees only the colors and notes nothing of their vivid reciprocity upon the canvas, sees as one sees only the superficial qualities of things. The one and the other see nothing of the work of art; the peculiar suspended quality of the art object does not exist for them, and they do not experience the phenomenon of appearance as such.

The sensible contact with the subject matter, even the deepest participation in the lives of persons and their destiny (as represented in a dramatic work) does not in itself turn vision into artistic vision. In artistic vision, the act of seeing forces its way through the pictorial element as through a medium that one leaves behind once one has done with it. Only where the picture as a sense object as such is comprehended and held fast as one sees through it, and then only without it interfering with the act of seeing-through, can the relationship of appearance come into its own. Only then are we sensible of it along with all else – we see the sufficiency of the picture for allowing the appearance of the non-sensible and the non-pictorial. And this means that only here does it become an artistic vision, for which alone the artwork exists.

This account of the matter may also be traced to perception – of the aesthetical kind. For if the picture given to the senses is not present in aesthetic perception as an object, then there are no ways and means to bring the non-visible to genuine givenness, not even, for example, by reenacting it subsequently in an act of reflection. Let us just try to represent to ourselves a concrete picture of the psychic life of a person as it is given in perception or in a well-done portrait, in some other way – much as we would like to be able to do when we want to describe to another person the impression someone has made upon us. We arrive quickly at the limits of what words, and even carefully formed concepts, are able to render. It is simply impossible. What the sensible picture can achieve is absolutely irreplaceable.

d) The guidance of perception in the aesthetical relation

Many other phenomena can be described in this context. In everyday perception our eyes do not pass over only the "picture" of the perceptual object as a whole, but over its details as well, at least in those cases where they do not stand out because of some particular practical interest on the part of the perceiver. The details that our eyes skim over are quickly forgotten; at most they will be held fast for a while in the pictorial perceptions of the "eidetic" philosophers, so that the one or the other can be specified later on. (59)

Even this matter is different in aesthetic perception. Here the detail rises to the level of the essential; not all details, of course, but still an amazing number of them. The picture that offers itself to aesthetic perception contains a richness that is foreign to the more vulgar form of seeing and hearing. There is no question that this richness depends upon a heightened intensity of perception itself. In aesthetic perception, the power of apprehension possessed by hearing and seeing goes far beyond what it is capable of in everyday life. This is true in a special sense, and not only with respect to heightened acuity. The sailor has sharper eyes than the painter does, and the hunter's ears are sharper than the musician's. But both of them see and hear only certain determinate things in the symphony of the perceivable; everything else is suppressed and left unnoticed. Aesthetical seeing and hearing are intensified in another dimension, where they are qualitatively extended: they notice the unnoticed, which the senses normally glide over. In this way, they make us conscious of another form of diversity. One can enter a room and see only the person to whom one wants to speak; one can also see the ray of sun that shines into the room, see the play of darkness and light, or the play of colors and highlights that fill the room.

One wonders again what such phenomena are based upon. And, in wondering, one may come across another basic phenomenon of aesthetic perception: apparently, this form of perception is also subject to a kind of guidance, and this guidance is fundamentally different from what is found in our everyday relationship to objects.

In everyday life, seeing and hearing are guided by practical considerations, and with time they are sharpened more and more in the direction of this guidance. This is not only true in such extreme cases as that of the sailor or the hunter, but also in our informal social contacts. We hear, for example, a word spoken in a whisper emerge from a loud conversational din, because we have an interest in the person who is speaking or a concern to hear what is said.

Aesthetic perception is subject to a different kind of guidance. In a Dutch still life it is the reflections of light, the shading and tinges of color, which otherwise are hardly noticed, that emerge as the essential objective detail – and do so entirely for their own sake. In the landscape, and not only in the painted one, we become conscious of perspective, which, in everyday perception, is absorbed entirely into the objects that are given in it, because perspective is subject to the familiar phenomenon of re-objectification.[36] This is true for both geometrical and

36 For the nature of the phenomenon of re-objectification, cf. *Aufbau der realen Welt* [*The Construction of the Real World*], 2nd edition, 1950, Chap. 38c, and also *Philosophie der Natur* [*Philosophy of Nature*], 1950, Chaps. 8c and 15f.

aerial perspective; both are comprehended together, or, even better, seen together.

The same is true of course in endless numbers of other cases. It is true for the timbre of the sounds uttered in speech, as it is for musical instruments; it is true even for the sound of the human voice and it is true in life as in poetry about the gestures and behavior of human beings. All of these things become essential, important, accentuated; the poet lifts them out of their unnoticed obviousness; as soon as they are (60) brought into the light, they become expressive and revealing. But then, too, the man who sees beauties in the living human being and in nature lifts them in the very act of looking and listening into consciousness and makes them his essential focus.

One may ask: what is it that does the guiding when aesthetic perception is subject to it? Why do the sensible details appear in them in this way and become the central focus? One might first answer: because what is not noticed in everyday life deserves to be noticed. It is itself beautiful, and it only disappears from view only because we usually pass over it quickly; the aesthetical perspective, and especially art, reveals it. Revelation as the standpoint on value is the guiding principle. In this way, aesthetic value, purely as such, would be called upon to answer our question. The aesthetical perceptual field must be pre-selected under the aegis of values of this type – in the same manner as the everyday perceptual field is preselected under the aegis of practical values.

There must be something unchallengeable about this answer. However, it leaps over many components of the problem that are presupposed by it. For aesthetic value is dependent upon the relation of appearance, and yet our reflections are still upon the level of one of the conditions of this relation, namely the act of becoming conscious of sensible details. We must therefore look for another solution.

In the essence of the details, there is a further aspect that offers itself as a guiding power: the small details that are given in sense experience have, once we become conscious of them, a significant mediating power. This is true in two senses. They always draw further details into the light of consciousness, and thus function as points of crystallization for perception; and they allow the appearance of the non-sensible, that is, the background – animation, human states of a psychic and a moral kind, but also the element of the universal as such in the physical world. This means, however, that details are capable of revelation to a greater extent than the sparsely differentiated content of everyday perception.

Where we have a case of a relation of appearance, the power of revelation is the decisive element. And where this power is most forcibly applied, aesthetic perception is drawn in that direction; here we can hence grasp a determining element of guidance, which occurs only in acts of aesthetical vision. What appears by its mediation is quite far from being absorbed by the detail, and even less by individuality and uniqueness. It is quite capable of including the element of the general, and not only generalities about human beings, but also about nature. Thus, a particular play of light upon something that is given through the senses may reveal the miracle of light in general and colors and even of visibility in general, and they become knowable as such. Such disclosure is unpredictable. But aesthetical experience teaches us that such things happen in fact, and that they are not at all unusual – they happen in the viewing of a work of art as well as in the freely roving eye of the person who perceives aesthetically. (61)

On the other hand, the paradox appears here that precisely what we think of as closest to perception and first noticed in it, viz., the purely sensible detail, is rather the thing most remote from it, and is discovered only by the spiritual consciousness when it is at a very advanced stage of maturity. For that reason, aesthetic objectivity is chronologically the last thing to be achieved, and most often it had to be first discovered by the eye of the creative artist.

The secret of this phenomenon of guidance may accordingly be located at the line of demarcation between everyday and aesthetic perception. This line always goes directly through our "perceptual world," and usually it is blurred; only in the most realized and thoroughly accentuated work of an artist does it become visible to us. The careful observer may find it announced, as it were, in the midst of everyday things: he notices it when something unimportant and superfluous somewhere in his perceptual field captures him, moves him, and holds him fast; when what is ephemeral becomes enduring, when what is trivial becomes important, when the colors and highlights of things begin a play among themselves that has nothing to do with the things upon which they play, or when the most serious events of human life, with all their cares and aggravations, suddenly, as though by nothing more than a simple change of direction, display for us a smiling face, and allow us to smile also.

Then the detail becomes visible and objective; and then we see its peculiar power to change the direction of our focus; indeed, the appropriation of the invisible depends upon it. That which requires the most differentiated power of expression can express itself only in the most differentiated detail, even if what is expressed is an entirely different thing from the detail, and similar to it in no respect. For that reason in aesthetic perception the emphasis lies always in the first instance upon the external, the unimportant, and the secondary. The poet loves to lead his reader along pathways through the merely external features of the behavior, activities, and speech of his characters toward what is most inward and heavy with meaning. We are shown their self-revelation and their efforts to conceal themselves, their eternal self-deception, and the unexpected moment when they get things right. One almost wants to believe that the smaller and more insignificant the detail, the greater the disclosing power that lies within it.

One may accordingly always respond by asking in return how it is possible that the function of mediating and disclosing, which after all presupposes that a given detail is already an object of consciousness, could nevertheless turn perception toward it. Such a question is quite logical. Yet it fails to consider that we do not have here a simple order of temporal succession, that in intuitive consciousness everything is conditioned and influenced reciprocally, and that all exchanges between levels and phases of acts of viewing objects involve a passage back and forth between them. It also fails to consider that every content that arises in consciousness immediately casts its shadow before itself, and that through which it is evoked then draws it after itself, and raises it to the light of full consciousness. Given such modes of psychic interrelatedness, what is temporally posterior may well determine (62) that which is immediately prior, because its origins lie in what was previously imperceptible, and what was imperceptible can only now unfold itself.

Our modern psychology has seen these things only slightly, and has dealt with them even less. They may also be hard to grasp before one has developed the categories of psychic existence. Given the state of inquiry today, and the direction of current academic interests, such an achievement is still quite distant.

Chapter 3: Pleasure in Beholding

a) The conservation of the dynamic-emotional element in aesthetic perception

What was treated in the first two chapters under the collective title of "perception" does of course not pertain to perception alone. Everywhere elements of a higher form of seeing entered, for example those of dwelling-upon, taking pleasure in, appraisal, and many others. They all remain tied to perception; they have a common point of departure in it, and do not break away from it as they develop further. Even the higher form of looking that now enters the process remains in its character close to perception, indeed related to it.

Perception plays for all of them the role of the primordial phenomenon. But it is already apparent that precisely as a primordial phenomenon it is not yet aesthetic perception. And even the primordial phenomenon in it is not an aesthetical one as such. The main thing about it is not its distance, not the objective relation, not even the passive looking, but the connection to, the integration within, the vital responsiveness of the organism and the psychophysical whole. Thus we have the dominance of the emotions, the elements of excitement, anxiety, and desire. The organism extends itself in an active-reactive manner in the environing world, it exists in exchanging substance and energy with it, and perception is the organ that permits its orientation within it.

Perception is not in itself pure looking; it is not uninvolved. It conveys to human life a sense of things as "effective." Looking is secondary; it is based initially in the disengagement of the emotional element. Perception is inherently as little theoretical as it is aesthetical. It becomes both only when it is released from actuality.

But while in theoretical "observation" responsiveness is completely disconnected, it appears that something of it is preserved in aesthetical experience. For the tonality of feeling of perception, the pleasant and the unpleasant, is essential to it. The tonality of feeling is, however, conditioned by the attitude of responsiveness. The light and the heavy in the object are felt; the inhibited and the free, the playful and the cumbersome, the fullness and the needful, strength and weakness, are made present to our senses. The decisive dynamic Something is the carrier of these (63) elements. Yet they are given in perception in the form of something felt. In this sense, therefore, – that is, in an entirely objective sense – the emotional element is not yet eliminated here. Correspondingly, the readiness to feel has not yet been replaced in the perceiving subject by the act of looking. The stimulus makes itself felt as it does in children. But it is no longer the dominant factor, *a fortiori* not the ruling one. The vital earnestness of the threatened creature has been transformed into joy in the unknown, in the attraction of curiosity. Or else even the entire relationship is just simply a play with all those things.

Of course, even that does not quite capture the truth. Rather there occurs here a synthesis of opposed perspectives: in the act of looking, which now begins its work, genuine distance to the material is achieved, but on the other hand, the emotional and dynamical elements of the original perception has not been destroyed, but merely "neutralized." This neutralization is sublation in the Hegelian sense: it is "no longer" what it was, it is "retained"; it is simultaneously "elevated" into something new. Hegel's three characteristic elements, i.e., negation, retention, and elevation, are clearly present, and are essential to the new circumstances.

One finds them all still tangibly present in the perception of a beautiful human body. The body is first practically recognized as such (in its performance) and admired or desired (erotically); this relationship to it is neutralized in the perception of form as such and thereby put in brackets, and yet at the same time elevated in an act of pleasure of a higher order. There is absolutely no contradiction that the feeling-tones of the first level are retained while the actuality that arose out of them is lost and in the end entirely disregarded. The warmth of the sensation is not identical to the original reactivity or with the vital urge. The perceiving consciousness has become contemplative; it interrupts the response, and lets it disappear while the spiritual feeling-tone remains attached to the object.

b) Perception and beholding

With the isolation of details and the extended graphic quality, we have already passed beyond the range of perception. To specify its exact limits is not possible. But we need not be concerned with that question; barriers do not separate the levels of conscious acts, for they pass imperceptibly into one another.

Nonetheless, a different type of experience now comes into play. And it is what forms, without break or alteration, the continuation of the process of grasping complexity, which began unnoticed in perception itself. This other form of perception is no less concrete, yet it is no longer sensory, that is, its object is not given to the senses; it is directed upon what was "given" in perception "along with" it, which, however, (64) is not a perceptual object in the strict sense. It is directed rather at what "appears" in the perceptual object, and, again with reference to the object, at what is "disclosed" in it. And in that way, it takes on the character of revelation.

In a certain sense all seeing has the character of a revelation, and thus we are saying nothing new here. Language, however, ties "revelation" to the notion of the discovery of something or other in life that has been hidden, especially where the play of fantasy has long cloaked it in mystery. The dark presentiment-laden tie to an unknown object hidden behind a thing is largely already present in perception; in the phenomenon of co-givenness one may find all levels of this relationship. In the higher or cultivated beholding there begins the process in which what was indefinite becomes definite. Then it is directed upon everything that begins to present itself as phenomenal behind what is given to sense: upon the living state, upon the activity of the soul, and upon what is akin to soul in the background, upon the secrets of nature and of the cosmos, to the most general secrets of man and world themselves. No limits are set to it. For that reason, religious objects have been since time immemorial so close by; and thereupon rests the fact that everything that is true for divine revelation demands irresistibly some artistic representation. This is nothing other than the power that self-revelation possesses for everyone, and especially for things that not everyone can bring to concrete givenness by himself or herself. It is not by chance that great art throughout history has grown out of and has taken its themes from religious conviction. One may not, however, conclude that its historical origins set limits to it. Such an origin, from the perspective of art, provides only a temporary preferred direction to its activities.

At this point, we meet already with the first main element of the higher form of seeing, or beholding. It is directed upon what hovers before consciousness as the most meaningful and signifying element, what appears to come from above, laden with meaning and value. It receives its direction not from sensory impressions, but from another sphere. And in this sphere, other forces reign that have seized consciousness in a different way. Even at this point commences, in the last analysis, that mysterious directness of perception in the aesthetical realm about which we spoke earlier, for this one is directed primarily at the detail, unnoticed in everyday perception and present in the sensory material, which are most capable of transmitting what is laden with meaning.

It is clear from this that the higher form of looking is always present in aesthetic perception and not subsequent to it; and it is clear why this is so: perception, appearing as tied to it, is already directed by it. It comes to be as this looking of the first order only with the looking of the second order, which simultaneously takes off from it. And one can assume, in a preliminary way, that only by means of the second order is it made (65) capable of the detailed graphic quality by means of which it distinguishes itself from vulgar perception, which is integral to responsiveness and is directed by it. Quite possibly we can glimpse here the basis of all aesthetical phenomena in which the object stands out from its connectedness with reality and the viewer becomes lost in reverie. But that would anticipate a later inquiry, and we may put the matter off for a while.

The inquiry is closer at hand as to what constitutes the positive content of the higher form of looking, or beholding. Very little can be determined from the perspective of the act of looking. Because the content appears first upon the object, only the analysis of the aesthetic object will be able to inform us about it. An attempt at an anticipatory analysis of the act would be useless labor, at least before the being of the object is clarified. Even more, only from the side of the object is it possible to understand how the higher form of looking works, and in what it essentially consists as an act. Any analysis of the act that is left to its own devices will fail. The real miracle that takes place on the side of the aesthetical act is the firm binding to perception of what is grasped and the interaction between the two kinds of looking, which are superimposed one upon the other and yet appear simultaneously.

Meanwhile, this much may be said in advance: all ideational content of the aesthetic object is relative to the higher act of beholding and is entirely grasped by it; and this, moreover, is indifferent to whether the object presents itself as "realized" in a real object – as in human and in natural beauty – or simply as magically placed before one's eyes, like the work of an artist. Then there is no question here of knowing something real. All "intuition" simply as such can be cognitive or spontaneously creative. That is true also of the higher levels of aesthetical appreciation. The ideational content of the aesthetic object, and everything that is determined along with it, can also very well be grasped in a synthetic and productive act and thus exist only by virtue of the act – quite indifferent to whether it is a question of the original productive act of the artist or of the act of observation that follows it.

It may be said further that the higher vision need not be simple or without parts. It can itself have levels, such that an entire hierarchy of acts of increasing elevation arises behind and above perception. Perception is here only its first link. The levels of intuition that lie closest to it are still similar to it, and appear therefore to belong to it; the higher levels, which contain ever more elements of thought, distance themselves from it, and the spontaneous and productive element in them increases, and leads to the creation of form. When a certain level is attained, the vision approaches again the level of knowledge, yet comes into conflict with it, and can become tied to it in a confusing way. But its nature and the direction in which it is looking remain different, even though they may share with it a claim to truth. And finally, it distances itself from knowledge, and leads beyond it. Then at the top are located (66) the genuine forms of "intuition" in that pregnant sense of *visio*, which in all historical epochs were considered superior to the *cogitatio*.

For that reason, it makes sense that the last forces, working from within outward, down to the level of perception – beyond all forming of the particular substance – which direct, select, and dominate, are feelings of value. For if the values given to value consciousness are grasped as an object, they are grasped intuitively, not in the form of understanding, but in the form of seeing.

This is a connection – or, perhaps better, a kind of lawfulness – that is not peculiar to the organization of the aesthetical act, but to all human consciousness, provided that it is affected with values. This law is most familiar in a practical context, but of course without regard for the kind of values in question. As phenomena of moral consciousness, we know in principle the directive power of values quite exactly; we know also the highly nuanced reaction to them of our feelings of value. Moreover, we have observed the extremely peculiar pathways upon which what can be intuited of the essential content of values comes to be out of forces that are merely felt. These pathways are not those of later analysis, the way taken by the phenomenology of values, but are forced open in the midst of life and under the pressure of real situations, and always in these cases the appearance of content-laden values is itself intuitive in nature.

The foundational schema of the upward march of value consciousness is the same in the aesthetical act. Only the kind of intuition is different, and different too are the occasions that cause it to function. It too extends into various peculiarities that are not available to vision upon the practical standpoint.

However that may be, this much results in any case for the organization of the aesthetical act: the value-elements in it do not separate themselves from it, but are rather completely integrated into it.

c) The role of vital and moral feeling of values

Meanwhile, the feeling and seeing of the values themselves that are here in question are in no sense aesthetic values. They are rather all those that reign in practical – and even in theoretical – life. Most basic are the vital and the moral values, but the wide sphere of commodity values are included here; that sphere is simply more concealed as self-evident behind the others. None of these values should be confused with the values that can be felt in aesthetical "appreciation," in the enjoyment of beauty, and in the elevated reverie of the observer.

Let us begin with the most familiar things. In sculpture and in many cases of natural beauty we are concerned with such values as (67) the strong, the vital, the healthy, the burgeoning, and the fecund, with physical capacity and purposefulness; we are not concerned with grace in movement, or the poverty or the harmony of form. Similarly, we are concerned in poetry and in our observations of the ways of men primarily with kindness, love, and faithfulness; with honesty and justice, the capacity for sacrifice, courage, and chivalry. One must add here that there is of course also a concern with their counterparts, with the negative values: with injustice, thoughtlessness, dishonesty, and underhandedness. For the whole of human life in all its aspects come into play here. Poetic figures can be understood without such components of value and disvalue no more than the other elements of life. The courage to make sacrifices belongs to the hero, and he must be given a feeling for values, for otherwise neither the audience in the theater nor the observer of life could recognize the hero as hero.

The most important feature is that this value-content constitutes for aesthetical appreciation only the presupposition of the aesthetic value and not its content. Vital values are and remain vital ones; moral values are simply moral ones. But they must be felt in a living manner if the quite different aesthetic value is to appear on the object. In this sense, one may say: the aesthetical consciousness of value is conditioned by the capacity of the observer to perceive the non-aesthetic values. And with this point, the highest level of intuition in aesthetical looking becomes unambiguously clear. Intuition shows itself so dominant in the nexus of acts of looking that all the lower acts are conditioned through it, even down to the direction of perception itself. Just this direction is the steering of attention upon that visible detail, which allows what is significant or consequential among such values to appear. We learn how true this is from life itself via the fact that value feeling is enormously strengthened and sharpened by aesthetical looking, and is even in many cases first awakened by it.

"How" in detail aesthetic value superimposes itself upon ethical and vital values – upon one and the same object and in one and the same act of seeing – that belongs to the analysis of aesthetic values and will be examined in its proper place. We must for a time stay with the fact that a conditional relationship exists here, which is determinative throughout, including the act of seeing itself. In the representational arts, this act is always first directed at the content that comes to appearance. The content is the formed material. With respect to the material, there is in turn a law that the entire manifold of Nature and Ethos, including its laws and its value-qualities, constitute its nature. However, the new form must be superior to it – just as the aesthetic values are superior to the practical and vital values. Here we find one of the reasons why all of the representational arts begin with "imitation," but then, as they progress, grow beyond it. But this again anticipates what is to come. (68)

d) Pleasure, delight, enjoyment

The place of pleasure is not to be separated from these things in the structure of the aesthetical act. It is the subjective reverse of looking, and indeed on all its levels. Nevertheless, it is merely "subjective" only as a pure tonality of feeling; what we obtain by it and what it shows us is something quite objective – precisely what forms the content of "judgments of taste." However, a judgment of taste expresses only what the pleasure he takes in looking says to him who judges. Pleasure thus has a central place in the structure of the act.

Despite this fixed relationship, pleasure is in its nature a completely independent element in the aesthetical relationship. It cannot be reduced to anything else, and for that reason it may be subjected to an independent analysis. Among the older thinkers Kant, and among the more recent ones Moritz Geiger, each dedicated penetrating inquiries to it, and the results they obtained belong to the best that has been achieved in the realm of aesthetics. Nonetheless, there is a danger that just this independence of the element of feeling in pleasure leads the analysis into the realm of subjectivity, and in this way, aesthetics became shifted to one of the psychological pathways that by the nineteenth century had been shown to be failures.

The genuinely aesthetical element in pleasure first appears when we examine its relationship to the object. For the peculiarity of aesthetical pleasure is that it is not less "objective," that is, related to an object, than is the act of looking. It points to values, indeed to the aesthetic values exclusively. True, as such this pleasure is the authoritative announcement of values within the structure of the aesthetical act. There are no others besides it. One could also say: it is the primary or immediate form of aesthetical consciousness.

A broad range of aesthetical consciousness becomes apparent here, and an entire segment of the manifold of values, ones not smaller than the manifolds of objects and acts. But we must note immediately that this consciousness is open only to feeling and not to thought, and that the fullness of the phenomena given through pleasure cannot be captured by means of analysis, and can be translated only via inadequate and approximate verbal expressions in concepts and theories. Here philosophical aesthetics stumbles upon impassible barriers, of which it must be aware and of which it must be respectful.

If upon reflection pleasure and value cannot be separated, even though the first belongs to the subject and the second to the object, then (69) the same is true mediately of pleasure and object. For a value depends exclusively upon the object. For that reason, the element of pleasure in announcing the presence of value becomes apparent only in its relation to the object. A strict order of subordination rules here, and it is just this aspect of the feeling of aesthetical pleasure that is important.

The more objective concepts of "delight" [*Wohlgefallen*] and "enjoyment" [*Genuss*] do justice to this order (Kant preferred the first concept, Geiger the second). One can feel delight only "in something," and one can only enjoy "something" The first expression like the second implies by this relationship not just a cause, whose effect would be the feeling, but an object explicitly intended in delight and in enjoyment. The proposition, "aesthetical pleasure is delight (or is enjoyment)" means primarily that pleasure attributes itself to the object, turns towards it, orients itself upon it, and is determined by it, and in this sense is "objective."

This may seem obvious to a person with artistic sensibilities. Whoever reflects upon it, however, will soon see something puzzling within the obviousness. The puzzle lies in the character of feeling itself, a character that also belongs to pleasure; one might say it lies in its condition, all the more because one cannot deny to enjoyment and delight the character of a condition.

Yet evidently, it is just this being a condition that is secondary in aesthetical pleasure, while its reference to the object is primary. That is psychologically essential for the special form of this condition itself, and requires its own phenomenological analysis. Considered from the standpoint of aesthetics, what is specific to the structure of the act in the consciousness of the onlooker lies in this displacement of weight. It is a question of the character of feeling as an announcement of values. And this is possible only when the condition of feeling in it has its weight outside of itself, in some other thing that is given to him in that condition.

Aesthetical delight is not a feeling turned upon itself, and aesthetical enjoyment is not an enjoyment of itself. To the contrary, where it flows into self-enjoyment (and that happens often enough) there is no longer aesthetical enjoyment, and the artistic feeling of value carried by the object is obscured; the latter may even be drowned out. Now we have no other standard of value, and certainly no other consciousness of the value of the beautiful than the peculiar enjoyment of, or the delight in, the object. Therefore the entire weight of the aesthetical feeling of pleasure lies on its objective side, that is, on the character of feeling as an announcement of value. This side is expressed in the relative depth and the qualitative distinctiveness of the enjoyment that looking upon the object triggers.

e) Kant's doctrine of aesthetic pleasure

In the *Critique of the Power of Judgment*, Kant taught three things about aesthetical delight. They are contained in both the first principles of his Analytic of the Beautiful, and here we will present them in an arrangement (70) we have freely chosen so as to cohere with the points of the problematic discussed above.

1. Aesthetical delight is "subjectively universal" (intersubjective) and necessary. That does not mean that every person necessarily feels delight when the object is given, but rather that anyone who has met the conditions of understanding the object must feel it. This subjective universality is valid in the case of the complete indivisibility of the object, for it is not a question of transference to other objects.

2. It is delight without a concept, without subsumption under something universal or under a rule that must have been grasped as such. Its own universality (the "subjective") is least of all a conceptual one. This implies the radical exclusion of intellectualistic aesthetics. Therefore, delight must appear without a concept, because it is felt directly in perception and in the pure act of looking upon its object. One may add to this that just because it possesses no knowledge of a universal element, no cognition, no insight into law, it is not knowledge at all. Thus it possesses no criterion beyond itself or above itself.

3. It is "disinterested delight." This famous formulation does not imply, of course, that the person feeling pleasure has no interest in the aesthetic object as such. One may very well have an aesthetical interest in it, even to a high degree, without losing the correct disposition. So for example one can have the greatest interest for an artist's work in progress, just as well as one can for the finished product and its fate of being understood or misunderstood by its contemporaries. None of this is intended here, for such interest is already conditioned by the aesthetical pleasure one receives from the object; it is the consequence of that

pleasure. What is intended is solely the interest that, for its part, determines the feeling of pleasure, the practical interest in the object as it occurs when the object serves as a means to something else. Thus interest is excluded from aesthetical pleasure; it is interest for the sake of an extra-aesthetic value. The one who enjoys knows no such values, even where it is a question of values that have the highest moral worth.

The first of these Kantian principles, the intersubjective universality, points clearly toward a rootedness in the object of delight. Whoever is able to look upon the object in an aesthetically adequate way will necessarily feel the same pleasure as anyone else whose acts of observation meet the same conditions. In this respect, what is convincing about aesthetical pleasure is similar to what is convincing in the practical and the theoretical a priori; for the latter too is subject to the same conditions: even the truth of a mathematical theorem can be apparent only to a person who is capable of understanding it.

In contrast, the second principle shows us the difference between a judgment of taste that announces itself in pleasure and apriorism. The latter is tied to an objective universal, thus (according to Kant) to laws and concepts. (71) There is nothing of this kind contained in the phenomenon of aesthetical delight, just as the object of pleasure is always an individual one (thus not objectively universal). Therefore Kant says, "The judgment of taste does not itself *postulate* the accord of everyone [...]; it only *ascribes* this agreement to everyone."[37]

Finally, the third principle is of an entirely different type. "Disinterested delight" means the independence of the judgment of taste, its freedom from determining factors of a non-aesthetical sort, in short, its autonomy. And when it announces itself in pleasure, what is meant is the autonomy of aesthetical pleasure in the object. Here it is already a question of the peculiarity and the irreducibility of value feeling, and indirectly of the aesthetic values themselves.

If one understands these Kantian principles in the way set forth here (which, to be sure, abstracts from the idealistic presuppositions of Kant's system), we may find in them insight of the greatest consequence. Because of material value-ethics, we are accustomed today to glimpse the chief authority for all values given to consciousness in the feeling of value. Kant, however, connected for the first time the consciousness of value in an aesthetical context (the "judgment of taste") to delight (or rather pleasure) as its authoritative mode of givenness. Thus here – long before the development of the phenomenological concept of value – we may

---

37 [Translator's note:] Kant, Immanuel, *Critique of the Power of Judgment*, translated by Paul Guyer and Eric Matthews, The Cambridge Edition of the Works of Immanuel Kant, Cambridge and New York: Cambridge University Press 2002, p. 101.

find the real starting-point of the entire later theory of value. Then pleasure and delight are understood here unambiguously as the kinds of feeling that intend values – and in fact they intend them along with their peculiar objectivity and universality in subjective dress.

On the other hand, in Kant's expulsion of all extra-aesthetical interests, the freeing of aesthetical consciousness from the contexts of life again receives a clear expression. "Interest," in the Kantian sense, is to be held captive by the state of current affairs and the situation; an attitude devoid of "interest" means release from both. The soundness of this point is strengthened when one introduces the concept of enjoyment: in enjoyment we grasp more clearly the element of pure devotional appreciation of the object; and where the enjoyment is deep, it becomes a state of transport, in which the observer is released from his real environment and his everyday life. We speak in such cases of being "forgetful of oneself," but we do not consider that such a state is rather one of forgetfulness of the real contexts of life and of the demands made on us by the present moment.

This state of release, a kind of floating condition, as it were, is experienced as pleasure, and can be enjoyed, but it is attributed to a miraculous power in the object. For as long as the act of looking is genuinely aesthetical, it – the object – and not one's own state, is enjoyed. That which transports us and not the transport is the "beautiful." It makes sense, therefore, that to the state in which we are transported out of the real contexts of life corresponds to the transport (72) (or transference) to another set of circumstances – into the world to which the object opens us.

In this way the Kantian principles lead one quite beyond themselves without one having to depart from them. For pure pleasure in the object is, despite its "objectivity," entirely directed toward the participation of the self; it always takes place as a kind of self-fulfillment. And here we find the limits of disinterestedness. It is experienced in aesthetical enjoyment as being drawn to an object, and can develop to the point of becoming spellbound by it. This participation of the self is at the same time quite far from eliminating the distance from the object. The latter is and remains essential; the object stands ineliminably over against the subject – no less than the relationship in pure cognition, although in a different way.

Aesthetical enjoyment never cancels the attitude of seeing. Seeing, however, presupposes that the object remains over against it. Aesthetical enjoyment is not an "absorption" in the object, not an identification with it, a mystic unity. That does not happen even in music, where the soul's resonance with the music is an essential form of its appearance. This fact does not contradict the phenomenon of being grasped by the object (in contrast to the mere grasping of it), of being moved, being carried away, and not even being elevated and transported into the world of the music. These notions all express that there is no loss of our sense of standing over-against or of being at an aesthetical distance; they express only an inwardness of strong feeling and the "intimacy" of feeling, which is the peculiar quality of pleasure uniting itself with the pure act of seeing.

In aesthetical pleasure we have to do with a synthesis of aesthetical distance and the most inward state of emotional engagement that bridges this opposition between them. Language has no words for this relationship. No doubt we can talk around it dialectically with the Hegelian notion of sublation. The emphasis in such sublation of aesthetical distance must, however, lie on the second meaning of the word, that is, "remaining contained," while the third meaning "being uplifted" into a new kind of relationship expresses the synthesis, but is no longer conceptually determinate.

If one grants the validity of this kind of synthesis as not cognizable, then the meaning of the Kantian notion of disinterestedness shows itself once again on a new side. Interest is necessarily conditioned by values. Extra-aesthetic values, we have seen, are represented almost in their entire manifold within the content of the aesthetic object. Yet they do not determine aesthetical pleasure; they merely play the role of conditions. More accurately, the correct feeling for them is a condition of feeling aesthetic value. Aesthetical pleasure is not the pleasure we take in the conditioning value-components, neither in the ethical nor in the vital values, although these are also given to consciousness in the form of feeling pleasure (as positive responses to values).

Thus even here we are dealing with a sublation-relation. Aesthetical enjoyment does not aim at these conditioning values, however high they may be; since, however, they remain contained in it and are its presuppositions, (73) enjoyment also remains tied to them in its object, but it lifts itself beyond them and immediately orients itself toward the aesthetic value that is carried by them. Aesthetical enjoyment is superimposed upon the extra-aesthetic values. The element of pleasure in it forms the synthesis of their being sublated (neutralized) and their continuing containment, and it stands out unmistakably from them.

For aesthetical enjoyment announces the presence of values only in the case of aesthetic values. And this is of central significance in the structure of the aesthetical act, because we cannot experience and sense aesthetic value in any other way. For that reason what is specifically aesthetical about pleasure cannot be broken down into component parts – no more than into specific feelings related to form, although these feelings are certainly present and can be identified roughly, as with the conditioning feelings of pleasure of an extra-aesthetical kind.

If we change the perspective of this discussion a bit and return once again to the general relation between value and pleasure, the entire situation will appear as follows.

All affirmative feeling of value has the character of pleasurable enjoyment: the everyday pleasure taken in things and states of affairs, vital pleasure (especially apparent in sexual matters), and ethical pleasure-taking (in joyful agreement, recognition, promotion, admiration, enthusiasm); similarly negative feelings of value have the character of aversion (rejection, depression, contempt, disgust). All acts that announce values (value-responses) have the form of pleasurable enjoyment and painful aversion, however varied they may be. The characteristic components of pleasure in the structure of the aesthetically receptive act are thus not a single thing.

What is special about aesthetical pleasure first enters through the observational (contemplative) attitude. This attitude is that of looking, in particular the higher kind of beholding, but within certain limits also the kind of looking that is typical of aesthetic perception. If looking at a thing could be separated at this point from pleasure, we would find ourselves dealing with a very loose relationship among acts. That is precisely not the case; looking at an object is essentially pleasurable, and pleasure is essentially the pleasure in looking. The appreciative devotion that occurs just in beholding, the intensified fine sense for imponderable details that are weightless and always overlooked in everyday life, is provoked by pleasure; this, however, is a feeling of value, and in fact of aesthetic value, which overlies all practical value. Aesthetical beholding, with its peculiar indwelling stance on its object, is made capable, by means of its unity with pleasure, of that synthesis of becoming lost in the object and yet maintaining distance from it, which, as we have seen forms the unity of elements in this spiritual stance that otherwise can not be unified.

If the state of appreciation was directed towards the conditioning value-components (the vital and the ethical), it would have to cancel the act of looking, for it would cancel the phenomenon of distance. Then pleasure would be produced by interest. By means of eliminating interest, in which, however, the feeling of value with those value-components is conserved, the relation of beholding (74) to its object may also be conserved, because it has been lifted into union with a value feeling of a higher order.

Finally, we must add there a word about the shifting of aesthetical enjoyment into enjoyment of oneself. The agent is able to enjoy the former as a state (one's own state). The reasons have already been given why this self-enjoyment is not aesthetical pleasure; similarly why this phenomenon is found with greater frequency among introverted persons, and why it interferes with genuine aesthetical pleasure in the object – and, along with it the relation of looking-at to objects – or suppresses or even falsifies it. If we bring together this shifting into self-enjoyment with the contrary, shifting into taking pleasure on the conditioning values (the ethical, the vital, etc.) we may see how genuine aesthetical pleasure holds itself on a narrow tightrope strung between two neighboring but totally different forms of pleasure, both of which are neither able to extend themselves to the Kantian sense of "disinterested" nor fall under it. For in both cases they lack distance, in both cases the object is not the same, and in both cases the characteristic aesthetical synthesis of pleasure and beholding is not produced.

Seen from these two sides, a high challenge is directed at the observer of the beautiful, a challenge that must be met in his attitude: he must make himself free from taking pleasure in the practical value of the content of the object, and to make himself free from valuing the condition in himself as an agent. Perhaps this double inward freedom is rarely achieved completely. Yet surely we do not often see in life this shift towards one side or the other. So it happens that we are easily deceived by the purity and genuineness of our own aesthetical pleasure.

The challenge remains, however. The work of art demands in all strictness that it be met with by the observer. The created work, even the most masterful, has only limited power to determine how well the challenge is met. The elevating power that emanates from it does not seize everyone. The capacity of devoting oneself to the object, with all its spiritual conditions, must be provided, on his side, by the observer.

Second Section: The Structure of the Aesthetic Object

Chapter 4: Connection to the Analysis of the Act

a) Two kinds of looking and two strata of the object

The provisional analysis of the structure of the act was clearly occupied with preliminaries alone. It nonetheless became clear in that context that the analysis had to confine itself each step along the way to the elements contained in the object and its values. That is not surprising, since to every act-element there corresponds an object-element. This is a relationship, however, that can be evaluated in other ways, of course, when we know more about the object. The analysis of the act is (75) not yet closed. But it can win new perspectives only when the analysis of the object is undertaken.

Therefore let us enter the most central inquiry with the question of the structure of the aesthetic object.

This procedure is not in tension with the introduction to the preliminary analysis of the act. The act simply offers clues, and is, in the present state of the discussion, the better prepared side of the whole. Hence the elements of the problem are as such more clearly visible in it. But these problems are not solvable with reference to it alone. Many puzzles point to this fact – perhaps most of all the mysterious appearance of pleasure "in" certain elements of the act; this is again identical with the synthesis of looking and enjoying.

Therefore a new kind of inquiry must begin here. In order for this to happen, we must first learn in what regions we may begin our attack upon the object. The first hints to such regions come from the structure of elements in the act. 1. Two kinds of looking are arranged one upon the other: perception and the higher beholding of something imperceptible – where the beholding impels itself toward the imperceptible, 2. The perceptible is a real presence, while what is given in the higher looking or beholding is not real, or does not need to be real; it is additional to the seen, and, indeed, possesses an element of spontaneity.

These facts are a clear sign of the stratification in the aesthetic object itself. The mere division into two members tells us as yet nothing about how the strata are constituted, how we may distinguish one from the other, and how they are tied to one another.

The idea stated in this general form is very old. And just as old are the answers to the question about this "other" that stands behind perceptible objects. Plato taught that the other is "the Form," and that this is what is grasped in the higher act of beholding. What is meant by this term is the universal as opposed to the real thing, and it has the nature of a primordial picture, which exists prior to all else in its purity and perfection (ideality). Accordingly, only the Form is genuinely "beautiful"; in the physical individual case it shines dimly forth. If one could free oneself entirely from perception, one would necessarily be able to grasp the beautiful as such, unmixed and pure.

The tendency of this doctrine suggests the exclusion of perception and its existing object. The case is similar in Plotinus and his much later disciple Marsilio Ficino[38]. The task of the observer is the same, to exclude perception and climb upward from the sensible to "intelligible beauty," thus to elevate oneself inwardly to the "pure" vision of it, one not mediated by the senses.

This doctrine obviously conflicts with the sensible element in aesthetical cognitive acts. This element is, however, essential to it, and (76) ought to be understood in its own peculiar nature. The entire relation is interpreted [i.e., Platonically] here according to the relationship of knowledge to its object and viewed intellectually, as though it was a question in aesthetical beholding of insight, of the intuition of an essence and nothing else. To this corresponds the vague meaning of καλόν among the ancients; it is just as much the Good (Valuable, Perfect) and the beautiful, and is hence not congruent with the meaning of the aesthetic object. The intuition of ideas does least justice to the aesthetic object. In the genuine aesthetical relation it is precisely the sensibly given that appears as "beautiful." The beauty of the Form, if it exists, is thus not at all beauty in the aesthetical sense.

German idealism first led the way out of this dead end. How Kant prepared the way has already been shown. Schelling and Hegel pursued this concept further. Now we say: it is not the Form itself that is beautiful, but the "sensible shining-forth [*Scheinen*] of the idea."

This formulation is by Hegel, but the thought may be described as the common possession of the idealists. Even Schopenhauer maintained it quite consciously as an "improved" Platonism.

What is new about this "sensible shining-forth of the idea"? We may summarize it under three rubrics. 1. The Form is not the beautiful, but rather the "shining-forth" is; and if it is the shining-forth of the "Form," then beauty is no longer the Form itself. 2. The shining-forth is sensible; with that, the object is recognized as an object of perception, and even an act of beholding does not separate it from perception. 3. Since the Form itself is not sensible, but appears in something that is, the object must have two parts; it must consist of sensible thing-like constructs

---

38 [Translator's note:] Marsilio Ficino (1433–1499).

as its foreground and the "Form" as the background. It is not especially surprising that the background has (or can have) a different ontological nature than the foreground, as long as one remembers its nature as an idea.

With this, a decisive transformation in the problem of the beautiful has been achieved. It is a question no longer of a high-flying metaphysics of the beautiful, but rather of a phenomenology of the beautiful, which makes fewer demands upon us, but is far more difficult to carry out. And immediately we discover the double aspect of the aesthetic object. Only now can we begin in earnest with the analysis of its essence. The quintessence of beauty is already visible: it lies in the relationship of appearance [*Erscheinungsverhältnis*].

However, we have thereby only made a start. Questions immediately arise: 1. What is the idea that appears here? 2. What does the appearing [*das Erscheinen*] consist in? Among these thinkers, "idea" was still understood as some general thing, and something like a principle (more or less in a Platonic way); the supposition behind it is again that nature and humanity are formed according to ideal primordial models (Schelling, Schopenhauer). But do (77) such things really exist? Even this thought, too, is just a remnant of ancient metaphysics that has been carried over to us unawares.

If we now assume that even beauty is no longer the perfection of such ideas, it still remains tied to the appearance of perfection; and, provided that is so, aesthetic value is left hanging upon the value-character of perfection – in poetry, for example, upon the nobility of the hero and the moral excellence of the great man. But that is precisely the error in this theory. What characterizes the essence of the beautiful is not that what appears is something perfect (a primordial model, an ideal type) but rather that it "appears," specifically 1. That it appears in a "sensible" form, and 2. It appears as indifferent to reality and unreality. What the appearing entity must have as content is not yet clear; that is still in question.

Yet what the other question about what the "shining-forth" [*Scheinen*] consists in, we can say immediately that the expression is not a felicitous one. To appear always suggests deception and illusion, and just that may lead us astray here. For, as noted earlier, nothing is simulated here, neither perfection nor a primordial model, nor even the reality of what is unreal (in poetry, the reality of the characters and conflicts). Rather something is thrust into the realm of the sensibly visible that otherwise is only accessible to the higher form of beholding, in such wise that this beholding is tied tightly to perception. But this linking neither simulates reality where there is none, nor is anything presented thereby as to "what" this element, which is accessible only by the higher kind of beholding, must be.

Thus neither "idea" nor "shining-forth" is entirely accurate. Both must be replaced by concepts that are more accurate and fitting.

b) The necessary correction of Hegel's "shining-forth of the idea"

A second correction of the definition of the aesthetic object must therefore be introduced. The first one, which Hegel made of the Platonic definition, is insufficient.

If one simply removes the "idea" from the "shining-forth of the idea," one is soon forced to recognize that the correction is not adequate. The "idea" of the idealists had not just been pulled out of a hat: there are in fact ideas that play an important role in the arts. The most familiar example of this kind is taken from religious ideas, which historically encouraged most of what we possess of great art: the early images of the gods, the Madonnas of the Italians, the temples, churches, hymns and oratorios and, yes, even tragedy. The same must be valid for many moral ideals, such as we find in heroic poetry, in drama, in portraiture and even in music.

All that is and remains essential. But it is far from constituting on its own the content that shines forth in a work of art. Much more belongs to the work, specifically that which precisely does not have the character of an idea, (78) but which is individual, unique, and even typical, and which, because of that character, are far from being absorbed into to the universality of the ideational. Here belong the characters of poetic figures, which are not given to the senses, but rather are only mediated by the senses, and appear without any claim to reality; they belong to the appearances, but they are neither absorbed by general ideas nor by the typical. Scenes acted out on stage are entirely so; the conflicts, fates, actions, and passions appear primarily as those of individual persons, and are so understood. It is similar with the persons represented in portraiture, even with the figures and facial expressions in freely composed scenes, and even when they have not been taken from life.

That is all essential, and not only for the arts. But it belongs without exception to what shines forth; in the arts, even to what is unreal; it is given only to a higher form of beholding, and only provided that it is seen also, is everyday perception lifted to the aesthetical level. Further, only provided that it is also "seen along with" can the higher looking or beholding begin, by mediation, and then proceed to the universal, to ideas that are religious, moral, etc.

In the stratification of the object, Idealism overlooked an essential member; perhaps even several of them. As in the stratification of the receptive act a connecting member of the act of beholding must exist between perception and the intuition of an idea, so in the aesthetic object a connecting layer must exist between what is sensibly given in it and the content of ideas, which is to be strictly distinguished from perception. And this connecting stratum must, just as in the latter case, belong to the appearance, and nevertheless like the former, be concrete, intuitive and individual.

Seen in this manner, the correction undertaken of the "shining-forth of the idea" is given a quite significant weight. The formula of the Idealists was still much too simple; it yoked together the oppositions contained in the object, and failed to concern itself at all with the many things that made up the connecting links. The extremities do not make the whole. In contrast, the real fullness that in fact lies in the aesthetic object is, of course, exactly this whole. On the side of the object there must therefore also be more than one connecting member, and the riches of what is beheld may lie just in the colorful manifold that is filled out by this rich domain. A new pathway to analyze the structure of the aesthetic object now opens up to us, and it lets us see in advance that the real essence of its structure can be most quickly grasped in the relation of the strata to each other.

We cannot see in advance how far this discovery may lead us, whether, for example, it is possible at all to proceed along this route to arrive at the essence of the beautiful. We can see even less our way toward an exhaustive account of it. But since as of now the route has hardly been taken, it may nevertheless promise new discoveries. (79)

The other side of the "correction" is less central. It states that it is not really a question of a "shining-forth," [*Scheinen*] but rather of an appearance [*Erscheinen*]. This shift in meaning lies in a resistance to the use of "shining-forth" because this term suggests an element of deception. But it is not that alone. Behind the Hegelian thought of "shining-forth" [*Scheinen*] there is hidden the remains of the old intellectualism: appearance implies an element opposed to truth. Truth exists only in the realm of knowledge, thus appearance exists only where there is a question of knowledge (as a limit, or as a failure of knowledge); or the opposite: only where it is claimed "that something of such-and-such quality exists" can there be appearance, deception, or a leading astray.

But here it is not a question of that kind. Whoever is unable to free himself, in reading a fairy-tale, a ballad, or any story whatever, from the question of whether "it really happened that way" does not grasp at all these literary works as such, he does not regard them aesthetically, but in a naively realistic or childlike way. Now just this realism hinders seeing, appreciation, and enjoyment, and misses entirely the elevation above the real world they offer. Such a person places a lead weight upon his capacity to be elevated; he does not give scope to the free, unattached state of beholding.

In contrast, "appearance" as such is quite indifferent to the real and the unreal. What appears at any point does so without the weight of reality, without any responsibility for the true and the false, without any claim to truth. That is why it is understood only as appearance. It is, of course, entirely an "object," but only an intentional object, that is, such that it is entirely absorbed by its being as an object, and thus is not an object of knowledge, which transcends the intentional act.

The claim to truth that nonetheless is made by poetry, as by all representational arts, refers to something quite different. We will speak of that matter in another context.

c) The place of aesthetically autonomous pleasure

With this, a new light falls upon the relationship of appearing. We see now that the phenomenon does not rest upon the structure of the act alone, but more importantly upon a structural relationship in the object. But that is not the only fact that attracts the attention here. The interrelationships in the act also appear in a new light, one that falls precisely upon the most difficult of its aspects to comprehend: pleasure, delight, and enjoyment.

We saw that pleasure does not depend upon the thing that appears, not even upon what is sensibly given "in" which it appears, but rather on the phenomenon of appearing itself. We can supplement this observation by noting that pleasure also does not depend on the content of an idea, and for this reason it is not a value-response to values other than aesthetic values, but rather depends exclusively upon the way in which the appearing phenomenon (including its value-components) presents itself to consciousness. Now pleasure is the factor in the nexus of the aesthetical act that genuinely announces values, that is, it is through pleasure and through it alone – that is, in the form of pleasure – that being beautiful as such is given. (80)

That fact is also misunderstood by the aesthetics of Idealism, although Kant saw what the problem was about. As long as one holds to the idea of a "shining-forth of the idea" to the senses, one cannot fully assess the value and meaning of "disinterested pleasure." It always seemed that there must be a more perfect cognition of beauty than one that is conditioned by the senses, i.e., "sensible shining-forth." This is why Hegel ranked philosophical-conceptual thought higher than aesthetical vision. A certain odium remained attached to "appearing" – a deceitful form of knowing – and the form of seeing proper to aesthetics had to be elevated to a state of pure cognition. Thus it was assumed that what appears must be "cognized," just as if it were an entity that in its appearance had not yet come into its own.

When Hegel came to understand the aesthetical relation to the object as intuition, he sensed that something must be disdained in this formulation. It would have to seem so, as long as one assumes in general the model of cognition that has always been a theoretical model. For that reason he valued concepts above beholding, and demoted pleasure to a lower level.

Now pleasure is a different kind in the aesthetical relation from pleasure in the theoretical one, and quite naturally it is different in the practical one. It is not only that in the former, pleasure is related to quite different values. It is also autonomous in a different sense. It first makes the object into an object of value. The value of practical success or of theoretical advance retains its validity even without taking pleasure in it; the value of a work of art exists only "for" a subject that beholds it and in the act of beholding enjoys it. Pleasure thus contributes to the constitution of the value that it points to and for whom it is intended. In this sense, aesthetical pleasure is autonomous. The observer endowed with spirit belongs to the appearance; for it is "to him" that something appears. Since however aesthetic value does not depend on what appears, but upon the event of appearance itself, the observer who takes in the appearance thereby takes part in aesthetic value. And since the same observer feels the aesthetical pleasure, its autonomy does not consist in the autonomy of the value given in it – as in other areas – but rather in its own participation in the creation of aesthetic value.

At this point we cannot yet grasp the relation entirely. We will come to grips with it later in the analysis of the object. But the phenomenon forces itself upon us already: aesthetical feeling of value is – what other value feelings never are – at the same time constitutive of values.

However, the phenomenon can be easily demonstrated. Aesthetic value cannot be anticipated; it does not exist before its appearance on the single object. It is also not objectively cognizable without an act of looking that is simultaneously taking pleasure in looking. It does not exist at all until it comes to be in the act of looking. For that reason it is so tightly tied to the singular case, and, strictly speaking, not only to it but even to the particular act of looking at it in one unique examination; on a second examination it may (81) be different, for each is a new execution of the synthesis that constitutes the phenomenon of appearing. Aesthetic value depends upon appearance as such.

Another indirect piece of evidence for this lies in the fact that language has almost no descriptive terms for these values. The images we use to describe them to each other are all inadequate, and do not reach what is unique in them. Aesthetical meaning is a latecomer to the human mind, and language was already in a finished state when it first appeared. Language is oriented towards the practical; for that reason also aesthetic values remained undiscovered and were long misunderstood, scrambled together with ethical and vital values – one thinks of our sense of human beauty, whose value-content has not been explicated – and they disappeared behind these latter values, while in autonomous pleasure the vital and moral values disappear behind aesthetic values (because they are mere conditions of pleasure).

From here it is possible to draw some conclusions about the character of aesthetic value. They may be expressed under the following rubrics.

1. They are not values of a self-existing entity, neither of real objects such as goods values, nor of something that is in the first instance merely ideal, such as moral values. For that reason no ought-to-be is attached to them. Rather they are the values of entities that exist "for us." They are, to be sure, genuinely objective values, that is, values of the object as such; but the object itself does not exist in itself, but only for a subject that understands them aesthetically. If the object existed only as what is given through the senses, then that would not be true, but the aspect of the object that is sensibly given is only a part of the aesthetic object, and this part alone does not make it one. For what appears belongs to the aesthetic object and this entity does not have to be a real existent. The aesthetic object is the whole of these. This whole thus exists only "for us" provided only that we look at it rightly.

2. Thus, one may also say: aesthetic values are values of being-an-object as such; neither the values of acts (whether that of looking, or of pleasure) nor of an existing entity as such that is made an object for an onlooker by means of his acts, but only values of the object as object. For that reason they exist independent of reality and even of the realization of appearance.

3. This means that they are tied to the relation of appearance as such, but also just to it as a whole. The members of this relation are of course found separate from each other, but then they do not form an aesthetic object. For that reason, aesthetic values are conditioned by the subject, and, in fact, in another sense than other values (e.g., as goods values, which also exist "for" a being to whom they are useful). The meaning of "being for us" is in this case not a thing's becoming useful, but an object-being that exists only "for us."

4. Thus these values are not objectively general, as are the vital and moral values, but rather individual values that are specific to each object, and unique to it alone. (82) There are, after all, a limitless number of ways of appearance; the way is different for each "material" and for each substance; it is different in each "performance" of the same material in the same substance. There are of course universal features of all things aesthetically valuable; they correspond to the universal or typical features of the relation of appearance, but they make up only schematic and, as it were, "thin" genera of valuable objects. The genuine values lie in the unique specificity of the object, and all that is of a comparative nature in the realm of the beautiful remains tied to the mere surface.

The kinds and types of the arts, and even the styles that connect one to the other, pertain in the first instance to the structure of the objects and only secondarily to aesthetic value. Then, too, general value-characters are often common to very different kinds and styles of art. Genuine aesthetic values are hardly touched by such differentiations, and surely not understood.

Nonetheless the character of aesthetic values – the state of being beautiful and its differentiations – is tied to the structure of the object, indeed to the whole with its many strata. The road from a preliminary fragment of the analysis of the act leads, therefore, over to an analysis of the structure of the object; we best come to the analysis of value by that road and by it alone. The analysis of the structure of the object is central to the purposes of aesthetics, and the most important information both for the further problem of the act and for the problem of value – so far as we can approach it, given the current state of research – are found there in the first instance.

Chapter 5: The Law of Objectivation

a) The role of "matter"

The previous discussions have led us towards the problem of the being of the aesthetic object. It was revealed to be an error to attribute an independent being to it (a "being in itself"), one not dependent upon a subject. On the other hand, we saw that a part of it indeed exists independent of a subject. Thus we have the problem of establishing the kind of being that belongs to it. To solve this problem is an ontological undertaking. This undertaking precedes all further questions and must now be addressed.

The task belongs in its broader context within the general problem of ideal being. For just as the aesthetic object exists only "for" an intellectual being, there is also contained in it some kind of intellectual content, at least a definite way of looking or understanding. In a natural object that is not immediately apparent, but it is in a work of art. We will speak therefore at first exclusively of the artwork, for it is certainly evident in this case that we are dealing with an intellectual product that possesses within itself something of the productive mind that created it. (83)

Generically the work of art belongs to a specific form of ideal being, the "objectivated spirit." It is objectivation, that is, the realization of an ideal content in objective existence. Objectivation does not refer only to the work of art, but to any other product that the human mind creates, from tools to invented apparatus to literary works. Everything that belongs to the spirit of earlier times, which thrusts itself historically before the quite different spirit of today and is understood by us as a witness to that earlier spirit, has the form of objectivation. Literary works play the greatest role here. But we need not be thinking of a work of art. Even a simple chronicle or a scientific report has the same fundamental form and ontological type of objectivation.

Now it is a fundamental law of ideal being that it cannot exist freely floating in the air, but can appear only resting upon some other kind of foundation. The personal spirit of individuals is carried upon the vital psyche, this again upon the life of an organic body, and this latter upon inorganic-physical being. A chain of conditions rule here "from below to above," according to which the higher entity is borne by the lower; and since intellectual life is the highest stratum of being, it is carried by the entire series of the lower strata. What is true for personal spirit is also true for the historical objective spirit, which constitutes the common spiritual life of entire peoples and epochs; it too rests upon, is carried – by the mental life of the individual as by the life of human tribes, and therefore finally by the entire series of levels of being or (as the ontological phrase expresses) by the entire stratified structure of the real world. Ideal being can simply not exist without the levels of being that bear it up from below.

What is true for the two forms of living spirit (the personal-subjective and the historical-objective) is valid also for the objectivated spirit. Objectivation is the third fundamental form of spirit. It is, to be sure, not living spirit in itself, but simply spiritual content, a product of the human spirit, a spiritual creation. In this capacity it stands in a certain sense detached from "spiritual life," and indeed from both personal and objective spirit and life; but at the same time it is lifted out of the spiritual life and is thus exempt from process of change to which that life is subject, and the objectivation can therefore have an existence of its own alongside of it.

The strange thing about spiritual creations is that they extend themselves temporally beyond their creators – the orator, the thinker, the writer, the poet, or the artist – indeed they not only outlive them but their epoch and its objective spirit as well. The change of generations and centuries passes them by, but they are not drawn into the fate of all that comes to be and passes away. They are capable, however, of such endurance only when they have been stamped upon an enduring real medium, a material possessing different (84) powers of resistance than transient human life. But in that case, the objective spirit is also a spirit that must be carried, that must rest upon an existent work that is itself not spirit, yet in the temporal measure of its enduring, it is superior to spiritual life.

Objectivation consists accordingly in the creation of an existing work that endures, and in which spiritual content can appear. In this way, the aesthetic object enters into, so far as human beings create it, a large set of phenomena; it forms a special class of objectified spirit. Thereby it falls entirely under the law of objectivation.

This law has a twofold form. It assets first: spiritual content can only endure if it is banished to real sensible matter, i.e., if it is tied to matter by its unique form, and is thus carried by it. And it asserts, second, that the spiritual content carried by informed matter always requires the responsiveness of a living spirit, a personal one as well as an objective one; for it depends upon a consciousness that beholds it – one may also say: upon a consciousness that comprehends or recognizes it, and to which, through the real medium it informs, it can appear.

In the aesthetic object, the material varies with the character of the art: stone, clay, or color upon a canvas, words, writing, or sound. But these all would be dumb, however they are formed, and could not be bearers of spiritual content – without the responsiveness of the living spirit. This consists of recognition (ἀναγιγνώσκειν), i.e., in understanding. What is sealed in matter and deposited in it must be once more extracted, freed, made to flow, made living again; it must be taken up into the living spirit. That can be a complicated process, and many conditions must be fulfilled for it to become possible. The living spirit is not always capable of it, and, if it is, then only at a specific stage of its maturity. Many writings of earlier times were forgotten or banished for centuries without anyone resurrecting their spiritual content – until one day they are excavated, rediscovered, and awakened to new life. The objective spirit simply cannot exist without a real, spiritual life. For it does not possess a life of its own; it must have a different life, one that is lent to it. For the living spirit from which it is derived may have perished long ago; it has been released from that spirit and can no longer return to it.

For the work of art, naturally, this is especially true. The law of objectivation is also its law.

This state of "resting upon" of the objectified spirit is simply different from that of the living spirit. The latter manifests the strata of being that run through it from below to above: matter – organism – psychic life – spirit make up a single irreversible series of carrying and being carried. The chain of strata of being is not found in objectivation; in the works of literary and plastic art (12785) the spiritual content is immediately tied to the lowest stratum of the real, viz., the material. Of course it hangs upon a very definite construction, which itself is the achievement of the living spirit; but one cannot say that it alone bears a spiritual nature. The chain of strata is thus leapt over, for the middle strata are missing. So, at least, the relation appears at this point, and only by the mediation of the living spirit are the missing strata filled in.

The entire relationship in the objectifying spirit is thus threefold. In the work as such, the informed matter and the spiritual content are tied to each other by the act of informing – but not tied as such, but only for the living spirit, provided that it brings with itself the needed qualifications. The living spirit is the necessary "third member" through which alone the other two are tied together. Without this member, the spiritual content in the matter cannot be reawakened. This threefold relation cannot be reduced or simplified.

The complex ontology of objectivation flows from this immediately: it is only in part a real objectivation; that is, only the matter in its formation is real. The genuine spiritual content remains unreal; moreover, it is not realized by the living spirit, but rather comes to be for the living spirit only as appearance. We see clearly from this that we are dealing in the relation of appearance with something far more general and not with the work of art alone. It is not a question of the special ontology of the aesthetic object but of the ontology of the objectifying spirit. We will still have to show what the difference is between the relation of appearance in the work of art and that in the various other kinds of objectivation.[39]

b) The spiritual content and the living spirit

This model of the tripartite relation is still incomplete. In reality, the living spirit appears (both as personal and objective spirit) in it in two ways. For the informing of material and the bestowal of spiritual content are in themselves the actions of a living spirit, and, in fact, they are precisely the original, creative acts. However, they are the acts of a different mind than the one that receives and recognizes them; a mind that may have perished long before his work manifested itself to the epigones.

We must therefore supplement our model and build the role of the creative spirit into it. Then the model becomes fourfold. The producing spirit informs the material; in that way it gives the spiritual content along with form, but also encloses it within, so that the receiving sprit can "disclose" it once again, that is, he has to win it back from the material. Clearly, the receiving spirit on its side must also engage itself spontaneously: it must, by understanding and beholding it, (86) allow what the producing spirit had made to rise up again; he must reproduce it. This engagement and this achievement first make it possible for the spiritual content to "appear" to him.

This fourfold relation is not an equal one. As the productive spirit does not know but must reckon blindly with the reproductive one, so the latter also is hidden from the former, for the creator is not contained in the objectified spirit; and where the epigone is not able to know of him in other ways (historically), he can imagine him only vaguely through his works. Of course the creator can represent himself in his works, but that is an addition of another kind, and one

---

39 For a detailed analysis of the essence and ontology of the objectified spirit, cf. *Das Problem des geistigen Seins* [*The Problem of Spiritual Being*], 2nd edition (1949), Chaps. 44–49.

must already know of the producer as such in order to understand the representation of him. He cannot decide whether, as Greeks of later centuries believed, Homer presented himself in the figure of Demodokos, and it does not affect much our reading of the *Odyssey* if this should not be so.

In fact within certain limits every representation of a work is also a representation of its creator, even when it speaks only of its object; any sculptor giving form to some material always involuntarily objectifies within it some part of himself, if only as a way of seeing things. No doubt this is especially true for artistic representation. But this kind of self-representation accompanies all communication and is not peculiar to genuine objectivation (of a lasting kind) as such. For example, in life every person continually reveals himself in his speech, his gestures, and in his behavior. Whatever he may speak of, he involuntarily gives something of himself away.

The picture we have drawn seems in a way to have turned about upon itself. At first it appeared that the objectified spirit had been freed from the living spirit, drawn out from him, allowed to float freely. But now we see that it is continually tied to one and another living spirit, and, moreover, tied back upon the first one, i.e., the producing spirit, such that the creator is still recognizable in his object.

Neither of the two is important in principle for the objectified spirit, but they are essential precisely for the aesthetic object. This too – the work of art – exists only in relation to an appreciating subject that possesses the conditions requisite to grasp it rightly, and otherwise for no one, and least of all in itself. The productive spirit – the sculptor, the poet, and the composer – remains, always within certain limits, recognizable in it, even when one knows neither his name nor his life. And much stronger than our ability to know of him is our assimilation of him to ourselves: the beholder can be drawn by the power of the work into the way of seeing things as the artist did, it can take him by the hand and teach him new ways to see.

Here it is necessary to reach back in our discussion even further. Perception remains important above all for aesthetics, and with it the sensible object that has been given a form in which a spiritual content has been objectified and in which alone it appears. One might think that this construct must have been from the outset in some way akin to the spiritual content. But more careful observation (87) teaches us the opposite. For this, too, we must orient ourselves on the simple non-aesthetical forms of objectivation. The most familiar form of objectivation that we encounter in life is useful here: words and writing.

Language belongs to a certain level of the living objective spirit. So long as this spirit "lives," that is, so long as it is in fact spoken, it is the "living speech" – in contrast to the dead languages, which are no longer spoken. The spoken word, as an element of language, plays a role on this level as a means of coming to an understanding with others; it is also the means of exchange in the spiritual market-place. For that reason its life is short; it serves only the momentary situation and disappears as such behind the "circumstances" that are in question. It is forgotten.

Yet it is nonetheless a case of objectivation, and displays its two characteristic levels of being: the level of existing reality, i.e., the audible sound, and the spiritual content, the meaning, and the "sense." Only both together constitute the "word"; one or the other alone is nothing on the plane of speech.

We see from this especially that the living spirit itself may constantly use objectivation, but without holding on to it or storing it away. The living spirit needs it always for its own temporary needs, the creation and maintenance of the common realm of spirit, in which its life consists and in which it moves.

But every word and every expression, along with its unique wording, can be kept and stored in the memory of the living. That happens often when the meaning of the utterance appears to have great weight, as has happened from olden times in the case of the story. The spiritual content is carried forth and it becomes a common treasure, just because it has been made objective in the written word. This process is enormously strengthened by writing, for it is of the essence of writing not to be transient, like the spoken world, but capable of being kept and maintained, because it is a permanent existing work. The extensive literature of stories passed down by the ancients is an eloquent testimony to that permanence. The truth-content of these anecdotes is not a matter of significance (and is, after all, no longer verifiable); the significance is rather simply in its preservation of the transient as such.

The philosophically remarkable thing about this relation is the profound heterogeneity of the strata of being in objectivation. For that also the most obvious examples are language and writing.

Sound and meaning are not only incomparable phenomena – they do not have a close common genus, and they also have a quite different ontological character. Then, too, they are to a great extent independent of each other within common constellations of words, as one observes upon the diversity of languages and even of dialects; and their constituents do not vary simply in concert with each other. Meanings are rather tied to phonemes entirely by convention (the occasional onomatopoeia are insignificant exceptions). (88) That fact makes possible both translation and multilingualism, even the variety of possible expressions in one and the same language. The real limits of translatability have a deeper basis; they lie in the disparities in the objective spirit itself, in its forms of intuition and habitual modes of thought in different peoples and epochs.

What is true of spoken language is even more so for the written word. The incommensurability of the form of the writing and its meaning, even the form of writing and the word is more immediately apparent here, even with respect to both their structure and their way of being. To a certain extent even the most naïve writer in his normal use of writing is conscious of these differences, and only habit conceals from him their great strangeness.

What is positive in this relation is apparently only the fixed nature of the order of the relation that exists between the audible sound and the meaning, or between the form of writing, the audible sound, and the meaning. On this relation depends the understanding of what is said and what is written, not upon any structural relationship or any other kind of similarity. The strangeness consists in the fact that an association of this kind functions most freely and most perfectly where it is merely external, conventional and "contingent," and not influenced (one might almost say not distorted) by similarities or structural correspondences between them. For given the fixed nature of its elements, such an association will have to have the greatest flexibility in order to be amenable to the indefinitely varied senses it must carry; that can be achieved most quickly when it is a mere relationship among symbols and is not hindered – even in the slightest – by the ambition to "copy" what it conveys.

The most telling example of this at first strange-sounding fact is the great superiority of the alphabet (with its relatively few basic symbols) in analyzing the sounds of spoken language over pictographic writing. The reverse side of this superiority is that "recognition" (i.e., reading) is tied to the mastery of the fixed association of sound and symbol, just as the understanding of what is said is conditioned by the mastery of the current correlations of sound and meaning.

In this way we return to the law of objectivation, i.e., that all appearances of spiritual content depend on the reciprocal performance of acts of the living spirit, so far as the latter brings to them the conditions of understanding.

c) Being in itself and being for us in the objectivated spirit

As with words and writing, so it is also fundamentally the same in all other objectifications of spiritual content. However, the forms of objectifications themselves are very diverse – detours (89) over symbols and correlations are by no means required in all cases – and, accordingly, the independence of the entire objective construction is modulated in a variety of ways, and with that also its capacity for preservation throughout history, as well as its chances of reappearing in the living spirit of later ages. That all depends on specific conditions, and most importantly in the conditions set by the material, its capacity to be worked, and its durability. Yet after all these are met, there is the dependence on the unpredictable decree of fate as to the return or continuing absence of living spirits capable of grasping its meaning.

The material condition is generally satisfied by the written word, but in the spoken word, it is not. The essence of what is spoken is its impermanence. What is written "in black and white" is completely different in its capacity to persist through time. It continues to exist even when it is not being looked at; private letters that were written only for the passing moment may be preserved through peculiar circumstances and after millennia bear witness to a life that perished long ago. So was the case with remnants of papyri from Egypt's desert sands.

Whether impermanent or permanent, the law of objectivation is met: our entire model of it has two levels, which in fact manifest the characteristic heterogeneity of the strata with respect to both its structure and its ontological form. For only the foreground, the material sensible form, is real; the background that appears in it, which forms the spiritual content, is unreal. The material exists in itself, along with its form; the background, in contrast, exists only "for" a living spirit ready to receive it, who contributes to it his own nature, and reproduces its content as he grasps it.

The foreground is always a sensibly apprehensible configuration. The background can to a certain extent be apprehended by the senses and therefore appear as it is drawn into an act of perception, as is the case with many works of art, e.g., in sculpture and painting there is a living bodily presence. The expression "spiritual content" must therefore be used with care. The background need not be ideal, neither as a thought nor as the ideal object of intuition. Its content also need not be taken from a higher stratum of being (psychic or spiritual being), nor be an imitation; it is sufficient that it be spiritually intuited originally, and that the way of beholding it is maintained in the manner of its appearing. The background is rather "spiritual content" only in the same sense as in reference to spoken words and writing: it is merely that something is expressed or described that is not contained as real in the object as a whole and also not deceptively presented as something real. For the ontological nature of the background, it is sufficient that it be called forth in the consciousness of the comprehending hearer or reader as a represented content.

The great difference between the different kinds and levels of objectivation is contained in its other elements. The differences are observed, for example, in the various degrees of its concreteness and detail, in the degree of abstractness and in the symbols merely external to it, with all of which the representational content presents itself to the receptive beholder. There are an incalculable number of subtle variations in these (90) features. In this respect, they are given great scope even in everyday speech, and entirely in the case of writing.

In contrast, in the work of art, the object that appears is always highly concrete; it possesses a wealth of content, and its ties to the real foreground are strong and deep. This is true even when the represented content, understood as spiritual in nature, is very general and ideal.

What is mysterious in the nature of objectivation is always and in all cases this: "how" can, then, the sensible thing-like construction that constitutes the foreground become in fact the carrier of a content that possesses an entirely different mode of being and that is there only "for" a receptive consciousness? For the relation between the two is so ordered that this content can be glimpsed in the sensible construct and can be at any time won back from it. It must therefore be in some way contained in it. For whatever else may be in the world, the well-known rule holds, that only a spiritual being can "have" spiritual content – however this act of having may be constituted.

The provisional solution to the mystery may be found in the consideration that in fact the spiritual content cannot come to be in the configured material without the agency of a living spirit. For the content is not the material in itself, but is there only "for us" who comprehend it. And it is only placed in the material by its creator "for" the spirit who comprehends it, but not stamped upon it independently of the nature of the material. Rather, the form really stamped upon it is itself only the material form, that is, the material of the sensible foreground.

If we substitute in this case the fourfold relation we developed above, the circle closes: in all cases of objectivation of whatever kind the appearing background stratum exists solely "for" a living spirit; it exists only by force of the reciprocal relation to it. That is the meaning of "being for us." This way of being is a quite relative one that divides the foreground from the background, although the original creative spirit who formed the whole is a real being who can appear in the spiritual content of his creation; he appears along with it, but not as an existing presence.

d) Foreground and background

These two elements of the objectivated spirit have thus an entirely different ontology. As a consequence, the real existence of a unity of the two would immediately appear to us as an oddity. Moreover, they vary freely, for the most part, with respect to each other. The greatest range of variation, however, exists within the unity they form with respect to their connections to each other.

Some objectivations have a merely conventional interconnection of foreground and background. The spoken word and writing are of this kind. Even more important is that the same may be said of concepts. Even the concept is an arbitrary form, one that in fact always receives its own content not from itself but from a (91) definite relationship in high style, i.e., from an entire system of concepts. An isolated concept is nothing in itself; it is neither definable nor able to be given content by intuition. In short, concepts are not autonomous, any more than an isolated word is. In practice, neither word nor concept ever appears alone; they exist only within speech, that is, within a context of interrelated thoughts.

The product of a constructed concept is the specialized term; but that says in itself nothing about the spiritual content. One must know that content from some other source in order to use it correctly. One needs to fill out its content by intuition – for its nature is to be the means of a higher kind of beholding (either by looking-through or looking-with it) – that is, not any form of intuition at all, but rather with the right kind of intuitive act that is appropriate for the concept. The concept of "planet" is grasped only by one who grasps intuitively Kepler's[40] ellipses and the conditions of motion of the bodies in elliptical orbits. This intuition must be produced so that the concept can come to function in one's own thought. That is what Hegel meant by the "exertion [*Anstrengung*] of concepts."

But from what source may we obtain the intuition? It is easy to see that it can be obtained only from a larger context that can be readily scrutinized. Scientific thought is always contained in a system of concepts already at hand, which, even if not complete, exists within the limits of the current state of scientific knowledge. One cannot separate the individual concepts from such a system without losing its spiritual content. But such a system of concepts can, as objectified in scholarly written work, maintain itself across the centuries and be resurrected at a time when people no longer think with the same concepts and intuit matters in the same way.

The conceptual system of Aristotelian metaphysics, along with its individual concepts – Form, material, *Eidos*, dynamics, energy – which are no longer our own, may still be won back from the preserved documents, and that so precisely that one can distinguish consistencies from inconsistencies in it. But that is possible only on the basis of the entire work, not of the individual concepts, if one were to take one by itself. The individual concept has its meaning and content only from the whole.

The conclusion we may draw from this is simple. A concept, understood by itself, has its essence outside of itself. If one severs it from its context of interrelated concepts in which it is rooted, it collapses, loses is content, and can be distorted to the point of incomprehensibility. Such a collapse occurred to concepts developed in the ancient world innumerable times throughout history: for example, to the Aristotelian ones mentioned above. To be sure, one can win those

---

40 [Translator's note:] Johannes Kepler (1571–1630).

isolated concepts back to comprehensibility, fill out their void; but one must then recreate their entire original context of ideas, and that can of course be done only on the basis of the historical sources (92) – by holding rigorously to the texts of Aristotelian metaphysics. And it is difficult to do so; it requires a long course of study.

The stability of the concept as an objectivation is otherwise not great. Concepts change over time – a claim quite in opposition to the teaching of the old logic, which attributed a super-temporal identity to them – for they have their own history, and their meaning changes for the living objective spirit. By this change we must not at all understand a decline. With every new growth in knowledge, new characteristics are rather added to the concept, and since this growth in knowledge may be extended across centuries in which our opinions concerning the same object may change fundamentally, the history of this concept may lead to the complete transformation of its content, even when it keeps its old verbal expression and still denotes the same object. In this case, in fact, the objectivation itself is altered, according to the understanding and the reach of the living spirit.

The amazing mutability of the concept – perhaps nothing in the world is as changeable as it – is not a weakness, but rather its unique capacity to follow the restless growth of knowledge. But this capacity is at the same time an eloquent testimony to the looseness of the tie that binds the term to the spiritual content in the concept.

It is very instructive to make these points clear by means of the example of the content. For only in the contrast we see here does the nature of the objectivation in the work of art appear in the correct light. The work of art has precisely a different kind of stability, an incomparably higher capacity to endure through time. The reason for this lies in the strong and independent tie in it between the foreground and the background. For here the tie is neither a conventional one nor one conditioned by externality (that is, by its extensive systematic relationships), but is rather a purely internal tie created by itself alone. For that reason, it addresses not our comprehension but our intuition and, within intuition, it has the form of a tight relationship between the sensible looking (perception) and the higher form of beholding.

With the bestowal of form upon a real object of some kind, a work of art gives the entire detail in which the spiritual content appears. For that reason, the content can always be recovered in the foreground detail without any need to reconstruct its far-reaching relationships. It is precisely the foreground, the material, and the sensibly real elements with which the work of art is richly adorned. Such adornment is not found in concepts, and for that very reason nothing in them can appear out of the concept itself, but it is instead dependent upon the relationships that lie above and beyond it. The work of art is dependent upon nothing of this kind; the fullness of the construction of the real object is sufficient to allow a spiritual content to appear to the beholder. That means that in the work of art the connection between the foreground and the background is a "close-fitting," tight, and independent one. The knowledge that one brings to the work (93) does not open one to the spiritual content, rather the act of beholding it does; and if this is no longer a sensible looking-at, it remains tied tightly to perception. Without it, it cannot bring what appears in it before the eyes of the beholder.

We can express this in a formula: the work of art has its essence in itself; the concept has its essence external to itself. The concept, taken in itself, is not a closed whole; the next higher unity above it is not to be found in it. The work of art is a whole, and so tightly closed upon itself, that the beholder does not have to rely on any of its possible external relations for its contents to be fully available to him. The richness of the sensible form in its foreground is sufficient to awaken by itself all the necessary interconnections for the appearance of the background. Even more: the work of art is not only independent of interconnections that it might not itself contain, but also to the contrary it is lifted above the real relations of life, of knowledge, and of comprehending; it is wafted beyond them and rests only upon itself. That is why it has the power to lift the viewer up along with itself and transport him into the quite different world of appearance.

Therefore, the work of art is not liable to a "waning." And as for the mutability in the living spirit, the work is subject to it only to a limited degree. It may happen that new content is revealed to the different – perhaps more mature – spirit in later times; but even this eventuality remains within the limits of what was once made objective in it. Upon what, however, depends the extraordinary power of the bond between the ontological strata of the work of art, by means of which it preserves its identity throughout history? That can be decided only by the analysis of the relations among the strata themselves.

Chapter 6: Foreground and Background in the Representational Arts

a) On ordering the problem and its investigation

Even in the act, which is itself a stratified beholding, we can perceive the twofold strata of the aesthetic object. Now that we have oriented ourselves in the opposed forms of objectivation, we are able to place all of these elements in a larger context of phenomena. Then the question of how the aesthetic object differentiates itself from other kinds of objectivation, which we just now discussed, takes on a greater weight. The reference to the greater strength of the inner bond, to its independence and its autonomy, is at this point insufficient. We must observe more closely the individual forms of the aesthetic object.

The following may be ventured in a preliminary manner to orient us within the domain of these phenomena. All aesthetic objects are stratified, to be sure, but not all of them are objectivations. Only the works of art that (94) are created by human beings are objectivations. In them primarily can we grasp the relation of the strata, their essential oppositions and their ties to each other. We must therefore exclude from this first attempt at the analysis of our material anything that is not a work of art, i.e., beauty in nature and in the human being. Later we will inquire into the extent to which what we find in the work of art may be transferred to those other domains of the beautiful.

Additionally, we may make another preliminary restriction. Among the arts, the most important ones for the aims of our inquiry are those in whose creations a spiritual content as a material structure stands out and presents itself to the mind. These are the arts that represent a "material," a subject, a theme. This group is comprised under the "representational arts." They are sculpture, painting, and the art of literature. Here we will inquire into the extent to which what we discover in them is found also in the objects of non-representational arts, especially music and architecture.

We may for the sake of our inquiry retain the well-known division of the arts in terms of the "material" in which they work: in stone or clay, in colors upon a canvas, in words, or in tones. It has already been shown why these divisions are not external ones. Not any content can be depicted in any material; or, expressed in a positive way, each material permits only certain kinds of content. Even if, in an extended sense, it is the same content, some kinds of material will touch some of its aspects rather than others. This is because each kind of material allows only a certain kind of construction, and in that kind only certain contents can be captured, that is, brought to "appearance." The background of the work of art is of course not determined by the foreground; the foreground is much rather determined by the background; but still the "kind" of possible constructions of the foreground prescribes limits to the construction of the background. In that way, it exercises some influence on the selection of the material (its themes), and its influence on the construction of the material is total. The selection thus extends itself to what can in fact be represented.

The peculiar kind of aesthetic value that a creation can have is indirectly dependent upon the material of the foreground, for beauty lies in the form of appearance.

b) Stratification in the plastic arts

The entire problematic of the order of strata can be read off from Greek sculptural art at its most developed. In the upright figure of Apollo nothing is sensibly given except the external shape of the body in a momentary pose. The left arm is lifted, the right lowered. The head is turned to the side toward the lifted arm. The sculpted marble is still; it does not move or live, to say nothing of it carrying out some definite aim. And yet we see much more than this if we stand before it and behold it in the manner of an artist. We see movement, we see (95) life in this human body, and we see the action that, though it is already executed, still expresses itself in the pose. The "far-darter" has loosed his arrow. The extended left arm still holds the bow; the eye follows the fleeing shot. Thus something quite different from what the construction of the material alone can make visible is given with the object and represented by it: the entire action of the bowshot, the pulsing life of the figure, the dynamics of the action and its resolution, and, still more, the superior bearing of the god, its gravitas and its powerful freedom.

The plastic arts all have these features, regardless what phase of a given motion is represented. In the case of the discus thrower, the body is caught in the moment of greatest exertion, just at the last turn before the throw, and only the external form of this moment has been made permanent in the stone. But to the beholder, the entire process and its dynamics appear, including the toss of the disk in the palestra. This is true also for wrestling, for the dancing satyr, even for the David of Michelangelo, where what is shown is his calm and calculating bearing just before he slings the shot. The opposition of the strata is apparent: the stationary real construct and the movement of the appearance. The steed of Colleone stands motionless upon its pedestal and canters at the same time. We see the state of rest, and we see the motion; the one does not disturb the other, does not contradict it: to the contrary, the one makes the other visible.

How is that possible? How can what is moving and alive "appear" in what is motionless and lifeless? We are so used to this appearing, and it comes to pass so easily when we behold an object aesthetically, that we hardly waste thought on it. But the puzzle is merely covered over by that attitude, not resolved. For it remains the case that what is really before us is just the motionless stone; it remains also true that motion, life, and the meaningful execution of action persist in what is unreal. Nonetheless, it is also true that motion, life, and action are beheld in full concreteness; these are given in a manner appropriate to them, and do not at all have to be added by thought, deduced, or inferred. Moreover, the viewer never blurs the limits separating the real and the appearance, although he sees them as one, and yet clearly distinguishes and never confuses the two. It would never occur to the beholder to imagine that the clay moves or the stone is alive, or, even less, to address the person represented as a living fellow man.

The relation of the two heterogeneous strata in its entirety is not intended to cause deception but is rather an accompanying consciousness of appearance as such. And from the nature of works of plastic art we can now list, clearly and in a reasoned manner, the four elements of the relationship within the phenomenon of appearance. 1. The real material foreground in a purely spatial construction; 2. The unreal background, appearing with the same concreteness, but without the illusion of reality; 3. The tight bond of the latter to the former for the beholder; 4. The maintenance (96) of the opposition of the two forms of being in beholding – without loosening the tie that binds them and without any reduction of the concreteness in the non-real element.

We see most clearly in this the contributory role of the beholder in the construction of the aesthetic object. The background "appears," of course, "in" the foreground, but only to a viewer adequate to the task of looking at objects aesthetically. The stationary material foreground is transparent only "for" him. This transparency of the spatial form is for him obviously what is genuine in the relation of appearance; it is that towards which the entire work of art is directed, for the sake of which the spatial composition in its lifeless stillness has been given to the material stone. But without this peering-through by the observer, it could not come to be. Without the contribution of the beholder there would also be no aesthetic object at all.

There is at the same time much else that comes to appearance in the plastic arts. Just think of the rider on his "galloping" steed who is poured bronze upon a pedestal; the motion of riding appears along with it. It cannot take place upon the pedestal, also not even in the appearance; more crudely expressed, the rider does not appear at all as if he was riding on the pedestal; no such nonsense appears. The rider gallops naturally over the free range, in a field; the field, however, is not present, so it must appear with the galloping rider. Thus there appears accordingly a different space in which Colleone rides, a similarly unreal space that is not congruent with the real space in which the sculpture stands. And the beholder, to whom it appears, does not confuse it with the space in which he is standing as he beholds the rider. Real and appearing space do not get in each other's way, any more than the static form of the bronze and the movement of the rider do.

With wrestling the situation is similar, as also with the Olympic Apollo and the discus thrower. This similarity is shown with special clarity in the latter. The toss, and with it too the phases of the thrower's motion, are nonsensical if we relate them to the space of the museum where the figure stands. The toss needs a large space, it requires the palestra, and indeed it belongs there. The palestra appears with it. What appears in the ontologically unreal stratum of the work of art is therefore not only motion and life, but also the specific space that belongs to it. Perhaps one may say: there appears also an entire segment of the world that is inseparable from the gymnastic life of ancient athletics.

And now we must look in the reverse direction and draw the conclusion: only provided that movement, life, ideal space, indeed an entire world in miniature with its hustle and bustle, appear in the silent stony form of matter can we call the plastic constructions in matter a work of art. We behold works of plastic art in terms of this appearing, we stand lost in them and enthralled by them, ourselves transported to this world that appears before us. And again only provided that we maintain in that transport a clear consciousness of the stone shape in the foreground as such, and experience with it the appearance as a pure appearance of what it also is, are we (97) experiencing aesthetically; and only then is the aesthetic object there for us as a whole. In its wholeness it has no other existence than this existence-for-us.

Consider the question we raised above: how is it possible that movement and life can appear in an immovable and lifeless form? If we cannot answer it as yet, we can now bring us a step forward towards its solution. Our sense of vision is in life adapted to the comprehension of moving bodies, of legs, arms, and figures in motion. We perceive life along with living things, although life as such is not visible. The plastic arts make use of these capacities by freezing a phase of motion in static spatial form and presenting it to our sense of vision. We, the beholders, recognize it in our own life, but we do not know it as a static state but as a phase of motion; we see along with it a bit of motion itself. If we look with our senses at a phase of motion, we immediately grasp inwardly the entire motion, or at least a bit of it: the dance, the toss, and the gallop. And as beholders we are drawn into this world of appearance, of animation, of life, of humanity.

So it is, at least, when form is imposed upon the stone; the phase of motion is seized and frozen plastically and true to life. For then the motion is recognizable as such to our beholding eyes. We then say of the sculpture: "It is convincing." But what we really mean by that is the power of letting-appear. We just do not know that this is what we mean. For it announces itself to us only by the joy of beholding it.

And yet we sense the distance of the appearance of motion from the static form of matter. For that reason, we retain our awareness of the sensible material as such. The reverse of this awareness, however, is our knowledge of the unreality of the appearance and of the artistic achievement in the sculpture. This knowledge is just as unreflective as our joy and the act of beholding itself. That knowledge accompanies it directly.

If we now consider that the fundamental condition of beholding and appearance is that the frozen phase of motion be represented in a true-to-life manner, we can understand how, given an adequately prepared beholder, it is that all else –

including the highest levels of appearance – depends upon the intelligible form bestowed upon the real material object. For that reason, everything artistically essential lies in this bestowal of form, including the technical details of its execution.

c) Drawing and painting

When I stand before a Dutch seascape and my eyes become lost in the distance just as if I were looking upon a real beach, it does not occur to me to believe that the wave-tossed sea is really there, and I need only to take a few steps to have it wash over my feet. The painting is not intended to cause such deception; it does not cause the illusion of reality, even when (98) it is very realistically done. What it in fact offers is something quite different: not what is represented, but the "picture" of what is represented.

Here too the two main strata may be distinguished: indeed, here they are more heterogeneous, more dissimilar to each other than they are in the plastic arts, and we are for that reason more easily able to distinguish them. Only the canvas and its spots of color belong entirely to the existing construct – in the case of drawing, the paper and the lines – but what is seen is the landscape, the scene, a person, a bit of life. All those latter elements belong to the background, and they are entirely unreal, and the observer, too, does not think them real.

The artist can directly create only the real element; everything else he creates only indirectly, by allowing it to appear through the forms of the foreground. But he can arrange lines and spots of color so that the entire fullness of the background comes into appearance within it – not seldom into what is in principle entirely unreachable by vision – human life and character.

The greater heterogeneity of the strata is already visible in painting (and in drawing) in the two-dimensionality of the surface of the canvas or paper, for it belongs essentially to the "picture," while the appearing background has extension in three dimensions just as physical objects do. The first and greatest accomplishment is thus just the appearance of the third dimension into which we peer. The distinctive means of the artist to this end is the invocation of perspective – which in the everyday perception of objects is of course already there, although unnoticed because it almost entirely disappears in the act of reobjectivation.[41] The effect of drawing begins by being made objective. There are other artistic means for the production of the appearance of three-dimensionality.

---

41 See the footnote on page 65.

However, what is essential in all this is that these means do not disappear in the objective element of the appearing background, but instead remain visible and affect us as achievements of art, just as the two-dimensional surface of the painting should also not be lost from sight in artistic beholding, but seen along with the background. If it disappeared completely, the picture could no longer affect us as a picture. It is the same relation, shifted a bit, as we see in sculpture: in the latter, the frozen phase of motion in the worked stone is still seen along with the appearance of motion. There, as in painting, the real foreground as such also remains objective.

Another implication of these facts is that the "picture space" into which we peer is entirely and only an apparent space. For that reason, it separates itself unmistakably from the real space "in" which it appears – that is, from the space in which the picture hangs and where the observer stands before it, thus from the room with its walls or from the exhibition space at the museum. No one looking at the seascape imagines that the sea really stretches beyond the wall on which the picture is hanging, although the beholders (99) who sink into the deep space of the painting might suggest that. That is all so self-evident to us that talk of such illusion seems ridiculous. But the obvious in this case, as so often in life, is what is genuinely remarkable. For it is only possible because when we behold a painting the appearing space is never confused with the real space in which we find it, nor are the two spaces felt to be one, but rather as different.

That is even more remarkable as the space that appears is not quite independent of the real one. The "picture space" only appears properly when the actual position of the observer in relation to the picture surface is correct, that is, when he is at the right distance from it and is properly oriented to it – as a rule in a "central" position – otherwise the order of space in the picture will appear distorted. Even as distorted, it remains of course of a different order than the real space, but the distortion itself is dependent upon the latter.

In every case, however, the "other space" appears along with its objectified realization; it does not appear integrated into the real space but lifted up and released from it, without blending with it and without any actual transition. This is the same phenomenon we encounter in the plastic arts, out of whose figures too a different space appears. Here, however, the separation is more palpable and obvious. This obviousness is given by means of the appearance of the unreal space through a two-dimensional canvas surface, which is of a completely heterogeneous kind. For the canvas surface is consciously seen along with the apparent space; it is thus given objectively. In the sculpted figure, in contrast, the spatiality of the standing figure is of the same (three-dimensional) kind as the apparent space.

We may say that in a certain sense we peer through the canvas surface into the apparent space, into the landscape or an interior. This surface has for the act of seeing aesthetically the peculiar "transparency" of the thing-like foreground for the appearance of the third dimension, of the landscape, or of the arrangement of objects. But still this seeing-through, like transparency, must be taken only metaphorically in this case; for we peer through the picture not as we would peer through a hole, and what appears "shines out" not as it would through a ground glass screen. Both cases would suggest a blending of real space and apparent space. Rather, transparency is only a symbol for allowing something to appear; peering-through is to be understood entirely as non-spatial – in the sense of how one looks into the soul of a man through the expression of his face.

A second distinguishing element of the strata is light. The clarity with which we perceive represented objects rests essentially upon the opposition of light and shade, and even color-tones are given different shades by the conditions of light. For light and color are complementary. (100)

Now the "light in the picture" that falls upon the represented objects and makes them appear in different degrees of shade is not the same light as falls through the window or the ceiling of the real space that surrounds the picture. We may thus distinguish between the real space and the space that appears in the picture, and between the real light and the apparent light. The latter can be focused light (in the style of Rembrandt), or it can be sunlight, the light of torches, the diffused light of the setting sun and, accordingly, the things and figures represented there will be given shades of color, clear or vague lines, or simply suggested by flecks of color and shadow. Moreover, the light in the picture has its own source, one not identical with the source of real light. The source of the light in the picture does not have to be visible, for it makes itself clearly known in the play of light and shade upon the objects in the picture, and does not need to be similar to the real source of light that illuminates it.

Only in one respect is the appearing light dependent upon the real light: the latter is the condition of the appearance of the former. If no real light falls upon the picture, the light in the picture disappears; if it is too weak or poorly positioned (such that reflections appear on the canvas), the light in the picture will be distorted. Yet even in this state of dependency, the apparent light remains a different one from the real light. It maintains its independence in agreement with the laws of stratification.

We see in this a similar relation of dependency as that between the real and apparent spaces. Yet even the independence of the apparent from the real light is the same as that of the apparent space from the spatial position of the observer.

We could conduct the same analysis for the entire manifold of the appearing objects as we did for space and light. We will refrain, however, from that task here, on the one hand because evidently the same is as true for the appearance of things as for the appearance of the space and light in which they are placed; but also on the other hand because much more can appear in the picture than they, such that the unreal background may open itself up further. Of that we will speak in another context. For the present, we are concerned only with the relation between the strata of reality and appearance in general, and this relation is, in the work of the painter (or draftsman) fully and sufficiently comprehensible by the elements of light and of space. These are the decisive elements for visual experience.

We may add to this one thought: the setting-off of the background from its existing surroundings is of special importance in an easily intelligible work such as painting. For it is the same act of seeing that perceives the real and the appearing things, and indeed, with respect to its kind, in the same three-dimensional space (101), the same perspective, the same plastic effects rendered by light and shade, even the same brightness of color. Here is also the source of the inescapable element of "imitation" (*mimesis*) that is peculiar to all painting and that remains with it however much it grows beyond it.

In painting, this setting-off requires an accentuation external to it, a strengthening of the setting-off as such. This is achieved in giving special prominence to the limits of the picture, i.e., the visible and prominent frame. We do not have to think only of the gilded wooden frame; the white edges of the paper used in drawing will do as well. The effect of the frame is essential, however it is achieved; and it is a kind of test of the relation of appearance in the created work: it does not just set off the content of what appears in the picture, which is assimilated precisely to the visible real objective content, but it sets the appearance as such off from the real as such: we might also say that it sets off the appearance of reality from reality, what exists for us from what exists in itself.

For that reason, the presence of frames in painting is not extrinsic to it, but essential. It serves to create a sense of unreality; it works against the creation of illusions of a non-aesthetical sort. It allows the represented figure or scenes to set themselves sharply off from reality, as it allows the pictorial light to separate itself off from the real light. Without a sense of the unreality the picture is not an artistic work. If one willfully blurs the boundary that separates it from the real environing world – which is almost achievable by certain effects of lighting (think of the effects achieved by the wings in realist theater) – then it becomes nothing more than a feigned reality.

The frame is the simplest means to work against the fetishism of the object. Painting has other means to the same end. The best known is the process of selection. The painter does not put all the visible detail on the canvas randomly, he puts only what is appropriate to his representation and to the kind of looking that is demanded of the observer, that is, that which draws him into this definite way of beholding.

For all observation is selective. We may think of the way our field of vision is biologically determined. There the determining elements are the practical orientation of our interests, and, in the end, the practical values that guide our vision. Artistic vision makes its selections according to other principles; the value that conditions it is the appearance of what the artist sees in his mind's eye and what the everyday person does not see, or sees only inadequately. This is true for the smallest detail of the drawing or the painting. The picture can limit itself to a few lines or to the most frugal specks of paint – it may in just this way direct our vision toward something definite that is supposed to appear, and direct it away from all else. To attempt such leading of vision, to follow its lead, is to understand the artist: specifically, to learn to see what he sees, and not only intuitively in beholding his work, but also autonomously in life itself. (102)

The result of the selection is the de-actualization of the object. It too allows the emergence of the distance between the appearance and the real. It thereby forces the relation of appearance into the consciousness of the observer.

d) The fundamental relation in the art of poetry

Poetry is similar to the fine arts in that it is also representational; it handles themes, and begins with the imitation of the real world. But it is not "constructive" in the narrow sense, because it does not build its themes directly into some material upon which they may then appear to the senses, but takes a detour over words and, through their mediation, addresses itself to the imagination of the reader or the hearer.

To this distance from the visible there corresponds another circle of themes, and in fact, considered as a whole, a much larger one. It includes all of human life. Things of the mind and spirit dominate it. The material in which this art works, however, is not only other than, but also of an entirely different kind from the material of the fine arts – and it possesses a different power. It is one not culled from nature but a material made by humankind: language, words, and writing. We have already spoken of how language and writing already have the character of objectivation and rest upon systems of symbols and classificatory principles. Now in poetry, words are the material of a higher kind of construction, and in physical forms of writing this form is preserved and receives permanence, the power of resistance, and durability. In that way, poetry, as a work, comes into greater proximity to objectivations of a non-artistic sort, to the great realm of creations of the spirit that can be collected under the title of written works. For no sharp boundary separates prose from poetry; we see this in the narrative art of the oldest writers in history, in the biblical narratives, or in the Norse sagas; in the same way we see it also in the poetic means used to represent the purely theoretical treasures of pre-Socratic philosophy.

Of course at the same time verse is only an adornment of speech, belonging entirely to the sensible foreground and to what is audible. But it is essential to the poetic construction; it keeps the ear of the hearer tied to the foreground and prevents him from entirely slipping past it and from sinking freely into the depths of the appearing background. Verse, as an external form of speech, can for that reason also become entirely dominant. We are especially sensible of that possibility in lyric poetry. Something astonishing occurs here: the process of bestowing form reaches over the sound of speech into what is expressed by it; it places itself, like the sparkle of highlights, upon the meaning of the words, emphasizing and intensifying them. Although it emerges from the visible and in fact belongs to it alone, it serves the internal and most intimate parts of what appears in the words, it takes part in the shaping of the background that is eventually represented, and this is an essential element in the representation. Thus the musical shaping of speech can in the best case complete, (103) indeed contribute – contribute in sensible concreteness – precisely what common words in their conventional connotations (which are always general) cannot offer.

How that comes about is a question that aesthetical analysis no doubt cannot answer in all its implications. But the phenomenon is unquestionable.

In its fundamental nature, the phenomenon of the opposition of the levels that appear in the art of poetry is a familiar one. No one would confuse the human spirit with the letters of the alphabet. Words can be heard and read, but the arrangement of words gives us the real shape of poetic creation. What the arrangement expresses is something quite different: the very embodiment of the human world – the fates and passions, the acting figures themselves, persons and characters. That is all background, that is, mere appearance.

A very naive reader (especially in childhood) will take what is told as "true events," and perhaps become all excited about them. Such a reader is not adequate to the experience of poetry, he is not a kindred spirit, not in the sense of aesthetical vision; he enjoys the tension, the sensation of what is narrated, but not the poetry as such.

The material of speech receives in poetry a revaluation. The natural attitude takes what is said as true. For the meaning of speech is to tell what is or what was true. The natural attitude takes false speech as a misuse of this sense of truth, as a lie, or at least as a harmless fraud. In contrast, in poetry there appears a meaning of discourse that is beyond the gravity of true and false; it does not concern itself with this opposition, and, in any case, stands before us without the ethos of denying or bearing witness to the real world. This understanding of speech lets us allow things to appear for the sake of appearance alone, to "tell fables," to genuinely "poetize." The element in which words exist, their sound, is not affected by this – perhaps only in that its use is freer – but the meaning of speech is changed. It stands to everyday speech as dreams to waking.

Yet in this respect speech is like shaping space in sculpture, and like the magic of colors in painting: it does not feign reality, it does not lead us to an illusory world. Therefore the poet works also with certain techniques to create a sense of unreality. The use of "metrical" lines is only one of these techniques; there are many forms of stylized speech that limit what our sense of reality demands of speech.

The effect of these techniques is that words – which usually serve sober practical interests – become capable of a construction of another order. And by means of these it achieves great transparency, which enables the revelation of what in life otherwise cannot be said. Such a heightened transparency is made possible only by poetry's indifference to the true and the false taken literally.

This remains essential even where poetry derives its material from reality. Its being put to use and its redesign are reserved to the poet. (104) We understand the unreality of the human lives, actions, and fates portrayed there, and we assume that; we grant to the creator of the material his poetic license to operate with it. In that way he first obtains the necessary latitude in which to move about.

The opposition of real and unreal in relation to the levels of material is thus intensified in poetry, as opposed to the originally practical use of speech. The opposition is not limited to the usual distinction between sound and meaning, which belongs to all speech, but reaches far beyond it. It releases, so to speak, language from its original function of bearing witness to reality.

The freedom of play in poetry depends upon this release, as well as the specifically artistic achievement of language. The setting-off of the appearing background from the context of reality returns again in poetry; it is more evident in the content of speech than in painting, even without the presence of a frame. Poetry allows a whole human world to appear before our inward vision; we can familiarize ourselves with this appearing world, we can, to a certain extent, live along with the characters that appear there. We see people acting and suffering, and we live along with them just in the same way as we do with others in real life.

Yet it is not our own and genuine real life in which we do these things, but another, an appearing one, a poetized and confabulated one. That does not make it any less meaningful, rather it is often enough superior to real life in the content of its meaning, and in the case of "great" poetry this superiority is what is essential to it. But the relation of appearance is not for that reason turned backward, towards our familiar relation to reality; reality is not simulated. That is true even when its themes are current, and drawn from problems of present-day human reality.

The form of existence of the background, with the entirety of its colorful scenes, is and remains in suspension, i.e., it is appearing existence. The figures called forth by the poet "are" never and nowhere than in the poetry. Therefore the slice of life that appears there stands isolated and set off from real life, confined, as is a painting, within a framework. But this framework cannot be understood to be real, but is contained by the ontological space of the language over against the figures. For it is not when we look away from and beyond words, but only through their presence to us, that we peer into the appearing life.

Correspondingly, this slice of life stands with fixed boundaries around it; it is closed within itself, a unity of life *sui generis*, with a comprehensible structure that is felt as a whole in an act of beholding; a segment that does not flow over into our environing life, but is clearly set off against it. Even here there is a different space in which it appears, and a different time; for poetry is essentially a temporal art. Figures, fates, actions and passions "play" within this apparent space and (105) apparent time. In reading, listening, or "watching" we are "transported" into the other spaces and times, and we do not confuse these with the real here and now in which we read and hear.

That is even the case when the material of poetry is taken from one's own present times and from one's own environment. Yet it is still the no-man's land of appearance, the "world of the poet" in which the events "play out." And, conversely, it is part of the power of poetry that it may allow the otherness of human life in historical times to appear in the concrete form of present-day life and experience. We see, as it were, through the frame of the written world directly into a life that is foreign and no longer really present to us.

e) The objective middle stratum of poetic works

In one respect the art of poetry is oriented quite differently from the plastic arts. The latter are turned directly toward the senses; and the stratum of being of the foreground, through which the background appears, is real and perceptible. In poetry that is not the case, at least not in an immediate way. It is not that poetry lacks a real stratum, but that it is an inadequate one. Only the spoken word or writing is given as real and sensible; and in fact appearance begins there. But still the figures, their character, actions and fates, do not appear directly in the words, but are mediated once again by something else, one must say: by a middle stratum.

With reference to this fact, we must correct one of the elements in the relation of appearance that we introduced at the outset. It does not cancel at all the fundamental relation, but it modifies it. What constitutes the particularity of the phenomenon of appearance in poetry?

We arrive most quickly at an answer by means of the following reflections. The poet rarely speaks in a direct manner about the psychic events that concern him, that is, about the inward life of the persons whom he presents. He prefers primarily to keep to the externalities, to that which in life offers itself to the senses, that is, to the gestures, speech, and movements of people, to their visible actions or reactions; he presents people as we would understand them in everyday life, i.e., from their expression, those that are voluntary and those that are involuntary. In this manner he creates figures capable of appearing to intuitive apprehension. But these external details are not what are essential to the human life as it appears in poetry; they are not congruent with the inward events, human activity and passivity, the intentions, the decisions, the successes and failures, not to speak of their congruence with attitudes, passions and fates. These are what really are at stake in poetry.

Why do poetic phrases not say these things directly? In everyday life we do this sufficiently when we speak to someone about a third person. Thereupon we see the simple answer: because in direct speech (106) about things of the psychic life words are abstract and clumsy, and they express only generalities. What one says becomes abstract and unintuitive. Only what is intuitive affects us immediately and convincingly. That is why poetry attempts to bring us to "see" the inward life of men upon their external expressions as we normally see the moods, attitudes, excitement, and passions of our fellows without them telling us about them. For every person reveals himself continuously in his visible action and inaction and also in his audible speech (whatever he may say). He does this involuntarily; he "gives himself away." Poetry puts this to use: it lets its figures reveal themselves, it lets them give themselves away; it places them in changing situations and lets them reveal their character in their behavior. What poetry achieves are not the plastic qualities of this behavior of theirs, but their psychic interior qualities, their fears and hopes, their nervousness and suspicions, or whatever else it may be.

Poets do not speak of such things as psychologists do; they do not dissect the psychic life in a laboratory. Instead of sharply defined concepts, their concrete images emerge from the lives and scenes they place before us and the situations in which persons show themselves. Poets help themselves along with conceptual abstractions only rarely. Anyone who uses them continuously is no poet.

In this way a peculiar intermediate stratum arises in poetry that is unreal, just as the background itself is, and, taken strictly, it also belongs to the latter; but just as the sensible stratum this stratum is immediately visible, even though it does not address itself to the senses themselves but to the imagination. It makes possible the appearance of concrete images of the characters to the imagination. It constitutes thereby a kind of foreground that plays in the entire poem the role of what is present to the senses. And precisely such an intermediate element is needed for poetic representation.

This element is nothing less than a stratum of appearing perceptibility. It is an appearance, because its perceptibility is not real. In fact, it is first produced by the existing stratum of words, but not by the latter alone; it is produced spontaneously and reproductively by the imagination. To that extent it belongs to the appearing background. But it belongs to the foreground with respect to its function, and is also felt by the reader and hearer as still belonging to it, although that is not possible at all, given its mode of existence. Nevertheless, it is directly tied to language, and the tightness of the bond is determined by the strict arrangement of the sounds and meanings of the words. The bond becomes loosened only when the language is not familiar to the reader. Now since the language speaks immediately of the objective multiplicity of this intermediate stratum, the miracle occurs of an entire world of things, persons, and events arising in the imagination, a world that is as concrete as perceptible objects, without, however, being perceived. (107) This intuitable objective multiplicity is the realm of appearing perceptibility.

This intermediate stratum is essential to poetry, even when its concreteness – depending upon the artistic capacity of the poet – may come in many degrees and, at times perhaps, shrinks to a bare minimum. When it completely disappears, the poetry passes into prosaic exposition, and its speech becomes conceptual, dull and abstract. This does not exhaust the function of the stratum of appearing perceptibility. But now it consists for its part rather in allowing what is not perceivable to appear, that is, the psychic and intellectual life of persons with their entanglements, situations, conflicts, etc. – just the same as in painting the visible colors let this life appear on canvas.

That is an advantage that the representational arts have over the art of poetry. Poetry cannot address itself directly to perception – at least not with the colorful fullness of objects, in which they make the experience of life "experienceable," but instead has to call upon a substitute stratum, where imagination takes the place of perception. For the real foreground in works of poetry, the visible script and the audible words themselves, is in comparison pale, schematic, and abstract.

This disadvantage of poetry is no doubt compensated for in part in that the imagination of the reader, which poetry calls to exercise itself autonomously, is in many respects richer than perception, and is free to move in a significantly larger arena. The displacement of the sensible foreground stratum in its concreteness to the unreality of mere appearance (thus really of the background) has also the advantage of greater freedom of movement and multiplicity. In poetry art moves a step further from imitation.

True, the element of abstraction in speech, which forms the only foreground proper, can never be eliminated. Words are and will remain concepts, after all; and concepts have unintuitable and inartistic effects, even though it may be true that what remains of their original nature contains some pictorial elements. This original element has just been forgotten, vanished, in a worn-out means of communication. But the unreal foreground (the intermediate stratum) is in need precisely of clarity and distinctness. The one who shapes poems knows how to work against this inadequacy by freeing the conventional meaning of words from their torpor; he makes them flow and come to life.

There are many means of achieving this effect, just as in life emphatic or very personal and sentimental speech uses them. Unique meanings of a special sort can be given to words by means of a unique blending of phrases; every word is supple in its meaning, regardless of the fixed arrangement required by their communicative function, and in the subtle nuances of words (108) the sense of each is altered according to the meaning of the entire verbal context. There is also the possibility of drawing out the pictorial character of the words from desuetude. Both means are well known and familiar. They constitute the peculiar transparency of poetic speech. But the special creative power of poetic expression is needed to raise them above mere playfulness and to make them expressive and suggestive.

f) Theater and the art of the actor

The disadvantage of poetry that we have just discussed is balanced out in the dramatic arts – but only so far as a second art and a second artist is placed between the poetry proper and the reader: the performing art and the actor. For then the intermediate stratum is transformed into reality; the reproductive imagination is removed and replaced by real perception. The "unreal foreground" is realized; the stratum of the object, in which poetic figures arrange themselves in space and time and speak and move expressively within it, becomes visible and audible, and can be the object of immediate experience. Readers become an audience.

This changes much. The first of these is the appearance of the art of interpretation itself, which stands between the mind that created the work and the audience that sees it. It is a second-order art – but not in a negative sense – that is quite close to the poetry, but is of a different kind. The poetry is dependent upon it, and must take notice of it, must reckon with it (with the capacity of the stage, the conditions of realization, the effects of scenery); it requires actors, directors, supporting mechanisms, a stage, an apron, a backstage – in all, a theater. Every dramatist knows what this dependency means, especially a beginner: he cannot put himself before the public directly; he must be called to it by the theater. Thus he first learns of the tightly wound world of another guild, represented by the so-called producers.

The second element to change is the work of poetry itself, which takes on a new form of appearance. The external mechanics of the stage creates a peculiar framework, causing an effect related to that of the frame in painting. Literature as a "performance" requires a more radical disconnection from the real contexts of life, just because it makes poetic figures visible and their speech audible. The "boards" themselves produce such a disconnect; they "are" not the world, they only "mean" the world. The apron is an unbridgeable border; it is never crossed in the play.

For these reasons one may say that the relation of the strata in poetry is not complicated by the production but rather simplified. Now for the first time the work of poetry – in its merging with the work of staging it – (109) stands exactly parallel to the work of fine art: it is no longer dependent upon the imagination of the observer (as reader), but addresses itself directly to the senses of sight and hearing; the appearing perceptibility is replaced by real perception.

With this a third element appears: the work of poetry is dependent in its content upon the art of the performer. For the realization of the intermediate stratum is not the work of the poet, but that of the actor. To him, the performer, is given the entire composition of the sensibly perceivable details. He has a free hand with these countless imponderable specifics. He becomes the co-creator of the work, even almost a co-poet; he is also a creative artist in his own way and within his own limits.

The poet cannot determine every perceptible detail of the action in the way, for example, a painter can present every last detail of a visible scene (within the limits he has set for himself) – his material, that is, words, is too intractable for that. The poet needs a sympathetic performer to take what he has put into speech, but only halfway, and realize it fully by bringing it to life. The performer can do that only by adding the details that the poetry lacks, and, indeed, according to his own best lights and his own spontaneous empathy with the spirit of the work (with the "role"), but only if he also "plays," acts, and makes the material manifest through the commitment to it of his own entire personality. His personality becomes an instrument, his action the medium – through which appears the new acted-out character whose shape was beheld and intended by the poet.

This means that the actor is a "performer" of the work, and that further implies that his achievement is a genuine creative work. We see this most clearly in the case of a failed production: for not everyone who masters his trade is an artist. We might say then that the role was "unconvincingly" played, and we would mean that the actor did not properly represent the character as the poet understood him. Just because the actor has genuine freedom to shape the role as he will, he can play it poorly. The great actor is the one who has sympathy with the piece, who is able to shape the imponderable details of the role through an unfailing sense of its spirit.

Furthermore, it is just the great acting talent in whom the freedom of creative writing becomes visible. A play is different in every performance. In this way even the identity of the work, so immutable in the other arts, is lost to poetry to a certain extent. Its identity is divided up into the string of its performances. What is remarkable about this fact, however, is just that this identity does not disappear at all, but maintains itself untouched behind the diversity of its performances and is unmistakable by every lover of the "piece." (110)

The enormous differences in the kinds of objectivation correspond to the conditions of performing theatrical works. The poet and the performer objectivize the same events, conflicts, passions, fates, and the same characters. But the poet gives his works only partial concreteness; even in the epic and in the novel the poet is dependent upon the imagination of the reader for supplementation. To that end he puts his creations in an enduring material, for nothing is more enduring than writing (which can be copied and reproduced without understanding it); he creates, as it were, "for eternity." The actor creates by "performing" what was merely written and confided to the imagination, that is, realizes what is realizable in it. Thereby he finishes to the very end what he took over from a thing only half-created; he gives it full concreteness and sensible clarity and distinctness. But he creates in a transient material, in audible speech and visible movements, gestures, and facial expressions. That is the most transient of all things transient: in a word, he creates only for the moment.

The fate of any performance is the incapacity for permanence. In the cinema, of course, a certain permanence of what is otherwise transient is achieved. We should not undervalue this fact just because the cinema is a recent invention or because it loses much of the vital quality of the stage. But it shows that transiency is not a product of the material alone; taste and a performance's power of insight may vary also, and the theatrical sense of an epoch is similarly changeable, for we seek new ways of interpretation, even though the poetic work itself endures unchanged. The individual performance gives way to ever-new ones just because it gives shape to every last detail.

Thus the art of the performer is and remains the art of a moment and "posterity gives no laurels to the actor." Along with the interpretation the actor offers, the work of the poet remains untouched in its "half"-concreteness and offers always the possibility of new readings. The poet, for that reason, is the lone survivor in the minds of posterity. The permanence of his name, as always in art, is tied to the permanence of the created object, thus in the end to the objectivation.

g) Actualization and de-actualization

To all of this one may object: in the performance of the actor, it is rather the entire plot of the poetic work that is brought to life, that is, translated into real events. If that is so, there is no longer any room for an unreal background that appears within the real. Then the law of objectivation, and with it the relation of appearance and the existential condition of the "beautiful" – thus of the entire aesthetic object – is lost.

This objection can be met. It rests on a complete misunderstanding. First of all, even in the case of a perfect realization of the action on the stage there is still much room for an ideal background. Second, however, only a fraction (111) and never the whole of what is acted out in the play is presented as real, and thus drawn into the foreground.

A plot is not externally visible action; its essence lies behind it, in the realm of the invisible. The plot proper, the "drama" as such, remains unreal in its performance. What are real are only the spoken word, the facial expressions and miscellaneous movements of the characters, the gestures, and the dialogue, in sum, what is visible and audible on stage. What is "on stage" itself, understood as a part of the plot, remains unreal. As always, the plot belongs to the appearance, and what is visible and audible is only that within which and through which it appears. It is consummated on the level of the psychic events, situations and decisions, loves and hates, successes and failures, of the destinies of its characters and of the ways in which they are lived out.

That is obviously happening on a different level. All of these events are thoroughly unreal and are not at all intended to be real. The performer does not love or hate, he does not suffer, and the destiny he portrays is not his own: all that only "appears," it is "played," acted out. And therefore the performed work is called a "show" and the artist as the performer a "showman" [*Schau-Spieler*].

In the same sense the poetic figures met onstage – Wallenstein, Faust, Richard III – are not real but only portrayed, "played." What is real is the living actor with his speech and gestures, but no one in the audience would mistake him with the kings, heroes, or intriguers that he portrays.

Precisely in the art of play-acting and dramaturgy what is decisive is neither the characters themselves, nor their destiny, nor the plot – thus all that is central to it – that is performed. And only for that reason is it possible for the audience to appreciate the art in the acting, indeed to notice it at all. If the members of the audience wished to take the events on stage for reality, the achievement of the actor would disappear entirely for them.

What is perhaps even more important: if the members of the audience were to take the events performed as reality, it would not be possible for them to sit quietly watching and serving as witnesses of clever intrigues or even of murder and manslaughter, or of the deep mental suffering of the characters. The stage would also make an entirely false presumption about its audience. The meaning of a tragedy would be falsely changed to one of moral brutishness, of a comedy to heartlessness. No theater imputes this to its audience. All theories that speak in this context of "illusion," that is, of the simulation of real events, are entirely false, they have disoriented us aesthetically, and almost destroyed the meaning of dramatic effect. The infantile mind that actually falls victim to the illusion of the theater is not an aesthetical consciousness.

The truth is the reverse: the self-evident knowledge of the unreality of the events being acted out on stage that accompanies all looking and hearing (112) is the necessary condition of the aesthetical and contemplative attitude of viewing and enjoying them. One can observe the entire situation from the perspective of "play": namely, what is real in everything shown on stage is only the play itself, and what is acted out in it is not taken for real, it is only "playing." That gives what is performed the character of weightlessness. For the action itself is entirely in earnest, but the earnestness is acted. Only in that way is it possible for the sense of the play to be serious and meaningful, even sublime, without the play ceasing to be a play. The staged play is therefore totally different from children's play. The latter is to a great extent entirely in the realm of illusion; the child does not keep his distance from what he is playing, he enters its realm entirely.

We find a clear confirmation of this relationship in the need of all stagecraft and performance for a limitation of realism. To achieve this, the ancients introduced songs that were developed at length, and processions between the "episodes." They also had the chorus, which accompanied the play but had no dramatic effect, and the dialogue was in verse. They banned from the stage all violence and terror, allowing such things to transpire only "behind the scenes." The dramatic arts have long retained much of these techniques, so also the use of verse, which is the most effective means of linguistic form.

A significant step further was taken by modern opera. Music is no mere accompaniment – for example, as "illustrating psychic states" – as many have assumed. Music is rather the most radical means of limiting realism. For music as such is essentially undramatic and nonobjective; it works against objective reality. Moreover, it introduces an element into poetry that is somewhat foreign to it, one that does not belong to it; for it is another form of art, and its synthesis with poetry opens a new chapter for aesthetics.

In general, every curbing of realism in theater – even by the stylizing of its external elements – is to be understood as the artistic fostering of the sense of unreality, in principle even when it works with questionable means. For it works consciously against the element of "imitation" (thus against *mimesis* proper). This can be taken too far, and can extend itself beyond the limits of dramaturgy. This appeared early, in the ancient comedy of manners, but most clearly in the modern world. These limits are breached in farces, as in the popular figures of Pagliaccio and Harlequin. The dramatic quality gives way to drolleries, to the farcical, and it disappears entirely in jest and fanciful nonsense.

It is important to recall in this context that in serious modern dramaturgy de-actualization [*Entwirklichung*] no longer involves the performers "playacting" as such. Realism maintains a free hand here – a clear sign that the appearance of psychic and inward states cannot do without a certain convincing faithfulness to nature. It may, however, also be a sign that the danger of a modern audience falling prey to illusion (113) is past, or at least not likely. The power of expression of the great character actor, which reaches far beyond what is merely typical in the character he portrays, demonstrates this most clearly. For every living human character has in it something unique and individual.

If we place these features of stagecraft alongside the stylized gestures of Chinese dramaturgy or even the restrained playacting in cothurnus and masks, as in the Attic stage, we may see the vast number of options available for portraying different degrees of reality and unreality.

As a whole and in general, in staged plays we find the same series of strata that govern the fundamental principles of all poetry and of all the performing arts. Only with respect to content is that order displaced. The "play" is the displacement of the "appearing perceptibility" toward reality and perception proper. The first segment of the background, which still lies close to the senses, moves thereby into the foreground. But only the first segment: everything else, the plot itself and the enacted characters, remain mere appearance. And when the play as such is understood also as appearance, the plot becomes clearly separated from the foreground and seen as unreal.

Chapter 7: Foreground and Background in the Non-Representational Arts

a) Free play with form

Perhaps one should say rather that there are no non-representational arts. Humankind represents something in all artistic construction – itself.

We must not understand that too narrowly. What appears in a work does not have to be the person or the artist himself; it may be the general type of person he is, and whatever special and intrinsic character that type has with respect to country, people, and epoch. It is always something of this kind. But this something is not what one means when one speaks of "representational art." With that term, one refers to the specific theme, its *sujet*. The same artist can treat many different subjects without his own nature, which speaks along with them, changing at all.

Moreover, the personal nature of a writer is not explicitly represented but appears only with what is represented and often primarily only for the ones who stand far from it, his descendants. His nature is simply not made a theme. And if it becomes one, as in a self-portrait, it is again still just one theme among many possible ones. We cannot say that because of this one phenomenon all the arts are equally representational. For involuntary self-portrayal is ancillary; it comes along after the conscious treatment of the theme.

We can treat separately each of the following arts: architecture, music, and ornament. For in their cases the situation is quite special. To be sure, that is true in music only when we ignore songs with a text and so-called (114) program music. Why one can and must do that will be discussed later. At this point the reason suffices that text and title are, as a matter of fact, not music. Therefore we must not make light of extending representational considerations to music. There is also such a thing as "pure music" that has no extra-musical themes in it and does not need them. The lack of such themes is precisely what the three arts we named above have in common, however much they are otherwise different.

In any case, that is only the negative universal in them. The additional affirmative element is not so easy to determine. Even in specific forms of matter, one can glimpse it only where there is a pure though not always free play with form, and then only in a provisional way, with no guarantee of its correctness.

The matter in question is in one case heavy mass; in the other, tones. Naturally each of these allows quite different kinds of play with form. Form itself is determined only as to its kind by the matter, primarily by means of the dimensions in which the form is extended; the opposition between art that is constructed in space and that in time distinguishes the two dimensions of artistic creation, but this alone is insufficient to define their peculiar natures. Poetry, too, is a temporal art, while the fine arts are essentially spatial. Within the limits of what is possible for the matter used, the constructive activity itself is entirely autonomous.

For here begins what one is tempted to call "free play with form" as such. It is a pure play done for its own sake. For "representation" is tied to objects of a non-aesthetical sort and begins as imitation. It must be "true to its *sujet*," but it can also be "false" to it. Yet the pure play with form knows nothing of being true or false – not in this sense, in any case – for no pattern, no model, no perceptible shape is given by it. It is based upon no previously given form. For that reason, the endowing of an object with form, as in these cases, is entirely an autonomous activity; it is a different and higher freedom than we encounter in the representational arts. It is pure production without an element of *mimesis* or reproduction, pure "creation out of nothing."

This freedom is paid for in architecture and ornamental design by accepting a certain unfreedom of a different kind.

Architecture serves practical ends that in themselves have nothing to do with beauty. Even where the ends are of the highest and most ideal kind they possess always a nature that is external to aesthetics, as in the construction of temples and churches, and also of palaces and the like. As the former serve religious services, the latter serve political power and its aura. In a simple apartment building practical ends dominate most markedly. But strangely this does not, as a whole, interfere with the aesthetical element and its value; rather it bears them. It operates here as a kind of precondition, and where the formal beauty of the house is achieved, it absorbs the aesthetical element completely, without bargaining anything away from it. (115)

It is otherwise with ornamental art. In itself, it does not serve practical ends, but rather the objects upon which it appears; architecture, practical implements, the patterns of carpets. Thus it is a dependent art so far as it is incorporated in a formal whole that it cannot violate, even if these provide only a framework for it. Within that framework, however – for instance a surface that it must fill out – it is relatively free and may, moreover, approach the status of a fine art. When it does so, it accepts many elements derived from the circle of themes within the whole. But such does not belong to its nature, which is absorbed entirely in the play of lines, colors, or spatial motifs that are there only for themselves alone.

Only music is truly free, and then only pure music. For it, too, can, in a sense, serve ends. In pure music the principle of "play" becomes completely independent. Music as a play with tones, melodies, harmonies, timbre – exists in a kind of matter that divests itself, to a high degree, of all aims external to aesthetics. For that reason it is the most free of all the arts. Moreover, it is free in two directions: it is just as free of themes or *sujets* external to aesthetics as it is free of aims external to it.

For that reason the question of creativity is a peculiar one for music. A level of productivity, unknown in other arts, is reached here. Composition is based upon invention – on an inward discovery and creation – to the extent that even a musical "theme" is freely created; it is purely a product of musical fantasy.

Now the question of aesthetics, one that touches profoundly the nature of this art, is this: are we dealing at all in music with the same kind of beauty as in the representational arts? Or does a second kind of beauty appear here?

The latter is what we should expect. If beauty in the representational arts lies in the relation of appearance, thus neither in the real foreground nor in the unreal background, but only in the appearance of the latter in the former, then the situation changes at the point where the opposition of these strata does not exist. Where there is no *sujet*, none can appear. Is there still another type of beauty that consists in nothing more than a pure relation of form?

There are two reasons for that conclusion. The first lies in the character of pure play with form, although only in specific material; the second can be understood by analogy to beauty in nature and beauty in the human being, where obviously no theme (*sujet*) belongs to its nature. Those are the points of departure of two more serious arguments raised against the concept of beauty in the relation of appearance. Perhaps all beauty is of the same kind? Or is all beauty fundamentally of different kinds, and the assumptions of an aesthetic of pure form would be true in a new sense? (116)

b) Beauty in music

The circle of questions just touched upon clearly has music as its central concern. Music is the art that is "free on two sides." We must therefore attempt here to grasp the fundamental problem.

We need not immediately ask whether beauty in music is beauty of an entirely different order. It is sufficient to ask first whether a relation of appearance exists in music and whether, if we can demonstrate that it does, it is capable of bearing the phenomenon of the musically beautiful. To this end we must set aside all program music, even the simple song, which is already a case of combining two arts (poetry and music); and we must not be led astray by the fact that the very beginnings of music are found in song. It is incorrect to judge a highly developed domain of the spirit and its great achievements simply upon its primitive origins. Those later achievements may have left their historical sources far behind them.

Further, we must not fail to take this question seriously just because music lays claim from the outset to psychic moods (pain, joy, courage, wantonness, longing, etc.) as background elements, which are undeniably expressed in it. That cannot be permitted precisely because moods constitute a further stratum of the whole. Besides, one would then pass quickly into the domain of program music. That transition must be postponed until we arrive at a later stage of our analysis.

In the meantime we can demonstrate that even in pure music – and, in fact, this side of all psychic content – a stratification and a relation of appearance is found. Obviously, it also is found in any and all other music, even in the composition and arrangement of works of poetry. But there it does not come into question, as it surely does in pure music.

We must assume that the audible tone constitutes for music the "material" that is given form by the composer. Then we must count the sequence and interrelation of tones as the ontic stratum and the foreground of music.[42] One may ask therefore: is there in music something that lifts itself beyond the sensibly audible sounds, something that hovers above it, and can that something be grasped by a person capable of understanding music? Or, to state this in the image we used earlier: is there something here behind the sounds that stands out against them, but that constitutes in this way a background that appears through the sounds in just such a way as to remain the genuine and true musical content?

It can be shown that indeed this content exists. We need only to seek it where it can be found – not far beyond the domain of sounds, but rather close to that domain and still within its realm. (117)

For music itself – a "piece," a composition, a "movement" – is not simply what is sensibly audible, for above and beyond that there is always the "musically audible" that requires a synthesis by the consciousness thatreceives it, one that is quite different from what can be produced in a purely acoustical perception. This musical synthesis is a greater whole, and creates the background, which is no longer sensible. What can be "heard" together in a purely sensible way is a narrowly restricted tonal structure: a sonata, a "movement," or even a prelude is far from appearing in such structure. Of course we hear (purely acoustically) as a sensibly real unity a limited series of tones, similarly we hear a series of harmonies, but only so far as our capacity extends for acoustically retaining (the lingering "after-echo") what has just been heard. Retention does not extend beyond a few seconds, less when the music continues and new sounds continuously wash over what has vanished in time.

Moreover, to hold together (sensibly and acoustically) the great mass of tones and harmonies of a "movement" is musically impossible, for it would cause an unbearable disharmony. Hearing is a sense conditioned by time, and music is an art conditioned by time. A "movement" is extended in time; it consists precisely in succession – a succession that is extended far more than the reach of retention.

Consequently, the movement is never present at any moment of its temporally extended performance. The movement needs time, it marches past our ears, it has duration; in each moment only a segment of it is present to its hearers. And yet to the hearer – at least to genuine "musical" hearing – it is not torn to pieces, but is apprehended as interconnected, as a whole. Despite its separation into its

---

42 We must not take the reality of the real stratum as literally as we do in the case of the material substance of poetry, that is, of words, which is also a construction out of sounds. Sounds are not real in the strict sense, because they exist as such only for the hearer. But we can ignore these facts here. For what is essential about the "real stratum" of a work of music is always the sensibly given, that which exists for perception, and this givenness to the senses is realized in the full sense of the word.

temporal stages, it is still apprehended as a coexistence of its parts – not as parts that are temporally simultaneous, but as belonging to each other, as a unity.

This unity is, to be sure, still temporal in nature, but not a simultaneity. Even a series as such can be a unity. However, here the unity is not produced in sensible hearing, but rather only in the execution of a synthetic act that must occur in musical hearing. Indeed, in the execution of this act musical hearing as such first comes to be – in contrast to sensible hearing. For it is not the instantaneous sound, but only the whole in the unity of its succession, that constitutes the musical organization of the movement's tones. Only out of this whole do the details that were built into it – the elements that can be sensibly heard together – acquire a meaning.

Perhaps one might object that all this is entirely obvious, for there could be no music at all that did not allow the drawing together of temporally separated elements, allow, as it were, their being heard as one. This objection is just a confirmation of the thesis; what is musically obvious is precisely what is meant. The situation is here as it is everywhere: philosophy is first to note what is remarkable and meaningful – perhaps (118) puzzling – in what is obvious. For a thing is blindly accepted as long as it is thought to be just what is generally accepted and reflection on what it really is has not yet begun. Even aesthetics has, up to now, not consciously analyzed its fundamental condition, and therefore has never noticed what is problematic about it.

But what does this problem consist in? We must reach as far back as the categorial analysis of time. Time is in fact the drawing asunder of all real elements in the stages of temporal succession. A man, for example, is at no moment of his life present to himself as a whole, for what he was he no longer is, and what he will be he is not yet. Only in intuitive time (which is not equivalent to real time), i.e., subjectively, is it possible, within limits, to grasp intuitively one's life as a whole, because in intuitive time consciousness has something that no thing or process has in real time: freedom to move. In life our apprehension of an activity is always tied to the momentary or narrow segment of it. But it is different in art.[43]

Now music creates precisely a unity and closed wholeness in what, in the temporal series, is drawn asunder. This synthesis is produced in the process itself of musical hearing, a process that passes far beyond the narrow limits of hearing tones in unison. But it is not produced all at once, but rather successively in the

---

[43] The relation of music to time can be understood only by means of a categorial analysis of time (and, moreover, of real time as well as intuitive time) in which their structural and ontological oppositions can be worked out clearly. This task has been undertaken in *Philosophie der Natur* [*Philosophy of Nature*] (1950). For the notion of the state of being drawn asunder [*Auseinandergezogensein*] of real temporal elements, cf. Chap. 12; for the nature of intuitive time cf. Chaps. 14 and 15.

process of sensible listening-to, and on the basis of a very definite inward unity and completeness of the musical work. For it is just this that constitutes an objectively structured interconnection of elements, a construct in which every detail refers forward and backward from itself, and these references are themselves also apprehended, of course unreflectively, but with complete clarity. For only so far as these references are apprehended do we sense the wholeness as such in the changing flow of sounds. And only so far as it is sensed, do we understand the work musically.

For in fact the musical unity of the work itself has the character of a synthesis; that is, it is a "composition" (*compositio* in a simple translation of "synthesis"). Such a unity is not heard by the senses. Therefore it is a genuine appearance and specifically one that appears through the sense of hearing. It therefore belongs properly to the background of the piece. Taken objectively, however, it is the synthetic unity in which the sound that has at one point died away and is no longer sensibly heard, is yet retained, and thus forms, as something still present, an essential component of the whole that is successively built up in the process of listening musically.

The hearer himself must execute the synthesis. As such, he is also active, imitatively, in the process of composition. (119)

c) The phenomenon of the background in music

Consequently, the fundamental peculiarity of the musical work of art consists in the fact that in its temporal unfolding the listener is able to hear from the inner interrelationships of its elements the compositional unity of such a structure, although that unity is not sensibly audible. For its unity is not present in any of the stages of its acoustical performance, but it is nonetheless what the composition is really about. A musical work requires the listener to anticipate and to recall, and, in every stage of his hearing of it, to have an expectation of what is coming, to anticipate the specific development that the music requires. That is true even when the actual development of the piece reveals itself as a different one than expected. For the resolution of the tension aroused by the music can be different from the one expected, and the exploitation of unexpected (innovative) musical possibilities is an essential element of surprise and enrichment. In music, such things are no different from poetry (e.g., an unanticipated development of the plot of a novel or drama).

It is well known that a composer can go too far in presenting an effective moment of surprise. His music can then seem to be striving after sensational effects. But excess does not destroy the basic phenomenon, for the playing with the disparity between anticipation and what really happens is constitutive of the unity of the composition and the musical structure of the whole, which, while overarching them, comes to appearance in the sounding-out and the dying-away of the momentary musical details.

The synthesis achieved by the hearer can be thought of as follows. As he apprehends what is momentarily audible, he is still inwardly aware of what he has just heard, even of what has long died away, and yet at the same time he is already present at what is to come. For in music each passage is directed beyond itself, both forwards and backwards. If one considers a passage isolated from the others, it loses its musical sense. This sense is tied to the whole. That is so true that in the contrary case, where the discerning listener, who by chance overhears a few bars of a piece, involuntarily supplements them and thereby apprehends a fragment of the whole – regardless of whether what he apprehends supplementarily truly characterizes the actual composition or not. What happens in his case is no otherwise than with a person trained in the plastic arts who beholds a fragment of a ruined sculpture.

The artistic miracle of a musical work lies in building within a temporal succession the unity of a collective structure; it fills itself out piece-by-piece, rounds out its parts and unites them as a single structure. By listening musically we experience the music's lofty climb, its growth, its towering up and out of itself; and this entire construction, rising ever higher, is then completed and unified only just when the audible succession of sounds has come to a close, i.e., has died away. The final (120) bars of a logically constructed work of music will then be apprehended as the conclusion of the structure and its crowning moment.

In fact one hears more than what is sensibly heard; one hears a construction of tones of another magnitude that is impossible to hold together acoustically in one's ears. This other construct is the music-work proper; it is the composition, the "movement," the fugue, the sonata. And this other construct constitutes the "musical background." Of course, we mean only the musical background, for much more belongs to the complete background of the music. Of that we will speak at another place.

Listening to music transcends sensible hearing. The entirety of the music that appears in a movement is not sensibly given as such. Acoustically it is unreal, that is, not even realized in the playing of the music, for it cannot be realized all at once. One hears it "throughout," for the sensibly given series of sounds lets it appear, although its phases cannot be held together; those sounds have the peculiar transparency that lets something else, the structure that cannot be reduced to it, appear to an attentive listener.

What appears is thus an unreal background in the strict sense of the term. All characteristics of unreality are valid for this structure. Consequently, in music we have the same two strata of the object as in the representational arts: the same two levels and kinds of opposition in their nature, the same phenomenon of appearing in sensible material, the same transparency of the constructed foreground. In the same way too, an identical role is given to the apprehending subject, for only to an observer who meets the conditions of musical discernment can the unity of the work appear. The entire situation with its four members, such as is characteristic of the mode of being of the objectivated spirit, we find here once again.

Of course, only these basic features coincide. We ignore here completely all further stratification. In contrast, the special kind of tie between the strata is quite different in these [representational] arts, perhaps just because in music the foreground and first background are more similar, and are more like each other in kind. For that reason in music, too, people long misunderstood the dual nature it possesses.

But it is clear how in the composer's work the foreground is determined by the background, how the unity of the internal shape of the composition determines the organization of what can be sensibly heard down to the smallest details. Here again the musical work of art is comparable to the works of poetry and painting.

If these points require further proof, we may turn to negative examples, that is, to failures in music. There is a kind of composition in which the details do not seem to the listener to come together, but instead fall asunder. The details may have a pleasant effect, they can root one to the spot, excite one, arouse anticipation; they may even point ahead to some whole. But when the whole is lacking, when the appearance of structure does (121) not develop out of the music, we experience it as lacking uniformity, as insipid and without character. No inward interconnectivity is felt; the piece lacks the unity of an inner form.

One may also say that such works lack genuine composition. For composition is "synthesis" of unity. The work affects us only externally, playfully; it makes the musically attentive hearer listen in vain; no unity appears to him. The contrast between "serious" and "light" music has nothing to do with this lack. Even superficial music, if it is done well – and that means that it is beautiful – does not lack unity and therefore it also does not lack the appearing background. Unity is in such cases of a different kind structurally, and it governs the rhythms and sounds of the foreground in a different way. But in its own way such music may well be musically beautiful.

d) Composition and musical execution

In a manner similar to theatrical performance, music demands an art of a second order, which alone allows the composed and written music to be audibly heard. The written composition needs such an art even more: after all, anyone can "read" a play, and, if a person has a little imagination, he can "see" the piece inwardly. To "read" a piece of music is quite different; it requires a specialist's professional training and a great deal of practice. Ordinarily an amateur musician can "play" the music before he can "read" it without playing it. Despite occasional exceptions, it is much harder to hear the music "on sight" than it is to sight-read a piece.

However that may be, the musical public requires the audible reproduction, the presentation, or, in the case of great works, the "performance" – if it is to understand the music at all. In this way, the art of the performing musicians in reproducing it becomes an aesthetical necessity. Here, as with drama, it is an art of "execution" [*Spiel*], and many of the characteristics of the art of dramatic performance apply: of course, only *mutatis mutandis*, for the kind of execution is different.

In no wise is it at all a question of representation. For that reason, the person of the musician does not present itself as an "instrument" – as does the actor, who employs himself as the medium of the representation – the singer does not, either, although he employs the human voice as a natural instrument. We must exclude too the opera-singer, not because of the music but rather because of the dramatic stage he inhabits. In pure music, after all, no objects are represented – at least no objects external to music. Therefore, the question of realism and the circumscribing of reality vanish entirely. In song, no doubt, both are present, but only by the introduction of the text as an extra-musical element. (122)

These are all only negative, limiting elements, however. In contrast, what is positive and foundational is as follows. Even in music, an ontic stratum of the artwork, which remains unreal in the written composition, that is, it is not given to the senses but is left to the imagination, is transposed to reality by the secondary art of "execution," and in that way it is driven into sense-perceptibility and into the foreground of the entire work.

The "reality" that comes in question here is exclusively the acoustical reality, the realm of the sensibly audible. This is true even where the "visible" energies in the movements of the musicians who execute the piece, or even those of the conductor, make an essential contribution to our understanding of the music. These visual cues, which assist us in listening musically, are a chapter in themselves. But they do not affect what is foundational, even when they reach into a level of deep psychic connections to the personalities of the musicians. Let us not forget that it is precisely the profoundly sensitive listener who will look away from these physical gestures so as not to be disturbed by them. To just such a person they may be too dramatic, obtrusive, or distracting.

To this we must add that the "realization" of the music by the musicians – including the amateurs who play it – is so obvious that in fact everyone calls the realization alone music, whereas the printed score in black and white is thought to be a mere expedient. We may not claim, therefore, that the reader becomes a listener (as in drama a reader becomes a member of the audience); the musical reader is the exception.

As a consequence, music proper arises objectively only with the secondary art of the musician. The organization that belongs to it is by nature not as large as that of the actor, it limits itself to the instruments, but it can, in the case of symphonic works, grow radically in size and contain a whole orchestra of artists for whom the musical accompaniment consists in their uniform collaboration – that is, in the achievement of the conductor.

No question of strengthening the effects of the frame arises here [as in drama]. Music as played and heard does not need to be set off from its ties to the environing reality; it is set off more than enough by its acoustic material, because this material, as a tonic series, appears nowhere other than in music. It is true, however, that a strict analogy to the fine arts appears only by means of actual performance: only through the audible performance is there a sensible foreground that is not dependent upon thought; the musical work first addresses the ears, and not the creative imagination of "readers" (who are rare). What is merely an object of thought is replaced by what can be perceived. (123)

In this way, the analogy to the actor's art appears in its correct light; music is dependent upon the performance by the musician. For here, too, there is an intermediate stratum where the performance is realized. The realization is no longer the work of the composer but that of the musician who executes it. The musician has a free hand in the shaping of the endless details of the most imponderable sort, which cannot be written in the score, but upon which the shape of the whole depends. He is promoted to fellow-composer, and is in this sense not just a "reproducing artist" but rather quite creatively productive – no less than is an actor in a play.

The composer, for his part, requires a congenial performance. The musician has received from him a work that is shaped only in part (still in a relatively general way), and he completes the process. He fills it with life and soul, according to how he thinks it was intended to be. But he does not proceed through the medium of his own person, but through the instrument. For he is not, like the actor, "representing" characters, but is the interpreter of music.

Yet it is also true of music that it is altered in each performance. The reading by the musician is always added to the composition, and that reading can be very personal and unique. Within certain limits the integrity of the music may be lost in this way; it is broken asunder by the qualitative variety of the interpretations.

Nonetheless, the greatest disparity between written and performed music consists in the type of objectivation. The former owes its permanence to the durability of writing material – *aere perennius* –, it is given concretely only by a half, it is true, but at the same time it is given a structure for all time, offering itself ever again to new interpreters. The musician, in contrast, gives the music a realized concreteness and clarity, but only in the most transient material; he completes it, but only for the moment. The higher objectivation cannot be maintained; it fades away in time along with its unique performance. Of course, within certain limits, the music can be recorded by means of modern technology (recordings), but that technology does not reach to the finer details of the music, and it changes nothing regarding the multiplicity and diversity of the renditions. The individual performances, despite all recording, will always be replaced by ever-new interpretations.

The art of the performing musician remains essentially the art of a moment. For him, too, future generations weave no laurels. And, next to his achievement and towering above it, the written composition in its half-concretion stands immovable, at each instant available for possible new consummations, and its creator survives in the memory of posterity. –

One might venture the opinion at this point that, similar to the actor, the performing musician draws into reality the entire background of the music, including its high spiritual content, so that there would then be no further space for an "unreal" background that could appear in the real. (124) In that case, the fundamental law of objectivation would fail and with it the ontological conditions of beauty.

That would be a complete misunderstanding. In no sense is the whole work of music made real but rather only the first and nearest stratum of the background, that which is sensibly audible, the tones and harmonies. Just these play the role of the intermediate stratum. They alone are acoustically realizable. That is no small matter, but it is not the whole of music. All the rest remains unreal, as before the performance, and is produced only as the achievement of the minds of the hearers. This is true for the entire psychic content of the music, whatever else it may consist in. We have not yet spoken of this matter, but it is easy to anticipate that this psychic content must consist in the later series of strata that constitutes the depths of the background. As in the art of drama, the plot proper, with its loves and hates, remains unreal, so too the moods and feelings in a musical performance.

But that is not the end of it. Even the entirety of the composition remains unreal in the performance of the musicians. The synthesis involved in holding together what one hears as a unity cannot be achieved for a listener even by the most accomplished interpreter; he can surely bring him nearer to it, can lead him to it, but no power on earth can take from the listener the construction in successive order of the whole of the piece in the process of musical hearing. One cannot "hear" for another person, just as one cannot think, grasp, or understand for him. For, as we have shown, the unity and wholeness of a piece of music exists nowhere but in musical hearing. It is therefore clear that everything that we said above about the "appearance" of compositional unity refers precisely to the audible performance of the musician, and not at all simply to the written music.

In this regard it is also clear that only the middle stratum of what is "sensibly audible" is realized in the here and now of the unique performance. And that means that in the performance what is genuinely musical in the music remains appearance. Of course one may not take this being-as-appearance too lightly; appearance can be itself genuinely objective, it can be compelling, cogent, and shock us deeply; it can, to our amazement, pull along violently an audience of listeners and unite them in the unity of "one" artistic experience. But for that very reason it still remains appearance and does not become an objective reality. It is precisely and only in this way that the foundational conditions of the "aesthetic object" and of what is beautiful about it are fulfilled.

It is hardly necessary to add to this that also no element of illusion is found in performed music. As the musicians make no pretense to the reality of their feelings, so also not to the reality of anything other than the varying comings and goings of the tones – not to the whole, which requires synthesis, and not to the psychic element at all. The performance remains performance, and the earnestness of what appears in it and irresistibly sweeps us along remains appearance. The relation among the strata with its contraries of real and unreal is maintained. The relation works here through other (125) means than in the representational arts. Its apparent removal rests simply in the fact that pure music has no themes external to itself, that is, it is not representation. But what it really transmits to the listener through the foreground cannot be expressed at all in words and concepts.

e) On the appearing background in architecture

What the non-representational arts have in common was defined as a pure but not always free play in specific forms of matter. This play is carried on purely for its own sake, but it is limited by the material substance of which it is made (to certain dimensions, the possibilities within the substance, etc.).

Those arts are free only from a "*sujet.*" For that reason they may be quite lacking in freedom from some practical end. Music revealed itself to be free in both ways. In this, architecture forms the contrary opposition to music: it is subject to ends that are external to aesthetics, and to such an extent that if such an end were lacking, architecture would cease to be. An art of erecting buildings that did not give service of some kind to human life – regardless whether it serves everyday life or that of the state or of religion – would be wanton, empty, merely a backstage.

The chief question of aesthetics with regards to architecture is whether it possesses a relation of strata, or, more precisely, whether in architecture an appearing background exists behind the real presence of the visible foreground. And since nothing like a theme is present in it, the question is not easy to decide.

At first it appears as though the question must be answered in the negative. For among the fine arts architecture is surely the least free. It is bound in two ways: (1) by the nature of the practical ends it serves, and (2) by the weight and intractability of the physical material in which it works.

We may ask ourselves how a "free play" with form is even possible, since form, after all, has other tasks to perform and, even more, free play with form takes place in this instance in coarse matter. And how we are to suppose the appearance of an unreal element? To respond, we must first clarify two phenomena relating to architectural effects.

The first of these phenomena is found in an analogy with music. As in music, where a larger effect arises, one that is audible only to a musical ear, behind what is sensibly audible, so also in architecture. Behind what is directly visible a greater whole appears that can be given as such only in bringing its elements together in a higher kind of beholding. What is directly visible is always at any given moment only one side of the construction, a façade or even somewhat less than that. It is precisely the same when one stands inside, whether it is in a house or the spaces of a church. The whole of the organized structure cannot be seen from any given point – at least not by the senses. Yet the observer has an intuitive sense of the whole; and that sense develops quickly and surely as one wanders through the various interior rooms of the structure, or as one (126) changes one's position while observing the uniform interior spaces or the external shape, so that the various perspectives, sides, and component elements are taken in one after the other.

This succession of views is no doubt random, and not a process of being led through some objectively given series, as in music, but it is nonetheless a temporal succession of individual pictures, each giving way to the next one, and which, optically, are quite different from each other. Aesthetical seeing, however, occurs when, standing out from these varying visual aspects, a whole with an objective structure appears, a physically unified composition that is as such not visibly given and cannot be seen from any given point, but rather first appears in the work of synthetic mental representation, and is to that extent "unreal."

This is no doubt true only when one places great weight upon the idea of "the senses." For the whole of the building is present before us as ontically real, but it is not sensibly visible in a single act of observation. The relation of appearance is displaced in this case, and approaches the phenomenon of appearance in natural beauty, where the elements of the entire vista are also genuinely together. Of this phenomenon we will speak later. For that reason we will leave at present the unsettled question of this ontological inconsistency.

Meanwhile, the inward artistic way of seeing is clearly distinguishable from sensible seeing. The object of this inner vision, as in music, is something larger, the composition proper. In viewing successively the parts as they become visible to us, the individual views become interlocked in a total picture. And as in music the individual tones cannot be heard acoustically as one, so in this case the individual views are not visible as one.

This phenomenon has not been taken seriously enough, probably because it seems so obvious. But in such cases, the main issue conceals itself in its very obviousness, that is, the genuine phenomenon of seeing architecturally. In it, the appearance-relation is hiding. –

In contrast, the second phenomenon is well known and often described, and yet it is difficult to describe it adequately. Apparently something more is expressed in the appearance of a building than the spatial and material form. We see this with special clarity in more ancient structures upon which an entire past civilization is visible. One need not know of the civilization from other sources; one senses it rising up before us even absent such knowledge – of course with varying grades of forcefulness. Very definite forms of human life are tied not only to churches, temples, palaces, to open stairs or battlements, but also to half-timbered homes or farmhouses in a local style. As a free-standing sculpture is encircled by an apparent space, so is a building placed within an apparent time and an appearing life-form, even within its cultural background: its forms of piety, its power and freedom, its ethos, its citizenry, peasantry, or lords. Something of all these "appears" in works of architecture, no doubt (127) in a very graduated manner, and most of them are present only darkly, as a living background, yet still satisfying and animating the architectural form. To the reflective observer, all that may become concretely present.

There is no exaggeration in these observations, and what they give us is not a mere picture. Something of this appearance-relation allows itself to be described matter-of-factly. A house stands to the domestic and personal family life of people as clothes do to the public person. We know that clothing constitutes the public and usually conscious self-presentation of a man; it expresses how he wishes to appear, and thus is the expression of his idea of himself (therefore fashion plays such a pronounced role in it). The lack of independence of individuals from the demands of style changes nothing. But a house is, in a certain sense, the garment of the individual's most intimate life within the community (family, relatives, domestic life); for that reason it is an even stronger expression of his self-understanding – one might also say his self-consciousness – within his larger circle of friends and associates. And that is all the more true because a house is less ephemeral than clothing; it is built to endure even for generations, and receives for that reason something like the character of a monument.

In this way historical peoples and epochs "appear" in their architecture, and by no means only in the monumental ones; these are simply the ones that endure the longer. Many historical periods appear in buildings in the most marked fashion – also in their goals, desires and ideas. The latter we find impressing themselves upon us through their monuments.

This is important in yet another respect. The analogy with fashion in dress is obviously architectural style. However, there is hardly another art in which the element of style plays such a dominant role as in architecture. The reason for this may lie precisely in the element of practical use a building possesses; not everyone needs to write poetry or to paint, but all of us must have a roof over our heads and may therefore come to a point at which we must build one, and to do so without being an artist. Even the average building engineer is not yet an artist. He can build only "as one does," that is, he falls back into the architectural style of his times. Thus it happens that men living in architecturally productive times become almost fixated on the current style; in that way, that particular style becomes characteristic and dominant, and we recognize it everywhere as the expression of its epoch.

An entire world of the appearing background is thereby given in architecture.

f) Practical purpose and free form

That much alone may suffice as a demonstration of what is in fact present in a work of architecture. But the problem lying within it is not thereby settled. Architecture is bound on two sides, that of the intractable material and that of practical purpose. Are these elements compatible with creative freedom in architecture? Here we encounter a clear antinomy of freedom and unfreedom. (128)

The solution must lie in a synthesis, one specifically engaging the two sides. The practical task of the building must be entirely integrated into the uniform composition and in such a way that it is visible along with its solution, i.e., it "appears."

Considered in this way, the practical purpose is not a troublesome element, something that we would prefer to see eliminated, but rather an affirmative element that cannot be dispensed with. The practical purpose, along with all other specific architectural tasks that arise out of it, plays a similar role here as the extra-aesthetical "theme" (*sujet*) in the representational arts, although in fact it is not such a theme. Architectural purpose is distinguished from the theme in that it is not freely chosen, but is taken from the given needs of life; indeed they mark it out. Architecture is not a free art but an art that serves us, indeed a good half of it is pure technical science; only in great architectural undertakings does it rise above it. It is also the only one of the five fine arts whose works remain tied firmly to practical life, for its creations are not isolated and separated from that life. However, we are not prevented from seeing them as closed unities and as wholes.

This last point has its limits in the close propinquity of buildings along a street or in a townscape. But then they may be integrated into larger wholes.

Moreover, the practical purpose in architecture is distinguished from a "theme" in that it is not "represented" in a building; it is instead realized, is implemented by an actual construction. One may say only in a qualified manner that in its implementation it also represents itself.

Accordingly, the practical end is a positive condition and is content-bearing. The formal beauty of the architectural work absorbs that end in such a manner that it consists in and exists along with the technical elements of the work's execution. The "elegance" of the solution of an architectural problem, even when it is quite prosaic, constitutes an essential element of architectural beauty. A building without a practical end would seem inorganic and unconvincing.

No doubt the conflict between the practical and the beautiful continues unabated even into the details of the design, and it may be impossible to force a truce upon them. But it is just here that a demand is placed upon the architect: he confronts the task of discovering a synthesis. And genius in composition, that is, in the art of architecture, may consist precisely in the degree of balance achieved by an eye that is both a builder and a creator of forms.

Something similar is true for the other side of the constraint upon architectural form, its connection to the substance of which it is made. This constraint is of some importance, for this is the coarsest and most unwieldy matter that we encounter in the arts, and its shaping is a real struggle. Sculpture, which must deal with similar material, is easily able to choose whatever suits its aims, and in some cases, produce it (129) synthetically – as with metal alloys, which obediently take on any form desired and hold it fast.

Not every form is possible in any material, but only certain forms in specific material; that is a fundamental universal ontological law. It is valid for all of nature, for every human construction, in all technology. It is valid also for the arts. But in architecture, it is like a decree of fate. A building must take material upon itself despite its weight and at the same time achieve stability of form, and the material must turn itself to account in structuring the interior spaces. That is only possible for certain types of construction. The greater portion of the work is technically determined by necessities of this kind; one might think of architectural technology as one great struggle with matter. And the solutions given to these problems, especially when they concern great size or generality, are so many victories of spirit over heavy matter. Schopenhauer saw this condition in his aesthetics; the result was a dynamic interpretation of architectonic form – a much more significant and profound interpretation than in modern art-historical theories, which understand all form exclusively from the perspective of construction in space.

This is especially remarkable where a structure is executed in the most durable of all materials, stone, which is also the heaviest and most inflexible matter. Overcoming weight in the roofing of the interior spaces is the main achievement of construction. This principle is already apparent in the form of Greek columns, which must support themselves as well as the architrave, the gables, and the roof. They direct thereby our mind upward to the phenomenon of juvenescence and make it visible. Weight itself appears to the senses in the form of space; it is of course actually present, but not visible as mere presence. It becomes visible only as form. Yet at the same time the overcoming of weight by the form of the structure also becomes visible. Well-known examples of this are formal structures such as the arch, the barrel-vault, the cupola, and the ribbed vault. The most evident example of this fundamental phenomenon may be the principle of the buttress, because its lines reveal most obviously its dynamics, its absorption of the side thrust of the building and the unbroken transmission of that force downward to the earth.

We find the greatest achievement of formal construction of heavy matter in the high-vaulted inner spaces of a church. Here weight appears clearly to the senses as the vault hovers and is held high above us in empty space. We are used to this sight nowadays, and our eyes pass carelessly beyond it. Originally, however, this floating over space was thought a miracle. The real element in it is the architectural construction – if you prefer, the technology – but the aesthetical element in this real relation is that the construction, and, in it, the victory of spirit over matter, "appears" in what is visible and becomes intuitively apparent.

With every new architectural invention there is a change in what appears and becomes evident in the visible – that is, there is a change in style. For the (130) style of a building in its formal structure is dependent upon the kinds of solution required by an architectural undertaking. Here is a further reason for the peculiar dominance of style in architecture. For here we do not have a free play with form, but rather an inner conditioning of form and the appearance of this conditioning in the formal elements.

The beauty of an architectural structure, as far as technical capacity makes it possible, comes to light when the overcoming of weight is actually made visible in the play of lines. This visibility is, however, no longer merely sensible, but is a beholding of a higher kind. One may therefore say the other way around: in technique and construction, provided that they condition the formal structure, it is a question of an appearing background. The content of this background is the intellectual achievement of the architectural composition.

g) The place of ornament

Ornament can no longer be counted among the great independent fine arts – as the name [*Ornamentik*] itself indicates. Nevertheless, for the sake of its kinship with the non-representational arts, it must be treated as an adjunct to them. On the one hand, it is freer than architecture, because it does not serve practical ends directly and it works usually without any great struggle with matter. On the other hand, it is not an independent art because it merely attaches itself to a building – or to some lesser human construct – and thus never possesses its own artistic effect.

Looked at positively, however, this lack of independence is its incorporation in a greater formal whole. In such a whole, the ornament has the function of decoration. If it is assimilated entirely to this function (as, for example, in richly decorated types of capital), then it also is drawn entirely into architecture, and becomes just a part of it. It is otherwise when an ornament lays separate claim to, and indeed possesses, an effect of its own by lifting itself out of the architectonic forms as something quite different, or even develops motifs of its own and thus again makes a new whole in itself.

This possibility of such a thing can also be aimed at by a building – just in order to allow the forms of the architecture to stand out against it. The ornament then has an effect similar to a frieze behind columns, which, as the latter, functions as an independent work. For the most part we will be speaking here of ornament in this last sense. It is not possible in any case to draw a sharp boundary between them.

Ornaments of pottery, vases, tools, and weapons play a relatively dependent role. But the origin of ornamentation may lie precisely in such cases. No doubt the oldest ornamental works we still possess (prehistoric ceramics) are of this kind; they are perhaps even older than the other arts. Precisely for that reason such dependent ornaments are not without high interest for aesthetics. Even in its origin, they are clearly a play with forms – even where they are forced into the service of a utilitarian object.

Nonetheless, each ornament can be regarded in itself, not otherwise than a picture or a sculpture. And that they permit this treatment (131) is essential to their art. Arabesques, for example, form a play with lines, which almost provoke such viewing. They are closed wholes and geometric schemata, and quite often possess symmetry and easily take on traits of a pictorial kind. One should not overrate their relative rank for this reason; still, within their modest limits they possess aesthetical independence.

The essential problem with ornament is whether even here there is an interconnected arrangement of different strata, and whether even here the beauty of ornament is dependent upon it. One must perforce question whether there exists in this case something other than the sensible real stratum in the fore-ground (the physical substance), in which the play of lines, the design, the fantasy of spatial forms, is each developed.

Now everything seems to indicate that we are at this point past the relations of strata and appearance. And that is true in a certain sense. In any case, we may find it difficult to trace the pleasure taken in an ornamental pattern to such a relation alone. Yet we must not dispense here, because of that difficulty, with what is a foundational relation for aesthetics. It is indeed contained in ornamental works, although it is concealed here. But it does not lie in the so-called motifs. The "turnip-pattern" on a Bukhara carpet is as such only a kind of occasion. Similarly, chain, vine, and animal patterns are exploited only as motifs. They are not represented objects, and hardly have any content that can produce an effect. One cannot glimpse anything appearing in them.

What is immediately surprising is the repetition of the motif, and also the spatial rhythms in the repetition. The same is true of other similarly formal elements: the arrangement, the symmetry, and variations of the motifs, and the coming together of the whole in a unified form that can take on pictorial character.

In this way, we are drawn to the other element in the essence of beauty, which lies in free play with forms. This element manifests itself, forces itself forward, and makes itself dominant. This process is similar to that in music, only with other materials and less rich. And again, something of the creative spirit appears here, though only indirectly, in its manner of seeing and its sensibility. Certainly at least something is there of its taste, its sense of form, its need of unity, its way of indulging in fantasy, and in its passing beyond the useful to create something of beauty.

No doubt, one can see clearly from this how the beautiful does not reduce itself to the relation of appearance in the ornamental arts. Play with form proves itself here to be an entirely autonomous element. And that means that there exists an autonomous enjoyment of form, one directed precisely on the free play with it.

This too is manifestly a genuine aesthetical enjoyment, although one less profound than one that is tied to the relation of appearance.

We could trace this enjoyment back to the pleasure we get from play in general. But that alone tells us little. That would depend upon (132) the objectivity of form in play, and this objectivity cannot be understood in that way. It will rather become necessary to return to much more primitive foundational elements, ones that belong to visible form itself, such as contrast, harmony, intertwining, interlinking, or overlapping: in short, to certain structural elements that are sufficiently general to have a categorial character. In fact, with such catchphrases as these one approaches the most elementary categories that all existing things and the content of all consciousness have in common. It is here in particular that one encounters the relation of unity and plurality, whose variations in the strata of existing objects is in any case extremely rich and truly dominant.[44]

This much may be offered as a view upon these matters; we will keep the question open. However, if this view is later confirmed, the entire play with form will be integrated again within the relation of appearance. For the appearing background in ornament would then be nothing less than the realm of the fundamental categories themselves.

---

[44] On the role and character of these elementary categories cf. *Der Aufbau der realen Welt* [*The Construction of the Real World*], 2nd edition 1950, Chaps. 23–34.

Third Section: Beauty in Nature and in the Human World

Chapter 8: The Living Human Being as a Thing of Beauty

a) Human beauty as appearance

The last problem discussed, which concerned the limits of the relation of appearance, will become very significant when we pass from art to beauty external to art. An artwork is a human work, one that is made to serve the aims of beauty. Clearly, the aim of the artist is to present, by means of an outward construction, something different. Nature works without such intentions; it is without any sort of aim, and without consciousness. It can therefore put nothing in its productions in order that something may shine forth from it.

The same is true of humankind, as it is and lives. It is true also of the entire world of events, upon which we stand and with which we work to form objects. Man is not the work of man, and the world that we construct is only to a limited degree the work of man.

Is there an aesthetical relation of appearance outside of works of art?

In the sense that nature might want to "intimate" something to us with it – half concealing, half revealing what it is – that can obviously not be. (133) But a state of being intimated even without a will to intimate, a self-concealing and a self-revealing without intention and purpose, is found in limitless ways everywhere.

This is well known from human life. Every person betrays something about himself in everything he does and lets be, in his speech and behavior, even when he does not desire it and even when he fails to notice it. In that way he may become transparent to an experienced or disinterested observer – down even to his secret and purposely concealed intentions and attitudes.

These are things that are usually difficult to express in concepts, at least not with the peculiar nuance with which they appear. That means, however, that these are matters that are revealed to us only intuitively, that is, to a higher vision and not to the senses. He who is experienced in the ways of men is practiced in this kind of vision, and has gathered many experiences; to him a picture of the soul of a man is always given along with his external appearance.

This capacity for seeing through a man, tested in practical life, which is always directed at the practical evaluation of others, may develop without any practical aim. And then it comes close to aesthetical beholding. Before the intuitive eye there occurs an appearance of the psychic inwardness of a man in his face and behavior, which rises up above all practical interests of the observer:

something like the shining-forth of honesty, simplicity, mental purity, or perhaps kindness and a willingness to self-sacrifice.

These are of course purely moral values. But the way they appear to us is different from what they are in themselves. They can be clear, obvious or impressive; they can dominate the general impression of a personality, they can penetrate or transfigure his face and figure. Such an appearance, intuitively present, of what is noble and good about a person, we experience as the beauty of the whole person. And that is beauty in the relation of appearance in its genuine aesthetical sense. The appearing values are of course not the value of the appearance, but only their material presupposition. Thus they do not coincide with them and, when they appear elsewhere, they can be understood in a different, more rational form.

In this context one thing must be made clear from the outset: what "appears" here is not reducible to the relation of appearance, it exists even without the relation in the actual person; it exists even when no one recognizes it, either intuitively or otherwise. For this is a matter of the real moral character of a person, and exists in fact along with its value-qualities: it is a matter of his real attitudes, his real inner demeanor. Whether these characteristics needs must appear in some manner we may leave unsettled. What is alone of importance is that if they appear, they are not reducible to this appearance, but exist in themselves independent of their becoming visible.

But then the relation of appearance is different in this case from the work of art. In the work of art what appears is unreal and exists only for the one who beholds it; (134) in the case now under consideration something really existing reveals itself. But the appearing in something else, in something external that is given to the senses, is, as such, the same. And just for that reason this is a genuine relation of appearance. That alone establishes the connection between human beauty in a real living person and beauty in art. And, on the other hand, if that is true, the relation of appearance is not other than that in the work of art. What is different is only the mode of being of what appears. But for the phenomenon of appearance as such that makes no difference.

Therefore, it is not necessary in this case to relearn from the beginning the nature of the relation of appearance. It lies in the nature of appearing that what is real can appear as well as what is unreal. In life that makes a great deal of difference, but in the aesthetical context the difference is less, because here we are not concerned with understanding what is real (knowledge), but rather with the concrete intuitibility of the appearance itself and also with the close tie it possesses to what is sensibly given.

The test of this example of the understanding of human beauty will be the disturbance of such an impression by the appearance of characteristics that betray something quite different. Take, for example, the case in which a face that otherwise arouses our sympathy breaks into a laugh or begins to speak and thereby causes a movement of the lips that reveals treachery, resentment, malice, or even just dullness. Such things as these are sufficient to convey an inharmonious impression; the movement breaks through the harmony of the stationary features and disappoints us, for, beneath the clear lines of the general impression, pettiness or weakness has become visible.

Again, these are moral elements. But the appearance in the visible is not an ethical matter but one that disturbs the sensible impression as such; it is therefore a negative aesthetical event. This disconnect in a person's appearance we experience as not beautiful, and when it forces itself upon us, as ugly. A harmony has then been disturbed, a unity broken that we had already discovered within it and welcomed aesthetically. And this broken unity is precisely that of an appearing background – of course one that is real, but one that presents itself in the external form. This self-presentation is the appearing. The break in unity operates in the sensibly visible foreground and it breaks its unity and also even disturbs its harmony.

Ugliness is when there is a disconnect between the inner man and his external appearance, so far as it betrays itself.

b) Beauty in relation to moral and to vital values

The problem in this relation is not quite as simple as it appears at first sight. It is clear that the content of what appears here of the inner life cannot be confined to what is morally valuable. What is contrary to value must also be considered; after all, it is not upon the ethical values themselves that what is aesthetically valuable depends, but (135) only their appearance to the senses. Why should negative ethical values not also play a role in appearance, if they too belong to the same sphere of human inwardness?

We are always in danger here of repeating the errors of ancient aesthetics and confusing aesthetical and ethical values. The ancients made this error in their concept of καλοκάγαθία. They said also "Animus sanus in corpore sano," a naturalistic turn of phrase, meaning a beautiful soul in a beautiful body. Here the beautiful as such is already assumed, and in fact in both levels. It cannot itself therefore be traced back in this manner to something more fundamental that underlies it. Least of all can it lie in a relation of appearance.

We should not speak at all of the soul as beautiful. One refers by such beauty to moral worthiness alone. Originally, genuine beauty is visible appearance in the transparency of physical form and in the dynamics of the living body. And, in general, we possess a fine sense for it.

Moreover, even a person whose morals are questionable can be beautiful. It is what we find so irritating in the phenomenon of human beauty. One may think of Alcibiades, a highly gifted man but also wanton, selfish, and unfaithful, and of the strange love of Socrates for him. He was in his way a quite unified character, a character that is marked distinctly as integrated and easy to understand in his outward demeanor. One may also think of the beauty of the youthful Nero. And the Homeric figures already demonstrated such discrepancies; not all of them were like Hector, fully accomplished both in his external appearance and in the depth of his inward stance.

Strength, heedlessness, or frivolity may express a pleasant devil-may-care attitude in a human face, while moral scruples are seen in dullness, being over-burdened, or restrained. Beauty is not the expression of moral qualities; it is far more the expression of inner unity and wholeness. Yet both, the highest moral greatness and unity, may also not be stamped upon one's external appearance, but hidden under an appearance that does not measure up to them. In this very simple and unambiguous sense, Socrates was the ugliest of men.

The beauty of a human face is entirely a question of the relation of appearance. And in this case, the relation – since what appears is something real – consists in the relative adequacy of the inner and outer form, in the becoming-visible of the one in the other.

Nevertheless, we have even now not yet plumbed the depths of the nature of human beauty. We must extend our vision over the phenomena, and we must carry over what is fundamental about the relation we have discovered to other things that can appear in a person externally as surely as moral values. To these belong above all the vital values. Man is not only a moral being, but also – and even before all else – an organic being. (136)

It is easy to forget this obvious fact when one assumes it to be merely trivial. But for aesthetics it is nothing less than trivial. Vital qualities can at times be obscured, but they can also be convincingly expressed by external appearance so as to seem to be given through the senses. Nothing in the entire field of aesthetics is so vulgar and common as the concept of human beauty as a well-shaped body (by no means only the face); perhaps this is even the oldest and parent concept of beauty.

This vulgar concept of beauty is largely connected to the sexual response. In the case of feminine beauty, it emphasizes the element of softness, tenderness, and youth; in the masculine form the elements of strength, firmness, and fearless-ness (the last not understood morally as yet, but as the feeling of power). It would be quite false to reject such dependence as external to aesthetics. It is a necessary constituent of the natural feeling of beauty. But it is just as little identical with beauty as are the elements of moral value; they are rather preconditions of it, a mere element of the content of the appearance in the aesthetical relation of appearance. Aesthetic value lifts itself above them and is of another kind. Of course, the confusion of them by an unenlightened or immature aesthetical consciousness is quite common. We must gradually learn to make distinctions here just as we must in the case of our feeling of moral value.

The parent concept of human beauty may well be tied entirely to the impression of the strength and fullness of life. These elements make up the preponderance of what has remained in the concept up to highly cultivated epochs. A strong vital feeling lets itself be heard in it, even where it is no longer sexually determined. Only slowly do we come to separate the feeling of form and movement from the natural feeling of life and from the opposition of the sexes; that then awakens a sense for spiritualized beauty, for the face of old age, marked with richer lines of experience and the voice of destiny. The ancients found this kind of beauty early on in the masculine face and only much later in the feminine face.

All that can be understood only from the long and uncontested dominance of the vital feelings and the relation of appearances based upon them. The richness of form of faces cannot justify it. For it the face of old age is simply richer in articulate forms.

c) The appearance of the type

But this is not a matter only of a man as an individual; it is just as much a matter of a man as a representative of something else.

Each person represents a kind of human being also; whether pure or mixed, he bears characteristics held in common: those of his time and of his people, of his social class or of a more narrow human kind or type or milieu. (137)

These more universal elements usually play an obtrusive role in his outward appearance, at least insofar as they are distinctly marked on him. For that reason, they are also essential in the relation of appearance that bears the opposition of beautiful and ugly.

We must remember also that we normally see the individuality of people only superficially, and are satisfied with a relatively general impression of the people whom we meet (think of our tendency to look rapidly for marginal "similarities"). This role of the typical then becomes quite understandable: we always attempt to "fit in" the individual person somewhere, to place him in a ready-made filing system.

In itself, that tendency has only a practical purpose, and is a kind of economizing. But it predisposes an observer in an aesthetical way also. A person is inclined to remain fixed on what is familiar to him or on what seems to him to have a certain universal validity, thus on what vaguely appears to be typical.

The supposed typical features of a person need not always be what we think to be essential characteristics; quite contingent associations may play a role here. But unknown and dimly suspected generic features of humankind may also strike an observer, perhaps a distant ancestral type that is unfamiliar but that announces itself in the face and demeanor of a person – in certain circumstances even in those of a child – and makes us take notice.

The question of the typical forms of human faces – similar to a person's build, his manner of moving, etc. – is peculiar: we have no concepts for such things, no words; we can communicate such things to others usually only by quiet suggestion (only creative draftsmen can reproduce them). And yet such things accompany our sense of human individuality even in its details; indeed, that fact is so universally valid that they determine our feelings from the outset when we "encounter" a person unknown to us, whom we see for the first time. Once we have a type in mind, it anticipates actual experience; we immediately expect a corresponding way of speaking, of gestures, facial expressions, even a certain way of behaving: in short, a character of a certain type. And, despite all, we are often quite right. The psychic type usually corresponds in some way to the outward form.

Since these formal types announce themselves purely intuitively, and are in no way tied to the practical interests of the observer, their appearance in an individual easily obtains an aesthetical character. This means that the appearance itself is the main motif. The individual with all his peculiarities affects us as a foreground that becomes transparent for the beholding of something else. This something else is the type, and it is all the same whether it is the type of a people, of an epoch, or of a more narrowly defined human type. The type shines through the peculiarities of the individual and gives to it a super-individual significance. (138)

In this manner, the workingman appears to us in palpable concreteness as type: the miner, the farmer, the sailor, the businessman, the officer, the intellectual: he appears even when we have no further interest in him. So also with the representative type of some people: the Englishman, Spaniard, Romanian, Chinese, or Indian. Incalculably many features belong to such national types: the character of the form of life, the style of life, the milieu, and even definite social circles. That all appears in a certain dependency upon one's own sensibility; it appears even where it is felt to be alien and perhaps personally disapproved of by the observer.

But always something forces itself upon us in these cases, something we respect for itself alone as appearance, and, no doubt, just because it makes an impression upon us as a strongly defined and closed formal whole, while the individuality itself with its superabundance of individual characteristics easily slips away from us. When we stand before such a complete character, the details may seem to us to be nothing more than "extraneous and secondary."

This last judgment may be a rather subjective devaluation. But we humans are liable to it, because we cannot do justice to the limitless multiplicity of the individual. Most men penetrate in their concept of the human only rarely to the individuality of a person.

A sharp distinction between the practical and the aesthetical concept of humanity is therefore hardly possible, but it is also not necessary. The one passes into the other without our taking notice of it – just as is the case with the boundary between the vital and aesthetical attitudes towards the physical human body.

Characteristic of both the practical and the aesthetical in our concept of humankind is the continuous transition from the non-aesthetical to the aesthetical. We begin with practical intent, and we are drawn by the weight of what comes to appearance into the aesthetical stance. The practically interested man becomes an observer; he open-mindedly partakes in what appears, and in that partaking loses himself. He experiences a change in his perspective to one of "disinterested pleasure."

There is nothing astonishing in this. Something similar occurs always in the passage to the theoretical point of view; there too in the detection of what is typical we forget our immediate purposes, and turn to the appearance just for its own sake. With the aesthetical attitude, this is far more often the case.

Here we have one of the essential points at which the foundation of the aesthetical attitude – and its object, the beautiful – becomes tangible in the context of life. Not all aesthetical beholding is entirely pure, for there are transitional forms of all kinds. We encounter such transitional forms in other areas of beauty also. Only in the arts is the separation clear and distinct. (139)

d) Situation and drama in life

There are other things that "appear" on human beings – of course not in their personal appearance alone, also not in the individual person as such, but rather in the community of several persons in their planned and unplanned meetings. When one realizes that there is a kind of dramatic art that consciously stages such things (even the epic ones), it seems almost obvious that even in life itself this being-together must appear objectively, although situations and conflicts are not perceptible in the strong sense (are not given to the senses), just as little as are the mental states of individuals.

We may call this the "drama of life." The expression is taken from literary works, but that is quite proper, for the poets first discovered it; – "discovered" it, in the sense that they first taught others to see as such what was always there and sensed in various ways, and therewith made the aesthetical element in life tangible.

For it is nothing less than obvious that this drama is seen as such, still less, perhaps, than the landscape about us is obvious. A very definite point of view is essential to seeing it, one with a certain distance from the hustle-bustle of human affairs, which the man immersed in practical life does not have and cannot appropriate very easily. One may call this point of view the art of aesthetical experience. The experience is not equivalent to perception, although it is carried by it throughout and is dependent upon it. But aesthetical experience passes also beyond it, because it reaches beyond vulgar experience. For the latter is experience in harness; it is drawn along by practical interest or by one's participation in the witnessed events.

In everyday experience a man is harnessed to a situation, he has a role in it or accepts a role with all subjectivity and passion, and with his own sympathies and aversions. In aesthetical experience he leaves all that behind, lifts himself above it; he leaves, as it were, the realm of practical interest and his role in it. Beholding, he takes his place "next" to life, to which he of course is existentially tied, and takes it all in "from the sidelines."

Much belongs to this state, to the achievement of which a man rarely can bring himself. Two quite distinct talents are required. A distance from one's own fortune and misfortune is only one; the other gives him the capacity for seeing events in the round. The first makes him an observer of life, the second gives him clear-sightedness, comprehension, and penetration. There may of course be causal connections between the two. But that does not cancel the essential difference in these two capacities, and their meeting occurs not as frequently as one would think. For that reason most of the drama of life that surrounds us passes us by along with the fullness of its appearance – not because we stand too far away (140) but because we are too close to it. For from the first we stand right in the middle of it.

The infrequency of the aesthetical stance in life and toward life, the isolating heights of the state of serenity it presupposes, should not hinder a person from recognizing in them the great aesthetic object that lies always at the ready before him and awaits only the maturing of his receptive consciousness. For the drama of life consists in the unbroken chain of the situations in which a person finds himself and in his efforts to master them.[45] All human plans, all success and

---

45 One may compare in this regard the more detailed analysis of the situation in *Das Problem des geistigen Seins* [*The Problem of Spiritual Being*], 2nd edition, 1948, Chaps. 1b and c, especially the intertwining of freedom and unfreedom.

failure, all ephemeral activity with its consequences, which themselves cause unanticipated situations, all foresight and all failure of foresight, all understanding of the situations and attitudes of others, as well as all misunderstanding of them, all entangling of oneself in the interests and undertakings of others, all guilt and innocence, true and false, censure and apology – up to the far greater developments that approach us like strokes of fate – all belong to the drama of life.

The richness of this tremendous multiplicity, which makes life what it is, is not calculable. All of moral life, understood as both positive and negative, belongs here. It reveals itself as the "stuff" of an inexhaustible aesthetical realm. But what this is as an aesthetic object is not what it is as a moral one. For example, it is precisely the small, the petty, the hollow, that which is ethically meaningless or despicable, that which is too shallow to spend even a second in contemplating, that can become aesthetically meaningful when it casts a ray of light upon the inner life of a person, or upon current tensions between man and man. And that occurs with what is small and negative just as with what is morally great and positive. That depends upon the force of the letting-appear.

The manifold of a man's inner life that appears in such cases is no less than what appears in his external appearance (in the face and demeanor of an individual person). It is in fact still larger, for it has grown with the dimensions of the community.

In these matters we must hold to the following: it is not human value that is beautiful, not fate, tragedy, the greatness of a man or his struggles; and the comical is not smallness, weakness, or triviality, but entirely and only the appearance of all such characteristics in some given experience. One may thus say: only the transparency of what is immediately experienced in all of these things, which are not in themselves aesthetical (they are rather practical, for the most part), makes up the aesthetical element with which we are concerned.

One matter is to be especially noted: it is not only a rare talent to be able to see life dramatically, it is also a talent that cuts two ways. It turns easily into unkindness when it pursues (141) ruthlessly its own aesthetical enjoyment. The aesthete who "enjoys" for its own sake every conflict in life (usually not his own), or the humorous person with a developed sense for what is comical, behaves toward what is in fact happening as an audience toward a stage play. He is able to forget, for the most part, that this is not play but something serious and bitter, and the struggle and suffering of the involved parties is genuine; he who stands so amused before it is heartless. And a man who goes through life with this aesthetical attitude and enjoys all the activity about him as mere play is disoriented; his feelings are not morally healthy. Indeed, he lacks the precondition of all genuine aesthetical evaluation of life and therefore he destroys in the end precisely what he is seeking: the precondition of it is just the intact and inerrantly correct moral sense, that is, the correct evaluative response to everything we experience.

In this way, the inward attitudes of persons turn themselves towards immorality and cold-heartedness, towards mockery and scorn, and take on a pretense to superiority and cheap skepticism. The true humorist does not feel this way. Even while laughing he does not forget the earnestness of life, indeed he senses it, perhaps with greater warm-heartedness just because of its contrast with humor. Here, too, maturity and moral strength is required, and a bit of genuine superiority.

To see and to sense the comical in life is relatively frequent; often we find it even in the immature child who heckles his teacher and is amused at the sight of his weaknesses. Such crudity is no doubt morally wrong, but the taste for the comical in what appears (let us say in the indignation of a pedantic teacher) can be entirely genuine. Even for the mature man it is not always easy to fix the proper limits of his amusement at the all-too-human in life. But that changes nothing regarding aesthetical enjoyment and the appearance of human weakness as a matter of fact.

The aesthetical enjoyment of what is serious in human life, of what is tragic in it, or of moral greatness and heroic overcoming, is much less frequent. It is more difficult to achieve, because we are ourselves drawn toward and into such serious events by our own responsiveness to them, by our sympathetic interest, by pain, or by becoming uplifted by them. Whoever has in such cases the proper moral attitude cannot at the same time easily become an impartial observer of them. On the other hand, a man who keeps his distance from them and achieves a state of quietude from which he can observe them passively must still also maintain a morally open heart for men and situations, because both are real and not play-acted. Thus he must – here is the antinomy – simultaneously take part and not take part, must be drawn into the events and yet stand over against them as an observer, be able to evaluate them morally and yet to evaluate them aesthetically.

This posture is close to the superhuman. It demands two souls in one breast, two heterogeneous kinds of experiencing. Such capacity is perhaps given only to poets, whose art respects the earnestness itself of what is seen and justifies itself in that way. But that is precisely art, and is no longer the beauty that is contained in life itself.

(142) Such a posture is not impossible in life. For does not man have essentially the wonderful freedom to be able to see himself from the outside even while immersed in his struggles, his actions and passions, to laugh and to cry and at the same time keep the eye of self-knowledge alert? How could he not have just as essentially that same eye for other persons and their lot?

Chapter 9: Beauty in Nature

a) The beauty of living things

When one thinks of beauty in nature, it is tempting to think of lovely "scenery," that is, of sea and land, of mountains and valleys. But it is precisely there that difficult aesthetical problems are to be found, because the forced entry of subjectivity, that is, of what imagination has added to the scene, is so much stronger than with natural objects, and also because mixed within our responses to such scenery are feeling of repose and recreation, which are no doubt pleasant but not aesthetical.

For those reasons we must begin with a different phenomenon, one in which the character of the aesthetic object is more easily understood. This is the beautiful as it appears to us in almost all living things.

We must hence step back one level in the series of aesthetic objects that are not the products of art, from human beauty to the beauty of fauna and flora. This is no mere pedantry; the process is the natural entranceway to the problem. Man is also an organism, and all the beauty delivered by the vital feelings that we see in him is itself the beauty of the organism. We can hardly say that the organic beauty of an animal speaks to us less softly than that of man. The pleasure we take in a beautiful animal is something that is universally human. We often enjoy beauty in animals in a less inhibited manner than we do with men, because in the former we rarely meet with features that repel us. With animals the entire question of morality is lacking; we not only know that animals are innocent, we feel their innocence in our immediate apprehension of them.

No doubt here too we have a case of purely vital enjoyment, a kind that is in no way aesthetical. The soft fur of a kitten addresses itself to us vitally in our touch, so too the attentiveness of a faithful dog, the touching way he openly keeps to his master, his joy and exuberance when his master responds to him, all speak to us in a no less purely vital manner. In such cases we lack the distance needed to look upon them as objects, which is a condition of aesthetical enjoyment.

But in the very center of this situation, which is a vital phenomenon or very close to vitality itself, distance of the right kind can also set in, and suddenly the pictorial conditions of the aesthetic object are fulfilled: a movement, or a phase of movement, the grace of a leap, an (143) expression of tension in the stance of the animal strikes us, and lets us peer beyond it to something different that is really there but invisible. This other phenomenon is nothing less than the natural miracle of organic life itself – and indeed in its peculiar nature: its kinship with us, and yet its foreignness.

For in fact both are contained in such a looking-through at what is well known to us, what our own vital feelings deliver to us, and what is different from us, that is, uninhibited animality disturbed by no conflict. One might also say that we see what is convincingly instinctual and certain of the accuracy of its response, where the animal is superior to human beings.

The sensing of these things usually takes the form of a dark premonition of profound interconnections, not to say of a great wisdom in the structure, the organization of the members, and in the way the animal nature acts and reacts. And, if we pursue this thought further, then – expressed theoretically – we may say we contact in feeling an amazing and, by its perfection, superior matching of means and ends that expresses itself in the whole of organic nature.

The truth in this is precisely the objective element: the aesthetical enjoyment of animals quickly leads, oddly enough, to a deep astonishment before the great metaphysical puzzle of organic life. For this puzzle lies in the inward adaption of means and ends, which holds together all the parts and all the expressions of a living thing and appears to us as an extraordinary harmony. This at first has nothing to do with theoretical investigations or reflection, although scientific inquiries may also begin with such impressions. Rather the impression is given to us immediately and intuitively, and the feeling of standing before the miraculous is involuntary; it forces itself upon us just in the sense perception of it. We do not reflect, for our standpoint is nothing more than one of free surrender, and, often enough, what is decisive about it is the element of surprise. A man cannot escape the feeling of standing suddenly face to face with the miracle of creation.

Sensations of this kind are a genuine aesthetical enjoyment in beholding, one given through a relation of appearance that is also quite perceivable by us. At the same time the depth of enjoyment varies to different degrees depending on the objective inscrutability of what appears to us. One can feel the miracle of organic nature profoundly or superficially, but it is always a case of seeing-through what is sensibly given and a feeling-through to something that is not sensibly given.

Further, it is important that the attitude of admiration not be confined at all to cases where we start with the vital feeling of sympathy. The examples taken from our trusty house pets may lead us astray in this matter. But they are one-sided. The same attitude extends equally well to cases that are distant and strange. The (144) perfect elegance in the leap of the squirrel at the tops of the trees high above us can bring it about. The flight of the swallow, the circling bird of prey, the energetic movement of the trout as it glides through the water, the playfulness of the dolphin as it leaps from the water – they all affect us in the same way. But they are foreign to urban man today; he does not get to see them so often. The deepest impression is perhaps made by what comes as a complete surprise when one first glimpses it – for example, the floating of the pelican as it glides upon waves of air, drawing himself along with the waves of the sea below. One does not grasp all at once what is happening in such a sight. The pilot of a glider knows the entire process, but the pelican carries it out with infinitely greater virtuosity.

But the phenomenon reaches even further into the alien and strange. There are creatures that seem sinister and threatening to men, to which they frequently feel a vital aversion, whether they display or conceal it: snakes, frogs, spiders, and great lizards. Behind such feeling are concealed instinctive fears that arose in early human history, when the threat from such creatures was real. And now that we have learned to distance ourselves from them and to look upon them objectively, there may arise in us a joyful admiration of what is alien and strange. The feeling itself turns about, and we see the kingly pose in the snake's erect head and neck (even fairy-tales speak of it), and we feel some satisfaction in the movement of the garden-spider as she weaves her web. Herder believed that the "essentially ugly" forms of animal life were botched natural creations ("the hideous crocodile"), but in truth there is nothing to that belief beyond our incapacity for creating distance between them and us, and the remaining traces of ancient fear. Nature is, in the end, not created for man.

In this way one descends further into the organic world. The same relation returns ever again. It is the same with the magnificence of butterflies, of jellyfish and medusas, of radiolarians and infusoria. The miniature world of organic life is full of "artistic natural forms." And naturally that is so also for the entire vegetable kingdom. Here beauty in general is given to human feeling in a more uninhibited way – although, or perhaps because – plants stand at a greater distance from the vital emotions of man. The contact with familiar organic life possessed by the human heart is much weaker in the case of plants, and for that reason aesthetical distance from them is correspondingly less disrupted by our vital feelings.

One need not think immediately of the fabulous glory of flowering plants – added to that is much vital joy in their colors or their adventurous shapes and also a bit of all-too-human symbolism – rather, within certain limits we seem to sense in every plant in its developed form something like a work of art. That is true of the slender reed with its golden spikes hanging obliquely from it, or the flossed form of a spruce, beech, or birch-tree, of the "angry" veins in the bark of an old oak, of the massive flowery stem of the agave, its leaves (145) protected by needles. Something of the mysterious purposefulness of living things reveals itself here also; something of the systematically arranged and mutually attuned organic functions and its unfolding; its life-urge, its capacity to assert itself, and its independence, adapted to the inorganic forces of its environment.

We see the same again in entire groups of members of some species, collected together: the mossy lawn, a bed of thyme, the meadow, the heath, a copse, and the forest. Here aesthetical feeling passes into another kind, however; it becomes joy in landscape.

An elevated aesthetical charm is formed about the obvious vulnerability, endangerment and exposure of an entire realm of organic forms – in their relation to the harmless indifference and, as it were, the ignorance of the organism, to their precarious hold on life. They offer themselves imperturbably to fate, become by the thousands its victims, and another thousand blossom in their place. One has a deep and dark sense of the cruel severity that rules the lives of species – severity towards the individual in the name of the species-life – and one feels amazed, involuntarily, at nature's waste of its own precious works.

This too is a relation of appearance, and has nothing to do with reflection or understanding. For what is strange about it is that we also sense intuitively the balance and harmony in the economy of living nature.

The calm naturalness by which the individual, beautiful in its form, bears this lethal severity has for human feelings something touching, something requiring love as a response. And in fact it is a kind of love in which the human heart, by means of aesthetical experience, embraces the grandiose richness of form in living things.

b) Beauty in dynamic structure

It would seem possible that one could, with the same principles, probe even further – to inorganic structures, to the point, therefore, where there are no longer living things. There are many thing-like forms that offer us genuine aesthetical enjoyment, if not as many as one may think. For most of the "things" that surround us in life have been worked over artificially, and thus of course no longer count among things of natural beauty.

Here we find one of the reasons why beauty is not as familiar in inorganic nature as in the organic world. Moreover, the primary and most independent among those dynamic structures that might be first to capture our aesthetical sense are normally not available to us because of their order of size; they are either much too big or too small to be given to our vision through the senses. Examples of these are the stars in the skies and their star-systems, on the one hand, atoms and molecules on the other. The median spheres, those that can be directly perceived, (146) are almost entirely swept clear of them. Nonetheless, there are also a few examples of them within this sphere. The most familiar are the peculiarly regular structures of crystals. When we do not know the geometric laws of these structures (the system of their coordinates), in simply looking upon them we still have a clear sense of the presence of such laws and of a hidden tendency of the parts to "line up" with each other according to those laws. In this there is unmistakably a relation of appearance.

The class becomes larger if we include in it some ephemeral phenomena. For example, we have the mirror-like surface of water, the closed shape of a drop with its natural spherical form (no doubt in many cases it is hardly visible); there are the circles of waves that extend themselves concentrically upon the surface of the water, the symmetry of a vortex whose flow is restricted, or even the phenomenon of the bounce of a drop upon ending its fall. More familiar is the regular play of the waves and that of the light-rays borne by them; not even to speak of such striking phenomena as thunder, the rainbow, or cirrus clouds wafting in the blue sky.

With phenomena of the last kind, it is no longer a question of dynamic structure. But even among these there are some that can be made visible, even if indirectly (as by a telescope or a camera). Even then, they do not lose their power to impress us aesthetically. Among these belongs the lunar system of Jupiter, with its four great moons, and Saturn with its wonderful rings. In these figures something of an interrelated dynamic of things appears in their external form; an inward one, that is not visible in itself, becomes apparent. Observers have always sensed as much, and said so.

In his idea of "world harmony," Kepler went much further. The relations of size, which he established by observation and calculation, were organized within a general theory, which he experienced as the great beauty of the (invisible) planetary system. The optical techniques we have today have filled out the content of this system. They have made the spiral galaxies visible, whose outward forms have no doubt allowed us to recognize the unity of their dynamic structure. The same is true for star-clusters and for cloud-forms. Notable in these examples is that these structures are not validated just by science; intuition, specifically immediate aesthetical intuition, anticipated them.

If we pursue Kepler's way of thinking further, we find our aesthetical vision extended to all natural dynamic structures. It remains tied only to certain conditions of preliminary scientific inquiry, which no doubt the majority of men do not meet. Thus, for example, the laws of atomic physics can fit nicely into the aesthetical way of beholding, although they are entirely mathematical in nature and abstractly formulated; the consequence of this is that the construction of atoms is itself brought closer to intuition. (147) This is of course expressed with an almost excessive clarity in what are no doubt hypothetical atomic models. Mathematicians no doubt say that these models are at some distance from intuition, but only because, as intuition, they do not allow anything to count in them as sensible beholding. That is one-sided. All indirect knowledge has a tendency towards a higher form of beholding and realizes it; even the concepts that it makes use of are nothing more than helpful means to that higher vision. Concepts become alive only when they are genuinely filled out by intuition. For that reason the element of intuition in them at all times makes again manifest its aesthetical side.

In general, relations of size happen to have an intuitive-aesthetical side that is well known in geometry. What is it about the beauty of an ellipse that so many have called attention to it? Only this, that a law becomes visible in its form, and we can sense it intuitively without grasping it with the mind. It contains a relation of appearance.

The mystery of mathematics' attraction for us may lie here – reaching all the way to the myth of the "most perfect science," which has always surrounded it: the unification of pure play with form and with the relation of appearance that intrudes from within it.

c) Beauty in landscapes and related phenomena

The last observations anticipated what was to come. They wandered off, moreover, into derivative phenomena and into the border regions of the aesthetical – whose placement can be disputed on principle. We must return to more immediate phenomena, which form the central elements of the entire series. In the realm of natural beauty, that would be beautiful scenery, the landscape. After that, there is of course much more: the rough sea, the clouds scudding across the sky, the ever constant starscape.

It happens that "our hearts rise up" before such things, we rush to them from our everyday business, from the noise of the great city, and, so to speak, throw ourselves into them up to our necks; we try to lose ourselves in them.

But just for that reason, these things are not simply aesthetic objects; they are just as much – and perhaps primarily – objects of our vital feeling, and, in that respect, must be sharply distinguished from aesthetic objects. To do that is not easy, since we are beholding the selfsame objects. Moreover, in this context, vital feeling tends to change into aesthetical enjoyment without any specifiable limits – exactly as we have just seen happen in the case of the beauty in organic life. The difference is only that in beholding organic life our vital feelings identify something that is objective, but in the case of the landscape there is much that is subjective, that is, what is felt in the object is influenced by what is peculiar to the observer and to what goes on within him.

The yearning of urban man reaches after the cow stall and the vegetable garden, as much as for the heath or the mountain snow (148), but they generally do not rise to the rank of aesthetic objects. A limit must be drawn here, even if it cannot designate a sharp distinction. Yet one cannot draw such a limit that follows the object alone, because even in the cases of mountain and valley, forest and meadow, vital feelings are close by – the yearning to escape from the sea of houses and buildings, the noise of the city and its grey everydayness. The wish to immerse oneself in nature and to be absorbed by it has the same vital character. This is, quite obviously, taking vital joy in oneself, not to speak of indulging the need for fresh air, relaxation, and for variety through contrast.

In all these cases, the element of distance from the object is lacking. The observer rather feels himself as standing in the landscape, and not merely in the spatial sense. That standing-within is apparently essential for his sensibility; he sees himself taken in, welcomed, surrounded; he seems even to bring with him a tendency to become one with nature. Therewith is cancelled not only the aesthetical quality of the experience, but the entire environing nature loses even its being as an object.

Only over against this primitive entering into nature does the aesthetic objectivity of the landscape begin to appear. How this happens is secondary. But it comes to pass, and a primary element in this process is the observer's dwelling upon individual picture-like impressions. For example, a perspective opens up framed by nearby reeds and branches. The dimensions of the heights above us reveal their structure; a village lies in the hollow of a valley. The whole affects us as a "picture," without any effort or desire on our part, and perhaps completely surprises us.

In this state, the beholder has been lifted out of the landscape and stands opposite it. He is only now genuinely a beholding observer, and thus enjoys the scene aesthetically. This happens to him also with respect to a segment of forest interior – now he sees objectively the dark green shadows, the playful rays of the sun – or it happens at a clearing, at a group of people, at a spring, at a cluster of trees rising before a sheer cliff. The essential in this is the pictorial character, the boundless view, and the separation from it. What comes to pass in the mind is a different kind of absorption and affection, a different kind of pleasure and enjoyment.

As difficult as it may be to isolate completely this stage – the vital feelings do not have to be disengaged to do it – we can at least demonstrate clearly the presence of one proper feature of aesthetic objectivity – the relation of appearance.

But what appears in this case? Is there something that could reveal itself to us as a unity and wholeness in what, seen objectively, are only random bits and pieces? Could, for example, that something reveal itself in the way in which the secret of purposive organic life can reveal itself and does in fact reveal itself when a living thing is beheld?

We may answer simply: yes, there is such a thing. For in the whole of nature too all things are adapted to each other; what occurs in concert is only what can so occur; (149) clearly not just anything can occur in concert with anything else. Species of plants may displace each other; they compete with each other, and that is essential for their way of being and the forms they take. The forest and meadow grow only when the soil allows, and they are dependent upon the available measure of rainfall. Lacking it, they are replaced by naked rock or dry sand. Of course, the observer knows nothing of the relation of mountains to rainfall, and cares little for it, and the changes in plant life determine the scene that offers itself to him, but these features stamp themselves upon his view of the landscape as that which in his eyes is not understood. He comes to sense these interconnections intuitively, precisely through the changes in the scene-like segments.

Whoever is accustomed to viewing landscapes exclusively from the perspective of painting – or even from specific examples of landscape art – is far from experiencing what we have just described. He looks at nature from an art-historical perspective, and lacks the natural attitude towards landscape. It is far otherwise when a person who has freed himself from a poor education approaches the inexhaustible pictorial riches of form and color that the face of the earth displays to us. To such a person, these pictures speak in an erudite language; they reveal and conceal, they tell stories and pose riddles. Light, the azure, the far distance, are all active in them long before their activity is understood as such. For man does not first look upon landscapes as upon a painting, but as an object.

Think of the landscape of a coastline with sparsely grown dune-grass and a low wood whose branches are bowed by an ocean wind, of shifting dunes with their undulating profiles, the sharp angle of the sides of them that face the land, and of their traces of now-lost woodlands. Or think of the tree line of the dark timber-forest in the high mountains and the snow stretching above it. It is not otherwise on land with dome-shaped polished rocks left by ice-age glaciers, or with the flat lake-country with its many islands created by those glaciers. One step more and we are at a uniform landscape of marshes left by ancient lagoons but now displaying scanty trees, heath and meadow.

Added to all of this is the fact that human life is imbedded in a landscape of individual farmhouses and villages. They bear witness to man's struggle with the forces of nature and with natural conditions. In this context belong the peaceful scenes of well-tended farmland (as Schiller described in his poem "*Spaziergang*"), the kind of scenes that suggest work, happiness, and both achievement and failure in the struggle for life and sustenance. At the same time there is the more profound sense of a native people becoming one with the land upon which they work, produce, and thrive, of home and of feeling at home.

The further the uprooted urbanite has distanced himself from it, the more the sense of home becomes a kind of hidden yearning in the back reaches of his mind. But even without such portentous yearning, the case is everywhere the same in principle: in the sight of the modest fishing-village with run-down huts and boats and nets on the beach; (150) the same when one gazes at mountain pastures and herds of cattle.

It would be quite wrong to separate the appearing content from the pictorial and sensible element, as though it were a question of two distinct things, just as it would be wrong to separate the dominant scenes of castle-ruins in the west of Germany, with their impressive recollections of a kind of life that has vanished, from the gently sloped hills in the surrounding landscape. For it is just this entanglement of the two that is characteristic. But in this intertwining, the relation of appearance between what is given through the senses and what is not – even for the observer who knows nothing – is essential.

In such cases the pictorial element, possessing only the character of a segment, is not at all isolating, but adds emphasis and intensity. The changing perspective, the alteration of the scene with every change in standpoint, the changes in light and season, produce concreteness and immediacy as they produce in us always an accompanying consciousness of appearance as such.

d) Natural beauty and art

It has been said perhaps too often that art first discovered beauty in nature. That is the claim made by the history of ideas. One thinks primarily of painting, for it first opened the eyes of humankind to the aesthetical secret of the landscape.

There is no doubt that painting achieves that opening by "painting" the landscape, that is, it represents it. In this way it teaches us to see. The ancients did not see it as yet, the Italians built their representations of scenes in their frames – in that art, landscape is grasped only slightly and secondarily (and, correspondingly, often in an artistic manner) – the Dutch made of it an independent theme, and the French Impressionists won for it the autonomy of light and color. To every stage in this process corresponds a new stage in the human capacity to see the actual landscape.

Stated in this form, the observation is quite right. It is strictly analogous to the discoveries made by art in other realms: the dramatic poet discovered the dramatic element in life, the comic playwright the comical, the satirist the ridiculous and perhaps even the amusing. One might ask whether the epic poet discovered heroism, or the religious poet the gods and religion.

Yet it is precisely the last analogies that remind us that we must not beat the principle to death. Highly intellectual thought can cause confusion when one exaggerates its function; one must reduce it to its appropriate dimensions, just in order to evaluate it correctly. Heroes are admired even without their poet, and men pray to gods, also, without their presence. But the heroes are idealized and made eternal by the poet; they are brought into the realm of the visible (151) and are humanized. But that is not the same as being discovered.

In all of these matters we must not mistake the enormous influence of the artist upon the development of the aesthetical way of apprehension itself, whatever object he is concerned to represent and in whatever material he works. The leading role in opening up our aesthetical sense for the human body must be attributed to the art of sculpture and, at a much later phase of its development, to the nude. Perhaps portraiture plays a similar role for the aesthetical sense of human physiognomy. But how we are to mark the dimensions of this role, which extends through all areas of representation, is a quite different question. To say that the arts alone have discovered the aesthetic object would be to say too much.

But why, precisely, is that to say too much? Surely not only because there are areas in which the proposition no longer applies. There must rather be here some fundamental principle that puts a limit upon it. We find such a principle in the simple reflection that the eyes of the creative artist must already be awake to a new kind of object if he is to make it the theme of his efforts to represent it; afterwards he may well be able to teach others to see it. The natural object as an aesthetic object must therefore have already presented itself to the artist if he is to be able to discover features in it that he will work to emphasize as essential in his representation – in the drawing, painting, or poetizing – of it. This means that in the artist's beholding and in his enjoyment in beholding he must become conscious of what he can objectivize in the act of creation and present to his contemporaries.

This is a relation of dependence that one cannot upset for the sake of a theory. If one does that, one falls into a ὕστερον-πρότερον ["later before," a rhetorical device] that will someday avenge itself as inconsistency. This is not contradicted by the fact that the artist is constantly experimenting, that is, there is a reciprocal effect of seeing and creating. Even in its individual stages of development, the artist's progress must lead his observation, or else experimentation would be reduced to blind hit and miss, and that would be just the opposite of the activity of a genius.

Understand this rightly: it is quite true that the artistic eye discovered the landscape and made it aesthetically accessible to others. But it is by no means true that artistic creation discovered it. In the artist himself there is no creating; it is rather observation that is primary and decisive, and simultaneously with that, the intentional act of enjoyment. Perhaps one may put it better in this way: in the artist what is primary is the aesthetical attitude towards the environing world. He is creative only secondarily; primarily he is a discoverer. And his discoveries come only within the limits of his time, or just a step ahead and beyond them. The means and the avenues of creation are, in comparison, only the vehicles of the execution of the work. (152)

If there is an antinomy here, it must lie in the nature of the artist and neither in his relation to the laity nor in his creative standpoint on the object. But at bottom there can be no antinomy. We are too accustomed to see the man of genius simply in terms of his capacities as a painter, and our habit of looking upon art from the standpoint of its history has led to reducing that capacity to the mastery of a variety of techniques. But then we forget that the techniques rest upon the ways of beholding, and that genius essentially consists in the manner of seeing. Every new manner of seeing, even those that seem merely to concern themselves with technique, produces new ways of letting things appear.

A wonderful example of this phenomenon taken from painting is the discovery of light – with its transformative effects upon the use of color and, in the end, with the disappearance of contour (the latter, for example, in the later Rembrandt). Here especially we can comprehend the extent to which new ways of seeing allow new things to be brought to appearance: the shading and "mood" of a landscape, dark interiors, even the peculiar qualities of human character. The concreteness of the represented objects and the selection of the details in the picture that have been drawn from life become as such fundamentally different. And that is achieved in part with the scantiest of means. From these facts we can explain the phenomenon of the "leaving out" of details that would have been given in everyday perception – or simply letting them disappear.

The same is true of the poet as the discoverer of the human. We have for too long considered the poet to be doing nothing more than forming and shaping his materials, in some case primarily as one who shapes and creates language. The poet is primarily a "seer," the clear-eyed one, the discoverer, the man with an open eye for all that is active in life, for whom therefore the conflicts and the characters on the stage of life take their places as objects seen from an aesthetical distance.

Chapter 10: On the Metaphysics of Natural Beauty

a) Formal beauty in nature

Among the ranks of the arts the beauty of appearance presented itself alongside formal beauty. The former was covered over by the latter in all great creations and, with that, disappeared behind it. On the lowest stratum, however, where the relation of appearance itself disappears – in ornamental work – it stands for and achieves for itself a certain independence. It will be shown again in the more detailed analysis of the strata that it retains its independence in all cases.

This formal beauty also plays an integrating role in the aesthetical natural object; human beauty no doubt also plays such a role, but it is still more concealed. We have already indicated what it consists in: it announces itself in a kind of free play with pure form of a visual and spatial kind, (153) but also of a tonic-audible kind, their play with color and tonal color, with rhythms, etc. So, at least, in the arts.

In nature it is no otherwise, at least in principle, only that here it is not a case of the mind disporting itself. The play with forms is involuntary, but not for that reason entirely random. Just for that reason we take note of it, it surprises us, it attracts our attention, it demands that we pause and take it in. We refer here primarily to the numerous forms that possess a remarkable regularity, as we noted above in the case of organic beauty. These are striking in heifers [Equisetinae] and shave grass, in grasses and conifers, just as in starfish, jellyfish and cuttlefish; they show themselves in the streamlined forms of fish and birds, in the forms and design of insects. In those cases it was, of course a question of the appearance of the organic purposiveness, or of its unknown lawful behavior; now it is a question of the play and effects of forms themselves. No doubt it is not possible to separate the one from the other. Nonetheless, we must distinguish between them; for neither does the variety of forms reduce to what is expedient, especially for the person who considers the matter unreflectively, nor can the line be effaced between the diversity of elements that are within themselves indivisibly intertwined and the different quality of aesthetical effects.

What is perhaps more important is that in these cases we are not dealing at all with special forms of peculiar regularity, but precisely with those that are lacking some ordering principle, or that are entirely opaque, possessing irregular forms that are scattered and seemingly random. The great example of this is the starry sky, such as one sees it naively, without a purpose to one's observations and without instruments. And yet, perhaps, there are very few things in nature that have so often stimulated the hearts of man to aesthetical beholding as the night sky; that it alone is the "most beautiful and perfect" of all things that the eyes of man can behold is a very ancient idea.

The truth of such assessments can be disputed, but not the fact of their occurrence. What are they based upon? One turns here to the many traditional metaphysical interpretations of the stars (where gods were seen within them) only with hesitation; these theories are no doubt determined by the aesthetical idea of sublimity. We may turn instead with more confidence to the movements of the fixed stars, which, long before the beginning of scientific observation, were thought to possess the highest perfection. But this too is most likely of secondary importance for these assessments.

The primary factor is, without doubt, the wonderful scene of groupings of the luminous stars themselves and their quiet undisturbed passage through the night sky – an unknown realm to nearsighted persons or to those men who never leave the big city. What is essential here is the complete lack of any kind of regularity of form. Regularity is so much lacking that humankind ordered the groups arbitrarily, ascribing to them the shapes of animals (154) or of heroic figures. These, of course, varied with the conceptions of peoples and epochs.

That is the same lack of lawful order that occasionally speaks to us from landscapes in curious tones, for example a landscape with pools and groups of trees in a marsh. In general, we must assign a positive aesthetic value to this element of irregularity in nature. Just the impression of "randomness" – not to speak of irrationality – can have its own charm. This is so notwithstanding the fact that regularity is also a positive aesthetic value. The formal value-elements in natural aesthetic objects are in fact diverse; they need not encroach upon each other, even when they are antithetical to each other. That fact coheres well with the formal elementary categories of unity and diversity, which always and only appear in and with each other, and may be seen to be just as fundamental in aesthetics as in ontology. The opposition of regularity and irregularity as such can, just an affirmative structural element, affect us with its peculiar charm.

Another good example of this state of affairs is the "song" of the birds. A great effort has been made to find musical accords in it – music in the human artistic sense, with its peculiar nature, an order grounded in musical scales. All was in vain. There are no doubt certain analogies here, if one isolates individual intervals; but genuine musical principles are entirely lacking.

Yet the character of each species of bird is marked upon the sound of its song. The figures, the rhythms, the melody, however nicely formed they may be, still do not make any musical unities; they are in fact comparable to the scattered constellations. The songs are a play *sui generis* with forms of sound. But as such they possess great aesthetical charm.

b) Indifference, quietude, unconsciousness

Play with pure form and the enjoyment taken in it make up in themselves a metaphysical element in natural beauty of which we are also sensible as such. For form is not in nature for the sake of play, and play is not there for the sake of enjoyment, as is always assumed in the case of works of art. All three simply coincide, as though we had organic purposefulness without a purpose. Even when one believes in a cosmic creator as a great architect, the being so conceived remains unknown and unimaginable; its notion in this context is merely an anthropomorphic expression for what is metaphysical in natural beauty.

But that is only a prelude. The metaphysics of beauty in natural structures, which are not there to provoke an aesthetical impression, goes much further. This metaphysics has nothing to do with the philosophical metaphysics of beauty that has so often been drawn up, neither of the idealist kind nor of the Platonic-Schopenhauerian kind (metaphysics of ideas), nor even with theological metaphysics. Rather the backgrounds that are decisive here lie very close to the phenomena, (155) and are necessarily given along with them to aesthetical feeling.

To begin, there is the wonderful indifference of natural objects to human beings and to our feelings – even precisely when they are aesthetic objects and thus awaken certain feelings in us. While we perhaps are consumed by suffering or yearning, spring blossoms out all around us; while blows of personal and historical destiny shake and overwhelm us, the stars in the sky still float by in their entire splendor. At times, we experience this contradiction almost like an antagonism against us. For we relate the beauty of natural appearances to ourselves. In the strict sense, we have a right to do so, for their beauty as such exists only for us. We exceed that right only when we extend what exists for us to the shapes and qualities that exist in themselves. And yet we know with equal immediacy of their immense indifference to us. We sense that indifference as a kind of barrier against us, as their alien quality, and this indifference is, perhaps, painful to us, yet we sense it also as the sublimity of the great theater of the world in which we stand.

We may call this the self-sufficiency [*Autarchie*] of nature, self-sufficiency in everything it offers to us. For the offering itself is made indifferently, unconcerned whether what it offers finds a subject to whom it may function as an aesthetic object. When a person senses something of this kind within the offering and takes it as the elevation of nature above the inconstancy of human life and feeling, a relation of appearance of a grand kind comes into its own and asserts itself in aesthetical beholding as a general cosmic feeling. Something very subjective and something very objective are mixed in that feeling in a peculiar way, yet without disturbing each other. A feeling for nature and a feeling of oneself are tied together in a unity that does not weaken their opposition, but takes it into itself as its essential condition. As man humanizes everything, so too does he humanize even the indifference of nature and thereby in a certain sense its inhumanity. Man experiences this indifference as a kind of attitude, specifically an attitude towards himself. But at the same time, this attitude is alien to him in the very depths of his soul. For he, man, is not capable of such indifference. And thus he senses this attitude of nature as directed against himself – that is, the inhumanity he senses in the act of humanizing it – as its foreignness and opacity, as something in nature's attitude that he cannot sympathetically experience.

That phenomenon stands in sharp opposition to the ancient mythological sensibility according to which nature – naively humanized – in all its manifestations "wants to do something to man" (wants to inflict something upon man): in the storm, the lightning, in the sunshine and rain, in the spring and the fruits of the earth. It is opposed also to the belief, manifest in early world-views, that found a *telos* in nature and fancied that nature both manifests and conceals itself. Both the mythical view of nature and the teleological view, which latter lasted long after the former had vanished, are really quite far from being what people very often mistakenly took them for – as an aesthetical view of nature. But it lacks saturation with the sublime indifference of nature. (156) Man has purposes, man manifests or conceals himself, man puts on masks and poses so that he may strike from a position of concealment; man lies. Men attributed all of that to nature. But nature knows exactly nothing of those things. Men were endlessly distant from natural aesthetic objects, indeed much further than from theoretical objects.[46]

This is not a matter of mature insight – realizing that nature does not lie, does not conceal itself, wears no purposes on its coat of arms – but only a matter of our feeling ourselves free from all such sensibility, even unreflectively, in our way of looking upon nature. This is the mystery of its indifference, a mystery for which we must have an immediate sense along with the two opposed elements that are contained within it. Nature must, unavoidably and unwaveringly, be present to our mind, indifferent and uninterested.

Of course the person who beholds nature aesthetically need not know this. That is a matter of insight. Insight can also lead him to the aesthetical way of beholding, but he does not need it at all. The beholding and appreciating observer, giving himself over to what he sees, has only a dark sense of the constancy of nature, or perhaps a reverential suspicion of it. Yet it is a suspicion that makes him feel blessed, just because of his consciousness of nature's indifference to him.

A further element in the natural aesthetic object is its unobtrusiveness, its stillness, and its gift of peace – that is, that nature leaves man in peace when he has no practical intentions of his own towards it.

That too is where nature stands in a palpable opposition to man, in its foreignness and its distance. Man is talkative, busy, and intrusive; he can hardly keep to himself. Language, the great tool of community and of the spirit, is also the most dangerous instrument for coming too close to things and imposing upon them. And not only does the silence of nature stand in opposition to the living human being, but also to the eloquence of human artifacts, to the objectivation of

---

46 This interpretation of mythic consciousness stands opposed to the usual view. It was always thought to be close to the aesthetical consciousness; it was felt to be related to poetry. The element of "poetry" in it is unmistakable. But not all poetry possesses an understanding of beauty in nature. A sense for poetry is an historically early phenomenon; a sense for beauty in nature, in contrast, came extraordinarily late.

spirit. This objectivation speaks of itself, of creation and of the creator; in it are contained treasures of the spirit, which demand recognition; with these treasures objects present their demands to the living spirit.

The natural object approaches man with no demands. That too, is part of its indifference, stillness, and unobtrusiveness. There is in fact just no intellectual content in it that might be recognized. For there is no one placed or represented within it; therein consists its radical difference from the work of art. Instead it shows humankind something else, the face of a puzzle, as it were, which anyone who has once given himself over to it in beholding it feels compelled to solve. But solving the puzzle does not seem to him to be a task for reason, but more as a miracle (157) for human feeling, one that we accept while beholding it and reverentially losing ourselves in it, so that we may remain before the miracle and enjoy it as such.

This element of stillness comes in degrees. It appears first on the faces of people, especially young people, people, that is, where speech inadequately expresses what is within them. It is intensified in animals, who do not have speech; it is dominant in plant life and present in its entirety in organic structures. But even in landscape there is perfect stillness; the whisper of the wind in the forest or above the sea is not experienced as speech directed at us, and what we perhaps otherwise call the "eloquent" in the shape of a landscape is a metaphorical expression for one's fantasy, which thinks itself inspired by it.

Moreover, it is peculiar how much men confuse silence and eloquence in their feelings for nature. Think of a thousand-year-old oak in a forest that has outlived generations of younger trees. A contemporary man stands before it, imagining past peoples who gathered about it, perhaps to dance and to celebrate festivals, and it occurs to him that the old trunk "tells stories" of those days. That is all very poetic of him. But the tree remains silent; it tells him nothing. In the Metropolitan Museum of Art in New York there is a huge section of a redwood tree with two thousand rings, one for each year of its life, and the dates of historical events are inscribed upon them. Towards the center, inscribed at a rather narrow ring, is the "birth of Christ." This causes the illusion that the tree could tell the story of history and what it has "experienced." The tree experienced nothing; it tells us nothing. It is wonderfully silent.

With that, we have arrived at the third element of the natural object. This is unconsciousness, in most cases even the absence of feeling, which – from the perspective of a person – is so alien to him, and he cannot quite enter its nature empathetically, for it is prohibited to him to enter into naked, harmless being-in-itself that is not being-for-itself.

This is not to say that anything simply as a being in itself is an aesthetic object, or just an "object" as such. The general law of objects – that is, no existing thing in itself is for that reason an object, but only "for" a subject that apprehends it and that brings that determinate perspective to it – is especially visible in the case of natural beauty, because the figured objects of nature display such a wonderful indifference to the subject that apprehends it.

It is just because they are silent and closed in upon themselves, although they are not actively closing themselves in, that they seem to have so much to say: not just about themselves, but about us and our relation to them, and not only about what is objective in that relation, but also about what is subjective there also. (158)

The paradox is only apparent. The valid law here is that just where an existing thing is devoid of all meaning, it is given meaning by its opposed number, i.e., by the third element in the relation of appearance: that is the mentally observant, comprehending subject, who values as he enjoys.[47]

In "being for us" the natural construct achieves a completion that it does not have as a mere being in itself. Nature in the aesthetical sense – that is, in the higher sense of beauty – first arises through man, arises "for him," by means of his enjoyment of it as an object. For that reason it is perverse to ascribe to nature as an ontological category all of what first comes to it through man as its "being-for-him": consciousness, mood, shades of feeling, animation. What is entirely alien in its nature is the fundamental condition.

c) Perfection, security, unfreedom

From its very beginnings, aesthetics connected the concept of perfection to that of beauty. It appeared that the highest completeness of a thing must be beauty just in itself. So the ancients thought, and so too Leibniz[48]. However, the equivalence goes too far. It implies that every realization of some other value – a vital or moral one – would also have aesthetic value. And that would obviously mean a confusion of the realms of value as well as of the kinds of satisfaction.

Yet there remains some truth in the relation of perfection to beauty. One must simply analyze it correctly. The first point is to see that we are not dealing with perfection itself, but with the "sensible appearance" of perfection; better stated, not with an understanding or cognitive grasping, also not with any appearance whatever, but with one that is only sensible – thus in a genuine relation of

---

47 On the role of this third member in the relation of appearance, see above, Chap. 5.
48 [Translator's note:] Gottfried Wilhelm von Leibniz (1646–1716).

transparency, in which the foreground is the one that is perceptible, but the background is communicated by it.

If we base ourselves upon this concept, the real world manifests a well-known series of steps in which man stands at the top as the highest being, and the inorganic objects at the bottom. Between them are extended the ordered steps of flora and fauna. We may now say about this widely extending series – and of course (159) still from this side of all aesthetical beholding – that they are steps upward to higher levels of being and downward to decreasing perfection.

This is a thesis that is usually misunderstood; indeed, it is often turned around completely. People believed the height of being itself to be a mark of perfection; they thought that plants are more perfect than an atom or a crystal, an animal more perfect than a plant, man than an animal. But the reverse is the case. Man is certainly the highest link in this chain, but not the most perfect. The reason for this, if we were to express it in a brief formula, is that the simpler the existing entity, the more easily does perfection (completeness, finish, self-sufficiency) come to it. The more complicated it is, the more difficult for all of its conditions to come together. The strictest natural laws apply to inorganic nature; thus we have in nature the lowest but nonetheless the most perfect creations. In the organic world, there is already great freedom of movement, especially when considered phylogenetically. For that reason we also have the detours and dead ends in the history of species of animals and plants under varying conditions of life. Man is, however, even as an individual, "free" in his decisions; as an individual he does not fall under laws of his species that would decide for him. Thus he is in his nature the most endangered species, because he is the most loosely tied, indeterminate and imperfect being. Freedom itself, his highest capacity, is what endangers him.

Let us now apply this relation found within the ontic series of created things to the "appearance" of perfection. We see immediately that it is not so easy for perfection to appear in man, not, at least, as specifically human, for example as a moral being; it appears more readily, perhaps, in a natural being. But as we go further downward through the levels of beings, perfection increases. It makes itself apparent in the forms of unity that become more integrated as they become more simple, under which unity a collective multiplicity of elements, though manifesting conflict, is kept under control. We do not see this relation when we behold natural forms aesthetically, but all the more we sense the perfection in the appearance without any reflection – we sense it as an internal peace, as constraint, security, infallibility and unfreedom; and the last strangely affects us in a comforting way, as exactly the opposite of our own nature, which possesses none of this infallibility. For our freedom is our insecurity, or hesitation, or constant liability to error and failure, our ability to be deterred in our projects.

Man is always immediately sensible of these things, but far from all comprehension of them: the instinctual certainty of the animal, its safe home within the domain of the laws of its species – perhaps felt even more strongly in the plants – but not so obtrusively, because they are more distant from him. This phenomenon is just as forcefully present in inorganic forms, whose lawfulness we sense without knowing what it is. In contrast, this standpoint does not extend to the "processes" of nature. For only "constructs" affect us aesthetically, a series of events usually does not, or does so simply in connection (160) with such constructs. But it is only such constructs that are given directly to the senses and as an intuitable unity. Out of them alone, even if they are given to us only in segments, the harmony of the whole speaks to us directly.

Behind this last phenomenon there is much else that the sciences have taught us to see: the special ways in which the sensible forms are conserved, the principle of their construction, the attunement of energy and function to each other. In the stability of most forms in nature not subsistence but rather a mysterious consistency reigns, which asserts itself through shifts in energy or in elements, and which contrives its own forms of self-regulation. The man who beholds aesthetically senses some of this behind the phenomena, without knowing just what it is. But it touches him as the miracle that it is.

The aesthetical theories of the Romantics held to an inward quality of nature that appears in nature's expressiveness. But it also held that we re-encounter in this inward quality man's own nature. Think, for example, of the veiled painting or of the youths of Sais [Friedrich Schiller]. That is surely poetry, but it is the poetry of an anthropomorphic metaphysics of nature, whose errors were presented above: it does not ever touch the genuine demonstrable appearance-relation in the aesthetical feeling for nature.

Of course we cannot defend ourselves from the metaphysical shapes that appear in the aesthetical beholding of nature. But the genuine demonstrable act of beholding takes different routes. It is more modest and yet also richer in content than the poeticizing imagination, which is, in truth, just a play with ideas after the fact. The phenomenon makes precisely the opposite apparent: in the unshakeable feeling for the complete otherness of nature, its foreignness, and its perfection, denied to humans.

For this is the remarkable thing: only where perfection as the secure being-in-itself of some construct "appears" in its external form and becomes apparent, only where it is visible, perceptible, and accessible to feeling, there alone in the world is this appearance experienced as beauty, and indeed without any regard for its distance from or closeness to humankind.

To be sure, the desire for a metaphysical revelation continues ceaselessly its inquiry into what in fact has been experienced as beautiful in such objects. There is a simple ontological answer to it that is sufficiently clear, although it will hardly satisfy that metaphysical curiosity: what is experienced as beautiful is everything whose sensible exterior presents itself intuitively to the beholder as the simple expression of an inner constitution. It is just in such objects that we sense a perfection that has grown naturally.

What is decisive here is that it is not necessary to understand the ontic situation in order to do this. One senses the inner meaning of the form, even without reflection, directly (as in the case of the organism) from what is visible. That was what was intended in an anticipatory way by the ancient doctrine of the *Eidos* as the form of perfection in every living kind. It presupposed erroneously however that this "inner form" was comparable to the external one. Because of this invalid reasoning, the ancients failed to find the solution to the puzzle. (161)

d) Creations of nature and creations of art

We see clearly from all of this that the relation of strata in the aesthetic object, which we developed above, has proven itself true for the entire series of phenomena. There is first a foreground, given to the senses, which is physically real, and then an appearing background. To be sure, in the natural object the latter is equally real, at least when we understand by it the determinative inner constitution of the object that gives expression to the outward form.

To that we may yet add: it is just this real inward constitution that appears, but not precisely as that which it is – not as a lawfulness, consistency, or adaptation – but usually as something quite different, for example as ideal form, as purposefulness, as secretive meaning, yes, even as intelligence. And just for that reason we must note once again: the appearing background is not real at all, but is merely appearance.

For that reason it is appropriate to formulate matters more carefully – we cannot of course easily dispense with formulas –: the dark awareness of being ignorant of the true nature of the background is just itself essential for the specific quality of the aesthetical impression, despite its appearance in a determinate form. Of course we sense that the background has its reality in the object, but for us its spectrum lies between complete indeterminacy and an appearing arrangement of elements, while we, even at that very moment, sense the definite real nature in it. And just that belongs with the peculiar appeal of natural beauty. It is the appeal of what is hidden, what will not let us go, and what still lets us find peace because it offers us further tasks for aesthetical beholding.

Here a yawning gap opens between the creations of nature and those of art. But from another perspective the two may approach each other again. It is characteristic of the arts that in the beholding of the object the beholding person disappears from his own view. He still feels himself in a state of enjoyment, but at the same time he is, just in his enjoyment, given over to the art object and is, as it were, lost to himself.

More precisely, the situation is as follows: the subject's stance must place him over against the work of art, it must put him at a distance from it; if he melted into it, his enjoyment would no longer be an aesthetical one, indeed it would approach an enjoyment of oneself. But in standing over against it, the subject can still forget himself and in this way disappear from his own view. One may now ask whether this is also true for the act of beholding the natural aesthetic object.

Some have believed that this question must be answered in the negative, because the natural object does not have the same power to draw the observer into the aesthetical realm, to distract him from himself, and concentrate his attention upon the pure play with forms and the relation of appearance. Is that true?

What is alone quite true is that in the case of the natural object we lack the artist, who leads the eyes of the beholder; the natural object is not concerned with making an aesthetical effect. (162) It is also true that there are natural objects that have far more power to seduce the observer into enjoying his own self, that is, to the enjoyment of his own feelings, than do works of art, and thus they work against the act of aesthetical beholding. Among such things are, first, landscapes and things similar to them, especially when one enjoys oneself while strolling within one. Here too the disappearance of the self need not be lacking, yet it is only too easy for a state of contentment to assert itself that engages even the purely vital feelings.

We have already spoken of the impossibility of drawing sharp lines between these phenomena. But in the end, is this not a question of the sharpness of the edges? Even those items that are not entirely separable from others maintain their unique qualities. As soon as the pictorial seeing arises the transformation is achieved and the act of beholding approaches that of the kind we find in the case of painting, that is, artistic beholding. The beholding subject vanishes from consciousness, it falls victim to the same forgetfulness of self before the work of art – and no doubt because the subject turns itself over to the object beheld. The subject is, as it were, overwhelmed and extinguished by it. The distinction between it and artistic beholding is weakened, and can finally disappear entirely.

The metaphysics of natural beauty is of course the aim of reflection, but just for that reason it is not simply a reflection after the fact. Kant brought reflection entirely into aesthetical beholding itself ("reflecting judgment"). He may have gone too far with that idea; but to exclude entirely the participation of reflective thought in beholding also goes too far. In fact the line between the two is again a blurry one. Aesthetical beholding not only challenges our reflective capacities, it contains often enough in itself its initial elements – and, provided that this is so, reflection belongs to the natural aesthetical phenomenon.

The unusual parallels between nature and art have occurred to philosophy down through the years. Creations of both kinds are able to offer us a veritable cornucopia of beautiful objects. And if their beauty is merely something for a human intellect that has learned adequately to look at them, there still must also exist something in themselves that offers itself to this intellect in an analogical way.

This is the problem that led Kant not only to treat the power of aesthetical and teleological judgment together, but also to place them together under one and the same regulative principle – perhaps he understood them too narrowly, but, in essence, he expresses correctly the metaphysical problematic that lies at the foundations of these phenomena.

As a result, many things that can be read off from the phenomena have manifested themselves, and what stands behind the relation of appearance in the natural aesthetic object may be seen: the determining inward side, the consistency, and the dynamic and organic features of the structure with its lawfulness and formal arrangement.

In olden times, people believed that God stood immediately behind the forms of natural objects as their creator; and with that, the situation appeared to suggest that art was the means by which man became like God. For here (163) man too becomes creative – even if essentially only imitative – and thus in fact God in miniature.

Today we tend to turn this theme around, for we begin with man's aesthetical creativity as the only warranted one: the non-artistic aesthetic object is the only point at which unconscious nature is equal to the inventive and creative human spirit. Stated in this way, we see the paradox more clearly. For what is truly amazing is the arising of structures in which the relation of appearance exists in full transparency for a human observer, although in its arising it was not destined for such a function. (164)

Part Two: **The Bestowal of Form and Stratification**

First Section: The Series of Strata in the Arts

Chapter 11: Opening up the Background

a) Modes of being and structures of content

The analysis of objects up to this point has been very sketchy. It has already shown the most important characteristic of the aesthetic object: the opposition of strata and, in the case of the arts, the ontological oppositions also. Further, it pointed out the way the strata are mutually interlinked and the significance of this fact for the relation of appearance. The results we have gleaned were shown to be valid within the domain of the arts – to a degree that found its limits only for a marginal phenomenon, that of ornamentation. They did not fail even in the case of natural beauty. Then too, the results afford, at least in principle, latitude for a different type of beauty, free play with form. Whether this is consistent or not with the beauty in appearance is as yet undecided.

These results are of course valuable, but much too general to do justice to the phenomenon of the aesthetic object in all its varieties. A second front of inquiry is therefore needed. It will have to confine itself to the arts for the most part, for in them the problem becomes more concentrated, as the background is not real. The arts no doubt can be unequivocally classified according to their "matter" [*Materie*], which in the case of the representational arts will yield indirectly essential distinctions with respect to their "material" [*Stoff*]. Since it is in these arts precisely a question of giving form to some artistic content in matter, the greatest importance lies upon the manner itself in which form is bestowed.

And at this point a further problem finds its source, one that we cannot approach with the mere distinction between two strata and their mode of being. Giving shape to some material is a question of "form." But with reference to form one stands before the much disputed question of what in fact distinguishes form as such from form as an aesthetic value – a question that seems so simple from an artistic point of view but is so completely opaque when one attempts to grasp it intellectually.

Aesthetics must in some way take up the problem of form. It is no doubt already apparent that the entryway to it lies in the stratification of the object. (165) But the two-strata relation developed above is obviously insufficient. What are we lacking? Where is the theory biased?

The bias lies first and foremost in the fact that the analyses of these strata terminated in the ontological opposition of foreground and background and essentially remained there. This opposition is, ontologically considered, the most remarkable thing about the art object: the inseparable whole of reality and unreality is a uniform structure, ontically no doubt a piece of nonsense, but one made possible only by the decisive participation of the third element, the receiving subject, which, as it were, itself stands outside the stratification.

For the aesthetic object in general, this peculiarity cannot be decisive, if only because it does not hold true for the natural object and for human beauty. What is decisive is real in these cases, and therefore the difference in the modes of being does not apply. And yet we still catch sight here of the relation of appearance. We cannot, therefore, make the essence of the beautiful as such depend upon this opposition. If, on the other hand, this opposition is essential for works of art, even for what is genuinely remarkable about the arts, still, even for works of art, beauty as such cannot lie in the ontological opposition. The opposition of the strata – above all that of the sensibly given and of the appearance – cannot be assimilated to the ontological opposition.

But this remarkable feature is not the whole. The stratification reaches further – towards the interior, and certainly without further opposition on the ontological level. This means that the unreality of the background, once it has been reached (at the stratum that lies closest to the front) vanishes no longer from sight towards the "rear." It continues on within the other inward levels of the object. We still must immediately provide evidence for this point.

To express the matter positively, what is decisive here is that next to the ontological opposition, a distinction of strata of a content-structural kind asserts itself. This distinction is just as important, but it does not limit itself to an opposition of two elements alone.

This other opposition cleaves the background into an entire series of strata. This implies that in the case of the work of art there appears in it not a simple background stratum, but rather a whole series of strata arranged one behind the other, all of which have the same unreality and are present only in the relation of appearance. They exist only for the beholding subject, and as content and as structure they stand out clearly from each other.

This opposition, in contrast, leaves the real foreground untouched. The foreground remains uniform. So it is at least in the primary arts; in the secondary arts – the "play" arts, in theatrical arts [*Schauspielkunst*] and in musical play [*Spiel*] – it is split up. But this splitting up is only an apparent one; in fact it is rather displaced than split up, that is, displaced toward the nearest stratum of the background: in the theater (166) the genuine play moves to the place of the written text, while in music to that of the audible sound.

In contrast, the appearing background arranges itself in a descending series of steps into the twilight depths of ideas, not immediately but mediated by other strata, which are just as unreal and just as essential for aesthetics. Here the main element is that this generality appears not abstractly and conceptually, but concretely and intuitively, not secondarily in reflection but immediately and at first sight, even if it is veiled in many ways.

We may summarize the entire situation regarding stratification in the following way: with respect to its ontological nature the art object exists essentially as two strata, but in respect to the collective structure of its content – and that means in respect to its inner form – it possesses many strata.

Both have great significance for the essence of the art object. The first is the ontic condition of its historical being, its continuing existence in some durable material, its capacity to be rediscovered and reawakened, its return to the living spirit even centuries later, and also its power to affect and modify that spirit. The second – the plurality of strata of the background with respect to its content – is the aesthetical condition of its profundity and richness, its fullness of meaning and significance, but also, and not least, the relative height of its aesthetic value, of its beauty. For along with the series of strata grows the concrete richness of the whole; the state of transparency continuously and evenly grows from stratum to stratum and with it the miracle of concretely intuitable appearance. On this the beauty of the object depends.

Those are the two fundamental functions of the work of art in man's spiritual life, i.e., the great consistency in its existence and its aesthetical charm. It is important to make clear that both depend upon the stratification in the work of art, but not on the same stratification; further that there is without a doubt a starting-point where the second stratification (the aesthetical one) hangs upon the first (the ontic one), and that the second stratification would be an impossibility without the real foreground.

b) An example: The portrait

Before we continue our examination of the fundamental principles, we must attempt to exhibit the series of strata upon a concrete example.

The task is difficult, because it must appeal only to the beholder's own aesthetical intuition and, where possible, avoid fixed concepts. Concepts are entirely insufficient here. Everyday language has no words for it, and science does not create any concepts for it, for the kinds of distinctions that function here are foreign to them both. These distinctions are given only to aesthetical beholding itself. (167)

We select our example from painting, specifically the portrait. We may consider one of Rembrandt's self-portraits in old age (these portraits are more tangible in their inner strata than many others). The series of strata may be sketched out in the following way.

1. The only thing given as real in the foreground are the specks of color on the canvas, which are arranged entirely two-dimensionally (the real light falling of the picture counts here indirectly, as does also the real space in which we take our proper position in face of it).

2. There then appears through the foreground the first stratum of the background: the three-dimensional spatiality, another unreal light with its (usually invisible) source, and also the physical shape of the represented figure with a portion of its environment.

3. We may take as the third stratum that of movement: the living bodily presence. This belongs – in the portrait it is limited naturally to the expression of the features – no longer to what the painter can make visible directly, and it is in that way and to that extent set off from the apparent spatiality, and yet is the foundation of all else.

4. For something else at once appears along with the third stratum: the man with his inwardness, the nature of the man; there appear traces of struggle, of success and failure of the man, of his fate in life; not the external fate, of course, although this too can stamp its traces upon a face, but more so the internal fate, that is, fate as it is determined by one's own personhood. This stratum is extraordinarily rich, or at least it can be. It is what perhaps touches us so deeply in beholding it. It is essentially beyond what can be seen with the eye; it lacks spatiality, color, and physicality, in the same way that this stratum is also not visible upon a living person. The artist is able to make it appear only indirectly – as it appears in the real world only upon the external features of a face. Of course there the appearance of this stratum is made easier by the visible movement of the features.

5. But what is most amazing is that this stratum, which does not appear physically or through the senses at all, has yet the power to be transparent for something more. In a man as he is there may appear a man he is not at all, but rather as he should be in his very essence and nature. That is, his individual Idea can appear – in the way it appears in life – only to a loving glance.[49] This achievement is one of the most remarkable capacities of art: the intuition and appearance of the moral core of personhood both in its uniqueness and its ideal nature at once (of, as it were, his intelligible character). This achievement is not within the capacity of the student of human nature, who never sees more than what is typical. Here the eye peers all the way through a man to what is unique and singular in him; it is precisely this that makes the portrait (168) a proper

---

49 For the notion of the individual Idea, cf. *Ethik*, 3rd edition (1949), Chap. 57 [English edition: *Ethics*, George Allen & Unwin 1932, Vol. 2, Chap. 32].

"likeness," [*das Ähnliche*] that is, literally a premonition [*das Ahnende*]. Every person has fortunate moments in which his individual Idea appears. The artist grasps at such a moment and holds it fast. In this way he holds fast the Idea's appearance.

6. And then there is yet another thing that can appear, something just as much part of the background; a thing unfathomable yet tied to the inward nature of a man: that which is universally human, that which anyone who beholds it recognizes as his own. It stands in strict opposition to the individual Idea, which cannot be a stand-in for anyone else and which must affect every other person as alien to himself. But here there shines forth something that concerns everyone, something that shows to everyone his own soul. In the arts one calls such things the Symbolic. And we cannot deny that it first gives genuine weight to individual persons, even the specific quality of their life and fate. Great works of art receive precisely from this final deep stratum their greatness and their permanent significance. That is quite understandable, because this is the universal, which addresses all men ever again in all epochs of history. We must simply make clear that there is no further expression for this something than the artistic expression: to let appear. There is no name for it: those that some have introduced – the Significant, the Idea (often only one's own religious convictions were meant), or the Deep Meaning – tell us nothing about its content. It is given only in what can once again be concretely recognized in what appears, and there it is unmistakable.

c) Some discussion of this example. Implications

What we demonstrated by reference to this example of a particular art form, indeed of one of its branches, is valid for all the arts and works of art; and beyond them, for most forms of beauty in the human and in the natural realms. It is valid for all things that are beautiful through an appearance-relation. It has its limits only where the relationship of appearance ends.

But this does not mean that the series of strata are everywhere the same, or even just as rich in content. The series takes many different forms in the arts, and is in part variable even within any of the arts. In painting, the strata of the background that are found more deeply within the work are quite different in the case of landscape or still life. This means that the order of the strata, and even the number of the strata, vary with the material. But they vary additionally with the way of seeing and its corresponding way of fashioning of the material – thus with what we call style.

It would be more correct to say that variation in the series of strata is an essential and foundational element in the distinction between materials and styles. For materials are chosen with reference to this variation, but the kinds of fashioning are developed out of them. This will be apparent when one reflects that everything unique in the bestowal of form upon objects is determined from within, that is, from the deeper strata of the background, and that these are the strata whose appearance, in the end, is the purpose of everything that is more towards the foreground. That surely does not exclude (169) a certain reaction from occurring in the coexistent strata. But the fundamental relation that has been specified remains clear: from inner to outer.

An additional spotlight falls upon the entire principle of the order of the strata in art when one considers that this order possesses the character of a series, that is, in it the relation of appearance is a graduated one. It is no longer a relation of only two members, as it originally appeared to be, but is a relation with many members that continues from stratum to stratum.

In this step-like relation only the stratum closest to the front, that of the sensibly real, is not one of appearance and only the most inner stratum is no longer transparent, or one that allows deeper things to appear. All the others, which lie between them, are both: they themselves are appearances and also in turn allow things to appear. They are, after all, the middle strata, and connected to others on both sides. What is aesthetical in this relation manifests itself from the reverse side: each of these strata, as an appearance, is carried by one that is further forward than itself and is itself the carrier of an appearance of one in the deeper background. Thus the relation of appearance continues step-wise and structured from the real sensible foreground into the last, hardly palpable structures of the background.

It is clear from this analysis that the entire weight of the ladder-like structure in which phenomena come to appearance falls, in the end, upon the real sensible stratum of the foreground. This is the only level to which the artist can give shape in a direct manner; all fashioning of the later strata must be achieved indirectly, just by letting them appear through the first, and the process is led precisely by the bestowing of form. And since this bestowal of form is at the same time the leading of the observer, the process can itself be understood by the observer in this way: the entire direction of inner vision – of the representational faculty, of fantasy, of intuition – begins with what can be perceived of the real foreground. Through it there appears in the next-deeper stratum, which is already unreal, only what "can" appear on the basis of the visible forms; again through this appearance there appear out of the next stratum after it only what "can" appear on that basis, and so on through the series.

Accordingly, what we have already seen from the character of aesthetical beholding is again evident: it is a beholding that is tied to and carried by perception into the depths, which are removed far from all physical sensibility.

d) Dependency of appearance and dependency of composition

This sequence of dependency in the continuing series of the relation of appearance must, of course, correspond to something similar in the composition of the work of art. And this latter must also have a reverse direction: from inner to outer. For in the creative work of the artist the appearing stratum must always determine the transparent one, through whose fashioning it is to appear. (170)

In the activity of the creative agent, the aim is always the "bringing to appearance" of what is beheld. That means that from stratum to stratum the background determines what stands further in the foreground. That in which something should appear must always be directed at the appearance of what is beheld, that is, it must be correspondingly fashioned. How the artist does that is and remains the secret of his art; the "law" of this process is precisely what he can obey – perhaps can even make, but never specify. For he knows as little as the observer.

Now not all works of art have the deepest background strata, for example the two last ones that were specified above; but some of the "further" strata are always there. This implies, however, that the outer is always determined by the inner, even if, as surely happens at times, in a contributory way. This determination is passed on from stratum to stratum until it takes on itself perceptible form in the sensibly perceptible foreground.

Thus there flows a dependence of the structure counter to a dependence of the appearance. Both pass through the entire series of strata but in opposed directions, the latter from the inner towards the outer, the former from the outer to the inner, and just for that reason they are the opposite sides of one and the same relation. The opposition here is similar to the one we find in the domain of knowledge between the *ratio essendi* and the *ratio cognoscendi*; however here it is not a question of being and knowledge, but of appearance and beholding.

As clear as these main features may be, there is always something puzzling about how what is ideal or just merely universal in a human sense can extend itself into the sensible matter of the foreground and still offer itself there as appearance to the eyes of the beholder. We cannot limit ourselves here to simply ascribing everything to the secret of artistic genius; it is not a question of the peculiar way the artist fashions his work, but of the fundamental principle that what is in the background and fundamentally different from sensible vision can yet appear within the visible.

Let us stay with Rembrandt's self-portrait in old age (perhaps the one in London).[50] In the sunken face and its heavily hung features there is something in

---

50 [Translator's note:] Hartmann may have in mind Rembrandt's self-portrait at the age of sixty-three in the National Gallery.

the gaze of the eyes that, once we seize upon it, will not let us go. We will have difficulty in saying what that something is, but it is there, it forces itself upon the beholder – and all at once we comprehend the suffering and overcoming in the man's life, comprehend something of the inner fate of the genius, comprehend perhaps directly the individual law of this nature; immediately we grasp also the universally human, and the tragedy of him who wrestles with the highest things. What is entirely invisible becomes "visible" in the play of color and form upon the canvas.

We can vary our example as we wish; we get always the same results. Think of the smile of Leonardo's *Anna Metterza* [*The Virgin and Child with Saint Anne*]. It is perhaps the most ephemeral thing that a man can grasp. It is held fast (171) upon the canvas with all else that transmits it – perhaps just a little trace in the corner of the lips, but yet a thing that is completely present. Even the faded colors could not efface it.

The power of letting-appear fetches the smile up and out of the deepest background and brings it to the sensible foreground, passing through the entire series of strata. Turned around, the appearance itself leads the observer from what is given by the canvas to the senses into the most inner depths of the essence of man. However not everything about this enigma is insolvable. Something of it can be resolved. What art brings about here occurs in life also – in the way in which men encounter and see each other. For they do not see each other only via the senses – they see also into the very soul of the other, but always through the sensible impression. And this seeing of the soul, this other form of beholding, is in fact the way men see each other in life; it is for the sake of that beholding that men look upon each other. Usually such seeing does not go very far into the depths – it does not easily pass to what is individual in a man – but in principle it is the same looking-through from the sensible into the psychic, which the painter also turns to his own use.

We find only two distinctions here. 1. The artist banishes what he sees into the realm of durable matter; he "objectivates" it so that it may at all times be beheld by an observer. 2. The artist beholds more than the profane eyes of a man in everyday life. The latter's eyes pass over and past most of what is to be seen, most easily over what is deeper and more hidden, for he does not have time to engross himself in such matters. The eye of the artist begins precisely with what others overlook.

e) Filling out ontically the series of strata

For this reason, the opening up of the background, which first appeared to be uniform, into an entire series of strata is central to aesthetics. Without it, the miracle of artistic revelation would not be possible. How far we may follow this principle into the arts themselves and into beauty other than that of art remains to be established. First, however, the situation has a further aspect.

When we spoke here about the law of objectivation (in Chap. 5, esp. b), we came upon a fundamental peculiarity of all spirit. Spirit appears as free and unattached in none of the three and only three forms of spirit we know of, but only as spirit that is carried ("resting upon"). So it was in the case of living spirit, of personal spirit, and of objective-historical spirit. And, moreover, it is always the entire ontic series of strata that carries it, for even psychic being is carried by organic being, and this latter again by physical and material being. There are no exceptions to this principle in the domain of real spirit. How is it, however, in the domain of non-real and non-living spirit, i.e., that of objectivated spirit?

In the first stage of the analysis it appeared to be clear that spiritual content was carried by a physical and material stratum of being – by material that had been fashioned, i.e., that of the foreground – but not by the mediation (172) of the intermediate strata. Psychic and organic life seemed to be eliminated. But then it became incomprehensible how spiritual content can tie itself to material being directly.

This problem is by no means a difficulty that was resolved artificially. May not what is not possible in the real world not only occur as such in the appearance-relation, but also be convincing? It is wonderful enough how from stratum to stratum higher being can be supported by lower; this great heterogeneity in the natural relation of two neighboring levels is already considerable. If the intermediate stages were passed over, say perhaps two at once, the bestowal by spirit of form on matter would be completely incomprehensible. For the most heterogeneous entities that exist in the world rest close upon each other, so that in fact the highest has to appear directly in the lowest.

This aporia can nevertheless be very easily resolved. Any absent intermediate members must be able to manifest themselves in the relation of appearance. One could draw that conclusion simply from the role of the beholding observer, who is necessarily contained within the total tripartite relationship. Yet it is important to demonstrate the presence of the absent members even in the series of strata in the aesthetic object itself. And to do that, we now possess the key.

That key is just this: the law covering the splitting open of the background in the work of art asserts that the intermediate strata appear also – and appear, specifically, in the same order and the same dependency (as one being supported by the other) in which they would have to appear ontically if the object were entirely real. The relation of ontic dependence of the strata is also maintained in the series of the appearing members. The most inward features of a man, which always bear large traces of his spiritual life, are not, as it previously seemed, tied directly to matter and its fashioning, but rather first to psychic life, then to organic life, and this last one alone is tied to matter. Only in characters in art do love and hate, pain and joy appear; otherwise such things could not be made visible to the senses or even imaginable. And again, only on the level of love and hate do human individuality, character, personality, and even more, genuine conflict, fate, or other such relationships of meaning appear. Only in a preliminary examination, in which the manner of being was central, could we be mistaken about this return of the natural condition in the entire world of appearance of the work of art. In the context of the manner of being, there are only two strata. Only the inner differentiation of the appearing background throws light on the real nature of this relationship.

This solution of the aporia is important for another reason. For it is here that we can in addition reveal the actual basis of the differences in the kinds of objectivation, which is decisive for a more refined understanding of the position of works of art in our spiritual life. (173)

Let us remember that on the one hand, we have words, concepts, and writing expressive of thought; on the other hand, we have the work of the artist. Both are fragile and subject to decay with time; words suffer changes in meaning, concepts fall "out of use," scientific documents are subject to misinterpretation and liable to reinterpretation. A special difficulty is posed by a single concept that has lost its original context, for it is difficult to return to its original foundation in intuition. Its fate is peculiar: it loses meaning and it withers away into abstraction. In contrast, the work of art holds tightly to its historical background; it lets that background appear through epochs and cultures wherever and whenever a beholding subject adequate to it appears.

We can account for this difference in kind only by what was said above: the work of art contains in itself its own concrete detail, while the concept has such detail outside of itself; the latter must be supplemented always and only by some larger intellectual context, that is, they must be filled out with intuition. This explanation is to the point, but it does not reach as far as the genuine problem. For one may yet ask: why do concepts (and everything built up from them) have their detailed context external to themselves?

To that the answer may be given: concepts have their detailed content outside of themselves because within the concept there is no effective guiding of intuition from the technical term itself (from the foreground, which is audible or visible in writing) to the intellectual meaning (the background) in which the intellectual property, the spiritual content, consists. Such guiding can occur only where the objectivation contains the entire series of strata from the sensibly given to the spiritual. This is absent from the concept: here the "thought" is tied directly to the concept, and there is no trace of the intermediate strata, which otherwise could appear. There is given no genuine appearance-relation. One cannot "intuit" the thought.

The situation is similar, *mutatis mutandis*, for entire pieces of writing that convey thought. However, in this case, the relationships among the concepts give us some starting-point for efforts to recover an intuitive understanding of them. The larger relationships help us to overcome somewhat the absence of direct appearance; here an indirect appearance takes over. But the means it offers are not intuitive. The isolated single concept, however, has the content that would be needed to satisfy it entirely external to itself.

Apart from the aesthetical effect, it is therefore the strength of the objectivation in the work of art that it can produce and conserve the entire series of strata in itself, and, correspondingly, it is the weakness of the concept and all conceptual expression that it does not produce the series of strata in itself. One may express this more concretely: what constitutes the strength of an artistic objectivation is the relation of appearance. Its essence consists in the letting-appear of spiritual content in sensible material. A concept, however, cannot make any of its content appear to intuition at all, at least not by itself alone. In it, then, the tie is an external and conventional one. It fulfills its function in (174) thinking only as long as the meaning given to the technical term is already known and can be executed intuitively. For if the concept is not filled out by intuition, it is dead.

The work of art is fundamentally different in this respect. The relation of appearance itself is carried out for the entire order of strata. That does not change the fact that in the How of appearance many kinds of mysteries still abound.

Chapter 12: The Order of Strata in Poetry

a) The self-testimony of the art of poetry to its middle strata

Painting, the one example we have given, is, to be sure, much too narrow to survey the relations among the strata and their consequences. Now that we have opened up the background, the first phase of our analysis (Chaps. 6 and 7) must obviously be taken up again and extended to the other arts.

Naturally, the way through the labyrinth of appearances must first be found. It must again lead through the entire list of the arts, but in so doing, it does not have to take the same route. Such a complicated relation as that of the "continuous appearance" can best be approached where the manifold of the strata is most clearly visible. To that end, the example of the portrait was chosen (in Chap. 11b). Now we must begin the second part of the analysis with those arts in which the strata can be most easily distinguished and where at the same time as many strata as possible can be found.

These conditions are best met where an art is not only representational but where the emphasis is placed on the side of thematic. That is most frequently the case in poetry. Poetry is the art that possesses the greatest range of material: everything that makes up human life, with its events, conflicts, activities and fates, belongs to its domain. For that reason it was once considered by the Idealist school as the highest of all the arts. But we must not forget that poetry is, from another perspective, the art that reaches least into the realm of the senses. For its matter is composed of words.

To this we must add something else that helps along our analysis. To pick out an individual stratum of appearance, to express its peculiarities in words, thus to describe it, is not easy; indeed it is always a risky enterprise. Concepts clash with intuition. This difficulty is well known, and aesthetics has always felt itself limited by it. For the ineffable, which is given, if at all, only in the relation of appearance, must be expressed in words, in a medium inappropriate for it.

It is obvious a priori that this can never be done. Such description does not even pretend to be successful in such an exacting endeavor; but it must nevertheless attempt to approach it, (175) that is, at least to set forth a few characteristics of the essence of the object that make it distinguishable from others. And here is the point at which the work of poetry meets the demands of such description.

For poetry speaks out in words that which philosophers cannot pronounce upon adequately. Up to a point, at least. Its matter is words, and what it cannot grasp by them – directly or indirectly – it can not grasp at all.

However poetry grasps very well the background of human life. It must therefore make articulate that in which it will allow that background to appear. But that means that it must give expressiveness to the intermediate strata. Then by means of their transparency the poet can allow human inwardness to appear. This fact can be turned to use by aesthetics.

Naturally the aesthetician does not find what he seeks simply expressed in concepts. The poet does not speak at all in concepts as such. Even when he uses concepts that are current, he transforms them in their meaning, emphasizes their pictorial origins, and, by means of context, places accents upon them that we would not otherwise recognize. However, that does not at all prevent the poet from giving voice to what people do not know how to say in their everyday language.

Poetry bears witness to itself in this way. It itself lays bare the principles of the construction of its product, the work of poetry. Its pictorial language is entirely sufficient for the aesthetician; indeed for its purposes it is superior to every other. For the aesthetician is not now primarily concerned with concepts as such, but only with a certain capacity to describe. And for that nothing can surpass the description in the language of the poet.

We must now try to choose examples so that one or another of the middle strata can best shine forth with a certain independence. Poetry has many such instances that serve this purpose. It addresses itself to the concrete imagination, it points always and initially to the external doings and activities of human character by means of words, which alone constitute the foreground – just in fact as things manifest themselves in life.

b) Poetic concreteness

Let us put together a few simple examples that will immediately allow two middle strata to become apparent. The first will be "There was a king in Thule."[51]

Of what, really, do these few verses speak? We see the "old rake" at the hour of his death upon a cliff overlooking the sea, how he drains the golden goblet for the last time and then throws it into the sea, thus denying it to his heirs. Behind this another picture emerges, about which nothing is said, which simply shines through: the picture of a young love that could not be fulfilled – perhaps because of the ancient fate of princes, who could not choose the woman they loved – of a love, however, (176) that had followed him through his entire life, and now, at the point of death, it is the one holy thing in that life.

Or the verse from Sappho: "The moon has set and the Pleiades; it is midnight, and time goes by, and I lie alone."[52] A brief fragment, and yet everything is contained within it. We are told directly of the sleepless night in a lonely place and of the setting of the stars; we see the west-facing window and the night-blue sky through its opening. Of the yearning of the lover lying there nothing is said. That appears only in the picture of the lonely woman upon her couch. But poetry cannot help the person who does not hear that yearning from within it.

This is characteristic of all poetic art: it does not speak of what in fact is of most concern to it. For what concerns it, if spoken in everyday words, would seem

---

51 [Translator's note:] Goethe, Johann Wolfgang von, *Faust. A Tragedy. Interpretive Notes, Contexts, Modern Criticism,* translated by Walter Arndt, ed. Cyrus Hamlin, A Norton Critical Edition, New York and London: Norton 2001, p. 75. (Goethe, *Faust* I, "Es war ein König in Thule," lines 2759–2782).

52 [Translator's note:] Campbell, David A. (ed.), *Greek Lyric: Sappho and Alcaeus,* Vol. 1, Loeb Classical Library 142, Harvard: Harvard University Press 1998, p. 173.

crude; and moreover it would not have a living intuitive effect. How is art to render the essential? To that question one can only repeat: it renders it in the same way that fate, suffering, and life are given to us in real life, in the external behavior of people.

Art also needs, as the examples demonstrate in certain contexts, only a very small segment of the external behavior and the specific circumstances in which it moves. It is not a question of more or less, but of how material is chosen. All human behavior betrays something of the agent's inward state, whether or not he wishes to reveal it. What is decisive is only that the chosen segment of his behavior betrays precisely that which is to be shown. This betrayal is identical to the relation of appearance.

If one asks why the poet takes this detour, we must answer: because only in this way can he really "let be seen" what he wishes to show – seen, of course, as understood in the sense of second-order seeing. If he were to speak directly of hate and love, jealousy, envy, fear and hope, he would sound like a psychologist, who calls everything by name, not as the poet does; and what emerges is not an intuitive picture, but a concept, which must be satisfied in some other way by intuition. It is well known that bad poets psychologize.

We do well to place next to the above examples some others taken from poetry of a more complex kind, that is, from the novel or from dramatic works. As different as these two forms of literature may be, they are still similar in that they both work with more complex materials, that is, they present a larger slice of human life with its conflicts, resolutions, and fates. They lead us into a whole sphere of humanity, and within and out of that sphere individual characters take shape. If the poet subjected his characters to a preliminary analysis, he would bore us. If he tried to tell their entire story, he would lose himself in an ocean without boundaries. He lets them appear in their acts, their speech and their reactions to things – but within a sharply limited selection of details. He lets them characterize themselves in a short sequence of scenes, lets them "betray" them-selves, just as people do in real life. (177) And it often happens that we do not guess rightly or see through him at once, but at first see the character from only one side, similar to the one-sidedness of a picture offered of only a part of some action; and that is just the way it is in life also. Just in this way the entire picture of what is inward takes on life; it sparkles colorfully, it includes contradictions, and these are essential for the progressive revelation of the inward lives of the characters.

A wonderful example of this last idea is Prince Harry (in both parts of Shakespeare's *Henry IV*): how he presents himself in the scenes with Falstaff on the one hand, on the other in the scenes in which he is king. What strikes us directly is how unconcerned the poet is with the unity of these oppositions in one person. Clearly this affects the audience in a much more concrete and lively manner the less it is thematized as such on stage.

But even without this phenomenon of opposition, a single small episode, presented without the slightest explanation, can give us the most profound insights. Think of the malicious little scene about the aunt's hat in Act I, Scene 2 of Ibsen's[53] *Hedda Gabler.*

The great writers follow exactly the same lead. Of course, many things are described quite simply; but what is essential in the work is not found there. Dickens[54], for example, allows almost all of his characters introduce themselves in scenes in which they bear the action. The description that precedes them is concerned mostly with externals. Hamsun[55] often lets his characters speak of matters of little consequence; what is important is not what they say, but what they do. In general, what is important is what is imponderable. It is not that the content of a speech is always unimportant; it is obvious that it is. But it is not the center of concern. That concern remains always what is unsaid and inexpressible.

The details that become transparent in this way are always more tangible when the poet allows his characters to speak directly. And there the strata in the poetic work are made directly apparent. Our analysis can begin here. In a sense we need only continue.

c) Distinguishing the strata in poetic works

With what strata of the poetic work are we concerned? Obviously not with the real foreground, with the words. But neither are we examining at the start the last and most deep strata of the background. Rather we are concerned at this point exclusively with certain middle strata. We must not attempt to describe these in detail and set them off from each other; only then can we appreciate properly the positive relationships between them. Now this relation is the relation of appearance.

1. The one further forward of the two strata considered here (and the two are nothing more than appearances) is clearly the one that in painting and sculpture corresponds to what is immediately and sensible visible; it is also the one that is pressed into the realm of the visible and the audible (indeed into that of reality); it is further the sphere of physical movement, (178) placement, facial expression, in

---

53 [Translator's note:] Henrik Ibsen (1828–1906).
54 [Translator's note:] Charles Dickens (1812–1870).
55 [Translator's note:] Knut Hamsun (1859–1952).

a word everything externally perceptible upon a person (one may compare in this way the above examples).

2. The stratum behind it, which appears through it, is not at this point entirely inward, but rather primarily just that of the elements of plot, the external behavior, the actions and reactions, the successes and failures of the characters. Among these one may also count indirectly the intentions, conflicts, and resolutions, then again also the situations – as far as they cannot be assimilated to the external contacts among the characters but rather include the tensions among clashing purposes; yet the motives and dispositions are still excluded.

3. Even with that, the series of strata with which we are concerned is not concluded. Only now another stratum begins, which, however, already appeared in the previous ones. We may describe it as that of the bestowal of psychic form. For only by observing the way the characters act may we peer through them at the unique moral specificity and character of men, at what is already established in a man's psychic life and is a prominent feature of his nature. From this standpoint, we distinguish the frivolous person from the sensible one, the egotist from the considerate man, the heedless person from the reverential, the coward from the bold. This stratum (it is already the third of the background series) first reveals to us the ethos of men, their merit and guilt, their accountability and their awareness of responsibility. For that reason, the depths of the conflicts, which lie always in the felt value-conflicts, first open up to us here; similarly, the moral side of the situation: that in which freedom and necessity are fatally intertwined – as the necessity of deciding freely.

One may think of the way in which Dostoevsky introduces his Dmitri Karamazov. We first learn some facts about his youth and career, which are reported as matters of fact. No one would feel on this basis genuine sympathy for him. The situation changes from the moment where, without premeditation, he lets the troubled Katerina Ivanova visit him, but then chivalrously lets her go off with his money, captured, as he was, by her great confidence. We are won over by her great faith in him. He thus wins with a single blow not only the heart of the girl but also the heart of the reader, and not all his later madness can efface that.

4. But then something quite different attaches itself here, once again a new stratum of objects. This stratum no longer concerns the inwardness of man, but rather the whole of his life. For even this whole cannot be given directly; it contains too much detail. The poet lets this whole appear only at certain points, in scenes or episodes; he shows it to us with the aid of its inward integrity, and for that the presuppositions are some characteristic conflicts and actions and the interlacing of responsibility and guilt.

This whole we may call destiny, whether it is that of the individual character or the mutually interconnected destiny of many persons. One must not, however, take "destiny" literally – as one determined for men (179) by a higher providence – rather it is usually the fate that one prepares for oneself, and is often a fate for which a man himself bears the guilt. The *Nibelungenlied* offers a lovely example of this. Siegfried prepares his own doom by allowing himself to deceive and break faith with Brunhilde, and then does not have sufficient resolution to destroy forever the trophies that betray him. As an example of a fate for which a man is guilty himself, the *Nibelungenlied* stands much higher than epics of otherwise the same rank.

The appearance of destiny is a large and significant event in epic and dramatic poetry. From a certain standpoint, it is the point from which all other matters, including the characters, receive their illumination. It is what we usually do not see in life, because we are too immersed in individual events. The job of poetry is to break open this narrowness of vision and point out the totality that appears within it. But poetry does not do that by speaking directly of such totality; it allows the inexorable consequences of decisions and actions to speak for themselves. In this way, the destiny of a man becomes concrete, picture-like, and intuitable.

d) The most inward stratum. Limits to what can be uttered

We have deliberately spoken up to now only of the middle strata of works of poetry. In them, we see clearly the step-by-step progress of the appearance-relation. But we must distinguish the last background strata from them.

What is there still, beyond character, guilt, or fate that could appear there? In the last chapter we demonstrated what there is by means of an example taken from painting, for the entire series of strata is similar (in cases where a person is represented): these are the strata of the individual Idea and of the universally human, both of which are of an ideal nature and superempirical, and yet they are different in nature.

1. As for the first of these strata, we have little to add here. Every man realizes that what lies within his nature is only partly realized in life. He can miss it entirely – through a bad schooling, a poor education, the imitation of alien personalities, and so forth; but some part of it still exists, and can be visible in him even through its many vicissitudes. When we realize that every man in every decision that he makes in life cuts himself off thereby from possibilities that originally were open to him though yet undefined (ontically they are of course only in part possibilities), we come to understand immediately at what an enormous distance a living person can find himself from the potential riches of his original – or we should say ideal – nature.

We normally do not notice that about a man. To do so, patience and a deepening observation of him are required. Everyday life does not leave us with leisure for such looking. But someone who loves a man personally often does; he is seeking the particular nature of the one he loves. Possibly he loves only because he sees the beloved (180) in the light of his idea of the beloved's personality, in the ideality of that what he is precisely in distinction from all others. The peculiar thing is that the poet, too, is capable of such beholding. In that way he is like the lover.

The difference between them is only that the poet in his capacity is not limited to a single person, and that what he beholds of the ideality of a person can be shown to others, so that they may also be able to see it. The lover cannot do that. At bottom, the kind of vision the poet possesses is of another kind.

What kind of vision could that be? We might think it to be a form of the intuition of values [*Wertschau*], indeed genuine ethical value-intuition. This does not suggest an intermingling of ethics and aesthetics; moral values are in any case the presupposition of the understanding of those conditions, situations, and conflicts that make up the stuff of poetry (in the third and fourth of the middle strata). There is no good reason why we should take the values of individual personality as an exception to this. To the contrary, since these values are concrete and various, they have special weight among the materials for constructing a work of art. Recall also that concepts are not at all adequate in the case of these values; as instruments, they are much too coarse; our living feeling for values, when it turns to concepts, easily loses itself in what is indefinite and blurred.

What is needed here is sharp, sculptural beholding. That arouses the poetic eye. Recall once more the example mentioned above of Prince Harry. The figure of Hamlet is individualized even more adequately in its Idea; no human type is sufficient to encompass it, but the man Hamlet, characterized by his empirical life, is also unable to reach the idea of him. Another figure seen in its intelligible idea is Alexi Karamazov. As Dostoevsky depicts him, he is not that in all respects, but only just as far as in life itself the ideal essence of a man breaks through into reality.

Not all poetry enters into this realm. Playing with the idea of a personality is a dangerous game. It can turn into a mere construction, in which case the work fails. The elevation into the ideal may affect us unnaturally, as artistically invalid; it may lack the power to convince. The majority of poets hold themselves back from such attempts. But there are works in which the highest ends are achieved in just that way.

What is contained in the "constructed personality" is easy to describe. It is the ideal of the individual invented by the inexhaustible fantasy of man – and not by following the genuine intuitive personal idea, but rather following a set of general ideals. A pale figure that affects us little emerges in this way: the fairy-tale prince, the knight without fear or blemish, the angelic maiden, the wise old man. Those are of course extremes; they are outworn figures from folk-tales. The descent into the unpoetic is palpable in them. Only the genius masters tasks of this elevation. (181)

2. It is quite otherwise with what is ideal in nature, which has a universal character. This kind of entity forms a further stratum of objects everywhere the object concerns human things – not only persons themselves. Whether in this case it is always a question of the a deeper stratum is uncertain, but in one sense it is so in all cases, that is, here we deal with things that are more distant from what is concrete and intuitive.

In life also we frequently see in the destiny of an individual, in his struggle or his guilt, an image of our own life; we identify with the hero while reading a novel – whether we do so rightly or not – we thereby enter into his world, we win or lose with him. All that rests upon a certain kind of generalization, upon the inarticulate knowledge that "so it fares also with others."

The poet cannot of course rest content with such obvious generalities. There are generalities lying far more deeply hidden, and which do not open themselves so easily to everyone. That, for example, "happiness" more easily comes to him who does not pursue it; that one's own action "brands" the one who did it; that people's loving sympathy is not measured by the advantages and abilities of one's own person but by our sympathetic participation in their lives – those are things that one never stops learning. They do not engage a man when told of them by a person of experience. But they reach out to him when they become intuitively visible in the image of a human life.

The poet does not express these general truths in words – that is, he does not "pronounce" upon them – he lets them appear in his characters. Only in that form can they affect us concretely and convincingly. The poet moves, in a certain sense, between two perils with such generalities. If they fail to meet the mark entirely, or if they are hardly recognizable as such, the poetry seems "flat"; it lacks what concerns everyone and what is important to all. But if he puts them too far in the foreground, and makes them explicit themes, if he in fact pronounces upon them, they seem unpoetic; that means they will not affect us at all, however profound they may be.

The genuine poet allows these truths to appear only upon persons and events hidden behind the eloquent details presented in the middle strata. That means: he presents them just as life also at times reveals them (when a man knows how to choose his words), in the image of the single case, often in the form of a puzzle, so that the reader has something to puzzle out. Thus in mature years we read many works of poetry with a quite different understanding and even with different aesthetical enjoyment than we did in youth. (182)

e) Ideas in literature

General ideas conceivably play the largest role in literature. They belong most authentically to its "material," and the specific, concrete materials are often chosen with reference to them. However, it is by no means the case that one should have to express them as a kind of principle; that happens rarely. The general or universal also need not have the form of a moral idea, as in the above examples; it can be of a much darker, irrational kind. It can, for example, take the form of a metaphysical disquietude, a living anxious fear, an inexplicable sense of uncertainty – something like the feeling of impotence before the countless and incalculable powers that affect one's fate.

A great number of general ideas in poetry are of a religious kind. This is because much great poetry in earlier times, like the other arts too, grew upon the soil of religious sensibility. And here, too, it is true that the average poet directly utters these ideas of his, while the genius allows them to appear in the destiny and in the attitudes of is characters (he lets them have faith, doubt, go astray, find the way back, "wrestle with God" …), and that is quite different from expressing one's convictions. Naturally, general world-views of all kinds function here. They may work themselves out even as far as the characters' love life and create harm or blessedness there.

Such general ideas may extend to absolutely all areas of life, even to the political sphere. One can find many important examples where the idea of the freedom of a people forms the very backbone of a literary work. It makes no difference whose freedom is at stake or against whom one is fighting; what is alone important is that sympathy be awakened for the oppressed and hate be felt for the oppressor.

These political ideas are especially instructive, for we can see in them clearly that it is not primarily a question of playing them off against each other, clarifying them, or even just uttering them, but merely of making them accessible to feeling. And that happens not in the course of their analysis, but in the action: by means of the injustice, heedlessness, and scorn of the powerful; by means of the indignation, rage, impotence, and despair on the side of the weak.

No art utters so many ideas as literature. And, in contrast, what the man of intellect, or even the philosopher, has to say about them is quickly forgotten. But we still may ask: why in contrast do they disappear so completely? The poet is usually not a thinker; he is not the one to grasp ideas most adequately and deeply. How does it come about, then, that the poet utters them most adequately?

But that is just the whole thing: he does not utter them at all; he just lets them appear. It is hard for the philosopher to utter general ideas; he has to hit the bull's eye, to show their parameters (define them). He must, especially, draw out of them the objectively universal as such, and make it (183) evident. The poet requires none of that. No one calls him to account. He needs only to point them out, but not point to the universal as such – each person can easily discover the universal element for himself – but point only to certain characteristic features of individual happenings, of personal feelings, passions, decisions, etc. That is sufficient to him.

It is clear that this frees the poet immeasurably from such burdens. After all, one can point to many things whose universal meaning one can darkly sense without naming them by name or even without being able to explain them. The poet not only does not have to do the latter, he must hold himself back from explanation. Explaining is not his business. The universal idea the poet has in mind should remain veiled, half in secrecy. Only out of the events may it speak. The poet does not have to "know," in the strong sense, about it. Just this element of ignorance makes him capable of allowing it to speak out of the poetry, without him speaking of it.

But let us not now turn the spear around. We are not saying that the poet has it easy. In a certain sense, it is precisely the height of human capacity to integrate characters, events, destinies, passions and actions, so that the meaning of general ideas springs forth from them – and, even more, without obscuring their concrete individuality.

This capacity is not given to everyone who can create rhymes or fit together dramatic scenes. Scores of youths try their luck in the poetic arts, but produce pieces often with little beauty. Why is it that so many give it up later, even though they have learned to measure themselves against greater poetry, even though their own expectations have grown? There is only one possible answer: because most of them are wise enough to recognize that they lack ideas; they mark well that they have no insight into the depths of human life, and that at bottom the pleasing shapes they trace are hollow inside. Or: they have ideas, and they have beautiful language, but the former do not appear in the latter. The gift of looking-through upon what is significant, and the capacity to speak it in the language of life – that is, the language of acting and suffering, of hate and love – is and remains a rare gift.

f) Toward a survey of the strata

Overall, we have counted here seven strata of literature. Only literary works could contain such riches. But this is true only for works of the high style: the epic, the novel, and the drama. And even there it is not always the case that all the strata are developed in the same way.

In literature of a more modest kind, the case is often simpler. Lyric poetry does not develop a plot; no conflicts, etc. appear in it – none of that belongs to its (184) type. It leaps directly from the sphere of the external (perhaps from the surroundings, etc.) to the stratum of feeling and moods; it is able moreover to let us know something of the nature of fate (as in the fragment of Sappho) – perhaps even something universally human – but it has no need of such things.

Lyric poetry fills its function entirely simply with this lesser aspiration. No doubt, it fills it often in a more perfect way – perhaps just because its aspiration does not aim so high. This idea is connected with two things: 1. with the very tight framing of the poetic work – so to speak, its miniature size –, and 2. with the peculiar external organization of its language, which the lyric permits in these dimensions. In these ways a certain concentration arises, both of what can be said directly and of what cannot be said and can only appear.

In general, this compression of thought to the most extreme brevity seems a challenge to the reader or listener to evaluate the transparency of the little that is said. No harm is done to the work if, with this concentration, all the background elements remain fixed in a certain vagueness – or at least in a state of ambiguity. What is vague, what has been only tacitly suggested, contributes rather a positive element to the lyric poem. The verses speak, as it were, like a person overwhelmed by feeling to which he cannot give voice; he keeps to things of little importance while yet hoping that they will make his feelings comprehensible.

One may survey in this manner the genera of literature – in part their conventional names, as the distinctions between them are. That would take us too far afield. Another matter is more important. When we have grasped these strata rightly, we must not use them to engage in pedantry. We should not insist, in the case of every literary work, even the very greatest, that they all can be clearly distinguished and, as it were, their nature can be distilled.

These are only principles that are generally valid, not literary straitjackets in which everything can be dressed by force. No doubt, one may say about the drama and the novel (the good ones) that all the strata are always present – up to the penultimate (that of the individual idea). But the order of appearance is not for that reason always the same, especially not in the middle strata. "Destiny," for example, can appear directly from the manner of the action (as is usual in Schiller[56]), or even just from the inwardness of psychic structure and the subjectivity of individual sensibility. Naturally, both need not be strictly separated; they cannot be so in any case, because in life the two are interlinked. Yet it makes

---

56 [Translator's note:] Johann Christoph Friedrich von Schiller (1759–1805).

an essential difference to the kind of literature whether the one or the other is dominant.

We are not considering the possible absence of a stratum, at least not for the middle strata. This is conceivable in the case of the two final strata, and even more of the sixth. The middle strata are tied so tightly together in life that it would seem (185) to do violence if a poet wanted to eliminate one of them entirely, just where he intended to represent active life. In simpler forms of literature the situation is otherwise, that is, where only mood, feeling, pain, or yearning are represented. For that reason, lyric poetry has much more freedom of movement – but of course, on the other hand it is tied to much more strict external elements of style. It is thus by no means, as some poetasters believe, the easier art. But that is simply more a question of the bestowal of form in the strata, and no longer one of the stratification itself.

What we may draw from the series of strata by way of a strict law is the non-exchangeability of the strata, or, perhaps more correctly, the laws of their place in the whole. The poet can allow a stratum that is clearly intuitable but which is still close to the foreground (for example, movement and gesture) to come off badly. That will seem unpoetic, but in certain cases, it may be necessary. But he cannot allow this movement and gestures of his characters to "appear" out of the plot (the genuine and inner one) or out of their psychic life. Where that appears to be the case, something else is at play: the inner person appears in the light of her actions, or her emotional reactions to events, and the fantasy of the reader, departing from these appearances, paints the corresponding facial expression (amazement, horror, etc.) upon the otherwise pale color of the characters.

By close examination, however, we may confirm this as nothing more than a device of the writer. For in reality it happens that the emotional responses become concrete only via a detour through allusions to psychic life. And if we ask why the writer takes such a detour, we may respond: because language is relatively lacking in direct pictorial expressions for bodily movement, just insofar as such movement is intended to be expressive, and gestures are relatively rich in expressions for changes in feeling. If the poet speaks of amazement or of fear, the reader sees directly the corresponding facial expression. ... This seemed to be a reversal, but it shows itself to be more a question of verbal expression.

Chapter 13: The Series of Strata in the Fine Arts

a) The order of strata in sculpture

The richness of the strata in literature does not extend to the other arts. That is so, on the one hand, because of the limitations their material causes them; on the other because of the medium and its circle of tasks; and yet again because of the special artistic means that are available to them. It is and remains strange that the least concrete matter, as is used by literature, in the end leaves open the greatest possibilities. It is the only matter that is not sensible. One could therefore make the inference before all other complications (186) arise, that sensible matter affects us in a limiting way – not only in the choice of themes, but also in the emergence of the strata. We will not try to anticipate here a judgment on whether that is so. What is important for the time being is that this relationship announce itself at this point.

The fine arts are close neighbors of literature – just as "representational" arts, but also because the circle of their materials overlaps to an extent. That would not be the case if, for example, sculpture went no further than the representation of movement and bodily presence, and did not touch the psychic being of man. It touches psychic being in fact, and lets it appear in the object – although not, of course to the same degree as the poetic arts, but unmistakably concrete and visible to intuition, as only art can let a thing appear.

Yet the first great epoch of Greek sculpture – its "classical period" – manifests characteristically little of this. True, it brings us as far as the sublime posture of the gods, but not as far as their active physical life. The aims and will of the artists are directed towards different ends, their tasks are more simply defined. And perhaps just because of this, this epoch in the history of art achieved its peculiar perfection, which people later called "classic." The law we enunciated above concerning perfection is adhered to here in the most clear and evident manner: the simpler work is more easily brought to perfection. That means, in this context, that the work of art with fewer strata achieves the greatest heights that are possible for it, given its level and the means at its disposal.

How can we express these matters in the language of the strata? To answer this question, let us return for a moment to the case of classical Greek sculpture: what strata are in fact present there? It seems that, despite all limitations, we can reckon with four distinct strata. 1. The sensible real stratum with its visible form gives us the foreground. 2. There follows the stratum of movement and rest, for bodily rest is in the broad sense an element of movement, for example, temporary repose. This stratum is already beyond the real. 3. Then behind the second appears the living quality proper of the represented human body, that which distinguishes it from a lifeless body, that is, the dynamic power over itself that is indirectly made visible. 4. And finally there appears – leaping, as it were, over all else – the power of divinity, the superior peace and sublimity of the gods, far above puny men. The same is true of representations of demigods, heroes, and nymphs.

Naturally, one may ask how such a leap is possible. The answer is quite simple; even the purely vital power, if it is sufficiently intensified, appears super-human; that is expressed very primitively, but it can be shown to be so. Think, for example, of the speech of Zeus to the assembled gods at the beginning of the Eighth Book of the *Iliad*, where he challenges the gods to take a rope and drag him down from Olympus. And the gods – (187) they are amazed by his talk, but they accept it, and do not dare to contradict him.

That changes greatly later on. The warlike spirit, fear, anxiety, suffering, the sense of being marked by death mark themselves on their features; these become transparent; the psychic element appears behind them. From thence, it is a long way to the psychological forms of expression known to Michelangelo (the *Bound Slave*, the *Pietà*, the *David*). But only the depth of feeling and the power to act increases; at bottom it is the same here as formerly.

It is similar to marble busts, wherever a personal "resemblance" is genuinely striven after. To speak more accurately, they strove after an understanding of what is personal in a man. What appears here is not simply what is externally individual, but what is inward or psychic – occasionally in rich detail. Of course, one cannot have the second without the first, but what is noted is the element of the psychic-personal (for example, in the late Roman portraiture).

Old Egyptian portraiture calls for much reflection in this context – with its mixture of conventional forms and highly personal treatment of the features, which maintain the sense of individuality. A man as an individual is seen as having two faces, the universal and the personal, and nothing mitigates the opposition – for example, where the face is individualized, but the rest of the body is understood conventionally.

A step further and one reaches the sculpture of our times. Its greatest representatives – no doubt very few in number – have reached a new level. Here the psychic and inward is brought to expression in certain figures just for their own sakes, but not an individual element at all, but rather something universal – that is, a kind of middle level, not the universally human but rather the typical.

A good example of this is Rodin's *The Thinker*, as with many of his other works. There is something strange about them: how can an artist represent a process like "thinking" in stone? That is, in something that is most foreign to it? And yet the impossible is made possible; one sees the effort of thought in the stance of the figure. Of course, we do not experience "what" he is thinking about; but that does not affect the matter itself. What is grasped is precisely just that which can at best be shown by way of a detour over the dynamics of the body. And that this becomes possible is the miracle of art. The detour, however, passes over the middle strata: one might say indeed over the psychophysical relation that makes psychic effort visible in the living body.

b) The exterior strata in painting

We have already spoken (above in Chap. 10) of strata in painting with reference to the portrait. The large number of strata was clear to see in this case. The parallel to literature, on the one hand, and to sculpture on the other, has also been pointed out. But painting is not (188) only portraiture, it includes a variety of other general types, as literature does, and we will have to inquire how much of what we have done here earlier will carry over to the other genera.

Sculpture and painting have two things in common: first, the matter they use is entirely physical, and second they have access to the very highest material (the kind of objects that can be represented) of which human beings are aware. The latter is apparent from the fact that there is just as much religious sculpture as painting. And this fact has had further implications throughout history, when we recall that great epochs of both art forms have grown in the soil of a highly developed religious life, and their most important themes are found in ideas of a religious kind. Thus the sculpture of the Egyptians and the Greeks; so also the painting of the Renaissance and to an extent that of the Dutch.

As far as sensible matter is concerned, we should observe from the aesthetical standpoint that these two arts, the "fine" arts, are the only ones that are "representational" in concrete matter, and thus bring themes, objects, and *sujets*, before the intuitive eye. Literature is also just as representational, although not in sensible matter; and music of course works as much in sensible matter, but music as such is not representational. That music can be representational, though in an indirect manner, is another matter.

Additionally, we note of course an extreme contrast between the materials used by the two arts. On the one hand, we have pure spatial form, which is indeed capable of being structured even to the finest details. On the other, we have spatial forms that can be reduced to a two-dimensional projection, but still offer all the gaiety of color; and where these are not found, as in drawing, there is still available the play with degrees of light and shadow. People have argued over which loss is the greater: the relinquishment of color by sculpture, or the relinquishment of full spatial form in three dimensions by painting.

Yet both arts have from this perspective their limitations. Sculpture is before all else limited to what is near, alive, and almost even to the human body. With respect to its diversity, that is no small area of competence, but it is incomparably narrower than that of painting, which also has access to the human body as an object. Its superiority lies indisputably in its capacity to deal with distant objects, and it even knows how to unite what is far and what is nearby in one "picture." This union does not require compromise; distance in space is not suppressed or deceptively made to vanish, but treated precisely with emphasis, and quite objectively represented. ...

One cannot hold back from drawing the implication that the direct imitation of spatial form is far more limited, with respect to the representation of spatial configurations, than a form of space that has separated itself from three-dimensional form and represents its objects by a detour through a picture surface of two dimensions. The latter is the spatiality of the "picture," regardless of whether a drawing or a painting. In the mastery of space, painting is (189) superior to sculpture, and this is so just because it has detached itself from the sensible immediacy of spatial form. Seen from the outside this seems a paradox. Yet right here we find the key to the diversity of possible representation in art.

This fact is not without importance for the order of strata in painting. For in a spatial art form, the circle of themes is determined in it by spatial range and the uniformity of perspective. Both clearly extend much further in painting than in sculpture. Themes such as landscape, ocean and sky, cannot be treated by sculpture; indeed not only such matters, but also farmyards, the interior of living quarters or of churches, etc.

The discussion up to now has also taken drawing into its account, which, if we set color to the side, is close to sculpture. However, with color begins the great qualitative richness that in life, too, marks the distinction between seeing and other forms of perception. Painting makes use of this special "distinction." For the manifold of qualities – with its inner lawfulness, oppositions, and constant blending into each other – is used by the artist as a language whose meanings are endlessly refined and which, if correctly applied, may express the most imponderable things.

This is not to say that individual colors have "meaning" – people have made up such games on occasion, but they fall far from the mark. Single oppositions, contrasts, the blending of colors, do not yet give meaning. That becomes possible only in the larger contexts, which always manifest structured themes, where the combinations of colors appear that are of concern to us here; they are unique, and serve the transparency that, perhaps by chance, allows living energy to appear.

It is important to be clear about this matter, for again certain kinds of themes in painting depend upon it – and, with that, the specificity of the relationships among the strata of a painting. There are in fact kinds of themes in painting that are determined primarily by the play of colors. This is well known in "still life";

we see it precisely in the work of its greatest representatives. It is true also for representations of interiors. But what is even more important: it is also generally valid for the landscape. As landscape is such a large branch of painting, the relationship we speak of shows its entire force.

We noted above in this context, that the eye of an artist in fact discovered the landscape, however not in painting but rather in seeing. Yet what is it, then, in the natural landscape that captivates such eyes? Of course, it may be several things. But there is one that must always be present: the bright colors, one after the other, just as they appear to us while looking, for example, past the trunks of trees into a clearing. They surprise and convince us, they are unsought-after and yet put in order as though by an invisible hand. And we should add: just as they not only contrast with each other and close up together to form the unity of an image, they are also different in light and shadow, and against the horizon are tinged with blue. (190)

For a person whose eyes have once been opened for these things – and for many others related to them – they do not easily let him go. For the entire world is what in fact has been opened to him. For that reason, the eyes of the painter return him so often to the landscape. It is as though one has discovered in it the adumbration of the principle of the picture – of course after separating it from deeper backgrounds, for a landscape does not need them. Perhaps also the transparency of color is greatest for these kinds of objects: this applies specifically to works of art that do not represent thing-like objects or structural unities, but give us only selections from the bright world about us that themselves may possess pictorial unity.

c) The inner strata in painting

Up to now, our discussion concerned only the external strata of painting: Those, specifically, that stand very close to the real foreground. We have here, corresponding to the distinctions made earlier, the appearance of space and objects, and the appearance of light. Here we must also include the level in which movement and animation appear, and it is perhaps fitting once again to distinguish these two, for "life" may appear in a picture in ways different from motion as such (the latter also appears, for example, in a wind-swept landscape).

But now we are already standing in the inner strata of painting. For without doubt the living quality that appears here belongs to a middle stratum that one must count among the inner ones. Perhaps the same is true even for the appearance of movement. For we must not forget that painting is similar to sculpture in that it can portray directly only what stands still; the speck of paint upon the canvas moves no more than carved marble, and from the radical stillness only the one narrow route of letting-appear leads to movement. Nevertheless, that route can open up considerable riches.

We must moreover consider that painting is the prototypical art of sensible vision (most likely the image of "aesthetics" was originally taken from it), and that the physical substance it uses permits that role, but also limits it more strictly than other arts are limited by the matter in which they are realized. The painter is quite right to remain in the sensible world, or at least not to depart from it too far. One can say that in the same sense and to the same degree about no other art form. For that reason, the artist is always drawn back from all supersensible visions to the sensible world and to color. It is almost as though he feels himself to have sinned when he distanced himself from the visible.

And yet painting does achieve the representation of what is psychic and inward in man. We spoke of that matter above in connection with portraiture. But this is by no means true of the portrait alone. For there exists an abundance of themes about the human condition that force themselves upon the artist, of scenes (191) that extend from everyday life to the miracle and mystery scenes of religion. The Dutch have demonstrated that every harmless occupation of men and women at home, or scenes of eating and drinking – and many other all-too-human matters – have their painterly side. This was a very strange discovery that no one before their times would have believed.

Even when it was not originally intended, some of the psychic life of men came to be represented, even if nothing more than taking joy in life. And – given the human condition – this something forces itself forward and becomes the main object. That occurs, for example, in historical scenes, but it happens also in the once much-loved mythical scenes. It occurs especially in religious scenes – whether these circle about the figures of Maria and the Christ, or about God the Father and the creation of the world, as in the ceiling of the Sistine Chapel.

By close observation, we will find here again all strata that were familiar to us from literature, but only in a much-altered graduated series and indeed in a different manner of appearing. But it is by no means the case that the last and most background elements come off badly. The limitation in force here is rather of a different kind, namely one that is drawn beyond the limits of what is static and only momentarily visible, i.e., drawn beyond a limit that belongs to the foreground and is rooted in the physical matter of painting.

One may not object that the painter of scenes is simply excluded from the natural circle of themes in painting! For the role such painting has played in the development of art is too great. No doubt, this issue is tied to the "commissions" of an extra-artistic kind, especially in the case of religious scenes. But can one seriously just think away the abundance of biblical scenes that have fixed themselves among the themes of painting? The group-scenes of Raphael and Leonardo, the long lists of Madonnas and Crucifixions? Or just Rembrandt's scenes from the Old Testament? They all belong within painting. And just as the technique of color, light, and the way of seeing develops in and through them, so also there develops the expression of inward human psychic life.

If we now summarize what painting aims at in the representation of the human world – we leave out pure landscape painting at first – and ask ourselves quite soberly what the series of strata in force here looks like, we may assemble the following points.

1. The level of the real elements, with its visible specks of paint, form the foreground.
2. Behind it, three-dimensional spatiality appears, things, and the light within the picture.
3. In this circle of things, there further appears motion – now made intuitively visible in a phase of movement or in a pose. (192)
4. The living quality of the figures appears in their state of motion, a quality strongly underscored by the "lifelike" color.
5. In the living quality of the motion appears further the human psychic realm, man's inner life. There appear segments of the situation, the passions, the dispositions, and the plot.
6. In unusual cases, something of the idea of the individual appears (in portraits of unusual depth).
7. And finally, there appear various kinds of ideal universalities. Often this is consciously made part of the theme, as in religious scenes, but often it is also completely camouflaged. Knowledge of the meaning of the scene, of the "legend" behind it plays an independent role here. Oddly, such knowledge usually does not reveal much that assists us in viewing the object aesthetically.

If one compares the list of strata in painting with those of sculpture, what immediately strikes one is the richness of content in the former. With sculpture, one can distinguish clearly only four strata from each other. The reason for this difference is found, on the one hand, in the quite different relationships of the material in which they are realized (there was no need in sculpture for the detour through the two-dimensional planes; with that is eliminated also the first intermediate stratum); on the other hand, however, we find in sculpture a very limited appearance of the psychic and inward elements. Similarly, sculpture does not permit a separate stratum for the appearance of inanimate objects, for it is limited to what is living.

The result of a comparison with the strata in literature is quite different. We saw that literature also has to do with seven strata. But in part, they are not the same strata. Immediately behind the level of words began that of movement and gesture along with the words spoken by the characters – the dialogue. The intermediate place characteristic of painting that is given to the appearance of spatiality and the appearance of activity and gesture is therewith eliminated; more accurately put, they are not properly eliminated but are entirely taken up in the stratum of activity and gesture; and in this same stratum belongs the appearance of the quality of life. The strata two to five that were listed for painting thus constitute only one stratum in literature.

Why this is so can be answered without difficulty; Literature is simply concerned only with people and their conditions in life, their actions, and the like. Any other miscellany of the world outside is treated by it as a garment or as decoration. Thus it passes over the sensible structure and draws it to itself only according to the measure of its transparency for what is psychic. In contrast, painting has in this preliminary theater of the human scene its most powerful thematic material. For that reason, it tends to rest awhile with them, render them in detail, and allow the psychic elements appear indirectly by means of them. For painting is most strongly bound to the visible, and, in general, it is the art most tightly bound to the sensible world.

Thus it is when we compare the middle strata. When it is a question of the deepest inner strata, we find the poetic art significantly superior – simply because it is a temporal art: it is not tied to the unique (193) moment, and can follow up on events, situations, developments, actions and their consequences, and the unfolding of a destiny during an entire lifetime. For that reason in a literary background a series of strata are inserted, which painting either fails to render entirely or is able to let appear only by way of suggestion. These are the strata: first, the situation and the action within it; second, the bestowal of psychic form and character; third, destiny and the manner in which it is borne.

Here the boundaries of painting can be clearly stated. These boundaries do not mean, as was already said, that it cannot enter the last background element of the human situation. These come forward as entirely comprehensible universal ideas, occasionally even as the idea of an individual. But they are limited to the sidelights.

Painting – corresponding to its entirely sensible matter – is the art more tied to the objective strata of the foreground, but within those limits it is inexhaustibly variable; literature is more attached to the background strata, and is therefore less sensibly given and concrete, but in return it is the art that dwells at the depths of human life and exhausts its contents quite differently.

d) Painting and natural objects

In one respect, the order of strata in painting that has been presented here does not do justice to the greatest potentials of its nature. It took explicitly as its sole purpose establishment of its representation of humanity. That is justified insofar as here alone the deepest strata can be made objectively present, and here surely is where its greatest tasks lie. But the entirety of painting is not thereby exhausted, and it is still possible that certain general traces of its nature have been overlooked.

What is still left is all painting that consciously limits its concerns to natural objects. There remains thus the entire large domain of landscape painting. One may wish to include here the still life and the nude, and that has a certain justification. As to the first, it belongs here although one can still sense the hand of man on the object; as to the second, it may be included only if the painting renders only the natural physical figure.

How does it stand, then, with the painted "landscape"? Let us assume that in it the deeper strata are in fact lacking because they do not belong at all to the object: if so, what makes the painted landscape so impressive, so full of content, so near to man, so akin to mind? Historically the "pure landscape" – without any people in it – appears relatively late. It seems as if man, for whom a landscape should be something quite specific, would still have to be in it – as though the painting would hover in the air without him. This is, of course, a naïve error. But a nugget of truth is concealed in the error. That truth consists in the fact that the landscape, viewed aesthetically, (194) is there only for the beholder. And, indeed, only for a beholder that is viewing it in a certain way, namely by letting it register in him and letting himself enjoy it. Through this detour, man in his entire psychic nature enters again into the landscape, no longer as a component but rather as a condition of the object – and that in a very special manner.

These thoughts are not to be understood in all generality, as they are understood for all things that have being as an object, even for the theoretical ones, such that something can become an object only "for" a subject (the law of standing over-against [*Gegenstehen* or *Objektion*]); rather they have a very specific meaning: aesthetically, the landscape does not consist in formations of land, woods, and fields, but first in the definite pictorial standpoint that permits the viewing of all of those things from a specific point in space. But with the slightest shift in the latter, in the specific point in space, the "landscape" is changed; it changes similarly with changes in light, the position of the sun, the weather – not to mention seasonal changes. The painter thus captures a momentary, quite ephemeral effect.

This is not like the observation of an animal, a flower, a human face, where, no doubt, the details are altered according to one's "standpoint" but are of the same fixed type as a whole: one returns to them after hours, days, or weeks, and finds there the identical "object."

In "landscape" the situation is quite different. A cloud formation draws up, and the picture is changed. Or, for example, the artist does not find the point from which he previously painted, and everything in the picture shifts. Here is the reason why in landscape the person of the viewer – his chosen point in space and time – plays such an important constitutive role. Just the role by itself of perspective in landscape art would be sufficient to demonstrate that fact. For without one taking a point of view there is no perspective. This is true for other themes in painting: interiors, groups of persons, scenes. But with them, it is not as much the point of view that is the determining element.

Thus, it is not necessary at all to aim immediately at backgrounds expressive of feeling in order to find man, in his subjectivity, included in an "aesthetical landscape" – whether enjoyed in nature or in the painted landscape. What is always also represented in the work is not only "what is seen," but also the beholder's way of seeing; in fact, much more belongs there than we have named. What we said above (under b) belongs there, that is, the great qualitative riches of light and color, the effects of contrast and shading, the infinitely subtle language of transitions and mutuality of effect, for which effects of light and color no other descriptive means would be adequate.

Here are the roots of the circle of themes in painting that are determined by nothing else than the play of color. For that reason every discovery of some pure possibility in painting is epoch-making for new developments (195) in art itself; that was the case with the Dutch landscapes, with French impressionism, with modern en plein air painting.[57] Before all else, painting is a "life in seeing," an art that is rooted more deeply in the senses than the other arts, and where even with themes of the most elevated kind the sensible element remains prominent.

In this manner, for example, is a vista upon a broad plain with hills ranging in the distance, framed by what is near and close by, perhaps a large foreground with grasses and hanging branches, the tight pictorial propinquity of near and far, which are seen as spatially separated but in fact are all simply seen together. That and how one can render such things in line and color is not immediately obvious; we recall the discovery of aerial perspective, painting en plein air, aerial painting, and the spatial placing in painting of figures in front of and behind each other: all depend upon discoveries in ways of seeing. And thus it is with foliage

---

57 [Translator's note:] *Hellmalerei.* Literally, "bright painting." Hartmann perhaps means instead *hell-dunkel Malerei*, which translates chiaroscuro; that, however, is a Renaissance development.

painting, dewdrop painting, highlight painting, with the colorfulness of shadows and the disappearance of the colorless (black) from the field of view.

It would require an entire chapter on the technique of painting to do it justice. For technical means are not external to painting; they are largely tied to the ways we see. And when we just think for a moment how every new way of seeing is also a new kind of intellectual openness, even a new feature of the psyche in itself, we may realize the nature of the interconnection between man and landscape in the aesthetical sense. Only by means of this detour can we return to the question of the background in the painted landscape: namely to the question of the deeper background strata, which really pertain only to man as his own object.

People had correctly seen these things in the element of "mood," and had seen beyond this phenomenon to more specific emotional content in landscape. But they had also included in aesthetical theory things that do not hold true. It neither is true that landscape itself possesses moods (cheerful, gloomy, chilly, cozy) nor is it true that we, the observers, simply project our moods into it (theory of sympathy). Rather the secret lies in the painter's way of seeing, provided he finds the technical means to prescribe moods to the observer and thereby draw him into his way of seeing.

Mood of course belongs to the observer, not the one he arbitrarily brings with him, but the one that is objectively required by the art object: the mood that has been made objective in its sensible detail. In this sense one may, with good cause, assert the opposite: mood pertains to the landscape itself, it is its own; and the mood that appears upon it is its "own" provided that it is the landscape "seen thus," as it is seen through the artist's way of seeing.

This relation cannot be presented in any simpler fashion. But only its capacity for articulation (its definability) is what is complicated about it. It itself is the simple consequence of the ontological qualities of aesthetic objects as such, (196) provided, to be sure, that everything not actually sensible in them exists only relative to a subject that beholds it adequately. That is, of course, true of all works of art. Here it is especially palpable, because it does not refer to a mediated higher form of beholding alone, but to sensible vision itself. The artist intensifies this, far beyond the way we see things in everyday life, and upon this painterly addition to sensible beholding depends all else – including even the most subtle moods.

Something here must still be developed. Recall what was said here at the outset (Chap. 1c) about the emotional content of perception. As everything that is seen and heard forces us to go beyond itself, to apprehend something else that is not perceptible (our apprehension of men, of faces, etc.), so in natural and primitive consciousness perception drives us toward affective elements: the unknown, the uncanny, the terrifying, fearsome, or, this too, the familiar, trusted, salutary, even toward endearing kindness.

Our perceptions of nature especially are filled with such accents; we are touched by the warm sunshine, by the flickering air on a summer noonday, the tender azure of faraway horizons, the dark wood, and the cool of the evening. We are not indifferent when faced with what we see, we sense it as approaching us, as though "it demands something from us" – whether good or evil; everything affects us in a calming or arousing manner. Even in a consciousness made wise by age, where these affects have been inhibited, they do not disappear entirely; under certain circumstances they can become quite noticeable. To an artistic consciousness, these accents emerge by their own effort and give to what is seen the colors of moods tinged with color: the "cheerfulness" of a colorful meadow with its flowers, the "secretiveness" of the green forest half in darkness, the "uncanniness" of deep shadows or gorges, the "freshness" of the trees blowing in the wind.

The emergence of such primitively felt elements is almost identical with the withdrawal of an attitude centered upon practical objects. This withdrawal, however, is characteristic precisely of the aesthetical beholding of a landscape. Thus, the emotional side of seeing becomes alive at the same time as color and light. It is as if the emotional elements in everyday awareness had been artificially locked behind closed doors; yet as soon as this kind of awareness is separated from artistic beholding, the bolts spring open, and the whole colorful blaze of affectivity comes forward and paints over all visible color.

This is no doubt only a point of departure for greater and deeper feelings and their contents, but this beginning shows nonetheless how the affective element is tied to what is seen – to a definite way of looking. For between such experiences and the deepest immersion of the self in the forms of nature is only a difference in degree. (197)

Chapter 14: Strata in Musical Composition

a) Levels of musical unity

The inquiries conducted in the First Part (Chap. 7) demonstrated that there is some difficulty in exhibiting the structure of strata in the non-representational arts. If that was already the case for the rough distinctions between the real foreground and the unreal background, how much more will that be true for the fine distinctions that begin with the splitting up of the background?

Or, perhaps, in the end no splitting up of the background takes place? The two arts with which this question is concerned are music and architecture. In both we find the situation regarding "appearance" complicated. In contrast, in ornamental art, where the situation is simpler, there is no longer a question, because the deeper background strata are lacking.

In music the situation allows everyone to assume without further ado that they have access in feeling to its background elements: it is after all apparent that the sounds and melodies are not there for their own sakes, but for the sake of some psychic content that does not just express itself in them, but pours itself out and "enjoys itself" to the full. Note that this latter phenomenon is an essential element, for much of our emotional life finds itself otherwise inhibited by life, and cannot enjoy and express itself to the fullest.

That is not simply the opinion of musically elevated persons who have been educated in musical performance or in music theory and criticism; it is also that of the musical dilettante who makes music a part of his life, hums a little tune as he walks or works, and lets himself be drawn into better music for the sake of relaxation.

Naturally, there is something understandable about this conception. The question is only what it is, what it consists in, what psychic contents are at issue here. Further, how can these contents be translated into music, if in fact they can, or how can they "appear" in the substance of sounds – and even whether we have then a genuine appearance. For in genuine appearance one must be able to recognize whatever it is that appears.

Thus far, we are still dealing in a very rough way with the aporetics of music. A more refined form, however, appears just behind it. This depends, on the one hand, upon the position of the first background stratum, about which we spoke above, which forms a tonal whole in a great style, but which cannot be heard all at once. This stratum – or are there several? – is not as yet a stratum with psychic content, but the leap to that psychic level must be taken from upon it.

On the other hand, a group of aporia appears as soon as we move from pure music to program music. Since the latter forms a significant part of the total mass of extant compositions, one cannot pass over them indifferently as with inferior music, but one must consider their problematic along with the others. (198)

As for the first of the two questions, one may quickly appreciate that program music itself takes on a certain analogy to painting. As painting, with its world of colors, gives scope to inexhaustible possibilities, so also does music, with its world of tones, sequences (melodies) and harmonies. The dimensions alone of musical structures remind us of colors: the height of a tone, its dynamics, the chord, the transition to another key (modulation) and rhythms (time-value, tempos, changes in tempo).

One is correct to expect at this point that in music as in painting a group of more "outer" background strata will appear that are all closer to the sensible material. That means that the stratum characterized above, i.e., of the musically audible whole, splits itself up further, and does so this side of the psychic elements that are present within it. This splitting up is difficult to follow, because the thematic handle we find in music is often lacking in the representational arts.

Nonetheless, it is possible to point out some features of the process. Clearly, it is a leap when one – as happened in Chap. 7b – passes directly from an audible heard sequence, as far as the mind can retain it, to the unity of a movement or an entire composition. Something with which to form tighter unities is set between these two, and a reference is thereby created upon which the greater whole can be built.

For example, there is the well-known law of four beats to a measure that under-lies such forms of unity. No doubt there are others that could take its place, but in such cases there will always be smaller closed unities that are developed musically as such, and are used as elements in the construction of a piece. In classical music, they are often emphasized by a return to the tonic. Such unities come close to what can be retained by the mind, and they affect us like sensibly heard unities, although they are in fact no longer strictly capable of being heard together by the senses. The whole, which is spread out in time, begins to close up in them.

The return of the main theme belongs here also, along with variations upon it, in which it can be recognized but still experienced as different. Here is rooted the principle of variation, which can reach into the consciously designed *"thema con variationi"* – a fundamental form of musical structure that can dominate just as much in the *"Lied"* as in a sonata. The classic form of the "first movement" is built upon it: the repetition of an entire section and, after the insertion of the "development," the variations, then two strophes and a coda. The addition of the "trio" in the scherzo serves similarly as a structural principle: these forms relate to almost all chamber music – quartets, trios, sonatas – and also to symphonies. We encounter them again in choral music.

Upon this is erected the "character of the movement proper," the unity of the larger construct – for which those elements that were analyzed above are most genuinely valid: the retention of what has faded away; the music's (199) foresha-dowing what new things are to come; its pointing forward; the continual expecta-tion and surprise, as also the holding together of the whole "at the last measures," when the piece is finally done.

An enormous growth of this "structural whole" takes place again in so-called polyphonic music: individual phrases are written into each other in such a way that they produce the harmonies of the whole only in concert with each other. In this process, the harmony contains a kind of inner necessity that is clearly audible within it.

The "fugue" is the most extreme of all musical structures. It possesses a unity and wholeness of a higher order; in it the phenomena of rising up out of its own resources and of steady growth in size while in a condition of purity are present as nowhere else in music. That fact is most apparent when one compares to it the relatively loose unities that larger compositions (those in several movements) possess: the harmonic connections between the movements in a symphony or a sonata. And there are even looser intercorrelations, for example in the "opera," where extra-musical themes determine the music to a great extent.

Therefore, if one wishes to do justice to this phenomenon of the step-like structure of musical unity, one will have to split open the stratum that inserts itself behind the sensibly audible into several strata. It is not important to determine how many of them there are, but in any case, one may, without risking much, distinguish three or four.

1. The stratum of closed musical phrases (the "law of four beats to a measure").
2. The broader "themes" and variations.
3. Musical "movements" (here we find the strictest unities).
4. The harmonic interconnections between movements in the large "opus" (less strictly bound unities).

But it is not the number but rather the kind of ordered step-like structure that matters.

It is possible to make finer differentiations.

b) The inner strata of music

The other side of these aporetics lies in so-called program music. In order to evaluate them, we must orient ourselves toward the inner strata of music. For it is upon these, and not the strata of musical unity, that the possibility of giving music an extra-musical "content" depends.

There is no doubt that as one approaches from the music's external strata and passes to the inner ones, one makes a leap, a μετάβασις εἰς ἄλλο γένος [leap to another domain]. The external strata have to do with the design of purely musical forms, the "play with tones and harmonies." There is no question there of feelings and moods. But with the inner strata begins something quite different, something that belongs to the ἄλλο γένος [other genus]. This is a highly subjective (200) element belonging entirely to the psychic life of man. The former is the most objective element that one can imagine; it is purely a composed structure that is subject to analysis and is objective. What appears in the inner strata, the psychic element, is never entirely objective; it exists solidly within its subjectivity, is difficult to grasp, hard to name (at least not adequately). It is there only for the devoted listener, and apart from itself it is scarcely imaginable.

We could say: it exists only in the experience of it; but then listening to music is characterized as experience. Once this experience has passed, the music done, the hearer's efforts to force what has been experienced into the present moment are in vain. For it can be grasped nowhere except in music, precisely in specific music with its specific ordered unities, although to the hearer they seem entirely heterogeneous and external.

We should not be surprised that, in any strict theory of music, all concern for "psychic content" is rejected as mere sentimentality. Accordingly, one becomes quite rigorous: music is a strict architectural construct; it has its own laws, which are purely structural in nature. It "can do quite nicely without feelings," and the structural features of the gay color of its musical elements – timbres, transitions, modulations, etc. – are rich enough to allow a world made entirely of tones to emerge.

When people defend such theories, they are pleased to point out the most strictly architectural kind of composition, i.e., the fugue, and when they do so, it seems as if the purported autonomy of contrapuntal music is sufficient proof of the superfluity of all the feelings men "project" into music.

And yet the master of contrapuntal composition, J.S. Bach, is absolute proof of the opposite view. Take, for example, the first four pieces of *The Art of the Fugue*, or the ricercar of *A Musical Offering*, or any fugue at all from the *Well-Tempered Clavier* – as soon as one grasps the technique of listening to them properly, one will find in them, beyond the pleasure one takes in the structures, something quite different appearing: the elevation that devoted listening produces of itself. And, in fact, this is a genuine elevation of the mind, in which we sense ourselves lifted up to another world, one of purity and immensity.

This other element is experience in objective form. It belongs objectively to the music, as a thing existing in it and yet as something that thrills us most inwardly, in short, as something that appears genuinely in it, appears, more specifically, immediately in the hearing of the musical unity; it shines transparently through it.

All characterizations of this experience are weak and overly general. We have no expression for it. We say, for example, it is "solemn" or "sublime"; we speak of the "dark depths," of the "radiant," the "ravishing," "exciting," or "lofty" ... But it is easy to see that these are all only images, and in fact weak ones. For here it is not a question of pale echoes, but of a powerful force (201) that takes genuine possession of our souls – a force that pulls us along and fills the souls of the listeners, and that nonetheless stands objectively over against them in the work of music as it maintains its aesthetic distance.

Such descriptions as those we offer are merely weak images of the mystery that takes place in the devoted hearing of a musical work of art. They are entirely insufficient for determining the objective strata themselves, on which the mystery depends: the inner strata of the musical work. One sees only that these are not simply present, but are what is of significance in the work – one might say what is metaphysical about it. How, of course, the sounds and the sequences are able to make the most inward phenomena of the life of the soul appear, those beyond all verbal expression, has not yet been touched upon in the slightest.

But let us leave this question for the moment. We see at least this much, that theories of musical form are insufficient in this psychic context; here we must in fact reckon with psychic conditions that are far deeper. Music is not a chess-game with tones. Without its background in the human soul, it would be.

Music is rather a genuine revelation, and indeed, of a kind that can be expressed in no other language. This last remark is crucial. We always feel ourselves in a predicament when asked what is revealed by music; that does not argue against such a revelation, but rather for it. One can say also: music is a proclamation, one that acts by awakening the soul of the listener – to come along, to dance along, to enter a great inward vital life, to give himself over to feelings that cannot be put under categories. And in this way, the miracle of a community of listeners in the emotional experience of music takes place. Indeed, they become as one, despite their individual psychic differences – a thing that otherwise in life is scarcely possible. This is the phenomenon of the concert-hall, one, to be sure, that occurs only when a musician of true genius is playing. No doubt, all the arts have the power to unite men; they reorient souls, dress their ranks, and attune them to one another. But none has this power in the same measure as music does.

Phenomena of this kind begin no doubt always with the act of listening, but they direct us unambiguously toward the object; for they presuppose the corresponding stratum of being in the composition that is related to the being of our souls; this shows how tightly woven are the analysis of act and object. In this respect, music stands alone among the arts. Of course every work of art requires of its audience an inward correlative movement or execution. Painting and sculpture require us to look towards what the artist "sees"; literature requires us to picture along with the writer the way he pictures things. Such an effort can grow to the point at which the reader is carried along. But in music, such things take on an essentially different nature: the process of being seized, of being drawn along, is in music *a limine* [at the outset] the main thing. Looked at subjectively, we can describe it as having one's own psychic life taken up by the movement of the work and being drawn along in its mode of forward motion; it communicates this motion to the hearer, and, when he executes that motion himself, (202) it becomes his own. Thereby the relationship to the object is in fact ended and transformed into something else: the music penetrates, as it were, into the hearer, and, in his listening, becomes his.

This state of being drawn along is experienced as a kind of psychic abduction – to an order of things that is otherwise not found in one's own life, but yet to an intelligible order, an ineffable perfection, harmony, and a floating rapture: the work, the achievement of the composer, disappears – for everything about a masterly performance seems easy – and the enjoyment of the state of devoted appreciation masters the soul, tension increases and decreases, and in that way we are rescued from a state of effort and the sense of being cramped.

This is not true only of the very great compositions, which quite often demand much effort and attention on the part of the hearer. It is true also of lighter and more flirtatious music – of dances and marches, of a jolly little song or a capriccio – but in these cases the heaven to which one is abducted has fewer pretentions. Yet the music can be just as pure, just as soaring. Only the depth of enjoyment is of a different kind, and so also the stratum of psychic life that is laid hold of by the music.

c) Composition and psychic life

Nevertheless, music is always objective. How is that possible? There lies here an antinomy that we must solve. For as the listening self is absorbed into the music, the sense of standing over against the music disappears. But then how does this over-against maintain itself? And how can the inner strata into which we feel ourselves carried and ravished, nonetheless remain the objects of our reflection, which always also preserves the required aesthetical distance?

There are two ways of enjoying music. The first consists in letting oneself be lulled or swept along by it: this increases in the case of certain pieces of great music to a point at which the hearer melts into the motion of the music, in effect swims in it. A good example of this is Nietzsche's[58] description of a "submitting to the mood of *Tristan*." Such a listener misses the structural niceties of the composition. He makes it easy for himself. The other kind of listening holds the listener more tightly to the construction of the musical work; he penetrates into it and gives himself over to pleasure only after he has mastered the structured and perhaps complicated whole.

Aesthetical enjoyment proper is only of the latter kind. Only such listening penetrates the music – it runs through the entire series of strata and appreciates the composition. The first kind, in contrast, leaps over the structural elements of the outer strata, burrows immediately into the simpler emotional hues, and ends

---

58 [Translator's note:] Friedrich Nietzsche (1844–1900).

with enjoying his own feelings, the feelings of his excited states of mind. With that, the aesthetical relation is abrogated, or at least becomes much distorted. We might call this a musical pseudo-stance. In the case of popular music, it aims at luxuriating in sound. It never does justice to music, even to the greatest and most powerful, for the hearer seeks only to wallow in it (203) and hardly concerns himself with the compositional structure. Many say this directly: there are some specific passages in great works for which they run to the concert-hall – passages that are just barely accessible to them, yet they never genuinely grasp the deeper content.

We find in this phenomenon access to the question of how a composition maintains its objectivity. The "wallowers" are those that hear falsely: the object, the composition, disappears from their view; only their own feelings are left to them, and, to be sure, these feelings, as the work communicates them, are not pure but unclean, for they have been dragged down to the marshes of the hearer's smallness.

The aesthetically correct standpoint is the reverse: it does not anticipate, led astray by certain "effects," but goes along with the composer, step by step, lets the structure of the work arise in his inner hearing, and only through that structure does the psychic element appear – of course, also as something experienced, something that carries him along, but carries only in the definite direction which the tonal structure points out to him.

The antinomy is thus solved. The inner strata of music have the means to take possession of the whole man, and, in the act of enjoyment, let him become one with the music. But the external strata have the means to focus his attention and even to shape the object of his attention itself. The structural elements of the tonal composition are what hold him firmly at a distance and in a state of contemplation of what is objectively present. Indeed the object-like nature of the compositional structure is so powerful in great works that it also holds the inner strata continuously in a certain objective position.

This does not mean that the objectivity of music depends upon the "external" level, that is, it does not suggest that the music proper begins only on the psychic level ...! That would be as if one were to say about a "landscape" that what is genuine in it is only the "mood," the rest just "technique." As with landscape, the sensible elements have their depths, and the mood only appears in them, so also here: the world of tones in music is never a mere externality that one may dispense with. It would be a mistake to leap over any of its strata, for in fact one would never gain access to the inner strata at all.

But let us return to the other question (on p. 216). How can sounds and sequences bring about the appearance of the inner strata, i.e., those that express the most inward and ineffable affairs of the human soul? Sounds and tones are, after all, quite different from human feelings. The question was put off when it first arose, but its significance must now be recognized at least as far as we can look into it. The answer to it may nonetheless be given in part.

First: the world of sounds and that of the soul are not as heterogeneous as they may appear to be at first sight. Both are non-spatial (not thing-like or immaterial), both exist as a flux, in transition, in motion, and both are developed in a play of conflicts (204): of excitation and relaxation, of tension and release. In fact, these are three ways in which psychic being differs essentially from the external world. And this much is clear: if there is to be material for art that can express this [psychic] being, it must be of the same kind: in its bestowal of form, no things or bodies may result; it may not consist of objects, but exist only in the execution – it must consist in nothing more than temporal flux, flowing, being moved and moving – and it must be able to flow along the dynamic lines of psychic events.

To achieve this purpose, the world of sounds and sound sequences has an unusual capacity: in that world, all is movement, all is excitement and resolution, surging and pulsing, tender dying away, quiet whispers or dark rumblings; wild roaring, storming, pursuit and escape, and also the taming of unchained power in musical form.

These images are not merely allegorical. They are no doubt very thin in content and are undifferentiated in comparison to the inexhaustible riches of all of what, moving and animated, is heard in music. But they point unambiguously in the direction in which these riches unfold. Here, in any case, we find the reason that music is capable of pronouncing the secrets of the soul without introducing objective themes – more precisely, letting them appear in sound. The arts of the visual sense cannot do this, or only indirectly, because they depend upon the seeing of objects and this seeing does not embrace the phenomenon of dynamics.

Second, in the tones of music an emotional content exits that is more power-ful than in the elements of the visual sense. We spoke of the latter in connection with the external strata of painting. In the case of tones and sounds, however, this content achieves an extraordinary intensification.

Let us remember once again what was said above (Chaps. 1e and 2a) about perception. There is an emotional side to all perception, which is repressed by adults only upon the physical-practical (objective) standpoint. It appears again upon the aesthetical standpoint. But it is tied more firmly to the auditory sense than to the visual sense. The evidence for this is the richly differentiated character of the human voice, in which we, without being clearly conscious of it, "hear" with great subtlety the traits characteristic of the person who is speaking or his momentary state of mind – and we do this independently of the content of his speech. The tonal color of almost all heard sounds, both the natural and the artificial, takes us far beyond that – sounds that are piercing, dull, rumbling, howling and whistling, the soft rich tone, the chirping, warbling; sounds of jubilation and woe.

Music takes on these emotional elements and consciously intensifies them by means of the timbre of instruments, and perhaps most of all by melody and harmony. Here is the place from which these emotional elements (205) pass directly into the motions and dynamics that unfold as a musical structure (cf. this chapter, c). Its secret is just this, that even the "matter" alone of music bears in it itself the foundation of all expression of feeling – even the higher ones. The situation here is just like the intelligible foundation of the act of seeing color: the most elevated "represented" contents are also not separable from the sensible foundation. Here it is the same: only in a meaningful language of tones, which is based in the senses, but not outside of them in some other language, can the psychic content be grasped. Therefore, one can "show" that content to no one who is not capable of extracting that content in the hearing of it. One "speaks" about it in vain, for one never says what is genuine and real about it, yet one can sit down at the piano and "hammer it out" – in a moment, it is there as if by magic.

In these two elements is rooted the inner connection of musical composition (structure and formal unity) to the psychic life that appears in it. The connection is a puzzlement, but it is quite axiomatic for all genuine musical listening. Since, however, the psychic phenomena in music are related to the structural and compositional elements as a continuation of the series of strata, one wishes to know even more about them: how many inner strata are there, and which strata are they? Naturally, we must not become pedantic with respect to the strata. We can distinguish only a few things here, and only with respect to the depths of the psychic phenomena to which music gives expression.

Thus, we may distinguish three background strata in music.

1. That of the immediate resonance experienced in the listener. This begins in the beat of dance music, but it belongs to all music. Its effect is similar to being spoken to and led off, and it can increase so as to give us the sense that we are being carried away.

2. The stratum on which the listener, by this means, has a deeper penetration into the composition and is gripped inwardly by it. This is not the case for all music, but only for works of a certain depth and elevation. This stratum causes psychic agitation; it reveals and proclaims. It raises what was hidden out of the depths of the listener's self. Almost all serious music works within the pathways of this stratum. It is extraordinarily differentiated and highly individualized.

3. The stratum of the Last Things, or what one may call the metaphysical stratum, in the sense that Schopenhauer gives to the appearance of the

universal Will. It need not quite be that, but it has always the character of an encounter with dark, dimly sensed forces of destiny. This stratum is rarely exhibitable in fact.

Of these three inner strata of music, the third and final one – despite its rarity – is the easiest to prove: it is present, overwhelmingly large and convincing, in religious music, – in a kind of music that of course is not religious as a composition, but was made so by the occasions for its composition and the (206) themes of its program. But it achieves in fact the deepest revelations, for the metaphysical treasures in its ideas carry it. These revelations are not really dogmatic, but rather those of the human soul. Yet they have entirely the character of metaphysics.

Moreover, there exists also a great amount of "profane" music that manifests the same phenomenon of the third inner stratum: symphonies, quartets, sonatas – if not as a whole, then in individual movements – and we must not forget the "concerti" in Handel's time and also the preludes and fugues of Bach. As for the latter, with respect to their metaphysical depths they stand completely alone.

The first and second inner strata belong to more serious music. Both are presuppositions of the third, for without getting into the beat of the music and without grasping the musical construction, the last and deepest inward strata could not appear. Before one can achieve the highest musical enjoyment, one must do the work of penetrating the construction. For compositions differ from each other depending on whether this grasping of the structure of a piece is present or not. For this constitutes a radical difference – both in the listener and in the composition itself.

In the listener: according to the depth to which he has penetrated the structure, the composition proper emerges for him; but tied to the strata of the composition is the appearance of the psychic elements. From the most superficial external strata, we are led only to the first inner stratum; from the deeper strata, where the structural elements lie, we are led to the second. This process is itself again graduated in a variety of ways ... that is, within itself it can lead on to ever more profound depths.

In the composition: not all have a larger and organized structure; rather the ways divide here between superficial yet pleasing, and serious or great music, where the "greatness" is purely inward greatness, a condition that can be found in seemingly smaller works. Only where there is a sufficient higher unity and a structure throughout the tonal composition is it possible for the second inner stratum, that containing the deepest riches of the soul, to appear clearly and distinctly.

A kind of law functions between the external and internal strata in music. The appearance of the deeper inner stratum depends on the corresponding deeper external stratum. Or, put otherwise: the greater and more rich the tonal composition, so much more of psychic life can come to appearance within it.

There are countless musical dilettantes who do not realize this, or who do not wish to believe it, who think they can leap past the compositional side of a musical work. They are mistaken, and they cannot see the mistake because they do not have the capacity to compare what they experience when they merely swing along lightly with the music and what an intuitive understanding of the construct would allow them to experience. They know only the surrogate. That is the reason why early miseducation in music is so destructive. There are (207) some composers who make use of this public prejudice and create music that speaks to us in simple tunes and makes no large demands upon musical understanding. These works lead many to seek simple relaxation and amusement in music. For that they have a certain justification. But one seeks in vain in such music for greater psychic content. It affects us superficially, and, when it creates the illusion of greater content, it seems hollow, empty, sentimental, fragile, arbitrary, and amateurish.

d) The place of program music

We need now to accommodate program music. Why we cannot simply pass over it has already been mentioned: there is too much genuinely great music of this kind to deny its significance; and there are entire classes of music – the *Lied*, choral works, and the opera – which present themselves entirely as program music. One might reject the opera for artistic reasons, but can one reject the choral song, the quartet, can one reject the *Lied*?

There is something peculiar about music that lets itself be used as a "second art" – by a primary art, i.e., literature. Here "second art" means about as much as dependent, reworked art – in many cases even nothing more than an art that interprets, serves, and illustrates (the undercoat ...).

The relation of music to literature is quite different from that of stage drama to literature. Music does not "represent" the content, it does not represent at all – for music cannot imitate literature – rather it lends to it its ability to "sound forth" pure tones bearing emotion, because literature as the mere art of words cannot do that. Moreover, it is not necessarily the case that a finished literary work is taken and then set to music. The composer at the very least chooses texts that can be set to music. There are also occasional cases where text and music are produced together, or the text is produced for some music whose character is already present in the mind of the composer.

But these are merely secondary questions. The main question is how music can take on such specific content that has been borrowed from human life and then present it. The content does not consist at all in pure emotions, but of persons, events, destinies, conflicts, etc.

One may go along when the composer "entitles" his work after things and human events, when he writes at the top, "Garden in the Rain," or "Spring Murmurs," "The Spirit of Morning," "Lone Wanderer," or when Beethoven gives titles to the movements of the *Pastoral* Symphony. But one may not expect that a hearer can guess the title from the music. For the theme named by the title cannot become the theme of the music itself. One must have stated it beforehand. Anyone who has not had it stated will most likely follow the piece with quite different expectations; the music can express only the tone of the feeling carried by sound, and the listener can extract only those tones accurately. The tone of the feeling expressed by the sounds, however, is something much (208) more general: one can extract from the "Spirit of Morning" perhaps "Magic of the High Mountains," or from "Spring Murmur" "Love's Rapture"; from "Lonely Wanderer" "Secret Sorrow," and the like. Music as such can only say what can be said in tones. And that is never any given content-laden theme. But music can, given any content-laden theme, express the feelings appropriate to the theme – and no doubt with an adequacy greater than what can be achieved by literature.

The possibility of putting poetry to music rests upon this, especially in the case of the *Lied*. It approaches the peculiar character of lyric poetry, where feeling and mood are the primary content. These can be taken up by music and made to appear. True, music can also achieve this end in very different ways. It has complete freedom to decide which musical themes (motifs) it will light upon and how it will treat them. When Löwe[59] and Schubert[60] set the same poem of Goethe to music, they chose the same thematic tone; of course, they emphasize thereby also different emotional tonalities of the poem, but they stay with the subject. Upon this fact rests the possibility of setting the same poem to music in different ways.

Within the limits of this freedom, program music is entirely justified. One may not only see in it a close affinity between the musical motif and the literary theme. Every further burdening of musical themes with meaning is arbitrary. In comparison, all musical "recitatives," all dialogue set to music, are quite questionable, especially where these are strictly tied to specific objects, to persons, to situations, and the like, e.g., where it becomes dramatic.

It is easy to see from this how a questionable principle infests the "opera." Much is amalgamated there in a way that creates difficulties for unifying poetry

---

59 [Translator's note:] Karl Löwe (1796–1869).
60 [Translator's note:] Franz Schubert (1797–1828).

and music, especially the element of drama; but in a theatrical piece, the drama is precisely what is primary. Now music has a tendency to draw the events that it is intended to accompany into the lyrical, and that is not easily compatible with the plot and the dramatic dialogue.

The older opera, which was built upon Italian models, accommodated itself to this fact by reducing the dialogue to "recitative" set to a kind of "half-music" – rather arbitrary melody without dividing the measures and with only slight accompanying harmony – and was to that extent more generous with the time that it gave over to the development of lyricism, that is to arias, occasional duets, terzets, or choruses. The drama in this way was resolved into a series of musical "numbers" (that is, more or less independent "set pieces"), which then tended to appear frequently in concerts. In this manner, the "plot" was covered over by style to such an extent that it served merely as a kind of occasion for an order of things quite external to it. For that reason, this kind of opera was able to last. (209)

But dramatic sensibility demanded more, and therefore a new direction took hold at the end of the eighteenth century. Now people wanted to put the plot to music, or, perhaps better said: to dramatize music itself. Composers had already set assertion and response in melodic form where possible, such that the character of what is asserted is reflected in the music. Now they proceeded more realistically; the harmonic underbody of the melody was articulated by the orchestra with lively timbres, and the melodic part was structured emotionally in the manner of the *Lied*. We can follow this process to Mozart[61]; it is almost complete in Weber[62]. The final step in the process was given by the operas of Wagner[63].

In fact, dialogue here was as much musically dramatized as is possible for music. But despite all these subtle differentiations, it seems in the end monotonous and boring. For the stage apparently does not take easily to music's waste of time: characters stand idly on the sidelines and do not know what to do with themselves while another sings. This is not due to a lack of "drama," it is unavoidable, and is caused by the nature of the opera itself.

Another means used by "dramatic music" is the introduction of motives determined by their content (Wotan-leitmotif, Notung-motif, Siegfried-motif). We must note that this does not occur in Wagner externally (i.e., not put in writing, as for example, in the music program); the hearer is brought, in a way natural to

---

61 [Translator's note:] Wolfgang Amadeus Mozart (1856–1891).
62 [Translator's note:] Karl Maria von Weber (1786–1926).
63 [Translator's note:] Richard Wagner (1813–1883).

music, through appropriate repetitions, to a set of specific associations. That is still entirely a musical possibility, and that is true although the content associated with the motifs is not at all expressible by music, and, besides, no listener could recognize it in the music as such.

The difficulty that such associations call up is of a different kind: drama requires, according to the specific features of the content, reminders offered by the motifs; music, however, has to form a structural unity, and cannot take up motifs randomly at all possible instants. This results in a drastic conflict of two requirements, one dramatic and one musical – and, indeed, within the composition itself. One cannot deny that Wagner's genius solved this problem at least partly, for the most part by choosing at the outset an appropriate selection of "motifs." Yet the compositional element suffers from it. It is possible that here the limits of program music have been violated.

One can furthermore ask whether all music that "accompanies" poetic themes simply brings something of this conflict upon itself. Can any text be so constituted that its cadence and rhythm respond to the genuine demands of music, that is, without doing violence to it?

With reference to many Lied-compositions, this must be affirmed (Hugo Wolff[64], Brahms[65] ...). But it is not true as a rule, and indeed it could not be. Either music, with its own peculiar necessities (210) goes its own way without a concern for text and voice – as with the practice of coloraturas of the eighteenth century – or the text becomes a schoolmaster of the music, as in many operas. One may also recall how large choral parts in many voices were set to a dry scanty text in sacred music, e.g., Lotti[66] set the words "crucifixus et sepultus est." In such cases, only the general dark emotional mood holds text and music together. Here too, there is a limit to program music, although, of course, a quite different one.

e) Strata in musical performances

We must say a word here about the art of the musician who executes the music. What was proposed in reference to it in Chap. 7c is insufficient once the splitting open of the background has taken place. It is a question of the second art next to that of the composer; the former brings the first background stratum, that of the tones themselves, into reality (audibility). In a way quite different from the

---

64 [Translator's note:] Hugo Wolff (1860–1903).
65 [Translator's note:] Johannes Brahms (1833–1897).
66 [Translator's note:] Antonio Lotti (1667–1740).

performance of a play, it makes the composed music accessible. For the composed music as such is more or less inaccessible to the public. For that reason, there is a large role given to the performing musical amateur.

Obviously, the performer gives us only the external strata of music directly; in fact, only the first of them becomes entirely and sensibly real. But that does nothing to change the fact that in his playing, the whole of the series of musical strata "appears." This does not distinguish the written music from the performance of it, and just as the actor is attempting precisely to make the inner strata appear, so naturally with the musician, if he is not entirely a superficial "technician." So, at least, is the meaning and goal of all genuine musical performance.

This does not mean that the performer really brings out the inner strata and allows the psychic element to appear. His talent may fail him on the technical as well as on the psychic side; he may lack sufficient maturity. For the right effect, two conditions must come together: the technical mastery of the instrument and also one's own musical voice, and his congenial appreciation of the composer.

Accordingly, one can distinguish two types of reproduction. At the far reaches of one side stands a trained musician. He has technical mastery, but he is lacking the inward spirit of the music, because he does not have the needed depth to experience it himself. Thus it usually happens that his choice of pieces for his performance is based on that fact: he chooses those concert-pieces that allow him to shine. At the far end of the other side stands the amateur. He has a musical sense and can hear the deeper psychic content in the piece, but he does not have the technical ability to let it be heard. Between these extremes, there are innumerable steps of all kinds. Only rarely do both types meet at the same level. In the first case, the music seems empty – it shines, but only superficially; in the second it is bungled (it seems inexact, unclear, and perhaps full of feeling that easily becomes sentimental ...). (211) Both may approach kitsch, yet each may also have its own special qualities. In both cases, the law of the strata is offended. This law maintained that the appearance of the inner strata depends upon the fulfillment of the outer strata – specifically so that the deeper external stratum allows the deeper inner strata to appear.

However, the deeper external stratum – the one, for example, that consists in the unity of the movement – cannot be brought out without a certain adequacy in the lower-lying outer stratum. This is what the amateur does not understand. He attempts, by leaping over the middle strata, to render immediately what he feels, but the compromises he makes in executing the piece frustrate his efforts. For the whole can be constructed only one level after the other.

Here is also found the reason why a certain kind of musical amateur generally prefers program music: it reveals to him, in an extra-musical manner, what the music should be about, and that is what he needs, because he cannot easily find his way through the external strata and the mastery of the instrument that they require. He does not notice that much is eluding him. For program music, too, cannot simply leap over the structural elements. This attitude comes in degrees, up to the attitude that is at bottom unmusical but that wallows gladly in feeling – which in reality leads only to a very superficial enjoyment of music.

The odd thing, however, is that in this manner two kinds of music come to be. There is music that is damaged to a considerable degree, if not entirely destroyed, by the slightest amateurishness; similarly by a technically weak performance. Of this kind are Beethoven's sonatas, and also works by lesser masters as Chopin, Grieg, and Debussy. And there is music that is hardly damageable at all, that even in weaker or superficial renditions can reveal something of its deeper content. Works by Handel and Bach and many of the older classics are of this kind.

Why is this so? The answer can again be given by means of the theory of strata: where the musical structure is more rigid, that is, where the external strata follow in a strict series, the inner strata appear even in an imperfect rendition. The higher wholes put themselves across by themselves in the process of listening alone, and out of them, the deeper inner strata appear. When such rigidity of structure is lacking, only the most meticulous performance of the content of the outer strata can let the psychic element appear.

Finally, we must not forget that the composer does not compose down to every detail; written music remains relatively general, and only the performing artist composes it in all detail. This is the same situation we have seen in the case of the dramatist and the actor.

The question is simply: in which strata of the musical work do we find a lack of definition? And in which, therefore, does the performing artist have to complete the composition? The answer: in principle, in all strata. But the emphasis should lie upon the external strata, not only because they bear all further appearance, but also because the inner (212) strata, despite their hiddenness, may yet be less "general" (undefined).

That may sound strange, but it rests upon the fact that psychic content – feelings, moods – reveals, if it becomes at all tangible, a well-known structure of its own. Well-known, namely, from one's own or another's psychic life. Yes, the soul possesses an accurate anticipatory function precisely where one's own experience of life is wanting. And those things that are experienced, known well, or simply anticipated in their peculiar individual character, then step in as a totality.

This extends so far that the deep-souled composer can lead the inexperienced man into psychic depths that are entirely new to him, without running the risk of becoming liable to distort the music. It is the same with the interpreter: he can, as he plays back the composition, be carried away far beyond his own psychic sensibility. For that reason the playing of untrained but highly musical persons – for example, youthful ones – has a power to enter the music sympathetically in a way that fills with amazement more experienced and mature listeners. The purity of such sensibility, heavy with its own future, replaces the knowledge and the power of those whose souls have grown rich. The condition of this is merely the clean and respectful treatment of the structural elements in music's outer strata.

Chapter 15: Strata in Architecture

a) The outer strata in buildings

We agreed in Chap. 7d that architecture is similar to music in that it is "free from a *sujet*," but against this we noted that it is subject to some practical purpose. Further, a relation of strata exists in architecture also, although its double determination, by the practical end and by the weight and inflexibility of the crude matter in which it works, clearly conflicts with the situation in music. We saw that even here we could speak without hesitation of a play with form, and the resistance of matter in architecture forms precisely its essential dynamic element.

What comes in question is whether in architecture the background also opens itself up and produces a series of strata; also, whether it is possible to establish a difference between the outer and inner strata, as was found to be the case in painting, literature, and music. We can say immediately that both questions must be answered in the affirmative. To both arts, however, belongs a special inquiry.

Recall how matters stood previously, as we distinguished only between the real foreground and the unreal background. On one side, we could demonstrate the intuitive (no longer sensible) consciousness of a greater whole, of the composition of the work of architecture, which includes many rooms and partial views of it. Here we see in our imagination, as it works synthetically, (213) what the artist sees set off clearly from what is seen by the senses; that this whole is a physical reality changes nothing, for it cannot be surveyed by sight. On the other hand, in the viewing of an architectural work something more that this whole is expressed: it lets a kind of life appear along with itself, which has been placed within the building and to which it testifies. To be sure, certain psychic peculiarities of this life are reflected in the building – in the church, the temple, the palace, or the private residence. For men build their structures in a way that expresses how they understand themselves, their life, or their ideals (e.g., religious ones). In that way, the individual nature of peoples and times can appear in their buildings, and even in their ruins.

In both of these phenomena are clearly reflected not only the splitting up of the background in architecture, but also the opposition of the outer and inner strata, similar to the opposition we found in music. Let us stop for a moment at the outer strata. If one assumes that every architectural work fills some practical end, moves within spatial proportions, and at the same time must struggle with the resistance of unyielding matter, then we may distinguish these outer strata in it:

1. The practical layout (most clearly seen in the floor plan);
2. The spatial layout – the proportions, distribution of masses (intended to enhance the view and the impression it offers);
3. The dynamic layout – the overcoming of matter and the utilization of laws specific to it.

These three levels do not in all cases constitute a clear series. In a certain sense, the first is prior to the two next ones, but it may be that these develop beyond the first.

To 1: *The practical layout.* We have already shown how the practical end is far from being a merely negative or limiting element in architecture, but that it rather takes over the role that is played by the theme (*sujet*) in the representational arts. An architectural work that has no practical function is unimaginable, and would be in fact like a poem without a *sujet*. It must be given a task, and it is precisely in the solution of that task that art must manifest itself (for example: an apartment building with so and so many units, so and so kinds of fittings, and so forth).

Every layout that proceeds from some pre-given conception of form must fail here, because it will necessarily come into conflict with its task. Only a solution that begins entirely with practical matters and only then chooses, from the perspective of aesthetical form, among the possibilities that these practical matters allow, can be genuinely organic, and constructed from inside out.

For that reason, the layout that is intended to realize ends is the first in the order of strata – and also in the order of appearance. For an impractical work that fulfills its tasks imperfectly seems even with regard to (214) appearance unattractive – at least for the eye that grasps it intuitively. Insofar as that is so, the aesthetical shaping of the work begins here. It is therefore not entirely true, as was just said, that standards of aesthetical form are chosen only from the possibilities that the practical ends allow; rather, in the treatment of the ends, those standards are already at work. That is not nonsense, because the end plays in this case the role of the *sujet*, and must therefore be entirely taken into the organic composition of the architectural work.

To 2: *The organization of space.* This is the stratum that is treated most extensively in the history and theory of art. It is of course important, but it is not the only thing of concern. One must not imagine that there is no leeway for the shaping of space if one's first concern is with practical ends. One who is inexperienced with blueprints does not see the abundant possibilities that still, as a rule, remain; and, especially, the inexperienced person has no clear picture of how, with small means – such as small changes in the dimensions that are insignificant for all practical purposes – relatively significant spatial effects can be achieved. For example, if one moves the roof down a small degree, the character of the house becomes different. It is similar if one alters the dimension of height, etc.

The art of the architectural genius consists to a great extent in his discovery of such relatively small means regarding the relations among sizes and in his cleverness in putting them to use, especially where powerful effects of spatial form depend upon them. That is true as much for the external architecture of the entire building, given the principles according to which it divides its elements, its structure, and its distribution of mass, as also for the internal forms of individual rooms.

Where it is a question of monumental structures, the effects of sheer size are added. These do not depend as much upon the actual size of the structure as upon the organization of space: there are enormous structures that do not seem big (skyscrapers), and there are some with very modest dimensions that affect us with their largeness (the Berlin Hauptwache and other works by Schinkel[67]).

To 3: *The dynamic organization.* Architecture is an art bound on two sides. The bond with the practical end is only one; the other is with matter. Now all arts are no doubt bound up with matter and limited by it, but the matter to which architecture is tied has a particular weight and stubbornness; it is crude, physical material – no doubt there are abundant choices among them (for the most part among wood and stone; also clay, only later iron girders arrived on the scene) – that will depend upon its purposes, but still it offers always only limited possibilities.

Not all spatial layouts can be carried out in every material. And, given some specific materials, they cannot be done in any way at all, but in ways specific to them. For that reason, the structure is from the very outset dependent upon the dynamic composition. The history of architecture is essentially a (215) history of building techniques: for example, the art, not just of piling up masses of stone so that they do not fall, but to fashion them as covering for the interior rooms (barrel vaults, ribbed vaults, domes).

The various building styles, one replacing the other throughout history, are essentially limited by the technical capacity of the builders. Here we see that in

---

67 [Translator's note:] Karl Friedrich Schinkel (1781–1814). Hartmann may be referring to the Neue Wache, designed by Schinkel and erected in 1816–18.

every dynamic layout in fact an aesthetical stratum functions in the building and not just a technical one. The important feature here is, specifically, that the beauty of form does not lie as much in the spatial proportions as it does in the dynamic meaning of the forms: it thus lies where the weight of the material and its overcoming by means of the construction is made present to the mind in its visible form.

Fine examples of such visibility are the flying buttresses of the Gothic, in which the outward force of the wall is absorbed by the ribbed arches leaning upon it at great height, and also the construction of the ribs themselves. ... Schopenhauer used ancient columns as an example of this, where the upward tapering sensibly expresses double weight (that of themselves and the roof).

We have spoken of all these things earlier. What is significant here is only the splitting open of the background in its external strata. In fact, the dynamic layout is quite different from the spatial layout and entirely different from the practical design.

b) The inner strata of architecture

That there are inner strata at all in architecture is not as obvious as in other arts. This fact is connected to the lack of freedom with which the practical ends, which are very much external and inartistic, can be pursued. If we stand before an apartment building from the 1890's, it is difficult to believe that it possesses inner strata. If we stand in a small western German town before a framework house (from about the seventeenth century), things seem a bit different. The case is similar with Westphalian or Upper Bavarian farmhouses. We become entirely convinced when we see old castles, palaces, estates, or even churches. Here there are obvious distinctions to be made: not every architectural work has the deeper background strata, those that speak of the life and psychic being of the people who built them. But the mere fact of age, that is, the temporal distance from the observer, will also make discerning of the background difficult.

What, then, will make up the background? We cannot force our way into this mystery. But we can see it in a negative sense. The contemporary apartment building with its many units is a product of an economic trend that demanded speed, cost-cutting, and, more than anything, effective use of allotted space. For the spatial design and dynamic layout, there remains, no doubt, some leeway, but there is no thought for these, no possibility for their development, no love. Never (216) is the practical layout developed with sufficient thoroughness and clarified by experience. Think of the dingy inner court, of the rooms that are too high and too narrow. Tradition is wanting, as too the connection with a life having a particular form and a particular style. The result is that the building lacks style; and that means as much as a lack of form; the design is purely external; it is expressive of nothing.

One sees from this that what matters is the connection of a building with human lives that develop themselves in definite ways. Only where this connection is found can the life and the nature of man appear in his buildings. One sees further that a close connection exists between the outer and inner strata of a building: for not only do we lack the inner strata where the connection with a form of life is wanting, but the outer strata also. And one may expect, accordingly, that this connection might be still closer – that is, that with the deeper outer strata deeper inner strata will also appear.

One may, accordingly, distinguish the following three inner strata of a build-ing – but not, to be sure, in assuming that they are present in all buildings, but only that a certain order is present in them; at least the deeper strata never appear without the ones that are less deep.

1. The spirit or meaning in the solution of the practical task: one could also say the kind of solution, within which again all kinds of compositional variation is possible.
2. The total impression of the parts and the whole – resting upon the second and third outer strata, the spatial layout, and the dynamic layout; but in reality the former already determines the latter two.
3. The impression of the will to life and the style of life, which is usually unconscious and always in a certain opposition to the practical ends pursued (the impression, therefore, of something impractical, of an idea). It can intensify and reach up to the level of a world-view, and it relates always to the self-cultivation of human life according to man's understanding of himself.

To 1: *The spirit or meaning of the solution in the composition of the practical ends.* One can attack a practical task from very different sides, and, correspondingly, can solve it differently. The choice depends on the standpoint that means the most to someone, and that standpoint is usually given by the character of life, especially that lived by a community. The frame houses of the waning Middle Ages drew their meaning from the need to save space within the tightly drawn town walls – the extension outward of the upper story, the low ceiling, the small windows; the meaning of the Westphalian farmhouse is drawn from their de-signers' efforts to hold everything tightly together under one roof: living quarters, stalls, pantries, etc.; but one can also separate rooms having the same functions in one large courtyard with multiple structures – as it is done in other places, and both solutions offer the possibility (217) of further arrangements. In building a church, the aim of holiness is achieved in effect in different ways in the system of equally high multiple-naves and in the basilica. Both allow for different forms of execution. But the spirit and meaning is of a different kind both in the way the inferior space is conceived as also in the external shape.

Every kind of solution to the practical task of construction lets its own principle be known. And with every principle, a preference is given to one aspect of the problem over other tasks. Which side is given the preference depends upon the style of life or the taste that then predominated. And here – already in the first inner stratum of the building – the style of life is connected most tightly to the building style.

To 2: *The total impression offered by the parts and the whole as resting upon the spatial layout and the dynamic layout.* As it is impossible to achieve the practical end without at the same time pursuing a definite idea of the structure, so too is it impossible to realize a spatial and dynamic layout without giving the forms thereby created a certain expressiveness. There is of course no name for expressiveness of this sort, and it is therefore difficult to achieve any agreement as to what it is. But it is felt everywhere we face a true and well-executed construction; and the expressiveness is extraordinarily varied.

We tend to divide this phenomenon into certain formal types, which we name after peoples or epochs that created them, or from whom these types are known. Thus we speak of the Pompeian villa, a Byzantine church, a Tyrolean farmhouse, and a Chinese temple. And we mean by such designations the inner character of its architecture, which is exhausted neither by its purpose alone nor by its spatial form and its dynamic layout alone. But, beyond all that, it brings to expression something of the character and the common essential nature of the people who, in the long passage of generations, created these forms. For the peculiarity of such forms of construction, which express their human quality, is that they do not arise out of the fancies of individuals, but are formed gradually out of long tradition.

In such structures belongs also the experience of life. That is seen in their daily presence and their use, in their very familiarity and in the continuing need to make everyday reality bearable and engaging –, that is, just to shape forms that satisfy a higher psychic demand, forms that themselves reveal something of the psychic existence and inner attitudes of their creators. Perhaps the situation is such that just those forms that are bearable and engaging to a certain psychic type also reveal something about that psychic type. For in the end the peculiar nature of the human frame and its forms of life are characterized by nothing so much as by what speaks to him in its daily presence. (218)

To 3: *The construction as bearing the character of a will to life and a life style.* One can also call this inner stratum that of the idea in the structure. In all cases, it has distanced itself entirely from the sphere of the practical. But this stratum fulfills the purposes of the structure wherever these are also ideal – as in temples, churches, cultural centers, palaces and similar architecture.

Here we now find something of importance. The ideal purpose of a monument is not identical with the human idea that is marked upon it. This is clearly visible in the magnificence of temples and churches. These have been erected to honor some specific divinities, but they survive the centuries and, when the time comes that no one attaches a meaning to the name of the deity, they still stand before us in their ideality, that is, they will still be felt as the expression of a will and a greatness that extends above and beyond all human capacities. Extending beyond humankind and pointing toward an ideal is quite well understood apart from all knowledge of its dogmatic and cultural purposes. And indeed it is understood intuitively in the visible impression of the structure, or even its ruins. The situation is the same with religious music, painting, and sculpture: only the themes are dogmatic; the artistic creation is independent of them, and it speaks just as independently to the non-believer.

For these reasons, we may speak in this context of a stratum of the world-view in architecture – and, if we may, of a metaphysical stratum also. For in fact here is put in question the metaphysics of man: how every kind of monumental architecture articulates something about the self-image of man. We showed above how a simple apartment building relates to the tight social circle of families as clothing relates to personality: as an expression of that self-image and as a conscious effort to give shape to one's life. In that way, a mere apartment building testifies to the essential character of man. Monuments, however, give testimony to what keeps his own ideal before his eyes, to what specifically he wants to be and of what his dreams are made.

And, if that is true, we may call this inner stratum in architecture that of the will to life. One must only understand that expression in its entire depth – not individualistically, but historically in the sense of a living human community with a common nature peculiar to it, common ideals and yearnings, in short, in the sense of a real-objective spirit. In this sense too, the phenomenon is quite well known: it is precisely that which draws us irresistibly to structures of great inward style, ones that have grown out of a genuine tradition. Only we usually do not know what it is that attracts us in this way.

c) Community, tradition, style

We have spoken often about how architectonic form does not grow out of the soil of individuality, but rather requires community and tradition. No doubt one may correctly say the same of other (219) arts, but those are much more free in their movement and allow the individual artist greater flexibility. Connected to this point is that the dominant role of style in architecture is especially strict in many epochs – in such a way that the architectural sensibility of men is entirely anchored in a specific formal character.

Why is this true of architectural sensibility? To this the first and most simple answer is: because a house is a practical object that offers itself to everyone in a striking way, a thing that sets the tone for its entire town. A house must fit into the whole of its environment, and, if it does not, its presence seems disturbing and vexing. In short, a house is a matter for everyone; it is privately owned, yet it still is an object of public concern.

Moreover, a house is an enduring entity; it is, once built, a form of capital, and therefore cannot so easily be done away with and replaced with another. The single individual does not, no doubt, grasp that readily, when he builds a house; he does not have to think about it as long as he is rooted entirely in the taste of his time and place. But it becomes a real question when he, as an individual, withdraws himself from that standard of taste.

Those are matters that distinguish architecture radically from other arts: no one is forced to look at a painting or a sculpture, or to read a poem or listen to a piece of music. One does not have to live with them; they belong in no universal contexts of life. They are, to the contrary, quite removed from them; and, if one wishes to see works of their type, one can normally just choose to do so. In any case, there is ordinarily no compulsion; works of art of these kinds are of no public concern.

For that reason, even in the communal life of the objective spirit to which they belong they are not a direct concern of a community. Rather, they first become of such general concern where their meaning has high spiritual significance. Precisely for that reason a house, even one of little significance and poorly constructed, is from the start the direct concern of the community. That is the reason why, in a highly creative architectural epoch, the sensibility of the community determines architectural form. This determination takes the form of the "ruling taste" or the "sense of style." To the persons who built it, these need not be manifest. He simply walks the well-trodden track in architecture – in architecture as in the other realms of life. The track in this case is the sense of style into which he has grown and which, of all others, is alone familiar to him.

One may therefore ask further – for behind all forms of community there lies originally an element of history – why architectural form grows only in the soil of tradition? To say merely that this is the case in all the arts is insufficient. For the case is not the same. Tradition has a greater influence in architecture, and for (220) the creation of architectural form it is more essential – at least as long as one builds out of the common sense of style (that is, as long as the point just made is fulfilled). This sense of style grows only slowly over the course of generations.

One may express the matter in the following way: the spirit out of which form is developed is from the start a communal (objective) spirit; that means that it does not begin one day in the life of some specific generation, but arrives from faraway historical regions and out of small beginnings; thus it is transformed only very slowly. Speaking concretely: when a son builds a house, he wants one like his father's, as he knew it throughout his childhood and found to be befitting his social standing. Stylistic traditions, and the traditional sense of style, are maintained because the latter is itself held tight by the former.

This means that the individual cannot extract himself voluntarily from this sensibility; he is trapped in it as in a communal spiritual form that thinks and acts for him. He knows it no other way. If he knew his situation in another way – from abroad or from the distant past – and wanted to imitate those forms, the effort would disorient him, lead him astray, and he would easily begin to misunderstand the foreign forms and come, disastrously, to confound them with his own.

The same is entirely true for the third inner stratum in architecture, that of the ideas, which beyond all else address man. Naturally, we limit ourselves here to building in which an idea plays a determining role – as with monuments. Within certain limits it is also true of private homes, so far as they allow something to appear of the self-image of the owner (within his close community). Ideas of this kind are in fact genuinely super-personal, or possessed in common. The best examples of this are religious ideas, which lie at the root of all temples and churches.

This is also true of religious ideas just because relatively important moral ideas stand behind them, when, for example, in paying reverence to divinity, one's own reverence for the πόλις [the state] is manifest. That, too, is a community matter, and is felt to be so; and something of the same is placed within the structural features of the temple. We need not spend much time on these matters. If one has grasped the nature and function of ideas in the background of architecture, its foundation in the objective spirit becomes self-evident.

We still should note that what is genuinely stable in architecture is precisely the inner strata, and perhaps this is most evident in the last and deepest of them, that of the ideas. This does not mean that the outer strata do not possess an independent constancy of form. But what is most characteristic is that the external structure is still held fast from within, held fast, indeed, by that imponderable psychic satisfaction that connects itself tightly in human sensibility to visible material forms. Here tradition rules absolutely. (221)

Second Section: Aesthetic Form

Chapter 16: Unity, Limits, Form

a) Multiplicity of form

One encounters the concept of form everywhere in aesthetics. It is unavoidable, because form is that to which beauty is attached. Just for that reason, the concept of form becomes so easily incommunicable for aesthetics, for it is form in all its kinds that constitutes the aesthetical question. In this sense, we rejected, in the Introduction, the idea of an aesthetics of form as almost tautological, because the opposition of "form and content" cannot be maintained: the artistic content is essentially itself form.

But now it has become clear, from various standpoints, that one must nevertheless take the concept of aesthetical form very seriously. First there is the opposition to matter: since every art has its specific matter, and every kind of matter can have only certain kinds of form bestowed upon it, so it is apparent that here there must already lie a foundation for further distinctions within the concept of form.

Second, the representational arts are concerned with the bestowal of form upon a "material" (themes, *sujets*), and this is apparently quite different from the forming of matter – though it stands in a very definite reciprocal relation to it, as the treatment of specific material is not possible in every kind of matter.

Third, next to beauty in the relation of appearance there is another beauty in the pure play with form. We encountered this idea of beauty in ornamental art – yet not only there, but also in music and architecture, and even in certain forms of natural beauty. (We will see that its limits are thereby also drawn too tightly. This kind of beauty plays a large role otherwise, but that still remains to be studied.)

A problem has already been encountered as to how it is possible for two kinds of bestowal of form to be given upon one and the same work: one upon the material, and one upon the matter. Both must obviously be quite different kinds of form. Nonetheless, the most intimate relation of the one kind of form to the other must exist; for, since the dispute about the "Laocoön" it is no longer argued that not any material can be given form in any given matter. But how are we to understand this tight connection between them?

Apparently, the situation must be such that the bestowal of form upon some material is at the same time the forming of matter; otherwise, one could never speak of the "forming of material in some matter." But that means that we have two opposed elements of *one* act of bestowing form, thus with two domains of what is unformed and needful of form, for both are also easily distinguishable, as in literature: the bestowal of form (222) upon language and to thematic material. What are given form are, on the one hand, characters and their destinies, and on the other, words, sentences, verses.

Here it is no longer a question of the unity of a multiplicity, as otherwise in all kinds of bestowing form, but of the unity of two manifolds, indeed quite heterogeneous ones. We have arrived now at a problem that immediately brings with itself some further implications. For in fact the two named kinds of form are not the only ones; there are more of them.

We can see already from this point in what direction we are moving. Clearly we are headed toward the conclusion that in a work of art – and perhaps in every aesthetic object – each stratum has its own kind of form; and then the next question would be: how this form, graduated in various ways, is structured within itself, i.e., how this heterogeneity of different forms, each lifting itself over the one before it, is able nonetheless to constitute a unity that is moreover able to make itself felt as such in the act of beholding it.

We should not assume that this is a simple matter. It might appear at first that we have here merely an opposition of ontological modes – the real foreground and the unreal background, corresponding to the bestowal of form upon matter and the shaping of the "material," but, as was shown in the previous five chapters, that turned out to be an oversimplification. Rather it is a question of the entire splitting open of the background down to its most inner regions, and, consequently of the entire series of strata in the aesthetic object, where apparently each of these strata is subject to its own shaping – one not dependent upon the others, but yet peculiar to itself.

This must be true just as far as the stratification of the object reaches. For there are also very simple non-stratified objects (as in ornament). And it is clear that the complexity of the problem of form grows with the increasing richness of the series of strata; thus, it would be at its greatest extent in literature, for example.

From this, it is immediately evident why the aesthetical problem of form has produced so few results up to now, although much ingenuity has been devoted to it. The failure of theory has perhaps been felt nowhere more painfully than here. At the same time it must be noted that, even with a new procedure that begins with the entire series of strata of the work of art, we cannot hope to obtain a quick solution to the problem of aesthetical form. We must not get our hopes up too high.

Why is this so? Because we cannot follow the various features of aesthetical form through all the strata. We have done much if we are able to point out single characteristic elements of them in individual strata. Artistic form itself, in fact – even if this were true only for one single stratum – is inaccessible to analysis. We can say only a few things about it, and, in general, only in the case of the external strata. Why does just this particular form – purely in itself, without any further transparency – seem beautiful, why does the slightest (223) alteration of it destroy the impression? Aesthetics cannot hope to provide an answer. It is just in this that the imponderable mystery of art consists; it belongs in a region whose laws even the artist does not comprehend, but he can adhere to them only out of the reliable and certain feelings of his genius.

b) Unity of multiplicity

What is at stake here is precisely the unity of form. The nature of the problem lies in the fact that with every increase in the depth of one's analysis of the problem of form one sees oneself drawn increasingly into the multiplicity and away from the unity. But that is of course quite to be expected. For all unity is unity of some multiplicity, and it is not possible to understand such unity when one has not learned how to understand the kind and the dimensions of multiplicity whose unity it is presumed to be.

Now there is a categorical law that a unity is all the more powerful as the multiplicity, which it is to master, is richer and more diverse. To understand this thesis correctly, one must consider all the categorial levels of multiplicity and unity. One begins with the simple mathematical unities, rises then to the structural unities in nature, to organic life, to species-life, to the unity of consciousness, to the unity of the community, of the objective spirit and of historical life. Everywhere there appear different multiplicities, and they are mastered in different ways.

Naturally, at the same time, the complexity of the multiplicity is continuously increasing, and it becomes more difficult to master its elements; and the kinds of unity that is to master them become correspondingly higher and more subtle. But along with the "height," its capacity to become disrupted, to be led astray, even its fragility, increases. Organic unity is more fragile than mere dynamic unity; psychic unity is more easily disrupted than the unity of the living body, and so forth.

But that means that with each higher level, the unity of a structure becomes ever more imperfect; and the highest kinds of unity are not the most perfect, but rather the least so. Categorially, that is the way things stand in general. We have already encountered the reciprocal relation of height and perfection from another perspective.

For aesthetics, we may draw the following conclusions. No one can doubt that the aesthetic object stands fairly high among the constructs belonging to this series. We need only ask whether it obtains this position due to its perfection or its ontological height.

Think first of perfection: it is the "beautiful" object that we affirm and enjoy because of its form; and how could that be otherwise, if its unity were not the most perfect mastery of multiplicity? Yet that is not so. For in all regions of beauty we deal also with the ugly! Nowhere, neither in the arts nor in nature are things so constituted that (224) all may be "beautiful," that all conforms to laws of form and unity – steadily and inviolably.

This phenomenon is best known to us in the case of man, whose ugliness often strikes us because we are especially sensitive to it. But the same is true also, even in the arts themselves, which consciously strive to create only what is beautiful. There are failures even there.

What does that mean at this point? It means, if we may express it in the categories of unity and multiplicity, that artistic unity by no means always knows how to master the multiplicity that it is dealing with (e.g., that of some given "material"). There are cases in which the multiplicity runs through its fingers – the painter who loses himself in details, the poet who brings together a huge mass of details, material, amusing tangents, but who neglects the composition of the whole. Even in music, we find the same phenomena: the music lacks a clear layout, lacks form and unity.

It is clear that aesthetical unity, through which a thing becomes a work of art, must in all cases be created. Art does not exist in multiplicity – which is quite different from nature, where entirely unintegrated multiplicities are rarely to be found. In return, art is also a unity of a different kind, a different type – and, in general, a higher type. To create this unity of a higher type is the job of art. As opposed to what is merely given, this unity must be beheld intuitively; indeed, it must be invented (intuited) in the inward act of beholding.

In the non-representational arts, that is immediately apparent; here the multiplicity is not taken from any given material, but is produced as a free play with form itself. Then even its unity, that with which it is held together, must be produced along with it. In any case, the intuited unity alone makes itself felt here also as a principle of selection. In the representational arts, we come across a different relation to multiplicity, because the latter is given with the theme. But since the material is taken from life, and life is unlimited in its multiplicity, the intuited principle of unity must engage in the process of selection in a new and different sense, that is, it must determine the segment of the whole that will be given direct representation.

c) Selection and the setting of limits

Thus the third essential element in this context has also been sketched: the element of selecting and limiting. What is specifically required is a selection from among the multiplicity that is immediately given, or otherwise provided (by the imagination), and a limitation of what in reality are the limitless interconnections of a thing. It is one of the first features of the aesthetical standpoint, that in it the art object separates itself from the contexts of life, leaves them behind and creates new contexts for itself (Introduction, § 5); this has proven valid in all art forms (a different space, different light, a (225) different time and a different life ...). But limiting in aesthetics does not refer to these alone.

For these all are merely external limitations, only a separation over against the given real context; the work of art conjures up a different piece of the world and places it before our eyes, and therefore requires the phenomenon of a frame in order to intensify the fact of being extracted. But it is not merely a question of that. The work of art requires still another limitation of multiplicity; we may call that the inner limitation. But this is meant only as a figure of speech.

Any material for representation, whether it be given through the senses or by the imagination, brings with itself a vast multiplicity; and the more concretely it is understood, so much richer it becomes. This multiplicity cannot be taken up completely by the work, for it would burst its bounds, confuse it, rob it of clear intuitive unity, and thus make even its shaping into a unity impossible.

This multiplicity can be dealt with in only one way: by a selection of what is essential for the work of art – that is, of what is essential for the appearance of the additional inner strata. This artistic phenomenon is called "omission," and it refers to the leaving out of detail. That is strange in itself, for of course the strength of a work of art lies precisely in the fact that it contains details, and speaks of nothing except by means of them. We recall that this is in contrast to the nature of the concept and to many philosophical theories, to which details are external.

This is just what the arts do in fact: they limit themselves – always from within quite specific perspectives – to broad lines, and of course to those that matter. The sculptor does not imitate every small irregularity, although these may very well contribute to the living quality of the work. The painter chooses certain qualities of light and shade, and neglects thousands of others; he does not paint every little speck on a tree, not every blade of grass in a meadow, but rather indicates such forms with miserly strokes; he can on occasion employ only coarse strokes such as we never "see" in real life. He can just rely upon the eyes of the viewers: their eyes will easily be able to fill out the tree and meadow, if they follow the artist's intentions; and what has been indicated with frugal means will satisfy the viewer.

We find an extreme of this kind in the drawing technique of many great draftsmen: often just a few lines are needed to make an entire figure in motion appear, or even to present a bit of landscape with traits that are entirely characteristic (Rembrandt's etchings).

The art of filling-out or supplementation in perceptual cognitions is of course quite essential in such cases. Without it, omission of features would be merely negative, a *modus deficiens*. But the opposite is shown to be true: we see this fact in the urge to add to a thing, to complete it. Here the sole matter of significance (226) is that the artist retain the leadership role in his suggestive sketching. Otherwise, the process of synthetic presentation would lose itself in acts of supplementation, make itself independent, and thus no longer be the work of the artist, but something quite different.

The process of omission is even more prominent in literature. How is it at all possible to encompass a large piece of human destiny within the space of just a few scenes? Destiny consists, after all, in a series of continuous events passing from moment to moment through months and years. A play, however, and within its larger space a novel, forces these events together in a narrow series of scenes – a series so narrow as is never the case in life, when measured neither by its concentration nor by the coherence of its content.

The two last observations are important for understanding the situation: life draws events – which cohere closely in respect to their meaning – far apart from each other, and thereby a person (the living observer) loses the sense of the interrelatedness of the events that are there before his eyes. In contrast, the dramatist gets rid of everything that is not essential in these interrelations that could impede the understanding of them. In this way, he makes poetic the course of events; he lets their unity stand solidly before us, in short, he "shapes" them from the inside out.

Here, too, the "shaping into unity" is essentially a function of omission and selection: that he selects in a certain way is precisely the compositional phase of the dramatist's art; he selects in such manner that within the most limited theatrical space the largest and richest set of possible interrelated events are made to appear. Much pertains to this effort, for example, that the background story be woven into the scenes so that they may appear along with the staged events, without having to be "recited" in a pedestrian way. For similar reasons, the events taking place between the scenes must be expressed in a recognizable way during the performance. This is true not just of drama alone.

One should not imagine that this inner "limitation of multiplicity," the process of "omitting," etc. is as negative as the terms used suggest. All limitation that proceeds from the essence of the material is at the same time a kind of fixing, which is a positive determination. That is in general true in the ontological sense, but here it has a particular meaning. What is positive here lies in the supplementation by means of cognition in the intuitive consciousness; one may say: in the appearance of that which is not given directly to the senses. There are equivalent expressions for the same state of affairs.

Yet how does it come about that different observers, who each must make up for what has been left out, do not supplement different things, but instead one and the same things, e.g., scenes that are not represented or narrated are still concretely before one's eyes by means of hints from the creator? For this is what is at stake here, and only when these conditions are met does the literary work affect us each as one and the same entity. This question is very elementary, but it is obviously a central one. (227)

There is only one sufficient answer: the guiding of the supplementation must proceed from the artwork itself, and it must be strict and certain – at least when the artist can count on the viewer's possessing a corresponding maturity and a high moral and cultural level.

That a work guides the viewer at all is not obvious. Think of how we depend in life otherwise on such supplementation, specifically in what we "sympathetically experience" of the destiny of other men. In reality we experience only very little of such things directly, and we must continually make up a picture of events, basically out of what we experience, hear, and dimly suspect. And how often do we in this way draw ourselves a false picture? Why, that is more frequent than not!

We must remember when it is a question of the guidance of the process of supplementation in our reception of the work of art that what we most lack in life, the drawing of attention to what is essential, is present with amazing force in the work of art. And if we were to ask further what it consists in, we could find, no doubt, that it is not possible to pronounce the last and truest word about it; only so much as this is easily apparent: omissions of detail that have been correctly distributed draw us on to other things. This is the affirmative contrary of the apparent *modus deficiens*.

But it is not that alone. Recall how the poet places certain happenings (or also simply intentions, unresolved sentiments, *ressentiments*, etc.) precisely in the center of interest by holding them for a long time in the shadow, and by that means compels the imagination of the reader or spectator to occupy himself with them, to puzzle over them, to figure them out.

Do not think that this is a mere artist's trick, a means of creating tension. It is rather a drawing-out of the imagination as it supplements what it sees, arousing it to great tension and autonomous action – not to mention making the spectator a confederate of the writer as he poetizes and creates. In fact, the poet in this way imitates life. For our own experience shows us human conflicts – always half in shadow, half capable of being guessed – drawn apart and thrown together with thousands of things that divert one's attention. The writer shows us the same tokens, but concentrated and cleansed of all disturbances, and with that, he draws out the imagination that it may supplement what is seen in a well-directed and clear manner.

The entire situation is clearly integrated into the succession of strata in a specific way. We may ask, therefore, how it is integrated, and which strata are peculiar to it.

The answer cannot be given uniformly, for the arts – even if one considers only the representational ones – are not the same with respect to each other. The levels upon which selection, omission, concentration, etc. take place is purely sensible in the plastic arts, but in literature it takes place on the level of representation, specifically the representation that is guided by words. (228)

It is closer in one respect to matter, in another to the "material"; in the first it belongs rather in the external shaping of matter (color, light, shadow, in the case of painting) and in the second more in the inner shaping of the material (the series of scenes in drama). Yet something their meanings have in common can be discerned that probably is also true *mutatis mutandis* for the non-representational arts: selection takes place in the middle strata of the work of art, and it belongs therefore neither to the real-sensible foreground nor to the most inner parts of the background, but rather is found in the outer strata of the latter.

This fact can be seen immediately in the case of poetry, where the "material" is limited, curtailed, and condensed by this procedure; here the selection occurs in the stratum in which the scenes are given form, and on the next stratum, in which the material has already been brought to a state of greater unity regarding the story and the destiny of its characters. These are precisely the strata where concreteness, vivacity, closeness to life, and clarity are most at stake.

But this is also true of the middle strata (the outer strata of the background) in painting. For there the background already begins with the spatiality and physicality that appear on the canvas; it is here – even more with respect to the "light in the painting" – that the choices be made and the shaping of the objective elements, as the painter sees them, take place.

Especially important about these reflections is this: the point is reached where the analysis of the strata becomes attached to the analysis of form. For it might appear at first sight as though the two stood obliquely to each other. That is clearly not so, and it is not by chance that in our very first steps we insisted upon the importance of the middle strata.

It is simply no longer possible, when one has grasped the principle behind the order of strata, to go a step further without encountering form and strata repeatedly.

Chapter 17: The Hierarchical Bestowing of Form in the Arts

a) The peculiar character of bestowing form in art

These observations are nothing more than a prelude. The main question that now appears asks: what, indeed, is bestowal of form in aesthetics, what kind of thing is it – in contrast to other kinds of shaping, to the ontic kind, for example, or to the subjective shaping of our ideas; and, perhaps most in contrast to the active shaping of things by practical human activities, such as the shaping of the conditions of life?

If one takes off from the representational arts, the first thing one will encounter is that here we have to do with a transforming: the material that art takes in is not simply reproduced but transformed into something else. That is the reason (229) why all theories of imitation are wrong, even though the earliest beginnings of the arts may have consisted in the imitation of some given thing.

The previous chapter developed a conception of the way "transformation" is to be understood. There we found the elements of selection, omission, and the guidance of all acts of supplementation through the work of art itself. But it is apparently not the transformation alone that takes place. Rather there stands another transformation behind it, one that is more fundamental and that already plays a determining role in the process of selection.

For this change of structure, the following points are characteristic, which in part may be derived from the previous analysis, but in fact also leads us beyond it.

First there is a change in structure of the human psychic elements into the non-psychic and non-human: into the matter of art (words, colors, stone); or, where there is no question of a psychic element, as in certain themes in painting and sculpture, at least something alive is given shaped in lifeless matter.

This kind of transformation is identical with objectivation as such. Just it alone is tied to the reshaping of content, and this is so only because not every kind of shaping is possible in every material form.

One forgets that point quite often – namely that even this kind of transformation takes place – because of the malleability of "representation." But it is obvious in itself that the "head of stone" is something different as that of the living human being who was perhaps the model. And no one would make such a mistake. Similarly, the person represented in literature is something different from a living man. The "transformation" begins with such simple things.

Secondly, this is a transformation into something unreal. It may appear that this contradicts the first point; for precisely "matter," in to which the subject is transformed, is entirely real. How then can a transformation in material be at the same time a transformation into something unreal?

This can be explained in the following way. The shaping of something in material substance is not a realization, a making real, but only its representation, and this does not negate its otherness at all. The figures that the poet creates are not made real by him, any more than the things that the painter shows us: they all remain unreal, and make no pretense to reality.

It would be much better to speak in such cases of removing reality, specifically in the twofold sense: 1. The releasing [of a thing] into a new sphere and at the same time setting [it] apart from reality; 2. Alteration or leaving aside many details, without which what is real could not be. But what is represented must be carried by some kind of matter; otherwise it would remain tied to a subjective picture, and could not enter the sphere of objectivation [*Objektivation*]. But of course, it is with this latter that aesthetic objectivity [*Gegenstänlichkeit*] begins. (230)

We can perhaps express this idea in summary form: with the realization of form – one that has already been selected – in matter, the material loses its reality. Or, while form becomes real in matter, the thing represented becomes by that process relieved of its reality and is placed over against it.

The third element is that this is a transformation resulting in greater intuitive clarity. This element is not equivalent either to the first or to the second. Matter is no doubt available to clear intuition, but only in the sense of the first kind of seeing, i.e., perception, and in that case it no longer is involved in the bestowing of form upon the "material" – or, if so, only as a means. The realm of the unreal, however, is in general not at all clearly intuitable; a special sort of formal construction is required for that.

For art works of all kinds it is precisely this aspect of bestowing form that is of special importance. For in most cases "material" is not inherently clear: we have in life no doubt intuitive knowledge of mental and organic things – the latter are deeply concealed – but only incomplete knowledge, and even that knowledge is in part like a dark sense of something without concrete intuitable content.

The poet, the painter, the sculptor, yes, even the musician, each lifts these objects out of their shadowy vagueness and makes them "indirectly" visible, audible, imaginable; they let them appear in the shape of concrete scenes or in the inward stance of a portrait, or in the waxing and waning of volumes of sound.

The decisive element herein is holding strictly fast to the unreality, or, perhaps even more, to a tangible deprivation of the sense of realty. This last phenomenon does not conflict with a thing's clear intuitibility. It manifests in this case the fact that the close connection of reality to clarity that we normally assume in life does not retain its validity in the realm of art. There is a clear intuitibility of a higher order, such as only art can produce to such a degree. Objectively it is identical with the "second seeing" or "beholding" that attaches itself to perception, but there it enters into immediate opposition to it, and has the advantage of inner freedom of beholding what is not real.

If we take these two points together, viz., the transformation into unreality and this into clear intuitable presence, then one is still inclined involuntarily to seek something positive that could genuinely connect them. Such things cannot be adequately grasped; yet anyone at all who asks this question has seen this phenomenon, and most have characterized it as "idea."

This notion, no doubt, has often been understood too simply in a Platonic manner as a certain purity or perfection; but then again, the universality of the "idea" is usually not absent. However in this last case we see the confusion, for then we would lose the element of clear intuitibility. (231)

One must rather take one's point of departure from the ontic nature of ideal being, as is familiar from mathematical or axiological structures: they are indifferent to reality and unreality, but they open us to greater possibilities than the real.

Structures as those that arise in the strata of the background do not have such ideal being; for example, literary characters, for otherwise they would be capable of being grasped by anyone independently of the work. This is obviously not the case. They also do not really possess eternal timeless being, but are very much dependent on their historical fate (the preservation of the text and the availability of minds adequate to them).

True, these figures "appear" in a timeless reality and are raised into an ideal realm. And that is quite obvious, for they possess nothing at all but the form of being we call appearance – with all conditions that belong to it (one should recall here the "tripartite" and four-part relation, Chap. 5b). To be perfectly accurate, we should say that structures of this kind have of course been raised to the ideal dimension, but only in an appearing ideality. And that is just sufficient for the figures of literature and portraiture, etc.[68]

For this appearing ideality unites the elevation above time and above connectedness to reality and the most concrete intuitive clarity. And this is what is at stake in this region. As such, we see something of what is genuinely correct about Platonic intuitionism: no doubt, it occurs in a very different type of beholding, as, for example, was the idea of Schelling and Schopenhauer.

---

[68] For more on appearing ideality cf. *Das Problem des geistigen Seins* [*The Problem of Spiritual Being*], 1933 (1949), Chaps. 50b and 51d–f.

b) The hierarchy of form-bestowal by strata

The previous points demonstrate clearly how closely related is the problem of the bestowal of form in the work of art to that of the succession of strata upon which it is built. The "appearing ideality," which comprises the first four elements of "transformation," is a function of the appearance-relation, as it governs from stratum to stratum – as far, at least, as the stratification reaches in the aesthetic object.

It is now necessary to evaluate this "function" with reference to the problem of the bestowal of form. If the possibility existed of analyzing "structurally" the entire phenomenon of aesthetical form purely as such, we could take a direct route here, in such a way, for example, as biology describes and analyzes organic forms or as ontology does for formal structural organization. But this possibility is not given: it would as such be equivalent to the revelation of the mystery of artistic production. This revelation is prohibited to philosophical inquiry.

What remains is the description of the conditions prevailing between the strata of the aesthetic object with respect to the bestowing of form. The following theses are most decisive. (232)

1. Every stratum of the aesthetic object has its own kind of formation, one that does not merge with any other stratum.
2. But there is also contained a dependency in this independence: the formation of the "prior" stratum must always be sufficient to allow the appearance of the next inner stratum.
3. In the total effect, then, the most external formation, i.e., the sensibly given one, is in the end determined by what is most different from it – by the element lying deepest in the background; it is the task of the more external formation to allow the most internal to appear.

An entire program of research is of course contained in these three theses, that, to do them justice, would have to be carried out with all the arts. Here a few remarks will clarify the matter and leave the issue open to supplementation later on.

The first thesis concerns the specific formation of every stratum. In poetry the bestowal of form upon language (thus upon the "matter") is obviously different from the formation of what is spoken by it; and this is so, no doubt, even when one takes the latter simply as that which "appears first of all" (that is, as the most external outer stratum of the background), thus as what directly manifests only the movement, gesture, and speech of the literary characters.

And yet the formation of the "manifested" movement, gestures, and speech (reproduced in the theatrical presentation) is different from the bestowal of form upon situations and actions. As the author can choose his words in very different ways in order to present the same movements and gestures, so also can he select the elements of movement and gesture – or even the dialogue – of his characters very differently in order to reveal indirectly to intuition the inward sense of the specific relationships among men, of the situations and actions. Compare with each other the ways different storytellers place before our eyes relatively similar situations in life. The independence of the forms in each of these strata will quickly become apparent.

This relation can be pursued: when there appears behind the level of situation and plot a level of the mental character of individuals or of an entire social milieu, there must also appear on this level some elements of form of a different kind – in fact both in the selection and the guiding of ideas. The poet cannot analyze a character with all his tricks and guises prior to his appearance; he can only let him show himself just as the external events in life show him to be from time to time: by highlighting his individual traits, illuminating his typical mannerisms and his social status. But the poet has the freedom to select the social status and mannerisms that are appropriate to his purpose in this "showing." In this way, he preserves the concrete clear intuitibility even in what cannot be given directly to everyday vision.

And so it stands also with the further stratum of the entire human lot, which the poet can in fact give us only in small segments; here too (233) form is bestowed upon a larger whole out of certain individual parts – but in such a way that the parts interlock within the whole of the poet's vision.

This is only an example. For in other arts the order of strata takes a different form than in literature. Moreover, the order of strata in literature has not been exhausted by the analysis thus far; there still are the last inner strata to consider. But it is nevertheless easy to see that a similar account applies there also, as, e.g., for the idea of personality, and not less for the universally human.

We can easily compare this with the situation in painting. The "technique" of painting (the treatment of color, the brushwork, etc.) is a perfect example of form-bestowal, but in a direct sense only upon the real foreground. The organization of three-dimensional space, the "light in the painting" and the physical objects are genuine form-bestowals, but obviously ones of a different kind, which, in comparison to the former, can be freely varied. Again, the representation of motion produces form of a third kind; and behind this stratum stand the further strata in clear intuitibility: that of the plot, of psychological states, moods, attitudes, or that of a character's individual personality, etc. – they are all, in the same picture, formal structures of an individual kind, transformations of something seen, or of ideal entities beheld in the mind –; but there are just as many different formal structures that never flow over and into each other, because each one has its own meaning, incorporating selection, condensing, and the power to draw attention to itself upon its own, and only on its own level, having nothing to seek on another level. For example, one cannot give form to spatial depth or lighting conditions on the same level as the one in which psychological states and attitudes are represented; or to give shape to the ideal of personality that is visible in a portrait where the concern is with movement and animation. Each must have its peculiar form bestowed upon it within its stratum.

In non-representational art, the situation is also at bottom no different – at least provided that stratifications govern in them. We can see this clearly in music; there, especially, the outer and inner strata are widely separated: each move entirely within the hierarchically arranged unities of the compositional structure, each unity entirely in the psychic world of feeling and moods.

Just this heterogeneity – which creates the miracle of music – is sufficient to make unequivocally clear the absolute otherness of bestowing forms upon sound and on the psychological realities that appear there. We recall how in the *Lied* the same human psychic themes can be set to music in quite different ways, without our being able to say that only one musical setting is "right" for the text. And, on the other hand, we recall how one can interpret, under certain circumstances, works of "pure" music very differently with respect to its spirit. And even where this plurality of meaning has its limits in what are purely matters of feeling, the formal structure of the music is quite different from the psychological content and its specific form. (234)

We can see the same conditions within the outer strata. A movement's "structure," for example, is not determined in the slightest by the "musical theme" (the smallest unity). This is true also the other way around. The theme has to be correctly chosen if it is to build a certain kind of movement (e.g., a finale written to a specific tempo), but it is never the case that only a single appropriate motif can be found for it. In certain circumstances (to make the point sharper), it is possible even to write the same "movement" around another theme. This conflicts only with the cant of musical theory, which does not distinguish sharply in this context between theme and structure, and therefore calls a movement written to another motif *a limine* a "different movement."

What this all makes clear, besides the implications we have already drawn, is this: the main weight of this independence, with regards to form, of the strata of an object is felt in the middle strata: in the case of the real foreground this is almost self-evident, for perception has independent laws for all areas of the senses, and these must be satisfied if there is to be an aesthetical effect. For the last strata of the background, however, the independence of the process of bestowing form is no longer as important: the ideal aspects tower up from their narrow confines – even the purely aesthetical ones – and usually enter into the realm of the moral.

Neither the foreground nor the final and deepest storehouse of ideal content is for itself an aesthetical structure. In all respects, the crucial phase lies in the middle strata: in the deeper outer strata and the less deep inner strata. The concrete riches and the intuitive clarity are played out there, and in them, therefore, lies the greatest variety in the way form may be bestowed.

Here one should always keep in mind that the enormous riches of content of works of literature, painting, music, and the like, rest precisely upon these strata and primarily upon the fact that the forms lie thickly arranged one upon the other. This has its great charm, moreover, in the independence of each of these superimposed formations as they rest upon each other.

The "heart" that is once raised to the level of this inner – higher – beholding is initially overwhelmed by the multiplicity of forms. The heart peers through one and immediately comes upon another one standing behind it. It finds no peace, and is drawn from one act of beholding to another.

c) Connections in the giving of form within the strata

The second point above maintained that independence always contains some form of dependency, such that the forms given in a prior stratum are sufficient for the appearance of the next one further down. Now what kind of dependency is this? And how is it compatible with the independence of form in each stratum?

We may first answer: it is the same dependence that we recognized in the relation of appearance generally. Every (235) stratum is thus so constituted as to allow the deeper stratum to appear. What is new about the relation of appearance is only that it is now a question of a relationship among the formal structures.

But then how is this a relationship among formal structures? Up to now, it has always appeared that relations of form and of appearance were opposed to each other. Yet we may earnestly ask whether next to the kind of beauty that consists in appearance there is not still another kind that is entirely assimilated to a pure play with form. And, at least with respect to ornamentation, that could not be disputed. How does that fact cohere with the dependency of formal structure within the sequence of strata in the work of art?

It is obviously false to separate widely the phenomena of form-bestowal and appearance. In fact, they are closely related. To begin with, the difference between them is only of a methodological sort: we cannot really "analyze" aesthetical form in any of its strata, for that is and remains the secret of art; it can be characterized only as to certain of its external traits. But we can of course analyze the relation of appearance. For that reason, we placed its discussion early on, and treated it independently, as though there was no relation to form. This methodological opposition cannot, however, be taken as absolute, or as founded in the very nature of the phenomena.

Most importantly, we must once again warn ourselves before proceeding not to confuse the opposition in question with that between "form" and "content." The latter is in part merely apparent: "form and material" can be clearly distinguished, but unformed material is not the "content" of the work of art – in fact, not in any of its strata – but only that which has been given form. For that reason, there is little that can be done with that distinction here. It is still true that the "content" – if one insists on using the term – always essentially consists in form.

The evidence for the relation of form concealed in the relation of appearance can be, however, derived only descriptively from the construction of the artwork's strata. For this, we must again appeal to a selection of phenomena, which, to be sure, cannot be complete, but seeks only to approach the distinction where it is relatively attainable, thus one that is relatively arbitrary.

Let us begin with sculpture, where the bestowing of form upon matter in the foreground takes place in real space. How does the sculptor allow movement and life to appear, while his figures are at rest and thus lifeless? In this question, there is also a concern for the relations of the real sensible stratum to the two that follow it, the outer strata of the background. For movement is not yet life, and life "appears" only in movement as something distinct – which, no doubt, may also be absent if the skill of the artist fails him.

We cannot, as we have noted, identify the very nature of how the sculptor does it. But this much is visible. He brings life about by mans of bestowing form upon the foreground (that is, the real matter, clay, or (236) stone) in a peculiar way. There is no other way to let movement appear, or, *a fortiori*, animation.

The sculptor "gives form," to be sure, directly to the momentary position of the limbs in that phase of their motion that he has chosen, for example, that of the wrestlers at a single moment of their match; but he chooses the phase such that the movement indirectly expresses itself, that is, he gives form to the phase of the motion of the struggle that he wishes to show us by shaping the phase statically. And to achieve this, he must make visible in that phase everything that is characteristic of that phase of motion (position, the play of muscles).

The situation is the same in the relation to the next stratum: animation. Life is no longer something spatial, in the proper sense, while movement of course still is. But life expresses itself in movement; therefore, one may also express life in movement by art. The sculptor does that by showing us the tension and effort of the entire body as it goes about its work. He can hammer out these two by giving spatial form to the phase of motion.

The element of bestowing form upon the foreground, which produces this miracle, is extraordinarily subtle. It may lie in the smallest measures among the spatial relations. Our analysis cannot penetrate these subtleties of form; it may only appear to the living aesthetical beholding on the part of the viewer. One may stand before the Wrestlers and ask which details in the group allow tension, struggle, and life itself, to appear. One will be able to find and specify many things, but one will not exhaust the riches of form, as long as it lets other elements of form appear (movement and life). One senses here with greater assurance how the appearing form is tied to the visible form, and how the work of art consists precisely in the fact that the latter is sufficient for the former.

And how does the composer succeed, when he wishes to express "passion," or a "solemn silence," "hidden sorrow," "yearning," "awe-inspiring greatness," and the like? Remember that none of these examples is taken from program music; they concern the psychic content, i.e., the inner strata of pure music.

There is no doubt: the composer, too, is simply free to give form to the outer strata of music such that they allow the given psychic forms to appear. There is no other way for the musical expression of human inwardness.

But now the outer strata of music are those that allow of no psychic [seelische] themes, but rather move in pure tonal musical formations and have their own "themes" in them. How, then, can the musician make psychic forms appear in the formal design of a musical structure?

The answer was given above (Chap. 14c), but without consideration of the problem of form, in the following way: music is fundamentally related to the life of the soul; both are extended in time, both exist in a flow, in constant transitions, in the motion; (237) both are found in the reciprocal play of tension and relaxation, of excitement and calm.

That constitutes the opposition of the life of the soul to the external physical world just as much as the opposition of music to the plastic arts. And therefore music, with its flow, its transitions, its agitation, can map at such great proximity and with such distinctness the flow, transitions, and agitation of our psychic life (the surging, the rising and falling, the dying away, the roaring and rushing, pursuit and escape ... and the taming of these unchained forces ...).

These elements are contained in musical form itself, they co-constitute it and are heard as such from within it. More accurately, they are contained in all three outer strata of the musical background – from the musical "theme" to the "movement" and to the sonata. It follows from this that they do not need to be added to the design of the structure, but that rather the purely musical-compositional design is what allows the psychic design (excitement and the like) to appear.

One can follow this relation further into very fine details – for example, into the succession of the motifs, the sonic effects of modulation, the unexpected appearance of new "development" or even a mere pianissimo. ... One may also follow it from within the outer strata from stratum to stratum, and similarly from the deeper outer strata to the deeper inner strata, and so forth.

But with that, nothing else new has been said. What is alone important is just the indicated foundational relation itself. And it is clear proof of the dependent status of form in the series of strata; proof, that is, for that hierarchy of the levels of formation, each one independent in itself, by means of which the deeper formation, in regard to its appearance, is tied to the formation directly before it.

As a third area of study let us now take literature. It shares with music the temporality of the main dimension in which it operates. In it are also the movement and the flow of the psychic life, which give the middle strata their wealth of content. But the similarity is merely apparent.

We see this immediately when we pass from the appearance-relation to the form-relation. Music can directly "paint," as it were, the movement of the soul by tonal agitation and stress; literature cannot do that, or it can only in a very limited way, by the sound of words. Literature must rather make the same detour here that our knowledge of our psychic life does: it passes from movement and gesture to situation and plot, and from there to the character and inward moral life of persons, and again from there to large collections of events, that is, to the whole of human life and destiny.

To what extent may one say that in this case we are dealing with relationships of a formal sort? Or, to restrict the question, how does the poet bring it to pass (238) that such inward things like situations and events in the plot appear in the movements and gestures that are presented spatially and external to them?

He proceeds no differently than in life itself. He bestows form upon what is external and visible, and lets it so appear by means of words, as we would see it in life as eye-witnesses; but through this bestowal of form on what is external – with all the writer's means of selection and guidance – he allows at the same time the internal to be reflected in the external, and the idea in it to "appear." For gesture and movement are revealing, and always tell us indirectly something about the human soul, something, most likely, they were supposed precisely to keep silent about and to conceal.

Thus the poet indirectly gives form to inward matters by bestowing form upon external things: upon the situation, provided that it is touched with psychic tension, and the plot, with its uncertainties, its struggles, and its climactic decisions.

The process of giving form proceeds correspondingly in the series of strata: within the plot, the poet gives form to the character and morals of his figures; and within the last stratum and all the earlier ones together, he draws the shape of an entire human destiny.

d) Determining form from within

If we keep these ideas before our mind, it becomes clear why the attempts of aesthetics to solve the puzzle of beauty with a uniform analysis of form are condemned to failure. One thought of the form of a work of art as something uniformly comprehensible. However, it is not. Form is hierarchical in nature, and yet upon every level it is independent, although containing at the same time a certain dependency. No one had imagined such complicated conditions to exist within it. Nonetheless, the element of dependency has still not been exhausted.

The third point set forth above claimed that in the total effect the most external element of form is already determined by what is most heterogeneous to it, that is, by the one furthest in the background. That seems, at first sight, however, to conflict with the previous point. That claimed that the bestowal of form upon the anterior stratum always must allow the appearance of the one next deep, in which case the appearance of the posterior would be dependent upon the anterior. But if so, then in the final effect of the entire series of strata the most external forms could not be dependent on the most internal ones, but rather the internal ones are dependent on the external ones.

This aporia rests upon a confusion. It can be resolved in a manner similar to the resolution of the theoretical confusions of *ratio cognoscendi* and *ratio essendi*: in the appearance-relation the form given upon the anterior stratum is always conditional for the appearance of the posterior one; in contrast, in the conditions of composition of the work of art, and in the conditions of the work of the artist producing it, the situation is the other way around. The giving of form on the posterior stratum is conditional upon that of the anterior. For what is in the foreground is formed in just such a manner that it permits the form given to the background to appear. The deeper inner strata therefore determine it. They are the ones for whose sake the (239) outer strata are there. And in this sense even the bestowal of form upon the sensible foreground is, in the end, determined precisely by means of the last background stratum.

This is a relationship among conditions that takes on very important forms in many of the arts, and it is also a very concrete one, such that one immediately senses from where the principle of selection in the middle strata has been taken, namely from the last background stratum, from a universal idea, perhaps, that is intended to appear concretely in the work.

In literature we find famous examples of this type, even when they do not quite make their point strongly felt at all: the determination of small external details by means of the "idea" of the things. For example, Schiller's *Luise Millerin*. Idea: the struggle of the oppressed for freedom from the despotism of the nobles. This idea runs through the characters and their destinies, which have been selected for its sake; it penetrates into situations and behavior, and further into speech, movement, and gestures – and from there as far as the written text of the play. Such interplay is perhaps even clearer in lyric poetry, where the forms of words directly express moods: for example, [Goethe's] "Über allen Gipfeln." The sense of impending death resonates with a certain directness from the verses.

Such self-interlinking of the first with the last link in the chain of artistic form may be felt everywhere in successful work, if one is attentive to it.

In the case of painting, it may be especially noticeable in portraiture, at least where real skill applies itself to something genuinely individual. The skill consists essentially in grasping and making visible this individuality. In great masters, it extends beyond empirical individuality – to the "individual idea."

How does the painter express such a thing? In no other way than in the way life occasionally expresses such things and "betrays" them: through small features of what is visible – a shadow at the corner of a mouth, a pair of light spots in the eyes – there is no other way. But this is in reality the passageway over the entire linkage of strata in painting, a passageway that cannot be shortened. For every omission of strata in the continuous process of the bestowal of form threatens the entire work with a lack of uniformity and comprehensibility. A portrait can have a harmonious effect only if it contains within itself the unbroken succession of the formal elements.

One can take examples from anywhere at all – always assuming that the final inner strata are present. In music, for example, it is almost entirely obvious that the ideal is directly determinative of the tonal elements, which are its building-blocks. Thus, the festiveness of [Beethoven's] Ninth Symphony is apparent, and that mood can be followed into its themes; these are determined by the fundamental mood in which its idea is rooted: broad, full-hearted love of humanity. The same can be said of the youthful, (240) untroubled heroism in [Richard Wagner's] "Forging Song" in *Siegfried*. And how much more must this be true of Bach's late fugues (*The Art of the Fugue* and the *Ricercar*), of which everyone senses the metaphysical horizons! No one can say just what these elements consist in. But it is determinative of the pieces up to the purely sonic foreground. And only the people who hear them from within are able to hear these works rightly.

In these reflections, we have omitted reference to architecture. It is more difficult to demonstrate these points in its case. But the last point is clear: provided that universal ideas are present at all at the roots of a work of architecture, so much is valid: they co-determine, with special purity and directness, the external shape of the work. We see this everywhere in monuments; in churches, the reaching of the spires to the heights corresponds to no practical ends. But even in the structure of a house, there is a synthesis of the feeling of home with family pride. All of that is visible in the external form.

Chapter 18: Appearance and Form

a) The dependence and independence of form

The most striking thing about the inquiries in the last chapter was that independence and dependency in the process of bestowing form accompanied each other through all strata. This interpenetration is nothing new in itself; we know it also from another system of strata, i.e., the categorical stratification in the structure of the real world.

What is of positive value here is that a mutual relation of supplementation and support passes through all strata, and, indeed a relation of forms – although, notably, each form is different in kind in the various strata.

What is here of primary importance is that the giving of form on a single stratum, seen as isolated and taken in itself, is not at all aesthetical form. The aesthetics of form has always misunderstood that. It thought to take to itself a definite kind of formal element, i.e., that of some one stratum, for example, the stratum in which literary material is treated, and to investigate just as such its intrinsic "laws." That may be possible, but it fails to achieve its purpose, for in this way one does not arrive at aesthetical form at all. For that begins only with the succession of forms of different kinds.

Here it is a question precisely of the mutuality of supplementation and support of forms, a kind of reciprocal conditionality that yet allows a relative independence of the formal elements of individual strata. For that reason a content peculiar to each stratum appears to careful observation: in the middle strata of literature, for example, we see the colorful multiplicity of events, of situations, or perhaps also of a whole scene – each according to the given level – and, within certain limits, one can enjoy each "content" of such kinds and let it have its peculiar effect. And, one may add (241) here that the more content a work of art has in the middle strata, the richer and more accomplished it is. This content is entirely formal in nature.

We see from this how things stand with regard to the interpenetration of independence and dependency within the strata. It is quite noteworthy that the rear strata shine through the ones more to the front, and it is just in that fact that the aesthetical meaning of the bestowal of form for the latter consists: in the task of allowing them to shine through. Nonetheless it is for that very reason not true that the meaning of the forward strata is entirely exhausted in that task.

To the contrary, every stratum, along with the artistic shaping that it has undergone, has its own weight, and this weight will be felt by the understanding viewer as possessing its own content – "content" of course not as opposed to form, but rather in the above sense of content [*Gehalt*], for which the formal element is the chief thing.

One can identify this phenomenon quite precisely. Let us return to the middle strata of literature. The verse, "Wie er sich räuspert, wie er spuckt,"[69] is essential here; similarly the way a man quickly looks about himself for possible witnesses, before he opens a shut door, or glances upon a piece of writing that is not intended for him. This is the stratum of movement and gesture. The same is true of the next stratum, that of situation and plot: think of the way a person caught in a lie tries to extract himself – he may go about it very thoughtfully and even succeed in it, but he may also get himself caught in contradictions and stand there ashamed. In both cases, apart from all transparency of the traits of moral character – thus for the next stratum – the bestowal of plastic form upon this variety of material has a value in itself that is also felt as such: specifically, as colorful, rich, abundant, human, and as true to life.

It is not possible to demonstrate these matters except by reference to examples like these and by appealing to the aesthetical enjoyment of this concrete richness. It is at least conceivable that a great deal of detail not be necessary for the appearance of character and destiny. Yet such richness of detail would still be justified, for it has a weight of its own: it gives a breadth and resonance to the work that is not unimportant.

Only in this way may we properly approach the relation, which still hangs in suspense, between independence and dependency in the hierarchy of aesthetical form that exists in the strata of the artwork. In fact, precisely in respect to aesthetics the thorough bestowing of form upon details in every stratum is done on the one hand entirely for the sake of some other detail, but on the other hand, it is there entirely for itself alone.

It is not excessive to express the matter so sharply, because on both sides of this apparent autonomy there is a separate aesthetic value. The details of the form given each stratum – especially in the middle strata – (242) create the riches, but the relation of appearance creates the depth and uniformity of the work of art.

But the unity of the whole will seem "thin" despite all depth, if it lacks the completeness of form bestowed on a variety of details in the middle strata; and

---

69 [Translator's note:] Friedrich Schiller, *Wallensteins Lager* [*Wallenstein's Camp*], Scene VI. Hartmann adds the "sich" to Schiller's text. The passage in question has been translated as follows. A hunter is speaking to an army watch-sergeant, who claims to have learned a great deal of manners from his superior officer. "How he hawks and spits, indeed, I may say / You've copied and caught in the cleverest way," says the hunter, implying that the sergeant has not learned much of the deeper spirit of the man. (Schiller, Friedrich, "Wallenstein's Camp," in: *The Works of Frederick Schiller. Historical and Dramatic.* London: Bell & Daldy 1871, p. 147).

similarly the riches of a colorful abundance of content will seem flat, if the full growth of detail does not allow its other face to be shown, that of transparency.

We can illustrate these matters with other arts. They are expressed with special clarity, for example, in painting; we saw already that here the greatest weight lies more heavily than elsewhere upon the purely sensible and visible, that is, upon the outer strata.

Why is that so? Hegel's aesthetics was anxious to respond: because painting is a sensuous-superficial art, and does not aim at the inwardness of things, as literature does. We have already noted the distortions of this thought: it is true neither that the painterly arts lack inner strata, nor that its attachment to what is visible is mere superficiality. To the contrary, it fulfills with the greatest exactitude the task of art to let everything – even what is of the nature of ideas – to appear in sensible form; just that is called "aesthetical."

Naturally, therefore, the emphasis in aesthetics also lies entirely upon the sensible element, by which we mean: upon the outer strata. Therefore, too, it is obvious that all details that fall under the light internal to the painting have a weight of their own. Just by themselves alone, they tell us something about this apparent light that we might not have noticed in life – and, they do that, indeed, apart from what features of life and motion ought to "appear" just through this light. For it is a question here too of the riches and abundance of what is visible, of their value for themselves alone – thus a richness lying quite beyond the limits of what is a necessary condition of this appearance. Despite all the variety of the circumstances, this is at bottom the same relation as in literature. What is new here is only that on both sides – that of independence and that of dependency – the character of the form on each stratum emerges more clearly.

It is no different in the non-representational arts, although here the independence of the formal elements in individual strata is more strongly apparent. True, this is not valid at all for the external strata, but that much more valid for the transition to the inner strata.

This is clear in music. The outer strata include the compositional elements, and these unfold their richness of form on each single stratum with convincing independence: it is a pure play with form, and is felt as such. The unfolding of the "themes," their variation, development, extension and recapitulation, their combination with other themes, submersion in them and then their return – those are all things that have their meaning and their laws entirely within themselves, and these latter do not draw upon whatever psychic content that appears in them. (243)

This does not of course prevent such psychic content from still appearing in just this hierarchical bestowal of form upon the compositional elements. The one is wonderfully compatible with the other; the dependency does not encroach upon the independence. A model of this relation is, again, contrapuntal music: its riches of form can be valued and enjoyed in themselves; it can also offer us a psychic background of amazing profundity.

b) Pure play with form

One thing becomes clear from the example of music: There must exist a kind of pure formal beauty that does not rest upon the appearance-relation. Otherwise, such a pure independent play with form, as we find in music would not be possible. More precisely, it might be possible, but it could not have such an unambiguous claim to an independent aesthetical effect.

We begin this section with this claim; it does not limit itself to music. We encounter it again in architecture, and it reaches its highest point in ornamental art, for there the play with form appears just for itself alone, without any relation of strata or transparency. But at this point, the problem of form becomes again more complex.

One thing must be clear before we proceed: if there is beauty in a pure play with form – without stratification, etc. – it is improbable that it be quite absent anywhere. We would thus be forced to seek out once again its laws, even in the representational arts. Of course then we might be dealing with a great variety of graduations in the phenomenon, and these could very well explain a disappearance behind the texture of stratification and of relations of appearance.

First, we direct the question at the non-representational arts. In their case, the appearance-relation is less central from the very outset. And, no doubt, the question concerns for the most part ornamental art, although this art does not stand on the same level as the other arts, and even with respect to the pure play of form it reaches the value of music or architecture only in a limited way.

We have already shown (Chap. 7e) how the play with form achieves in ornamental art a certain independence, which, however, comes about only in a limited way through the inclusion of the ornament in a greater formal context, for example, that of an architectural work. The remainder of the appearance-relation, which nonetheless might be attached to it, should be left out of consideration here.

It remains to be seen how something similar to what occurs in the external strata of music can be found in ornament. A formal motif, a "theme" as it were, is placed at the foundation and then is freely and imaginatively transformed, repeated, interrelated, placed in opposition, and in these transformations laced together to form a new and greater whole.

This schema applies fairly well to ornament. Of course the process need not be so simple; there can be an interrelation of motifs of different (244) kinds. They can also be varied together or independently of each other; in this way they can lead to greater multiplicity. In that case, the mastery of the whole by means of an inclusive formal unity will mark a greater achievement and a higher synthesis.

This play with form can be carried out on a variety of grades: it can be very primitive – both in the motifs and in the treatment of them – it can also rise to considerable complexity and then offer to our eyes the task of tracing its lines or its chains of repetitions, of puzzling out the twisting play, of finding the unity of the whole, which cannot be taken in a clear view immediately, but which is still within reach, or of tying together its various entries, etc.

The pleasure given the viewing subject when he is drawn into such "tasks" is clearly of a unique kind, although less profound than in the other arts. In any case, there is a stimulus here and excitement *sui generis*. One thinks involuntarily of the "play of the powers of the mind" that Kant recommended so highly, which begins its work through the perception of relations of line and form of this kind. In fact, much can be inspired by a complicated ornamental art: contrast, harmony, Arabesques, the intertwining and unraveling (of lines, for example), overlapping, the interruption and the continuation of what was interrupted.

Those are elements that we also know from the middle strata of music, and there, too, we have a distinct autonomy, a case of speaking-for-itself – without referring beyond itself to something else. And if such independence is possible in music, where, indeed, the appearance-relation is dependent upon it, how much more must it be possible in ornamental art, where this relation is absent.

No doubt, formal beauty of this kind is more various and sublime in music. Why is this so? The basis for it must lie, in the end, neither in the greater workability of the audible "matter" (tones and sounds), nor in the greater variety of its possibilities – in both respects the "visible matter" is at least similar – but rather because a tone does not express any physical object, and thus is free from motifs of a different kind, while the visible form falls captive to physical themes when it branches off or becomes complicated. (Or we should say: the height of a tone has nothing visible analogous to it, as color corresponds to timbre. Does music thus have an additional dimension?)

Thus it occurs that ornamental art has to worry about shielding itself from concretization. Concretization inhibits free play with form – although, on occasion, it may also give such free play new ideas. But such stimulus should lie in the background; it must not become intrusive. For this reason in all ornamental art that makes use of plant or animal motifs, there is a clear tendency towards stylization. That term means in this context approximately the same as deconcretization: the natural form (245) becomes conscious, and is expressly transformed into something else. This other thing is the image, which fits itself into the play of lines, the patterns, or the twisting shapes upon which it is visible.

We see this phenomenon clearly in the leaf and tendril motifs of the ancients; similarly in dolphin, lion, snake, or fish motifs. We see it still in the demon and monster motifs of the Gothic, which no doubt stand already at the limits of sculpture and ornament.

This entire tendency, which represents a kind of flight from formal realism, is only a variation of what we have already encountered in a more general form as an element in making an object less real. But here it is not a question of a mode of being, but of form itself. These objects should no longer affect us as a real animal or a real plant, but as something entirely different, something that does not appear in the real world in such a manner, for example, as musical "themes" never occur in the real world outside of music. The multiplicity that arises out of the play with form is intended to be a world unto itself; it should never, therefore, count as the imitation of something real even of its parts. Here we can grasp the opposition between ornamental art and painting.

It makes sense, therefore, to orient the problem of the pure play with form precisely towards primitive motifs. These still stand entirely on this side of all thing, animal, or plant motifs. One can perhaps describe them most simply as motifs that are spatial combinations of sorts or even as "geometric." The latter expression should of course not be taken in a strictly mathematical sense, but only in the sense of a geometric way of looking at form.

It has long been remarked that certain simple geometrical figures exert a definite aesthetical attraction, which can be rightly classified with aesthetical pleasure, enjoyment, etc. Often in past times this attraction was praised as the "beauty" of pure geometry. The ancient belief that the circle was the "most perfect form," and, perhaps even more, the sphere, did not rest at all upon speculative considerations alone, but rather more on the obvious intuitive simplicity and the clarity of the figures, which themselves were originally felt as "beauty."

We can feel that immediately even today. Perhaps the shape of the ellipse or the hyperbole seems even more "beautiful" to us; and in this a dark sense of the lawfulness that inheres in it speaks to us clearly. Further examples of this are the spiral, both the Archimedean and the logarithmic. One can follow this series further downwards – to the rhombus, the rectangle, squares, and triangle; only here the human sense of aesthetical form is not so universal. But in other areas, that is also true.

If one is sufficiently advanced in this play with form as to see into these primitive beginnings, one may draw the conclusion (246) that a single great line of gradations leads from them to the enormous riches of form in music and also to the middle strata of other arts.

One should not spoil this insight by an assumption that an inscrutable opposition exists between the beauty of appearance and the "beauty of form."

Rather, our examples from geometry show precisely that absolutely continuous transitions are present here: to this bears witness the presentment of the laws behind the figures felt by the naïve viewer, that is, a person that is not scientifically oriented. For in this presentment the remainder of the relation of appearance is clearly recognizable. One may recall here Schopenhauer's doctrine of the intuitive character of geometrical insight.

But it is the same the other way around. Even aesthetical joy taken in the play with form never entirely ceases, even in a person trained ever so much in the representational arts. We already demonstrated that in the case of music; it is almost as clear in the middle strata of poetry and painting – specifically wherever the multiplicity of details reaches a magnitude that renders it aesthetically independent. For detail is genuine bestowal of form – and indeed one far beyond what is needed for appearance to take place.

Thus, the attachments on both sides are tangible, and the continuity of gradations in the interpenetration of these "two kinds of beauty" is entirely complete. One should not forget in this context that the principle of the one and the other nevertheless remain completely different.

c) Shallow and profound art

This scale is also one of depth. One senses before all reflection that ornamental art is a "shallow" art; and no one would ever think of placing it alongside the literary works or compositions of great masters. The continuity of the scale thus extends from the shallowest to the deepest aesthetical effect. And the problem that appears here is just this: what is the relationship of the relative depth of aesthetical effect to the relative preponderance of the appearance-relation or of the play with form?

We must first make one thing clear: anyone who thinks seriously about art is often disposed to consider only "great art" as being worthy of his consideration – indeed, as art at all. But such art can only be profound art, where one understands "profundity" without bias as that kind of art in which the inner strata dominate, especially the last, which always contains intellectual elements.

This insight may do honor to its representatives – it tells us they are very serious about art – but it is incorrect. There is also such a thing as (247) shallow art; we usually call it "light" art. We associate it with novels intended for amusement, with dance and the operetta, with funny caricatures. True, with such "light" art the danger of being derailed is greater than in the serious and profound arts. But it is wrong to draw the conclusion from this fact that it is not genuine art at all.

The situation is rather as follows: within light art, there is also good and bad craftsmanship, for example in operetta, in dance music, in novels intended to amuse. Naturally, such works, even when they are well crafted, are directed to a superficial sensibility, observation, and enjoyment: they serve to distract, to give pleasure, to amuse. But they can do these things in an artistically accomplished manner or artlessly. And only in the latter case will the connoisseur respond to them as failures – as "kitsch." We may understand kitsch as the attempt to cause certain effects cheaply – for the most part, emotional effects, which can be justified neither by their moral structure nor by the appearance of something from within them.

Of course, it is true that it is much easier to produce shallow works than profound ones. For simply less originality is demanded of it, less genius. Yet there are works of genius in shallow music: light, but with great beauty.

The scale of shallow and profound works exists within each art with the exception of ornamental art. But it exists also in the entire domain of the arts: the profundity of poetry and music is achieved by no other art, at least not in their great works; painting and sculpture may be for their part superior to architecture with regard to depth. So it is, at least, when one surveys them all. Of course, the scale is much larger within the arts.

What does this scale consist in? What is shallow art, what is deep art? We may begin with the act of appreciation: there are superficial and profound effects – upon the human soul. The participation of the self is from one occasion to another a different one: to be gripped, to be seized by, to be deeply shaken – or simply to be touched, to be inspired. ... As amusement is distinguished from joyful elevation, so are the strata of our psychic life touched on levels of varying depth.

All this is merely a sketch of what is contained in the object itself by way of stratified formal elements. For the difference lies here: in what stratum or on what strata does the enjoyment of an artwork lie?

And yet on the other hand, it is simply not so that the superiority of the deeper objective strata corresponds always to the deeper reaction to it of the human soul. That would be to conceive the matter too simply: for a novel written abstractly would then have the greatest artistic effect because of its psychological effects upon the mind. But such a novel cannot do that, because it lacks elements of clarity (248) and closeness to life; those things lie in the middle strata, to a certain extent also in the outer strata and even in the sensible foreground. The same is the case in painting: deeply meaningful mythical figures that lack sensible vivacity, animation, and the power of color and light, cannot have a strong aesthetical effect; the deeper sense of their symbols would be unclear to intuition.

What, then, is this relation in reality? Beauty in the arts is indirect in multiple ways. The eyes pass through a series of strata, of which each allows the next one to "appear," and in every stratum it is the specific form given to the content that brings about this appearance. Beyond that, however, still another multiplicity playfully gathers up all that comprises the riches of the artwork. This is all a recapitulation of what was said above. But it contains the basis for an answer to the question we posed. For the greater beauty is the deeper one.

But that beauty is the deeper where the eyes pass through a longer series of strata. It does not matter so much that precisely the last and deepest strata be present, or even that they have had their formal elements clearly shaped, i.e., the two innermost strata in the background of poetry and music; more important is the series of the strata itself, its dissimilarities and its variety, and also the variety of the detail in them. These details, however, come under the purview of the pure bestowal of form or of the play with form.

Depth, therefore, does not depend at all upon the opposition between the relation of appearance and the play with form. No doubt it is true that the latter always seems shallow, considered in itself; similarly, that all deeper beauty depends on the relation of appearance. But the play with form can possess an extraordinarily deep sense, if it is itself stratified and each stratum displays independence. Also, the force of letting-appear is, in its case, tied in each stratum to the form-bestowal that is proper to it. For that reason, the main element in the effects caused by size and depth of a beautiful object is not so much the "absolute depth," but rather the depth of the serial interconnectivity, one after the other.

This depth is thus the relative depth of the appearance-relation. But the effects it produces are not indifferent to how many varieties are contained in each individual stratum. In other words: their aesthetical meaning is also a function of the richness of the play with form. This was precisely what was demonstrated by the middle strata of music and literature in the richness of detail. And in painting, the situation was the same, only shifted somewhat to the external strata.

But we must in contrast establish that the aesthetical meaning of a multiplicity that has been given form in some specific stratum – one of the middle ones, perhaps – is in no manner a function of its independent beauty taken for itself. That might be conceivable in itself, for if there is at all beauty in the pure play with form, apart from the appearance-relation and independent of it, then it is reasonable to assume that, in the series of strata through which our eyes (249) pass, each stratum would have to display an independent beauty of form; and then one might also think that the result of formal beauty, in one stratum or in several, would have to be the diminishment of the aesthetic value, or even its complete elimination.

That would be an error. What is essential in its entirety for the aesthetic value of the whole is only the richness and variety of the details in the individual stratum – also, naturally, its unity – but not the independent beauty of form in it. This thesis is of course valid only in the representational arts; there it is well known. These arts can also very easily represent what is ugly, and they must do so when dealing with those themes that fall into its realm: in painting, primarily with the portrait, and in literature primarily with the description of characters and social settings.

In these cases, the middle strata may be filled with ugliness, so that for the supersensitive reader aesthetical enjoyment will vanish; but ugliness as material does not impede the beauty of form in other strata, and certainly does not impede the beauty of appearance.

d) Form and content in the structure of the strata

We said earlier that "form" and "content" do not drive themselves apart; indeed, they can hardly be brought into opposition. In fact, form itself is the content of the work of art, as is everywhere visible. What remains is the double opposition of "form and matter," on the one hand, and "form and material" on the other. About these two, we saw that the bestowal of form on some material always takes place in matter, such that there is no question of two kinds of form-bestowal, but only of one.

As long as one understands "content" as "material," there is no objection to putting "form and content" together. However, then the expression "content" extends also to what is universal in the final background stratum, which is never reducible to "material" without remainder.

As for the identity of form and content, which has often been asserted: the correct meaning of this assertion is a very simple and harmless one, but which has just always been falsely expressed. The content (material) [*Stoff*] of a work of art exists just only in the bestowing of form by the artist. What stands this side of the artistic bestowal of form is not at all the content of the work of art, but rather a kind of raw material to which the artist will bring life.

It is without doubt easy for non-artists to imagine the productive creativity of the artist. As little as one may really be able to understand that process of creation, one thing should be clear: even the creator does not bestow form only *post hoc* on the material he chooses, but is rather already testing himself in shaping just by his choice. And for the observer the material exists entirely "in" the form that is bestowed upon it.

That is verified once more when we apply here what was agreed upon earlier: the aesthetical bestowal of form upon some material is possible only by means (250) of extracting from the context of the real world that which has been torn asunder and muddled together by life by selection, omission, and condensation. That is itself already a bestowal of form upon material. This latter does not thereby become "identical" with form, but surely inseparable from it.

This corresponds also to the fact that we do not experience a piece of literature or a painting as having some sort of double nature, as form and content, but rather entirely as a closed whole, as a uniformly formed content, in which the two aspects cannot be distinguished as such. The distinction is made by an interpreter; quite often not even by him, but by a theoretician.

Only the theoretician makes us conscious of what we called transformation. This word means that the material already possessed form when the artist took it on. This form is stripped from its material and another form is bestowed upon it. Only by this means can this material become an element of the work. But it is just that fact that only the reflective person knows; the mere observer does not know it, and the creator does not need to "know" it. In his case, the inner eye simply "executes" the transformation.

In the non-representational arts, the situation is quite different. It would be false to let the content of music begin only in the inner strata, i.e., with the psychic element; rather it begins already in the compositional phase. But there it is identical with the bestowal of form.

We can say the same *mutatis mutandis* about architecture. The purposive composition and the spatial composition, and the dynamic composition, too, are eminently cases of the bestowal of form; but just these three constitute at the same time the essential content of architecture. Nothing is changed by the fact that there exists in architecture another "content" – an ideal one – beyond the first. But this other content too is one that, in the architectural work, has had form bestowed upon it – and not only "formed in stone," but also formed upon its own level, i.e., as psychic content.

We need here to return once again to the question of ugliness as material of beauty – thus also as the "content" of beauty. Up to now we have shown, but only by means of some examples, that the arrangement of the strata and their transparency in series, one after the other, requires in no way that the bestowal of form upon each individual strata, seen each in itself, must be beautiful. In the representational arts, at least, certain middle strata – just where the riches of the content are unfolded – are compatible with a considerable dose of ugliness. This is true in the portrait, in the novel, and in drama.

The first explanation offered for this fact was that in these strata the richness of detail is at stake and not beauty of form; for the depth of beauty grows with the number and the riches of the strata through which the eyes pass. But this explanation is not sufficient – it is not, for example, for the fact that, in the arts that we have named as relevant, the appearance of ugliness in certain middle strata can have an intensifying effect, specifically giving depth and space for the beauty of the entire work. (251)

For this phenomenon, there are plausible reasons:

1. All content is subject to the phenomenon of contrast, and for that reason ugliness placed next to beauty lifts the latter into the light.
2. The representational arts must create a sense of real life; if not, they lack truth. Real life is only possible by admitting ugliness to one's material.
3. A certain type of realism produces a sense of richness and abundance, whether or not for its beauty or for the lack of it. The question is only of building realism into a tightly framed space.

These points speak for themselves. What is important is that they are just as valid both forward and backward in the series of strata. In painting, for example, what is at stake is a beauty that is very much sensible and in the foreground – perhaps in a portrait of a notably ugly man. The ugliness in the bestowal of form upon the inner (deeper) stratum does not injure the convincing beauty of the ones further forward, for example, the shaping of space, light, color and motion (Franz Hals[70], Goya[71] ...).

In literature, the reverse is usually the case: in the strata of motion and gesture and those of plot and situation a great deal of ugliness may be contained; that may be true also for the stratum in which what is pertinent to character is given form. That does not prevent a background beauty from becoming apparent in the next stratum in the series – perhaps that of human fate. Or again, it may appear deeper in the last strata. Here we are reminded of the characters of Raabe[72] and of modern realistic novels, and also of Shakespeare's or Ibsen's characters. They are repulsive in many particulars, but precisely through them the total picture becomes colorful and rich and the lines of human destiny run deeper.

Of course, what is normal in literature is that aesthetically and morally repulsive elements do not appear in too great a measure in the middle strata – nonetheless, when they do, it is usually mixed with genuine traits of ugliness. We must be clear about this: as a rule, what in life is "morally ugly" (so we frankly call it) affects us also as aesthetically ugly. Among examples of this phenomenon belong licentiousness, weakness, slovenliness, inconsiderateness, and coarse egoism.

One could draw from this some support for the Aristotelian theory of φόβος [fear] and οἔγες [dread]. Both express the idea that our feelings may flow along with the suffering of the literary character; however, it offers us too little, and one

---

70 [Translator's note:] Franz Hals (1580–1666).

71 [Translator's note:] Francisco Goya (1746–1828).

72 [Translator's note:] Wilhelm Raabe (1831–1910).

would have to add many other forms of this participation: hope, expectation, shared joys, shared loves and hates, anger, rejection etc.

Both the positive and the negative "draw us on"; they let us experience vicariously, and both are only transitions that allow the concrete pictorial appearance of something greater. This greater thing does not have to lie in κάθαρσις [catharsis], and certainly not in some process within the observer. It must rather lie objectively in the picture of life that appears there. (252)

Chapter 19: Theory of the Bestowal of Form in Aesthetics

a) Aesthetical feeling for form

During the past centuries, the idea of a feeling for form has played a large role in aesthetics – a role that was naturally strongest where one had little thought for the relation of appearance, and tried instead to trace beauty solely to pure play with form. On the side of the act, the prevalent conception was that art was a matter of feeling, and the aspect of beholding was neglected.

It was pointed out earlier that one might note the beginnings of a feeling for form in quite primitive cases of formal beauty, viz., in "geometric beauty." The examples given were the circle, the ellipse, the hyperbola, and the sphere – but also certainly rhomboidal or rectangular figures. We may rightly add the regular polygons along with stylized star-shapes.

There is not much to notice in these matters. If one is seeking a basis for the fact that such shapes are beautiful, one should not seek it in some far-off metaphysical or psychological subtleties, but in very simple and primitive conditions: for example, in the intuitively apparent and striking uniformity of the shape, in the readily apparent unity of multiplicity. Behind this also stands a dark consciousness of regularity or lawfulness, of which, however, the intuiting consciousness know nothing.

Thus far, we find nothing questionable about the idea of the feeling for form. Something questionable enters, however, as soon as one attempts to explain the phenomenon in a certain psychological way. And many such attempts have been made. They all commit the error of tracing the phenomena of beauty and the joy we take in it to considerations external to aesthetics.

Thus, for example, the point has been argued in the following way by (Eduard von Hartmann[73]): a broken line – perhaps one zigging and zagging – is more

---

73 [Translator's note:] Eduard von Hartmann (1842–1906).

difficult to follow than a curving line or a wavy one, and therefore has a more unpleasant effect upon the eyes. For that reason, it is felt to lack beauty, while the wavy line seems beautiful. The basis for this is sought in the musculature of the eyes, which are forced constantly to readjust themselves for the zigzag. Something similar is sought even for the straight line as opposed to one that is slightly curved (and to this idea can be traced the avoidance of straight lines in Greek architecture).

With this kind of causal explanation of the feeling of form, we have a total confusion of distinct elements, and this indeed in more than one respect. First, aesthetic value is played off against the value of the pleasant, thus against a much lower region of value. Second, the explanation is not even purely psychological, but rather physiological, and therefore cannot grasp in the slightest the genuine aesthetical element in the intended feeling of form, i.e., the genuine aesthetical pleasure. Third, the argument is (253) also false in regard to its content. The zigzag line is usually not in fact taken in by "following" it, but rather entirely as a unified figure, i.e., by surveying it; the same is true for the wavy line. There is no basis therefore for assigning in this context grades of relative aesthetic value. And, even if there were such relative value, it must have another basis.

As was said, the other basis is discovered by sensing out, in the dark, as it were, an inherent lawfulness. That is entirely sufficient to explain the feeling of form of such a primitive kind. We just must not think that this "sensing out" is an intellectual process and pretend that it gives us a kind of secret knowledge.

In order to confirm such a correction, we find in the same theories examples of a dynamic kind that renounce all psychologizing and physiologizing and bring to the discussion argumentations of the aforementioned kind. For example, the curve described by a tossed stone is felt as beautiful because we sense intuitively at each moment in its flight the balance of impetus and gravity. One may proceed in a similar way in other areas: note the striking streamlined shape of the bodies of fish and birds; and, long before anyone had a dark sense of streamlining, there was an intuitive feeling for the inner lawfulness of this form. ...

Such examples show clearly what the nature of genuine aesthetical feeling for form is: nothing of "pleasantness" or "able to be easily executed" stands behind it. Instead, there is an objective feeling that joins itself to an inward, fundamental, law-like state of affairs. One will not be mistaken in assuming that this kind of feeling leads us once again to the vicinity of the appearance-relation. One can just as well say: the law "appears" in the concretely intuited physical case; this case must therefore be transparent. And it might be conceivable that all this beauty in the play with form could in the end be traced back to appearance.

One can formulate this more generally: "form is felt to be beautiful when it allows a principle guiding form to be beheld." In this way, the thesis is expressed in its greatest generality.

But there is a phenomenon that speaks against it: there exists also a kind of form that in fact does not allow a principle of form to appear and yet is felt to be beautiful, a form in which lawlessness and disorder is the beautiful, and is evident as such. Examples: the townscape of older towns that have grown up in different epochs: the bright diversity of different kinds of things placed together, yet which is deeply attractive. ... Or: the form of a hamlet with red roofs lying in a green landscape with its irregular flowerbeds. ... Or: the overlapping of the lines of hills and forest in a landscape ... that is quite a disorder. Still more – mentioned earlier: the starry skies. Here we need to do violence to find a principle of order in the constellations ... just as men did with respect to the mythical figures.

The solution of the problem: even the "fortuitous" is not entirely without a lawful principle, even if it is simply the law of "scattering." This law, (254) which is traceable to the "law of big numbers," is visible only where there is a great quantity of cases; where the number is smaller, its presence is extremely slight, and merely suggested.

But so things stand precisely with the examples we mentioned: the hamlet affects us randomly, as a matter of fact; and it has a kind of principle only in the unified shape of the courtyards, and that shape can attract notice even when one is standing at some distance. The landscape is more concise: many objects, similar in their kind and style, collect themselves together. ... In the shapes of mountains and heights, however, certain oppositions of a material kind are set that speak to us precisely out of their apparent randomness (the lines of forests like flattened billows, distant lines of mountains with more or less steep ascents, slopes, and peaks ...). This can arise reciprocally. These cases do not yet contain examples of "laws of contingency" of a truly great size – as, for example, globular star-clusters, whose form conspicuously has high aesthetic value.

b) Empathy and activity

We see from all of this that there is something right about a feeling for form, if one grasps it in a way that does justice to the phenomenon. This way of doing justice, however, has been disputed. One might have lent support to it on the side of the object by means of the concept of the quality of form in the sense of today's Gestalt theories; but in earlier days, one did not yet possess such a concept.

And so some took risky detours. One of the strangest is that of the theory of empathy (Theodor Lipps, et al.). Taken strictly, the concept of empathy is an aesthetically extremely fecund one; it was only robbed of its value by a specific and much too complicated theory.

Consider: what can the artist painting a portrait do otherwise than "empathize" via the facial features of the person he is painting? Or the poet, who borrows from life a character for his drama? Any understanding that is analytical or psychological is insufficient in such cases, and it arrives too late on the scene. All depends upon intuitive vision, which, in passing, grasps what is essential by passing over it, and holds to its external signs. How does a man summon up such a capacity for intuitive vision, which simultaneously penetrates and lovingly extracts what is essentially human and valuable?

We know that in life such an understanding of another person is possible for one who loves him. The loving eye has an inward emotional tie to the object of his love. On this emotional side, everything depends; it is the element that opens and reveals in the act of beholding. It is no secret that the painter and the poet do basically the same. For even in their cases a certain love of the object, a willing submission and a devotion to it is a presupposition – only without the personal accent given in the real engagement with the person that genuine love requires. This kind of intuitive, strongly emotional appreciation, which lives, rejoices, and suffers along with another, but without real engagement with him, is the true sense of empathy. (255)

But in fact, only this sense is justified aesthetically. It corresponds to the first sense of the word: we mean by empathy with persons or with entire situations in life an emotional understanding with or a penetration into them.

Aesthetics should be satisfied with this analysis. For it is sufficient for the receptive act of the observer: one can say of him also that he "empathizes himself" into the characters and their social circumstances. And one ought not to let oneself be deprived of the good sense of such empathy. It is much to be regretted that this good concept of empathy, formed after nature, has been taken over by theories and disfigured. For there are arts where it is indispensable: music, architecture, and ornamental art. This is easy to see. Music deals with an inward, sympathetic vibration, an emotional moving-along with the dynamics of sound. Only in this way can the psychic content of the music communicate itself; for this content is nothing other than a pure emotional dynamic.

Music is the only art that penetrates human being in this way, directly and deeply grips him and makes him vibrate with the sound. A concept such as "empathy" is indispensable here. The one who listens to music genuinely "lives emotionally" with the music. In architecture one may at least speak of a felt rhythm of form ("Form" understood in the large sense as "composition"); and in ornamental art there is always a quiet engagement with the play of lines, a non-committal vibrating with them. Here also with form.

The addition "with form" is essential. For it is here alone that the concept of empathy belongs in a chapter on form. Here alone, too, one can extract it from its psychologistic disfigurement and, as it were, purify it!

The most powerful evidence that we are dealing with a feeling for form is found once again in music. Even a primitive feeling for music at least follows along inwardly with the rhythm of the beat: in dancing, in marching, even in working. Singing along inwardly or even aloud cuts more deeply ... motifs, themes, melodies, entire phrases, intensification. In such cases, empathy goes very far. And one notes its force when it fails us entirely, when one rejects inwardly some "theme," that is, one will not allow oneself to be gripped and moved by it; something in us resists feeling empathy, for example its tedium. Even moving in concert with the inner strata and their psychic content takes the entire pathway over musical form and empathy with it. It is just this last phenomenon that is itself at once empathy with the dynamics of feeling.

In the case of architecture, it is more difficult to state what empathy with form consists in. It does not have the general shape of an act of moving-with the object; architecture does not penetrate into us. Yet its forms engage us and draw us into a life that is not our own: we feel its dynamics, (256) feel its massiveness, feel its heavy weight that unfolds itself high above us, feel how it is kept within limits by its finely measured proportions, its overcoming of gravity, and its victorious superiority to it.

It is no different with poetry, although here the orientation of the reader towards themes and content clouds the feeling for form. In reality, the feeling shared with the hero is precisely feeling with form, but only with such form as constitutes the essential content of the character (the bestowal of form on character, on destiny ...).

To that extent, empathy becomes indistinguishable from feeling for form. The psychology of empathy did not stop at that point, however. It wanted more, wanted to explain the phenomena, and to that end it invented a schema: the receptive subject of art was thought to be active in the object (looking at a cliff, one executes an act of "rising up") – although it would then be difficult to understand how the enjoyment of one's own activity could at the same time be the measure of the value of the object "in which" the subject is active. Even the examples are, in fact, treated quite arbitrarily. What comes out of this at best is an explanation in terms of psychological causes.

The only genuine and earnest question in this context is: is there an activity of the receptive subject in the aesthetic object? This question must be answered in the affirmative, but in a quite different sense than that understood by the psychology of empathy. Specifically, this activity does not consist in placing or projecting our feelings into the object, but in a reproductive viewing of a higher order, a beholding to which the background of the artwork appears stratum after stratum. This function of the activity is nothing new. It is identical with the role of the receptive subject in the fourfold relation that is peculiar to all objectivation. Insofar as that commonality is so, it does not even possess anything specifically aesthetical. It is contained in all acts of reading and understanding, even those of an intellectual kind. The difference is only that in the receptive understanding of the work of art it is closely tied to intuitive cognitive functions and to the inward "emotional" feeling-with the artistic form.

c) The bestowal of form and self-representation

To conclude these reflections we must be mindful of still another side of the principle of form, one that is self-evident, but too infrequently noted. It concerns the bestowal of form as objectivation – one should rather say, as the aspect of objectivation in the aesthetic object. But that means that in the act of bestowing form, the making-objective as such first becomes possible. That is well known. In this case, however, it is a question of the connection of this state of affairs to the feeling for form and empathy.

This objectivation plays no essential role where objective themes are already present. There the bestowal of form – and with that, objectivation – is only transformation, superformation, as we have seen earlier. This is the case especially in the representational arts (257), even though in them the bestowal of form is not at all absorbed by them. The form bestowed upon them is in fact quite different and ideal in nature.

But the process of making objective is of great significance in the non-representational arts, in music and architecture; for there it is precisely a question of first making tangible something that exists in us in a non-objective manner by means of bestowing form and objectivation. In music, the structure of tones is such a process of objectivation by means of the bestowal of form – and, indeed, in this case by a freely invented process of forming that had never before been heard in the world. That which has been made tangible in this bestowal of form, however, is the flowing and surging of the life of the soul, its most tender and soft arousal, its vacillations and its sorrows, its strength and struggles, its storms and its defeats, none of which can be made tangible in any other way.

If one considers soberly what that means in fact, and what therefore is the essence of the bestowal of form as objectivation, one must say: it is nothing less than this, that man himself becomes visible – or, perhaps: that he comes to stand before himself, not that he simply experiences himself, but rather that he catches sight of himself. But he can become visible to himself only as an object; only as object does he stand outside himself. This being outside of oneself produces the objective bestowal of form.

In architecture, this making an object of oneself is a dark, puzzling process, but it is no less effective. What is incomprehensible about human nature expresses itself entirely in forms that seem to have nothing to do with man; yet precisely as his way of expressing himself these forms possess the traits of his nature and are thrust before our eyes.

"Visibility" can be taken literally. One may add: this incomprehensible nature is thrust into the most coarse matter and in the most intrusive and permanent manner thrust before our receptive eyes. Man is always building; when he builds his house, he builds himself: that is, he builds the expression of his own will to live, his ideal of himself (as with clothing), and even his mis-understanding of himself.

The same can be said, in a much weaker way, for ornamental art. In one respect the making an object of oneself here is perhaps purer: it is the mere play with form as such, and is further removed from practical ends. And even its obvious relation to playfulness, which takes its place here at a certain elevation, is revealing. It betrays the presence of man where he does not expect to appear. All play is transparent.

In this respect, the difference between representational and non-representational art in the problem of form does not loom large, as one would normally expect. The secret here is simply that man presents himself within all the arts, even when he is working to bestow form of a completely different type.

But we must understand in no way this "oneself" in a personal sense. The term usually refers to something more general, usually to a type of human being, but it can also refer to all that is human. This is entirely true even of the apparently individual self-representation of an artistic personality; e.g., of the self-portrait by a painter or a confessional novel (258) by a writer representing his own life. In the hands of a significant artist all material extends into a wider and impersonal context, and it is precisely for that reason that he can find the widest echo.

Here music has an advantage over literature. What it communicates in its inner strata about the psychic life remains always on a certain general level. People have called this the "indeterminacy" of music, and characterized it as a failing (Hegel, Vischer[74]). Yet it is also an advantage. For this is the root of its capacity for free interpretation; specifically, that one and the same piece of music

---

74 [Translator's note:] Friedrich Theodor Vischer (1807–1887).

can mean very different things to different listeners. The way form is bestowed upon it is not like that upon an individual object – a given human figure – but from the outset upon what is typically human. And that is the reason why in vocal music there is always something left over from the room to maneuver between words and music.

What is truly amazing about this is that concreteness is nonetheless not absent. The clarity of form in the realm of the audible is something entirely different from the realm of the visible: in the latter, it remains tightly attached to the individual object (material, motif) and cannot be separated from it; in the former, on the contrary, it is tied to the musical motif and to the structure of the composition. The "motif," however, bears the psychic material; it is never identical to it regarding content, for it transcends it with respect to its level.

d) Disengagement from the creator by means of form

Form as an objectivation of the selfhood of the artist – all the same whether conscious or unconscious – cannot be underrated, because upon it the elements of self-consciousness and self-understanding depend. The same holds, therefore, for what Hegel called the "being for itself of spirit." One may add to this that it was not incorrect of him to attribute the arts to the "absolute spirit" – if we assume that knowledge of itself makes spirit "absolute."

However, that absoluteness no longer belongs to the genuine aesthetical character of art: it is rather one of the general cultural functions that it has to fulfill; one could almost call it art's metaphysical function. For in fact there are things that humankind learns through art and only through it. Unquestionably, these learned things concern man himself. Aesthetics concerns itself with man only peripherally, and it was Hegel's error to pretend that this metaphysical function was the aesthetical essence of the matter. These were the remains, as it were, of an intellectualistic aesthetics.

What in contrast is important and central to aesthetics moves along a line opposite to this phenomenon: specifically, in the work of art the artist disappears, he does not speak and testify to himself there, but to something else entirely. From the standpoint of the observer, one could express the matter as follows: he observes the artwork in complete detachment from its creator. The work has disposed of the subjectivity of the creator; it left that subjectivity behind along with his individuality, his sufferings and struggles – it left behind also the sweat and toil he put into the work. (259)

One who is learned in history can of course recognize the peculiarities of the artist in his work; but that is no longer a form of aesthetical understanding but rather one proper to historical and theoretical comparative analyses. It is the science of art. For it is not the enjoyment of art, not to mention an aesthetical beholding of it.

This is also the reason why research into the personality of an artist offers us nothing that could open his works to us. No doubt, it can contribute to our understanding of the origins of the work, or to that of its subject matter; but it is neither an aesthetical beholding nor an aesthetical enjoyment. This is especially true for the question of "origins." There is nothing more indifferent to a measured aesthetical understanding than the history of the origins of a work – except insofar as one gets something of its history from beholding it aesthetically. This is true of architectural works whose elements were erected in different centuries, or where they have been continuously added to. When an art historian comes to us with a chronology and ties the history of the building to the fate of its community, we find him interesting and instructive, but this information has another kind of educational function. But why a certain structure seems beautiful, although people ventured upon its construction without concern for questions of form, while another structure seems disturbing in contrast – that one cannot explain in an art-historical way.

If we compare the detachment of the work of art from its creator with the element of self-consciousness and with the process by which a living mind becomes an object to itself, we are led to a kind of antinomy. On one side, the work speaks eloquently of its creator, but on the other, it is expressly silent about him. It reveals and it hides, it betrays and it keeps its silence. Both are clearly essential, even if they are not both aesthetically essential in the same way.

How may this antinomy be resolved? And is it one, really? One can deny the latter: the opposition is not an inward one, it is only apparent. The creator, in fact, does not speak of himself, he does not even portray himself in the genuine sense – not even when he produces a self-portrait – he is concerned even then with something else – but he does speak of or testify to the entire spirit of what he is engaged in, and out of which he creates. For no one, even the most original mind, creates simply out of his own subjectivity, as though he stood alone in the world for himself; every creator creates out of the objective spirit as it embeds itself historically in events into which he has grown, and as it creates within him. He also becomes creative when he himself has grown artistically out of and beyond that spirit.

Thus, the antinomy is resolved. The work, and the specific forms it possesses, is the witness of an historical spirit, now made objective; but the personality of the artist and its subjectivity has nevertheless disappeared into the form bestowed upon the material, even though that bestowal was executed by that personality. The latter point can be clearly appreciated from cases where it is not known with any certainty whether some portrait is a self-portrait (260) or not; similarly with events described in some literary work where it cannot be determined whether it has been taken from a personal experience of the writer or not.

The uncertainty of the self-revelation in a work of art corresponds to this fact. The genuine artist does not know what he does in bestowing form upon his material according to his way of seeing things, such that one may recognize that way of seeing in the forms bestowed, and even be drawn by it to learn how to see. The artist does not know how much he gives form to a part of himself in the creative process, and even less to his personal existence as part of a common life and as part of an historical epoch.

And in the same way, the observer of the work is ignorant of what he sees in the formal structure of the work when it gives to him intuitively something essential about the historical spirit of an epoch. It is easy for him to err in two ways. Either he takes what he has been given as the personhood of the artist, a very frequent misapprehension, or he completely misunderstands the spiritual posture, now become object and form, out of which the work has been created. Nonetheless, since he is the mere follower who no doubt reflects clearly upon his looking and enjoying, it is more likely that he and not the creator will know what spirit has been communicated to him.

This notion also corresponds nicely to the phenomenon of disengagement. It means only that the law of objectivation for a work of art has been obeyed. This law asserts the state of separation of the formed matter from the connection to the living spirit in which it had grown, and also its state of release from it. For in the fourfold relation of objectivation the mind of the creator is the most transitory, and the observer's mind, which lives in its own time and receives the objectivation, comes into its justified place – so long as it is adequate to receiving it. The objectivation itself, however, which makes this reception possible, consists in the bestowal of form upon some enduring matter, on the condition that this matter is transparent for the entire series of strata that depend upon it.

Chapter 20: On the Metaphysics of Form

a) Imitation and creativity

If we survey what has been said about aesthetical form, we will not be mistaken to think the outcome very small – in comparison with what we would like to know about it, and what constitutes its mystery. We sense clearly this mystery throughout; sense it behind all partial definitions that can be given of it. But it is difficult even to indicate just in what it consists.

The difficulty has its basis in the incomprehensibility of beauty: incomprehensible, specifically, in a way different both from aesthetical beholding and the value-indicators that pertain to it, i.e., enjoyment and pleasure. If we could also comprehend the beautiful as such in a different way, then the different way of comprehending would also have to be an aesthetical form of comprehending. But there is no second kind of aesthetical comprehending, but only beholding accompanied by pleasure. We must remember this in order to protect ourselves from false expectations. Aesthetics (261) cannot make the impossible possible any more than any other science can.

What would we have to know about form? Nothing less than why one form seems beautiful and the other one ugly. Thus we wish to solve the mystery of the beautiful with one blow. And, besides, we want the impossible: we want to comprehend with our understanding and its coarse tools, i.e., with concepts, what only aesthetical beholding can comprehend.

To make this situation clear it is sufficient to realize that making such demands of aesthetics is utopist. Aesthetics may not allow them, for then it would of necessity become metaphysical. The academic study of art can thus respond to these demands only partially, at least as far as it is dealing with those parts of the question that can be answered by reference to larger empirical materials. But this study, taken strictly, also leads us beyond facts, and therefore does not arrive, in the end, at the reasons for the beauty of certain forms and not of others.

It is hence understandable that aesthetical theories have stumbled when they treated these questions. Most of them become quite metaphysical in the course of their work, but other theories sought to extract themselves from metaphysics by genetic-psychologist routes. Some even wandered along mathematical-speculative detours, for example the theory of the "golden ratio," and also via the mathematical analysis of music. Some of these attempts were dealt with in the course of our earlier chapters and discarded. We dealt more recently with the psychological aesthetics of empathy, and at the start of our inquiry with the ancient aesthetical of ideas and its later influence upon German idealism.

We could not dispose of the latter tradition entirely, for there hides within it elements of reflection that even a more cautious analysis could not entirely dismiss – for example in the problem of beauty in nature and, more narrowly, of human beauty, specifically where it concerns the forms of living creatures. Yet in all the arts it fails totally, and it is just this failure that led aesthetics, quite logically, to the relation of appearance.

Of course, one may become suspicious when one sees that this relation still is not sufficient to account for all problems of beauty – suspicions that lead one precisely towards another mystery, one yet hiding in the form of the object. Here all further reflections are subject to a limit imposed by the fact that between the bestowal of form and appearance a much more narrow relationship becomes visible than one would expect at first. It has just been shown that in the work of art a relatively independent kind of form-bestowing governs from stratum to stratum, and in such a manner that all appearance of deeper backgrounds depends upon the preceding form in the series.

In principle, there are only two possibilities for treating aesthetical form beyond the phenomena already discussed. Either one may seek the foundation of the beauty of form in the object, even if entirely hidden in its backgrounds, or one may seek it in the subject. The (262) first tendency has led to a metaphysics of ideas, the second to the psychology of empathy.

We can press forward a bit on both sides without engaging in excessive speculation. In the direction of the object, we find the old theory of imitation, while in the direction of the subject that of autonomous creativity: μίμησις [mimesis] and ποίησις [poiesis]. Both of these theories have made little progress. Yet both of them contain a very serious core idea.

Μίμησις [mimesis] – we should translate it as "representation" – is based on the thought: no man can create objects more perfect than those in nature; he can only imitate them. The same is true of the human scene: no poet can contrive conflicts, destinies of deep significance, or greater undertakings than real life contains, he can only represent what he experiences.

In contrast, ποίησις [poiesis] is founded in the thought that there are spiritual creations that are otherwise foreign to nature and life. They are clearly present in music, in architecture, and even in ornamental art; and beyond them, also in poetry and the fine arts, so far as they manifest things that the layman does not see in real life.

These two foundational thoughts are justified each in its own way, and for that reason we must take them into account. Clearly, it is a question of establishing a unity among them. And perhaps from its very origins the error in them was simply that they appeared separate from each other.

What therefore can we recover from the idea of μίμησις? It will help to limit this question initially to the representational arts. We can in any case extend the question later as needed. Consider: to outdo the forms of living things would be manifestly the greatest madness of man: forms of human fantasy can hardly outdo the leaping deer, the circling falcon, and the diving shark. Therefore it cannot be the task of art to do so. So far as art "represents" such natural forms, it can only attempt to imitate them, where "representation" in itself is naturally something different. This is true also for the human shape, the human face, and its expressions (mimicry).

But two things must be noted. 1. Artists usually do not create forms of living things just for their sake alone; they are not competing with nature, neither in sculpture nor in painting. The first concentrates almost entirely upon the human body, the second upon man himself or upon the landscape, but there another principle of the bestowal of form effectively enters.

For to that must be added 2. Even the most perfect forms of nature, of living things and human beings, only become aesthetic objects when there arises a subject capable of understanding them properly. The act of the artist, therefore, as over against forms in nature possessing beauty, is precisely that of first discovering them. To "imitate" what is perfect is perhaps in fact (263) the lesser part of the aesthetical mission; the greater and more primary is to lean to see, to seek and find, to dwell with and learn to gaze lovingly.

In this sense it is true that the painter – and yet not before his art reached a certain level of development – was the first to discover "the landscape" and thereupon also taught the layman to see nature for himself. In the same sense it is true that the portraitist teaches us to look into faces, the poet into characters and destinies, the sculptor into the dynamics of the human body. If one, in face of all that experience, still wishes to be faithful to art as imitation, so be it. But it does not touch the essence of the case, to say nothing of the element of transformation, which was discussed above.

And what is of permanent value in the idea of ποίησις, understood strictly as "creative"? We have already referred to the non-representational arts, which bestow a kind of form that does not exist outside of art; this is seen most clearly in music. Here we find an enormous realm in which forms are created that are purely acoustical – not transformed, but a construction of new forms that is absolutely creative. The expression, "pure play with form" refers perfectly to this. It is similar in architecture, and to a much lesser degree in ornamental art.

It is of greater importance in this context that the representational arts manifest the same creative character in the bestowal of form, although they are limited to their "models," i.e., *sujets*, themes typically taken from life, and cannot dispense with this touch of imitation, with which our discussion of aesthetical form began (Chaps. 16c and 17a).

To "reconstruct," to "transform," – those words are much too weak. There exists also a purely synthetic bestowal of form in art that brings in something quite new: figures born from an idea, arising out of creative beholding, in opposition to reality and to everything empirical.

Renaissance painting created such ideal types in its Madonnas, saints, and Christ-figures. Michelangelo purposely created titanic figures that were larger than life. In the same line of development, we find the carved divinities of the ancient world, even their statues of youths. We can say the same for most epic poems: they are songs of heroes that contain a tendency toward the creation of ideal figures. And we cannot deny that such art – along with many missteps into the false and the unnatural – also produced genuine creations with an inner truth and power: figures that shone prophetically into the future and could instruct entire generations of a people.

We see, therefore, that the synthesis of imitation and autonomous creativity is not at all difficult to find. The two elements simply do not relate to the same features of the same objects, but to very disparate things. A fruitful art can never distance itself from life and from reality. For that reason, an element of μίμησις must always remain in it. It must always root itself in real (264) life, whose developed forms are also the formal motifs of its creations. Looked at otherwise: an art form can become great and tower above its own times only when it has traces of the visionary within it that lead beyond this real life; when it can creatively behold what does not exist and yet convinces because it points beyond this real life while yet being a part of it. No genuine antinomy, therefore, created the conflict of μίμησις and ποίησις.

b) The finding of form and the phenomenon of style

If one is convinced that, along with art's ties of dependency to the fullness of life, there is also in art's bestowing of form an entirely creative element, then the question of creativity becomes even more insistent. For we must locate the form that is creatively constructed. The main issue remains: how do we find it?

Once more, we stand here before one of those forbidden questions, where we know that it is beyond the capacity of our judgment to resolve it, but we also cannot restrain ourselves from asking it. What we want to know is just this: how the artist manages to find a form that is not given. We wish to look at the cards he is playing, wish to penetrate the secret of genius – that means: to penetrate to where the artist himself does not know the answer, to where his mysterious activity is beyond the reach of his consciousness and must await an epiphany. But even that event does not reveal to him what happened in him and how he brought it about; it reveals only what the form he was seeking is, and how he can hit upon it rightly in this given case.

We know of a silent maturing that the creative person cannot much alter by his will alone; at the most he can eliminate obstacles to the process. He can unburden or distract himself when he seems to have run aground, but he cannot alter the condition itself. We know also how, for a great master, the condition can be a torment: he can be filled with a sense of failure, with impatience, with pain. Schelling knew something of this torment and tried to express it: the artist bears a destiny within himself; the work yet unborn is that destiny. And what is strange is that after its birth, the work says absolutely nothing about all of that:

everything in it is settled; it presents the appearance only of a superior silent greatness.

All this tells us, once again, that we cannot penetrate the mystery of how the artist finds his forms: of why, of all avenues in aesthetics, the way to the penetration of the creative act of the artist is the least accessible. Nothing is more tightly closed to us than that. Here we stand directly before the "metaphysics of form," without being able to find our way into it. Nonetheless, a few elements – viewed from the outside – can be distinguished: the inward *telos* of the work, the accident of inspiration, and the springing up of style in history. (265)

The first element expresses itself clearly in the striving of the artist. But this striving takes shape only in the work itself. We know that the inner *telos* of the unborn work holds the artist in its power, it gives him no rest, drives him to experiments, sketches, new initiatives. But from what direction comes this *telos* that holds him in its grip cannot be determined. It arises in the mind of the artist, but only negatively: in the form of dissatisfaction with what his attempts have achieved up to now. What underlies his achievement bears the imprint of this vision at a certain stage of its development. But the workings of the artistic imagination upon its impressions cannot be specified. Only the striving towards new forms is conscious. The work of the creator is in this way somewhat related to a natural process, as real genius is a gift of nature. But the element of the *telos* distinguishes itself from natural processes decisively here.

The second element, accident, is in some respects easier to trace. It offers the inspiration, the material, and the *sujet*. But it does not explain why the artist takes up what he has been offered by a chance encounter, or how he recognizes his own aptitudes in it. We may assume that the *telos* appears before him darkly, and the inspiration "approaches" him. But how that happens remains in darkness.

In the middle of his daily life, he is struck suddenly by a scene, of which he has been the accidental witness, or by a living human figure or a peculiar destiny. Something inside him leaps to grasp it. But he takes what has happened not as it is, but shapes it into something different – in the sense of an inner picture that had already passed before his mind. And he is a genuine poet only when he knows how to give it form such that it transcends itself – not by becoming false to itself, but by becoming the revelation of a truth beheld in the mind.

The painter does the same: he strolls between forest and heath and suddenly a view holds him fast: a motif, which he immediately beholds inwardly as a picture; a face detains him. Think also of how the "accidental" framing of the view – the eyes pass through branches, or between the trunks of trees, or through an opening in an old wall – acts to shape images. We call these things "accidents." And it is only by chance that it encounters the artist; but the fact that he grasps it, values it, assesses it, that he paints it, is not accidental, but the work of the *telos* in him.

We see that *telos* and chance, although opposed to each other ontically, not only take to each other very well, but belong closely and essentially together, and supplement each other in the process of discovering form. The artist's purposive search for form is perhaps impotent without the helpful work of chance; but the favorable chance event would be meaningless and squandered without the purposive searching of the artist.

We must not be afraid to give "chance" or accident its due. One does not deny all value to genius if we do. In the end, genius is not the capacity to make use of chance or even to recognize its favors. Naturally, we mean here by "chance" the "unintentional," thus the opposite of *telos*, not the indeterminate. The accidental (266) in this sense is precisely what ontic necessity is. But this form of necessity does not concern aesthetics at all.

Style may be the most important of these elements. It consists in a certain formal character or schema that is not discovered by an individual. It is given shape by an entire epoch, but the individual is carried along by it in his own search for form. Objectively, it is for this reason also universal, and is not absorbed by any individual work. In times when a certain style is "dominant," it is what determines all individual form in advance – not totally, but it establishes a certain direction for it. Moreover, the phenomenon of style is differentiated: There are particular styles, folk-styles, local ones, those peculiar to stages of life, even the highly personal style of specific masters.

But the great epochal styles are most significant. They manifest the characteristic peculiarities of the entire objective spirit. For as long as they live within some creative activity, they belong to the objective spirit; only for its epigones are they attached to objectivation alone. Style has its foundation in the sensibility of human beings for form; only secondarily does it appear in works, released from the creative and observant spirit. Style is the element of form in aesthetical "taste," and therefore it changes along with taste. Styles grow up and disappear, and it is always individual artists whose creations bring about that change. But the individual does not create style; it works itself out in the creative activity of generations. And when it has been worked out, it dominates human sensibility for form, and the need for it.

We must think of this domination of style as the inability of a person who lives in its time and its way of life to ever think that people could create things in any other way. The prototype for this is found in architecture, from which the concept of style is taken and only subsequently extended to other areas. The reasons for this lie in the practical ends of architecture, and other factors (Cf. Chap. 15c).

It should also be observed that style does not refer only to the arts, but to the entire way of life of a people – down to its ways of interpersonal relations, of forms of speech and movement, not to speak of clothing and fashion. Thus we speak with some justification of a style of life. And one cannot deny that there exists an inclusive unified phenomenon of style in all these areas. The consequence of this is that there exist epochal styles that in fact include several or all areas. The Rococo manifests the same elegant flourishes in both speech and music as also in its forms of architecture and furniture or in attire.

We see from this that style is a concept that extends beyond aesthetics; it belongs to the further circle of phenomena of the objective spirit of history. Here we are concerned only with artistic style. And it is characteristic of this style that it constitutes a way in which form may be bestowed, or a general pre-determination of possible individual forms, which strips from the artist (267) part of his role in the discovery of form, and just in that way also limits his freedom of activity.

This and nothing else is what we refer to when we say a specific form "dominates." And, as with all domination of objective intellectual forms, we have here also cases of the individual breaking through the dominant form. When this happens, there can be confusion and formlessness, but the break can also offer a genuine roadmap for the discovery of new forms.

More than this cannot be said. It is only the great masters that achieve such breakthroughs, as also in other areas of the objective spirit, for example in linguistic innovation. Artistic style marks a limit to the free discovery of form, to the playful imagination that shapes form, but style is itself form that has been already discovered and marked as such. It is a type of form-bestowal.

What one wishes to know beyond this is how such new form is "found"; how the creative imagination first goes about shaping it, and why this specific type of form-bestowal becomes evident, pleases, and affects others. Analysis cannot determine any of that.

c) The great styles of art and fashion

The circle of problems that concern the bestowal of form, the finding of form, and the fixed types of form, becomes considerably larger when one relates these problems to the series of strata in the work of art. For initially all bestowal of form relates to one specific stratum. That is true also for styles. But because the bestowal of form upon one stratum is precisely what gives it transparency for other strata, and these in turn must have their own formal shape, forms – and also types of forms – link together, the one linking into the other.

One should compare to this what was said in Chaps. 17b–d and in Chap. 18a about the hierarchy of form. We learned there that in the overlapping of the strata, the bestowal of form on each individual stratum is both autonomous and dependent; further, that the variegated riches of a work depend on the element of autonomy in the bestowing, but the relation of appearance depends on the element of its dependency. Both are thus essential. But what will this mean if we relate it to the forms of style? To which stratum are the great styles attached? Are they attached to one only, or to several at the same time?

In the case of the painter, does the bestowal of form lie in the brush strokes, in the handling of light, in the ordering of spatial relations, in the dominance or absence of contours (in what pertains to drawing), in the manner in which animation and movement are made to appear, etc. – or does it lie in all these things together, or is there a preference for one of these elements? And if the bestowal of form lies in several of them, that is, if it is distributed through several strata of the painting, how do things then stand with the relationship among the acts of form-bestowing in the strata? Is one stratum given preference? And why?

One expects to receive a uniform summary answer to these questions. But such an answer cannot be given. Rather, the conditions of the dependency (268) of form in the strata come in various grades, and are once again isolated for individual strata and cannot be transferred to others.

Some of this can be demonstrated. For example, it is obvious that in a painting the treatments of space and light must be closely related, because space and light are indivisibly connected in natural conditions of vision; that in the foreground strata the application of paint still has broad latitude in contrast to the treatment of space and light. The same is true for the treatment of the contours of things that lie deeper in the background. Still deeper in the inner strata, the appearance of animation and life may be essentially co-determined by all the others. Correspondingly, in the work itself the relation of form in the external strata (e.g., the structure of space and light) must be already determined by a *telos* that aims at allowing motion and life to appear.

Aesthetics cannot follow into its details these relationships among forms. They are too complicated and subtle to allow it. It helps little to compare them to relationships in other arts. In literature, for example, the situation is similar – only that there the outer and inner strata are more clearly distinct from each other in the networks of form-bestowal that belong together.

In contrast one can certainly determine, though only within certain limits, on which strata of a work of art – either for the most part or entirely – style depends. Even this question cannot be answered in a uniform way, for it is precisely styles, understood as types of form-bestowal, which are in this respect different. As in life, too, we can speak in part of the style of a person either as a whole or in part as the style of his external demeanor.

This results in differences in depth among styles. First the well-known styles typical of an epoch stand out; it has long been noted how they include all sides of human life. We speak of "gothic man," et al. Of course such things can be considerably exaggerated, and that is not without danger; in any real historical human types are mixed many sorts of forms of varying provenance. Nonetheless, it is true that many aspects of life take part in these unities of form. It is likewise true that in the arts such unities dominate in more than one stratum.

It is not necessary to struggle to sketch out conceptually what is meant by these epochal styles. The essence of the bestowal of form cannot be expressed in any other way than the arts themselves do. It is entirely sufficient to point out the best-known styles. One cannot describe them to anyone who is not "familiar" with them, and anyone who is familiar with them does not need to have them described. It is left to the philosopher only to point out the inflexible form-types in them and to appeal to the aesthetical feeling for them. So we as epigones can easily grasp the unity of the classical Greek styles (with their subgroups) of the fifth century in their temples, their (269) figures of gods, their frieze-reliefs, and in their lyric and tragic poets. Beyond those, there are many others.

One can demonstrate, with reference to such styles, in which strata of the work of art they are primarily effective in determining form. Clearly, they function in ways that determine form in the entire series of strata; most visibly, to begin with, in the bestowal of form in the real foreground, but also no less in the deeper outer strata and the inner strata of the background – in many varieties and grades – but perhaps least of all in the final strata, which contain what is purely ideational in nature.

The reason we first notice the great epochal styles in architecture is because styles are most visible when they appear in the foreground: precisely in architecture, the foreground is a pure, almost detached, bestowal of form upon matter – without the pretense of representing anything. Whoever looks more deeply will no doubt note the style in the composition of ends and space, as also in the dynamic composition – and, beyond that, in the will to create and bestow form that drives the entire undertaking.

Antique tragedy impresses above all by its linguistic and choral forms (in the songs). Later we recognize the same type of form-bestowal in the movements of the figures, if not to speak of "play," and, behind this, in the way the situation and action are composed, and then even more forcibly in the bestowal of psychic form upon the persons (characters), and perhaps with even greater power in the working-out of the formal structure of man's fate in its entirety.

It is easy to see that the same is true of the literature of other times and other styles. One thinks of the great epics of the thirteenth century (Wolfram[75], Gott-

---

75 [Translator's note:] Wolfram von Eschenbach (c. 1160 – c. 1220).

fried[76], et al.), which are structured through and through by the styles of their epoch (the High Gothic) down to the content of their leading ideas – whether religious or chivalric. There are middle strata here, too, that show this best. The manner in which the figures move, grasp their situation, act within it; how their personality is shaped by these means (the figures of Hagen [von Tronje] or Rüdiger [Markgraf Rudeger von Bechelaren]), and how their destinies are marked out, etc.

This homogenous shaping throughout many strata constitutes the dominance of great styles. To a certain extent this is true even of the shaping of great art, but there, of course, exceptions are found precisely among the greatest creative artists, because they are also the breakers of conventional forms.

In clear opposition to this are acts of form-bestowal that have the same ambition but where in fact form does not penetrate the entire work homogeneously, and extends only to individual strata. What usually happens then is that form attaches itself only to the outer strata, or simply to the sensible foreground. We find such styles among individual artists, or tight groups of them. If they possess great genius, they may produce thorough formal structures throughout, but they may also end attaching themselves only to externals – for example, they many not concern themselves with imposing structure upon their material – and then, in the place of style, we have "fashion." (270)

"Fashion" is thus to be distinguished from genuine style – even from a very individual one – by the absence of formal structures that are related to one another through many strata, and whose nature is determined by and along with the inner strata.

This is true also of the imitation of styles by the disciples of some master. People have asked: why is it that architectural works produced today in the Romanesque or Gothic style do not genuinely affect us, but rather seem almost unharmonious and ugly? The answers given are all expressive of the thought that throughout them we sense something that is not organic, unmotivated, external, even misunderstood. That is true. But what does it consist in?

It is easy to give an answer when we follow the gradations of form in each of the strata. Imitation never begins by composing with the ends of the structure in mind, to say nothing of the spatial or dynamic composition; it starts instead by bestowing form upon the external formal motifs, whose meaning is not understood; thus, for example, with certain sections of the façade, or the arrangement of interior spaces. The imitators do not understand that the strata of the composi-

---

76 [Translator's note:] Gottfried von Strassburg (? – c. 1215).

tion determine these elements (according to practical ends, space, and dynamics). For their aims and building techniques are of quite a different kind.

Therefore, the best imitative work seems to lack organic integrity. The builder no longer senses the inner necessity of the form. He forces them upon a building that has been planned in an entirely different way.

d) A sensible interpretation of speculative theses

To conclude our reflections upon the metaphysics of aesthetical form we may say that we cannot trace to their very origins and solve the puzzles that are contained in their positive content. For that reason the nature of formal beauty is a genuine metaphysical problem. Still, we can, to a fairly large extent, point to the conditions that a metaphysics must meet, specifically with reference to the inner relations between the forms of various kinds that are superimposed within one and the same work of art.

But then what is most positive in what we are able to claim falls again upon the relation of strata and appearance. Moreover, much remains valid in what older theories of a speculative kind have discerned. Thus we have, for example, the old theory of unity in multiplicity, which no doubt is a theory of an ontological and not a purely aesthetical kind; however, it attains a strictly aesthetical meaning if we understand it as the intuitable unity of a multiplicity that is also just as intuitable.

There are many kinds of unities in multiplicity: every concept is one, every state of affairs, every heavenly body, every dynamic structure, every organism. ... But nowhere does the unity or the multiplicity depend upon intuition; in aesthetics, in contrast, we have to do not with a merely existing unity, but with the unity that we are able to feel in an act of beholding. That is what is new in it. And that in fact is true of all kinds of aesthetic objects, especially the works of non-representational arts (music, ornamental art), as much as beautiful objects in nature. The test by example (271) is the challenge made to intuition, or, one may also say, the effort that intuition must bring to the challenge – not only to conceive of form creatively, but just as much merely to understand it aesthetically.

The effort of intuition is inconsiderable when it is a question of superficial and simple art – but of course it can already be a considerable challenge to persons untutored by the Muses. In the case of richer and deeper art, in contrast, it can require a considerable synthetic achievement of inward reflection.

Examples of this will be found neither in ornamental art nor in light fiction; nor, perhaps, in architecture, also, except for monuments. Important works in the other arts are full of examples: Shakespearian characterizations of human figures demand the application of synoptic intuition, for the characters are not spelled out in advance, but are given to us in their actions and passions, and a person who does not possess a mature understanding of human affairs will not find his way into their inner being. Similar reflections apply to the portraits by Holbein[77] or Frans Hals.

This phenomenon is most familiar in music. Every larger "movement" of a sonata or a symphony requires of the listener a large-scale musical synthesis; and innumerable listeners, however much they may be moved by it, do not arrive in any sense at understanding its unity and inner structure (its construction, its structural autonomy). They lack a capacity for musical activity, that is, having present to their intuition the sounds just heard and those that are yet to come. This is most forcibly the case with fugal (polyphonic) music: that is why so many musically trained persons fail in their hearings of the creations of Bach. Most people, of course, do not know how badly they fail, because there is no entryway for them into the inner structure of the fugue, for the theoretical entryway, not the one "heard," does not help them at all; they therefore have no way of measuring what passes them by unawares. This latter point is true in all of the arts for all failures of synthetic intuition.

The old idea of essential form or ideal form retains certain significance in the context of the old notion of the unity of multiplicity, but no doubt also only with many exceptions. Naturally, it can no longer be a question of substantial forms, though they were once accepted as obvious, and thought of as metaphysically constant and eternal models. However, there exists in fact an ideal form for every formal type that is perceivable empirically, in which the type is marked purely, regardless of whether such a thing occurs in the real world or not. Artistic imagination can, with relative ease, take what it encounters as a type, lift it over itself, and direct it towards its ideal form (its perfection). That process is indispensable to art down even to the details of how art bestows form upon its material. For that process simplifies matters; it extracts what is essential and makes it intuitively comprehensible, reduces complexity, and those things that appear in real life as mixed and confused are given a certain plastic outline. (272)

Thus the antique tragic poets raised their heroes upward to the level of an ideal type of human being; the figures acquired in that way something lapidary, their elevation exaggerated; they stood spiritually upon buskins. And much that was vividly human remained in those types. One expects just such conditions in all heroic poetry. The epics of peoples is full of them, and sculpture too – even in

---

77 [Translator's note:] Hans Holbein the Younger (1497–1543).

works that claim a likeness as in portraiture (the "Pensieroso"[78]). Painting has such types also (the Madonnas ...).

These examples demonstrate that we no longer have to do with a metaphysics of form. Ideal forms of this kind are not taken from reality, not even from an already existing realm of ideal being, but they have been fully shaped by the artistic imagination.

Here we have a place for new productive work, the size of which it would be difficult to exaggerate. It is given to the artist to behold ideas, and to show what he has beheld to others. No doubt not all the ideas he has beheld (e.g., human ideals) will be groundbreaking for those who experience them second-hand, but there are always such that do so. And in that way the artist becomes a bearer of ideas. This is without doubt seen most vividly in the poet. In ages when a higher ethos begins to form in the minds of a people, it is always the poets – that is, the epic poets – who hold the ideal image of man and virtue before the people's eyes that define the ethos against which the people must measure themselves, and, in fact, do so measure themselves. These poets are the genuine teachers and shapers of whole generations.

This role of teacher is possible because the creative mind enjoys a freedom in his observation and his work that men in general do not have, not even in their ethos. This kind of freedom in aesthetics and art is quite different from moral freedom. For the latter is tied to commands (values), and, with respect to them, moral freedom is the freedom to decide only for or against them. Artistic freedom in contrast can be the pioneer in first beholding the values themselves, and placing them before the minds of others.

Such a freedom can reach as far as it wishes beyond real existence, for it is not its task to realize what it beholds. It does not act according to an Ought, it is not a freedom of necessity, as the Ought is.[79] Artistic freedom is the opposite, the freedom of possibility – indeed of perfectly unlimited possibilities – for, within its domain, which exhausts itself in appearance and does not strive after reality, nothing at all is realized. The direction of its modality is the offsetting of reality.

The real miracle of this freedom is its power to let appear concretely the idea it has beheld. The artist declares the idea to be neither morality nor a command, nor even an ideal. Rather, he presents it to intuition as a living figure, which he lets act and speak for itself before the eyes of the observer. And just in that way it affects us convincingly – leading us, as it were, upward toward the desired

---

78 [Translator's note:] Michelangelo's sculpture of Lorenzo de' Medici, Duke of Urbino.
79 Cf. *Ethik*, Chap. 23, especially p. 204 [3rd edition (1949), p. 216; English edition: *Ethics*, George Allen & Unwin 1932, Vol. 1, p. 305].

human type. For (273) in morality it is not moralizing, pedantry, or admonitions that affect us, but always and alone the lucidly beheld model.

This leading of vision upward is, of course, no longer an aesthetical function of literature, but one that is moral, political, and cultural. Yet it demonstrates how genuine art is closely tied to life. It remains puzzling, however: only after we dispense with all metaphysics of form does this simple, clear, and deeply meaningful freedom of bestowing form autonomously become visible. Here lies the meta-aesthetical mystery of all great art.

Third Section: Unity and Truth in Beauty

Chapter 21: Artistic Freedom and Necessity

a) Freedom and arbitrariness

Artistic freedom carries its dark side and its dangers in itself: arbitrariness. This notion concerns primarily the representational arts, for arbitrariness can set in where the foundation of an art is imitation, and what is creative in the representational artist tempts him to make things better than nature and life do. That temptation is always close by, for nature and life are also creative, and produce forms, figures, and destinies, which they offer to our eyes. Life informs us of them and we are used to looking at the world as a "creation"; but rarely do we become aware of the analogy between these two kinds of creativity.

It is not necessary for the assertion of creativity in nature to place at its roots a theistic world order. What is productive in nature is just as much a scientific concept – especially since the metaphysics of substantial form has been abandoned and replaced by the thought of a continuous evolutionary creation (descent) of organic forms. Organic nature is eminently creative – although it is not "development," for that precisely would remove the element of creativity. And human life is even more creative; its figures and destinies are far more numerous and diverse.

From these domains, however – inorganic nature plays only a small role here – the arts derive their "material." That means that the "materials" of the representational arts already contain elements of form that have a creative process behind them, and are derived from a production behind which stand generative forces that are quite comparable to those of artistic production, and are surely superior in many respects.

It is after all no accident that it is precisely these ontological domains in which, apart from all art, are found the beauty of the real world, natural beauty, (274) and human beauty. One is therefore correct to say that in the fine arts, "nature and morality [*Sittlichkeit*]" become the "material" upon which further elements of form are bestowed. "Morality" is no doubt too narrow a concept here; we should say, "nature and human life," for human life is not coextensive with an ethos. Otherwise, the thesis is correct.

Where there are productive forces that shape structures, there is also an achievement of high levels of unity and wholeness of form, plentitude, and also structures done poorly, missed possibilities, forms burst asunder. These are facts that we know sufficiently from the circle of problems concerning natural beauty. Consequently, representational art can also either succeed or fail in its efforts to depict the successful and, in their own way, unsurpassable creations of nature or of the human form. In other words, it can be "true" or "untrue."

And this is the place at which the freedom of art can become a danger; it can turn into arbitrariness and in that way fail in respect to the "unity and wholeness" of form that has already been built in nature. Then it sinks beneath the level at which it should begin as one of its foundations – even if only to make tangible the beauty that nature had created. We are in no way criticizing representational art for including in its material what is ugly, that is, misbegotten; rather that it can fail in this task also, for it is not falsely pretending what it has created is beautiful.

But can something seduce the artist into falsifying experienced reality? To this we may answer: he can arrive at such falsification for three reasons:

1. Out of impotence, lacking depth in imitation;
2. Out of idealism, because his imagination creates the illusion of something that seems "yet more beautiful" to him;
3. Out of moral compunctions, i.e., considerations not of an aesthetical kind, e.g., pedagogical.

The first of these is extremely common: not only notorious bunglers, even many serious artists "misdraw" figures they have in mind or encounter in reality, because their vision and understanding is one-sided, or because their technique of representation is inadequate to what is seen and understood.

These are two quite different cases, and both are found in all of the representational arts. At the start of a great artistic movement, when it is beginning to spread but has not yet matured, both may almost become the general rule. In such times, it is precisely the bold avant-garde that falls into such one-sidedness. Think, for example, of the unnaturally thin architecture of the Quattrocento artist who painted cityscapes, or of the period's artificially selected and exaggerated landscape-motifs, in both cases present only in the background but still thematic. If we look back upon the fully matured art of later masters, we see what is positive about their achievement, but also the limits of their vision. (275)

The situation is similar with literary figures and their conflicts on the threshold of new writing: the domination of certain types in drama and in comedy (comedies of character), behind which the fullness of living vanishes. Even the early Schiller drew stock characters poorly (e.g., Karl and Franz Moor, Fiesco, Wurm ...), and of course the works of second and third-class writers are filled with such, especially the dilettantish poetasters, who bring no genuine poetic standards to their work.

The second reason for bad writing and the exaggeration of what is given empirically out of a need for intensifying an ideal, is no less familiar. The tendency to begin with nature and life develops from the justifiable need to understand and to present the forms beheld with as much purity as is at all possible – precisely as ideal.

The Archaic Greek sculpture gave form to god-like figures in which all their musculature was exaggerated and all of the softer parts of the body were neglected and almost bypassed. These figures seem to us neither natural nor beautiful, but they once manifested an ideal of the human body that aimed at strength, tension, and high achievement. ... Gothic sculpture gave form, without fear of the unnatural and the ugly, to faces whose expression was intended to manifest piety and an ethos of devotion. In the rich tradition of the Madonna in many epochs we find a large collection of ideal female beauty, none of which merely reproduces the ideal womanly type then current, but seeks to elevate it towards an imaginary ideality, and just in that way loses naturalness or falls into what is somehow unconvincing. For ideals are not only subject to time, but are also abandoned to the subjectivity of the artist. Classical tragedy – already in the time of Euripides, and even more marked in Corneille[80] and Racine[81] – is full of idealized and exaggerated figures. The sad thing is that the oversized standards make, in the long run, the human type seem slightly puny, because they measure only single sides of man that are exaggerated at the cost of others. But in that way the characters are deprived of life.

The third reason lies in motives external to aesthetics. Usually, what lies behind the effect aimed at is of a moral or pedagogical kind, but it can also be political or religious. Because literature has the specific capacity to affect and motivate us morally, it is easy for such purposes to mix themselves into the intentions of the writer. However, this does not happen only in works intended to educate, which of course is not a purely aesthetical genus, but is also found among very earnest representatives of pure poetry. We may think of the novels about the education and development of a character, such as the later parts of [Goethe's] *Wilhelm Meisters Lehrjahre* or perhaps better [*Wilhelm Meisters*] *Wanderjahre!* Think also of [Schiller's] Marquis de Posa [in the play *Don Carlos*].

The idea of an aesthetical education is old, and it has quite frequently influenced the fine arts, and not only literature. In Christian sacred painting, there is a certain unmistakable trace of it. Here, however, it is not (276) easy to distinguish pedagogical aims from pedagogical effect, for the latter can be unintentional, and can appear without any falsifying tendencies. This distinction must, however, be carefully maintained. Otherwise we will not do justice to art.

---

80 [Translator's note:] Pierre Corneille (1606–1684).
81 [Translator's note:] Jean Racine (1639–1699).

b) The formation of aesthetical ideals

Genuine artistic arbitrariness occurs only in the second and third cases. For the first one rests upon a *modus deficiens,* and cannot be included within the concept of artistic ability. We can also ignore the third case, the pedagogical one, because it depends upon the introduction of motives external to aesthetics. What remains important, therefore, is primarily the case of the elevation of natural objects by aesthetic idealism, i.e., the desire to surpass what is given in the real world.

It is not easy to discuss this case. For there is also a justifiable tendency in art to place vivid images before the eyes of men. And these must essentially be exaggerations of human reality. Even from a standpoint external to aesthetics it is clear that a form of art – especially a literature – of such kind must exist; for living without ideals is not good for a people, and ideals can be put vividly before its eyes only by art.

Similarly it cannot be denied that this connection between art and life is both natural to and necessary for art, to the point at which an art that loses sense of it loses also the very ground beneath its feet. Here we encounter the highest cultural undertaking that art must fulfill, with which it justifies its existence in the life of a people.

The ancients sensed this, and their ideals were doubtless as fruitful for art as for life. A prime example of this is the ideal of the youth [ἔφηβος] as it was articulated in sculpture. It made men desire to emulate it, but did not harm the high art of sculpture. One may say similar things about the heroic figures in Homer, of which many are considerably exaggerated; no less is the figure of Socrates in the poetic Platonic dialogues. Similar things may also be said about the knightly heroes of the German epos (Parzival, Siegfried, Tristan); yes, even about the more simple figures of the Nordic sagas. Are matters any different today? Consider the case of Dostoyevsky's[82] "idiot" or of Alexei Karamazov? Of Wagner's Hans Sachs [*Meistersinger*], of Hamsun's Isak [in *Growth of the Soil* (1917)]?

The greatest difficulty is and remains only this: how are we to distinguish such fruitful and artistically justified ideal figures from the arbitrary and questionable ones? With reference to what qualities may we recognize them? To this we must respond clearly: for a later generation, the distinction is easily made with reference to the figures' success; for contemporaries no given measure is possible, and the distinction can at best only be artificially divined. (277) However, divination is uncertain. The first part of this sentence asserts nothing but the old saying, "By their fruits shall ye know them." That proves only that in the end the decision

---

82 [Translator's note:] Fyodor Dostoyevsky (1821–1881).

as to genuine and spurious is not an aesthetical one, but in some way determined practically.

And we must say to that: in this context the ideal figures are entirely moral, at least as far as their content is concerned, or at the very least they are closely related to moral ideas (as the Greek ideal of youth). It is an aesthetical ideal only with reference to form; for only art can bring ideals into our sphere of vision, whatever kinds of ideal they may be: art alone presents an ideal in the form of a figure filled with life.

If we are dealing with ideals whose content is of a moral nature, the answer is easy to give: those ideals are fruitful that (1) touch an actually existing realm of values, and (2) correspond to a real historical tendency in the moral life of a people. The latter is essential, for otherwise the sense of value of contemporaries will not be able to direct itself towards the ideals that have been presented to them. The poet who touches such a tendency and, like a visionary, grasps the values that all are seeking, will become the bearer of ideas for his times. But that, too, is a criterion that we can only apply in retrospect.

However, the two conditions of fruitfulness that we have named still do not suffice. An ideal may be true to its values and its historical moment, but that concerns only its content, that is, its moral aspect. It still also possesses an aesthetical aspect, and that too is a genuine condition of its fruitfulness. This aesthetical aspect is its concreteness, figurativeness, and clarity – its stepping into the realm of visibility to the senses. For only as an ideal that has become concrete, that is, as a living figure, can it win over our hearts.

It is easier to judge upon this aesthetical condition of fruitfulness, even for contemporaries. For it is precisely as a contemporary that one can experience its effect on oneself, that is, whether one is convinced by the manifest ideal or not. Objectively, this condition depends entirely upon the ability of the artist: whether the ideal he has seen has been understood in a genuinely concrete way, whether he understood how to behold, as a visionary does, just how a figure of some longed-for type must move and present himself. That can be achieved only with the highest powers of intuition, because the art of beholding in such cases must be creative.

Art has not always been successful in bringing its ethical ideal to complete and concrete expression in a figure. Medieval sculpture succeeded only very conditionally. It lacked a natural feeling for this living human body, and, when in the early Renaissance the needed forms were found, especially in painting, the medieval ideal of the human being was no longer of concern. There is a false tendency in the history of art, and even more in aesthetics, to justify all of the ideals that appear in history – usually by appealing to their relativity to the sensibility of their times. Rather, this sensibility consists itself in the domination of certain ideals, and it is at least determined by them. Such relativity (278) does exist, no doubt, but its existence has reasons, and the reasons lie initially with the formation of ideals, or in some cases by the lack of them.

One notes that here the problem of freedom and arbitrariness in art returns. Apparently it functions everywhere that art aims to create objects that reach beyond what is empirically given, i.e., beyond mere imitation. If one thinks of the examples of randomness, which were given above, and compares them to the legitimate ideal objects in art, one cannot dismiss the thought that there must be an artistic necessity that opposes arbitrariness. This precisely is its difference from arbitrariness – in practical matters also – that freedom is not a shot in the dark that meets with no resistance; it has to deal with a very definite condition, i.e., it must take steps to raise itself up and over them.

This appears to contradict the above definition of aesthetical freedom, which expressed a freedom of possibility (without necessity and "from" it). For in the arts we are concerned not with the realization of what has been beheld, but only with letting-appear. Nonetheless, in artistic consciousness – and in aesthetics – there remains the unmovable idea of an inner necessity that governs within the work of art and touches its concrete figurative nature. With this necessity no ethical task at all is suggested, no Ought, not even a practical requirement, but a genuine aesthetical necessity that is present throughout the work like a kind of lawfulness, and that organizes it as a unity.

c) Artistic necessity and unity

We would perhaps have by now abandoned everything to arbitrariness if artistic form did not have laws of its own. By this we do not mean a law that one could or must dictate, but on the contrary one that form dictates to the creative and to the beholding consciousness. Moreover, it is not a universal law; it is nothing more than the law of the individual work of art. Yet it is a law that holds the parts of the whole together, and prohibits substituting one for the other; an inner necessity that ties the members together in such wise that the one draws the other along with it.

Is there really such a thing in artistic form? No doubt there is: every formed object has its inner logic. To put it crudely: try to exchange the members of two sculptured figures (taking care to fill in all ruptures)! Only nonsense could come out of it. That is precisely the mystery of the torso: it seems to us to be a whole, because through its whole and partial forms the position of the arms and legs become implicit. That is clear, inner necessity, and in fact a purely aesthetical one. A special kind of charm is simply given off by the torso – for the observer – to intuit as he looks upon the whole work. This charm does not depend upon actually supplementing the form; it is restricted to (279) a synthetic play of fantasy, but it must be taken very seriously, for it offers strict rules to guide the given object. That would not be possible if there were not a tight inner correlation among the parts that extends as a form of necessity to the missing members.

We find the same aesthetical necessity in numerous other phenomena. So, for example, in the poetic structure of a human character. There are examples of characters that seem to lack unity, who seem not just to express a real disunity of mind, as existing persons may do, but are illogically composed and represented. This disunity we experience as a poetic fault – and then our aesthetical feeling rejects the work. Similarly, we may see a lack of unity in an entire poetic work, a drama, etc., when it "breaks apart" within itself, as it were, or "loses a clear development." This phenomenon appears frequently where the author loses himself in a multiplicity of details – especially in the middle strata where the composition of the material must take place.

This is also true of the non-representational arts, of music and architecture. In both there may be compositions without organic structure, of whose lack of logic one becomes sensible even without analyzing the works. This inner logic is felt most strongly in great musical works. Their greatness consists, after all, precisely in the inner necessity by which unfolds the whole of a theme, a phrase, a movement, an opus in several movements. The unity and wholeness of a composition rests upon this necessity, and on this again depends the appearance of psychic movement in the inner strata.

Naturally every art possesses its peculiar kind of necessity, one that cannot be transferred to another. Moreover, the situation is different in the representational arts from that in the non-representational ones; in the latter cases, a unity of form governs in every stratum. But that changes nothing regarding the law of inner necessity that exists throughout.

The necessity is "inner" provided that it depends on no external conditions, but rather – like "immanent truth" – refers to the harmony of the entire construct in itself, in such wise, specifically, that when some members of the whole are given, the others are co-determined, and cannot be eliminated at random. More correctly: it is not that everything about the other members is thereby determined, but that something in them is determined essentially. Necessity of this kind thus touches parts or members of the whole, with reference specifically to each other and to the whole. Whether one calls this lawfulness or not – since it is different in each work – may be just a matter of taste.

But in contrast, making this clear is important for the question concerning artistic "freedom." This freedom initially stands opposed as an antinomy to the necessity within the work of art. Freedom concerns precisely the play with form, the bestowing of form beyond the empirical, the process of selection and omission, etc. This antinomy is insoluble as long as we (280) understand aesthetical freedom as arbitrariness, that is, as permission to manipulate form in any way at all. But it is an error to understand freedom in this way.

Freedom here, as everywhere it appears, is not a negative, but a positive. It means neither lawlessness nor a lack of determination, but rather the beginning of its own autonomous determination and lawfulness. To express the idea with greater definition: in the domain of the creative bestowal of form there exist unique principles of unity and wholeness that do not occur elsewhere; these exercise a strict necessity in the work of art, but they are not for their part dependent upon other principles, whether those of being or of the ought-to-be. They themselves thus constitute the freedom of the creative spirit. And because it is not a question here of making real, but rather of its contrary, subtracting reality and creating mere appearance, these principles come in no conflict with any other principles. For that reason moral freedom is a great metaphysical puzzle, but aesthetical freedom is in no way one: nothing opposes it. And therefore with regard to content it is identical with aesthetical necessity. For the creative person aesthetical freedom may well be "the freedom to set forth wherever he will";[83] but he can wish only for what has unity and necessity.

d) The unity of the work and the freedom of creation

If one accepts this inner necessity as part of artistic freedom, it will be easy to distinguish freedom and arbitrariness: arbitrariness lacks inner necessity, there is no law and no principle of unity in it, on the basis of which images can be shaped. If we could always recognize at first sight whether law and a principle of unity were present, arbitrariness could have little latitude in the arts, and creations by people with inferior skills would immediately reveal themselves as such to everyone. But that is not the case in the world of art.

Experience teaches us, from the little light we can shine into the creative act, that in most cases the creator finds himself searching tentatively and with great labor after the convincing unity that hovers before his mind; he searches in many different ways, he sketches, he draws, tosses them out, and tries ever again. And it is frequently the case that only the agreement of the viewer convinces him. His

---

83 [Translator's note:] Hölderlin, Friedrich, "The Course of Life," in: *Poems of Friedrich Hölderlin. The Fire of the Gods Drives Us to Set Forth by Day and by Night*, selected and translated by James Mitchell, San Francisco: Ithuriel's Spear 2004, p. 25.

test bases itself on the example of someone being convinced by the work. But even this is no certain test: for even though the creator of the work may be unable to find the criterion of his success by himself, how much more must such an incapacity be true of a viewer whose judgment might well be backward, or inadequate in some other way! If he lacks all access to a special kind of beholding, he will misunderstand the work. Even entire groups of the artist's contemporaries may fail when faced with a new form of art. For the genius and his work stand isolated in their times, and it is the crucial test of his ability – better, of his belief in his ability – to hold fast to what he has beheld and feels to be inwardly necessary. If he does not pass (281) the test, he will lose confidence in his undertaking. The fate of a man unrecognized in his own times is tragic.

The same is true in reverse order. An art-going public can be gripped by the external effects of some novelty and be swept along by a work possessing no inner necessity at all. In such cases we have the pseudo-artist who causes a sensation, but whose fame is ephemeral. This is much like the historical phenomenon of "fashion," which is, in the end, artistic arbitrariness. It is not always easy even for a connoisseur to see through such a thing correctly and reject it at its very inception. This is a familiar phenomenon in times of limited originality.

Aesthetics does not have the task of finding applicable practical criteria. In this area, it must rather confine itself to the determination that such criteria are unavailable and cannot be found even in theory. That the systematic study of art may result in dogmatic judgments should not be allowed to lead aesthetics astray. That rests upon nearby border-crossings, toward which the desire for novelty or the subjective engagement with movements propels the individual artist. The individual is historically subject to suggestions conditioned by his epoch.

Even without the ambition to make decisions, aesthetics has an important task in this context, viz., to determine by analysis what in fact should be understood by the unity of a work of art, so far as it rests upon inner necessity and yet gives latitude to creative freedom. This question is an old one. Once, at the very origins of aesthetics, it was a living question in the dramatic arts and produced the doctrine of the "three unities," that of place, of time, and of action. That is viewed quite narrowly and to an extent also externally, but it is nevertheless a beginning of and an attempt at an answer.

Of these, only the unity of action is really central. It is quite essential, and in fact precisely with respect to the inner structure. However, it is not sufficient. For it affects only one stratum in the structure of the literary work. What we need, however, is a unity that encompasses all the strata. If we confine our study entirely to the middle strata, we must find, on this side of the unity of action, a unity of movement and gesture that perhaps also must include the mode of speech; it has to be something like the unity of lifestyle of the characters presented.

Similarly, on the far side of the unity of action there must be a unity of the characters: the preservation of the identical psychic form. And, even further beyond this: the unity of human destiny – which of course does not coincide with that of the situations and action. Only when one holds these unities, which belong to separate strata, together in a hierarchical series, does one approach the unity of the entire work. This too is itself hierarchical; it is a complex, many-dimensional unity.

But it is still a question whether even this much suffices. For obviously the unities of the individual strata of appearance are not (282) simply arranged alongside of each other, they are also dependent upon each other. This is apparent, because the rearmost stratum must always appear in the forms bestowed upon the ones before it. This uniform preservation of the style of the performance of the characters is the condition of the appearing of the unity of situation and action. Then too, a departure from the style deprives them of their integrity. This is the same for the final condition of the appearing of unified characters; and this again for the emergence of the unity of destiny, etc.

This relation of dependency in the hierarchical gradations clearly plays the role of a general law, and is also constitutive in all other arts for the occurrence of inner necessity and unity. In painting, the entire relationship of unity might be shifted more towards the outer strata. In architecture it is palpable in the interrelation of the composition of aim, space, and dynamics, and these three clearly make up a unity of mutuality by conditioning each other.

Perhaps the unity is most profoundly felt in music. Here it builds itself up in steps from relatively small elements into the great unity of a movement or of a work in several movements. Here we find also the inner necessity of the whole marked in the most plastic manner, because such logic is the condition of a unified effect. That is especially instructive, for music is the freest of all arts. It is free in two ways: from the "material" and from the aim. But it is just this most free of all arts that has the most finished type of inner necessity and unity. It cannot be more clearly demonstrated that the unity of the work and the freedom of creation are compatible with each other.

In addition, one can produce a comparative categorial analysis of unity. And since in art we have the complete unity of a created object that evidently has the character of a structure, it must in all essentials amount to a variation of the general category of structure. This variation is presented in the *Aufbau der realen Welt*,[84] Chaps. 33b–d. But by no means were all possible structural types enumer-

---

84 [Translator's note:] *The Construction of the Real World*, subtitled *Outline of a General Theory of Categories*. First published 1940.

ated there, e.g., in particular, not the structure of the work of art. Its analysis is made difficult by the fact that it does not have a uniform nature. But if one ignores that, one may at least venture that this structure possesses an especially strict composition, that is, it is held together by an especially rigorous inner necessity.

Recall that even in the foreground, a selection takes place that leaves detail to the very minimum – often with great economy – in contrast to real objects of a corresponding type, but what the relation of appearance communicates in this way can have a richness that is easily superior to the reality. From this it becomes clear that, in the act of beholding, a totality is constituted that is determined by the uniformity characterizing the structure. It is the same in literature with regard to the lifelike character of the figures, so in painting with regard to the psychic reality of the expressions of face and figure, so also (283) in a musical piece with regard to the superabundance of motion, suspension, and rapture.

One should recall that no general laws, rules, or principles are found here, as are found in structures of other kinds, e.g., with dynamic or organic structures, or with the fabric of families or of communities. For every work of art is strictly individual and what is typical about it is merely secondary.

The fact that the artist is not tied down to rules or models, but can create only in freedom, is tied to the individual structural character of art. This thesis, too, must be correctly understood. It does not mean that the creative artist stands in no tradition, or that he cannot learn from models. It means only that the tradition of his art does not consist of rules that he must carefully learn and use to direct his own procedures – that is what the dilettante always tries to do; and the model does not become a fetter when he manages somehow to go beyond it.

To create in freedom – that does not mean a random process of hit or miss, or the frantic search for novelty; it means rather the grasping intuitively of the inner unity and necessity of an entire construct – not that in one stratum, but a preparatory mental penetration of all of them – and then finding the external, sensible elements for bestowing form on one's material, that is, the words, the sounds, the colors, or the stones – finding them, so that from this point forward the series of forms bestowed on the background strata becomes transparent. We call "free" a creation of this kind, in the sense that it discovers and assesses a new possibility for letting something appear that was hidden in the background.

Chapter 22: The Claim of Literature to Truth

a) The false claim to truth

We must distinguish sharply the question of inner necessity and unity from the claim to truth that appears in the representational arts. This claim is not simply one of logical consistency, unity, and wholeness, and also not one intended as an analogy to the "immanent truth" of theoretical science, but rather much more as an analogy to transcendental truth. With this, we approach again the circle of problems that forms about "imitation and the act of creating" (Chap. 20a), but approached now from the perspective of the obligations of art to extant nature and actual human life.

The flourishing of "aestheticism" at the beginning of our twentieth century took this obligation very lightly: in the end, could not any inaccurate rendering of the real be valid as creative originality? Of course no one would dare to challenge entirely the autonomy of the artist's – even of the representational artist's – imagination. Imitation is opposed to transformation, and the artist has a right to the latter, otherwise he could not make appear (284) to others what actual life reveals only to him, the clear-sighted artist, in his interweaving of events, but is concealed from the masses.

Given this, how is art's claim to truth to be maintained, and, even more, an obligation to truth? One thinks again immediately of the binding of art through the givenness of things and through experience, and something is correct about this, only it must not be understood in the sense of theoretical truth, that is, the bare correspondence to real being.

But how should the thesis be understood positively? The problem is not to be solved with the principle of form-bestowal, although naturally we are concerned precisely with form in this context, the bestowal of form both upon matter and upon material, for the two are tied together, as has already been shown, such that the bestowal of form upon material always takes place "in" some form of matter. It will be useful to limit the questions initially – to one single representational art. Literature offers itself for this purpose, because without a doubt the claim to truth is made by it in the most principled way. "Poets lie too much," said Nietzsche.[85] He was referring to the effects that disorient, are too embellished, and impair our

---

85 [Translator's note:] Nietzsche, Friedrich, *Thus Spoke Zarathustra: A Book for Everyone and Nobody,* translated and edited by Graham Parkes, Oxford and New York: Oxford University Press 2005, Second Part, "On the Poets," p. 110.

sense of life. We may set aside the question. That poetry courts this danger, however, must be admitted.

We begin here immediately with the main issue. It is not a question of any sort of limitation of our "joy in pretending." Imagination is and remains the ultimate source of poetic creation. And whoever wishes to understand its claim to truth in opposition to imagination would misunderstand that claim from the outset. That can be proven a thousand times over.

For an example, take the ancient popular literary form called the fairy-tale. Founded in many kinds of beliefs and superstitions, the fairy-tale is full of wonderful, supernatural things. It is no matter if people once really believed in these things or not, for even today people gladly engage lovingly with fairies and giants, princes under a spell and animals that talk. It does not occur to them to connect these things to an inappropriate claim to truth. It is sufficient that people could believe in them at all and enjoy them. It is the same with legends and myths, with the popular epic poem, and even, to a great extent, with the high epic poems.

But even if we disregard such "tales of wonder," the material of a poem does not pretend, even within the limits of the natural world, to a truth in the sense of the real existence of its characters and the real happening of the events it describes. Neither Schiller's nor Shaw's[86] Joan of Arc corresponds to the historical figure. Yet both are extraordinarily effective dramatically. Only children read a story with the idea of its reality; an adult understands the unreality of what is narrated, or, perhaps better: he understands the indifference of poetry to reality and unreality. This is true for the novel and for the drama – even when real persons and (285) events, for example, historical ones, make up the material. The latter may have its limits where well-known persons are represented. But this limit is easy to get around in the selection of the material.

In all these matters, the poet has the greatest freedom. We may also express this in the following way: nowhere in the broad arena of the composition of material does the poet meet with serious limits to its free shaping, nowhere do we expect that people will hold him pedantically to correspondence with reality, and of course they do not hold him to it. It is sufficient if, when he is dealing with historical material, he has respect for the still living sympathies of his public. And it is easy to see that in lyric poetry this freedom is extended even further. Whether the poet, in speaking of the sorrows of love, refers to his own, or whether he speaks out of simple feeling for another's sensibilities, his verses, their beauty

---

86 [Translator's note:] George Bernard Shaw (1856–1950).

and their ability to touch our emotions deeply are not affected at all. Thus it is with all poetic expression of the emotions.

It is another question whether the poet can express convincingly what he has himself not experienced. This question has been variously answered. Perhaps it cannot be answered with any generality, because the gift of placing oneself into a situation and shaping it from an alien sensibility is divided among men in extraordinarily different ways. One may say at least that a poet who has had a rich experience has access to much more of what is human, and he offers the far greater likelihood of giving convincing shape to that experience than does one with a more limited personal experience.

Here we can make several more demands of the poet that are well justified. So for example, that he possess knowledge of life and knowledge of man – which are quite different from the richness of his own experience. The knowledge of humankind consists in the ability to see through what men hide; and to that belongs the gift of penetration, the critical eye. The satiric poet and the writer of comedies have great need for these gifts. But we do not ever say that their characters, just because they are taken from life, must really have been "so." There exists also a kind of mockery and scorn that is very unfair and untrue. Think of the treatment of Socrates in the νεφέλαι [*The Clouds*] of Aristophanes. Even the accent placed on specific values still has generally free latitude with respect to what is real.

Finally, we must not forget that we also expect just as surely a certain idealism from the poet: he should not give prominence only to weaknesses and other failings of human nature, but also recognize what is noble in them and separate that out from the dregs. But both of these matters concern the ethos of literature more than its claim to truth.

b) The requirement to be true to life

For the present, we have learned from this analysis only what the requirement of truth in literature is not. But we have not yet learned what it is in an affirmative sense. This must now be discussed. Here precisely we must try to be clear. (286) For we can look for the meaning of this requirement in the direction of an unrestrained realism or we can understand it in a quite different way.

To say it all in a word: what we seek in literature and demand of it is not factual truth but a truth that is faithful to life. What that word [*Lebenswahrheit*] means, however, it not easy to say, although we all understand it, up to a point. Even the witch in the fairy-story seems true to life when she is crafty and malicious, but her craftiness is set a certain limit; even Cinderella's helpful doves seem true to life, because they are reciprocating the love they received from her. The anecdote that people tell about some famous man may seem true to life, not as though "it really was that way," but rather because it characterizes him as he was, or as his acquaintances knew him. The ancients had a large literature of anecdotes – and these went quite logically into their historical writing, yet, on the other hand, they always remained related to poetry. An anecdote fails to be true to life when it lacks the image of the person, or in itself misrepresents or confuses that image.

Why do characters in novels, such as in those by Felix Dahn[87], Georg Eber[88], or Gustaf Freytag[89], not seem true to life – although they have been drawn correctly and clearly? Because they have been constructed within a set of features that have drunk from the well of opinion of the nineteenth century. These writers are scholars and have, in the end, no vivid ideas taken from the life they are trying to describe. For that reason, the characters, the situations, and the activities, even the destinies of men, do not turn out to be true to life. It is quite otherwise when the writer takes the historical material only as an occasion, and does not pretend beyond that to be drawing a picture of times foreign to his own. Thus, for example, Shakespeare's Caesar, Antony, Coriolanus, Henry IV, or even Macbeth. He draws from all life, from his vision of the life going on around him, and the characters and destinies seem true to life.

One may glean from this an approximation of how it stands with the difference between true-to-life and factual truth: the former, too, consists of a very definite correlation with real life, but not in singular and unique (individual) facts, but with what is fundamental and essentially human; yes, even beyond that, with what is humanly typical in diverse things – not with what all men have in common, but only with men of a certain stamp. And this means at the same time that because a type of human being is in itself a uniform whole, the requirement of truth demanded of literature becomes attached to the requirements, discussed above, of unity and inner necessity; indeed the first flows directly into the second. Such characters seem untrue that are not bound by an inner necessity to unity.

We may pursue this postulate of truth one step further into what is individual. For literature in its concreteness does not deal with types, but with highly individualized single characters. (287) Hamlet and Lear, Wallenstein, Tasso and Mephistopheles can neither be assimilated to a formula, nor even to an ideal type after which they are constructed; certainly such characters as Glahn [in Knut Hamsun's 1894 novel *Pan*] and [Dostoyevsky's] Myshkin [in *The Idiot*] do not, and also not

---

87 [Translator's note:] Felix Dahn (1834–1912).
88 [Translator's note:] Georg Eber (1837–1898).
89 [Translator's note:] Gustaf Freytag (1816–1895).

Gabler and Rosmer [in Ibsen's plays *Hedda Gabler* and *Rosmersholm*]. But the same conditions are valid for the unity of the individual character in its uniqueness. As to the type: it too possesses an inner law – however, the law of the latter is far more difficult to give than the former; it is too complicated. Nevertheless, we can sense whether the unity is maintained throughout the representation or not. Accordingly, the character seems to us true or untrue to life, it will seem complete in itself or disintegrated, something pasted together. That is something for which there is no criterion, but it is of great importance for every literary work.

Additionally, what is merely general about humankind and typical of men cannot achieve a fully perspicuous effect. At bottom, both are lifeless in their effects – for the simple reason that in life itself there are no pure types. Thus any mere stock figures seem untrue to life in the end. Comedies of the older sort, which relied on such types, even if they were much beloved in their own times, had finally to learn that fact: they outlived themselves as soon as their initial effects had been wrung dry, and they seemed to the next generation to be ossified and artificial, that is, untrue to life.

In the classicistic tragedy a similar process was played out, and only the element of high pathos could for a while conceal its slow downfall. The king, the court-intriguers, the hero, the fool, the pure maiden, the crafty servant et al., or other fixed types, dominated the entire literary form as though it were possible to create something only within its forms. In its greatest representatives, the early modern drama raised itself beyond those forms, but not without the example of Shakespeare, who still had these types in hand but knows how to fill them with a living individuality. What is significant in his achievement has not been well understood by many critics and literary historians. If they saw no stock characters that they could easily classify, they practically blamed the poet for their absence. But they were wrong to do so. Only what in a human character grows beyond the type is filled with life and true to it.

But the requirement of being true-to-life extends far beyond this. It refers in fact not only to persons, types, and characters, but just as surely to the situations, conflicts, and resolutions, the interweaving of kinds of behavior, the outcomes and surprises, the role of chance, good and bad luck. All that must be true to life. And not only that: it applies even to the entire milieu in which the action takes place, to the coloring, the background mood, and the style of life of the characters that make up the foreground, that is, to the style of life held in common in those days.

How seriously we must take this requirement can be demonstrated by the negative example of the "*deus ex machina.*" This appears when the writer can find no natural way to untie the knots that have been wound by some high authority and to lead everyone to a happy ending. Even the men of old laughed (288) at such devices and at their overthrowing of the living truth – its implausibility was apparent even to the simple-minded. But up to and including literature today we find the *deus ex machina*, perhaps in the form of a chance event that saves everything; and one cannot deny that it serves to relieve the seriousness of the situation, that it has a comedic effect: yet, foolishly, what is comedic does not lie among the lesser characters, but precisely among the powerful, who are supposed to rule over the comedy and to determine the fates of others. Here the requirement that poets be true to life is lacking on the level of fate and chance.

Only a bit more ridiculous is the vulgar "happy ending" that we know in a thousand variations from the cinema: the outcome attached inorganically to the series of events, an outcome that is not given by the development of these situations. It is rather simply patched on for the sake of feeling good.

c) The question of strata in the claim to truth

We see just from these extreme examples how much broader the problem of the true-to-life becomes, and how it eventually extends to everything contained in the bestowal of form upon material in a literary work. For if the characters are not alone in being affected by this requirement, then there are no limits to where the requirement must stop. It affects the whole of the composition of the material – in the saga and in the drama, in the novel and *mutatis mutandis* in the lyric poem (although there only intimations of it are found).

These matters will not be pursued in detail for the various species of literature, if only because they repeat themselves in them and, as a common feature, vary only in grade. In contrast, a new and more fundamental question now appears, which in a similar way relates to all species of literature. Upon what stratum of the literary work does the requirement of being true to life come into question?

After our initial reflections, it appeared as though the requirement of truth concerned only one middle stratum, that of the bestowal of form upon psychic material and upon the characters. This limitation has already shown itself to be untenable: characters are not indifferent to or isolated from the conditions of life in which they give themselves form; they therefore must be understood on the background of those conditions. And, conversely, the conditions of life are given form also by the characters.

This changes the situation fundamentally. One may now answer that out of the strata of a literary work at least the four middle ones stand under the requirement of being true to life. In just these strata – movement and gesture, situation and action, psychic development, destiny – lies the entire form-bestowed material; and our problem concerns the quality of true-to-life in the shaping of the material. If one looks a bit more closely, one finds that this response also does not yet suffice. Rather the foreground, with its ordered words, is also drawn under the requirement, for not every style of language seems "true" for the treatment of some specific material. Similarly, both (289) of the inner middle strata are drawn under it too. For there are ideal qualities that express themselves in the order of events, and may then be either true to life or not.

The final background strata can be left out of the picture, because they bear the ideal elements (the individual ideals and the universal ideal). But for the remaining strata it is essential to be convinced that they all stand under the aesthetical requirement of being true to life, and that they are in fact only aesthetically effective when they fulfill that requirement with a certain adequacy.

For example, in the stratum of movement, speech, and gesture, every step, every pose, every remark that falls outside the intended and portrayed style of life destroys or at least does injury to the picture of the character as integrated within a time and an environment. And the injury can be of such moment that the later strata, that of the plot, for example, are no longer able to appear correctly. Appearance is highly conditioned by the form bestowed upon what appears. In this stratum we may point to the characters in the novels by Eber, Dahn, and Freytag as seeming especially untrue to life. A notable example is the first appearance of Britannus in Shaw's *Caesar and Cleopatra*. Britannus speaks and acts as if he were quite the Englishman of our times, even down to his opinions. It seems as if all the characters of the drama had been drawn into the present and deprived of their seriousness, because what sounds modern works destructively upon the intended style of life. Within that style, it is untrue.

This fact is demonstrated even more clearly by the stratum of situation and action. Perhaps we reflect insufficiently upon how superficially identical situations are in fact not identical for a man of a different nature, who is the child of a different milieu; correspondingly, even the action in which a man reacts to a situation cannot be the same action, even if the character was the same.

One might perhaps say that great writers have always placed special value upon the plasticity with which form is bestowed in this stratum – knowing well that, for the most part, it is upon the clear understanding of situations that all else depends. There are novels in which most of the narrative must be dedicated to the unfolding of situations in life, such that, in comparison, the events that actually take place in them vanish. Long passages in Balzac[90] are to be understood in this way, as also many in Dostoyevsky, Thomas Mann[91], Galsworthy[92] and Hamsun. ...

---

90 [Translator's note:] Honoré de Balzac (1799–1850).
91 [Translator's note:] Thomas Mann (1875–1955).
92 [Translator's note:] John Galsworthy (1867–1933).

Plays must be more sparing in this respect, for they are strictly limited. They cannot draw out their descriptions at length; instead, they can work with the occasions offered by the course of events, as life itself does. What we mean by the development of a dramatic scene is a compact series of situations in which each is immediately comprehensible on the basis of those prior to it. On the other hand, the behaviors represented (more accurately, their proper motives) are only comprehensible on the basis of the situation. However, guilt, merit, responsibility, etc. depend upon these behaviors, just as the weighty decisions of a character do. (290)

This connection is evident in itself. And there is hardly a writer that does not understand it and has not operated according to its laws. For that reason, it is very difficult to give a negative example of it. Errors in the portrayal of a situation exist when it is not possible to understand, on the basis of the account, why one person behaves in such a way and not otherwise, where we can assume that his character has been stable throughout.

As for the stratum in which destiny takes shape, the requirement to be true to life has special importance: the writer who gives shape to some human destiny approaches astonishingly close to the role that divinity plays in the minds of believers. And when the poet comes close to the role and pretends to be a kind of amateurish god, what he produces is simply a perversion.

For such matters we have the examples, introduced above, of an almost ghostly sort: the *deus ex machina* and the *happy end*. They are gross examples, of course. What is characteristic is precisely that a fate, which is generally seen and presented quite realistically, is at some point turned toward something improbable or unnatural, for example, the conclusion of Zola's[93] *Rome*, where the intended effect was that the two lovers (the nephew and niece of the cardinal) die together, and the girl then really does die later than the beloved (of a "natural" death!).

This is bungling in the matter of destiny: we see clearly how the writer, relying on some favored idea, twists fated events unnaturally into unnatural shape. The literature of all epochs is full of such falsification; usually we do not notice them, because we are used to being indulgent to writers. Often the trouble is in the way the figures themselves act to determine their fate. We think to find the crucial point in the character of a figure; but if his character has been described as harmonious and wise, and nevertheless there suddenly appears stubbornness in him that fixes his destiny, then his destiny has been poorly drawn. Wiechert[94] (*The Simple Life*) [*Das einfache Leben*, 1939] allows his Orla to

---

93 [Translator's note:] Emil Zola (1840–1902).
94 [Translator's note:] Ernst Wiechert (1887–1950).

fail at the last moment to rush to meet the new life that is opening up before her – despite her wisdom and clear understanding – for the sake of a tragic and inauthentic idea of renunciation. This is the reversal of the *happy end*.

In the face of this, one may ask: what leads the writer so easily astray that he falsifies on the level of destiny? There is a clear answer that touches upon the following points. 1. Man is, in life, powerless in the face of destiny, for it consists of elements in his life that are dependent in no way upon him, his knowledge, or his desires. In literature, a writer has an opportunity to give shape to destiny; he grasps hold of it, and wants to show what he would do in place of Providence. This motive we can call the presumptuous consciousness. 2. A second motive is found in the aversion to chance and to the absurdity of events. Man tends to understand all human destinies as the real "transmission" of some providential power. We can call this the metaphysical-teleological motive. 3. A third motive consists in the tendency to see the transmission as aimed at some individual (291) into which the writer's own tendencies insinuate themselves. These tendencies are usually of a moral kind, or at least felt as moral: the wicked man should quickly meet his fate, the hero his reward. In tragedies, the situation is reversed. We can call this motive simply that of the moral "tendency" as such.

The second motive is the most innocent one. It is not without justice that destiny be presented as something that is "transmitted" to us, not because it is so in life, but because people think of it that way, and the characters in literature think it so also. In this sense, theology in the literary shaping of destiny is "true to life." What is least in keeping with art is the third motive: the moral accent in the shaping of destiny. This is quite natural and often joyfully welcomed by the natural feelings of the reader: his sense of justice, so often frustrated, "finally" is satisfied. The first motive is the most important, just because the writer, even the great writer, seldom becomes conscious of it.

d) The true-to-life in the first and last strata

We can see clearly the outcome: that this literary requirement to be true to life is firmly tied to the middle strata of the literary work. The requirement is, to be sure, divided more or less evenly among them. But being true-to-life is especially threatened on the level where fate is shaped, and the threat comes from poetic license and rests upon a basis external to aesthetics, one that is, in the end, metaphysical in nature.

But the picture we have sketched over several pages must still be supplemented. It lacks an account of the remaining strata, provided that the requirement of being true-to-life extends to them. In the first place, we have the foreground stratum of the written word. It has already been noted that this stratum can hardly be indifferent to poetic "truth." But how is its participation in such an ideal requirement to be understood?

The term "word" suggests more than its dictionary definition. It suggests, for example, the mood of the speaker, or perhaps even something of his attitude towards what he has said (perhaps a note of skepticism). One can speak of serious matters with seriousness, and one can also speak of them in jest; and, in certain circumstances, the contrast between them can have a especially resounding effect. That is true also to a great extent of the written word. For in writing, the possibility exists of adding nuances to dialogue and styles of writing that create the effect of the true-to-life – or of being false to it. This is by no means only a question of good taste in giving form to spoken expressions; it is just as much a question of giving the effect of truth.

He who affects the style of a fairy-tale in the middle of a contemporary novel will fail to convince. He who affects the tone of contemplation in some highly dramatic scene will not win over an audience. The word that fails to convince is the essence of the untrue-to-life. The layman says, "Such things (292) don't happen." And he is right. Just think of lyric poetry alone: one single inappropriate word can tear to shreds a piece of fine tissue that was woven transparently in the melodies of words. The art of the poet consists essentially in the perfect word flying to greet him at the perfect place for it – words fixed, naturally, in the depths of the background, which he thereby first made speak.

Another no less serious matter is the demand found in the last inner strata. We identified it above as those of the individual idea (of a single person) and that of the universal idea (*viz.*, of the universally human). The first idea we see in the sudden appearance of the idea of personhood behind the acting and erring person; the second in the tendency of a play, or in the inner, unspoken moral tone of a novel.

Let us dwell for a moment upon the latter. A literary work of merit without something universally human – its idea – in the background strata is hardly thinkable. But a literary work that is tendentious is endangered. It can be derailed on two sides:
1. The moral tone, the idea, the philosophical presuppositions can themselves be erroneous, that is, be in conflict with our experience of life, and
2. They can be represented incorrectly – too obviously, too insistently, or even too darkly, too veiled, misleadingly, unclearly – and can then be repellent or even simply disappear.

In both cases the universal idea will lack the power to convince us effectively: thus neither be true to life, nor felt as true. And both still have little to do with objective "truth."

The writer must allow his ideas – especially his moral beliefs – to speak only through the events, and to let them speak in the way life itself lets them speak, that is, as suggested by the destinies of the figures, but as always still needful of an interpretation. The poet must not give this interpretation: not only because to do so will seem prosaic, but also especially because then the interpretation does not seem true to life. For it then affects us as the interpretation of someone in particular. Such interpretations are subject to error. A moral or a philosophical vision that is expressed in words immediately loses its power, because it has not been exposed as a living truth by the narrative itself. No doubt a person who reads the work also wants to learn something, but he does not want to be instructed like a schoolboy; he wants to see for himself.

With the occasional appearance in literature of the individual idea the matter is easier. And this is because the writer's task with it is more difficult from the very outset: more difficult in the beholding as in the presentation. For it appears to him only rarely, and always only as a vision, which may come upon him when he beholds an actual human being. Even more rarely does he find the means to achieve its realization. Here is the difference: philosophical and moral ideas can be conceived and grasped in the abstract. (293) The individual idea, however, cannot be made up or constructed.

There are, of course, characters in literature that are constructed according to a prefigured idea: think of those typical of classicism and of comedies of character. But it is not the individual ideal that has been prefigured, always a general idea, a type. We may ignore them here, for they do not concern our problem. Nonetheless, it is true that many creative writers think they have grasped the idea of an individual person, but have only a type in mind. That is, of course, simply illusion.

Where individual uniqueness in its idea is understood – as often occurs in the characters of great writers, for example, the idea of Socrates in Plato – it is beheld based on a deep individual experience of a real person. It is not beheld empirically, but lies, rather, like all things having the nature of ideas, beyond the empirical; yet always beheld with the contours of empirical things and, as it were, in the extended direction of the form that it possesses. That is the reason why, in this effort, the writer does not quickly fall into the danger of arbitrarily constructing his figures, but otherwise succumbs to it where he is working with what is ideal. But just for that reason there are so few cases in literature of such exaggeration of individual figures.

Chapter 23: The True-to-Life and Beauty

a) The disclosure of life in art

One is driven by such reflections to the borderline region where the truth of a work of literature coincides with its aesthetic value as such, and this becomes identical to its beauty. The matter cannot be easily dismissed, because we are dealing with "representational" art proper, and this must necessarily contain some element of imitation, however much it may be reconstructed. From this point, there is perhaps only a short step to their complete identification.

Other facts support this identification. Literature is intended to reveal a part of the world to the reader, or at least a part of human life. For it is the nature of man to live open to the world, but this openness is a task that each person must accomplish for himself. Even the experienced man tends to be open to the world only so far as his practical need for knowledge of life and human affairs require. Beyond that, the mind tends to be closed. At this point literature should step in, and reveal entire regions of life to which we had no access.

This is much in keeping with what was developed above: that the first function of the artist is "beholding," upon which basis the function of pointing things out may follow. Teaching to see is the common task of all representational art. (294) Since literature has to do with the human being, should we draw the conclusion that it has the task of teaching us knowledge of man?

This cannot be the meaning of the requirement to be true to life that we place upon art. Not only because the tendency within it is understood too theoretically and is too much subordinated to practical ends. Why is this so? And what is the difference between the two requirements? What in fact should literature teach us, if not knowledge of man?

In order to answer these questions, we must clarify the nature of this knowledge of man, which, as such, does not belong to aesthetics. Knowledge of man is something that is quite prosaic and disenchanting. Its origin is not openness and penetration of mind, but rather distrust, which comes from painful experience. The man wise in human affairs tends to peer skeptically – perhaps even slightly pessimistically – upon the world. He surveys human life, but only with very specific things in mind: honesty, dependability, trustworthiness, all primarily in their negative forms. Knowledge of man is negatively oriented – and, to be sure, for practical reasons. For we always want to know what we can expect from others. What matters is orientation and practical vigilance, aimed at obtaining advance knowledge of how others will act at any given time and how they will react to our actions, in sum, how we must treat them with reference to our aims. To do that effectively, we must focus an unloving eye upon them.

Literature does not teach us such things. And when such knowledge comes out of it, that is merely incidental. Literature, as art in general, is oriented positively. It does not teach us to reject, but to appreciate, and to rest awhile lovingly while we gaze. Its way of looking is that of the searching, devoted, loving eye. It is the absorption in what others overlook. The eye of the poet is always aimed at hidden treasures.

What this eye discovers and teaches is, most properly, that treasures lie hidden everywhere beneath the debris of everydayness, and that it is worth our while to stop a moment to dwell among them for a while, to become absorbed in them. In this sense, literature is revelatory – it opens us to the world –; it reveals in its own way much more than the practical knowledge of human affairs, but it reveals something different for which, ordinarily, the man of the world never has use. The revelation of the values of things worthy of our love is, for the most part, irrelevant to practice, but it makes our vision of life rich, and enables us to partake of its fullness.

There is a further distinction to be made here. Knowledge of humanity is tied permanently to a certain universality of its insights. It does not aim strictly at the individuality of an individual, but only at the type. The individual for himself alone is not of interest to it apart from his relevance to some practical end. For such ends, it is best to ascertain general rules, and, even more, to have these rules at the ready. That is what (295) a man wise in human affairs does: he has the human type at the ready, and whatever falls under that type is thereby practical knowledge and done with.

The one genuinely wise about man is he who has at the ready a filing system of marked human types for sorting the persons who come his way, a system that has enough room to hold all the current cases. That is why his judgments are so superior, so quickly made, and so hard to deceive. Naturally, what lies beyond this system of types is given no attention. But that, precisely, is individuality. The good judge of man has no need for that, for he finds it an encumbrance, so he drops it, and considers it inessential. Such a judge of men is almost blind to human individuality. No doubt, his blindness is self-caused. We must recall that even the theory of personality extends only to types, and does not lead us to the real "person."

In these matters also, the attitude of literature is the opposite: what is essential is precisely what is atypical, merely unique, the apparently "contingent" element that is met in the individual person. The individual man is, for literature, not the representative of a kind of human being, but is important for himself alone, that is, with his individual peculiarities, his specialness, and his difference from others. And this is certainly not because his peculiarities are especially grandiose, but rather simply because the concrete fullness of life in the personality lies within this uniqueness, its riches, its clarity.

Literature, with its double tendency – to seek out what is positive and what is individual in man – leads to an entirely different depth of beholding and of disclosing truths about life, and it can be the headmaster to the awakened eye in a quite different way than can the practical knowledge of human affairs, which is always a kind of misunderstanding. The eye of the knower of men is a prisoner to a schema of types of men, and is always superficial in its beholding; it fails completely before the more intimate inwardness of men. All partaking in another's sorrows or joys or journeys is foreign to such a man. Fundamentally, he is cold. At precisely the place at which he leaves off or fails, the poetic eye begins its work – that is, by partaking in joys, etc. This eye is warm, searching, loving. Thus it is able also to penetrate the secrete depths of the human soul, which opens itself up only to a loving and searching eye. Upon this disclosure of man and of human life depends entirely both the richness of form of what is beheld, and the transparency of riches and depth of what appears before the beholding eye.

It becomes evident only from this perspective what the peculiar nature of the function of literature as revelatory is, and, at the same time, how the requirement of being true-to-life is related to artistic value (to beauty). Literature of course discloses both the nature of man and the profundity of life. But it does not do that the way knowledge does, and it is unlike knowledge in that it cannot be directed for practical purposes towards objects or aspects of them. The case is rather the reverse: literature, for its part, shows us what is important and deserving of reflection in life and in human life without consideration for other interests that might be brought into them. It shows also what (296) it beholds only to an eye that can behold along with it – in an image, in concreteness, without explanations, without speaking of the universal elements within, without whys and wherefores. It shows us things in their strangeness and mystery, and leaves them unmolested.

b) Realism and its limits

The person who wishes to learn from literature in the way a psychologist would has to draw his own conclusions. Literature will not do it for him. He will not draw much nourishment from it, because the information he receives does not lie in the direction of the questions he is asking. The writer does not "teach" in any other way than life teaches: through the events themselves. That there are no real events in literature does not make a difference in respect to the teaching. Only how events are drawn together, the selection from among them, the bestowal of form upon the material, makes the difference here, an immense one, but one that is quite different, and does not affect the general point.

Because of this, in literature – as also in painting and sculpture – we find an orientation towards realism. This means fundamentally nothing other than a requirement of being true to life that is distributed over many small individual characteristics: the narrated events and the narrated characters should, as far as possible, have the same effect upon us as real events and characters would have. Realism in literature, given this requirement, is a healthy tendency: in the novel, in the drama, even in the epic poem, it has been largely adhered to. But there are places where it reaches a limit.

Why is this so? Why must realism be limited, if realism is simply the correctly understood tendency to the true-to-life? Why does the dramatist use stylized language on stage – for example, verse? Why does the director soften the dynamics of rough encounters among the common people? Why does a self-controlled master storyteller dwell only upon sorrow and depravity? Why does the reader himself complain, when so much that is repugnant is placed before his eyes? Indeed, even when the milieu described in fact demands it? The time spent lingering among drunks in taverns and dives in some of Zola's novels was felt in their day as too much of the real, as too much "truth."

The meaning of art is not exhausted in instruction, in disclosing and making men wiser. Its original task is much simpler: to give pleasure. Otherwise, there would be no sense of speaking of "taking pleasure" or taking "delight" in art, and of "enjoying" it. The truth about human life can be quite unpleasant in given circumstances. It can even be oppressive and painful, can spoil one's (297) love of life, not to speak of one's love of a piece of literature that constantly leads the reader through unpleasantness and rubs his nose in everything shameful. It cannot be denied that there is a narrative strategy that does this with excessive devotion.

We can answer the above question summarily: the other requirement, which is opposed to that of the tendency towards being true-to-life, is the requirement of beauty. It should not be immediately objected that beauty need not lie in the "material" and that it ought not to lie there. For it is not a question at all of the material alone: the bestowal of form, the poetic presentation of the material is just what can overstep the limits of what is artistically tolerable. Realism in the arts is essentially a matter of form.

Here we come upon a very strange opposition. It now seems as though truth and beauty stood relative to each other as contrary value-claims directed at one and the same objects, such that the artist must, as it were, choose either the one of the other. This cannot be the final word in this matter. And yet something here cannot be simply dismissed: to find a correct middle way will always remain the task of the artist, as soon as he engages himself with material that is taken directly from the milieu of the common people and from human weakness.

However that may be, there are various matters to be considered in this context.

First, practical interests often are mixed in among the demands of literature, such as social conditions and political tendencies. Upheavals in moral values are always fermenting somewhere in our consciousness, and may commandeer literature for use as a weapon with which to carry on its struggles. To that end, literature must reveal stresses in the actual social conditions.

Second, different epochs are very different in their sense of this problem. An entire generation may be spent on one significant conflict. Our grandfathers put up with very little true-life material in a literary work; their senses were disturbed when something appeared in poetic material that was not in keeping with public morality and propriety, in conformity to which they lived their lives. That has all changed. We are more broad-minded. But we too close our minds to such unlimited realism – one perhaps become somewhat voluptuous – the borders have simply shifted.

Third, our tastes have developed from a kind of art that was, to a great extent, idealistic, and that stylized real life. Thus we have the high pathos of tragedy, the dominance of the heroic, the deep religious and chivalric mood of the older epics. Poverty and misery were quite muted in their effects. The capacity of the reader for realism has grown continuously since then. And it is hard to say how much further it may grow. But with it the capacity of literature itself for the hard facts of life has also grown. (298)

In this way we see that the limits of what one can expect of literature by way of realism are quite relative – to the artistic sensibilities of an epoch. For that reason we can establish no fixed norms.

People have argued over whether certain characters in Dostoyevsky are objectionable in a literary sense (Stavrogin [*The Possessed*], the elder Karamazov, or Golyadkin [*The Double*]). The imputation is well founded, but there are counter-values that balance the scale here. For there is greatness and beauty, moral elevation and the most tender blossoms of life that can be measured only from the lower depths out of which they grow. The writer cannot speak of them, cannot let them appear, without allowing the human swamp to appear also in the stratum before them. Under such conditions, it is a question of balancing-out of the two. Literature has the task of achieving a synthesis. A maximum of worldly truth, in the conditions its material requires, must be taken up in its appropriate forms, in order to allow the deeper element of meaning (values, etc.) to appear, but without destroying the artistic form.

To what extent this task can be achieved is demonstrated by the great realists among those authors who have uncompromisingly refused to engage in cheap idealization and prettifying: Dostoyevsky, Knut Hamsun. But this solution is the one achieved by art, and cannot be counterfeited on their model. But theory – in the sense of aesthetics – cannot in this way solve the problem.

c) On the dialectics of realistic representation

One should not forget that the literature of our time, wherever it may have achieved some degree of greatness, has just this realism to thank; but, on the other hand, literature is nonetheless mistrustful of it. The aims literature sets for itself becomes in this way higher: the greater the task, the higher the artistic aims. We may make this idea clear in the following way.

There is a tendency to tone down the impression of troublesome truths about life. For that, there are entirely external means to do so – careful selection, slight changes in color, and even giving shape to language. But all such means seem in the end to be falsifications, too; they prettify. As a rule, they disenchant even the naïve reader, for he notices that what is represented lacks seriousness, and if he does not notice it then he has been to some degree betrayed.

What can be demanded of an earnest and true-to-life literature is precisely the opposite: to find the form for all material, even the most unpleasant, through which the writer can present the affirmative value of that material. A compromise is not required – if we wish, we can call such measures a balancing of the books – what is required is rather a higher form that can take on the abhorrent and ugly and overcome it.

What does "overcoming" mean? It cannot mean simply letting something disappear, be destroyed, or denying it. One might think here instead (299) of a dialectical relation in the sense of Hegel: specifically, the "sublation" [*Aufheben*] of the thesis is negative only in the most superficial sense, in the antithesis it is rather a "preservation," but in the synthesis, an "elevation over itself." Beyond doubt, something like that takes place in literature. What first seems abhorrent is afterwards "taken up" in a whole to which it is indispensable as an element; and in the end it is elevated above itself, because it has shown itself to be an accessory to something far greater and far more meaningful. This is the dialectic of realism in literature. One can express this in a non-dialectical manner, as one can for every dialectic. But then one must begin from the other end, from that of the synthesis, thus, in this case, from the "elevation above itself."

In what direction, then, can the writer elevate in this sense something that was beheld at first soberly and realistically? Surely only to a place that he beheld as an idea beforehand. He must, therefore, have the "idea" in advance. This need not be a Platonic or Hegelian "idea"; it can be any superempirical and large idea, any ethical or even religious ideal.

But here we need not reach out immediately to the highest things. Rather, such is the condition of human life that the form of a situation gives the impetus and the circumstances for action; the deeper the actual situation is rooted in our condition, the closer we will feel ourselves to the acting character. And, again, the greater the unpleasantness the agent has to struggle against in his situation, the higher are his chances of achieving through his actions a satisfactory solution to this problem. We see this in the fact that even when he loses and blunders, our sympathies are still with him.

These are facts that shine a unique light upon the question of the justification of the abhorrent and the ugly in literature. It is apparent that the radiance of the humanly beautiful, great, and meaningful burns brighter according to the measure of those dark depths; perhaps they can be seen only on such a background. Indeed the comparison says too little: one must have the entire depths of human misery clearly before one's eyes in order to be able to see what is great and ideal in such small and quotidian human action, suffering, strife, and the like. But that brings us to a further result.

The ability to see what is great and ideal in what is small and quotidian is in fact the main function of art: the letting-appear. In this letting-appear we have the essential beauty of the work of art. If this is true, then we must also say: here beauty is conditioned precisely by the representation of what is ugly and abhorrent. Or, if one wishes to avoid the paradox, what remains is still rather peculiar: the demand both for something true-to-life and for beauty, which at first stand contrary to one another, seem to approach each other in such a manner that one might well almost think to equate them. (300)

But how? Has the difference between the relation of truth in literature and its literary quality been lost? One can perhaps respond: yes, the literary quality, its success as literature, is a question of form, but the true-to-life quality is a question of content! This observation is insufficient: literary form has a role in essentially determining the content; it is perhaps the most important element in it. Here we are dealing in fact with "inner form," that is, the state of having been formed from within outward. This kind of form-bestowal is precisely what makes the "content," (i.e., the material upon which form has been bestowed) true or false to life. It, the form, is what can be realistic in the content or simply an embellishment of it. It may therefore be that one and the same success with respect to artistic form can constitute the literary quality, the beauty of the object, and, at the same time, its true-to-life quality. We cannot rid ourselves so easily of the equivalence of truth and beauty.

One may ask the radical question: are there important literary works whose essential content, as chosen by their authors, passes reality entirely by, and is thus no more than sheer foolishness? Expressed a bit less starkly: is there such work whose essential content is insipid or superficial? We must answer: no! The lack of quality of the novels by Courths-Mahler[95] does not stem from a lack of immanent adequacy between the strata, but from a lack of poetic truth. They lack real quality because their intended content, consistently worked over in the inner form, lays claim to having made clear some essential content regarding this world of men, and yet they are unable to justify that claim.

This proves the inseparability of literary quality and truth. But the inseparability need not mean that they are congruent. Poetry at times may well affect us powerfully and yet not be true to life; it would lack only that one last satisfaction. So it is too in life; I can "see" some event incorrectly, but still with the greatest detail – and just such detail can also confuse us – and the same is true the other way around.

If we are to solve this problem properly, we must travel a middle road, and seize upon what is affirmative on both sides, while omitting what is simply negative.

d) The true-to-life and essential truth

The results up to now seem to be these. Two kinds of poetic truth overlap each other. The one is inward agreement, unity, completeness, consistency in itself; the other is the true-to-life, which has one pole of its nature outside of poetry, in the real world transcendent of it – but nonetheless is true not at all among its details or in its facts, but rather in its essential characteristics. So far as poetic quality is conditioned by both requirements of truth, one may now say: truth, too, is a transcendental relation. Literature that is not true to life cannot convince us, that is, it is not literature at all. (301)

Nonetheless, what is true-to-life and what is literary quality can differ from each other in a considerable way. The requirement of truth, for example, can come off in a literary work much more poorly than the way inward form is expertly executed and its beauty in appearance, animation, detail, liveliness, and unity of form. We have examples of such in some of the characters in Hebbel[96]: in his Golo [in *Genoveva*, 1841], in Herod [in *Herodes und Mariamne*, 1848], in Candaules [in *Gyges und sein Ring*, 1854], and even in Wilde's *Dorian Gray*. We find the reverse of this in the late Goethe (*Faust* II, *Wilhelm Meisters Wanderjahre*, etc.): there we have a surfeit of the wisdom of life and of the true-to-life, but at the

---

95 [Translator's note:] Hedwig Courths-Mahler (1867–1950).
96 [Translator's note:] Christian Friedrich Hebbel (1813–1863).

expense of a clear sense of the fullness of life and even of formal literary unity. We know how strongly Goethe himself had a sense of this.

These examples show that both the quality of true-to-life and literary quality may well become even quite radically separated. But then literary works also suffer quite distinctly from the corresponding defects. If one lacks the quality of the true-to-life, it approaches prosaic, unpoetic thought; and only the strongest external means can cover over these defects, and even then only a bit. The close ties and the mutual conditions of the true-to-life and clear perfection of form (the poetic quality) must not be allowed to seduce us into thinking them identical, but also not into positing an all-too-great independence of the one and the other.

Something else may be seen from these reflections. Certainly Golo and Candaules, and similarly Dorian Gray, are hard to imagine with their aestheticizing unscrupulousness, founded upon no motive. But in the first two, do we not meet with something that may lie in the nature of a certain kind of love? And in Dorian Gray is there not something that could motivate this frivolous man of high talents, given a bit of direction by others?

This something, an essential form seen at its outer limits, may be distorted, but one can see clearly the direction in which it lies, even if it does not occur in reality. In Hebbel's dramas, the wheels of dramatic form eventually spin idly – he does not succeed in giving form to what has been seen at its extremes, that is, in making the characters convincing. But are there not such extreme essential forms in man – of real men, though perhaps also of situations and destinies? But then there must be an essential truth as opposed to the true-to-life; and this might very well be contained in these characters of Hebbel.

If that is so, there must also surely be a requirement of truthfulness that is aimed precisely at this essential truth. And there may very well be an entire genus within literature that places this requirement – with the right to poetic license and bias – above all others. In this way, we can perhaps establish the success of dramas and short stories of this kind. We may think of the situation this way: a writer can represent a character whose forms are lifted up to a mythical dimension, and yet thereby enter an essential sphere, perhaps (302) even where it has the sense of a certain fanatical attachment to value, although what is true-to-life – human life as it is – is not attained by him in this way.

Such things must be possible for poets, because otherwise there could be in literature no higher escape from everydayness, no ideal types, no individuals elevated into an ideal realm. Ancient tragedy always had such larger-than-life characters; epic poetry had them perhaps first of all, and so too all literature whose material is drawn from myth. The requirement of truth does not in such cases correspond to nothing in real life, but rather to essential forms of real life that have been raised to the level of an idea. It follows clearly from this that essential truth is something different from the true-to-life, and therefore even in one and the same literary work the demand for one is not congruent with the demand for the other.

This can be expressed also in the following way. The writer can behold and shape faithfully certain essential possibilities of our peculiar human nature that are never realized in actual life. One may not draw from this the conclusion that every such transcending of the real is justified. Even the characters in Hebbel that have caused controversy show that to be true. But from where, then, shall we derive a criterion for what can be judged as essentially true and what is not, that is, is only constructed? Not every extreme can lay claim to being worthy of belief.

Perhaps one may respond in this way: criteria that one can place upon an object as one would a ruler do not exist in the entire realm of art and beauty. Therefore, we may not require any here. Yet the educated sensibility, possessing fine "taste" in art, is not for this reason entirely helpless before such a question. There are certain distinctive marks of it, but they cannot be articulated and taught like the rules of a game. Good taste can glimpse, for example, in the demand for a certain degree of essential truth the limits of realism in art and of the demand for the true-to-life in general. One will, perhaps, be happy to find in these requirements the counterpoise to realism's requirement of truth, and for that reason, good taste – a thoroughgoing idealistic one – will approve this standpoint to a certain degree.

Yet essential truth must be so conceived that the extension beyond the true-to-life, and the "idea" that indicates its direction, is justified from within a whole, that is, its legitimacy is drawn from that to which it belongs, and it does not draw its effects out of something external to the whole. One may concede this point in the case of the characters in Hebbel and of Dorian Gray. We encounter such figures to a much greater, more fantastic degree, in Cervantes[97]: the idealism in Don Quixote's tilting with windmills makes fun of the true-to-life, and seems ridiculous; but it lies consistently within the arena of blind chivalry that has been built for it. And even the complete unwillingness to see one's true situation, which here takes on a mythical form, is still something essential to human life.

It was demonstrated above (Chaps. 22c, d) that the requirement to be true to life extends to all strata of literature, although it is peculiarly intense (303) in the middle strata. But how do things stand with reference to essential truth? It is clear that things are quite different here. As a requirement, essential truth is always tied in the first instance to a particular stratum, and only secondarily does it extend itself from that stratum to others. We do not mean by that that it must

---

97 [Translator's note:] Miguel de Cervantes (1547–1616).

always be rooted in the rearmost stratum (that of the general ideas); that would be a mere tautology, for the requirement concerns the agreement with an idea. Rather the question is: in which of the middle strata does the determination by means of ideas assert itself directly and powerfully?

The answer can be given by reference to some very great examples. Take the first act of *King Lear*. Lear sets off the decisive conflict in the plot by asking how much his daughters love him. Here we have the key, not to Lear's character, but to the entire situation through which the plot moves: not only Goneril and Regan, but Cordelia, too, express their love for Lear in the same unconditional way, the first two deceptively, the latter with exaggerated scrupulousness; thus Cordelia's amazingly blunt answer. The play derives its inner necessity and its essential truth here. The true-to-life no doubt comes in a distant second; it appears in *Lear* more in the details, in the individual scenes.

But one thing is distinctly visible here: the essential truth is rooted unambiguously in a definite stratum – in *Lear* in that of the characters, in the character of a family, one may say. Only from there does the essential truth reach over to bestow form upon the situations and scenes on the one hand, and to give shape to destiny on the other. Shakespeare knew how to unite admirably all these things with the simplest true-to-life elements. In *Lear*, the entire essential content is presented in the situations, scenes, etc. With Hebbel's characters, a similar main stratum is lacking that can carry the weight of all else.

Chapter 24: Truth in the Fine Arts

a) Criteria and standards

Apparently we must deal cautiously with essential truth. Presumably every literary work will contain some elements of it. But the true-to-life, and the touch of realism that it requires, cannot replace it, because the former moves in the opposite direction, drawing its elements from a decidedly idealistic realm. One asks oneself ever again: can there be an essentially truthful measure of life that is nonetheless unattached to life?

Put so bluntly, of course, there cannot. Yet to the contrary, the examples mentioned above demonstrate clearly that, within certain limits, such a thing exists. And where it does, it is artistically evident. But one must not take this to extremes. For example, it is not true that the artist could put individual essential human characteristics through a sieve and, as it were, have each do a solo. (304)

The isolation of a few essential characteristics of the Marquis Posa takes place so close to the limits of what is convincing that he no longer seems to belong entirely to the stage. Pseudo-classical evil men, who are nothing more than their own wickedness, may be necessary in certain dramas. But if they are supposed to affect us as living men and to address dramatically the situations that their actions have produced, their wickedness must appear as humanly justified – by their having a certain essential nature, by the circumstances, or by some other specific motivation.

This has been achieved perfectly in more recent literature – not first by Dostoyevsky (one thinks of the figure of Smerdyakov [in *The Brothers Karamazov*]) but even earlier by the German classics; it applies even to Mephistopheles. And, looking back even further – perhaps to Corneille – we have the sense that it was not at all difficult to meet this requirement.

Why, however, is it not difficult? For this reason, that only the types that are entirely constructed seem untrue when they are put upon the stage just to achieve some end within a given conflict. It is sufficient for bringing them to life that they appear to be necessary by reference to some essential relation to the situation, that is, the requirement of essential truth is sufficient here. The more difficult requirement of being true-to-life does not necessarily have to be met.

But it is irritating when the two kinds of truth are separated in some obvious way in a literary work. If, however, the true-to-life is supposed to agree with essential truth, then it would have to be primarily in life itself; what is real should agree with the ideal essence that approaches its type. That it does not do that lies in the essence of the real as such. The higher we are on the great chain of being, so much more are the two kinds of truth separated, and only with much greater difficulty can an artistic construct come to its perfection. Recall the law: the higher the construct, the more imperfect it is on average. Height and perfection are inversely proportional.

Literature has to do with the highest construct, man. Factual truth and ideal essence cannot come together in a man and his life. For that reason, when he is taken as a subject of literature, the true-to-life and the essential truth are sepa-rated by a large gap. Thus it is easy to conclude that it is precisely there that a considerable part of the conflicts are rooted, out of which are constituted the chief material of epic, dramatic, and novelistic literature.

Since we are dealing here with the relation between two kinds of truth that only together constitute literary truth, we may locate literary untruth in all places where 1. one of the two founding truths is false; and 2. the relation of the two to each other is false. The latter, for example, is seen in the case where no essential truth "appears" in the true-to-life, or where the latter is not referred back to or founded upon the former.

The measure of the true-to-life is for that matter surely not life itself, but rather life as it is seen and (305) understood by the world of its contemporaries, especially by the writer, and as it is communicated through the specific form of the work – its genre. The first we have established above; for we can of course make measurements only upon what we see. The second point, however, requires a further demonstration.

The classification of the forms of literature exercises a selection of possible "materials" – and within any given material there is another selection of motifs and of details. We know that from the general analysis of form. Such selection is based upon content, largely; not all materials are appropriate for a novella, not all for a drama, etc.; and even where a material is appropriate, not everything about it will be appropriate.

At this point, the decisive role of the category of form takes another step forward; the same is true also for essential truth, and its analysis could be carried out independently. This implies that even the measure of essential truth does not lie without question within the ideal essential natures of things (in the sense of the phenomenologists), as they are in themselves, but rather as they are seen and understood – by an historical period or by the poet himself – and, additionally, as they are communicated by the specific type of the category of form in literature. There too the first matter is immediately comprehensible. The second means, however, that such categories of form as lyric poetry, the epic, the novel, etc. bear within themselves their specific selections of ideal essential relations, those, that is, that are appropriate to them. In this way the Ideal in *Kriemhild's Revenge* [1924 film by Fritz Lang] would not belong in a novella, and that Shakespeare's "Prince Hal" would not belong in a novel.

We might add to this one further remark: the genera of the forms of literature make up the gross outlines of a typology. In reality, it is a question of much more nuanced distinctions among forms, and, corresponding to that, a very differentiated selection of materials and selections within materials may be drawn. The French classicist drama was not compatible with many kinds of materials that the Shakespearean drama could access with relative ease, and upon which it could bestow form. The dramas of Lessing[98], Schiller, Kleist[99], and Hebbel – they all had not only choices of material peculiar to them; they also made corresponding selections within the themes.

With that we come to the special typical types of form in literature, which no longer belong to our circle of questions (those of general aesthetics). It is enough if we establish here that each of these very special types – differentiated even by the individual literary figures – have their own inner laws, according to which

---

98 [Translator's note:] Gotthold Ephraim Lessing (1729–1781).
99 [Translator's note:] Heinrich von Kleist (1777–1811).

their forms stand or fall. But that is only an extension of the question of the differentiations within the arts. We will have to catch up with these later.

b) The true-to-life in painting

The inquiry made in the last few chapters remained fixed upon literature, because in it the claim to truth is most easily understood. But such a limited survey remains of course one-sided. We must therefore now (306) supplement it. To do that, we must move over to the territories of the other arts. How do things stand with them in respect to the claim to truth?

The immanent artistic truth may be kept out of consideration here: that is only the inner unity of form, and, as such, does not generate any contrast with the remaining problems of form (Cf. Chap. 21). Artistic necessity already contains everything significant about it. But things are different with the transcendental claim to truth, as we encountered it in the poetic arts, and, in their cases, on both sides: on the side of the true-to-life and on the side of essential truth. But both are of direct concern only for sculpture and painting. In the non-representational arts a transcendental counterpart is lacking with which some kind of agreement might be discovered.

In an extended sense, no doubt, one can speak of a true-to-life quality in music and even in architecture, for both express psychic realities. Yet that is a *cura posterior* [of later concern]. The two remaining representational arts, that is, the "fine arts," as they have been called, have a greater urgency for us. With them matters are again very varied, because the circle of their themes is diverse. Sculpture is almost entirely tied to the human figure; painting extends itself to everything visible that can be captured in the form of a picture. Painting, therefore, offers richer possibilities for the problem of the claim to truth.

What do we mean by true-to-life in painting? One may almost wish to believe that its meaning must be identical with the beauty of appearance in the painting. "Let the creative art breathe life."[100] Thus, the more clearly the painting offers life as such to our vision, that much higher must be its artistic value. Does that mean, however: the more true-to-life, that much more beautiful?

Yet this is not quite true. If the thesis were unlimited in its applications, then, in general, paintings that depict their material the more realistically would be

---

100 [Translator's note:] Schiller, Friedrich, *The Poems of Schiller, Complete: Including All His Early Suppressed Pieces*, translated by Edgar Alfred Bowring, London: Parker 1851, p. 275. (Schiller, "Tonkunst": "Leben atme die bildende Kunst").

artistically the more impressive and the more perfect. But that is by no means the case, at least not to that extent; styles in painting are all essentially limitations of realism. They rest upon a selection from among the seen and given: not everything is placed in the painting that the eye may at best take in; rather only those things that the artist appraises as worthy. We must recall here what was said above about there being a certain degree of selective seeing as form is bestowed (Chap. 16c).

But so much is clear: all selection and all omission is, it must be granted, a kind of subtraction from the true-to-life. Much is in fact excluded from the reproduction and declared to be inessential. And yet the result need not appear to us as stunted – just because other details can thereby not only be brought forward, but can also be made to stand out more boldly.

The one replaces the other: the preferred element for that which had been excluded by the selection. But what gives the artist the right to such a rearrangement? How does he dare to change the place of accents (307) so willfully? Or is it not arbitrary? Might there be even here lawfulness and inner necessity?

Let us take a concrete case. Two artists are painting the same scene at the same time and from the same physical standpoint. A third artist passes from one to the other, making comparisons, and notes as the work continues that the two are painting different things. With the one, the shadows, the perspective, the ground configuration stand out. With the others, the dominant role belongs to colors, light, the brightness of the greenery and the fields, and the distant blue of the sky.

Who would maintain that one is "really" a picture of this scene, but the other is not? That would be possible only if the artist was a skilled painter but the other a rank amateur. But this was not considered here. Let us assume that both were "well" painted, and each convincing in its own way. But then we must seek a different answer to our question. What shall it be? Apparently, there must be a principle of selection that is sufficiently objective to lay claim to validity, and to justify the differing ways of seeing. Only then will the cuts in what is given not seem to be untrue to life and arbitrary.

Compare this with a much richer and well-known case: the portrait of the same man painted by different artists. There are many of this kind; they exist even today, and in each case, the extremely striking phenomenon of divergence is prominent: a divergence in the conception of the human, but also divergence in the painterly means and the selection of details (for example in the way contours are elaborated or veiled).

Nothing is more instructive than the extraordinary diversity of the ways of seeing, and the ways of accentuating what is essential. A portrait is a work of art with many strata, and upon every stratum, we see reference to this diversity. Here also one cannot easily maintain of the two portraits – even where the artists have comparable skill in execution –: this is really the person, that is not he. Rather one sees quite clearly that the one picture emphasizes different essential qualities than the other, indeed, that even in the sensible foreground it focuses upon other aspects of what is visible. The other essential qualities, for their part, may touch the physical details, the animation of the expression, or the play of color and light, the organization of space, etc.

But here, as with the landscape, there must be something that determines the diversity of ways of seeing the selections and omissions, etc. What is this determining element? It cannot lie in the *sujet* (the living person whose portrait it is) alone; also not in the artist alone, perhaps, that is, in his subjective attitude. If it were present in the first, then there could be only one justified way of painting; if in the second, the artist's way of painting could not convince and sweep along any observer.

What determines the way of seeing must therefore lie in something else – in a third thing. And there can be no doubt what this third thing is: it must be an essential element that lies in the represented object itself, and the fidelity [308] of the representation of this element – in one or in several strata – must have the character of an essential truth.

We may, accordingly, limit the range of artistic freedom to the selection of the essential element. For none of them can be created at will. But since there are many such elements in the painted subject, he may choose. But once he chooses he must be faithful to the essential element he chose, and then select from the true-to-life only that which is relevant to it.

c) Essential truth in painting

The results of our inquiry up to this point are at any rate remarkable. No art is so close to the senses and is so sensual as is painting, none is so oriented to the imitation of the visible, everything in it depends upon the way of seeing and the kind of letting-be-seen; thus no art ought to be attached so unconditionally to the true-to-life as it is. Nevertheless, we have seen that in painting, standpoints govern selection and the determination of form. These standpoints have not been taken directly from life, but are derived from an act of essential intuition [*Wesensschau*]. These acts transcend the empirical, and they select, according to the judgment of the artist, in a generally free manner. Are these two compatible? How does it stand affirmatively with the relation of the true-to-life and the essential truth?

If the standpoints, from which selection is made and which determine form, are taken from the intuition of essences, the question naturally arises about the nature of this intuition of essence. It may be answered in the following way. On the one hand, the intuition concerns the selection of contents in the *sujet*, i.e., in the character of the person, so to speak; on the other hand it concerns the formal selection from what is visible – from those aspects of what is seen that appear "painterly essential." To this latter are counted the choices of what in the landscape rivets our attention. As has been shown, neither the one nor the other is entirely necessary or entirely arbitrary.

The painter, just as the writer, can choose a collection of essential characteristics from which he makes further selections, but he can do that only from those that are really present in the object. He cannot freely invent and incorporate his inventions, for then he would produce something quite different from a portrait or a picture of a scene. So a person sketching in red ochre the face of his subject will choose those elements of the face that lend themselves only to outline, and choose only that play of light and shadow on the face that can be indicated with hatch-marks. Thus on the one hand the selection is made from what is purely visible, on the other hand from that which is given of the man: both occur within a range that has been determined by this selection. Only within this range – thus the range of the selected elements – can we have the true-to-life in the narrow sense.

That is important just because in painting even more than in literature the claim to be true-to-life requires a limitation. It needs one because the art of painting, right from the outset, is directed so entirely towards the "breath of life," (309) thus apparently dependent on the most direct imitation possible. Wise selection first makes imitation possible, for otherwise all would be confounded in unlimited excess and the visual image would be flooded. This is a fact that only a person properly trained in painting can measure.

We must additionally make clear that we proceed in a similar manner in our everyday life in the simple act of visual perception. No one takes in absolutely everything that a physical face or a thing, or a scene, presents to one. Each of us takes in only what is practically important for him – all the more in the case of things and persons – and this importance is already determined by the essential standpoints that we bring to it. What interests us in men is their psychic life. Even facial characteristics are taken in only superficially. Otherwise, we would not know how to deal with them effectively, for our minds move along according to our habits entirely by abbreviating our perceptions, but those abbreviations are steered in a certain direction, and are entirely practical.

The painter produces something that corresponds to this by not painting everything he sees, but only a part of it. He selects also – but no longer from among essential standpoints of a practical sort, but among specifically painterly, artistic standpoints. That is what constitutes the limitation of the true-to-life and the necessary ingredients of essential truth in his creative work. Naturally, this work is not exhausted in the process of selection and omission, but is first realized in the positive accentuation, in the making salient, and in the occasional super-elevation of what has been selected.

The truth of this can be best seen in extreme cases, for example, in caricature, or also in a drawing that does not resort to caricature, but gives us by a few well-chosen lines entire interconnections of motion and scene. Caricature can make just one essential feature of a person appear as a "solo," with very slight use of the means available to it. There is much about it that is not true to life; it exaggerates. But something in it is true-to-life even in all its exaggerations; it lies in that one essential feature, which had not just been called up arbitrarily, but was in fact found in the essence of the person – sought out there visually, as it were.

Here it is apparent how the true-to-life quality and the essential truth in "drawing" – and thus also in painting – are interpenetrated. For painting, it is not possible to be true-to-life, convincing, realistic, without establishing these upon an essential truth that selects and thereby also determines form. The most important thing, however, is that the activity of selecting and of determining form not be limited simply to the inner strata of the painting, but that it have an effect precisely upon the outer strata – up to the foreground, in which the physical techniques of painting play a role. These latter techniques can be seen in brush-work, in etching, etc., where movement immediately appears in the genial mani-pulation of line. One can see it in Goya's blotchy scenes thrown onto the paper, where behind the movement he chose as his theme, almost everything else disappears (contours, figures ...). (310)

That such may seem convincing, where the chosen essential characteristics are those of the object, that is, taken from real life, is, as was already noted, the condition of its justification. Moreover, here we come upon the reverse relation-ship of the two elements of artistic truth: at this point, the true-to-life is the condition of essential truth.

This may seem strange, because it is precisely the true-to-life that is supposed to be selected here, and that selection was to be carried out from the perspective of the essential truth. Yet the two do not contradict each other at all, but instead together make up a clearly judicious relationship of their mutual dependency.

The true-to-life – even as a mere claim – is not replaced in painting by essential truth, even less than in literature. It is rather merely limited and directed along specific avenues, which then function to determine form and style; essen-tial truth, for its part, is not drawn from fantasy, but from the essential constitu-ents of the object to be represented. Indeed, to the contrary, the measure of its essential truth is taken from these essential constituents. And that suggests immediately that the measure has a counterpart in the real world, and is thereby a matter of the true-to-life. We have here two opposed and independently varying essential elements. Obviously, both can function only together, not as isolated. There is nothing troubling in that.

When these essential standpoints are brought in arbitrarily, both the essential truth and the true-to-life quality of the picture break down, and from a style that determines form from within, an external and artificial fashion emerges, which causes the breakdown of appearance in the middle strata.

d) The claim to truth in sculpture

In concluding, we must add a word here about sculpture. It is easily predictable that we will find there that the true-to-life is so situated in it as in painting. However, that must still be shown, for the differences between these two fine arts are quite apparent. We must expect some deviations.

We must not forget that sculpture was once already quite developed in its capacities for grasping things in their essence and portraying them while painting was still laboring in its wretched infancy. One may think of the Old Egyptian portrait-heads and the contemporary decorations of walls and columns with conventional schematic figures, which, moreover, were worked up in the manner of a relief. What was the cause of sculpture's head start?

The question takes on more weight when we consider what enormous progress painting has made in the intervening years – especially since the Greeks – how, in painting, one discovery leaped over the next, and only in the last five centuries have its great and most important developments come to pass, while the greatest achievements in sculpture did not extend very far beyond the creations of the Greeks in the fifth century BCE. What caused this relative stagnation? It is of course not a complete stagnation, but compared with the development of painting, it is remarkable. (311)

The answer must be: sculpture was the first to have discovered a fruitful essential standpoint for true-to-life representation, of a kind that was truly derived from the nature of its themes (objects), and yet left sufficient latitude to permit its creative development.

It is not at first a question of great ideas here, but rather of something quite simple: for a very general example, just the fruitful thought of representing a head or a human figure, purely from its most external features, i.e., the forms of its surface – leaving out everything that it might harbor within itself (life, strength, awareness) – while at the same time discovering that, within certain limits, this life within can "appear" on the simple spatial external form.

That sounds rather silly when, many centuries later, some pedant pronounces it soberly. However, what is silly or immediately obvious is no less fundamental and decisive as what is complicated. Without question, this was once the epoch-making idea behind the first stirrings of sculpture, which then took on immediately the form of an essential truth. It is not axiomatic in itself that an external appearance, grasped only spatially, could also be the adequate appearance of something inward. We can look upon the abstraction from color as a second element. Such abstraction is also not immediately obvious, and the ancients did not continuously value it. In any case, the idea asserted itself later, and, when it did, it accompanied the greatest developments of sculpture.

These are conceptual elements that nature does not itself thrust upon men; they must discover them themselves. Nonetheless, they are simple and close at hand if one compares them to what is foundational in painting. Painting begins precisely with the projection of what is seen in a thing upon a flat surface – a leap requiring a different kind of boldness. It implies the renunciation of the direct bestowal of spatial form, and replaces it by transposing it two-dimensionally – yet in such a way that depth reappears in it. This implies also the introduction of perspective; and so on with the "other" spatiality that appears in it, the apparent "light in the picture," etc.

The basic idea of sculpture, in contrast to such bold essential elements, all of which work in the processes of selection and bestowing form, is in fact very simple: the basic idea is an essential truth that immediately has extremely drastic effects, because it excludes most objects as its theme, and in the end has almost nothing but the human body as its object. True, the sculpture of animals also has a long history (Egypt), and it has produced much of significance. However, in comparison to the sculpture of the human figure it did not play a leading role to the same degree. Moreover, we must recall that the latter represents in itself alone a region of great diversity.

This implies that even given all the differences between the two fine arts and given the clear superiority of painting, the fundamental condition of the true-to-life and the essential truth in them is nevertheless the same, and rests upon the same free choice of specific, limiting essential principles. These principles are simpler in the case of sculpture, however, and the process of selection is quite (312) different. Among the simpler essential truths of sculpture is that it is easier there to follow up the consequences of selection and bestowal of form. From this standpoint one can cast light on the entire history of sculpture: one will find many varying essential truths, but the foundational essential relationships remain the same. Under the spell of any of them, however, the orientation of the true-to-life takes its direction.

The degree to which one knows how to deal with motion even if only thematically, to say nothing of actually representing it, is extraordinarily diverse;

and, according to that degree, the region is established into which the true-to-life is drawn. It is similar in dealing with and representing psychic content sculpturally, and entirely so with whole scenes. At the foundation of these phenomena lies limiting and form-determining essential truth. However, it varies.

It may also be established:

1. Truth in art is a making-visible (revealing) of essential relationships pertaining to human life, to the real life of man and to the merely "possible" (fictional).
2. It is carried by the artistic bestowal of form, which, for its part, forms a perspicuous structural whole in conformity with the nature of things and of life.
3. This whole must be visible not only in every strata of the work of art, but also be realized in the unity of the series of strata. Only in that way can the true-to-life and the essential truth be unified in the immanent truth of the inner unity of form.

Chapter 25: Truth in the Non-Representational Arts

a) Limits to the question of truth

Can one speak at all of "truth" in music and architecture? Or even of a claim to truth? Are they not both pure playing with form, in which nothing is represented that could be correct or incorrect? Is one a useless kind of playing, and another a useful one? From these questions, we take our present point of departure.

There is a sense of "truth" according to which we can in this context no longer raise meaningful "claims." It is no longer said to be the case here of a "correspondence" to some real model. This fact constitutes a natural limit to the question of truth. However, it is primarily just a limit to the possibility of the true-to-life, not to the essential truth, or the latter only insofar as it limits the true-to-life in its process of selection.

But there is still another sense of truth. A city apartment house with many small apartments, narrow inner courts, a narrow and cheaply constructed staircase, may still have a façade like a palazzo and a correspondingly magnificent portico – such things seem to us to be untrue. The case is similar when the outer façades have been stylized with Gothic motifs, but the plan of (313) the inside rooms has nothing to do with them; or when a little tower is attached to a corner house that has no use for it, and the tower has nothing in common with the rest of the building. Why do all such things seem "untrue"? Because here something has pretensions to be what it is not in fact, and what the structure ought not to be: something far more powerful and lofty.

One may call these kinds of phenomena, of which our cities are full, straight-forwardly "phony architecture." But there is still the question whether this phenomenon can be generalized. Does music also contain phoniness of this kind? It cannot be of precisely the same kind, because music does not serve practical aims that it could, on the level of its external form, violate in a disharmonious manner. But, for this reason, there could still exist some inner discrepancy of a different kind: for example, when one sets a simple folk-song to music for a great orchestra and ends with a pompous finale, or when one sings it in the aesthetical style of the Italian *bel canto*. It is perhaps the same when one plays a piece for a solemn ceremony in a fast tempo that reduces its seriousness.

These examples are essentially lacking, in that the discrepancy appears between the composition and the performance. But there are also cases in which it appears from within the performance. The latter occurs in almost all performance by dilettantes, usually because what the performer can do and what he wants to happen do not correspond. But the former we find occurring in the compositions of talented imitators, in which much of the technique of construction of great masters is understood and imitated, but it is not filled with the corresponding psychic materials; or, also, when a genuinely original master with profound sensibility cannot find a means of construction that is adequate to his feelings, and helps himself along with a substitute. Such a happening is not as seldom as one should think.

What these examples have in common – those taken from architecture also – may be that the question of the genuine true-to-life does not occur in them. Their hold upon some existing state of affairs is lacking. But what then is in question when one still senses something untrue about these things, something that is not simply identical with the ugly or the disharmonious? Have we found here an absolute limit of "truth" in art, beyond which one can speak only in an analogous manner? Or is there an essential truth here that takes the place of the true-to-life?

The latter may not be impossible, although essential truth cannot mean the limiting of the true-to-life and setting it right; nor can it mean making a form of something alive or at all real in its ideal nature into a measure of what the artist is showing us. This is incorrect if only because the artist does not "show" anything but what is contained in the structure of his composition.

Given that, even essential truth would be left with just one inauthentic role – unless one draws it inward, and relates it to the artistic (314) form itself, to an "essence" of this inner form, which demands consistency, unity, and execution.

In fact, in the case of the representational arts, where the importance of the true-to-life was not lacking, we noticed a relationship between essential truth and specific forms of art, and, as it were, a relationship back from the latter, which itself had a decided influence upon selection. But at bottom, its effect upon selection is felt more by the essential truth itself, and the two could not therefore really be identical. Remember that the standpoint taken upon essence turned out to be relative to artistic form. From that fact, it becomes clear that here too we are not dealing with the essential truth in the work of art, but simply with the "immanent truth," or, more correctly, a question about what corresponds here to the immanent truth, of which we are familiar upon the theoretical standpoint.

What in this context corresponds to immanent truth? We spoke of it sufficiently in Chapter 21: it is the inner necessity or the artistic unity of the constructed object. This may also be called its inherent lawfulness. There belongs to it the consistency of its execution, its unity, and its rigid consolidation as a structured whole. There is no possible doubt that this is a universal aesthetical demand – it is also evident that this immanent truth is especially dominant in the non-representational arts, for it stands there alone – without any foothold in requirements transcendent of itself. But can one for that reason call it a requirement of truth?

b) The untruth in deceptions of form and in indistinctness

One cannot call it such without further consideration any more than one can, from a theoretical standpoint, pretend that the mere inner "rightness" is truth. Nonetheless, there are two standpoints from which we can speak of truth, even in the case of the non-representational arts. The one lies in the realm of immanent agreement and unity, the other concerns the psychic content articulated in the inner strata of these arts. As such, this latter is not as such the work of art, but rather plays the role of some material, even when its expression remains indistinct. With reference to it, even the true-to-life is possible here.

As for the former standpoint, there exists in fact a deviation of the artist from a formal principle chosen by him earlier, which appears to the observer as "untruth," or falsity; it is not an accident that the use of this expression has become current for designating it. The examples from architecture offered earlier shine a light on this phenomenon. For in those examples there really was a reference to a kind of feigning, or to a misleading of the observer.

But to be more accurate, one should not speak here of feigning [*Vortäuschung*], but rather of feigning of form [*Formtäuschung*]. For the observer is deceived about the form itself, and indeed by means of form. The form of the whole is in fact not uniform in itself, and the external form placed over a building, a façade or a portico misleads us about the real inner form. That the (315) expression is rightly chosen is shown by the fact that the deception is seldom unconscious, and almost counts as fraud. Therefore, in this sense one may indeed speak of an inner "demand of truth" in the problematic of form in architecture. However, from that it does not follow that we can universalize this demand and extend it even to music.

For conditions in music are quite different. It is the only art that is free on both sides: it is tied neither to a purpose nor to a *sujet* (material). Architecture has at least the tie on the side of a practical purpose. However, in pure music, at least, form-bestowal hangs in the air as pure play. What could correspond in its case to "deception" on the level of form? In architecture, it served, obviously, to misguide people for the sake of some practical end. Can there be in good music a kind of "misguiding"?

Surely not one of the same kind as in architecture. But perhaps of a different kind? Or is it possible that a composer, seduced by the elevated feelings expressed by some great model, would attempt to make something of the same grandeur, and to that end, in certain passages, perhaps in the introduction, he likewise touches a sublime tone – perhaps in the theme and the first development – but then loses entirely the sense of this style, and falls into either sentimentality or, banality, or into virtuosity (the latter is found often in Liszt[101]).

Such a case is somewhat similar to the confusion caused by the banal apartment building with the façade of a palace! In the latter case, no higher kind of composition, neither of the space nor of the purpose behind it, stands behind the advertisement that first hits the eye, so in our musical example, no larger musical composition stands behind the pompous passages in the introduction. Music in the nineteenth century, especially the later period, contained a lot of compositional deception on the level of form. The newly developed harmonies allowed even less gifted spirits to produce on occasion music that was pretty and appealing; often it was based upon a sophisticated musical idea, but it lacked a more profound finish. By that, we mean it lacked genuine composition. An entire musical literature was built from once-beloved salon-pieces, and it ruined musical taste thoroughly for several decades.

That is musical untruth in one of its two senses: the first belongs on the list of immanent disharmonies and irregularities. The other sense concerns the psychic material that is stamped upon the inner strata of music and that appears there – the liveliness, the impulse, the rising and falling, the tension and resolution, the joyous flight, ecstasy and soft passing into silence. ...

When it is in fact possible to capture these ineffable rhythms in the soul and to "let them appear" in the strains of music and in its sequences of tones, then it must also be possible to botch the process. That would mean that music would

---

101 [Translator's note:] Franz Liszt (1811–1886).

become untrue in its soul. Since the events and processes in the soul constitute the dimensions of real life, which alone can be expressed musically, one must therefore (316) conclude that we have to do here with the musically untrue-to-life.

If, however, there exists the musically untrue-to-life – in a sense comparable to that in the representational arts – then it would be logical that there is also the musically true-to-life. We would have to assume that there is a representational element that lies at the foundation of music: namely the representation of precisely these events and processes in the soul – those extending from simple excitement and relaxation to joyous flight and rapture. But then one can again doubt whether this assumption is justified. For even though a composition expresses such processes, and can make them very urgently, it is always questionable whether we can all this a kind of representation – in a sense comparable to the "material" of a piece of literature or of a painting.

There is a distinction here that refers to a dividing line that must be maintained in all circumstances. If one wishes the motions of the soul themselves to count as the "material" of music, one must still concede that music does not allow these motions to appear with the exactitude that are given to apperception.

In this case, the concept of "exactitude" [*Bestimmtheit*] is to be taken in a concrete sense: tender music with softly rising motifs can be understood as the expression of young love, but also as the expression of the dewy freshness of morning. ... The precise content of shifting feelings is not to be heard. In this sense, music, even just as far as it really arouses and communicates the depths of the soul's excitement, still floats upon an indistinct cloud. If the composer did not tell us in his title "what it is supposed to mean," the music, for its part, will not tell us.

What it really tells us is something more general: just the dynamic aspects of the heart's emotions, of the excitement, the fading away, the sweetness or the harshness, etc. It does not penetrate into more differentiated contents. Therefore, we must be cautious in accepting the assertion of theory that music "represents." And so also one should not speak here of "representation." One can bestow upon some stirring of feeling a dynamic expression without literally representing it.

c) Traces of the true-to-life in music

This does not prevent such giving of expression from being in fact correctly or incorrectly done; and that means only that it may seem to us, despite its inexactitude and generality, quite false to life. We can demonstrate this unambiguously by well-known examples from music. We must only not "force" these examples too much.

There are emotions of the soul that are too complicated to be made musically comprehensible without its thematic expression in words. The composer nonetheless attempts to express them musically – and the effect is that (317) the expression becomes untrue. Here the limits of exactitude in musical expression have been passed. That is always the case when the composer, "writes alongside" it what it is supposed to "be" by means of a title The listener, who hears the music and only afterwards reads the title, says, "Aha!", and means thereby that the music, in any case, had not told him that.

There is also a more serious case in which the listener can hear distinctly in the music sounds resembling a certain emotion of the soul, but who is then disappointed, because the emotion is not continued and is not intended. One finds such things in large compositions, in symphonic music and chamber music, where the introduction promises greater development and intensification, but the promise is not kept by the development (Dvořák[102]).

One can of course say that this breach is more concerned with the inner unity and necessity of a piece. However, there is also in fact its inadequacy with respect to the felt emotions of the soul. This of course can never be demonstrated with any certainty, but one is not deceived; one can hear it aesthetically within the music. Otherwise, it would not be possible that in highly pretentious passages we could have the impression of emptiness or of deceit. That is a phenomenon that cannot be further analyzed, and we are forced to rely only upon our artistic sensibility.

Whoever has the capacity to make nuanced distinctions will be able to hear such untruth in the music. No doubt, music grasps in a unique way the activity of the ineffable human soul, turns it to the senses, and offers it to the sensibility we have in common with others, but it does this only through the mastery of the highest techniques of compositional structure. And that demands much.

We may characterize the nature of classical music (from the seventeenth to the early nineteenth centuries) by its inclusion of relatively modest emotional expression in a rich compositional form, and by the imbalance of the formal over the emotional. Later this tendency toward imbalance turned in the other direction: the rich flowering of compositional form contracted, and the psychic elements that were to have been written to this form grew disproportionably large. The result was to overload musical form.

Such developments progress towards merely placing expressive tonal ideas alongside of each other: single harmonic series dominate; one looks for new kinds of harmonic structures, and thinks that in them alone one has already squeezed

---

102 [Translator's note:] Antonín Dvořák (1841–1904).

out and expressed the essential in music. That might be so if the emotions, in their nature, were incapable of reducing their response to music to a single striking moment instead of extending themselves in time, that is, running through musically an entire development. For that reason, structurally tight compositions are such superior expressions of what pertains to the soul.

From this perspective, one can obtain a deeper look into the essence of pure music. Here is the reason why pieces that are overburdened with feeling but relatively simple in their construction are not only of dubious quality but seem, in a direct manner, quite untrue. One who is musically adept hears the untruth in the music: the piece should, above all, affect us in a certain way – it is intended to be celebratory, uplifting, or devotional – and it is merely pressed into that service by certain external effects. Yet it cannot succeed (318) because the deeper regions of the soul's emotions, which were to be feigned, are entirely lacking in it.

That is a familiar phenomenon, and one found not only in third-class compositions. It has nothing to do with lighter, superficial music; it would be very unjust to confuse these latter sensitive and nuanced works with the former. "Light music" does not pretend to any profundity of feeling; it does not wish to be anything but what it is, a comforting and harmless play.

We see from this clearly that we are dealing with a genuine trace of the true-to-life in pure music. No doubt it is considerably paler than in the representational arts; moreover, this element of the true-to-life stands close to the frontier of "immanent truth" – more correctly, on the borderline of what we call the unity and inner necessity of a work of music. For that reason it is so hard for aesthetical theory to make it stand out clearly. For we can depend even here only upon aesthetical pleasure and displeasure, and never upon some assignable criterion.

In this respect, it is easier in the case of architecture; there we have a counterpart given in the practical purpose it serves (which can also be an ideal purpose). For since the first thing that the master architect composes is the purpose of the composition, and everything else reflects back upon that, there results freely a condition of true-to-life or falsity, depending on whether the composition of the rooms and the dynamic composition conform to the compositional purpose, or instead turn to additions, ornaments, or deceptions of form that are not organically related to it.

One must not in any case forget that architecture has deeper inner strata, and in that regard, it corresponds to those in music. In addition, there are high intellectual contents, which, due to their intangibility, force their way to the foreground and attempt to enter the realm of appearance.

For that reason we find in architecture still another form of the true-to-life in addition to that which relates to the practical purpose of a building. It can hit the mark or fail to do so. And with this true-to-life quality there is again tied an essential truth of a peculiar nature, for in the psychic background of architectonic composition there usually stand high essential ideals, which in their turn function just as much in selection as in determining form affirmatively. Everything else that can be developed here is almost a mere repetition of what was said earlier. In this respect, architecture and music differ only in degrees from literature.

d) The situation in program music

It is easy to understand that the situation in program music is again different from that in pure music. Here we again have themes with a definite content whose nature is external to music. With that, all inexactitude and relative generality are excluded. True, they are no longer musical themes; music itself cannot (319) represent them either, but only frame them; it expresses precisely in all thematic materials only the accompanying psychic dynamics – and everything that it might wish to represent beyond these dynamics would be condemned to untruth.

Here we are given great latitude for the true-to-life and for the essentially true, and for their opposites: in the *Lied*, in choral works, in the opera, in oratorio and in all other art forms that combine words and poetry with music.

One can set to music, for example, some lyric poem – and do it "beautifully" or in a highly interesting way – and yet one may fail to capture the character of the poem. That is not a rare occurrence. One can fail to capture it according to the tastes of a certain epoch, while another epoch will sing its praises. This relativity of hitting and missing the mark corresponds very well to the "inexactitude" of all musical interpretation of same given objective material; one can even set to music the same poem in quite different ways. For that reason, none of the musical settings need be off the mark. Yet one of the other may seem to have failed given certain temporally conditioned essential standpoints.

From this, we may extract two points
1. Where an "essential element" is brought in as a necessary condition of true and false, we have the starting-point for essential truth in music written to a text.
2. Where a difference between true and apparent success and failure of the text through the music can be demonstrated, then if differences in the spirit of the times govern here – even under essential standpoints – then our sense of "truth" with respect to it is itself relative.

These two suggest themselves in this context and are easy to survey, and therefore we will not at this point follow up their implications. What is important in them for our problem is only the fundamental presupposition, i.e., that it is a question of truth and untruth at all when a text hits or misses a mark because of the music, for this is not immediately apparent. Such things could of course also be cases just of "good" and "bad" musical settings, or of successful and unsuccessful ones – in short, of grades and degrees of artistic quality.

Then we meet again what we learned above: that there is a peculiar strong convergence in the representational arts of the true-to-life and artistic quality. One might think that the fundamental presupposition presented here is a verification of a certain congruence of the two. However, that is not so. One concedes too easily such identifications because the inexactitude of musical expression gives it support. What is the situation in reality?

One must first become clear how much or little of a poetic text can in fact be expressed musically. That was formulated unambiguously above (Chap. 14d): only the psychic dynamics as such are expressible, thus excitement or rest; what cannot be expressed is (320) everything that concerns the "about what" and the "by means of what" of the excitement and the rest. That holds without exception and limitation.

However, this condition is liable to produce the greatest illusions. The composer, like the performers (especially the opera singers and their directors) attempt involuntarily to put more into music than it is able to bear.

In that way, something untrue enters music – essential untruth, because the essence of music, of song, of the accompaniment and the framing of feelings is injured. Indirectly, so is the untrue-to-life also. For music brings to the text what the text, of itself, cannot have – deep immediacy in its expression of feeling. There are texts that do not take to such expression, for they say things of relative indifference, and cannot make use at all of such expression of feeling.

That is true e.g., of numberless passages in operas, in which the action requires some merely indifferent words, whereas the principle behind opera requires musical adornment. The effect is notoriously untruthful, and in fact more untrue to life, such as the stage can hardly tolerate. Almost all of our operas suffer from this, even the oratorios (recitative). The cleverest efforts to gloss over this difficulty (Wagner, Strauss[103]) change nothing.

We see that this is not a matter of a lack of skill on the part of individual composers, but of a fundamental inadequacy, the consequence of which is the ease with which essential untruths and the untrue-to-life appear. The specific

---

103 [Translator's note:] Richard Strauss (1864–1949).

errors of the composers and the performing musicians (the latter e.g., in realistic singing) are the first ones to appear and they make the situation as bad as it can get – so that for one finely prepared, the unbearable can occur. These inadequacies do not happen in instrumental music, because the inner inadequacy is eliminated that arises from two arts with very different inner necessities being grafted upon each other.

The fundamental inadequacy is and remains the following:

1. On both sides there is an excess that the "other" art cannot take on: on the side of literature, the specific content; on the side of music, the direct profound expression of the soul; the literary arts can have these only in modest amounts and only indirectly;

2. A real meeting of the arts is therefore possible only along a narrow pathway, that is, along the path where the soul itself is stirred in its living nature. There we find a harmonious concord between them. Naturally this is possible only when the composer has the needed empathy for what the poet has in fact created. Any deviation from this line results in untruth, both the essential untruth and the untrue-to-life.

3. This does not mean, however, that in a mixed piece, i.e., music written to a text, the two arts have no latitude over against each other. To the contrary, they bring to their presentations quite different sides of the composition: poetry brings an entire situation, characters, drama; the (321) music brings the tremor of emotion, the sense of overflow, of melting away, etc. Those things do not oppose each other ever, so long as the two, artfully joined, supplement each other at every instant. However, the lightest encroachment, regardless from what side, will result in the composition becoming untrue.

In these three theses lie the reasons why in great music it is relatively so easy to produce a successful *Lied* or a choral work that affects us with its wonderful harmonies (perhaps interspersed with solos, duets, and the like), but it is so difficult to produce an entirely faultless opera. It is especially hard there to keep to the "narrow pathway," upon which these heterogeneous arts should meet, just because the musical expression of feeling must accompany the drama of the performance. Yet the shifts in the dramatic situations do not allow any longish passages for the development of the music, as would be necessary for making greater profundities accessible. As a result, the older opera resolved itself into "numbers": recitative, duets, arias, etc., and did not attempt complete dramatizations. Modern opera has not found, up to now, an equivalent compromise. (322)

Part Three: **Values and Genera of the Beautiful**

First Section: The Aesthetic Values

Chapter 26: Peculiarity and Multiplicity of Aesthetic Values

a) The divisions within the problem and the basis of their classification

If a scientific aesthetics were so advanced today that the way stood open for an analysis of aesthetic values, then it would be appropriate to enter upon it immediately. In the chapters of the previous section, we encountered continually the expression "artistic quality" – in contrast to the truth-content. But what this "quality" might be, with which, after all aesthetic value proper is denoted, we have yet said very little. We must at least attack this problem and attempt to clarify it; we must put to a test what yet may be discerned about it, despite the difficulties that arise from it.

The state of aesthetics is not favorable to such an attempt, as was already shown in the Introduction. But fundamentally, the analysis of values in aesthetics, in contrast to ethics, is hindered by the fact that we cannot extract individual general values – such as would correspond to the classes of "goodness" (ἀρεταί) – but instead have to do with a large number of highly individualized values. For every work of art, and almost all other things that are beautiful, have their own peculiar value, upon which, no doubt, more universal characteristics (value-elements) can be found, but that value is not the sum of its elements, for it is something quite different.

Beyond this, there exists the universal element in the entire class of values, that is, the aesthetically valuable as such, in contrast to the values of the useful and of goods, of vital values and moral values. Here is a task that is solvable within certain limits, if one begins upon the foundation of the analysis of objects that was set forth in the two previous Parts. At the very least, we can indicate now the essential differences of the aesthetic values from other classes of values. Further, it will turn out that it is also possible to demonstrate a few essential laws concerning the value-relation between aesthetic values and certain other classes of value. (323)

The situation is different for the "special" values in the domain of the beautiful, which are neither those of individual works of art nor the universal of aesthetic values. There are definitely such things; but as classes of values, they do not play the same role as the classes of goods values or of moral values. One must try to grasp, classify, and categorize or describe them according to where they belong within certain types of object.

Up to now as a whole, what has been achieved is only a vague outline. This outline stands just in the middle between the universal and the entirely individual aesthetic values. While the two extremes are relatively easy to grasp – the one by means of the understanding and analysis, the other by means of the entire inviolable clarity with which aesthetic objects are beheld and enjoyed – the middle of the scale is not accessible by way of either means, and it can be reached, as it were, only by detours.

These values obviously represent a group of values, the classes proper of the beautiful, and they press themselves unceremoniously against the classes of the object or those of the arts and their special subdivisions, but finally against the kinds of aesthetical feelings and aesthetical responses. This results in three kinds of customary classifications. All of these have limits and contain an element of one-sidedness.

The first type of classification (according to the object) is the natural one for beauty in nature and the humanly beautiful: One distinguishes the beauty of a face or a figure from that of a location or of a scene that one has observed; in the case of the latter it would be better, no doubt, to speak of drama. Such distinctions, of course, may be transferred informally to the arts, as far as these arts, for their part, represent such diverse objects. In the case of painting, we speak of a "seascape," a "landscape," or a "character study," but we mean their representation. We distinguish strictly the kinds of value in them by analogy to those values possessed by the object. That means, in these cases, an analogy to the *sujet*.

The second type of classification follows the arts and their subgroups. The one-sidedness here consists in the exclusion of natural and human beauty. Otherwise – within the arts – the classification is entirely justified. For there can be no doubt that, depending upon the specificity of the art form – in music, e.g., upon whether we are dealing with a minuet, an aria, a saraband, etc. – the specific kind of artistic value will vary. This could not be otherwise, for the specific art forms are nothing other than tried and tested types of form, in which things of beauty may be shaped. They remain valid even if their multiplicity should turn out to be of a non-uniform or a merely external kind.

The third type of classification causes far greater difficulties. And yet it is the one that does the most justice to the problem of aesthetic values in all their multiplicity. It renounces all external support in the object, and relies exclusively on the value-response given by a consciousness that beholds its object adequately. In this way, this classification follows the method of the analysis of values that we are (324) familiar with in ethics, and which achieved very tangible results there. The principle behind it is the distillation of unique qualitative shades of tone (nuances) from the living reactions to felt values, and their treatment as a direct and immediate witness to similarly differentiated nuances of value. As to the justification of this procedure, there is fundamentally no dispute. We have no other source of knowledge of aesthetic value and disvalue than our feeling of values. Whether one calls this feeling of value delight, enjoyment, affirmation, or pleasure, nothing of its import is affected.

Yet something has been forgotten here: there is also a classification according to the main empirical-historical developments that have dominated – or predominated – in the arts. We usually call these main forms of development "styles" but we mean by that term only those styles that are sufficiently widespread formal types, thus primarily those that extend over several arts and characterize what is similar in each of them.

We are in general familiar with this usage at least from the standpoint of art history, and we cannot deny that this standpoint, too, is justified. But the notion of style shares with the second principle of classification, that according to the forms of art, an exclusion of natural and human beauty; yet it finds itself related to other cultural forms of the same historical epochs that no longer fall in the domain of the aesthetical, or at least are not absorbed into it. One speaks, for example, of the Gothic style of life, or the human types typical of the Rococo.

The concept of style is in one way too narrow, in another too broad, to enable us to grasp the differentiations of aesthetic value proper. To this must be added the consideration that the concept of style itself must first be determined, something that has up to now not been achieved without a preparatory analysis of value. Moreover, the concept of style has to be called upon everywhere that a fixed and similarly unique and definite idea of value has attached itself to the tastes and the vision of a specific style. In fact, there are various examples of that.

b) Differentiations according to the qualia of value feeling

It is necessary before all else to say a few things about the genera of beauty according to the third method of classification – that is, according to the type of the value-response and enjoyment. The multiplicity of aesthetic value viewed from this standpoint is quite considerable, but only a very few of this multiplicity are given clear designations; the most are ἀνώνυμα, that is, our language is not able to extend itself to them. Even the few designations that one can apply here always have something strangely indeterminate and blurry about them, partly because colloquial speech has eroded their meanings, partly because the concept of nuances of values was unclear or wavered in its meaning from the outset.

In the *Critique of the Power of Judgment*, Kant thought one of these genera of the beautiful, viz., the sublime, to be so fundamental that he treated it, on the same level as and alongside of, the idea of beauty itself, in a special "Analytic." (325) If we take a closer look at this analytic, we find that he himself, on the basis of his inquiry, would have been confident to count it as a variety of beauty. What prevented him from doing so was the somewhat too narrowly defined concept of the beautiful that emerged from his earlier Analytic of Beauty. (Compare in reference to this the Introduction, §3, where some of these genera were first enumerated.)

There was an early objection: why should not a similar special place be also given to the graceful and the charming, to the pleasing and moving, to the idyllic and the comical, to the humorous and the tragic? Then one would have to carry out an "analytic" for each of these genera. One could of course add to the list many other genera of beauty that raise the same claim, such as the grotesque, the fantastic, the capricious, etc. One could even suggest that in the same way the "lyric," the "romantic," the "classic" belong here, also. Of course, one would no doubt observe that one has gone astray regarding the forms of art, on the one hand, and in the types of style on the other – both of which no longer touch upon the immediacy of our feeling for aesthetic values.

When one shines a light from this position backwards upon the first-named genera, one sees that among these some have already been borrowed from specific art forms, especially from those of the poetic arts: for example, the comical and the tragic, but also the idyllic and the humorous. More specific poetic forms lie at the basis of the grotesque, the fantastic, etc. Apart from the sublime, there remains only the graceful, the charming, and the pleasing, as genera that have been derived solely from the feeling of value; for even the emotionally moving stands quite at the limits of artistic form.

The fact that precisely these three remaining value-genera are extraordinarily pale and blurry is calamitous. It is not even possible to demarcate them unambiguously with respect to one another; they flow over, one into the other. If we take them all together, they no doubt contrast sharply with the sublime. And if we take this contrast as our point of departure, we will discover also that it continues in the emotionally moving, the idyllic, the comical, and the humorous. This continuation does not, of course, proceed on a straight line.

This contrast with the sublime divides itself instead into several subgroups arranged in parallel fashion. It branches out. That develops in such a way that the subgroups lose their weight and independence, while the sublime, as the contrary common to each, gains considerably in weight.

Nonetheless, we should note that one of the value-genera that we enumerated approaches the sublime, and, in a certain version of it, could almost count as a species of it: the tragic. Without question, a genuine tragic effect cannot be achieved without at least a trace of the sublime. This is significant, because the tragic is not simply an art form; it is a value-genus that also appears in other arts than tragedy. A clear case is music, where it is notably bereft (326) of all drama. Then, too, it appears in painting (in certain portraits, etc.). The special position of the sublime is thereby once again considerably strengthened, and precisely in the Kantian sense.

We will then also submit the sublime to another investigation. In many respects it will be more essential than those of the other value-genera. But those too, each and all, demand their special study, regardless of whether one belongs in this or that classification.

It has already become obvious that a clearly arranged classification and comparison of aesthetic values cannot be obtained in this manner. There are no doubt genera of values to which a seemingly foundational feeling of values bears witness; yet they are neither derived from the feeling of values, nor are they in the same way identified and distinguished from each other by it. A secure foothold for a genuine entry into the realm of aesthetic values is not to be won in this way.

One may convince oneself even more of this impossibility when one recalls that there exist artistic values that do not fit into this series: the value of the drama is of this kind. It is not tied as firmly to the art of drama as one might think; it also belongs to certain forms of the novel, and we encounter it even outside of art in life itself, in the area of what is beautiful in man, if we bring an open mind to it.

Finally, we must recall that we also meet in life many of the genera we have enumerated even apart from their aesthetical coloring. The tragic and the comical are good examples of this. Terrible events easily seem tragic to us even when we attach no aesthetical meaning to them; much of what we witness by chance seems comical to us – in life, we laugh over many kinds of petty but all-too-human events, and often we laugh at ourselves. Both such events are on the near side of art. Most frequently a moral judgment is expressed in them. But that too is very distant from the sphere of aesthetic values.

The case is similar with the idyllic and the emotionally touching, perhaps even with the charming and the pleasing. For there exist "charms" that are of an entirely different kind than the aesthetical, even if they are related to them, or are distinct from them but not sharply so.

Very many things in life may seem idyllic to us without our actively enjoying them. A thing can be very touching without possessing the slightest touch of aesthetic value. Think how a scene where others are touched by something may easily appear comical to us. It is sufficient that the response be ever slightly too strong – relative to a more sober sensibility.

That does not prevent us from taking up and analyzing one of the other of these value-genera. People have tried repeatedly to analyze the sublime on the one hand, and the humorous on the other. Much of significance has been discovered by these efforts. Only we must not fall victim to illusion: we are always inclined to expect great things of analyses of this kind – new disclosures (327) about fundamental interconnections in life, and the like. Metaphysical aesthetics of the idealists and later thinkers have given impetus to dreams of this kind. For it readily seems self-evident that we are touching ultimate things when we have at the ready a metaphysics of spirit, in whose structures the role of bringing together and concluding widely interwoven threads of theory falls to Beauty, Art, Beholding, and Enjoyment.

Such unspoken metaphysical motives infect many theories, even up to our times. From that perspective, every more sober effort will seem unsatisfying, even superficial. Nonetheless, aesthetics must today take a more modest path. Studies of the object, the stratification, and the conditions in which form is bestowed have demonstrated that unambiguously. Our deficient orientation within the problem of value, typical of our situation today, only serves to confirm further this necessity.

c) The range of beauty

If we lay to rest the difficulties in the classification and arrangement because we can come to no final conclusion regarding them, there still remains another option: we can approach empirically, as it were, the individual genera of aesthetic value, as far as they present themselves and can be grasped. In this way, indeed, all past aesthetics has proceeded in practice.

We may hope along the empirical "way from below" to encounter those universal fundamental determinations of the beautiful, which our analysis of the object has produced. Where the two roads meet, we should at best meet with results.

But our expectations must be limited. It is still very questionable whether the beautiful is congruent with the sum total of all these value-genera. Its range as the foundation of general aesthetic values could extend far beyond them.

That is indeed the case. It is a simple matter to assure ourselves of this, even though we have no insight into the additional value-genera. Such an insight is not necessary for that assurance. We must not forget that we possess an enormous multiplicity of individual cases, each having an immediately evident character that is aesthetically valuable. The individual cases are the works of art themselves.

If we take one or another work that is recognized as a masterpiece and ask ourselves under which of the enumerated classes it falls, given the character of its aesthetic value, we will rarely find one that is exhausted entirely only by one of the genera. For example, under what genus should we place *The Brothers Karamazov*? Neither the sublime, nor the charming, nor the moving, is sufficient to cover it; not even the tragic, which extends a very thin thread throughout the work. What will we say of *Growth of the Soil* [Hamsun, 1917], *Wanderers* [1922], etc.? The ready categories of aesthetics are simply insufficient for them. Or [Ibsen's] *The Wild Duck* [1884], *Pillars of Society* [1877], *J[ohn] G[abriel] Borkman* [1896]? Even Shakespeare's major dramas cannot be placed under one genus. Are (328) things any different with Rembrandt's self-portraits? Or with the Dutch landscapes and seascapes?

What are the consequences of this? There is much "beauty" in the strictest sense of the word that is not exhausted by any determinable value-genera of beauty. In the place of these value-genera we speak instead of qualities that we think associated with a particular form of art, or we simply take from this art form the name for it and use it to refer to the artistic excellence of the work within that form. So we speak of the value of a "picturesque" quality, of the "dramatic" quality, the quality of the "staging," of the "narrative representation," or of the "sculptural" quality. Such terms may have a certain justification, but with these characterizations we refer only obliquely to what our value feelings tell us, and they do not say in what that feeling consists.

If we also set aside weak attempts to exhibit such differentiations among values, the basic fact remains that the quality of "being beautiful" – understood as the state of being aesthetically valuable – is not exhausted by all such genera, but that rather a multiplicity of beauties without number exist inside and outside of the arts, which are not to be accommodated "in that way." But this is with what we are really concerned when it is a question of the basic value and the value-genera of beauty.

In this context, it is by no means unimportant to attempt to make clear that this is not, let us say, a question of a broader concept of beauty, but rather solely a question of the aesthetic values in their strict sense. Such broadening is nowhere closer to us than where we are now, because in life we are accustomed to characterize a limitless number of things as "beautiful" that are merely useful for some given purpose, are useable, cause fun, are pleasant, or also are morally "good."

This misuse is so vulgar that it is not worth a single word to set it straight. Two things are present here that deserve special consideration. The one concerns the strange turning of meaning to the moral realm. How does it happen that a form of behavior – let us say a high-minded or a generous act – comes to be called "beautiful," while the predicate that really belongs to it is that of the morally "good"? And the same when we call the opposite of these acts "ugly"?

Three things are hidden behind this practice.
1. The tendency to conceal or to weaken the earnestness of morality;
2. The habit of allowing what is external and visible in the behavior of a person to substitute for what is inward and moral; for naturally the moral tenor, the

dispositions, even the general and fundamental attitudes of a man stamp themselves directly upon his typical visible appearance, his gestures, movements, manner and bearing;

3. The old prejudice, which traces to Plato, of the identity of the ἀγαθόν and καλόν [the good and the beautiful]. This point has been continuously strengthened through the expectation that groups and classes of values should all be traceable to an identical fundamental value. Such a value was understood e.g., by Aristotle as the καλόν. When he argues, "τοῦ καλοῦ ἕνεκα [for the sake of the beautiful]," the value of final appeal is meant, which is counted as the only one. (329)

It is not easy to confront such deeply rooted misuse. Another such misnomer is hidden even deeper, i.e., calling the psychic inner processes "beautiful" and "ugly" in themselves. We do this in a moral sense, calling a wicked act "ugly"; but in an extramoral sense we also speak, for example, of the "beautiful" peace and mellowness of an aged person, or of the "beauty" of the awakening of the love life in a young person, the blossoming of the understanding of the conflicts and conditions of the life of other persons. One may object: all of that is really beautiful, also, and precisely in the narrow aesthetical sense. One may wish to insist that there is a "beauty in old age," and, even more, the "beauty of youth."

The latter must be entirely conceded. But it is no objection. The beauty in youthfulness does not lie in its emotional excitation, its awakening, etc., but rather in its appearance in the external man, in his gaze, in the cut of his physical features, etc. So it is too with the beauty of old age: not the mellowness, but its appearance in the face and bearing, is where this beauty lies. The case of the "ugliness" of an action is different: in the action, there appears, no doubt, something of the inner man, precisely as a moral agent, but we refer in such case more to the moral deed itself, and there we go astray. It is erroneous in a strong sense to speak of a "beautiful soul," or of a beautiful heart, beautiful feelings, or sentiments. These epithets are false.

We may say in general: beauty is and remains tied to sensible appearance – or, as in literature, to an analogy with the sensible, that is, to our highly concrete and vivid feelings. The beautiful is not what appears, but only appearance itself. No doubt the appearance-relation can grow considerably in substance by means of various other value-contents – perhaps of a moral kind – of what appears and with that the state of beauty may increase in fullness of its meaning and its resonance; but such value-contents can never replace appearance or render it superfluous, and therefore can also never constitute the aesthetic value. The facts just established are no longer new ones. They are the precise implications of what was discovered above (Chaps. 4–10) about the nature of beauty. But of course, the significance of these statements becomes apparent only gradually.

Chapter 27: The Situation Today in the Problem of Value

a) Classes of values and value-aporia

Aesthetics does not stand alone as an inquiry into values. It attaches itself to other sciences of value, which were developed prior to it. Only ethics stood with real energy in the vanguard, and that too only in the last decades. For if aesthetics, which (330) had not yet gotten its bearings, had at least found a linkage to ethics, it would have received a significant help. The relative position of beauty to the other classes of values is easier to find, but that fact is rather strange, since these classes are still little defined. Yet the situation is more transparent here. The first thing to do is to cast an eye into the realm of values in general, at least so far as it has opened itself to philosophical analysis up to this moment.

The classes of values we normally take into account have no systematic principle and are examined partly empirically. For that reason, they also do not make up an uniform series – such as a clear set of stages – but fluctuate between precedence and co-subordination, even though there are only a few of them. Even the demarcations between them have not been indisputably established.

If we begin at the bottom, we can distinguish the following classes in the following manner:

I. Goods values, including all values of the useful and the instrumental, but also many entirely independent areas of values (those genuinely intrinsic); among such things, the broad class of the situational values.

II. Values of pleasure, or what in everyday life is usually characterized as the "pleasant."

III. Vital values – those are the ones associated with living things, and are arranged in a series according to height, development, and life force. All vital value has instrumental worth for whatever promotes life; vital disvalue, worth for what harms life.

IV. Moral values: Collected under the heading of the "good."

V. Aesthetic values: Collected under the heading of the "beautiful."

VI. The value of knowledge: Really only one value, the "truth."

It is easy to see that this series is heterogeneous. The three last classes of value stand in a kind of parallel arrangement to each other; this does not exclude the possibility that differences in rank are also found among them. For each of these classes of value, except for the last, contains an entire scale of values, some higher and some lower, as we know well from ethics. Similarly, there are also higher and lower aesthetic values. The consequence is that it is just as possible for there to exist ethical values that are "higher" than specific aesthetic values, as for there to be aesthetic values that are higher than specific ethical values.

These three last classes of values have been gathered together as "spiritual" values. So said Scheler. But not much is thereby achieved. One can attach still another class to them, that of religious values. But their actuality [*Bestehen*] depends on certain metaphysical presuppositions that cannot be demonstrated: without the existence [*Existenz*] of a divinity, those values would be illusory. It is therefore better to leave them out of consideration here – although in the history of humankind an entire domain of culture corresponds to them.

Among the first three classes of values, that of the values of pleasure [*Lust*] is not without ambiguity. In part, the group may be congruent to the class of goods values, for what is "pleasant," e.g., warmth in winter, is just for that reason a "good." The difference between the classes becomes clear only when we understand (331) the value of pleasure strictly subjectively, that is, as the value of the sensation of pleasure, not as the value of whatever produces pleasure, or what we usually also call "pleasant." But that is difficult to maintain, because we consciously understand pleasure almost exclusively as a sign of certain qualities of an object and then call it after what arouses it.

This is not the place to clarify and correct these and similar inconsistencies. Here it is a question only of how matters currently stand, and we find that even the borderline between the value of the pleasant and vital values is not clear. Specifically, the pleasant is in part unambiguously related to the functions of life; in part, it founds and expresses immediately something that promotes life – the way that the good taste of food teaches us what is nourishing and digestible – and in part it is something quite different, and what is pleasant can seduce us to actions that are destructive of life. The latter we find in all cases of excess, or in drugs, in alcohol, and the like.

The relation of goods values to the vital values is significantly simpler. Here we have at bottom a simple relation of foundation; specifically the goods values are founded upon the vital values, thus the lower upon the higher. A "good" is not a thing in itself, but only a good "for" someone; here we do not have to understand by "someone" a person, i.e., an intellectual being. There can be goods "for" an animal or a plant, i.e., for a living thing into whose possession it comes. But it must always be a good "for someone"; outside of this relation there are no goods. Everything that stands in a relation of utility to some creature has a goods-value, a usefulness for it, but also only "for" it, not in itself – thus a grain of seed is a goods-value for the bird that feeds on it, thus also air and light and the circulation of water for all life on earth.

In this way, the "for" is to be understood objectively: it is not tied to any knowledge of "being good," even when the creature for "whom" it is a good possesses consciousness and intelligence. Those enable him to understand it and to mark it paid by a responsive feeling of its value. Just so are for man air, light, water and much else like them the most necessary goods for life, but they can be felt by us only when they are withheld; even our "daily bread" – how few of us enjoy it with the feeling of thanks that its high value deserves!

We must not forget that this "being for us" of the goods of value to man has nothing to do with a crass value-relativism; it does not mean a dependency of value upon our holding things to be valuable, thus (332) also not upon our feelings of value or even upon our knowing about them at all. It suffices for something to be "good" for us, that it is to our benefit, even that it could benefit us if we thought to put it to use or just simply to discover it. The earth's storehouses of coal were a great good for man, even before men discovered and understood them as such; these goods were lying there at the ready; they had only to wait upon their exploitation.

Goods values for man are primarily those that relate to him and are to his benefit, but in no sense accessible to his intellect. This conclusion is important, because goods values play, for their part, a leading role in moral values. We must therefore modify the above thesis of foundation, such that the goods values are values only "for" living beings or persons – thus relative to bearers of vital and spiritual values – and for that reason founded upon the higher classes of values entirely, and not simply upon vital values. No doubt, the moral values are the primary ones that come into consideration here. Yet the reverse relation begins precisely with them.

We must note here also that in a certain sense it is correct to say that the values of pleasure are founded in the same way upon vital value. The pleasant does not genuinely exist in itself, but only as something pleasant to "me"; more accurately, pleasant to some living thing. The difference is only that here it is a question of pure values of subjectivity, of sensation as such, and not of values inhering in an object.

The class of goods values is very large. It begins with the lower values of usefulness for vital functions, but it climbs upward to the highest spiritual goods, where only persons or persons in relation to other persons can have them: friendship, benevolence, love, such as may accrue to us. These values are essentially conditioned by ethical values that relate to our behavior toward others; they are the goods values attached to moral values.

In part, these extend beyond the lower moral values in the general scale of values according to their relative height. This is one reason more not to distinguish the classes of values according to their relative height alone, a distinction correct only as a whole, not for individual cases. Here we must also recall that even aesthetic values display in large measure the characteristics of goods values.

Finally, we must say a word about situational values. There were just now counted among the goods values, but that is true only in an extended sense. "Goods values" were once defined (and were still so by Scheler) by the ontological character (the stratum of being) of their bearers. The thought was: only things, states of affairs, or natural states akin to things could be bearers of goods values. To these latter would belong, for example, the external conditions of life, those of human life, and of other organisms.

This definition has turned out to be too narrow. It is sufficient only for the narrowest needs, that is, as long as we have to do (333) only with the usefulness of things. It does not serve for the higher goods values; every configuration of events can have the value – or disvalue – of a good, and similarly every behavior of another man, regardless of whether it has moral significance or not. That is even true for every "chance" event, that is, one without purpose, and of every situation and state of affairs.

For entities to be valuable that do not count as things, but rather above and beyond things constitute entire sets of conditions, phenomenologists have coined the appropriate concept "situational values" – without any suggestions of an independent class of values. In fact, situational values belong under the rubric of goods values, if only one does not insist on understanding "goods" narrowly as things. Otherwise, it would not be possible to count such values as happiness and power among the goods values. For what constitutes "happiness" is rarely included in just one thing – as, in fairy-tales, a piece of jewelry, a gem, or a magic mirror – almost always happiness is tied to definite circumstances in life, that is, to situations. That is of great significance for ethics. For moral values are unambiguously referred back to the goods values that bear them, and indeed precisely to the situational values.

b) Kinship and contrasts among the classes of values

We can see from what has been said here and elsewhere that the attempt to define the classes of values according to their types of bearer of value is highly questionable. For the goods values, in any case, the situation is hopeless; one would have to say that anything at all can be a bearer of a goods-value, from things to the most refined behavior of persons. Something similar is found among the "spiritual values."

So, at least, when one considers the three classes of value together: moral, aesthetical, and epistemic. No doubt they all have ample latitude in the domain of the mind, but they do not have the same bearer. In the case of moral values, the human being as a person is the barer of values; only for him is it possible to be "good" or "bad" morally, as also only to him belongs the freedom necessary to be one or the other.

In the case of epistemic value, man is by no means its bearer, not even as a person, not even as a being that knows. For neither man nor the knower is "true" when his ideas correspond to the facts or "false" when they fail to do so; only his ideas themselves, his judgments, or whatever he deems to be his knowledge may be true (in reality, it is knowledge only when it is true, otherwise it is erroneous). That a man can "be true or untrue" means something quite different; its meaning is entirely ethical in nature.

For aesthetic value, the reverse holds true. Here "man" as the bearer of values is given not too broad a role, but one too narrow. No doubt a man can be beautiful or ugly, but then too, an animal or a landscape can be beautiful or ugly; indeed, the same holds of every object, every natural or living (334) phenomenon. To these we must add the rich multiplicity of art objects, which are of course all objectivations of the human mind, but not living, personal mind, not men!

Accordingly, we may say about aesthetic values something similar to what was said about goods values: any possible thing in the world can be their bearers – things, organisms, persons, world-systems or individual segments of the real world, but especially those things created by men to bear them. "Things" is for the latter much too narrow: fantasies, purely imaginary notions, all are such bearers also. However, they must be somehow anchored in things, that is, objectified.

If, on one side, aesthetic values display similarities to goods values – so much so that one might be tempted to count them among the highest goods values; after all, they often fall like gifts to humankind "from heaven!" – still, we cannot mistake their kinship on the other side with the values of pleasure. Has not aesthetics attempted often enough to carry over the shadings of the pleasant and the unpleasant to those of the beautiful and the ugly?

This kinship obtains grater traction if one recalls that the act of beholding and presenting values aesthetically is decidedly a pleasant one. Of course, for the feeling of pleasure itself that responds to these acts the value is not tied to pleasure, but rather to its object. But, after all, this objectification is just as characteristic for everything "pleasant and unpleasant": we call what causes pleasure "pleasant," not pleasure itself, what causes pain "unpleasant" (that which is bad tasting, painful, bitter).

What distinguishes them is the kind of pleasure and the kind of object. The act of aesthetical receptivity is sensual as looking, not in its pleasure. Pleasure begins only with the second act, that of beholding, the one that is higher, super-sensible. Accordingly, the aesthetic value of the object is not tied to the sensibly given, as with the pleasant, but to the appearance-relation – or to a formal relationship equivalent to it.

Now here is the point at which it is important to count aesthetic value among the "spiritual" values – by means of which it is drawn onto the level of the value of truth and the moral values. But for this it is not enough to hold onto the schematic form of the higher act of beholding. Here, precisely, we can give a better account on the basis of the analysis of the object.

What, specifically, do we mean here by "spiritual value"? It obviously does not mean that aesthetic value accrues to the human spirit; that may be granted to be so in the case of works of art, because they are "objectified spirit," but it does not hold for all other beautiful things in the world. The spirit is not in this case the bearer of value. What sense of "spiritual value" yet remains to us? In order to answer that question, let us recall what was said in Chapter 5 about the "law of objectivation," in particular about the role of the living (335) spirit in the being of the objectivated spirit, and also about the latter's "being for us."

What was in fact striking about these matters is the triadic relation – at bottom, it has four members – in the nature of the objectivizing spirit: the appearance-relation between the real foreground and the unreal background, which exists, however, only "for" a living spirit to whom something can appear – regardless of whether we understand the spirit as personal or as "objective." The "fourth member," then, is the creative spirit of the artist, who, of course, may belong to a long-ago past, yet be present behind the objectivation and can, to a certain degree, "appear" within it.

This last matter, however, plays no role here. It is absent from natural beauty and from human beauty. In contrast, the living spirit as the third member is essential for all aesthetic value, for this value of an object always pertains "to someone," but not in itself and without reference to a beholding subject. The essential role of spirit in the triadic relation of all things that can lay claim to being "beautiful" constitutes the character of spiritual value in beauty.

There remains to be said that here, too, there is an obvious kinship with goods values, and specifically a second kinship next to the first one presented above. There, as here, there is a reference back to a subject whose presence is a condition of the value. Only a secondary distinction is made by the fact that for the values of goods by a living thing, even without intellect, "for" which the value exists, must be present. The main matter is still the correlation: the "for" itself, without which the value cannot exist.

The difference is that only in the case of goods values it is a question of a real relation to a subject, without any concern for the relation being conscious. But here, in contrast, it is a question of a characteristic relationship of a consciousness. That means: a "good" thing is such for A, when it is to his benefit, or even could be such, without A knowing and appreciating it; but a "beautiful" thing is beautiful for A, when "for" his beholding and feeling there exists the appearance-relationship. Otherwise put: when the real foreground of the object becomes transparent to him and the series of strata of the background appears to him from within it.

The second "for" is characteristically subjective; it pertains to an intellectual consciousness. In that respect aesthetic value is as dissimilar as possible from goods values. We see from this how the weightiest distinctions are rooted in the unique and most nuanced relationships among the essential conditions that lie at their foundation.

c) Goods values and moral values

These last characterizations concerned, in a preliminary way, the place of aesthetic value. But nevertheless we have as yet entered only the front courtyard. To examine these values in earnest, we need to take a larger detour: we must bring, above all, the (336) moral values into the discussion, for the aesthetic values have again a special relationship to them. To that end, we need to start with a fundamental definition of the essence of the moral values themselves.

For the justification of what follows, we must of course refer to the *Ethics*. We can enumerate only the main elements here and recall the essential standpoints relevant to them. The primary points are the following:

1. Moral values and disvalues have only persons, or the actions, attitudes, and dispositions of persons as their bearers. They are decidedly the values of persons and their actions. The basis of this exclusiveness is that only persons have freedom, and their freedom becomes active only in their acts, attitudes and dispositions. For only that behavior has moral value that is not forced – perhaps by natural necessity – to be as it is, but rather could have turned out differently than it did.

2. Moral values are not relative to someone "for" whom they are valuable, as is the case with goods values. The "for" pertains merely to the goods values that are tied to them; these are values only for the one who benefits from them. But one must not confuse them with the moral values themselves: the honesty of A is a "good" for B, who has to live with him. B is the recipient of this good; the value of honesty itself belongs to A. This value exists independently of whether B makes use of it, sees it, recognizes it, indeed whether or not he understands it.

3. Moral values and disvalues accrue only to such acts, attitudes, and dispositions that have to do with persons in addition to things. They are thus tied not only to persons as subjects and as bearers of value, but also to persons as objects; as, accordingly, all actions that can be morally evaluated are "actions on persons," or more accurately: all control exercised over things with reference to the persons affected by them. The objection that one can treat animals lovingly or heartlessly changes nothing. For in that objection the opinion obviously functions that creatures other than man possess a certain degree of personhood.

More important than these basic essential facts is the relationship that governs goods values and moral values. This relationship is not exhausted in the distinctions and contrasts we noted above; similarly it is not exhausted by the appearance, just noted (in point 2), of the goods-value that is tied to them. This is rather a salient positive essential relationship, one that is constitutive of the moral values themselves. We can express it in the following formula: all moral values are founded upon goods values, and, moreover, every moral value has a specific kind of goods-value as its presupposition. Nonetheless, their own peculiar nature is entirely autonomous with respect to the goods values that found them.

One may call this the law of foundation of moral values. It still demands a justification. The first part of the law is easy to (337) establish. In what way does the action of the honest man differ from that of the thief with respect to the unprotected property of others? In this way: the first man respects the possessions of others, while the second man does not. But the presupposition here is that the objects possessed by another have a value, specifically a goods-value, for which one may desire them. If this is lacking, the urge to steal them is lacking also, and the behavior of the honest man is in no way different from that of the thief. The moral values, and likewise the moral disvalues, are thus conditioned by the goods-value, that is, they are founded upon it.

The situation is the same when I do a favor for someone, or please him: the favor or the pleasure signifies a goods-value for the other person. Usually that value has the form of a situation-value; for example, when I help someone or give him a present. The intended value does not lie in the value of the object alone, but lies rather in the fact that it benefits the person – it lies in a typical situational value. The conditional relation extends no further than the goods-value. The latter must be present and must lie at the foundation of the moral value, but otherwise the moral value is independent.

This fact touches the second part of the law of foundation. It may be summarized in three theses:

1. The moral value that is "founded" upon the goods-value does not contain the latter as a component (as an element of value) in itself. Otherwise expressed: The founding value does not recur in the founded one. The goods-value of some desirable object is not contained in the value of honesty, for that value belongs to the person of the honest man, and he cannot be desirable in the same way as the object. The moral value is thus autonomous with respect to its content.

2. The height of the moral value is independent of the height of the founded goods-value. The example of the "copper coins of the widow"[104] shows precisely why that is so. The highest moral value – the greatest capacity for sacrifice – can rise upon the slightest goods-value, and the reverse is also true – the greatness of the sacrifice is not identical to the magnitude of the goods-value.

3. The realization of moral values is independent of the realization of the goods-value (provided that one comes into question at all). More accurately: Independent of the realization of the situational value.[105]

A special explanation is required for the third thesis. When I want to give pleasure to someone and surprise him with something, but fully miss the mark, that is, I instead do something that is quite at odds with him, the situation is as follows: what I had intended (the pleasure that I wished to give him) does not occur, but the will, the purpose, the intention, is and remains morally valuable – just provided that it was genuine. (338)

This last point nonetheless implies that I had willed in earnest and not just wished. What matters is the real intention, the engagement. The result, in contrast, can turn out differently. To be "affectionate" as one readies a pleasure is entirely a matter only of the purpose, the disposition. The moral value can be completely realized by just that, without the intended situational value being realized successfully.

The outcome is that the entire dependency of the moral value in the foundation-relation is limited to the bare existence of the goods-value in the intention;

---

104 [Translator's note:] A reference to a figure in the gospels. In Luke 21: 2–4 we read, "He [Jesus] also saw a poor widow put in two very small copper coins. 'Truly I tell you,' he said, 'this poor widow has put in more than all the others. All these people gave their gifts out of their wealth; but she out of her poverty put in all she had to live on'" (*The Holy Bible. New International Version.* Grand Rapids: Zondervan 1986).

105 A closer study of these three theses is given in *Ethik*, 3rd edition, 1949, Chap. 60e [English edition: *Ethics*, George Allen & Unwin 1932, Vol. 2, Chap. 35].

but again the content of the moral value is determined neither by it, nor by its degree of value, nor by its realization.

d) Intended value and the value of the intention

This result is very strange. It carries with it a string of consequences that extend at first only to ethics, but later also touches aesthetics. To obtain an overview of these consequences is not easy, but for its sake we will have to treat of the first of these consequences, although they have nothing to do with aesthetics directly.

The foundation-relation demonstrated that in every ethical intention or action two quite different values are involved, a goods-value and an ethical value, and furthermore they stand in a definite relation of dependency. These two values apparently never coincide. But that, too, is only half true, and the other half lies in a second law.

In every action, in every act of will, in every ethical situation, the moral value or disvalue does not lie in the direction of the intention, i.e., it is not an intended value, not the aim of the action, but it appears first on the intention as its bearer, and is thus its value, the value of the intention. This law, Scheler's law, can be enunciated as follows: the aim of the action is not moral value, but rather the goods-value, or, more accurately the situational value. The moral value appears "on the back of the act." In this relation the intended value is the "founding" value, the value of the intention is the "founded" one. And since the latter is the moral value, this agrees exactly with the law of the foundation-relation.

The justification of this law is simple, but it does not coincide with the three forms of independence of the foundation-relation; it has a purely ethical character. A man who wants to give pleasure to someone does not act in order to be affectionate – to see himself crowned, as it were, with this value-predicate, but solely to give pleasure to the other person, perhaps to benefit him with the gift. He does not think of himself, but of the other, and desires also nothing for himself; and he is affectionate precisely insofar as he thinks of the other. If he thinks privately in some way of himself – whether on his advantage or on the way he poses himself morally – then his action is no longer affectionate. (339)

If a person acts for the sake of his own virtue, he normally does not achieve it. Virtue belongs to him who possesses the right intentions. To do so is to be oriented toward the situational value (the right kind, of course). A direct intention to realize the moral value will rather in fact destroy [*zerstören*] it, because the intention that has tied itself to moral action becomes disrupted [*gestört*]; in extreme cases it leads to the agent seeing himself reflected in a mirror, and to pharisaism. No doubt we should not carry this idea to extremes. For the direct intention of a moral value is not impossible in principle.

One can easily see one's way to this idea. Moral values are directly intended in all attempts at moral education. Whether education in morals can extend itself to all moral values is an entirely different question. Courage, love, the capacity for self-sacrifice are difficult to teach; hard work, constancy, love of order, self-control and discipline may, to a great extent, surely be attained pedagogically, and, within certain limits, surely also trustworthiness, fidelity, a sense of justice, etc. Thus, the number of moral values that may be directly intended is not small. The same is true even for all kinds of self-discipline, which may be done by an adult. It is true also for every kind of self-criticism, repentance, self-reflection, conversion, and for all kinds of conscious "discipleship." A man "wills" to become like his model.

Nonetheless we must also consider one more thing: the law is in force as long as the moral value that is striven after is not – or not completely – identical with the moral value of this striving. The teacher, perhaps, trains his pupil out of his awareness of duty, out of love, or out of some philosophical devotion to the people and the state. Those are not the same moral values that he seeks to create in his pupil – perhaps constancy, the love of order, etc. Here, too, the value of the intention is different from the intended value. And the same thing holds, to a great extent, for self-discipline.

At this phase of the discussion, all of that is not a mere digression. Rather, it shows how deeply the heterogeneous classes of values are tied to each other. And that is also essential to the problem of aesthetic value. For they, too, do not just float in the air, but are tied to other classes of values in a strangely tight and peculiar way.

One final point about moral values should therefore be mentioned. Although it does not lie in the nature of ethical behavior to be intended [*intendiert*], it is yet always intentional [*intendierend*] or purposive – morality is, after all, a collection of commandments that prescribe where our intentions should be directed. But then three questions remain to be answered:

1. What moral values can be commanded?
2. Which can be striven after in a meaningful way?
3. Which can be realized through striving after them?

The answers cannot be given summarily. Rather, they are differentiated according to individual values and groups of values. That means that already at this point no lawfulness within the realm of values is available to us; we are left empty-handed. (340)

To 1: Apparently only those of the values listed above that were teachable can be commanded – i.e., they are capable of taking the form of ought-to-do – such as hard work, constancy, orderliness, to a great extent also self-discipline, self-governance, and even honesty. Values that cannot be taught may be love, trust, etc.

To 2: Most of the moral values can in principle be striven after, but there is a danger in striving after them directly. The ethos can in such cases turn into its contrary, and they should not in general be striven after. What is really not attainable through effort is the value of individuality. That value must be realized by itself if it is to be realized at all in life. Whoever strives after it as a goal is always in danger of failing to reach it. It is more likely that other men will lead him to it. There are parallels in such cases in the domain of the goods values: for example, happiness can be striven after, but cannot be realized in striving. Whoever strives for happiness destroys his chances for it almost necessarily.

To 3: With the exception of purity of heart, almost all moral values can be achieved; purity of heart, or innocence, is not in any case to be realized in acts of striving after it. One can only lose it, but not recover it. The same holds for a few goods values of great magnitude: youth, beauty, and unaffectedness.

e) The metaphysical problem of value

We must state with complete clarity that in all these reflections we have taken pains to abstract from the metaphysical problem of value. This problem consists in the question of the nature of the being of values, of the meaning and the origin of their validity, and their absoluteness or relativity. This is not to say that these are not important questions, but they are just not decisive for the context of the questions we were discussing; they are indifferent to it.

The questions of being and validity are, for the lower classes of values, unambiguously rooted in the conditions of real being. A "good" is a thing that benefits a creature or a man, and an "evil" is what is detrimental or threatening to him. These are clear, objective conditions; man, whom they surround on all sides, is not able to change any of them. True, some goods can become evils if circumstances change, and vice versa. This claim appears to be relativism, but it is not. For when an entire set of its conditions has changed, a thing is not the same thing. This is true even more for situations. All things in life depend ontically on all others, and the single object is, what it is, not for itself.

This is the case with the goods values. Nothing like pure utility "for" a subject lies at its foundation. It makes no difference whether the utility is aimed at achieving something or not; it is the former in those few cases in which conscious activity stands behind it; the latter is the more usual, the accidental expediency – as in the way the seeds of certain grasses are not invented for man, but, when he grasps their nutritional property, they became for him one of the greatest "goods." (341)

The question of the being of the values of enjoyment is just as harmless. These lay in no way a claim to objectivity; in their subjective sphere, however, as pure values of feeling, they are sovereign and not subject to any relativity. For here any kind of relatedness can be only to the real stimuli of enjoyment and distaste; and the degree of pleasantness and unpleasantness varies considerably with the condition or disposition of the subject that experiences them. This relativity – that in the external relation – is immediately obvious; it in no way endangers the peculiar quality of the value of pleasure, or its autonomy and independence.

Even in the case of the vital values the question of being raises no difficulties. That such things as health, strength, elasticity, quick and sure reflexes, or firm and secure instincts have great value for the life of creatures, is as simple a condition of being and purposefulness as that of the goods values, and it requires, like the latter, no further demonstration. Taken strictly, these properties are nothing other than the inner natural goods of creatures. We could also count them among the goods values. At least we see from this how entire classes of values can pass into one another without sharp boundaries between them.

A genuine metaphysical problem appears only when one asks what it is that makes life itself valuable – so valuable that it is impossible to deny it, but to the contrary, all other existing things in the world are divided into goods and evils by reference to life. A thing that is valuable in that way is an intrinsic value. But intrinsic value can no longer be derived from ontic conditions; also not from considerations of utility. Intrinsic values cannot be derived from any others. And if they are truly intrinsic, then they are absolute.

Now there has been a lot of guesswork about this matter. The simplest seems to be a teleological justification: an upward-ranging foundation is given to life-values, such that one founds the life-values on the spiritual or intellectual ones, so in fact upon the intellectual life itself. But it is not very satisfying for ontology that life exists only "for the sake of mind," for life is there a thousandfold without mind, and it is entirely independent of mind.

For questions of this kind there are no further phenomena from which an answer could be derived. The truth is: we have no other argument for the value of life, we have no other evidence for it except our feeling of value, which affirms life unambiguously, while it denies death and destruction.

That is a fact that one may interpret subjectively just as well as objectively. Subjectively, because we are living beings, and all that is alive has an essential tendency toward self-affirmation; objectively, because living beings constitute the higher stratum of being as opposed to the stratum of the non-living, and it is also quite conceivable that the height of the value carried by some ontic entity keeps in step with the "height" that belongs to that entity.

But such attempts at interpretation are child's play in comparison to the bottomless difficulties which one encounters with moral values as soon as one asks the question about their ontological status and their validity. For here it is (342) no longer a question of the values that arise out of ontic contexts and are apparently the reverse side of them, but rather of those that posit themselves over against being and assert an Ought, and make demands that require absolute compliance by men, but which cannot be traced back to anything else.

And here, too, we have nothing but our feeling for values to stand upon. Yet the feeling of value does not speak under all conditions; it stirs itself only when it is awakened, when the maturity of men reaches the domain of values. It bears a different witness in youth and in maturity, in various peoples and milieux, but especially in different historical epochs. The relativity of this, our sole reliable witness to values, seems in the end to transfer itself to the existence and validity of ethical values and make these fluctuate. This assessment appears to be given justification by the plurality of "moral systems."

Here we find the metaphysical problem of value in all its earnestness, for the ethos of men stands and falls with the super-historical validity of moral values. Up to now, one solution has been found that goes only so far as to claim that a fluctuation in the feeling of values does not need to imply a fluctuation in the values themselves; all the more if it manifests these alterations only in the direction of the negative side. For the feeling of values never assets contradictions; it never disowns values that were once recognized by it, even in other epochs; and it never stamps a value as a disvalue – in that respect, Nietzsche's doctrine of the "transvaluation of all values" rested on a misunderstanding – but rather the feeling of values can "err," can turn itself off or become a dull instrument in certain cases or, as the phrase has it, it becomes blind to value. That explains abundantly the historical relativity. For apparently different times and nations are blind to certain areas of the realm of values, and are only "clear-sighted" when judging just a few of them.

The affirmative aspect of the problem, i.e., the ontological status of the ethical values themselves and their "validity," which is conditioned in more ways than temporally – insofar as validity must mean something other than merely being acknowledged – has not been made clear in this way. Here the metaphysical problem of value is left entirely without a solution.

Chapter 28: The Place of Beauty in the Realm of Values

a) An attempt to trace the problem

The essence of aesthetic values is, in many respects, easier to determine than the ethical ones. Most importantly, the pressure of the metaphysical element ceases for it. Not that its essence is without background elements and full of puzzles that contain many metaphysical (irresolvable) problems, but these are not pressing here, because the aesthetical (343) values do not make demands and they give no orders, and no controversies are created by its claim to autonomy.

Aesthetic value has the reverse relationship to man: it gives him a gift, it flies to him, and shows itself thereby to be a "good," no doubt such a peculiar one that we cannot simply subsume it under the heading of goods. However, even though it makes demands of the artist, once he beholds it, which are wide-ranging and can even take on the dimension of destiny, these demands are still not moral ones, and the artist is entirely free to choose other tasks for himself.

One-sided aesthetical theories – usually such that have been shaped by the poetic arts and their history – have attempted to trace as a matter of principle aesthetic values back to ethical ones. They rely ever and again on the idea that we are representing the human, and, indeed, the moral element in humankind (broadly understood) for the most part, and only that work is satisfying, in which the element of ethical value is handled properly. This must not be understood narrowly: in the drama and the novel, the good need not "win out" in the end, but its destruction must be represented in such manner that our sympathies are on the side of the good. Otherwise, the poet will fail also to create the effect of the "beautiful," and instead cause repugnance.

In our times, this conception has returned repeatedly, although it is usually hidden beneath an outward rejection of it. It holds on tenaciously because the argument just given for it is quite valid (sympathies must be on the side of the "good"). One does not notice, however, that the thesis has not been demonstrated. It may no doubt be very true that there is here a necessary condition for the occurrence of aesthetic value in literature, yet without this one condition being sufficient for its occurrence. To speak concretely: without sympathy for the morally right side, there would be no beauty in the literary work, but also none with that sympathy alone. Quite other qualities are needed in the literary bestowal of form for the achievement of that end, for which the correct moral feeling of values is only a presupposition.

Of course it is possible to argue more rigorously against such confounding of values and their "tracing" to other values. It is intended to be applied only to the very cases that most speak for such a reduction to ethical values. Further reflections lead us beyond, especially toward the reflection that there are, after all, other arts than literature and other beauties than in the arts. There are beauties that do not attach themselves to man, and just for that reason cannot be traced to moral values. For aesthetic values can attach themselves to all things that exist, but ethical values can attach themselves only to man. Or, when we look upon a beautiful oak tree, an old elk, the bank along a woodland creek, or a starry sky, must we behold a "hidden humanity" in them in order to see their beauty?

Here we quickly reach absurdity. And with that, the thesis is done with – without yet having to call upon the heavy armor of the non-representational arts. But we must observe that the relation of at least some aesthetical (344) values to the moral values is not thereby disposed of. But this relation is of a quite different kind.

In this context, we must again be warned about the Hegelian system of aesthetics. Although it correctly assesses the "appearing [*Scheinen*] of the idea," provided that it is a question of appearance, in its development the emphasis nonetheless falls back upon the idea, specifically upon the content of the idea. And if one looks more closely, one will find that this content is almost entirely of a moral kind. This leads us to the thesis that the aesthetical-literary values must be traced back to the ethical ones.

The thesis of Cohen's[106] aesthetics is better in many ways: "Nature and morals are degraded so as to become material for the arts."[107] In this idea is contained the conditions presupposed in both sides, without granting to the values on either side a superior position. Perhaps it was only because of the obstinate rejection of the concept of value by neo-Kantianism that the proper understanding of the fundamental situation, which had almost been attained, was delayed for so long.

The main thing in all of this is and remains: aesthetic value is not an act-value, but an object-value, while moral value is essentially that of an act. If within an aesthetic object certain acts also belong to the bearers of the aesthetic value, as with all levels of the drama, still the act is only a part of a whole, and its moral value or disvalue is not its aesthetic value or disvalue.

To conclude: not what is inner and psychic in man is as such beautiful, but purely its sensible appearances as something visible, or as visible to the mind (the latter is especially true for poetry). The same is true for a living face: its "beauty" lies in a certain play of lines or the rhythm of its movement, not because moral values of an inward kind peer out, or because an excellence of soul expresses

---

106 [Translator's note:] Hermann Cohen (1848–1918).
107 [Translator's note:] Translation E.K.

itself in them, but simply because a concealed inward life that has been given form appears within them, upon which both moral value and disvalue depend.

A common conception concerns the reduction of aesthetic values to expediency for some end. This idea does not derive from Kant. Kant drew it only into the transcendental realm, where he considered expediency "for" some subject, whereas traditionally the ontic purposefulness of a thing was thought to be in the thing itself. Tradition understood the latter as the perfection of nature – behind which, according to the generally dominant opinion, genuine, real purposive activity had to function. Naturally, they were thinking primarily of living creatures, and, among these, again of man. This inner teleology of creatures lay at the root of the *Monadology*, and with that, the idea was taken over by Kant from Leibniz (through M. Knutzen[108] and others).

At this point, the *Critique of the Power of Judgment*, belatedly but effectively, tried to put things in order. Only in that way can the connection between "aesthetical" and "teleological" judgment be understood: we cannot assume, just from the miraculous craftsmanship of animal (345) organisms, any purposes that constitute them, and even less can we assume purposiveness for the objects that we call "beautiful," which have, but only for us, the wonderful property of being able to force from us an enjoyment that requires of us no practical interest!

This idea has been subject to such rigorous critical analysis that one cannot add any objection against it. Whether Kant's further explanation by means of the "play of the imagination and the understanding" is correct, is another question. But it changes nothing regarding the principal thought.

It should not be concealed that this fundamental thought about the nature of beauty tells us very little. In fact, the role of purposefulness in the beholding and the enjoyment of the subject is self-evident. For it means that if no real determining aim lies behind it, then nothing else than what the phenomenon tells of itself is there: the object is so constituted that it captures the act of beholding it and calls forth that peculiar pleasure that is free from all other interests.

This peculiar condition of the aesthetical problem of value now becomes clear: even today we must, after careful analysis, agree with Kant's basic thesis, but we cannot conceal that hardly anything is achieved by it for the real problem of beauty. It does not help us to know that no superhuman understanding pursues its purposes along with us, all the more as in the arts the creative man quite surely acts to achieve purposes.

What will take the place of what was once believed to be the providential powers of nature, what kind of power governs nature's multiplicity and creates

---

108 [Translator's note:] Martin Knutzen (1713–1751).

the clear unities in natural beauty? We shall not learn that by means of this merely critical philosophy.

b) Uselessness of beauty and luxury in life

Among Kant's doctrines, one that is of use in the analysis of the value of beauty, is that of the disinterestedness of enjoyment. The only indications we have of the specific nature of some value are the kinds of acts in which we respond to it evaluatively, and we must gather the former from the latter. This is the way things stand. With the idea of disinterest, Kant identified a peculiar character of the act: peculiar character of the value must correspond to it. What is this character?

If we reflect that "interest" refers here to every kid of usefulness or usability for both practical and theoretical ends, then it becomes clear that to such disinterested enjoyment all goods values and all instrumental values for some ends, that is, all expediency, are denied entry.

The value of beauty is accordingly definable as that of something "purposeless" i.e., literally something "not there for the sake of an end" – and as the value of something "useless," or, to name it more precisely, of something "useless in itself." This last phrase is taken from Nietzsche, who used it for his "radiant" virtue [Cf. *Ethik*, Chap. 56].[109] His definition of this virtue applies precisely here. He compares it in a simile (346) to gold: it is "uncommon," it is "luminous," it has a mild luster, and "always bestows itself."[110]

All of that is characteristic of genuine aesthetic value, especially the "bestowing itself." Aesthetic value is without use for practical life; it stands there as something "beyond need," that is, necessary for nothing. If it causes joy and gives a certain luster to life, then that is something important, and perhaps it bestows meaning upon all of life, but still it is something "useless." The last term is understood literally: something useful for nothing else. For it lies in the nature of absolute intrinsic value that it serves nothing else at all. Otherwise it would not

---

109 [Translator's note:] In the Coit translation of Hartmann's *Ethik* (*Ethics*, George Allen & Unwin 1932), "radiant virtue" is used to render Hartmann's "die schenkende Tugend." – which is usually translated as "bestowing virtue." I have kept the phrase for the sake of uniformity. It is, in a way, the virtue or the gift of giving (schenken) wisdom: The gift of those who, usually as great teachers (e.g., Schopenhauer), give to others the force of their personality, one gifted with wisdom, and are thereby able to impart wisdom to others.

110 [Translator's note:] Nietzsche, Friedrich, *Thus Spoke Zarathustra: A Book for Everyone and Nobody*, translated and edited by Graham Parkes, Oxford and New York: Oxford University Press 2005, First Part, "On the Bestowing Virtue," p. 65.

be intrinsically valuable. For that reason, other things can very much serve it, and perhaps everything else.

When seen in this way, disinterestedness refers to nothing but the absolute intrinsic value of beauty, traceable or reducible to nothing further. That is simply a validation of what one silently assumes when one turns to aesthetics. Nothing new is thereby said. For that reason also, no genuine positive characterization of the fundamental aesthetic value is contained in it. Even from the encounter with Kant we emerge with empty hands. His analysis is formal and critical and it thereby points out a way; but it leads to no tangible goal.

Moreover, this negative characterization of aesthetic value is not without danger. People have understood it to mean that beauty, and with that, all of the arts, are a luxury in human life. From there, it is easy to interpret the situation such that all artistic life, along with its creations, is simply superfluous, that is, no longer in keeping with the suffering or the seriousness or the struggle of life. Then too, the aspect of "play" in the arts has this aftertaste of the superfluous and the frivolous.

In the face of this, we must stand guard: "uselessness" is not superfluity; precisely the highest things are useless *because* they are the highest. Anything that imparts meaning is in this sense "useless," even the intrinsic moral values, the highest more than all others. Thus the world is built up from the bottom. Life is not useful for lifeless nature, mind is not useful for organic life; but both, when they first come into existence, bring sense and significance into the world.

So beauty too stands before us in its peculiar value-character. It is useful neither to the life of the organism nor of the mind, though the latter finds in it a mountain-peak that radiates across its entire horizon. And, again, just for that reason the greatest achievements in the world of the mind can derive from beauty. For such things is the word "useful" much too puny. For it is a question of the giving of meaning. It is also insufficient to bring in the ideal of a certain "cultural function" (for example, in education) of beauty, as when one wishes to resist this idea of uselessness. There is something much greater going on here.

These analyses define the external aspect of aesthetic value. The uselessness – the "luxury of life" – corresponds exactly to the extraction and liberation of the entity that carries the value from all the conditions of life, to its isolation from them, its extraction from life, and to the phenomenon of the frame. (347) However, the meaning given in the self-value, which again benefits real life, corresponds to the deeper ties to life found in the creativity of the artist and in the acts of beholding and enjoying; it corresponds also to the fact that precisely the highest of its effects, those that have been most entirely liberated from the real world, are those that derive from the most potent and stormy elements of the life of the mind.

From the standpoint of our investigations in Part One, these are things that seem to be only its consequences. Nonetheless, one can ask: what do these consequences consist in? They lie in the following considerations: the beautiful object showed itself in Part One as a thing constructed in strata, where only the first stratum, the foreground, is real; all other strata are mere appearance. The quality of being beautiful depends neither on the foreground alone, nor on the background strata alone, thus neither on the real or the unreal alone, but in the peculiar interrelation of both, that is, on the appearance-relation as such. These theses are recapitulated here; they constitute the major thesis of the doctrine of the aesthetic object.

What conclusions may be drawn concerning the nature of the value of beauty and of the position of aesthetic value in the entire realm of values? The following: aesthetic value is not the value of something absolutely real or an existing thing in itself, as is the case for goods values, vital values, and moral values, but rather the value of something that lies only in appearance, thus a value that exists merely for us – one could also say: the value of something that exists merely as an object as such. Now that is again the simple consequence of what had been said earlier. But the formulation is so terse, and so central in its importance, that we must analyze its nature in detail. For what it asserts is something unique in the realm of value.

For all other classes of values, the realization of values is itself valuable, but for the aesthetic values that is not so; aesthetic values are not realized at all. For the object to which they are attached as their bearers are not real objects, but rather possess a mixed ontology. Only the foreground is real, but that is the least thing about it; all else – the entire series of strata reaching inward – is and remains unreal. But the value does not depend on this background at all, but only on appearance itself.

Thus the most extreme contrast lies in the nature of this value, compared to the value of something useful, or something good, of life and life-functions, of human actions and dispositions: everywhere the reality of the bearer of value is the main thing, and everywhere the value gives rise to propensities and acts that aim at its realization. This holds even for the value of truth. It is otherwise only for aesthetic value: It is and remains the value of an appearance.

The situation is no different even where the limits of the appearance-relation proper are found, i.e., in the external strata of the non-representational arts and in ornament. These limits do not suggest that (348) appearance entirely stops at them, but only that here there is no longer an appearance of a different kind of content. The expression "pure play with form" alone testifies to that.

The "play" is in contrast to earnestness (of practical life); it is not a genuine concern for reality, but for the unfolding of sovereign form in a material that holds this form fast. Reality is of secondary importance, and it extends only so far as the material does. Play is entirely a "luxury in life," even if it is also lovely and able to bestow meaning; it is a thing that is "useless" in itself. This is true particularly for pure aesthetical play with forms – that is, where it is not like vital forces that want to exercise, stretch, and unfold themselves. This "play" is therefore originally related ontologically to the appearance-relation.

c) The founding of aesthetic values upon moral values

What one is unable to determine directly in itself can be determined out of its connection to better-known phenomena that lie upon its borders. This is true for the aesthetic values, to a great extent, and particularly for its basic value, beauty. With it, as also for the moral values, there is, in addition to such roundabout methods, the appeal to value feeling. Thus we will study the relation of aesthetic value to moral and to vital value; and, in certain domains of the beautiful, to the values of goods and of pleasure.

Here we come upon a phenomenon that we would not have expected a priori: the foundation-relation again appears. We made an acquaintance with this relation in our study of the moral values. There it existed generally between them and the value-goods, and also among the situational values; its presence was rooted in the fact that in moral agency the value of the intention is never identical to the intended value, but rather "appears upon the back of the intention" (Cf. Chaps. 27c and d).

Obviously, this relation cannot appear here in the same form. There is no question in this case of a comparable intentional agency. The founding must therefore be of a quite different kind. Let us say just this much in advance: if it is true that nature and morality become material for the arts, then it must also be true that the values contained in the natural and in the human moral world become "material" there also. That is directly related to the problem of the independence of aesthetic value, which was our point of departure.

Let us recall that the error that suggests itself here consists in the false substitution of moral values for aesthetical ones. That happens everywhere that an art form takes as its material humankind along with its entire moral life. When in an epic poem the hero is represented in the radiance of his high-minded nobility, the reader almost necessarily falls victim to the illusion that this moral value of the hero is the artistic value of the poem. That is in drama everywhere the case, especially in (349) tragedy, where sympathy for the heroic man is intensified considerably by his downfall.

Here it is clearly a matter of a fundamental relation between aesthetical and ethical values. The illusion to which we have referred comes down to the identification of those classes of values. Yet that cannot be the case, for the same literary art forms also represent just as much the low, shadowy sides of moral life – otherwise they would not be true-to-life – especially the novel; and yet their artistic value does not suffer as a result.

What, then, is the genuine fundamental relation of the two classes of values? Let us stay with the drama. The aesthetic values of primary concern here are those of the dramatization itself, the liveliness of the production, the sculptural quality of the conflict and tension. Beyond those lie the intensification and resolution of the plot, the portrayal of human kindness, of heroism and tragedy, etc. Now if we ask ourselves: what do the moral values and disvalues that are proper to the material and that have been worked into it in the process of bestowing form upon it, contribute to the appearances of those aesthetic values?

Our answer must be: they are its presuppositions. The dramatic tension proper can be felt, if at all, only by the man who, with his sense of moral values, "stands on the side of rightness," who feels sympathetically "with" the excellent, brave, and high-minded characters, and also "against" the envious and malicious ones. If an audience member is in any way insensitive, immature, or blind to these moral values and disvalues, he will fail to see perhaps not only the moral of the story, but the dramatic situation itself, the tension, the tying together of the plot and, in consequence, the peripety or Aristotelian turning-point, in short, everything out of which the peculiar aesthetic value of the dramatization is made. He does not understand what is going on upon the stage; he cannot appreciate the artistic achievement of the actors, he lacks the key to everything. That is the simple meaning of the conditionality of an aesthetic value upon the moral values.

This conditionality is obviously related to the foundation-relation. As in a human ethos, moral value can "raise itself" [*sich erheben*] only "over" a goods-value as its basis, so too in this case can aesthetic value "rise" only "over" certain moral values – specifically, where these are felt and responded to in the correct way.

Now this relation is without doubt a much more general one.

First, it extends to all literature, and by no means simply to the drama. In the epic, in the novel, in lyric poetry the situation is the same, for everywhere aspects of moral value are at least worked into the material and are present there.

Second, it extends to the fine arts, at least in so far as some of them represent men and human conditions – for example, in sculpture the dying gladiator, in painting the character study. (350)

Third, it extends even to the non-representational arts, provided that psychic life appears in its inner strata: this occurs of course in an indeterminate manner that depends upon the entire tonality of the work.

Fourth, one can find the same relation again in human beauty, just where we meet it in life: for here too the moral assets and liabilities, which appear in the external features, must be at the very least be correctly felt and responded to by some observer in order that he correctly assess the beautiful and the ugly in its total appearance.

In this sense, therefore, moral values are a condition of aesthetical ones. But is that in fact a foundation-relation? To that question belongs, as we saw above, the independence of the founded values, their axiological autonomy – just as the moral values retain that quality over against the goods values. The dependence can in fact lie only in the presence of the founding values: thus, in this case, in the correct moral feelings of the observing subject.

Is that really so? This question can be affirmed unconditionally. And we can demonstrate, by analogy with the foundation-relation of the ethical values to the aesthetical, the three characteristic forms of independence.

1. Moral values do not reappear in the aesthetic value that has risen over it, neither as a nuance of valuation within it nor as a component of its value. That it constitutes the value-foundation for the aesthetic value refers to something else. The dramatic value of a scene is not composed of the moral values of the individual characters taken together; rather they are only its presupposition. Dramatic value is also achieved where the characters are markedly lacking in moral value (Macbeth's scenes, Mephisto and the schoolboy [in *Faust* I]).

2. The height of the aesthetic value is independent of the height of the founding moral value; the same is true for the importance of the moral disvalues. This is proved by the fact that from a group of insignificant and vulgar characters presented by a writer very interesting and highly significant dramatic situations can emerge. The older dramatists did not entirely grasp that; they required characters from elevated social milieux, kings and lords. Only the modern drama has descended to the bourgeois classes. In [Ibsen's] *The Wild Duck,* there is not a single important person.

3. The occurrence – we cannot use the term "realization" here – of aesthetic value is also entirely dependent upon the achievement of the founding moral value. This is well known: otherwise, there could be neither a tragedy nor a genuine comedy. For in the first the hero, and with him the righteousness for which we whole-heartedly side with him, is defeated, and the wicked triumph; but in comedy the character with high moral aims descends to pettiness and futility, and some annoying subordinate succeeds. In both cases the (351) aesthetic value, i.e., the dramatic, theatrical, tragic, and comical value, rises above the moral ones – floating over them, as it were –. That aesthetic value does not depend upon the "victory of goodness" – that is, upon its

"realization" in the content of the play's plot, but upon quite different conditions: upon the artistic bestowal of plastic form upon the characters and scenes, upon the structure of the whole and upon the concreteness of what appears from stratum to stratum.

What then is left over as the element of dependence in the way aesthetic values are founded in moral ones? Only this, that the ethical values and disvalues are present in the form bestowed upon the material; they come to their proper title, and are responded to by a correct feeling of value. This latter also has an analogy in the foundation-relation of the ethical values; for there, too, it is significant that goods are really felt along with their goods values, e.g., someone else's goods as things that are desirable.

It remains to be shown that the situation in literature is just the same in painting and in sculpture (as with the portrait or the gladiator); further, that the same could be shown for music and architecture, insofar as psychic life and an ethos speaks from within them. We may pass them by at this point, because the method of demonstration for them is everywhere the same as in literature. However, that demonstration turns out to be all the scantier and more formal, the more indefinite and general is the expression of humanity in those arts. As a practical matter, the demonstration of the situation in literature – where it is most tangible – is completely sufficient for its validity in the other arts.

d) The broadening of the foundation to include vital values

Up to now, the foundation-relation of the aesthetic values has been understood only as their foundation upon moral values. The question is whether that is sufficient, and whether other classes of values could be drawn into this relation. Before all else, we must inquire whether the vital values do not also play a founding role here; for "nature," too, and even more, living nature, are areas from which the representational arts draw their material. The values of goods and of pleasure may also be in play here, because, after all, they are touched upon through the "material." It is thus still a question of how far the foundation-relation reaches, and whether it remains the same throughout.

The founding role of the vital values is the easiest to see in the fine arts, as far as they represent the physical bodies of men or of animals, but the human body is of closest concern to us. There is a superabundance of elementary vital feelings, which speak out in an observer when he is placed before sculpted, drawn, or painted representations of the human body. A certain "empathy" actually dominates here – in the sense that one feels with inward immediacy the movement, the effort, the elasticity, the physical achievement, but also the state of rest, of release, of relaxation, and of the sense of well-being. Those are elements of the feeling of life that are tinged with values, with, specifically, those that are vital in nature. (352) This is true also for feeling sympathy with elements of disvalue, such as suffering, defeat, and failure.

The feelings tinged with sexuality belong here also; they accompany the sight of the human body. These need not be the same as sexual arousal, but that may on occasion happen. In innumerable cases the very most powerful and original vision of an artist was from the first accompanied by sexually charged emotions; only later did these achieve the purity of the aesthetical feeling for beauty. And just because in this case the two realms of value are so tightly woven together, such that the vital values first arouse aesthetical sensibility but then the artistic value decisively influences vital and sexual sensibility, it is appropriate to clarify the relation among the values that lie at their basis.

At this basis lies precisely a foundation-relation. Here aesthetic value is founded upon vital values, that is, the former is dependent upon the possession of the relevant vital qualities by the body represented by the artist and by the observer's ability to feel these qualities as they are by means of his own properly oriented sensitivity to values. If the observer has no sense of the strength and elasticity of the human extremities, then their beauty and plasticity will be a closed book to him, for they presuppose such acts of feeling. And if he also lacks a healthy sexuality, then the physical beauty of youthful bodies will be lost on him, for here, too, vital stimuli are the presupposition of its appreciation.

There exist theories boarding on the philistine that deny and in a certain sense scorn all intimations of sexuality, even everything erotic, in artistic vision. That is an exaggeration of a tendency that is justified in itself: naturally there cannot be an enjoyment of an artistic kind where sexual feeling dominates aggressively; for it is itself a vital feeling, and its elementary power displaces the finer and higher feelings of values. But if the observer is entirely without this natural vital feeling, aesthetic value is also closed off to him. He lacks the power of sensual arousal that leads us towards them, and he lacks an intuitive understanding for the deeper capacities and secrets of the body. We should emphasize that we are not at all speaking just of direct sexual desire for the opposite sex alone, rather for an emotional sensitivity to every sexual power, also to that of one's own sex.

For a more precise demonstration that this really is a foundation-relation, we must present those of the three forms of independencies that are in accord with those of dependency. These forms of independence are very easy to present, as soon as one has grasped correctly the kind of dependency that is involved here.

Clearly, the dependency is only one of being present: the vital value must be there, it must be given, just precisely in the sense that it is grasped and appreciated; without the correct feeling for it, formal beauty cannot be understood. The conditionality, however, is limited to this one point: in all others, the value of beauty is independent. (353)

1. It is independent with respect to content. The vital value does not return in the aesthetic value. In every respect this is the main point. The value of the vitality of the body does not return in its value as beautiful; the thought of its capacity for movement and control is entirely a simple presupposition of its beauty. Similarly for the value of the body's sexuality: it is excluded from the aesthetical feeling of beauty; it is, so to speak, allowed to return, but it is then clearly responded to as a different value that no longer extends to the aesthetical.

2. The independence of the height of a value is almost completely obvious. The artistic value depends on the representation and not on the material represented. The art of painting, especially, governs its material with entire freedom. Painterly values are effective much more in the play of light and color than in the material of the painting; they elevate even what is of little value to the luster of bright color and the enjoyment of seeing. But a trained eye for what is alive is, as always, its presupposition.

3. The value of beauty is also independent of the "realization" of the vital value. To show that, we need only point to the many scenes of crucifixions and martyrdom in painting. For with respect to their "material," we see in these genres the destruction of states of high vital value. In painting there is also an analogy to the tragic.

We see that this foundation-relation, here as elsewhere, is entirely complete; its characteristic elements all recur in aesthetics, as was first demonstrated in our study of the ethical values. For the theory of value this signifies the exhibition of a more universal law of value, about which the only question remaining to investigate is how far the law extends and how it is integrated into the still more universal stratification of values.

For aesthetics the consequences are not as large. Nevertheless their significance is considerable, when one realizes that up to now almost no doctrines have existed concerning the relation of aesthetic value to the lower classes of values. One must attempt here before all else to measure their consequences correctly. What we have said about those consequences is not exhaustive.

For by no means are the fine arts the only ones to be affected: vital values come always in play where the human and all-too-human are represented, especially in poetry. Everywhere that material contains a struggle with poverty, hunger, disease or other suffering. Where deep passions, instinctual envy, or a tender and shy awakening of love are brought onstage, the correct feeling of the affected vital values is the foundation of all other value feeling of a higher sort. Here the corresponding three kinds of independence can be demonstrated easily; for the relation is the same as in the fine arts.

We might go a step further and draw music into our discussion also. For we have no reason to assume that the dynamics of the human, which is articulated by the inner strata of music, concern only the purely psychic part of life; it could also touch at times (354) bodily states – from the external rhythm of the beat to the indefinable vital feeling of contentment, of urgency, of relaxation, etc.

e) Relation to the lower classes of values

If one has passed far downward to the realm of vital values, one cannot help but examine how the relation in question stands with respect to the still lower classes of value, those of goods and of the pleasant. For it could be that a foundation-relation is present there too – just for the reason alone that foundation depends always upon the "material," the material, however, only as far as it is taken from the sphere of human life, and is permeated entirely by those values. After all, the general field of perception in our everyday experience is already "pre-selected" by means of pleasure and pain.

It follows immediately from the fact that they found ethical values that goods values must also be foundational for aesthetic value; for since ethical values themselves have been shown to be foundational for some aesthetic values, the values of goods must also be indirectly foundational for them.

The drama and the novel depict situations in life within which characters act. Now action involves managing goods that have significance for persons. Thus only the man who grasps the goods values present in the scene with a correct feeling for their value will understand also a course of action correctly or correctly assess dramatically some human situation.

The same is true, *mutatis mutandis*, for the values of pleasure: to the understanding of a situation belongs the sensibility required to understand what is painful or sweet to the characters engaged in it, what they find attractive and what repulsive. All effort of will in life depends upon these elements of pleasure and pain; for that reason they must be correctly felt imitatively in their unique character as values and disvalues. Otherwise the situations will not be correctly understood, and also not the ways of acting, the characters, even their destinies. Out of the consistency of their "appearance" the beauty of literature is constituted. How can we appreciate a Dutch painting of a feast, if we have no sense of culinary values? Thus in the case of both the goods values and the pleasure values, we are dealing with a genuine founding of aesthetic values. So, at least,

382 — First Section: The Aesthetic Values

as far as we are concerned with the main positive point: the state of conditioning. It is important to see this conditioning by the values of pleasure clearly and within its limits, because aesthetic value also announces itself in the form of pleasure. We must distinguish the two.

It is not otherwise with the negative point, with the three forms of independence of the founded values. Since the difference in relative height of values is already quite considerable here, the presence of those forms is more apparent than in the case of the ethical values. (355)

1. It is immediately evident that neither the goods values nor the pleasure values recur as an element in the aesthetic values. That also follows directly from the fact that the situations are not real, but only apparent; but reality is essential for goods and for pleasure and pain; as merely imagined they may serve for the understanding of another's sensibility, but surely do not produce one's own.

2. One sees from the fact that the drama in human conflicts can easily be caused by insignificant events as well as by matters of life and death, and that the height of the value of some good or some state of pleasantness does not determine the "relative height" of an aesthetic value. The real mainspring of the conflict lies in the characters, in the passions of those involved in the situation, etc.

3. The realization of the goods values or of the values of pleasure has absolutely nothing to do with the "realization" of the aesthetic value. This is true if only because aesthetic values are not in fact realized at all, but are attached to appearance. Moreover, the destruction and loss of valuable goods and pleasures belong precisely to the meaning and aesthetic value of many elements in the plot and of various human fates. How the characters respond to the loss of them is essential to that meaning and value.

If we look back from this point, we will observe how the foundation-relation dominates the entire borderline separating the aesthetical from the other classes of values. Only the value of truth is omitted here, because in its case there exists a different and more complicated set of conditions, which we came to know earlier as "true-to-life" and "essential truth." These conditions, as far they extend, remind us of the foundation-relation too, because they play a role in conditioning aesthetic value.

The foundation-relation of the aesthetic values is distinguished essentially from that of the ethical values only in one point. The latter are continuously and necessarily founded upon goods values, and do not occur without such a foundation; in contrast, the aesthetic values are neither continuously nor necessarily founded upon vital values, goods values, or the values of pleasure, yes, not even necessarily upon any one of these classes of values.

These aesthetic values are founded upon those four classes only under specific conditions, namely when they are values of works of representational art. The law of foundation is thus valid only for literature, painting, and sculpture, but indirectly no doubt also for music (in its inner strata). It is difficult to find the law that functions in architecture, and it does not apply to ornamental art.

However, there is a point here at which beauty in art once more approaches beauty in places external to art. For apparently the foundation-relation plays a broad role in natural and in human beauty as it does in the representational arts.

This is easy to see. When at any point living nature takes on aesthetic value for us, the sense of the vital value is its natural precondition: the sense of power, suppleness, health, facility in movement, etc. This sense of vitality even passes almost (356) unnoticeably into the aesthetical sphere, but without the two becoming assimilated to each other. That is true also for our feeling of sexual values.

And this is as much true for the ethical values as for the goods values and the value of pleasure felt upon looking at a living human being: the sense of the drama of life, the comical, the tragic, etc., can accompany the events we experience only when our sense of human joys and sorrows has already been sufficiently developed and drawn out from the experience of life. To that belongs, however, a completely developed sense of the values of pleasure and the goods values to which the human heart is attuned; even more for ethical values, which are already elevated above the former.

The test of this by example is of a negative kind: the sharpness of vision for the corresponding disvalues – for displeasure, suffering, renunciation, unhappiness and moral weakness – allow the comical and tragic elements in real human life to flash out before us, indeed they first open us to the inadvertent dramas of life.

Chapter 29: Survey of the Value-Elements in Beauty

a) Values of the mere being of objects

When a person well versed in the arts turns to aesthetics with high expectations, he is disappointed when he learns that what we have said in the previous few chapters is almost everything that can be said about the nature of aesthetic values. Those chapters confirmed what was said at the outset: that aesthetics is a prosaic science, and in many respects a backward one – in great contrast to its rich and variegated subject matter, which it is unable to define exhaustively, given its current state. And here in this chapter also we will attempt only to draw a few conclusions from this fact.

All analysis of value is just feeling one's way into the proximity of the aesthetic values. We cannot grasp directly those values themselves in any other way than with value feeling, that is, in aesthetical beholding, enjoyment, and rapt contemplation. We "know" very well on the basis of this beholding that they are each unique, but we cannot express what their uniqueness consists in, at least not what constitutes their essence proper. For what we can describe are always mere individual traces in them, those of a relatively general character that are found in other instances: in a word, what is merely typical. But what is essential is in every case something unique and singular, that is, the genuine aesthetic value is individual; it is the value of one single object.

This is also true for the basic aesthetic value, the beautiful. Taken strictly, "the beautiful" does not exist in such generality. Rather, in the concept of the beautiful (which, naturally, one can and must shape as a generality) there exists only "something that is truly beautiful," that is, it characterizes what recurs, what can be held in common. It does not touch beauty itself. If one wanted to characterize (357) what beauty itself is, one would have to say it (1) with reference to the individual case – which would be too complicated, and one would have to say it (2) as the artist says it – not conceptually but as directed to our capacity for beholding and feeling – but then no concept would emerge. That is the basis and meaning of the irrationality of the beautiful and of aesthetic values in general.

One must not, therefore, demand the impossible of aesthetics. Just as we must renounce any attempt to produce an imposing metaphysics of beauty, so too we must renounce a description of its character as a value. All that we can do is limited to certain of its fundamental characteristics, which are in part derived from the analysis of the object and in part must be interpreted from their relation to other regions of value. One should not attempt to collect some of these particulars without a concern for the extent to which they may have appeared in the earlier chapters.

The first difficulty is related to the ontology of the bearers of these characteristics, for it is complex. The specific bearer of these values is neither the subject nor the act: that is, an emotional state, a state of the subject (beholding, desire, rapture), nor a being in itself external to the subject, for it is in itself what it is. Rather it is a third thing, one difficult to grasp and even more difficult to relate to the question of value. To speak concretely: it is neither enjoyment that is beautiful nor creativity (the "ability to make" art), but solely the object. Yet once again the object is not the thing, the man, the building as it is, but only as what it is for us. The result is as follows. Aesthetic values are not, as one might otherwise expect from its relation to pleasure, the values of an act, neither of beholding nor of creating. They are values only of the objects of these acts. For that reason, they are not the values of some thing that exists in itself, for a thing in itself does not need to be an object at all, it is above all being as object. The aesthetic object is not above all being as object, it does not exist in itself, but only as object of those definite acts of beholding and enjoying. Whatever is there apart from such acts is merely the real foreground, thing-like as other things are; nothing appears in it. Only to a beholding of a specific kind can the background appear; this belongs within the aesthetic object.

Consequently: an aesthetic value is the value of an object only as the object of these specific acts. The value is not tied to the naked being of the art object – as even the moral values are tied to the qualitative existence [*Sosein*] of man and his actions – but to these objects' "being-for-us" in contrast to their being in itself. That means: it depends on being an object for us. The object of knowledge is only *per accidens* an "object"; by nature, it is an entity, and becomes an object only by means of a knowing subject. The aesthetic object, in contrast, is essentially only an object; therefore, its values are the values of being an object as such, values of a mere "object-being" (the old sense of the *esse objectivum*). (358)

If one now recalls what the nature of this "essential object-being" is, we find it founded in the appearance-relation. If something appears in the foreground and then something else again from stratum to stratum, and what appears in its series of strata essentially constitutes the aesthetic object, then the value of the object must be a value of this appearing. It clearly does not suffice to call it "the value of the appearing thing" or even the value "of the appearing thing as an appearing thing." For it could still seem as though this were a question of the value of the "background" alone, without the foreground, which would contradict flatly the analysis of the object: only the background appears, stratum after stratum, but it could not appear without the foreground. Thus, the foreground belongs to the whole. And we must express the matter so: the aesthetic value is the value of appearing itself. With respect to content, it includes always foreground *and* background, and can be detached neither from the one nor the other. These are no longer new ideas; they were already the result of the analysis of the object. But only here, from the standpoint of the problem of value, can they be fully assessed.

b) The value of de-actualization

One easily recognizes once again in these matters the ontology of "de-actualization," of which we have often spoken. Clearly, the value of such things as aesthetic objects can only be a value of this process of making unreal. But we must understand it correctly; it may not be taken in the sense of the old doctrine of the "idea" or the "ideal." Let us recall in this context the Hegelian teaching.

Hegel meant by the ideal not an artistic (artificial) beautifying of natural objects, but "reality itself," understood, he thought, in a way that is more true and more profound than is possible under the conditions of quotidian life; "reality in its entire abundance of power and freedom." Accordingly, a character, for example, appears in life only as a "fragment," one bounded, limited, dependent upon a thousand trivialities; for that reason the heroes of heroic poetry had to be kings and lords, for only they are "entirely free." Opposite to their lives stands "common life," with its everyday miseries – that is, life "unpoetic and boring." Art must, he believed, lift everything into the ether of a distress-free existence.

This kind of de-actualization is not proposed here. It is not true in any case that this doctrine touches upon the genuinely "real" – that can be true only for Hegel's metaphysical concept of reality, which refers to the "realization of the idea" exclusively, and which in this context would be entirely tautological. Moreover, the elevation of all things "into the ether" means, in the end, an artificial beautification of them, if, perhaps, not a trivial one. In fact everything is lifted beyond the visible into a "shadow land of beauty," and there it is robbed of its power, simplified, made distinct, perhaps drawn with classical lines, but poor, lacking bright colors, weak and limp, in a word: lifeless. (359)

There is no question that much of the older poetry produced works like those. But are they worthy models, classics? Or did such poetry display the weakness of all initial tries? Was it the incapacity to reach into the real, full life of man? Certainly not always. We contemporaries have descended from this high pedestal into everyday life, into the lowlands, into the sphere of weakness and misery. And behold: life here is still richer, larger, and deeper.

The mystery of the situation is that one must "be able to see" this sphere of life, one must have an enlightened eye for it, must be able to penetrate it, to draw from it what is significant, what is always there. ... "And grip it where you will, it's gripping too."[111] We do not need to distance ourselves from what is real in the sense of an "ideal" when we look as an artist does, but only to distance ourselves in a different way. The question is only, In what way?

One grasps quickly the correct sense of de-actualization when one fixes one's eyes on the relation of power and impotence with respect to values, and compares

---

111 [Translator's note:] The passage referred to is the following: "Just reach into the wealth of human living! / Each lives it, those who know it are but few, / And grip it where you will, it's gripping too." Goethe, Johann Wolfgang von, *Faust. A Tragedy. Interpretive Notes, Contexts, Modern Criticism*, translated by Walter Arndt, ed. Cyrus Hamlin, A Norton Critical Edition, New York and London: Norton 2001, p. 6f. („Greif nur hinein ins volle Menschenleben, / Ein jeder lebt's, nicht vielen ist's bekannt / Wo du es packst, da ist's interessant." Goethe, *Faust*, „Vorspiel auf dem Theater," lines 167–69 spoken by a "lustige Person.").

them to the ethical values. To do this, one must recall some well-known features of ethics.

A clear sense of the Ought is tied to the moral values, but these values do not have of themselves the capacity to realize their own Ought-to-be. The real world does not measure itself according to them, for it has its own lawfulness, which it obeys, i.e., the lawful order of nature. The Ought demands something else, but it cannot realize what it demands by itself. Such is the impotence of the moral values. They are realized nonetheless, not by their own power, but by the power of man. For man is a real being, and only where a real being puts himself to work for them can these – purely ideal – demands be fulfilled, that is, become realized.

Ethical values thus have much less causal capacity than do natural laws. But insofar as they determine the will of a man – and they do that, when they become evident to him – their power to cause things to happen transcends the laws of nature; and, provided that happens, they are the stronger principles.

What does this point have to do with the aesthetic values? Aesthetic values are not made real at all, neither by their own power nor by the power of others. For the work of the artist is not for their realization, but only their appearance upon an appearance-relation. One may therefore say: aesthetic values are, in the real world, more impotent than the moral values.

That no longer seems amazing, once one has grasped that they are not the values of something real (being-in-itself), but only values of an object as object, or of an appearance as appearance. They cannot be realized at all; rather they remain the values of a "being-for-us." They exist, similar to the background of the beautiful object, only for a certain kind of looking -through. Aesthetic values are, to be sure, "banished into a real object," that is, they are fixed upon it. But that is not the same as realizing it. (360)

Nevertheless, there is a greater power, also, that corresponds to the greater impotence. For this impotence relates only to the real world; there, aesthetic values have not only nothing to "create" as do the ethical values, but also nothing to aim at. One may also not seek the domain of their power or influence in the real world. In their own sphere, in contrast, these values are anything but powerless. In that sphere, there is another standard of freedom. There are no obstacles here, no laws of nature opposed to them, and the creative person can shape things according to his own measure – and, where he "represents," he is bound only to care for the true-to-life, not, however, to the specific unique real conditions of possibility. Otherwise, he is free; what emerges from his efforts is a matter of his composition.

Moral values must set the dead weight of the real world in motion; their realization comes up everywhere against the resistance of the real. Aesthetic values come up against no resistance – unless against the "matter" in the real foreground of the objects – for they have no tendency to transform things that real. They merely allow something different to "appear" in them.

For these reasons, aesthetic values stand open before very different possibilities than those that may present themselves in the realm of the real: possibilities that are not tied to real conditions. Representation and appearance pass over without restraint the limits of what is possible in reality. Aesthetic values have, therefore, no resistance to overcome in their own sphere. Of course, there are laws in their sphere, but only their own, those of aesthetic values. There, they have no regulations limiting them, which they would have to overcome. Aesthetic values are thus not only autonomous within their sphere, but an autarchy, that is, they are all by themselves, are absolute, and have no gods seated next to them.

In this sense, they are values of what has been made unreal, de-realized, i.e., values of a kind of being that is far distant from real reality and with no pretensions to it. This "making unreal" rests upon a peculiar kind of freedom, in which the balance of possibility and necessity, as found in reality, has been suspended – but not to the benefit of necessity, as with the Ought, but to the benefit of possibility. Here we have a being-possible without a being-necessary, for it does not rest upon a closed chain of real conditions.[112]

For there, in the ethos, is the positive freedom of necessity (i.e., the detached necessity[113]), but here, in art, there is the freedom of the detached possibility, which is fundamentally without boundaries. Upon that freedom rests the power of art to let appear what is not. This is where the true role of "ideals" belongs. Naturally there are "ideas" which the genius first beholds inwardly, but he then gives them to humanity to guide its way. But he bestows them upon us not in a conceptual form, but intuitively, as a shape, living and pictorial. In that way, he convinces. (361)

c) Relativity and absoluteness

Let us touch upon the question of the extent to which aesthetic values are to count as "relative" and the extent to which they count as absolute. We refer not to the inner relativity, which is self-evident, where it is contained e.g., in the foundation-relation, but the external, historical relativity, as lies at the root of all talk about relativity. But we must begin with a comparison to the moral values.

---

112 On this matter cf. *Möglichkeit und Wirklichkeit* [English edition: *Possibility and Actuality*, De Gruyter 2013], Chaps. 35b–d.
113 Cf. *Ethik*, Chap. 23d [English edition: *Ethics*, George Allen & Unwin 1932].

So much has been clarified about the nature of the existence of moral values during the long disputations about it that the historical change in moral beliefs and in the consciousness of values need not to refer to the relativity of these values to the given conditions of some period; this change may also have a different real basis. This different basis is the narrowness of the consciousness of values and its evolution within the multiplicity of values, such that in each epoch contemporaries grasp only a segment of the realm of values. The epoch must then be blind to the remaining value.

The evolution of the human eye for value will in the meantime be determined by the very different actualizations of the individual value-domains. Every moral value appertains to a type of situation (to a περὶ τί). It can be real only if situations of this kind are frequent in common life, or if they become intrusive: so bravery only when men live in danger. But then it is not the values that are historically relative, but only their becoming actual, and, dependent upon that, the openness of the feeling of value for them.

That is a clear outcome, which recognizes fully the phenomena of relativity, but gives it a deeper meaning than relativism has heretofore given them. The question now is whether this outcome extends to the aesthetic values as well. This seems at first not believable, for nothing varies as much as artistic taste. One thinks of fashion, of the quick appearance and disappearance of fashions in art, of the great periods of art history in painting, poetry, music, and architecture, where in each the general direction of tastes evinced peculiar preferences.

These facts make the problem very complicated. Kant saw it in its more simple form, that is, unhistorically. His "antinomy of taste" in aesthetical judgment was designed to account for it. The antinomy concerned only the judgments of taste in individuals; moreover, it was limited to the question of whether the judgment is "founded upon a concept" or not. We would most likely say today: upon a general principle. But there could be a universal validity – intersubjective universality – for aesthetical judgment even without objectively universal principles. That universal validity might stem from the merely intersubjective communality of the entire human constitution, that is, from the conditions governing the senses up to the most ideal demands of rationality.

In a deeper and historically grounded form of the question the antinomy would be expressed as follows: in all the variations of taste, is there a firm basis for deeming a thing beautiful? Or can such a thing not be, because (362) taste in itself demands variety (as in fashion!), and always rejects what is already done and has become routine. It might also be that taste must change along with transformations in the conditions of life. If so, the situation would be strictly analogous to that of ethical values.

If one looks upon the matter in that way, then the scales seem to tip markedly in favor of relativity. How can one seriously put in question the variegated diversity of the sense of beauty in history, which in the human ideal of beauty in painting, in architecture, in music, in comedy, is so obvious? It is clear that this vacillation and this diversity in taste cannot be denied. The question is simply whether this is really a relativity of values, or whether it is in the end only a relativity of judgments of value and of the feeling of value – due to the fact that the heart does not open itself at all times to all values.

There is a phenomenon that must be recognized in this context that weighs decisively against value-relativism, namely the possibility that exists for recovering the meaning of once authoritative aesthetic values. One can – if one is sufficiently experienced, learned, and practiced – open one's own feelings of value to the specific values of works of the past by consistently taking part sympathetically in these works. This is possible only when these "specific values" are not tightly tied to their historical epoch and relative to them, but rather are valid and convincing to a much later and differently oriented mind, one that takes an appropriate stance towards them. But that means: it is possible only if they are absolute in a fundamental way, and the relativity in question – as with the moral values – is merely one of the temporary direction of preferences of the feeling of value itself.

And just think what an enormous role is played just in our times by the wonderful capacity of our feeling for art to orient itself! The sense for the tastes of past eras has in fact risen in our times. We are the living witnesses of a feeling for values that allows itself to be awakened even to the strange tastes of alien epochs. Only when that happened did the great surge in the systematic study of the history of art and the growth of our awareness of it become possible. So relativism cannot be the final word. The most convincing witnesses to that are found in the further fact that for us today the art of many past epochs has become as familiar to us as is our own.

To conclude, let us recall one question: what does the "claim to universal validity" really mean? This claim can be raised by something that is objectively individual and absolutely singular, as Kant correctly saw and insisted upon in his concept of "subjective universality." Every genuine work of art raises this claim, and yet it is never fulfilled in fact, but is met by the divergence of a thousand individuals.

The answer is simple. For it is the same as with the theoretically universal and the concept of the a priori. People usually do not reflect upon this: the universality of a mathematical theorem does not mean that any uneducated person can understand it. It means rather only that anyone who does understand it (363) must assent to it, because it is inwardly compelling precisely for the faculty of understanding. It can mean nothing more than that.

It is the same with the universal validity of the judgment of taste and of the aesthetic values in general. Not everyone who is unschooled in art or otherwise inadequately oriented towards it can assent to the value judgments of those who understand and are open to art, but only those who are themselves open and adequately oriented. Intersubjective universality means nothing more that the agreement of those who are adequately oriented.

Therewith collapses the antinomy that has confused his issue; similarly all presumed "relativity" of the validity of aesthetic values. Also historical relativity: for as often as an adequately oriented consciousness reappears in history, the same value is also again given recognition.

Second Section: The Sublime and the Charming

Chapter 30: Concept and Phenomenon of the Sublime

a) The domains of appearance of the sublime in life

The expositions of Chapter 26 have shown that the genera of beauty, and, along with them, the separation from them of the specifically aesthetic values, does not result in a clear series within any of the given standpoints; just as little a uniform principle of classification or even just an overview of them that would in some way inspire confidence. That is in keeping with the situation today in aesthetics, and must be accepted. We must nonetheless try to extract what can be grasped of it.

We saw already in that chapter how the sublime extracted itself from the series of value-predicates – as something exceptional, with greater weight than the others, and more singular. The sublime, alone among the others, stood uncontested, whether or not one subsumed it under the beautiful or, as Kant did, deemed it independent and equal. All later aesthetics took up the genus of the sublime – partly because of tradition, which extends back in time to the ancient concept of ὕψος ("height," "*sublime*"), whose nature was not yet purely aesthetical – and partly because every great and serious art approaches this genus, such that we always find ourselves referred involuntarily to the sublime.

For these reasons, people have also demonstrated that all other genera of the beautiful are found in other places in life, where one does not think of aesthetical enjoyment: the graceful, the sweet, the charming, the comical, the tragic, etc. One could not, therefore, claim that these have a value equal to the sublime. (364)

But in this way, the same objection could be made to the sublime: does it not occur in life quite without any trace of the aesthetical? When one thinks of the overwhelming powers of nature, such that we can crate no aesthetical distance to observe it, or of great human destinies to which we stand too close to view them aesthetically – in the face of death or in religious devotion – one may wish to believe that this objection is justified. In any case, we may assume here no clear separation from the other genera of aesthetic value.

In a different way, another kind of separation of the sublime from the other values occurs when one looks at the set purely in terms of content. The other genera of values – or at least the value-predicates – exhibit a broad similarity to each other and, specifically, they bring a kind of similarity to each other into their common opposition to the sublime. Of all of those genera, only the tragic is excluded. Further research will most likely place a few others alongside the tragic, perhaps from music: the *largo*, the *grave*, the *maestoso*, etc.

The graceful, the charming, the idyllic, the sweet or lovely, have quite obviously this similarity to each other, and this same opposition to the sublime in their very nature. And everything related to them must be counted among them also: the farce, the grotesque, the fantastic, and, yes, even the amusing. At a somewhat greater distance belong here also the genus of the comical, with all its species: the ridiculous, the funny, and the humorous. Out of this contrast the genus of the sublime becomes more precise; it is now unambiguously definable by means of its fundamental difference from these genera.

Here the real basis for this difference may lie in Kant's having thought the sublime to be of such fundamental value and having placed it "next" to the beautiful itself. One cannot defend him for doing that, and the theory by mans of which Kant himself tried to justify the idea is, although quite profound in meaning, rather one-sided and, in many respects, artificial. But it is understandable if one sees that Kant had a tendency to force "the beautiful" a bit toward the group of "simpler" value-predicates: towards the graceful, the charming, etc. We will speak in a moment of his theory of the sublime.

But at this point we must ask: where in fact do we come in contact with the sublime? This "where" asks after the domains upon which we make its acquaintance, and those are not only aesthetical ones. To this question we may answer simply: upon almost all domains where we encounter something enormous or otherwise overwhelming in its elevation: in nature as in human life, in fantasy as in thought. That the two latter are not real domains does not change the fact that in them, too, the great and the enormous are contained. The sublime is indifferent to its ways of being. This indifference also makes it possible for aesthetic objects to be sublime. For aesthetic objects are, with regards to most of their components, unreal. (365)

First of all, the sublime occurs in many kinds of natural phenomena: the storm, the surf, and the waterfall, in sheets of snow in the high mountains, the desert, the quiet of the heath, in the starry skies. Those are old and well-known examples. Many things of a different sort can be for a scientist genuinely sublime: the inner structure of the atom or the subtle changes in the nucleus of a living cell – just as much as the statistical laws of the stars in the galaxy.

The significance in these matters may be that nothing here has yet to do with the aesthetically sublime. For of course the sublime also exists this side of the aesthetical. For the aesthetically sublime first comes to be upon the standpoint of beholding and enjoying by a subject; for it belongs to the essence of the aesthetic object that it exists as such only "for us," assuming we bring with us the correct way of looking at it.

But the sublime approaches us in human life more forcefully and in a deeper sense; for these cases we usually do not have a sense for it. A person who calmly bears pain or great sorrow "is" in a notable way sublime – over pain and sorrow. Who sacrifices his life and health in some great undertaking "is" exalted over the goods of peace and comfort that he renounces for it. This "being" sublime has nothing to do with a "feeling" of the sublime; it exists absolutely in the person, regardless of other men's knowledge of it or feelings about it.

This is in itself not a thing aesthetically sublime; one could call it with greater justice the morally sublime. But if this were a case of truly great deeds, of heroism and high capacity for responsibility, the sublimity would be evident because we would respond to it in our hearts with spontaneous admiration.

We come to the aesthetically sublime only when we achieve some distance, alongside of our admiration, from which to gaze upon it peacefully and to allow its greatness, far from all its excitement and immediacy, to affect us.

We must not forget that the purest manifestation of the sublime lies in the domain of myth, of religion, and, in general, of world-views; also in that of philosophical thought or theorizing. For a long time people have had these phenomena in mind when they attempted to characterize the sublime without bothering to consider whether they were in fact characterizing the aesthetically sublime.

Naturally, such things are not only aesthetical, especially in the case of myth, where poetic forms are nonetheless clearly those of art; but here, too, there is a boundary to be drawn. In the domain of religion, the artistic representations of the sublime are, however, in no way identical to the sublimity of the objects of the belief themselves, i.e., with the Divinity and its dominion over the world. Religious dogmas bear eloquent witness to that. The dogmas stand in direct opposition to the clarity and distinctness of aesthetic objects, and could never be the bearer of their values. (366)

b) The appearance of the sublime in the arts

The wide domain of the sublime outside of the arts and of the aesthetical in general demonstrates clearly that it is not, like the beautiful, a specifically aesthetical appearance. In that it is similar to the graceful and the charming or the comical, as well as to the other "genera of beauty" that we have noted, which initially are not specifically aesthetical appearances. From each one we must first separate individually the cases that are aesthetical. But in which domain do these lie?

Without doubt, they lie primarily among the beauty that is external to art; it appears as much in nature as in human life. For our purpose, we may lay claim to all of those cases that we just named with respect to the non-aesthetically sublime; for it was readily apparent that all these cases become transformed into the aesthetically sublime as soon as the subject that grasps them obtains the required distance and the tranquility of contemplation. This we may accept as a fundamental law throughout, and it is demonstrated innumerable times in life, when one and the same overpowering event at first appears as merely oppressive, but which then all at once appears thrilling.

When Schiller says, "Man now loses hope at length, Yielding to immortal strength," he merely expresses defeat, and stands entirely on this side of the aesthetical; when he continues, "Idly and with wond'ring gaze, All the wreck he now surveys,"[114] the attitude has turned about, and the aesthetically sublime gives itself simple expression in the same event, a conflagration.

This distance is usually not so easily obtained in the case of the morally sublime. A violent emotion in the face of the forces of nature may well be the more intense, but it does not penetrate to the same psychic depth. The morally sublime – perhaps a convincing act of generosity or magnanimity – forces one's own selfhood to measure itself by it, and the admission of one's own incapacity to do something like it is oppressive. A man must deal with it inwardly. But when, out of the consciousness of one's own moral inferiority, distance upon it is taken, one's admiration and reverence is then that much deeper.

The aesthetically sublime occurs in life ceaselessly in the wake of the sublime in nature and in the morally sublime; obviously this happens only to the degree that a person – and even an entire epoch – is aesthetically awake.

Let us supplement this with a few words about the religiously sublime. Since in its domain lie the most powerful forms of appearance – most powerful because they involve philosophical world-views – it is to be expected that here, again, will be found the most abundant occurrences of the aesthetically sublime as it appears in the wake of those forms.

That is so true that Hegel's aesthetics – and no doubt that of the Romantics in general – identified the one with the other, or, at least, did not know how to keep them separate. People identified (367) the "divine" straightway with the "idea," which comes to "manifest" itself there; that God was thought eminently sublime is reasonable, but to hold without further ado that this same sublimity, which is purely religious and philosophical, was an aesthetical one (as in myth and dogma) is a failure to distinguish matters properly.

At this point precisely the relation of the arts to religion should have been given a better analysis. No doubt the arts originated from religious life, yet they

---

114 [Translator's note:] Schiller, Friedrich, *The Poems of Schiller, Complete: Including All His Early Suppressed Pieces*, translated by Edgar Alfred Bowring, London: Parker 1851, p. 222. (Schiller, "Das Lied von der Glocke": "Hoffnungslos / Weicht der Mensch der Götterstärke, / Müßig sieht er seine Werke / Und bewundernd untergehn.").

reached their highest flowering when religious life was already beginning to wane. They received their ideas from it, but they remained autonomous with respect to their power of sensible form, and transformed religious ideals into ideals of a conspicuously human type.

The arts no longer dared to approach the divine sublime itself. It was once forbidden to the fine arts (Do not make pictures!). Greek sculpture tried and achieved it – but only because their gods were very human; the same holds true for Christ in human form – in the great epochs that painted the "Son of Man." Only music, perhaps, is thoroughly permeated by the divine sublime. It was able to do so, because it did not have to work with the objects of religion, but could suspend it in vagueness.

For that reason, in the minds of its imitators the musically sublime could most likely sunder itself easily from the philosophical world-views about which it once wove its tendrils, and today stands before us purely as the aesthetical sublime. Not even the connection to a text (in oratorios and cantatas) is an obstacle to it. The parallel in pure music by just these same masters (Bach, Handel, et al.) demonstrates that clearly. Historically and with respect to material and thematic content, the arts, when they create something sublime, take their point of departure from the philosophical contents of the religious life. That may not be challenged, even if the process of separating the arts from religion has proceeded considerably, and other thematic domains of the sublime have come into fashion.

In which arts do we find not only the "aesthetically sublime" but also the "artistically sublime"? And, furthermore: in which forms of art within the arts may it be found? Upon which strata of the object does it depend? The first question is easy to answer, and it will serve as an introduction and as a guide. The last, in contrast, is difficult, and leads us directly to the most fundamental question: what really is the sublime?

Initially, one might be of the opinion that the sublime could be found only in the representational arts, because only there do we have genuine themes. But that is the first error: that the sublime might be tied to objective themes from which they cannot be severed. In truth, the sublime is rather independent of them.

With the exception of ornamental art, the sublime exists in all the arts, but in a graduated series. Its impact in painting is relatively slight, although it does not lack sublime *sujets* and there is no scarcity of ideals (368) of an exalted humanity (of the Titanical). Painting may in exchange be too tightly connected to the sensible – the purely sensible is quite distant from the sublime. The "painterly" effects proper are those of seeing itself, not of something standing behind it.

Where painting genuinely reaches into the sublime, as in the figures on the ceiling of the Sistine Chapel, something alien to painting enters – a combination of drawing and sculpture; and, perhaps, something that is humanly larger than life can be grasped authentically only in this way.

Of course in the art of the portrait there is an element of the profound-sublime, as we see in the late Rembrandt, where all of the magic of colors, rejoicing in the senses, gives way to what, standing in the background, touches the truly human.

The contrast of sculpture to painting in respect of the sublime now becomes clear. Hegel saw rightly that the former was the first to "form" the sublime in its figures of gods. Here in fact was created the ideal of human nature beyond experience and reality: it was inwardly beheld and, by means of creative imagination, given sensible shape as a model of perfection.

Literature is as much capable of expressing the sublime as it is of the other genera of beauty. It has the broadest scope in inner diversity. Even in lyric poetry the sublime is not absent; it comes powerfully to the fore in heroic epics, primarily in the characters, but also in their destinies; especially where their destinies becomes significant and tragic.

The situation is similar in tragedy. The characters that are marked by destiny fall under a grander law, and they experience its image in their own downfall. Whatever is great and uplifting in man reveals itself here in its purity. Then man grows beyond the measure of the merely human. But it is not true, as one may think, that "the tragic" as such is sublime (*Little Eyolf*).[115]

The sublime appears in its purest form precisely where it is least looked for: in the non-representational arts of music and architecture. Music presents it in the depths of our psychic dynamics, a place that representation cannot reach. Music can express the psychic-sublime because it allows it to "speak" directly and thereby produce a resonance in the hearer; it affects him emotionally and lets him sense it just as he otherwise senses only his own experience: as his own.

Architecture achieves as much the other way around; it displays a static sublime in quiet repose and greatness. So it has long been the case with monuments: in the Doric temple the sublime had already achieved a level – in a way that appears so simple – that has never again been reached: earnestness paired with an elevated and serene cheerfulness. In the great style of churches in the Middle Ages, a perfection of special and dynamic composition was once again achieved, and is best known in the Gothic. (369)

---

115 [Translator's note:] Henrik Ibsen's play in which the title character is a paralyzed nine-year old child, Eyolf, who drowns in the sea.

c) Kant's theory of the sublime

After this survey of "where we find the sublime," we can approach the question of what it is, or wherein it is distinguished from other kinds of beauty. This question does not yet incorporate the question of the value of the sublime, but that will become ripe for decision through the clarification of the first two. Kant developed the classic theory of the sublime, and we must begin with it.

Kant distinguished the mathematically sublime from the dynamically sublime. The first gives us what is great absolutely (the great beyond all comparison), and the second corresponds to the power of nature, viewed "as power that has no dominion over us."[116] This last point is true because otherwise the relation to the aesthetical vanishes, and only the "fearful" as such remains. Kant developed only the first point.

In both cases the perspective is quantitative: "*That is sublime which even to be able to think of demonstrates a faculty of the mind [Gemüt] that surpasses every measure of the senses.*"[117] In the apprehension of something so beyond all measure, a "feeling of the inadequacy" must arise in us, namely "of [the] imagination for presenting the ideas of a whole [...]."[118] Kant has in mind, as the whole that pertains to this experience, something infinite that is in fact impossible to grasp with any clarity. The first kind of sublimity is therefore a condition of "non-purposiveness" of conception for judgment.

At this point in Kant's analysis, the sublime could produce only a sense of displeasure, oppression. But then Kant introduces something else: the demand for totality that is made by human reason. Just the failure of imagination "indicates a faculty of the mind which surpasses every standard of sense."[119] In that way, the mind wins back its pre-eminence and experiences a pleasure of a higher kind, one conditioned by displeasure of a lower kind.[120] This pleasure is the feeling of the sublime. It signifies a lifting of the heart out of its depression. Apparently the most important thing here is the dialectic of the appropriate and inappropriate, of suitability and unsuitability, of pleasure and displeasure. Whereas in the "beautiful" (in Kant's narrow sense) adequacy, suitability and pleasure arise in us directly, they are conditioned in the sublime by their oppo-

---

116 [Translator's note:] Kant, Immanuel, *Critique of the Power of Judgment*, translated by Paul Guyer and Eric Matthews, The Cambridge Edition of the Works of Immanuel Kant, Cambridge and New York: Cambridge University Press 2002, p. 143.
117 [Translator's note:] Kant, *Critique of the Power of Judgment*, p. 134.
118 [Translator's note:] Kant, *Critique of the Power of Judgment*, p. 136.
119 [Translator's note:] Kant, *Critique of the Power of Judgment*, p. 138.
120 [Translator's note:] Cf. Kant, *Critique of the Power of Judgment*, p. 141.

sites, and the core of the matter lies in the overcoming of this opposition. But what always happens is that, in its final effects, man remains the pre-eminent being; aesthetical pleasure is essentially the taking of pleasure in this pre-eminence.

This is most important where the faculty of judgment turns to the moral nature of man, his noumenal aspect. And that is seen in its purest form where we are concerned with events in our moral life – the kinds of material that is worked upon in the arts. In art, we are concerned with a still greater pre-eminence, for here freedom begins in man, with which his intelligible nature first truly appears. (370) One may apply to just this phenomenon the definition: "That is *sublime* which pleases immediately through its resistance to the interest of the senses."[121]

If one surveys these definitions of Kant, they leave one unsatisfied with respect to two of its aspects. First, they remain tied, even more than the definitions of the beautiful, to the subjective: one hears too much of the effects upon the mind and not enough about the structure of the object. But the dialectic of pleasure and displeasure remains useful, so far as those two elements may be understood as indicators of value.

But second, really too much in the object is made to lay complete claim to infinity. This somewhat frivolous play with infinity stems from the early Romantics' tastes. But the subject does not require it; the first formulation, "the absolutely great," is the better of the two, if one may understand this term as referring to an "absolutely great effective force," without concerning oneself with how great or small it really is.

Thus, Kant's account of the sublime says little, although he is clearly groping in the proper direction. Perhaps one may, in agreement with the direction of the two of his points that we just specified, record the following two elements as essential parts of the concept of the sublime:

1. Two elements of feeling are in conflict with each other in the beholder, one functioning as a defense or as resistance, a feeling of impotence or fear, and the other as assent, of which the latter is founded upon the former. For this reason the value of the sublime is a value founded upon a disvalue – namely upon the former's coping with the latter.

2. A quite peculiar element of "greatness" appears upon the object. It is questionable whether anything at all quantitative plays a role here. It could be simply a question of something "superior to us." That would be entirely sufficient and in better agreement with the more severe appearance of the sublime, for not all cases of it lie in the domain of extension, but rather in that

---

121 [Translator's note:] Kant, *Critique of the Power of Judgment*, p. 150.

of moral greatness – wherever it appears in the living human being or in artistic representations. It is also in better agreement with the peculiar forms of the sublime that appear in the non-representational arts (music and architecture).

Chapter 31: The Structure of the Aesthetical Sublime

a) The special forms of the sublime

The sublime, as Kant saw it, exists without doubt. There is only this question, whether this is true for all forms of the sublime – even if that is so only for the ones touched on above, e.g., for the sublime contained in music and in architecture. In those there are found what are perhaps the purest forms of it. But where do we find the basis for this limitation? (371)

One basis lies in the forms of thought peculiar to Kant, which in many domains works with *pars pro toto* [taking a part for a whole]. For example, "duty" was seen by him as the sole ground for taking a position within ethics; within the concept of the sublime, he gave preference of place to overwhelming power, oppressiveness, and fearsomeness.

Both of these had the eventual effect that Kant saw what was overwhelming more than what was sublime, or rather he held the first for the second. It could not be denied that this specific form of the sublime exists, and Kant's examples, taken from nature and its ways, are entirely correct as characterizations of it. But they do not exhaust the type. They show a preference for that aspect of the problem from which Kant drew the relation of opposition between the pleasant and the unpleasant in the observer. As a result, the opposition appears artificially inflated by him.

If we further ask why Kant sought such emphasis, the answer must lie in his metaphysical convictions. To Kant, God is the absolutely sublime, before whom all creation is vanishingly small; this sublimity peers through all limited forms of sublimity in nature and in the life of the mind as infinity and unattainable being. This philosophical perspective led to a one-sidedness in his picture of the sublime.

Let us therefore look away from this one-sidedness! Much is left over when we do; especially if one puts to use the achievements of Kant discussed in the previous chapter, viz., the idea of the value founded upon a disvalue, and his refusal to understand the "absolutely great" quantitatively. We are able to grasp best the latter idea if we place the different forms of appearance of the sublime one next to the other, though, to be sure, in a more broad and open way than Kant did. To begin with, we must leave out of consideration the question of how the aesthetically sublime is to be demarcated from the sublime in life.

Thus, I present – without any claim to their systematic order or to the completeness of the list – the following species.

1. The great and the grandiose – both without concern for measurable quantities, only "great of its kind," in the way in which buildings may affect us with their grandeur, even when they are not large in size.

2. That which is grave, imposing, overreaching, profound or whatever seems inscrutable; grave in the sense associated with solemn ceremonies.

3. That which is complete within itself, fulfilled and perfect, before which one feels puny and needy (as often with the morally sublime); that which is mysteriously silent and still and may yet be sensed upon the surface of something dark and immeasurable.

4. The pre-eminent (in strength or power) – what in nature is the overwhelming, in human life is the morally superior, imposing and inspiring (generous, splendid, magnanimous).

5. The monstrous, the violent, and the fearsome – as something in life that overwhelms a man, and before which he (372) furls his sails, but also in artistic form as the lapidary, the monumental, or what in form constitutes the "flinty" and the "colossal" (Kant).

6. That which is touching or deeply moving – both found primarily in human destiny, but prototypically in literature.

7. Once again the tragic, distinct from both of the above – not only in tragedy, but also in other kinds of literary works, in music, and in real life this side of art.

These individual forms of the sublime form only a selection, and the series is not uniform; for example, the last two kinds are much more specific in their kind than the other five. Much about them still requires an explication; that is the case with the first three points, which deviate considerably from the Kantian conception.

Much of this can be made clearer by viewing it from the standpoint of the opposition itself. For every special form of the sublime has its opposite, which need not at all be negative (as, e.g., averse to all value, ugly); and often this counterpart is well known.

To 1:   What is meant is the "inward greatness," which in fact is not extensional in nature. That does not exclude the possibility that in special cases the term refers to something that is "big" in the sense of extension, such as the starry skies; yet the sublime is tied more to their undisturbed uniformity and inerrant reliability of their movements. The contrary refers to a being of small stature, petty, the ordinary man, the "nonentity." For the "inwardly great" – the "well-formed" –, the case of what is "grand and spacious" in the form of a building offers singular evidence. A good example of this is Schinkel's Old Guardhouse:[122] it is a vanishingly small structure between two larger buildings that it overshadows by means of the impression of size that it exudes. The same can be said of some very small compositions in Bach's *Well-Tempered Clavier* – preludes and fugues – only a few last longer than seven minutes (using a moderate tempo), but given the inward greatness of their structure, they can be measured against the greatest compositional works and still emerge superior.

To 2:   We must not misunderstand the species. The serious or grave has nothing to do with what is sad or melancholy; also little to do with the tragic, which, to be sure, always remains, for its part, tied to them. Seriousness need not dispense with joyfulness; the synthesis of the two is clearly found in solemn celebration. And we should observe that everything inwardly lofty, as long as it is not oppressive, has something solemn and celebratory about it – something of what is separate from everyday life and "elevates itself above" it, so that "celebration" is an exceptional state in life. Precisely here might lie the primary sense of the "sublime." It consists in this state of "elevation above." What is solemn and celebratory is in fact given its purest form in great music.

To 3:   The perfect (complete within itself) is not normally included in the sublime, at least not any more; but it cannot be denied that everything that is perfect (373) makes an impression of superiority. When the mysterious and the puzzling are added to it and fill the observer with a sense the something greater may be contained in it, the impression becomes considerably more intense.

The two forms of the sublime under 2 and 3 (within certain limits also 1) may well constitute the pure original type of the sublime, which stands entirely neutral in regard to emotional elements of other kinds – the tragic, the threatening, etc. This is in opposition to Kant, for whom the oppressive stood in the foreground, as his theory required.

For these two forms also the contrary element can be brought in as evidence. The contrast to the serious and the solemn is the banal and the quotidian, but in

---

122 [Translator's note:] Presumably Hartmann refers to Karl Friedrich Schinkel's Altstädtische Hauptwache in Dresden.

no way the simple and the superficial; to the complete and the perfect, the half-done and incomplete; to the concealed mystery, the vulgar and the vapid.

The next two points, 4 and 5, together make up to some extent Kant's sense of the sublime. The opposition they have in common is to the familiar and usual, those things with which we know how to get along in life.

To 4:   What is morally superior is related to the perfect (in the sense of point 3); one can doubt whether it must create an entirely oppressive feeling. It could produce a sense of being immediately swept along or ravished, as by enthusiasm. And that is perhaps only natural.

To 5:   Monumental structures pay a great role in the arts – and not only in architecture. Their weight is felt perhaps even more in sculpture and literature. In the case of the violent-fearsome, we are indeed on the very edge of the sublime proper: the feelings and the sense of oppressiveness become too strong, and the impression of size is diminished. Without distance from the object, its aesthetical understanding is simply not possible.

The last two forms of the sublime (6 and 7) are close to each other, and likewise both in turn close to the "fearsome."

To 6:   The deeply shocking is almost always tied to the fearsome; the former is the emotional side of the latter. What "touches" or "thrills" us stands at greater distance from what oppresses and torments us; it is again a more uplifting element. But this is possible only where something in the human characters is able to grow beyond the element of destiny. The states of being touched or thrilled already contain elements of admiration and mental uplift.

To 7:   In the tragic, the note of drama is predominant, or, perhaps better, the purely artistic in general. In being thrilled or touched the decisive factor is the soul's state of being touched; in the tragic what is decisive is the uplift of the soul, and the specifically aesthetical state of enjoyment in the audience. To this state corresponds the highly developed formal style of tragedy. That is, however, a special problem – not only for the drama, but for other arts as well. (374)

b) The tangible essential characteristics of the sublime

If we now cast a look back, we will see that the sense and essence of the sublime has become more precise. Indeed, we see only now how unclear is the traditional concept of the sublime. The series of its special forms brought the phenomenon not only to its correct dimensions, but also threw new light on its uniform nature.

It is by no means required to conclude our discussion with a formal definition of the sublime, which we could read off against the Kantian. All ambitions of this kind must be set aside.

What then has been achieved in general for the philosophical specification of the aesthetical sublime? It appears to be negative in part, but it is eminently positive, though only mediately so. The opposition to Kant's analysis concerns, moreover, only its specific emphases and its one-sidedness. The following affirmative elements remain.

1. The detaching of the sublime from what is transcendental and absolute, from God and all other specifically philosophical presuppositions. Affirmative: the absorption of the sublime by terrestrial and the nearby, by the natural and the human (this in opposition to the Romantics).
2. The detachment of the sublime from the realm of the quantitative: not because it cannot also be quantitative, but because in the great majority of the forms in which it appears, its superiority is of a different kind, indeed even its "greatness" is of a different kind.
3. The detachment from the oppressive. Of course, there can be elements of affliction and distress in the sublime, of fearsomeness and the catastrophic, but that does not constitute its nature. The primary element in the sublime is the elevation produced by the beholding of what is superior.
4. The elimination of its foundation in an element of disvalue (the "inappropriate," the "unsuitable," etc.); similarly of the corresponding displeasure in the value-response by the subject. Instead of its foundation in a disvalue, we arrive at its foundation in a value. This value need not lie in the subject. It usually lies precisely in the object, and indeed as its intrinsic value, provided that it is experienced as the absolutely great and superior.
5. In the place of what does not correspond and what is not appropriate, there enters a clear correspondence, one that lies originally in human nature, between the superiority of the object and some psychic need of the human heart.

The last two points are genuinely affirmative; this affirmation becomes apparent in the nature of the sublime. Yet there are still some things needing clarification. Specifically, it is not the case, as one might think, that a pleasure that is conditioned by some pain, or a value that is founded upon a disvalue, simply cannot occur. Both occur frequently; the first is familiar even in psychology as the law of contrast among feelings. The second we know from ethics, where the distress of a fellow man (a disvalue) founds the moral value of brotherly love. For that reason there should (375) be nothing to object to in the Kantian analysis of the sublime in respect of this relation. The matter is simply that this analysis does not account for the phenomena: more correctly, it accounts only for a part of the problem, and not for the central part. For the sense of the sublime does not, as a rule, begin with the oppression of our self-esteem; rather, the latter is a special case.

The fundamental law that applies here may well be this: man feels from his very origins drawn to the great and superior; indeed he may go through life with an unspoken desire for something great and imposing, and keep open a watchful eye for it. When he finds it, his heart flies to it.

That, at least, is the case for normal men who are not poorly educated or full of anxiety; the latter is frequently the case, as we can see in men who possess a certain faint-heartedness before whatever is extraordinary – and even greater timidity before whatever is monstrous or overwhelming. To be dismayed or humbled by what is overpowering is usually secondary, although when one is up against certain kinds of external powers that is quite natural. For in such cases, the origin of the discernment for the sublime occurs on a second stage, one in which some distance has been established from whatever is threatening.

One of the most appealing moral characteristics that can belong to a man is that he is drawn to things that are great and superior to him. This pull upon his heart is not of an aesthetical nature, but it is easily transformed into aesthetical beholding and the pleasure of admiration. In any case, as a tendency toward value it lies (as an ethical response) at the foundation of the aesthetic value of the sublime, and that constitutes merely a special case of the more general law of foundation of aesthetic values (Cf. Chap. 28c). This admiration of what is great is basically, we might even say, of a more general kind. The moral case itself is something more specific. There is a kind of primitive magic exerted by the "great"; it possesses a "magnetic" capacity, which draws the human heart to itself. We may express it in this way: the man unspoiled by a poor education carries within him the tendency to reverence, and to live with an eye directed over and beyond him.

Perhaps this tendency is rooted in a still more fundamental tendency, the desire to bring meaning into one's own life. For all that transcends us gives meaning through itself: man senses darkly the secret depths within him as one source of meaning. What the meaning of this transcendence consists in is a question only for later reflection, or even for philosophical consideration; in practical life, men do not ask such a question, and one's developing aesthetical perceptiveness does not ask it at all. For aesthetic perception is tied directly to impression. But impressions arise, as always in the aesthetical relation, from the senses. And the senses are light years away from giving an account of such matters.

The changeover to the aesthetical sublime begins as soon as the first "flight of the heart" to what is "great" has achieved a state of distance and contemplation. The pleasure of seeing (376) lifts itself above the passion of devotion and the longing that feeds upon itself; and then, immediately the aesthetic value of the sublime arises as a more palpable value in the object, one beyond its importance as a value that bestows meaning.

What is of the essence here (as was already noted in point 4) is that instead of founding the sublime upon a disvalue, we have its foundation upon a value. With that, the purely positive relation between them is reestablished. Kant and his followers did not see the founding value, although it was there to see; the element of human pleasure in it shows itself unambiguously. The value of everything that appears on very large scale attains an added weight just because it is significant and powerful; the weight of this value is most intensely felt where it is a question of non-extensional psychic and moral greatness. The attraction of the human heart to what is magnificent is so basic that it will indirectly accept elements of disvalue of whatever strength. That is the reason why we meet with the latter frequently in the sublime, and why they are so frequently and emphatically represented in it.

That Kant made these elements of disvalue into the main condition of the sublime must have been due to the fact that in those examples of the sublime in which disvalues are represented the opposition of the sublime to the remaining genera of beauty, that is, to the charming, becomes very prominent. This difference was troublesome to Kant. He thought it made the sublime different from beauty in general, and he thereby brought confusion into aesthetics.

c) Intangible essential characteristics

In this way, the opposition to beauty may be dropped from the usual list of the characteristics of the sublime. That does not happen because the concept of the sublime has been noticeably broadened, but because the element of conflict in the essence of the sublime has been eliminated. With that the foundational arrangement is justified, whereby all special genera of aesthetic value are subordinated to the beautiful. With that, too, the concept of the latter is now fixed.

According to this analysis, the sublime is that form of beauty that responds to the human needs for "greatness," for something "surpassingly great," and with that the resistance of the faint-hearted and the all-too-human is easily overcome. This definition also dispenses with the other side: that of the integration of the more general specifications of the beautiful, which must hold true where we are dealing with a subordinate form of the beautiful.

To achieve the correct supplementation among the structural elements of beauty, it is sufficient to introduce the appearance-relation, for if that concept fails, as it does in ornamental art, then the sublime would also have nothing more to seek. Now provided that beauty consists in the appearing of a non-sensible background, i.e., the sensible real foreground to the object, and this existence is an "existence for us," one can grasp the sublime (377) in the following way. It is that specific appearing of an unsensed background in a real sensed foreground of the object, which accommodates the needs of man for greatness, and, with the greatest ease, overcomes any resistance opposed to it.

One could leave the definition at that. But it is striking that this accommodation, of which we have spoken, depends structurally upon the appearing background itself. We can therefore simplify the expression, if we refer it from the start to the appearing background. Then it will read: the sublime is the appearance of what possesses overwhelming or surpassing greatness, which cannot be given through the senses, in the foreground of the object given to the senses, so far as this greatness of the appearing object accommodates the psychic needs for greatness and overcomes easily the petty human resistances arrayed against it.

The background is the surpassing thing itself that appears "in the foreground." This appearing is especially strange in this context, because of the incommensurability between foreground and background. This is not so only in the arts; it is found just in that way in the sublimity of nature, where it is also peculiar in a similar way. For there, too, what is given through the senses is only a finite detail (a view of the sea, of the starry skies). But just that is the mystery of the thing: how can what is entirely Other appear to the senses? Yet the puzzle is no greater here than it is in the case of the beautiful.

Herewith we must drop all dialectics of the sublime, which once was so popular. It was referred to in passing by Hegel, was spun out broadly as a theory by Friedrich Theodor Vischer, and continues in our own century – usually in such a way, to be sure, that one can see only dimly through to the antithesis. But the issue did not concern that antithesis alone. It was a question rather of creating a guide to the whole theory of art, whereby the arts and each of their more special forms, would be organized as a series. In this series, progress towards the next member could always be initiated by a [dialectical] turning-about of one of its elements. This genuinely Hegelian schema is cut at its roots when one finally abolishes the artificially exaggerated antithetic of the oppositions in the sublime. The consequences of this abolition affected immediately the entire structure of aesthetics. For all further [dialectical] transitions are built according to this schema.

Another question now becomes acute: how can, in fact, what is overwhelmingly great be represented in the arts? It must be represented in some form or other, for it is supposed to "appear." The foreground is always tightly limited, just because it is given to the senses and is intended to affect us as an easily surveyable whole. How, then, can something overwhelmingly great appear in it?

Since the Romantic era this question has been subject to an intensified antithetic. Back then, writers intensified the opposition from the outset by speaking of the "infinite in the finite," – an example of the bad disposition of the Romantics to elevate excessively everything that given, and to drive it into the Absolute. (378) One was forced by this tendency to return to earth before one could correctly understand the question.

What is in fact at stake here is simply the way the overwhelmingly great is placed within the narrowly limited realm of what can be surveyed by the senses. And that is strange enough. We have already pointed out that here we are faced with the far limits of imitation, and indeed on both sides. For no doubt nature contains things of surpassing greatness, but it cannot be imitated; and no doubt such a thing genuinely comes first to be as an idea, but it cannot be captured by any attempt to objectify it.

The answer is to be found in the more general nature of the beautiful. It is not at all a question of imitation or even of representation in the sense that something must be made real here. It is sufficient for the aesthetic object – even for the sublime one – to "appear." In order to appear, however, the surpassingly great need not be "produced" or "completed." It is enough that the idea we have of it stands perfectly clearly, peremptorily, and intuitively before our eyes. Otherwise, the question of making something appear presents here no more problems than elsewhere. The faculty of representation is similarly free, for the most part, in its creations.

Nevertheless, it is precisely the clarity of this appearing that is puzzling. For how can a thing that is out of the reach of the senses be brought to intuitive clarity? No doubt, in aesthetical beholding there is the "higher intuition," and it is not bound to the limits of the senses. But the impression of greatness must be maintained, for the observer does not know how large is his own contribution to the aesthetic object – thus to the sublime.

But this is where the key to the puzzle lay all the time: the appearance-relation, which one attributed to the object, could have been created only by the participation of one's own fantasy. The object in question, narrowly limited, can well enough be transformed into something overwhelmingly great by the work of the imagining mind.

Obviously, all representation of the sublime is incomplete and imperfect. But this incompleteness may be felt in the representation itself, and in that way the sublime is brought indirectly before us; thus, e.g., the morally sublime of a great deed or passion, and also the sublime in nature. In fact, the poet proceeds in that fashion: in offering to the senses concretely small phases of a life, he lets the sublime appear in the destiny of a person, and, in its appearance, it becomes aesthetically sublime.

The distance of the sublime from the senses constitutes the inward extent of its role as a mode of beauty. For beauty is appearance in sensible form. This opposition is never entirely overcome. It is not by chance that the art of painting, which rejoices the most in the senses and exercises itself entirely in the "magic of color," is least capable of the sublime, so little, in fact, that it draws even the most sublime religious themes (379) into the magic of the senses. Still weightier is the affirmative testimony of music and architecture: what is amazing about them is that these two "non-representational" arts prove themselves most potent in the representation of the sublime. Not because these arts are less sensuous, but rather because they do not actually "represent"; what they express instead in their autonomous bestowals of form is made sensible only in a dark, indefinite way, and in that way, of course, the magic of appearance has been transported far beyond the level of the senses into the realm of the non-sensible.

Chapter 32: The Place of the Sublime in the Organization of the Strata

a) The preponderance of the inner strata

The analysis of the structure of the aesthetically sublime has led to some intangible elements that are essential to it. For example, seen from the side of the phenomena these elements are no doubt tangible, but have not yet been brought to a point at which they can be understood. No violence will be done to divide further these extra- or super-phenomenal elements here. But now analysis may penetrate a bit further to some specific points that have appeared along the way.

Among these points, that most recently treated thrusts itself before our attention. It concerned the relation of the aesthetically sublime in the arts to the appearance-relation, which lies at the root of all beauty. This relation is, according to our recent discussion, a much more intimate one than one tends to think – indeed, more than theories of the sublime would be willing to grant. For it is more essential with these than with any other "materials" that in the case of "overwhelmingly large" the appearance be nothing more than "mere appearance." In any other way, the "representation" – or even just the "expression" of the sublime – would be impossible.

This raises the question: upon which of the strata of a work of art does the sublime depend? Or, if not upon any one of them exclusively, to which is it tied primarily? It would no doubt be conceivable that distinctions among the strata remain in this case quite external. The sublime could, depending on the nature of its material, be tied to every stratum. And it could be rooted in the total relationships among all strata. Both possibilities are improbable, partly because the arts take part in sublimity in different ways, partly because the "overwhelming" as such asserts its distance from the senses. We must rather extend our question: how is the sublime related to the givenness to the senses? And how does it stand in relation to the "play of forms"? The latter dissolves the appearance-relation at its very border. The former, however, is opposed to "overwhelming size."

Idealist aesthetics accused the sublime of being essentially without shape: otherwise said, formless. Such an accusation pretended to base itself upon Kant, who in this context spoke of the "unlimited" (F. Theodor Vischer). A further basis for this opinion seemed to lie in people's belief that the (380) "universal" was essential to sublimity; the latter opinion relied upon the quantitative notions of real space and time. Such ideas as Hegel's "bad infinity," or the "tedium," especially that found in nature, hovered before the minds of these Hegelians; so, as in a recurring example, the motionless open sea was tedious. As a counter-weight to this, they (such men as Solger[123]) demanded of the sublime a form of motion, a "sudden bursting forth," as Longinus[124] required such (περί ὕψους) for great rhetorical effects.

We see clearly in all of this a kind of tentative searching that finds no real point of contact. The "bursting forth" is obviously quite extrinsic to the sublime, and represents a disordered aiming at mere effect: how else could there otherwise be such phenomena as the "majestic" or "solemnity"? The "tediousness" is only a borderline phenomenon (about which will be spoken later). However, "universality" has been falsely imported here; individual literary characters contradict it completely. And the "formlessness" is a misunderstanding, but, as before, a quantitative one. Something that was really without form would be an aesthetical impossibility; such does not occur in the arts, and in nature it would not be beautiful, indeed not only not sublime but a nullity.

The truth of the last two elements is something quite different. What people have called the darkness of the sublime is a certain indeterminacy, a puzzling and mysterious quality that attaches itself to it, a depth or abyss concealed within that fills the viewer with a holy awe. Something alien, something standing at a great distance from us, remains in it. Therefore detail disappears: all that is trivial is excluded from sublime human figures (the trivial pertains to the standpoint of the "valet"[125]). Thus the poet reaches into the idealized times of long ago. Even the death of the individual seems to lift us into an ideal realm. Yet for all that the

---

123 [Translator's note:] Karl Wilhelm Ferdinand Solger (1780–1819).
124 [Translator's note:] Hartmann may be referring to the ancient author of *On the Sublime* by an unknown "pseudo-Longinos."
125 [Translator's note:] "To the valet, no man is a hero."

sublime is not universal; even less is it "formless." Rather it remains tied even here to the individual figure, and is only tangible in it.

Thus we have not been able to answer our questions about the part played in the sublime by the strata of the work of art, and also with that its position regarding the sensible givens and the play of forms. Since the first question was by far the most important, we will begin here with the two other ones.

1. The sensible givenness of the sublime is, as with all background matters, a conditional givenness: the overwhelmingly large does not itself enter the sphere of the sensibly given – that would be impossible – but only its appearance, and that is just as possible as it is possible for figures to appear.

2. The play with forms has a lesser role in the sublime, because, in general, details play a lesser role in it; and where alone such play has no relation of appearance (as in ornamental art), nothing remains of the sublime either. The sublime stands in an indissoluble opposition to play. (381)

3. Among the strata of the aesthetic object, it is without question the deeper ones – the inner strata – that emerge as the bearers of the sublime. Its appearance in the outer strata, which are close to the senses, is only partial. For that reason, "darkness" attaches itself to it, the indeterminate, the secretive, the concealed depths and abysses. That is obviously quite different from formlessness. Try sometime to give what is full of mystery a different expression! You will not find one. It can be given only in a veiled manner. This is precisely a bestowal of form, even if a conditioned one. What is "monstrous" naturally requires form of a different kind than other things. It can be revealed to the senses and to intuition only when it is largely hidden from them.

This can be demonstrated in a very specific way, as soon as one looks more closely upon the phenomena of the sublime in the arts with this idea in mind. Before all else, we see its perfect conformity with the trace of impenetrability that always attends the sublime: what is contained in the deeper strata of a work of art never allows itself to be adequately grasped except in the act of aesthetical beholding – and that means: through its appearance in the outer strata.

In drama, in epics, and in novels we never find the sublime, if it appears at all, in the outer strata. The writer can perhaps give it a bit of emphasis through his diction, can give it "weight," can point to the veils that conceal it. – But in those ways he can never make it clearly intuitable. Nor can it be at all self-contained within the work. It also can lie neither in the stratum of movement and gesture, nor in that of situation and action. In all of this, it can only "appear" if it lies in the deeper strata: for even the plot is essentially the mode of appearance of something else.

This other something consists in the psychic form bestowed upon persons, i.e., in the qualities of their character; similarly, in the next-deeper stratum, in the destiny of human life. Only here can the phenomenon of the overwhelming largeness come to be in man: it appears as much in goodness as in evil, as much in freedom and in the force of will, or in the passions; in striving and success as much as in downfall; as much in the inner struggle of a man with his better nature; as in triumphant victory.

These are in no sense the ideational strata. But they are nonetheless the characteristic inner strata of literature. Here the element of content is entirely concrete and its form is intuitively present; thus, it has no trace of the universal. And its indefiniteness does not lie in itself, but only in its appearance in the outer strata.

It is not much different with sculpture. We have Hegel's famous example of the sublime in the classic Greek sculptures of gods. How is it with the sublime in such cases? One seeks it in vain in the details of the figures' stance, and, with even less success, in symbols and emblems. Only the whole of its attitude expresses it: when illuminated as a whole, (382) what produces its effect is the facial expression of a superior kind of tranquility, of severity, kindness, and wisdom.

Think, for example, upon the way the Olympic Apollo holds his head, or upon the head of Athena in her Corinthian helmet: here the level in which the appearing divine-sublime is rooted becomes clearly visible. It is the last stratum, that of the universal ideas: great human ideals rise to the level of the superhuman and are beheld as in a vision and fixed in stone. But this fixing in stone is entirely brought to life; it appears provided that it can be placed in the spatial form of stone. And what remains upon it is darkly sensed; it is a profundity that can still be felt.

And where in music is the sublime found? It is hard to find in the pure play with forms of the outer strata, however deep one's understanding of the compositional structure of the musical piece may be. It can only be something other, a uniform whole – specifically a dynamic whole – that stands behind it; and that must belong to the domain of those inner strata in which the emotional turmoil of the psychic life unfolds.

Out of this originates the great power that we have concretely before our eyes in certain "first movements" of symphonies, quartets, or sonatas. That is no cheap sublimity, which one is free to ignore; rather, the situation is as follows: either we "understand" the music, and then we understand also what is sublime in its great style, or we do not understand it, and then what is essential in the music passes us by. This is so even more profoundly for the fugues of Bach: in their smallest segments we have the appearance of what is greatest and most profound. From there come the most sublime effects that no one could challenge, the "metaphysical" elements, as we often call them.

What is wonderful in music is just that it can produce in its outer strata an almost adequate expression of things other arts are not nearly capable of expressing. It is achieved through the absolute freedom of the play of forms in the tonal composition – even in the larger unities of entire musical works. On the other hand, it is achieved through the relinquishment of any real "representation": for the element of content, as much as one recognizes it as psychic emotion, remains hovering in a characteristic indeterminateness, and only the dynamic character comes to expression. This indeterminateness corresponds closely to the "darkness" in which the sublime appears.

Finally we have the same preponderance of the intangible inner strata in architecture – namely everywhere that it becomes monumental, that is, where its aesthetical effect is that of the sublime. Palaces and churches, ancient temples, even towers and city and castle walls manifest this type of formal composition.

Some inner rooms seem "intimate," and others are "uplifting"; we know the latter from Gothic cathedrals. The impression is that of overwhelming height and size. In the older Romanesque it is more a sense of massiveness (the Octagon of Aachen). But the "immensity," (383) that is expressed within it belongs to the sphere of world-views and originates from the last palpable background of the work.

This condition is even more subtle in antique temples, where the expression of size lies more in the external form and is represented by means of the contrasting play of columns and entablature. Perhaps the secret of size lies in simplicity – even if it is in part only apparent. Beyond this suggestion, we can analyze no further the fact that the Doric column has a more sublime effect than the Ionic or even the Corinthian column, which latter are more pleasantly built and more slender. And the situation becomes even more inscrutable when we notice that even with its smaller mass, the Doric column seems considerably "larger" than the others ... A pure example of the architecturally sublime.

b) The sublime in the tragic and its aporias

We have seen the preponderance of the inner strata in the aesthetically sublime object. We could perhaps demonstrate that preponderance still more convincingly, if we were to take account here of the sublime aspects of the tragic, for there is always sublimity where there is a genuine tragic effect. An inquiry of that kind would be too extensive at this time. In lieu of that, we may bring just a few thoughts into this circle of questions. The tragic, like the sublime is not, of course, merely an aesthetical phenomenon; in theoretical discussions of it many purely ethical issues have been drawn into it.

Among the few questions that may be raised about the tragic that really belong in this context, we may count only those that contain certain aporias of the sublime. They are questions such as these: how can there be sublimity in passion? How can what is morally evil be sublime? How can a mere human destiny be sublime? How can guilt and human weakness be sublime? How can the downfall of a good man be sublime? And how can the triumph of the senseless find any place at all in the sublime?

We see that these questions all revolve about the same point, and this point concerns precisely the essence of the tragic as such, that element within it through which it is distinguished from all other forms of sublimity. What this point is cannot be doubted; one must place it at the very top of the essential definition of the tragic.

The tragic in life is the downfall and ruin of what for man is of the highest value. To experience delight at such an event would be morally perverse. But the aesthetically tragic is not the downfall itself, but its appearance. The appearance of the downfall of what is humanly of the highest value may very well have aesthetic value and call forth a delight in beholding it – the shudder it causes us – without harming our moral feeling. This delight is, then a genuine feeling of the value of the sublime. (384)

Why does what is humanly great become especially evident and palpable, precisely in its downfall? One might perhaps opine that human greatness appears precisely in its limitations and its inconstancy. That is of course true, but what is strange is that the human heart ascribes these limitations to it as something positive. A psychological law lies at the root of this fact.

All goods seem to possess the greatest value just at the moment that they are stolen or taken from us: the pain of loss makes the sense we have of their value more intense. The negative value in the tragic appears in this form. One might also say: that is the positive meaning that the disvalue of destruction takes on. For the value and the aesthetical delight of the viewer is not tied to destruction, but rather to human greatness itself. But this human greatness is brought into the full light of our interest, of our sympathetic participation in it, and of our more intense feelings of value, only by the painful sympathy we feel for its destruction.

We may call this the aesthetical magic of the tragic. It is a kind of transfiguration of the human. It is like the rays of the sun turning everything visible to gold as it sets. In comparison, it is of secondary interest that in the structure of a drama the impending downfall gives occasion to the heroic in man to take upon a truly superior stance. Only the seriousness of what threatens him places a man before the highest challenge; such challenge first allows what is great in him to "appear." And the aesthetic value depends precisely upon appearance.

With that, we have already solved one of the above-mentioned aporias of the tragic: it is not the downfall as such of the Good that is sublime, but the Good itself is transfigured in its downfall, and becomes sublime. And the more clearly the downfall reflects itself in the suffering and the defeat of those who struggle, so much more is the magic of the tragic amplified, for so much more is the audience driven to inward sympathy. To this extent Aristotle's doctrine of φόβος and ἔλεος [fear and pity] is entirely correct; however, the affirmative element in it is developed too subjectively.

In a similar way, the other aporias are resolved. How can a mere destiny be sublime? The situation is the same as with the case of downfall. Not every destiny is sublime, and neither is every great misfortune, only the tragic ones – i.e., the destiny of some great kind, one that bestows upon that destiny the transfiguration of a downfall. The best example of this is the tragic denouement of a great love: one sees to what degree the destiny that separates the pair has an elevating effect upon us just by the ease and almost the necessity by which a happy end destroys all grandeur. One may in fact say: destiny as such is not at all sublime, just as little as a downfall; what is sublime is solely the human greatness that is amplified in it.

The same is true for the other form of the aporia: how can the triumph of what is senseless have a place in the sublime? It finds its place where (385) what is awesome in the appearance of human greatness is conditioned by its defeat. The defeat appears as the triumph of the senseless.

How can there be a sublimity of passion? And how can there be a sublimity of evil? These are two very different questions, for passion can also be a passion for goodness, for high endeavors. But in any effort to answer them, they belong closely together. There is a false resolution of these aporias. In the overcoming of passion, there may be sublimity, and there are poets who seek to find, in the self-overcoming of their heroes, the resolution of tragic conflict. But such resolutions are "rational," and leave us cold. They are intended as a "moral." Thus, they are poetically false.

The real resolution is a quite different one. The negative element in the sublime is by no means so general as Kant thought, but there are in fact certain genera of the sublime that really contain this element, e.g., the "fearsome" or the "threatening." To these belong, as was observed, the tragic. But the negative element does not necessarily have to lie in the external threats that endanger men. It can also lie within them, and it can even be attached just to those characteristics that constitute the human greatness in him.

It is at first indifferent to the nature of sublimity "what" grows up in man to overwhelming greatness, if only there is a power in him that is capable of true greatness. Passion in itself is neutral: it can be destructive, but it can also be constructive; its greatness makes it significant. In Romeo and Othello it is love, in Macbeth it is ambition and the desire for power. An audience may accept these passions for a long while, can even feel them empathetically in their aberration, and sense their greatness as impressive.

This extends much further in the case of the sublimity of evil. We reject it, we step back from it in horror, but we yet still sense the greatness in it: Richard III sweeps us along in such a way that we admire as such his boldness, his vigor, and we find his efforts to be worthy of a "good" cause (a better one). In that way, his well-known wickedness grows with his downfall – but does evil itself thereby become sublime? That cannot be true.

To this we must answer: in fact that is not the case, evil in man is not sublime, although the downfall of the wicked man contains tragic sublimity in itself. Rather human greatness as such is sublime, even when it turns itself to evil, yes, even when the decision for evil is taken in principle. This is developed, via the highest sublimation, in the tragic figure of Mephistopheles, who, in the end, is the one betrayed. Then, corresponding to this figure, are those forms of passion that evil wears: anger, fury, desire for revenge, and the outrage that burns up accumulated resentment. The greatness in all that is like that of a natural force.

The final secret in the tragedy of evil is freedom. There is no freedom to do good alone, there is only freedom to do good and to do (386) evil. Thus, freedom appears in an evil will – whatever may motivate it – and just as purely in good will. However, freedom as such, understood as willing as such, is the fundamental attribute of man, the emblem of his power – and at the same time it is the general necessary condition in him of morality, the capacity to be good or evil.

As the final aporia, consider the question: how can guilt and human weakness be sublime? This is not the same question as the preceding, for guilt is not the evil in man, but it is rather primarily a document of freedom. It is well known how men disputed a hundred years ago whether the true tragic fate is guilt by one's own doing, or whether it falls to a hero from outside oneself. Voices were not lacking to speak out for the latter, and, for support, they pointed to the ancient tragedy of destiny.

People believed that men were able to sympathize adequately only with the innocent, but that is quite untrue. A man in a conflict who is without guilt is hardly human. For, first, action in life, in some situation, gives him no time; thus, he acts out of passion. Second, real life situations are not such that a man can emerge guiltless from them; in the most momentous human situations, at least, that is not possible. One value stands opposed to another, and the will must decide which he will violate, and to which he will do justice.

That is the reason why even being completely guilty as such has something tragic about it. In the case of great guilt, however, one that is decisive for a man's life and places a heavy burden upon him, this tragic element is amplified to the sublime, because the measure of guilt is greater than the capacity of the man to bar it, and it can cripple him inwardly (Don Cesar)[126]. ... Then guilt develops into a destiny – in the form of an inward fate for which one has prepared the way. And the problem flows into that of destiny and downfall, which was already solved unambiguously.

c) Questions on the periphery of the sublime

We have introduced the tragic here not for itself alone, but only insofar as it represents a special case of the sublime. And that is only a part of tragedy. The other side of the tragic lies in the domain of the dramatic that makes up one specific sector of aesthetic value. For it is by no means by chance that tragic conflicts offer especially propitious conditions for meeting the requirement of highly animated and concentrated plots. That belongs to dramaturgy, which will no longer be treated here. What is more important for our general problematic is that tragedy also represents a marginal case of the sublime, which one apprehends upon the strong negative element in it.

The tragic is, in fact, not the sublime. When both appear in a character, such as in Siegfried in the *Nibelungenlied*, they still do not consist in the same characteristics: the sublime lies in the larger-than-life size of the unyielding power, of the immediacy, uprightness, cheerful security (387) and inner peace in the character; the tragic lies in the deceit to which he devotes himself, and the consequences that were his own doing. If the sublime appears only through these consequences, what is great and inspiring is still not attached to those consequences, and the tragic element remains in a certain opposition to sublimity. That is a trait that attaches to all that is aesthetically tragic. It is already given with the negativity of is preconditions alone.

In this sense, what is genuinely tragic also stands closely tied to the sublime, but opposite to it, and constitutes its counterweight. What is and remains most noticeable is that the feeling of value, too, reacts to these two elements in entirely opposed ways: it reacts to the errors and downfall with weeping and wailing, and

---

126 [Translator's note:] Don Cesar, character in *Die Braut von Messina* [*The Bride of Messina*], 1803 play by Friedrich Schiller.

to the greatness of what is thereby lost forever with enthusiasm and an inward sense of elevation.

Consider also that the tragic as an aesthetical collective phenomenon constitutes that form of the aesthetically sublime that concerns human and moral greatness. It is true that it is not the only form, but it is in fact the one that is most strongly marked by the sublime – if one does not consider the form of music, which is even more marked by sublimity, though it is indefinite. Literature, in contrast, manifests the tragic in completely objective individual definiteness. And if this form turns out to be in fact a phenomenon on the periphery of the sublime, certainly a peculiar weight would surely fall upon the phenomena on the periphery of the sublime. In the tragic, no doubt, this was never clearly seen. Only in well-tested theories, provided that they try to make room of the negative element, do we find something like a sense of this state of affairs.

A second form of the phenomenon on the periphery of the essence of the sublime is tediousness. It is a phenomenon that attracts less attention, and seems to have been rightly considered almost nowhere in aesthetics, although many thinkers have come close to it. At first sight it seems even unbelievable that there should be a direct transition from the sublime to the tedious – that the former should change over into the latter. And yet the possibility is not so strange.

Consider that the contrary of the tedious is the amusing, the distracting, and the gay. All that is lacking in sublimity, there is no concern for diversions, or, perhaps, they can be provided at times, as often happens in the musically sublime, but in the nature of the sublime itself it is not to be found, and there is a kind of sublimity in which monotony plays a major role. People have pointed to the example of the still waters of the high seas, where neither one's own animation nor the contrast of land and sea introduces some diversity. One might add to that the example of the desert, perhaps also the flat northern tundra.

With these examples, one senses immediately the borderline space between the sublime that ravishes us and the monotonous-indifferent: it seems as if a mere step would suffice to leave the one and enter into the other. That is a serious danger for the aesthetically sublime. For in tedium it is (388) eliminated beyond hope, because it lacks what is gripping, mysterious, attractive, and inscrutable.

The attempt to understand, as did the Romantics, the overwhelmingly great in the sublime as a kind of infinity has been shown to be false. But that does not exclude the possibility that in certain cases it is really a matter of an infinity – at least in the imagination, or in what imagination takes to be infinite, i.e., everything very large, whether extensive or not. Examples such as the still ocean, the desert, the tundra, are of this kind. But then there is no doubt that infinities of that kind, the Hegelian "bad infinity," are entirely tedious infinities.

One cannot avoid this curse of the infinite by reaching for the highest objects and calling immediately upon their sublimity as a hedge against tedium. Even God becomes tedious if one takes His infinite nature a bit too strictly, if, that is, one no longer looks upon Him, as the pious do, out of a deep living desire; thus in Dostoyevsky we are told of the blessed in heaven who sit to praise God for a thousand years, and then again for a thousand years, and so forth *in infinitum.*

Plato saw this danger to the sublime in the eternal seriousness of the tragic poetry of his time. He noted this danger, at the close of the *Symposium,* as a contrast to his famous insistence that the tragic poet also be a comical poet. Nothing but comedy can bring bright life and animation into monotonous seriousness. And that is quite natural: for so is human life. Shakespeare proved that Plato's insistence is not utopist.

The most weighty among the phenomena on the periphery of the sublime is the comical, or, as it is usually described, the ridiculous. "It is only a step from the sublime to the ridiculous." In this form, everyone knows the peripheral condition that is intended here. And, in life as in art, the scornfulness of uncreative men takes whatever is useful to it for "whate'er is bright to stain, and in the dust to lay the glorious low."[127] Such is the work of caricature, satire, and parody; such of travesty; such, as we see in life itself, is the work of the clever buffoon. They all bring laughter effortlessly to their side, and sublimity vanishes, is forgotten, is done for. One may think of Euripides in Hades in the work by Aristophanes (ληκύτιον ἀπώλετο ...). Or in the impersonation scene in *Henry IV*: Falstaff's joke on the king.

That is possible only where the sublime itself has already provided the toehold for it, i.e., where it lowers its guard. But how does that come to pass? It means that something is lacking in it. Why does the sublime find itself so easily lacking? Does it not have the highest pretentions? Or is the matter simply that people allow themselves to be led astray to the extent that they represent the sublime with insufficient powers? Perhaps even in their own lives they are able to realize it only in a foolish way? This latter point must be affirmed: say that someone wants to give himself an appearance of dignity that he does not possess. Immediately he makes himself ridiculous; (389) another man feigns power and confidence in his demeanor. Both fail on the first attempt.

And yet we find the sublime a thousandfold about us. Nature alone is full of it. Why is it not lacking in nature? Because it does not begin with pretentions as

---

127 [Translator's note:] Schiller, Friedrich, *The Poems of Schiller, Complete: Including All His Early Suppressed Pieces,* translated by Edgar Alfred Bowring, London: Parker 1851, p. 244. (Schiller, "Das Mädchen von Orleans": "Es liebt die Welt, das Strahlende zu schwärzen / Und das Erhabne in den Staub zu ziehn").

men do, and only that which is genuine and entirely fulfilled in it is alone what matters. Only man misses the sublime. Even in art works even in representation.

Why in fact is it only a step from the sublime to the ridiculous? Because the pretentions of the sublime are of a higher and more encompassing kind. It is easy to fall short of such pretentions; here the possibility of derailment is the greatest.

However, the nature of the comical consists precisely in such a derailment – a fall from things important and bitterly earnest into what is trivial and banal. That means that what is overwhelmingly great turns out to be some everyday human trifle, just when it was least expected. Thus when Diogenes says to Alexander, "Stand away from my sunlight," the sublime, which then collapses into itself, is that of "Majesty."

Perhaps no kind of human or tragic greatness exists that would not be liable to this derailment into the ridiculous, for anywhere the trivial can peer out of a chink in one's armor. Or does there exist a sublimity that was created by men but that is beyond all such danger?

No doubt there does: in the non-representational arts, in music and in architecture. Here, too, there are weaknesses and errors in form, but they remain attached entirely to the foreground – more correctly, to the outer strata – and, in the worst cases, they appear as miscarriages and have no comical effect. The basis for this lies in the neutrality of the tones and the natural forms, as also in the indefiniteness of musical and architectonic expression, neither of which are expressions of themes or content, but merely deliver the psychic dynamics. These latter are, of course, not only stronger and more direct than in other arts, but are rather also more perfect, which is alone possible precisely in the heterogeneity of their material.

One further matter must be noted here. For poetry of a high and heroic style, this third phenomenon on the periphery of the sublime is a truly fearsome threat. In its most inward nature, such poetry is endangered by an involuntary transformation of the sublime into the ridiculous – and it cannot protect itself from that fate very easily – not even where it is completely genuine and fully realized – because ingenious or vulgar mockery can at any time, by a slight falsification of the tragic, create a point of attack for the comical. The example from Aristophanes is close to being of this kind.

Is there any remedy for it? Can one actively prepare a barrier to it? Yes, there is a means, an infallible one, but it presupposes a poetic skill of the highest kind. The tragic poet can himself discover the ridiculous that borders him on all sides and absorb it into the negative side of the tragic. In that way, he breaks the point of the spear – he turns it (390) about, so that it does not point in the direction of the sublime – and he lets the tragic element be amplified by burdening the tragic hero, already burdened with bad luck and pain, with scorn, which is the heavy curse of the ridiculous.

A proof of this taken from a high example is the fool's scene in *King Lear*. The fool says to Lear, "for when thou gavest them [your daughters] the rod, and puttedst down thine own breeches" [Act I, Scene IV]. The "fools" in Shakespeare illustrate this point; and indeed Shakespeare, too, as a whole, in almost every tragic play. Thus one cannot make fun of him; he anticipated the ridiculous, which borders on the sublime, and uttered it more powerfully than the most malicious mockery could do. – Note here again also Plato's law of the unity of the tragic and the comical.

Chapter 33: The Charming and Its Varieties

a) Phenomena in opposition to the sublime

It was shown above how within beauty in general the sublime stands in a clear position of opposition to an entire series of aesthetic values and families of values (Chap. 30a), that is, to the charming, the enticing, the idyllic, the delightful, the amiable or kind, the sweet, the droll, the grotesque, the fantastic and the amusing. The series can be differentiated more extensively. What is more important is that the series is not the only one, nor is it homogenous in itself.

We have seen that the sublime has a certain special place within the realm of beauty in general – because of its significance, but also because of its uniqueness. To this special place corresponds the fact that it has, in a multidimensional relation of opposition, contrasting values of very different types and of very different importance over against itself. Each opposite number forms an entire group. It is sufficient, however, to characterize each of them in terms of their best-known representatives. Accordingly, we will distinguish here four contrasting or oppositional dimensions in which the sublime forms the common extreme: as such, the sublime stands in opposition:

1. To the quotidian, the usual, the neutral, to that which is in no way distinctive;
2. To the facile, the small, the insignificant, to what lacks importance, to the delicate – to these one might perhaps also count the idyllic, but surely the sweet and the droll;
3. To the charming and its various species: the enticing, the delightful, the amiable, the graceful; beyond them most likely also the amusing, the grotesque and the phantasmagoric;
4. To the comical: this term used in its broadest sense, with its varieties: the witty, the ridiculous, and the humorous. (391)

We will consider the comical separately. It perhaps constitutes the most difficult of the regions of aesthetical problems, and for that reason we must hold off discussing it until simpler matters have been resolved. The first of the oppositions that we named, the "quotidian" and the usual or normal, does not require any analysis here, because it has no aesthetical character of its own, but is neutral regarding aesthetic values. Of direct interest in this context are only the two middle values in opposition to the sublime: the "facile" and the "charming," both with their specific forms that are, moreover, closely related.

As for the first, the opposition is to the "weighty and the great" in the sublime. This aspect has been taken so seriously by some aestheticians that they have even counted the charming as belonging to this opposition to the sublime (Eduard von Hartmann). They thought that if the sublime is the overwhelmingly powerful and great, then the charming must be the "impotent," that is, a thing that has some-how turned out to be weak and small, and if one must look upward to the former, one must look downward to the latter.

If one looks more deeply into this relationship, one finds that two different oppositional dimensions have been confused with each other, the second and the third: that opposition of the sublime to the facile, small, and delicate, and that to the charming and delightful. That the two are not identical ought to be obvious from the fact that the differences in size can hardly determine whether something is charming or enticing – not, at least, where it is primarily of significance, that is, in man, with respect to both body and soul (and in fact they exist only as the two together). The "delicate" is, to be sure, just as much in opposition to the sublime as is the charming, but this is a different opposition. That is the reason why it lies in another domain of value as the group of values that make up the charming.

The parallel to the comical might make one think of a relation between the sublime and the charming similar to that between the comical and the ridiculous that was discussed above. If this is so, it would then be a question of another marginal phenomenon of the sublime: there would have to be a direct transition of the sublime to the charming, a switching over, just as the phenomenon of the "one step" [from the sublime to the ridiculous]. There is no question of any of this as a matter of fact. There is no continuous transition at all from the sublime to the charming, not to speak of an insidious switching over of the one to the other. And the reason why this is not possible is that in this case a much more abrupt and pure relation of opposition exists.

That may be additionally confirmed by the fact that in this opposition there is hidden something negative and exclusionary – something that makes it approach a contradiction. The sublime excludes charm as such, and the attractiveness or amiability that ties us to a person excludes, for its part, the presence of sublimity. If one only tries to imagine this, one will see immediately the element of mutual exclusion. This touch of the contradictory makes transitions and transformations of the one to the other impossible. In that way, it does not allow any suspicion (392) of a border region existing between them. On the side of the charming no threat to the sublime arises, nothing forces itself upon its domain, and nothing at all penetrates into that domain. Remember also that the sublime at least permits an element of oppressiveness – and of what is negative in general. The charming radically excludes such things. They would annul it.

It is impossible to say what the charming consists in; it is even more impossible to say what the sublime consists in. In the latter, at least, we can point to the easily comprehended element of "greatness," although it is not so simple to say what greatness consists in, when the quantitative element in it insubordinate. Some thinkers inferred from this opposition of the charming to the sublime that we must have a case here of "smallness," but then one confuses the charming with the delicate and the sweet – as we have already noted. From this perspective, therefore, we are unable to obtain an essential characterization of the charming.

b) Orientation to the nature of the charming

One might simply give up the attempt at this point, since it is not the case that all beauty must be either a thing sublime or charming; rather there exist very many other instances of beauty: in the drama, the novel, in architecture and painting, in music and in life. ... We also referred to this fact above. Nonetheless, something remained that now thrusts itself upon us as a problem, namely the peculiar opposition itself to the sublime.

This contrast has not yet been evaluated. And since the attempts to date must be considered failures, we must attack it from another direction. There are in fact three possibilities for such an attempt. The first consists in a direct description; the second in an inquiry into "where" the charming appears (in which arts, etc.); the third in the question, In which strata of the aesthetic object is the charming rooted?

For the first instance, let us consider description. The "charming" means that which "charms," and indeed whose charms attract us. That is what is intended. What is it then, for example, that attractively charms us in a landscape? That would be easy to say, if one stood before a lovely landscape or a picture of one and could point to individual details; but it is hard to do when all one has are concepts to reckon with.

Is it that the landscape must appeal to the needs of men in order to be charming? Hardly, for then one finds oneself in a context of usefulness. But if I say that the landscape breathes peace and cheerfulness, then I am as far as I was before, and must ask anew what it is that produces the impression of peace and cheerfulness.

To that one may reply: a softly rolling terrain, traces of people in the form of their houses, farms, and pathways; a water-course or the (393) mirror-like lake, the enticing variations in woods, fields, and meadows; above it a summer sun with little billowing clouds scudding by. ... No doubt, one hears something of the charm of the landscape in all of that. But is that universally valid for the charming? That cannot be so; this is only a special case, at best a type of charming landscape. Most likely, the element of variety is extremely general. The truth may be that the charming is individual, and different in every case. But there is nothing new about that; it is common to all things beautiful.

Is the case any different with a charming face? What charm attracts us here? The charm of expression, a slight smile; perhaps a wide-eyed glance, perhaps down-turned lids. ... Clearly, it may take quite disparate forms, indeed even change to different features in one and the same face can affect us with its inner animation, as infinite variety, as riches. ...

And even then, we have said very little. The genuine charm of a face or of a person lies in what shines out of the soul into the features of the face. Here we enter immediately the realm of ethical values; the aesthetically charming cannot be sealed off from that domain, for in fact certain ethical values enter into and condition – one could also use the term "found" (cf. Chap. 28c) the charming. There is nothing remarkable about that. They are also presupposed as foundations everywhere there is any question of the beauty of the human being or of the human condition.

But it is impossible to relate firmly any single moral value to the charming as its foundation, for there are always others to consider: on the one hand, shyness, modesty, innocence; on the other pride, a dignified self-assurance, rectitude, simplicity, unselfconsciousness.

And it need not be a matter of values alone. Disvalues can be foundational here, such as fear, dread, uncertainty, or the need for protection. A strong impulse can be generated by the expression of these negatives; indeed, precisely an aesthetical impulse in addition to the moral one. For the expression of them demands sympathetic interest and active help, and it affects us as a component of kindness.

It appears accordingly that in the domain of the humanly charming something more is to be obtained by means of the description of the relevant phenomena than those below the human realm. Perhaps that is because our attention here is directed by the phenomena themselves to the relation of appearance. With that, we already stand close to the second point of the inquiry: where the charming appears in the arts. We have asked similar questions with respect to the sublime, and from them resulted some distinctions among the arts.

With respect to the charming, there result also distinctions in the arts. For that reason, we must not allow any of the arts to be entirely excluded here. Even ornamental art can be charming, alluring, and attractive; similarly, architectural works can in certain cases have a charming effect, especially smaller ones that are harmoniously integrated within a landscape. Sculpture (394) is familiar with the charming in the stance and expression of its figures – from the grace of Aphrodite to the posture of the dancer (Kolbe[128]).

But the charming has much greater latitude in the domain of painting. The basis for this is profound. Charm exercises itself in the sphere of the sensible; whatever values may stand behind it as foundational, in itself it is entirely an affair of appearance. Painting, however, lays direct hold upon everything that is visible to the senses. It can hold every facial expression fast, even the most transient, and can allow everything that can be reflected in human features to appear in that expression. However, it is not so much the substance of the human being that makes up the charming, but the sensible play of the forms and colors themselves and the potency of appearance as such.

The content is developed much more effectively in literature. But even there the importance lies, in the end, upon the process of appearance. The endearing, the fine, good taste, come to appearance in the attitudes of persons; and this "appearance," upon which alone aesthetic value depends, is apparently also one close to the senses. The grace of Susanne (in *Figaro*), the captivating ways of Philine[129] appear in their stories, whether recounted or performed – not by gestures given visible clarity, as in painting, but by having the advantage of not being limited to a single instant. Since they are extended in time, they are capable of being followed along. In the case of human charm, that is a great advantage. In that way, the poetic arts can easily compete in their effects with painting by letting appear such subtle traits as that of the enticing, the fascinating, or the enchanting, although they do not attain the closeness to the senses of painting.

Finally, music: where there are nuances of the human soul that let themselves be captured without any definite content, music is in its true element. The greatest delicacy, flowering and swelling, warmth, clarity, brightness, buoyancy and purity – it knows how to bring everything to its adequate expression in its absolutely free play with form, which, in the nuance of the dynamic, knows no limits.

If one compares these results with the situation we encountered in the sublime, we get the following picture. Only music plays the exact same role for

---

128 [Translator's note:] Georg Kolbe (1877–1947).
129 [Translator's note:] The title of a poem by Johann Wolfgang von Goethe and a character in his *Wilhelm Meister's Apprenticeship*.

the sublime as for the charming, in that they both aim at the highest and most differentiated effects. In literature, the achievement is a bit unequal. It presents the sublime only in the limiting form of the tragic, while the charming is able to unfold completely in all its human forms. Sculpture clearly demonstrates a preference for the sublime, painting for the charming. Architecture is more capable of the sublime, and there it is able to rise to extraordinarily high values. In comparison, ornamental art, at least in one of its modes, is the master of the charming (the agreeable), but never of the sublime.

We see that when one places music on top, then descends downward past poetry and the fine arts to the level of architecture and ornament, one is moving along a line marking an increasing separation of the arts with respect to (395) their aptitude for the sublime and the charming. It has already been noted that this is connected to the relative distance of the arts from the senses – as that distance first appeared clearly in painting.

The next question is how we are to interpret this divergence. For that, we must enter the third of the groups of problems presented above, which concerns the part played by the strata in in the creation of the sublime and the charming in the work of art.

c) The predominance of the external strata

In which strata of the object do we find the charming? This question should be understood as strictly as in the case of the sublime: it is obviously not a question of isolating individual strata and in imagining that in them alone is the seat of the charming – that would be nonsense – but of identifying which levels have the largest part in the charming. That is a sensible question, and it can be answered.

We recall (Chap. 32a) how it stood with the sublime in this context: the inner strata were predominant in a decisive way. The overwhelmingly great is and remains a matter of the background and, in some cases, it possessed an intellectual character; and the negative element in it, which has been much discussed since Kant, consists in nothing more than that the senses fail before it.

Now the case with the charming and its varieties is somewhat different, and may be discovered at a place that aesthetics has long sought in vain, one that determines in a genuinely positive way the opposite of the charming: in charm, the predominant factor lies in the outer strata of the object. It depends on the superficial regions, to which it is tied – not the foreground alone, although the foreground takes part in it essentially.

Thus, in literature the attractive and amiable characteristics of the figures are neither tied to the stratum of destiny, nor even less to the stratum of the figure and his secrets; but hey are tied, only to a slight degree, to the situation and the plot, and much more obviously to the stratum of the movements and gestures of the persons and their external appearance and speech, which stands close behind the foreground. That stratum is co-realized in the stage play, because it addresses itself directly to the senses – more strictly, to sensible fantasy. One understands this immediately when one reflects on how great is the role of grace in fantasy. Then, too, values such as gentleness and sweetness, the enchanting and the attractive, are rooted here – close to the doorstep of the senses, and always extended into its domain.

That is, as it seems to me, the first and, up to now, the only affirmative determination of the charming to which aesthetics has attained. It was successful only through the distinctions among the strata in the structure of the aesthetic object, which were introduced here for the first time. Without it, we would lack any point of departure for an attack upon the problem of the charming. The proof of it can be gleaned from all areas of art in the exact same way as from literature. (396) Moreover, the proof is not limited to what has just been said: think of lyric poetry with its rich variety of sensible images, in which the special forms of the charming play a considerable role.

But the strongest witness for this idea is found in painting. It is in fact the art from which the sublime markedly withdraws – not because it lacks at all the necessary deep strata for it – those it indeed has, as we see in certain portraits – but rather because it absorbs too readily into itself the cheerful sensuousness of light and color. This characteristic partiality for the foreground is averse to the sublime. But it corresponds perfectly to the charming: for what is amiable or enchanting plays itself out on the level of the visible, and this dominates the art of painting like no other. The same is true for every kind of enchantment, of the blossoming, the fascinating: only the eyes are opened sufficiently for such seduction. In such full, concrete details, which are here in question, poetry cannot keep up with painting, although it has the advantage of process in time and can mark the changes in the features of its objects. Yet the smile of Mona Lisa can only be painted.

We should recall at this point the divergent tendencies in the arts with respect to the sublime and the charming: music is capable of both, but architecture and ornament are unfairly weighted, the first toward the former and at the second toward the latter. This divergence, apparently, has its basis in the way different strata dominate in different arts.

Music possesses a unique freedom. It can elevate the deepest material resident in the background to the level of immediate sensible feeling – of course not to a point at which it can be grasped conceptually, but that is not at stake here – and it can put in sound the lightest and most enticing melodies in an immediate series of ravishing tones. That is so essential to it that in "great music," that is, in works of several movements, it has become custom to interpolate a certain alteration between the sublime and the charming. That is the meaning of the entry, in the middle movements, of scherzo, minuets, and the like, while the first and last movements, but especially the first, manifest preferentially throughout the character of the sublime.

Upon this freedom of music – primarily pure music – which itself remains rooted in indefiniteness regarding its object, rests its wonderful capacity to accompany everything, and to surround with the right mood whatever is peculiar to the ongoing human life. Thus it is able to bring into the opera and oratorio, with scarce effort, the spiritually sublime in a form that can be comprehended and experienced, as it brings grace and sweetness, mildness and bright warmth into light songs, dances, and operettas. Music can make dominant, according to its wishes, the inner or the outer groups of strata. For that reason, it is more of a universal art than the others.

We might have shown further that even sculpture, within limits, is capable of both extremes – no doubt with a certain preponderance of the sublime. It thus manifests the preferences opposed to (397) those of painting. Can one now say that the condition rests upon a preponderance of the inner strata? If we look at the classic example of the Greek sculptures of the gods, where sublimity predominates, we will be able to affirm that. For this is the stratum from which appearance emerges, the stratum of religious consciousness. It is of course true of sculpture that it can do otherwise – only not with the same sovereignty as music. It cannot capture so easily the ephemeral and the light-footed; yet where it does so, it can hold tight to it. It can also transfer its weight to the external strata.

In this regard, the place of architecture is also instructive. A building, as a rather large work, is always something imposing in itself, and, as such, it resists the charming. On the other hand, however, the tendency to become monumental – i.e., to move into the domain of the sublime – is found even in relatively small structures. The monumental can at least express itself in the detail, in portals, open stairs, courtyard passageways in patrician homes. In contrast, the charming appears more seldom, and when it does, it is only where it is derived from an imitation of folk-styles and integrated into a landscape or a townscape that is in itself idyllic. Nonetheless, the charming is possible in such buildings as the peasant cottage, the timbered house, etc.

The final confirmation of this law lies in ornamental art, from which we saw that, in its case, the sublime does not come into question. It does not have any deeper strata that could appear; it exhausts itself in a free play with form. And it is characteristic of such play that it may very well have "charm," exert an attraction upon the senses, and even arouse directly an impulse to play with spatial form. Here we have the extreme, here the charming lies directly in the foreground. For a genuine background is not present.

Chapter 34: Peripheral Problems of the Charming

a) Compatibility of the sublime and the charming

A large collection of marginal problems accompanies the main problems of aesthetic values. Taken strictly, the situation is such that we are as yet not even certain about the main problems themselves. It may turn out one day that the analyses of the sublime and the charming are still insufficient, and that even its concepts and the relevant phenomena are not the central ones that must be attacked. Thus it might easily happen, as it often does with insufficiently developed areas of research, that from the marginal problems that no one had noticed the real, central questions may finally be developed. But such things cannot be anticipated. One may prepare for such an eventuality only by inquiring into these marginal problems for their own sakes. (398)

From among these problems, the first is directed at the issue of whether, and, if so, to what extent, opposed aesthetic values are compatible with each other, or more concretely stated, whether one and the same aesthetic object can be simultaneously sublime and charming.

There are two reasons why one would expect an affirmative answer. First, there are some arts that are masters of the sublime and of the charming, as we have seen – music and poetry especially – but the other great arts, too, although to a more modest degree. It is then difficult to understand why the arts should not be able to make both appear in one and the same work of art. And second: in life – as occasionally also in nature – the two are, after all, often united. The striving and struggling of a man can be genuinely sublime, all the more when he as a great resistance to overcome – nonetheless he may shine with the amiability of an old culture and the poised cheerfulness of a serene nature, no doubt to contrast with his earnestness, but not in conflict with it. But this alone says little. It is far more a question of how in principle this relation is given shape for the arts.

One may not shunt this problem onto another track. That happens, for example, when one assumes there is a relationship between "charm and dignity" – an assumption that is familiar to us since Schiller, but is of a different kind than the one we seek. For dignity is only related to sublimity, and has been falsely presented as one of its varieties. Dignity is too much an exclusively ethical phenomenon for it to be placed in service here; besides, theoreticians have understood it too much as "consciousness of one's own sublimity," where self-consciousness is in a dangerous passageway towards narcissism and the cult of the self.

At first sight, the sublime and the charming seem to exclude each other. Just because an object is sublime, it is not charming; just because it is charming, it is not sublime. To one belongs heaviness, to the other lightness, to one austerity and severity, to the other mildness and attractiveness.

But there are objects of a broader nature and a greater inner variety. Of this kind are man and likewise any segment of a human life, even more when the man in question manifests all kinds of complex interrelationships of any given kind. Figures of such a kind may well be sublime in one respect, and in another be charming. A man can possess amiability of the purest kind in his intercourse with others, and yet in his plans, his undertakings, and the energy with which he executes them he may be truly a man of grand format; that is not seldom the case in times of high culture, because there are great careers, political ones, perhaps, that are not possible to carry out without a degree of charm in one's external demeanor. And a slice of life, such as a writer cuts out for us in a novel can, as a whole (399) be full of fascination and charm, and yet from its depths lets us perceive the sublime lines of a larger destiny, a personal one, perhaps, or even an historical one.

If one reflects more exactly upon what this situation entails, one will have to confess that it must always be so with some truths about life in the representational arts. For in life, everything is in fact jumbled together. We must not forget here that the art of representation begins with separating off, leaving out, and isolating objects, i.e., with a process of simplification. That consists in getting rid of this jumble and thereby allowing individual aspects of things and their interrelations to appear vividly before us.

As a consequence, the unification of the sublime and the charming in the arts should be a limited one. At least it places before the artist demands that are not easy to fulfill, and the same is true for the viewer who, in order to assimilate such works, would have to have seen a great deal of life and bring to the work a broad and developed heart.

But with that, the question of the unification of sublimity and charm is not yet solved in a fundamental way. We see now, however, what form the eventual solution must take, and upon what it must be based. Thus, we return to our basic thesis about beauty, i.e., that beauty rests upon a relation of stratification and of appearance.

We have already seen how the main distinction between the sublime and the charming lies in a distinction in depth of the series of strata of the object: the sublime, where it appears, is rooted in the inner strata of the object; the charming, in contrast, in the outer strata. Now upon this condition also rests the unification of the two with each other. If they had their soil and roots in the same stratum, then they would have to encroach upon each other in the form of appearance peculiar to that one stratum. In an object, one and the same thing cannot be both sublime and charming, or grandiose and amiable; rather they must be of an essentially different nature. Thus there can no doubt be a thing that in its depths is sublime and yet charming in the direction of its surface – but not the reverse. And, moreover, that is all the more possible the more an object has a large number of strata and the further away from each other are the strata that bear the sublime and the charming.

For these reasons, such unification in the case of a living person can take place with relatively little resistance, assuming that the individual meets the conditions for it, and the same is true in the case of a literary representation of a character or a corresponding human destiny. But just for that reason the unification faces significant difficulties in the case of objects with fewer strata, both in nature and in art, and the number of cases sinks to a minimum in sculpture; or sinks to an external juxtaposition of objects, as in a landscape. That such may still be effective as an intended contrast alters nothing of substance. (400)

With this solution we put an end to an old bone of contention. That such contention about this issue could last as long as it did lies in the fact that no one could find upon any of the prevailing foundations a starting-point for a fruitful solution. In the end, the lack of clarity that enveloped everything did not affect the unification of the sublime and the charming alone, but also the inner nature of both. And this nature cannot be penetrated without appropriately resolving the aesthetic object into its strata.

A confirmation of this that lies close at hand to the new conditions, as they were made accessible by the theory of strata, is found in the gradation of the responsive emotions felt by the appropriating subject. Here it is a question of aesthetical pleasure, that is, of enjoyment. This enjoyment can possess very different forms, and that is in a certain way dependent upon which domain of founding values (moral, vital, or goods values) are at its basis. The deeper founding values belong to the deeper strata of the object; the moral values, for example, clearly belong to the stratum of inwardness of character. For that reason they are also the ones that call forth a deeper sympathetic participation on the part of the viewer.

That, moreover, means that the aesthetic values that erect themselves above the object are also arranged in a graduated scale: those that are tied to its deeper strata are also the ones that are more deeply felt, that is, those on which a stronger participation of the ego takes place. That means in turn that they produce deeper aesthetical delight, and a more serious and richer enjoyment.

Thus the sublime is marked by a greater depth of enjoyment and of inner sympathy – corresponding to its own rootedness in the depths of the object. And, inversely, the charming is marked by a certain effect on the surface of the object and by an enjoyment that hovers lightly above it – corresponding to its own rootedness in the external strata of the object.

The unification of the sublime and the charming in one object is consequently possible precisely insofar as the two kinds of delight, which conflict with each other (as they must, when they are felt in one and the same object), are able to stay out of each other's way because they belong to different psychic depths. As a clarification of this, consider that the heterogeneous feelings tied to the same object conflict with each other only as long as they concern the same level of psychic emotionality (one can, no doubt, respond emotionally to the same person both as exciting and as boring – for example when the person is thoughtful, but likes to repeat himself in a clumsy way ...).

b) Problems marginal to the charming

The marginal phenomena of the charming make up a further group of problems. They are not as distinctive as those of the sublime, but they stand, as it were, parallel to them. Moreover, the dimensions of opposition in which they operate are quite of another kind. The parallelism (401) consists only in subtle transitions of the charming to something contrary to it, or also, and not seldom, in an abrupt changeover. Among these forms of changeover, of which there are perhaps many, we will discuss three here, because they throw light upon the nature of the charming itself.

When we reflect that charm, grace, and attractiveness of all kinds lie in a certain perfection of form – although we cannot specify it in any detail – it becomes clear that in these cases beauty always consists in harmonious proportionality, or, more succinctly put, in restraint as such. This is in straightforward opposition to the sublime, which is rooted in the overwhelmingly great, thus clearly in a kind of excess. Excess in the case of the sublime is not a lack of measure, but in the case of the charming it would be, i.e., the opposite to the measured and to noble harmony and proportionality. In this case and for that reason, excess is destructive; it breaks charm to pieces, and something formless comes to take the place of perfection of form.

From this standpoint, we can already see in which direction the first marginal phenomena of the charming lie: in exaggeration. When an artist desires to create with special nicety things that are attractive and enticing, and amplifies them to a degree such that they are no longer true-to-life – or do not seem essentially true –

then the charming changes over into its opposite: it attracts no longer, because it is unconvincing, and it is unconvincing because it does not seem genuine. This "does-not-seem-genuine" is a lack of the true-to-life. What that means can be shown only by examples. Distortion to the point of exaggeration may easily arise from a genuine artistic urge to create the greatest impression by one's drawing. We often find exaggeration where it is a question of the nuances of value that surround the charming.

Nothing is more familiar than the over-rendering of the youthful hero – with all his admirable hot-bloodedness, his capacity for enthusiasm and his unselfconscious chivalry. To measure out such essential elements correctly requires the highest artistic tact and, at the same time, a fineness of feeling that has been matured by long experience. Otherwise, what we will have is an ideal figure much like a fairy-tale prince who lacks genuine living truth. Great writers have not always known how to avoid this, the young Schiller, among others.

A parallel example is the model of the angelic maiden in the Romantic novels of a century ago (beautifully brought out in Dickens). These figures correspond to an emotional ideal; however, they affect us as untrue-to-life, and appear to us today a bit ridiculous or, even worse, they bore us. A third example is offered by certain Madonnas – not only in the painting of the late Middle Ages, but also just as much in the High Renaissance – which consist of hollow purity, humility, and piety, and as a result, those qualities begin to strike us as bloodless and somewhat lifeless. Much good will is surely needed to overlook those qualities – as the art historian does, who is concerned only with the phenomena typical of an age. (402)

It is not by chance that these examples come close to false aesthetical ideals. The phenomenon of the derailment both of the charming as it becomes untrue to life and of ideals that have gone awry, coincide in a broad way. This is a fundamental phenomenon manifesting itself in very different kinds of problems at the frontiers of aesthetics.

Another marginal phenomenon of the charming, which is related to the preceding ones, and which also concerns "representation," is the generation of excess tension in immediate emotional effects without their being justified by the actual bestowal of form upon some material. Most of these special forms of the charming are capable of producing such emotional effects, and within their limits, they are entirely appropriate. Indeed, most of these forms are even known through such emotional effects; the "attractive," the "touching," the "enchanting," the "amiable," even the "charming" in general; for it means, after all, not what is charming in any way at all, but rather the attractive-charming.

However, these emotional effects have the peculiarity of making themselves autonomous, and then they overshoot the mark. The artist perhaps wishes to amplify them to some extent, but he may thereby spoil them. This occurs, at least, when a finely nuanced feeling for form and tact does not take care to maintain the proper limits. If not, what should be touching will be transformed into the sentimental, the soft, mild, and sweet into the cloying, the affectionate and gentle into the effeminate, and emotional strength and emotionality into mere sentimentality, that is, into a kind of swimming in feelings for their own sakes. And if the transgression of limits in one of these directions becomes quite noticeable, then there arises, instead of a work of art, the caricature of one, that is, kitsch.

Kitsch is nothing more than the inner derailment of an artistic will that lacks the means to bestow form effectively but that attempts to prevail violently by circumventing the requirements of form in order to achieve a certain effect that the artist has in mind. That is seen most readily where it is a question of a touching or otherwise powerful emotional effect. Kitsch is so dangerous and destructive in the arts because those who have no accurate sense of form and measure cannot see through it; it can therefore bedazzle whole groups of viewers and ruin them aesthetically.

Only the charming is threatened totally by kitsch and values related to it, not by the sublime. For when the sublime becomes vacuous, it falls victim to tedium or to comedy. The charming object is liable to dilettantism, to experimentation with insufficient skill. We might express this as follows: charm is more poorly shielded from the abuse of what is superficial and relatively easily learned in the arts. For such abuse can be done precisely with what is learnable.

Kitsch is encountered in the arts in quite varying places. The concept originated in painting, where the value-group surrounding the charming (403) dominates in any case. Here it makes itself felt as a lack of pure painterly skill: in the incapacity to understand the visible in an authentic way. The lack of skill in seeing is then replaced by flat and fabricated color contrasts – which have an effect that is unnatural, cloying, and flat. Kitsch may also flower in literature and music. In the former, by means of its treatment of materials (in the vulgar escape novel), in the latter, by means of a lack of disciplined execution in favor of individual effects tinged with emotion. Ornamental art is hopelessly exposed to it, because there we have a pure play with form without a background to appear in it. This freedom is dangerous; it tempts unskilled men to arbitrariness. Think, for example, of Art Nouveau.

A marginal problem of a quite different kind appears here in the third case. It lies in awareness or also in what is aimed at. It is to be distinguished radically from the two marginal phenomena we have just discussed: it does not concern the representation or the expression of the charming in art, but the charming in life, especially in man. It thus extends itself mediately to artistic representation, provided that the arts deal with man and human life; thus to literature, especially the drama and the novel, and along with that, to a lesser degree, to painting.

We may distinguish charm from the state of sublimity in man in that the former excludes consciousness of itself, for when it becomes fully conscious, it stands is at the point of changing into something quite different, whereas the sublime is compatible with a certain form of self-consciousness, and marks itself in the demeanor of a man as dignity. The latter is threatened only by conceit, arrogance, pretense, and the like, which, however, may easily be rendered innocuous by the curse of the ridiculous. Charm, in contrast, loses much of its force when it becomes self-conscious, and is often entirely destroyed by it. It cannot tolerate conscious reflection, and is dissipated by it. In its place there then arises the appearance of charm: affectedness.

This phenomenon is most familiar in the domain of the feminine-erotic charm, whose aesthetical aspect is questionable (when it is genuine). If, in this case, sweetness and amiability become aware of themselves, they turn to coquetry, that is, to an artificial and willed amiability. As long as the deception of the inexperienced man lasts, amiability has erotic fascination; at the moment it is seen through as "put on," its power is extinguished. But let us not split hairs! Naturally a naive and amiable coquetry exists.

Affected charm stands in a roughly parallel position to affected dignity ("sublimeness"). The difference is only that the latter seems comical, the former simply ugly; the latter belongs to farce, and can have a good effect there; the former has no place in any art. From this standpoint, one can better understand why charm and sublimity generally exclude each other. In order to unify the two, one must have an object of very broad dimensions and a versatile ingenuity. (404)

c) Other oppositions among aesthetic values

We cannot conclude our observations of the sublime and the charming without taking a further survey from our present standpoint. This survey will concern in part these themes themselves, and in part aesthetic values as a whole. But the state of the problems in aesthetics appears not to be propitious for such a survey. The material is not ripe for conclusions to be drawn, and we cannot expect anything except broad generalities to emerge from it. But one must attempt at least that much.

The opposed positions of the sublime and the charming require a further explication. We have already shown that this opposition neither exhausts the beautiful nor splits open the entire domain of beauty. But it is also not the case, as a few recent aestheticians have maintained, that beauty, which shows no preference for one or the other, must manifest a kind of indifference to the charming and the sublime. Such neutrality would presumably be quite vacuous.

To the contrary, the sublime and the charming form a polarity of two extremes, between which most of what bears the name of beauty can be easily arranged: everything in its nature stands closer to either the one or the other extreme. We can give many examples of that. No doubt, there are also cases of beauty in which quite different elements dominate – as, for example, beauty in the drama and in the stage setting of a play, that of liveliness in painting, motion in sculpture – for in these cases, any arrangement in such a graded series is external.

This seems disappointing. One asks oneself: is the entire opposition of sublimity and charm a purely external one? That can hardly be true, considering that the analysis demonstrated essential structural characteristics on both sides. But it may be that there exist still other value-polarities, and these too should be able to be made visible. Indeed, it might be that they form a more encompassing system along with the first opposition of sublimity and charm, a system of dimensions – for extended between any given pair of oppositions is a continuum – and it may well be that absolutely everything can be arranged in that system.

But, after some reflection, that too reveals itself as a false hope. Perhaps the problems regarding it are still not ripe for discovering a solution – as for so much other matters in aesthetics. And what "other value-polarities" – or simply structural polarities – are supposed to be in question?

Now one might think, for example, of the four oppositions in the sublime, among which the charming was only one, and which also formed a multidimensional system (Chap. 33a). But one can easily see that these three oppositions, viz., the facile, the quotidian, and the comical, stand in genuine opposition to the sublime; for if one removes this common opposed element, the entire relationship among them vanishes.

From the standpoint of the comical, one might right away think oneself to be grasping an independent dimension of opposition. For its opposite number is, taken strictly, (405) neither the tragic nor the sublime, but only the serious as such – said negatively: the non-comical. One could take this opposition as the more fundamental one and could of course arrange many others in its domain. Its only failing is that it is too contradictory. That implies that its opposite number is just negative, and as long as one cannot fill it in some way with affirmative content, the opposition remains vacuous, and useless for our orientation – that is, in a domain of values that consists exclusively of positive value, a domain, indeed, in which even disvalues have a definite positive content.

Thus here again we come upon the old calamity of aesthetic values. They cannot be grasped. One must be happy when one finds a point of attack anywhere at all.

With those observations, however, not all possibilities have been exhausted. In fact, one meets in aesthetics every now and then with attempts to introduce new value-oppositions. So, for example, the attempt was made regarding the opposition of "classic and romantic" (Hegel and his school); to be sure, the attempt was in vain, because this antithetic relates at bottom to a subordinate element, that is, not to a purely aesthetical element but one of a philosophical kind that here too belongs more to the material than to the aesthetical.

Another opposition, one emanating again from the material, might be taken more seriously: the opposition between material that involves conflict and material that is free of conflict. The justification of this is more deeply rooted, insofar as it brings with itself a large number of genuinely aesthetical consequences for form and composition. But it defines the region far too narrowly, for it can be related directly only to poetry, and, even there, only to the epic, the narrative, and the drama; it may still appear in an attenuated form, but only in certain branches of the fine arts. If one understands "conflict" more generally, so that we can also attribute to it the introduction of disharmony into music, then the concept of conflict becomes somewhat metaphorical and extraordinarily vacuous.

Finally, we may still think about placing at the foundation of all else the opposition that was developed (in Part One) between the beautiful as appearance and the direct and immediate beauty of form. This is, in any case, a very fundamental opposition. Beauty as "the appearance of one thing in another" is something fundamentally different from beauty as a "pure play with form." But this opposition concerns more centrally the theory of the aesthetic object, its structure and its conditions, and less centrally the kind of values. Rather the one is closely tied to the other in the majority of aesthetic values (as the discussions in Chap. 17 and Chap. 18 have shown). Their relationship in music and in architecture was especially profound. The only exception was ornamental art. But that is an art of second rank; it possesses no great depth. (406)

Chapter 35: The Giving of Meaning in the Aesthetic Values

a) The world's demand for meaning

One should not leave these questions of structure and value before having conducted a survey of the universal element in aesthetic value. This question can now be understood differently than was possible initially – more in the spirit of a philosophical world-view and with reference to the whole of human life. For these values play a unique role in that life. We could have postponed this survey until after the discussion of the comical. But the latter becomes easier, if we are able to presuppose the former.

The very least that our investigations into the sublime and the charming were able to tell us about aesthetic values concerns what is special about them. And this did not take us very far, because we are not able to pursue any further the differentiation of the values. At least the discussion tells us something about the nature of aesthetic value in general. The value was everywhere presupposed.

The truth, in fact, is that we can refer in the case of the more special aesthetic values only to our living sense of value. We can make an appeal to it, as it were, an appeal that may go awry just when we have concrete cases clearly before our eyes. That is true even for the sublime and the charming.

But, after one has reflected upon this limitation and realizes that it cannot be overcome, one may very well ask, in a new way, the question: what is the peculiar situation regarding aesthetic values as such? For it is not improbable that from an analysis of specific groups of values something will be yielded regarding the value that founds them.

Such an outcome has in fact occurred here. It lies in the character of both the sublime and the charming as givers of meaning. ... In order to show that, however, we must reach out a bit further – into matters of philosophy and of metaphysics, but not into a specific speculative metaphysics, but rather into the domain of inexpungible metaphysical problems.

Among these problems, one of the oldest and most peremptory is that of the sense and meaning of the world and of human life. So long as there was a belief in a higher power, the question does not arise, because it has already been answered through faith. If faith collapses, then the problems, arising as though out of nothingness, are suddenly there. And then they may straightaway become life threatening. For who would want to live a life that has "no sense"?

The Platonic philosophy, after the dissolution of Sophism, answered the question with its "Forms." The Forms constitute a realm of pure perfection, and everything in the world is oriented toward them, nature and man, with the single difference that nature adheres strictly to the commands of the Forms, while man, with his will, deviates from them. But the giving of meaning lies in the Forms. One may think in this way, at least, so long as one is not suspicious of the teleological metaphysics that one has silently assumed. (407)

In reality, two teleological principles active in the world are assumed by this theory, and the world itself is understood by analogy with man as guided by an understanding and purposive consciousness. For goals must be "posited" for some future, and means to their realization must be "chosen" antecedent to the goal. Both of these are possible only for a conscious mind, thus one similar to that of man. The ancient metaphysics of Forms miscarried on this hidden anthropomorphism, and with it failed not only the more vulgar (i.e., those that theologized) forms of the theory, but also the entire principle of optimism: the wish to found the meaning of the world upon teleology.

What then remains? A world devoid of sense? In such a world man cannot live, at least not in full awareness of its senselessness. One therefore looks about for something else that might bestow meaning upon things. But men always seek it in the same places from which they had been banished. They are tied, as it were, irresistibly to those realms. They silently assume two principles: 1. Meaning can lie only in the origins of things; none can enter the world subsequently. 2. Meaning can inhere only in the whole of the word and extend from there to its parts, for example to human life; but it cannot emerge from a part, or even less, to pass from a part over to the whole.

These two assumptions have determined the course of metaphysical thought for centuries. They resulted in a search for the source and bestowal of meaning exclusively in universal principles, never close to man, that is, in human life or in the activities or operations of men.

But here lies the other possibility, one far greater, of solving the problem of meaning. For the two silent assumptions have revealed themselves as prejudices. Our sense of meaning and value tells us that there are endless things in life, which, though limited and individual, are meaningful without recourse to principles or to a greater whole.

Thus every morally good act, every wise thought, every adequate response to a value, is meaningful and bestows additional meaning just out of itself alone. Out of itself alone: that means that it does not have meaning only for the sake of something else. Such is every act of benevolence, every participation in the spiritual and the inner life – every sympathetic understanding and every interpersonal involvement that breaks through icy loneliness precisely where a man wishes to be seen and appreciated – are meaningful just for themselves alone; yet they bestow a meaning upon other things, and a deep need of the human heart for the realization of meaning is thereby satisfied.

All of that is a realization of meaning arising from a part of the world that is empty of meaning in itself, a part, in fact, that is secondary and dependent. We see precisely here how there can be autonomy in what is dependent. This is a thesis that can be justified, even in all generality, by the categorial law within the doctrine of categories that asserts the "freedom of the higher construct." (408)

If man with his powers, his sense of values, and his occasional capacity for realizing values, is capable of bestowing meaning and value, then precisely the senselessness of the world as a whole obtains a meaning for him. For then it falls to his lot to be the bestower of meaning in the world. He would not be able to give the gift of meaning to a world hostile to it – it would resist it – but surely he can to an entirely "meaningless" world, one that is in itself indifferent to meaning but is entirely open to being given it.

The situation is precisely the opposite of what the metaphysicians took it to be: for a being of the nature of man, a meaningless world is precisely the only meaningful world. A world that, without man, was already filled with meaning would render him superfluous even despite his gifts for bestowing meaning.

These gifts are, before all else, those that constitute his moral nature: the power of self-determination, of decision (freedom); the capacity to anticipate (providence) and to posit ends of action (predestination), as also his consciousness of values (*cogitio boni et mali*), or, perhaps more correctly, his feeling for values. Also belong on this list are the gifts of sympathy, understanding, and moral appraisal of those whom he meets.

But that is still not enough. For his aesthetical gifts are also exemplary of the bestowal of meaning, that is, the gift of seeing the world as something beautiful, and likewise many items within it. And not only that: the capacity to create goes hand in hand with the ability to see. In his creativity, man possesses the power to experiment with unknown forms beyond those created by nature – to posit them next to and above what is natural.

b) The bestowal of meaning by men and by art

Now all meaning in the world is connected to values; indeed, it consists essentially in its reference to value, to the realization of value, and to the discrimination of values. This is clearly seen just from the forms of the bestowal of moral value. But the matter is not such that, as one might think, only moral values come into consideration here; the other classes of values, too, play a role, the lower (e.g., vital values), but especially the higher ones, thus those that are at least equal to the moral ones: the values of knowledge and the aesthetic values. It can be shown that the latter are no doubt less preemptory and immediate as the moral ones, but are especially pure forces in the bestowal of meaning.

The bestowal of meaning that comes into human life via aesthetic values consists fundamentally in nothing other than in the convincing feeling of standing face to face before something of absolutely intrinsic value – before something for whose sake alone it would be worth living, regardless of how the conditions of one's life stand otherwise. That is so, not least because it is a question of no practical interest in beauty, or of the desire to use it or to make it one's own, but simply because of the joy taken in the object; or the pleasure we feel in living in a world in which such glorious things exist.

This element – that most pure bestowing of meaning – is stronger in aesthetic values than in moral ones. And that is beautifully expressed (409) in Kant's thesis of "disinterested pleasure"; indeed it makes up perhaps its most genuine and deepest meaning. For here precisely nothing "practical" is in question, as always with moral values, whose demands, after all, concern human life.

In men who are artistically creative, this kind of bestowal of meaning is amplified considerably, as long as it is of a kind to bring forth consciously what is valuable – specifically absolute values that are intrinsic in nature. But these values do not depend on creativity alone. The viewer, too, carries the same bestowal of meaning to his part in life. To be able to "see" what is beautiful does much: without the viewer, there is no beauty, and, to be sure, he must be a viewer in a specific way. Thus are intertwined the three parts of the relationship in the aesthetic object. Accordingly, the man who beholds and grasps values is there also with the creator.

If we now reflect that there are an endless number of "beautiful" things in the world even this side of the arts and of human creativity, we see clearly the large role in bestowing meaning in this world that is played by the man who beholds aesthetically.

What is the highest value in life has something of the character of giving gifts. Nietzsche demonstrated that radiant virtue is like gold in that it is "uncommon and of no use and luminous and mild in its lustre"; "it always bestows itself."[130] These four characterizations apply properly to the aesthetic values. They too are "uncommon and of no use," and they elevate everything that takes part in them to something uncommon and useless. The latter term means that it no longer serves any purpose. And the first asserts its rarity; for to beauty there belongs the pure gaze of the beholder, and he is more rare than one commonly thinks. Not all of those who wax enthusiastically about beauty really know how to "see" it. Not all delight is aesthetical delight, and it is frequently difficult to distinguish whether it is or is not. There are many sources of counterfeiting of aesthetical delight and replacing it with other forms of delight. Correspondingly, there are many pseudo-aesthetical stances, and we will speak of them in a moment.

It is the same with "luminousness" and with the "mild lustre" and perfectly so with the "bestowing of oneself." Nothing is as much characteristic of aesthetic value as its having fallen to us as a gift from heaven – as happiness and grace may fall to us, and the love of men. Usually an element of surprise is also given

---

130 [Translator's note:] Nietzsche, Friedrich, *Thus Spoke Zarathustra: A Book for Everyone and Nobody*, translated and edited by Graham Parkes, Oxford and New York: Oxford University Press 2005, First Part, "On the Bestowing Virtue," p. 65.

with it; for whatever artistic ideas may arise in a man, they do not come when they are called, but ambush him when he least expects it.

For the truth of these things one may appeal only to the aesthetical experience of the artistically open-minded man. The philosopher can do nothing here either, except to appeal to the living aesthetical sense of values. There is no other witness to the miracle of the artwork than the human heart, which receives it with joy and thankfulness.

Seen objectively, however, this witness and this joy are already the effects of the aesthetic object, its radiance shining into human (410) life – in a life of compromises, of half-measures, and of distress. Just therein is reflected the bestowal of meaning, which emanates from beauty, from sublimity, and from amiability and fascination, such that this radiance penetrates the darkness of suffering and distress – it enters those places where other powers have lost their strength to succor us.

For what brings forth aesthetic values is no real change in things, but an inner psychic reorientation of a man: nothing is removed, yet a spiritual good is bestowed, things imponderable and immeasurable are given to us for our own. The power that expresses itself here is not real, but it is a power that grasps, validates, and justifies our real living heart, a power that extends as far as our philosophical picture of the world. Basically, all experience of beauty (the state of being aesthetically valuable) has philosophical significance just because it bestows meaning upon our lives. For without our seeing a meaning in our lives over the course of it, we could not live.

We should remember in this connection one basic phenomenon: the aesthetic object is lifted out of the daily bustle, out of the obligations in life that weigh upon us, out of all of permanent features of the everyday. Here the reverse manifests itself: the re-entry into our life of what had been lifted out of it – but not to assimilate itself to it, and thereby vanish, but rather to give to life what is for its needs of the greatest importance: meaningfulness. Perhaps one should put it more cautiously: it is the knowing or beholding of a meaning-content.

In all of this, aesthetic values are fundamentally different from moral values. The moral values are those that initially seem to place a burden upon us, give us tasks, call upon us to be responsible; they always have to "demand something, foster something, impose upon us," and thus their gifts cut both ways, although in the final analysis they can lead men to the heights.

Aesthetic values are quite the opposite in this regard: they burden us with nothing, they demand and foster nothing – unless simply this, that man behold and take part in them, and in taking part receive from them pure joy and a lesson in how to feel. They give to men only a gift. ... But however it may be with the giving of gifts: giving takes two, and there is something the recipient must supply:

the taking. To be ready to receive, to be open: these things men must bring to the giving, so that they may execute adequately the act of beholding. We need not interpret that in the sense of the deepest understanding of art. It is sufficient that a man be prepared to bring to it peace of mind and reflectiveness. Much is achieved just with that.

c) Pseudo-aesthetical attitudes

These demands are not hard to meet, at least not within the limits of what was in general accessible to us initially. For men cannot force aesthetical understanding. But bit-by-bit, as a person goes through life, such understanding may bear a variety of fruit for him, often when he least expects it. He may contribute to the process (411) by keeping himself inwardly open. But here, too, there is a danger of missing the mark. It lies in the pseudo-aesthetical attitude.

The pseudo-aesthetical attitude seems to be unimportant; almost nothing of real relevance in life depends upon it – and yet by it a man destroys for himself great revelations in life – those that have metaphysical weight, as does the bestowal of meaning. No, we would not condemn a person morally because he lacks a genuine aesthetical attitude; but when his life lacks all light and luster, if it contains nothing of the uncommon and the useless from which all illumination proceeds, then we could attribute to him a share in this guilt.

For that reason, pseudo-aesthetical attitudes are so dangerous: they act as a dissolvent, precisely where the decisive bestowal of meaning is present – there where one's own reflections can render even the nature of this giving of meaning comprehensible – as the gift and power of man. This gift is not meant only as the gift of creativity – thus of rare and favored men – but of any man who is led by a real inner yearning for beauty to the act of beholding.

What is the pseudo-aesthetic attitude? It is that attitude of anyone who does not enjoy the aesthetic object as such, but rather attributes some different character to it, and from that obtains greater enjoyment – and that is then of course a different kind of enjoyment. Of this type are the following kinds of attitude.

1. Enthusiasm solely for the material; or, if not enthusiasm, at least an interest in it. That is the usual situation with the contemporary readers of novels: they want to be entertained or distracted from their everyday lives; they are indifferent to the artistic quality of the work, and they hardly notice it. And when such quality is lacking, they do not miss it. Very immature people "read" in that way. They "gorge" themselves, are ravenous, insatiable. ...

2. Remaining on the level of cheap, superficial effects, which are parts of works that are in fact far deeper. Here it is a case almost always of relatively shallow

or vulgar emotional effects, such as the touching or sentimental. That is easy to find in poetry or music. In the latter case, there is still another kind of mistake: when music is misused for the sake of playing with fantasy images, or as a direct stimulus for them. Then music is in truth not appreciated and enjoyed, but rather one hears the ramblings of one's own imagination. Something similar is true for every other manner of letting oneself be stimulated by art works, for example, by events in plays or novels that have us dream of being in similar circumstances.

3. The inward concentration upon or enjoyment of one's own feeling of pleasure in the place of taking pleasure in the object. This is called the auto-aesthetical attitude in psychology. This too is quite common, perhaps most familiar from Nietzsche's description of how a "female Wagnerite submitted herself to *Tristan*." This boils down to a kind of swimming in one's own feelings; anything genuinely structural in the music – and even in the operatic plot – disappears. The case is similar – for auto-aesthetical natures – (412) in the other arts, too – painting, lyric poetry, etc. (in the sense of Geiger's *Zugänge zur Ästhetik* [1928]).

There are other pseudo-aesthetical attitudes, e.g., one informed by a philosophy that in fact comes down to nothing more than a picture of the world that is often constructed quite primitively. This is quite frequently a picture derived from religious faith, which the viewer wishes to see appear in the background of a work of art. Occasionally the world-view simply has been whitewashed over with philosophy.

In aesthetics (and certainly also in many ways of understanding art), the Romantics' popular metaphysical picture of the word, which once for many decades was thought very profound, was of this kind. It held that man rediscovers himself in nature and, more generally in all existing things. In those days even the poetic arts found this thought fascinating; many people went almost so far as to identify the thought with Romantic art. This is a great example of how disorienting such ideas can be; they can embrace whole epochs, turn into doctrine, and at last even come forth with the claim to be the measure of a higher kind of art!

Not few men live an aesthetical sham life because they continuously take a pseudo-aesthetical stance, whether by simply enjoying the material, whether by a cheap enjoyment of superficialities, whether by self-indulgence. The first type is still and all a natural one, although it is not aesthetical in nature; the second is a solvent, so to speak, a softener, but the third is a perversion of aesthetics and for that reason positively destructive.

There exist various other forms of pseudo-aesthetical attitudes, e.g., when one tries to make the arts useful in the service of some practical end – a political, religious, or even some material end. But that is really more a misunderstanding of art and of aesthetic values; it can no longer be called an aesthetical attitude, thus also not a pseudo-aesthetical one. Yet it causes the greatest damage to the arts if they do not resist it with all their power. For there are always some who let themselves be led by the nose. Yet then all bestowal of meaning that emanates from aesthetic values ceases.

Third Section: The Comical

Chapter 36: The Sense of the Comical and Its Forms

a) Heartless and hearty merriment

The comical, as a theme of aesthetics, belongs to a considerably narrower domain than, say, the sublime and the charming; it becomes dominant only in one art, literature. No doubt, drawing and painting are familiar with it also – think, for example of caricature – but it does not play a very large role there. It is essentially foreign to music and architecture; it slips occasionally into program music – but then only through the medium of words, whose accompaniment is music. (413) Otherwise, life, too – without art – is filled with comedy. But think: would we see it there without the poet's eye?

Within certain limits, we would. We have – so far as our eye for it reaches – much fun in life from the unintentional comedy of human behavior. Every clumsiness, every slip, every missed intention, can cause us to laugh. Laughter in such cases may be quite heartless, for the laugh is always on the loser.

What is mocking laughter? First, it is nothing more than taking pleasure in unintended comedy in life. Beyond that, it can become very unpleasant, if it deliberately seeks out weaknesses and enlarges them, and in that form abandons them to the laughter of others. Mockery is never fair.

But is the merriment with which we acknowledge receipt of the comical in life fair? Is it not also quite heartless and insensitive? An observer stands there and looks upon the bad luck of his fellow man – perhaps nothing really terrible, just annoying to the victim – and draws amusement from it. Even when that amusement has nothing of schadenfreude in it, it still contains rejection and destruction. Everyone knows, of course, that laughter can "kill." There are men who live inwardly solely by making fun of others. Every small mistake is magnified and made use of in a joke, and the victim is belittled.

One may ask, in the face of this situation: in the comical, have we really to do with an aesthetic value, is it at all an enjoyment of beauty, an aesthetical experience?

The answer is: yes! For the question here is not about the moral value or disvalue of an aesthetical attitude, but purely about its aesthetical character. This character can rightly exist; it can also have an entirely aesthetical character, even when the attitude has a morally questionable aspect.

Yet it need not have such an attitude. Merriment, such as the comical produces, can be entirely harmless. Take the phenomenon on its lighter side: the delight in the comical in life does not always have to tend towards schadenfreude – and perhaps it does that only among the morally immature; to a more mature man, a different nuance in this attitude is more natural. He looks at the matter, laughs a moment or smiles a bit, and then forgets about it. Those little annoying calamities are so very familiar! ...

That is no proof that delight in the comical is an aesthetical delight, but it does prove that it can be, that is, it shows how the proximity to a heartless and insensitive attitude does not prevent it from being an aesthetical one. As an aesthetical attitude, the heartless delight in a comical scene, may be different from a hearty and sympathetic one; aesthetical delight in the comical as such is, despite that difference, as much one as the other. The (414) difference in the attitude is primarily a moral one. This first tends towards frivolity and arrogance; the second displays a trace of wisdom.

The genuine aesthetical character of delight in both of those cases consists in its being purely objective and without practical interest. It is not aimed at the person affected, but at the phenomenon, the happening as such. Pity and schadenfreude, which also may be present in it, do not belong to the aesthetical phenomenon but to the ethical response to it.

That the latter is also provoked lies in the nature of the happening. What makes us laugh is always something out of the arena of human weakness, smallness, pettiness, or arrogance or stupidity (folly!); a bit of confused thinking suffices for it, especially when the thinking pretends to be deep wisdom. In short, every kind of nonsense may come in play here, with conceit, haughtiness, and pretentiousness in the lead; more harmless is simple clumsiness, and whatever else is tied to externalities and to chance.

If we examine these human weaknesses, we find that they are essentially moral weaknesses, and that they very well deserve moral censure. If in life a haughty man is brought down, a sophist or hypocrite revealed as such, the delight of the observer is not as heartless as it may appear, and the laughter such men inspire is justified.

In all such things, there is also an element of the tragic and the touching. For haughtiness, conceit, pettiness, confusion, may have very serious consequences. And, depending on the sphere to which they belong, they are heart-rending or horrifying – the essential matter is only that the same thing be looked upon here from quite different sides; these other sides lie in the extended contexts of life – in places where man no longer has the consequences of his actions under his control. They take on the weight of earnestness and of importance only through these consequences. The comical and the delight taken in it stay on this side of these far-reaching contexts. For that reason, we can take delight in the light side of the same phenomena: "light" literally, without the moral weight that is often attached to them.

Is man, then, an artist in life – without otherwise being one? The ability to see the humor in things is, after all, a specific talent that not everyone possesses, one that a man may perhaps be born with just as much as with genuine artistic predispositions. But an affirmative answer to this question must be taken with caution: among mature men with some experience of life there are very many who have this gift at their disposal – only in such a modulated way that we do not notice it at all in those who have relatively little of it.

Another thing counts against it, viz., a practical interest lies in close proximity – quite this side of all aesthetical attitudes (415) – to taking life on its lighter side: it allows a person to manage the entire miscellany that he encounters if he is not concerned in a close and personal way with it. In the bustle of everyday life, everything has both its earnest and its absurd aspects; it is no doubt morally comforting to remain focused on the latter, so far as that may be possible.

As soon as some event touches a man's own person, he loses his sense of humor. Still, until he reaches that point, he encounters many events that do not concern him personally. Then we have the attitudes of devil-may-care, of laughter, of thinking everything funny as a mode of coping, of having done with matters, of making life easier.

In short, behind this attitude stands a well-tested way of life. This latter gives an impulse to the gift of humor. Where this way of life meets with that gift, it strengthens it considerably. And what is peculiar is that this practical tendency often goes hand in hand with a genuine aesthetically autonomous stance toward life.

b) Unintentional comedy and humor

"The comical and humor" – the two surely belong close beside each other, but are not only not the same, they do not even stand at all formally in parallel. The comical is a matter of the object, its quality – if only "for" a subject, as is true for all aesthetic objects – while, in contrast, humor is a matter of the observer or the creator (of the writer or the actor). For it concerns the manner in which men look upon the comical, understand it, give an account of it, or put it to literary use. Thus, one does not bring the two phenomena, otherwise related to each other, into too close proximity. They are so as much unlike each other as music and musicality, the laws of mathematics and the art of reckoning (aptitude for doing sums in one's head.)

This fact has usually been overlooked in works on aesthetics. One is accustomed to place humor next to comedy as one would a second phenomenon of the same genus, or would subordinate humor to the comical as a species. Both assumptions are false. The humorist is not comical; one does not laugh at him, but with him at something else, viz., the object of his humor, and indeed because he is able to show us the comical in this object. In fact, humor itself in not comical!

It is exactly the same in the other direction: the comical man is not humorous; usually he lacks even the humor needed to see the comedy in himself. That, precisely, makes him even more comical – when he gets annoyed or enraged instead of laughing, as a man full of humor would. His comedy is inadvertent.

All genuine comedy that we encounter in life is unintentional. On stage, comedy is done willingly, where a man consciously makes a comical object out of himself; but it is an acted-out comedy. Such comedy can, when intended sincerely, be far superior to the unintentional variety, yet it is (416) something different, and is related to unintentional comedy as, in general, play to life. The actor requires for this a very peculiar gift, one that is not given to every actor: the gift of humor.

Of course, a humorist needs a certain kind of humor (representational humor), the teller of anecdotes needs another kind (entertaining humor), the observer of human folly needs still another (smiling humor), likewise the soldier who emerges with a jest from the debris a grenade threw upon him (black humor). But that is all a matter for a more specific analysis.

In the same way, the comedy of poetic figures in plays and novels must always be unintended comedy. For if in life only comedy of that nature seems genuine, so quite naturally it will also seem to be so in literature and in the theater. That the actor produces such effects onstage through his art changes nothing; just as little as the fact that the writer considers the matter and puts it in words. It is not a question of reality here, but of appearance.

For that reason, in literature and drama it is essential that comedy "seem" genuine. That means: it must seem as it would in life, if we could observe it there with the same intense concentration by which literature focuses us upon the comedy. Or, stating it as a principle: since in art we are concerned with an appearance that is intended to seem lifelike, the appearing comedy of characters (and situations) that are created by a writer must necessarily be of this unintended kind. It must seem as if it were not composed by a writer who "wanted" events that way, and even less by the actors who realize it artistically onstage, but as if it came about involuntarily in a chance coming together of diverse events.

On the other hand, there is a talent the writer needs in giving shape to the comedy of his characters and bringing them to appearance as though they were not created by him, viz., Humor. What kind of humor is needed here depends upon the kind of comedy that is at stake. He may need all kinds of humor, the cheerful, the dark, and the introspective. He must master the entire range.

We see more clearly now why the two related phenomena, comedy and humor, do not run parallel to each other, but are arranged in series in such a way that all humor initially refers itself to existing comedy and cannot come to be without it. Comedy, for its part, calls upon humor and, so to speak, requires it as the adequate response of the subject.

The relation that emerges in this way is related to the foundation-relation; only that it does not primarily concern values, but simply the state of affairs, i.e., the state of the affairs in the object and in the reactive conduct of the subject.

The tie between the two reciprocal elements remains an entirely one-sided kind. For quite obviously, there is no necessity that a humorist take on some piece of comedy; he may be lacking (417) an adequate reaction to it, or a subject may fail to produce it. There may even be no receptive subject present, though all the conditions for comedy are there in the object. Then the reciprocal condition for the comical as aesthetic object that lies in the subject (as the third member) would of course be lacking; provided that is the case, we may say that then the comical does not occur at all as object.

The comical in the strict aesthetical sense can also not exist without the element of humor. It requires, like every aesthetic object, the reciprocal work of the subject. The subject must bring to it something quite definite; and, in this case, that consists not only in a high-spirited and easy-going attitude, but also in a sense of the comical itself. This latter, however, is in the normal case essentially identical with humor. We can sum up: without comedy in the object, no humor in its reception (or, even more, in its performance); but also without humor in the reception, no comedy in the object.

However, the second half of the last assertion is not quite correct. No doubt some response must be given by the subject reciprocal to the comical as aesthetic object, and no doubt it must consist in having the right sense of the comical; but it does not have necessarily to consist in "humor," not, at least, when we take this concept of humor in its narrow and precise sense, in which there is also always an accompanying affirmative element that concerns the object. And this element could do the same reciprocal service as humor does, but in a different way.

In fact, there exist other ways to make effective use of the comical. They are related to humor in their openness to comedy, and in that respect, they are coordinated with it; but they are all very different from it, and in part, they are even contrary to it in their attitude toward the comical. Of these kinds, these are the most important:

1. The comical taken as empty amusement;
2. The joke – the use of the comical for the sake of a punch line;
3. Irony – the assertion of one's own superiority by the apparent belittling of the self; denigration in the form of apparent appreciation;

4. Sarcasm – bitter, mocking, destructive denigration – in the form of exaggerated appreciation.

The two last, it is clear, are sharply opposed to humor. For humor always contains – even when it is "black" – something good-natured in it. Irony does not of course need to belittle its object bluntly, but it may easily do so precisely by means of that which gives it the aftertaste of delicacy and distinction: by means of the inclusion of one's own self.

The same is true of the joke: as such, it does not have to be malicious, but it is not concerned with sparing people. Rather, it must intensify the comical element and to take care that the joke is on someone else. (418) Of course, the joke can only be on someone whose unintentional comedy is at stake. And, *mutatis mutandis*, the same must be said for taking "empty amusement" in the comical: it aims only at gaiety and merriment; it is indifferent to any injury it causes.

c) The ethos of laughter and its varieties

From the confrontation of these ways of appropriating the comical – specifically the joke and sarcasm – with humor, we can see clearly that an essential element of an ethos is everywhere involved, and that the opposition between them depends precisely upon it. It is not immediately obvious that an ethos of a certain kind lies at the foundation of humor. But one can exhibit and define it.

It is not a question here of a momentary stance or an attitude, as one might – or should – apply precisely in an individual case and for an individual object. A man's sense of humor is a gift, which, as also with other talents, may develop at a given stage of maturation, and then be maintained at a certain level of consistency; it often accompanies its owner to the grave. No doubt, a man may also lose his sense of humor, but then only through the influence of traumas that may reorient his customary attitudes.

Humor is an affair of an ethos, conditioned by character and reflecting one's entire picture of life; this ethos stands behind one's sense of humor, and probably that sense was first provoked by the ethos. In any case, the ethos is what gives it the characteristic coloration of one's benevolence and good humor. The ethos, which works here to give form and direction, is warmhearted, loving, placating, sympathetic, and, just for that reason, of a kind that is capable of seeing in the comical what is humanly touching and amiable.

One should not be put off by the fact that such an eminently ethical element works itself into what is otherwise a purely aesthetical relation. That is by no means a contradiction. We have seen sufficiently the extent to which moral values are foundational for aesthetic values (Chap. 28c), and this was traceable to the observer's having his heart in the right place, that is, that he stood with his own feeling for values on the morally correct side. Otherwise, the aesthetic value would pass by him unnoticed.

Precisely this is the fundamental condition of humor: he who does not see the appealing and the amiable in the foolish and the fatuous, will also not know how to appropriate its comedy from the outside – just as is true of empty, transient states of amusement. Humor achieves something here that is quite different: it excavates and lifts into the light, along with the comical, something profound.

One can call in brief this ethos, as it is concealed in comedy, an "ethos of laughter," although the term of course does not refer to laughter alone, but to what constitutes a man's entire attitude towards life. But is the way one laughs not also always a genuine expression of an entire (419) attitude toward life? And in life do we not often hear within each kind of laughter an attitude of some sort? All the things that human laughter can reveal! One needs only to bring to mind concretely "how" some given person laughs, and then to ask oneself in all seriousness what that laughter tells us. People laugh as differently as they act, as they move, speak, and remain silent.

Humor runs parallel to other ways of appropriating the comical, i.e., to empty amusement, to the joke, to irony, and to sarcasm. It cannot therefore be true that only in itself, and not in these others, is found the "ethos of laughter." Rather, there must always be an ethos present that determines one's inward attitude toward the comical, and, along with that, transforms the comical itself. It must be present precisely where the situation is morally ambiguous or where, perhaps, it is repugnant.

In fact there is an ethos in each of these ways of appropriating the comical. In general, it may lie, essentially and lawfully, in the character of all forms of our sense of the comical, that a specific ethos stands behind it. In the majority of cases, the ethos is of a kind that rejects and condemns – just because comedy rests upon human weakness and smallness.

The negativity in the "ethos of laughter" is characteristic of the four forms we listed: laughter itself is in them all, and having fun and making fun of is a means of disapproval and only of disapproval, of looking-down-upon and of feeling oneself superior. It carries the mark of that "heartless delight" that we spoke of above. Of course that is the case for the four types in very different and very differently graduated ways.

It is not necessary to pursue any further the specific types of this loveless ethos. It is sufficient to have grasped its basic nature. It is especially marked in sarcasm, which manifests a strange unsparing attitude in a person who considers himself to be beyond all criticism. But even the "jesting" use of involuntary comedy is at bottom of the same kind. It is just not concerned with wounding and being "mentally destructive," but only with the cheering effect it has. But since that effect succeeds more easily when there is less regard for the person caught with his pants down, the "joke," too, has at least mediately the same tendency to "mental destruction." And thus it can become, mediately, entirely malicious.

We see this in how the jokester goes about among men of a more harmless spirit. He pulls them along with him, and in that way seduces them to the same heartlessness as he; yet beyond a certain limit, he revolts people, because he does injury to their sense of justice. An uncorrupted moral sense rebels when it sees everyone laughing at the expense of one person.

The activity of the wit can reach a certain level of aesthetical genius, yet be at the same time morally questionable. This two-edged sword cannot be separated from pure "wit." This lies in its nature, insofar as making use of the comical rests necessarily upon what is negative in human behavior, pettiness, weakness, (420) folly, and bad luck. The condition of humor renders it a bit milder. But then it is founded on a different ethos of laughter.

People enjoy listening to a witty man, but do not love him. For they feel, given their own weaknesses, that they are not given support by him, but rather are unmasked by his ethos. The clever man will take care not to reveal his nakedness too openly to him.

The implication of what we have just said for the artistic – especially literary – exploitation of the comical is that all comedy already stands upon an ethos of receptivity. That is a consequence of the threefold relation in the aesthetic object, i.e., from the contribution of the apprehending or receptive subject to the appearance-relation.

Up to now, we have spoken only of the comedy in life and of the inner attitude of the bystander observing it, "for" whom alone it exists. In the case of the writer, the relations becomes more significant, because he gives to his own ways of apprehension the form of an objectivation, and thereby lifts the comedy out of its transitory existence into a state of historical permanence as an appearing ideal quality. In that way, his action becomes morally an infinitely more responsible one.

For that reason, the "comic poet" who desires to be witty or merely sarcastic has never existed in a pure form. His heartlessness would cry out to heaven. In life, sarcasm usually blossoms; wit, too, is used as a spice for seasoning in a larger literary context; a forceful witticism in a dark mood serves as a relief, for it shakes off burdens and creates for a moment a light-hearted "ethos of laughter." But whoever wishes to put together an entire book containing nothing by jokes will achieve the opposite: he will bore us. Boredom, however, is precisely what jokes are intended to stave off.

The true comical poet must have more than the art of amusing the reader, of irony, of wit, and of sarcasm: he must have humor. And that means that he must master a higher "ethos of laughter," one that is not aimed at its target in a purely negative, loveless and heartless way, but which, out of the fullness of our common humanity, can feel solidarity even with the foolish and petty in human affairs, to which he knows how to give expression in rousing comedy that sweeps us all away.

Chapter 37: The Essence of Comedy

a) What is fallacious and what is serviceable in theories of comedy

We approached the problem of the comical from the ethical side, and came to understand it as conditioned by the psychic attitudes of people who have a sense of the comical, who enjoy it and respond to it inwardly. That was preliminary work; necessary work, to be sure, but work that simply prepares the way. What the comical is in itself could not be explicated in that way. What, then, is the comical? (421)

Given the previous discussions, to say what it is may not be quite as difficult as many artificially constructed theories make it seem. These theories tended to set the task at too great a distance, and for that reason they were forced into a much too pale and general schema. Nonetheless, concealed in these theories are important insights.

If in this way the theories have been reduced to a certain sweeping simplicity, they have on the other hand made life more difficult by demanding too much in the way of explanation, and have thus became complicated once again. This criticism is directed especially against the idealistic doctrines of Hegel's followers, not so much against Hegel himself, who in regard to this problem generally failed entirely, but certainly against Weisse[131], Ruge[132], Vischer, et al. These all attempted to derive the comical from the presupposition of the "Idea" (of a Hegelian character), where the sublime is developed dialectically out of "conflict," and then is led on to a "comical solution," which, in a certain respect, is thought to be necessarily more complete of the two. The question of how much of this can be retained will not occupy us at the present time. The problem with

---

131 [Translator's note:] Christian Hermann Weisse (1801–1866).
132 [Translator's note:] Arnold Ruge (1802–1880).

which it was concerned was in the end a metaphysical (world-view) one, i.e., it was no longer purely aesthetical.

But what is important is precisely that the problem of the comical is in no way so deeply metaphysical, as, for example, that of the universal features of the beautiful; the latter is not entirely solvable, because it led to a final indissoluble element. The comical, however, is much more specific in nature: insofar as it belongs to beauty, a surd remains within it, but that is nothing new, and does not concern the peculiar nature of comedy.

In one respect, the situation with the comical is the same as with the sublime and the charming: with them, the special character of the genus can be identified with great rigor, and so too here. Then, too, the genus of the comical can be thoroughly analyzed precisely in the opposition of these two genera. We must only not place too great a weight upon it – the weight of theory and of a pretense to system, to a world-view.

Instead of over-complicated theories burdened by a pretense to a totalizing system, we shall allow the major theses of several less assuming doctrines to take the stand. They almost all concern the "definition" of the comical, but without always succeeding in their efforts to draw correctly the limits of this circle of phenomena. To correct this is in most instances quite easy. What is remarkable is that in many of its central issues all of the elements in the essential definition of the comical manifest a kind of congruence.

We can begin the series with Aristotle. His definition concerns, to be sure, only "comedy" as a genre, but it extends itself, as is quite natural, to all forms of the comical. According to him, comedy is the "representation of the weaker sides (in man)" μίμησις φαυλοτέρων μέν. But this is not so for any given badness, but only for the ridiculous. What then is the ridiculous? He replies: τὸ γὰρ γελοῖον ἐστιν ἁμάρημά τι καὶ αἶσχος ἀνώδυνον καὶ οὐ φθαρτικόν (*Poetics*, 1449a 32 ff.). "The ridiculous is a certain lack and (422) ugliness, but of such a kind that it remains free of deep pain and ruin ..."[133] "ἁμάρημά" may be translated as "weakness," but it is definitely determined by the φαυλότερον. In αἶσχος there is not necessarily an anticipation of aesthetical nuances; it is "ugliness" in its broad sense, the morally inferior, that for which a man is ashamed.

The "ridiculous" is thus given a moral basis by Aristotle – perhaps too narrowly, but it is accurately sketched within its primary domain, human "weak-

---

133 [Translator's note:] In the translation prepared under the editorship of W.D. Ross, the passage reads, "The Ridiculous may be defined as a mistake or deformity not productive of pain or harm to others." Aristotle, *The Works of Aristotle*, ed. W.D. Ross, Vol. 11, Oxford: Clarendon Press 1924, "De Poetica," 1449a 34f.

ness." Just as convincing is this limitation to the ἀνώδυνον, etc., for the comical obviously ceases where real pain and bitter suffering begin.

In this ancient definition, something very important is lacking, the subjective reverse of the comical, the role of the subject sensitive to the comedy. It was a long time before anyone noticed this. The thought that something else is concealed in comedy, that it "deceives" us, so to speak, but then reveals the deception where we least suspected it to be, appears only in the modern era.

Hobbes expressed the idea as follows: comedy is the appearance of the unexpected, but tied to the feeling of one's own superiority. Here the moral element is brought into the final clause and referred entirely to the perspective of the subject, a perspective that depreciates.

That is perhaps questionable, for it emphasizes heartless delight in a one-sided manner. Consciousness of one's own superiority does not necessarily have to follow laughter over others' weaknesses; where it does so, it no longer belongs to a genuine sense of the comical.

On the other hand, Hobbes gave an original formulation of a foundational element of comedy with his "appearance of the unexpected." The expression is, however, too weak. The mere state of being unexpected is insufficient; rather what is unexpected must be precisely the weakness or smallness in human behavior (the φαυλότερον) in a place where we expected something of far more grandiose and heavy significance. The descent from an expected significance to its insignificance, if it catches us by surprise, and hits us in the face, is the comical.

Both elements in this specification of the nature of the comical have been appropriated by many, reworked and, in part, improved upon. Only the latter part of it has turned out to be truly significant: the "unexpected." This idea, along with the Aristotelian definition – the φαυλότερον and the ἀνώδυνον – constitute the starting-point of all further formulations.

By the eighteenth century, those two elements of the comical became part of the vernacular. Wolff, Baumgarten, Eberhard[134], all understood the effect of contrast in the comical. Even the liberating effect of comedy (or of laughter) – from the bands of seriousness – was recognized in that era and articulated (Shaftesbury[135]). (423)

Even the formulations of Kant strike us as the mature flowering of these reflections: "In everything that is to provoke a lively, uproarious laughter, there must be something nonsensical (in which, therefore, the understanding in itself

---

134 [Translator's note:] Johann Augustus Eberhard (1739–1809).
135 [Translator's note:] Anthony Ashley Cooper, 3rd Earl of Shaftesbury (1671–1713).

can take no satisfaction). *Laughter is an affect resulting from the sudden transformation of a heightened expectation into nothing.*"[136]

One might like to take what Kant says about laughter and carry it over to comedy itself. It is not the "affect" that is important, but the objective strangeness of the object, which is able first to call forth an "heightened expectation" and then surprise us by collapsing "into nothing." Kant knew how to bring out in sharp relief that this, and nothing else, is the key here: "Note that it must not be transformed into the positive opposite of an expected object – for that is always something, and can often be distressing – but into nothing. For if in telling us a story someone arouses a great expectation and at its conclusion we immediately see its untruth, that is displeasing."[137] What follows is the anecdote about the merchant whose wig turns grey when he learns of his financial losses (as a counter-example of a good joke).

The other element of comedy, represented in Aristotle by the φαυλότερον, is found in Kant under the category of "nonsense." That is clearly a broader motion, for it is not limited to the domain of the moral; the example of the wig shows that there exists comedy without moral weakness. Thus we will have to broaden the ancient formula. When the nonsense is resolved, we clearly sense relaxation in our laughter.

The theory of comedy has stayed within these limits. Jean Paul[138] saw in the comical a "lack of judgment beheld through the senses" – an "action that contradicts the situation of the actor."[139] Schopenhauer is more rigorously Kantian: the comical is the sudden appearance of incongruence between what is expected and what comes to be – or between the concept and the real object, so far as the latter reveals itself as nothing. Here, too, the effect itself is the trailing-off into nothing. Schelling and Schleiermacher, two Romantics, made things too easy for themselves when they play off this contrast against the greatness of the idea and the nullity of the semblance. The element of self-resolution is more important, as Vischer and others emphasized. If what is nonsensical, cockeyed, or illogical were maintained, it would produce only confusion and annoyance; only when its contradictions resolve themselves is the tension eased, and this resolution, if it takes place suddenly, is felt as comedy. Eduard von Hartmann puts illogicality in place of weakness throughout (that is in conformity with Kant's "nonsense," but

---

136 [Translator's note:] Kant, Immanuel, *Critique of the Power of Judgment*, translated by Paul Guyer and Eric Matthews, The Cambridge Edition of the Works of Immanuel Kant, Cambridge and New York: Cambridge University Press 2002, p. 209.

137 [Translator's note:] Kant, *Critique of the Power of Judgment*, p. 209f.

138 [Translator's note:] Johann Paul Friedrich Richter (1763–1826).

139 [Translator's note:] Translation E.K.

is rather too narrow). Volkelt[140] says that the mere semblance of value presents itself visibly in its own self-resolution. (424)

b) The types of nonsense in the ridiculous

At this point, we have assembled a collection of the essential elements of the comical. They were developed historically one after the other, but only in assembly do they result in a complete picture. They are: nonsense (the φαυλότερον, weakness), the semblance of significance or importance (which must be there at least at the outset), the self-resolution of semblance (it vanishing into a nothingness), and the unexpected. These four elements are not always sharply distinguished; they flow into each other. They are well primed only for an artificially polished joke, which comedy can carry to extremes. For that reason, the joke also has a punch line, which a maladroit comedian may spoil.

Obviously, it cannot be allowed that the Aristotelian φαυλότερον be limited exclusively to the "illogical" (as in E. v. Hartmann). It may be true that in all the little moral defects that the great majority of comedies – in life as in literature – offers us, there is an illogical element, but that alone does not make for comedy, for that alone does not make possible the effect of the transition to nothing. The Kantian expression is better, i.e., nonsense, which cannot be understood in a merely logical sense. What is then alone of importance is that the nonsensical remain concealed at first, so that it may, if only for a moment, take on the illusion of meaningfulness, and be able to convince us of it.

One finds this analysis confirmed for the entire series of content-phenomena that yield the material of comedy, i.e., in everything that has the character of φαυλότερον. If one takes off from the obvious opposition of comedy and the sublime, it becomes clear that in the former we always are dealing with the small and petty in man, just as we deal with the overwhelmingly great in the latter. Instead of sublime excess, we encounter the deficiency of the ridiculous. But ridiculousness is not rooted in deficiency alone, but in the claim made by what is deficient to be in fact of a normal measure or even of an excessive one. And if comedy is to become vivid, the claim must first find a certain acceptance.

The phenomena of human life that fulfill these conditions can be divided into three groups.

The first group contains moral weakness and smallness that likes to parade itself as strength and human normalcy, and thus attempts to conceal itself, but it

---

140 [Translator's note:] Johannes Volkelt (1848–1930).

cannot prevent itself from betraying and thus completely unmasking itself. Of this kind are caprice, inconstancy, comfort, laziness, impatience, apprehensiveness and fearfulness, cowardice, taking fright, credulity and gullibility, lack of self-control, anger, blind rage; further, loquacity, love of gossip, pomposity, collusiveness – but also real pettiness, pedantry, tight-fistedness and greed. In these latter, there are significant moral defects.

This list is of course incomplete. But one sees in these examples what kind of human weaknesses function in comedy. These are (425) – according to Aristotle – those weaknesses that represent human lapses, none of which are very serious and do not bring about moral decay with them; thus they are failings that are still barely compatible with a certain endearing quality in their bearers – and that, no doubt, to very varying degrees. In the case of pettiness and greed, the limit has already in fact been exceeded.

It is well known that these kinds of weaknesses offer an inexhaustible circle of themes for comedy – in life itself, as in poetry and storytelling. Yet when one asks why this is so, the reference to the ἀνώδυνον καὶ οὐ φθαρτικόν is quite unsatisfactory.

What is genuinely comical about weaknesses lies in their tendency to mask themselves, and, where possible, to pose as their opposites. And the comical effect begins with the critical moment when the mask falls off, to the surprise of all, and the all-too-human is revealed in its nakedness.

Accordingly, laziness or the enjoyment of creature comforts is not comical itself, but surely become so when, behind a mask, empty fuss and bother are concealed, which were not seen through immediately. The case is similar when the weaknesses already manifest themselves openly, but then gravely offer deceptive reasons to justify themselves.

In the same way, gullibility is only comical just when it thinks itself to be merely very careful; a lack of self-control and anger, just when it thinks itself entirely justified, or wants others to think so; gossip is usually comical just when the gossiper thinks himself to be far superior to the chitchat of others; pomposity just when it believes in its presumed importance. ... Only in these ways is the self-annulment of the nonsense in all of this an inner and necessary one, just as the changeover "to nothing."

The second group has a strong component of intellectual defects, and is close to the element of illogicality found in nonsense. But here the weight lies upon the blindness of men to their own failings, or upon the tendency to conceal them.

In this group belong a careless unconcern for logic, stupidity and unreflectiveness, folly, prejudice and blindness; furthermore, always with a component of stupidity, are self-certainty, stubbornness, vanity, haughtiness, meddlesomeness; finally, the inflexible adherence to what is conventional – and, along with that, the entire objective sphere of conventionality, so far as it is obsolete, and suppresses what is justifiably natural; then, too, the artificial upholding of appearances (good manners) and, in general, of inauthentic moral tenets.

Many more things that bring out the comical in an especially graphic way might be added to this list, as, for example, foolish pride or foolish cleverness, the spouting of fixed opinions, the pompous wisdom of people who know nothing – moral defects with a component of absent intellectual power, which makes such inward nonsense especially apparent.

Here too, the most important thing is that something in the stupidity, in the lack of logic, etc. appears as wisdom and deep reflection. Then (426) simple stupidity is not what is comical, but only the kind that one can sympathetically understand and, within certain limits, go along with, or one in which one can empathize. Only from that position does the "changing into nothing" occur, which then produces the comical effect.

This is the reason why common stupidity is not so comical as one that is genuinely refined, that is, thought out in advance, of a kind requiring a certain amount of intelligence. It is especially noticeable in the case of folly, i.e., in that kind of stupidity in which after all reflection – perhaps quite carefully done – something central to the case is overlooked, though it is as clear as the nose on one's face, especially when the case lies in the moral domain. The resolution of the nonsense in the course of events takes the form of realizing that one was "taken in," which always is especially convincing, and which can be put to use artistically, because the very nature of coming to realize that one has been taken in is inherently "dramatic."

Thus, the liar is taken for a ride when he does not think through the factual implications of his swindle; so too the deceiver or the sanctimonious person, and other phonies in comedy (Tartuffe). The unmasking of a villain is an inexhaustible theme for the ridiculous, especially when it is the result of some agent's own innate absurdity, that is, when it leads to a self-resolution.

In this group, a special role is played by social conventions as well as by the tendency of men to hold to them as to a divine order of things. There is an entire world of illusion that is founded upon them: bogus virtue, bogus morals, bogus dignity, and bogus pride. Just where the genuine sources of our moral sense are dammed up – simple kindness, love, respect, forbearance – the forms of convention make the most space for themselves: ossified traditions, soulless ceremonies, false severity, zealous concern for social forms, heartless repression of the feelings of natural men (especially of youths).

In these cases, comedy lies neither in convention itself (etiquette), for there will always be such things, nor in their simple obsolescence, for then they would seem simply vulgar. It lies rather in the contrast that arises from simple and natural men assailing these things; all the more, when, with a stroke, the cloak of venerability is removed from the sacred rules and they reveal themselves as the work of narrow-minded men.

This phenomenon is closely related to the importunate demeanor of the man who would make the world a better place, although here we move in the reverse direction. The man who knows the better way desires to overthrow the world as it is, and considers all conventions obsolete; he believes that he is enlightened about what needs to be done. Such a man is always the newcomer to the domain he wishes to reform. His comedy is brought out most impressively where the way of the world itself, through the course of the smallest events (those lying in the "quiet corner") leads him to absurdity.

The third group is the most harmless. The defect that lies within it is neither that of intelligence nor in morals – although the two may play a role – it concerns a man who is out of joint, who possesses some incapacity. There are many men of these kinds, and their absurdity most likely lies in the fact that a normal man has always to a certain extent a corrective (427) to them at hand: as *homo sapiens* he can compensate for them.

We must include here all kinds of clumsiness and helplessness in practical matters, beginning with simple stumbling and stuttering and proceeding to constant hard luck, and, as a consequence, missing out on some simple need, though it lies ready at hand; further, the external awkwardness in appearance, the lack of social forms, not because one rejects them, but simply because one does not know any better. Consequently, exaggerated shamefulness, embarrassment, bashfulness, but especially also the fear of others and the wish to avoid them, while also giving constant attention to the opinions of others; finally, a lack of presence of mind, absent-mindedness, daydreaming of nothing, distractedness and the lack of a proper mental discipline.

All that can be rediscovered in the types of comedy familiar the world over. These are the more harmless cases of comedy, although, of course, they are also the ones in which our laughter may easily become unjust. With certain forms of awkwardness a man can simply do nothing about them. Wilhelm Busch's[141] work is filled with such comedy – which can rise to the grotesque – and therefore he tries to shape the material of the episodes so that a moral light may shine out from them upon the misfortunes he depicts.

For that reason, the deceptive appearance of superiority distances itself from these kinds of comedy. Only a shadow of it remains in the ignorance of the

---

141 [Translator's note:] Wilhelm Busch (1832–1908), German caricaturist.

comical character of the extent of his awkwardness. But that is sufficient to make possible the appearance of a punch line in the eventual turnabout.

c) The self-resolution of nonsense

Of the three elements of the comical, the first two have had their say, because the second, the "deceptive appearance of what is meaningful and important," cannot be separated from the first one, "nonsense and human weakness." For tied to every kind of human defect and nakedness is some specific accompanying way to conceal or to deny them, and these have their counterpart in in a vain sense of self, of conceit, etc. A third element is still lacking, the presence of which would allow a latent comedy to appear in full strength and establish its validity: the self-resolution of the nonsense.

Older theories held that it was acceptable to include the ugly among the other forms of nonsense that constitute the comic material. That was done basically for the sake of the theory – specifically, because the "system of the Spirit" had been so structured that anything of disvalue had to dispel itself and the world eventually to be "purged" of it, to which end the comical would provide the most potent means of such cleansing.

We purposely ignored this situation up to now. The ugly is a chapter itself in aesthetics, and has been touched upon in its place. The critical question is that of the *modus deficiens* in it. The ugly has only the one relation to the comical, that in it a discrepancy (428) exists, as it were, a kind of "absurdity," for example, a disproportionality of face or figure. But this sort of nonsense does not have the capacity to dispel itself; indeed, it does not lie in its nature to reach a point of intensity by some misdirection of its self-awareness. Thus we cannot find in it a case of a turnabout into nothing; the fall lacks sufficient height. For that reason, the phenomenon of the ugly was left out here.

What is the nature of this self-resolution? Everything absurd in life avenges itself somehow in the passage of time. It does not do that because some universal mind rules over all events and balances them out, but because the chain of its causal consequences cannot be limited. It does not always have to avenge itself upon what caused it, or what was responsible for it; it can also meet with other possibilities. But it lies in the nature of transgressions of this kind, to which a bit of responsibility of one's own is attached, that the "vengeance" indirectly and in its final effects falls to the guilty party. That is in itself a purely moral affair, to be sure, a quite serious one, often enough even tragic. It has nothing to do with comedy. To be sure, the mere self-resolution of an obligation, an absurdity, or a piece of nonsense is far from being something ridiculous.

What then makes it ridiculous? Usually, one at first answers the question as follows: it has the character of the trivial, small, or the meaningless within the three groups of the ridiculous, the ἀνώδυνον καὶ οὐ φθαρτικόν. The vengeance of the universal course of events, too, is therewith swept into the domain of the trivial, and with that, revenge is no longer subject to the seriousness of the ethos in the hard, real world.

But that is insufficient. A lack of seriousness alone does not make for comedy. For that, a special kind of effect is required, one with which begins the self-destruction of nonsense, or the revenge of events. This effect occurs when the absurdity at first conceals its nature, and presents itself as something quite serious and rational, but then suddenly, by means of the weight of its own consequences, shows its true face. That is that we called the transformation or "turnabout to nothing" (with Kant), the coming to an end in nullity of an affair that seemed heavy with meaning. It may also be simply the lightning-fast revelation of the absurdity, and with that, the resolution of the nonsense.

In fact, older theories had maintained that in the comical something must always initially make an impression of greatness, yes, even of the sublime, and this greatness must then collapse into nothingness. That was the opinion of the Romantics, of Hegel and Vischer, and also for Schopenhauer and some of the later idealists.

But this schema is taken from a specific kind of comedy, from the "joke," which no doubt depends upon an extreme augmentation of tension; here is the height of the fall the main thing. The more weighty the thing that is to fall "into nothingness," the greater must be the comical effect: the "joke" needs a "steep drop." Without one, we do not achieve the desired explosion at the end. For that reason, the "punch line" is so important for the joke that when it is lacking or is interrupted, the comical aspect is destroyed. That means that the joke (429) is spoiled when the self-resolution becomes visible even just a moment too early; it virtually depends upon a cue. To have an eye for it, and for the art of narrative that belongs to it, is a genuine artistic talent. There are many men who regularly spoil the point of a joke.

This relation, which defines the "joke," cannot be generalized. The great majority of things comical need no massive support from the sublime. The comical does not always need the "parturiunt montes nascetur ridiculus mus."[142] And if it is also true that from the sublime to the ridiculous is only one step, it is

---

[142] [Translator's note:] "Mountains will heave in labour and born shall be a ludicrous mouse!" Horace, *Satires and Epistles*, translated by John Davie, Oxford World's Classics, Oxford and New York: Oxford University Press 2011, p. 110.

not true because this step is a condition of all things comical, and that all comedy requires that it be preceded by the sublime. Most comedy is of a far simpler kind.

There is, for example, the annoyance over a minor mishap, the dread of imagined danger, the uproar caused by some misunderstanding or by something missing, the joy in gossip, and one's own even larger contribution to it, possibly even just as one expresses outrage over the gossip of others. Here we have no need of a prior "elevation" of some kind.

It is perhaps of greater foundational importance that honest good will can become ridiculous when it sallies forth with means that are entirely insufficient for its ends, or because of a naïve understanding of the good. The former we see in the case of the immature and inexperienced; the latter in the case of the unsophisticated idealist or weekend politician.

In this group, finally, belong the large number of persons whose otherwise moral good will is invaded by egotistical and well-calculated motives that are at first concealed from the willing and acting agent himself – that is, motives that he is, at least in part, not really conscious of, but motives that are in part also willfully concealed and even appear, as it were, masked before his own consciousness, although a dark awareness of them continues to exist. Thus there is a kind of self-deception for which one bears responsibility. The first kind occurs, for example, when one gives a gift to a person for whom one has good will, but where there is no lack of some calculation about the obligation caused to this person – for that reason, the giver may feel outrage at the person's failure to be thankful for the gift. The latter case is with public "charity" that in reality is meant to serve one's own standing in society.

In all these cases, one thing is characteristic: this comedy does not require a "steep drop," for there is no explosive effect intended. There is of course the contrast between the spheres, the opposition of earnestness and nullity; yet, comedy occurs without such amplification and, especially, without assembling all its elements at some moment crucial to the "turnabout," and thus also without any real "punch line."

Just the annoyance expressed by a man trying to dress himself quickly as the button on his tie pops out is comical in itself. The contrast between the importance of what he is doing and the nullity of the object is also ridiculous without any amplification; and the self-resolution of the nonsense is sufficiently given in the uproar and despair of the victim – when the (430) time he has lost does not have fatal consequences. It is the same with the secret egotism of the calculating gift-giver, with the nervous impatience of a man who waits in vain, the quickly provoked jealousy of the man in love, the self-induced dread that torments a man awaiting an imagined calamity, the easily distracted prayer of the sanctimonious worshipper.

For this reason, the famous definitions of the comical, at the head of which stands the Kantian "turnabout to nothing," does not have to be lowered in rank. It is only natural that the inner essence of a peculiar phenomenon will be first discovered in its most acute form. That has happened in these cases, for the form of real sharply-honed objective comedy is the "joke."

Nonetheless, it would be an error to carry over this characteristic acute form to all remaining forms of the comical. The important thing, rather, is that there be a great many grades in the intensity of the tension and of height of the "drop" – one might describe it as the phenomenon of "contrast" – and that our emotional response to the ridiculous extends here into very mild mixed emotions.

We do not always need explosive effects, but not even acute tension. No doubt our human sense of comedy is similarly graduated in multifarious ways: a coarser man always first appreciates the coarse effects, to which belong many kinds of increase in the "drop" (artificially, if not otherwise); the man of greater nuance will, as a rule, prefer the quieter, more psychological, or more deeply hidden elements of the comedy.

The two genera of the comical that have often been noted correspond to this perfectly. The crude comedy, which quickly degenerates into the grotesque, burlesque or the spectacle; the finely wrought comedy, which – always in association with the charming – manifests the opposite tendency, i.e., to pass into the playful and the intellectual.

d) Superiority in humor

One need not alter any of the essential elements in the definition of the comical because of the above limitation. In reality, it is a question rather of the abrogation of a limiting condition, that is, of the expansion of the sphere of validity. Nonsense, apparent importance, and self-resolution, remain where they are. Apparent importance, however, can be put on a lower rung of the graduated scale in such a way that it is no longer felt as apparent. Nonetheless, something analogous to it must be left over, some presumptive weight, or at least the belief that it exists.

It is characteristic of humor – in life as in literature – that it does not, for the most part, move within artificially exaggerated oppositions, but holds more closely to life, and draws upon steeper drops only where they, as it were, offer themselves.

This coheres well with the inner nature of the eye that seeks out humor. This eye is not disapproving, cold, or loveless, as that of the (431) jokester, who welcomes every occasion to laugh when the joke is sufficiently potent. The eye of the humorist is fundamentally full of love and sympathy; he even shows favor to the human weaknesses he reveals. Therefore, he exaggerates neither the weaknesses themselves nor the contrast in which they appear. And before all else, he does not inflate a presumed "sublimity" as a background for these failings.

Comedy that is seen as humor is a milder comedy. Just for that reason, it speaks to a more refined audience. There exists in life a deep need for this kind of comedy among those who are always under stress and always earnest; it makes their hearts leap a bit, and loosens the tension they are under. That capacity has its basis in the peace and composure of the view of life that the genuine humorist brings to his work, and which, within certain limits, he also transmits to his readers.

This peace gives a man a certain distance from the eternal busyness of life. It cannot protect him from what fortune may confer upon him, but perhaps from the many little and petty events that, because of their great number, can seem to crush and overwhelm him. Humor has a beneficent effect on us, whose nullity might, as it were, be clearly demonstrated *ad oculus* [visually]. Despite its exposure of the small failings of men, humor is still the genuine benefactor of humankind.

No doubt the enjoyment of this beneficence is no longer a purely aesthetical enjoyment. We have here rather a moral consequence of the aesthetical phenomenon. In this way it also corresponds to a precondition of genuine humor, a condition that, even more than it, is rooted in an ethos.

For that reason the true humorist is superior in life, while the man without humor is his inferior. That does not refer in any way just to the peculiar gift of producing humor, which is, after all, not frequently encountered, but above all the sense of and receptivity to humor, the simple broad-mindedness and inward disengagement that everyone is capable of – if not at every moment and in every situation.

The sense of humor is a genuine aesthetical stance, but one always resting on an ethos. This ethos must, of course, be summoned up, must, as it were, be erected from within. For it signifies the overcoming of inhibitions, or at least the willingness to do so. Neither is self-evident. For everyone, in some areas of his life, has his own inhibitions – his own obstinacy, his pedantry, things that annoy him, or his conceits – and only through a genuine self-overcoming is a person able to break through them into laughter. If, in the humor placed before us by some humorist, quite different inhibitions than our own are at stake, still one's own are really targeted also, for they are all far too similar to each other such that they all could not be uncloaked and exposed by one.

The humorless man – meaning the person who does not even have a passive sense of humor – is therefore a truly morally defective man; he is too inhibited even to want to free himself. At bottom (432) he can easily be taken as a man who, with some justification, fears humor, because he senses that it is directed at him. That means, in turn, that he thinks of himself as the butt of some comedy, or at least imagines himself as one of its targets.

The man without humor is, accordingly, himself a perfect representative of comedy. Inadvertently, he puts in the hand of the humorist the best example of it. For the aversion to humor is with such men identical to fearfully holding fast to gravity and dignity, behind whose deceitful appearance stands pure "nothingness."

The test of the example of human superiority (the purely inward one, not that toward other men) has always been whether a man can laugh at himself or not, or, more innocuously, whether he can hear a jest aimed at himself or not. Not everyone has the taste for that, and most people cannot put up with it. For the ability to put up with such a thing does not consist simply in grinning and bearing.

These phenomena – together with their characteristic antitheses – were observed early on. They were noted by Aristotle in his *Nicomachean Ethics*. He sketches two types of κακία [vices] in the deportment of men, between which an "unnamed" ἀρετή [virtue] lies. The περὶ τί is the jest, and the types of ἕξις [habits] concern the attitudes of a man towards a jest he is told. At one extreme is the βωμολόχος, the "rogue," who makes everything he touches seem ridiculous and will allow no seriousness; at the other extreme is the ἄγροικος, [boor] who understands no jesting and takes everything with bitter seriousness. The latter is obviously the humorless man, who immediately becomes furious at a joke aimed at him. If we also consult Theophrastus[143] in this matter we realize that the ancients themselves saw this type as highly ridiculous. But that is precisely what we are concerned with here: he who cannot laugh along at human weaknesses, some of which are or come a bit close to one's own, makes himself precisely into an object of comedy.

Chapter 38: The Comical and the Serious

a) Metaphysical aspects of comedy

In itself, comedy has not much to do with philosophical questions. Those stand closer to its antithesis, the sublime. So, at least, matters appear at first sight. But after more careful observation, the situation changes. The ethos alone, which

---

143 [Translator's note:] c. 371 – c. 287 BCE. Successor to Aristotle in the Peripatetic school at the Lyceum. Hartmann may be consulting *The Characters*, which is attributed to Theophrastus.

determines the kind of sensibility required for comedy, points to its deeper roots. Apparently a man possessing humor must somehow have or secure a footing on a philosophical platform, even when the philosophy does not penetrate his objective consciousness. Those are facts that, with reference to certain forms of literature, can be demonstrated precisely. (433)

The distinction is well known between gentle and mordant satire.[144] The opposed attitudes, one that affirms and one that condemns life, is hidden in them, one half optimistic, amused, enjoying itself, that "lives and lets live," and the other markedly pessimistic and able to amplify itself to the point of bitterness towards life in general. The subtle humor of Horace's[145] satires is a lovely exhibition of the first phenomenon. In the second genus, such high achievements are no doubt impossible, for the sought-after effects are of a coarser harshness, and the view of life that stands behind it is too negativistic.

Even when we omit reference to such markedly extreme cases, a certain philosophy of the world and of life always stands behind the eye for the comical. That means that this eye has a metaphysical background – no different from the sense for reverence and matters of faith, or for human love and human hatred. And, very often, the world-view that lies at its base is one and the same for all these domains – often even for that of knowledge. It does not have to be so, for the philosophical perspectives of a person are rarely thought through uniformly. But there is always a tendency towards such uniformity. For that reason, all sense of the comical, especially its deeper form, i.e., humor, always has a moral, metaphysical and – if you like – a religious side, too.

This is what we sense so strongly in the great humorists among the poets: Jean Paul, Raabe, Reuter[146], et al. They do not have to step out of their personae and demonstrate their view of the world to us; we receive it much more concretely and penetratingly from the way they see and give shape to the comedy in life.

There is an additional interconnection between metaphysics and comedy. It concerns specific characteristics in the structure of the world in which we live, so far as we are able to respond emotionally to the world-structure as comical. And it is understandable that men find such characteristics more readily where their own place in the world resides and their own integration into the great processes of the universe is at stake.

Many subtle metaphysicians have found tragedy in the place of humankind in the world, and given it a pessimistic expression. But such thinkers have also

---

144 [Translator's note:] The distinction Hartmann is referring to is usually expressed in English as that between Horatian and Juvenalian satire.

145 [Translator's note:] Horace (65–8 BCE).

146 [Translator's note:] Fritz Reuter (1810–1874).

found comedy in the same role, and in both cases for almost the same reasons: for example, for the reason that men cannot help but seek their own "happiness" everywhere, but in so doing they discover malice in the constitution of their own nature and of the way of the world that builds barriers along the road to their happiness. Metaphysical theories of this kind are, for the most part, eudaimono-logical,[147] and the fact of man's eternal betrayal in the "balance-sheet of pleasure and pain" plays a determining role in them.

We know this from Schopenhauer, who, in the development of such theories, usually unfolds a grim humor. The entire state of the world – beginning with a "brutal will to create a world," which produced an (434) intelligence that later "abrogated" it – seems like a huge joke.

Friedrich Schlegel introduced the joke into philosophy, but on a quite differ-ent basis. His procedure is related to the dialectic of Schelling and Hegel, for which the element of the turnabout is also the essential element. A trace of jesting can be heard in many of the clever and ingenious formulations in Hegel's system.

One may also find essentially aesthetical forms with which to develop a metaphysics of the comical. In his day, Schelling had made progress in adapting the aesthetical attitude entirely to philosophy by making of it a universal organ of metaphysical knowledge. Only second-rate minds, however, considered this ex-ample worthy of imitation. But in aesthetics itself it found a few counterparts.

The Romantics found a profound irony in how man is thrust into the world, while in truth he stands behind it and plays a role in determining its nature. Man will never succeed, in their view, in rediscovering his own nature in a world that appears alien to him, and thus we have the tragicomedy of man failing to grasp his own nature in the nature of the world. Novalis went a step further with his "magical idealism": this permits man to create a world according to his own wishes. He must have a magic wand, that is, he must control the "central organ," just as the artist controls the senses: the painter takes control of the eyes, the musician of the ears.

An idea of St. Schütze[148] (*Versuch einer Theorie des Komischen*) seems a bit more specific. According to him, comedy is a game that nature plays with man all the while he thinks he acts freely; thus it is a game that nature plays with human freedom. This idea, which in itself is perfidious and truly satanic, is softened a bit by understanding it as claiming that comedy is at bottom only the "perception or representation" of such a game. However, this changes little regarding its tragico-

---

147 [Translator's note:] Schopenhauer used the term, "ευδαίμων λόγος," "doctrine of happi-ness."
148 [Translator's note:] Stephan Schütze von Steinacker (1771–1839).

mical betrayal of man, with respect to his responsibility, accountability, human dignity and ethos, in a highly ridiculous and metaphysical way.

Others have praised this idea (Vischer), but it was clear that it is too narrow for a definition of the comical. Then, too, it is obvious that there are very many other things that are comical and comedies that are less harmful and have nothing to do with such a fundamental betrayal of man.

One great example of a metaphysics of man persists and takes on the form of a grandiose joke: man struggles to be honest and good, believes that he is guilty of every fault, blames himself and listens to his conscience, bears up under what he takes to be his guilt – and in fact it is not his guilt, but, without his knowing it is instead determined by a chain of causes that worked its way through him, and that is infinitely indifferent to good and evil. (435)

In this "comical" picture of the world, not only the person is degraded to the level of a mere thing, in fact to a mere plaything in an irrational game of an eternal mechanism, but also even the high aims that men honestly take to be their own are branded as mere nothings, and replaced by very banal motives of a petty, egotistical kind.

The case of metaphysical comedy, which is tied to all teleological world-views, is not much different. It becomes amplified where the world-view is openly anthropomorphic, or takes to itself only anthropomorphic characteristics. The first is the case where one catches sight of will and predestination in the world-process, the second where man stands before us as the highest meaning and purpose of the process, and everything appears to be directed towards him. The grotesque comedy here lies in man, who lovingly constructs this picture of the world – with the intention of structuring the world in a way that is especially favorable and lovely for himself – but who achieves precisely the opposite: he robs himself of the only dignified and meaningful station in the world.

How that happens is really a chapter in the book of metaphysics. But the essential thing is as follows. Man has his special place in the world, as possessing a "higher nature" in comparison to the animals, thanks to two higher gifts, the capacity for purposive action, and the capacity to decide matters by acts of free will. The person who assigns purposive activity to the entire world as a form of determinism denies and trifles away these two gifts. The first is denied, because man can realize his ends only through means (such as natural energy) that allow themselves to be harnessed without any resistance to his aims; but such neutral means can be found only in a world that is determined by mere causation, never in a world determined by final causes, in which every object brings with itself initially a "directedness toward something or other." In that way, man injures himself, he makes out of his own active nature one that is condemned to passivity. The second gift, however, that of freedom, is trifled away because in a word determined by teleology there is no more latitude for "free" decisions. In such a world, even the decisions of man are predetermined, and his freedom is only an apparent one.

The "comedy of teleology" can be traced through the entire long history of human reflection and inquiry; in everyday life, in myth, in religious thought, in philosophy: almost all philosophical "systems" are indeed teleological. It seems as if some secret power has drawn men ever again to deceive themselves.

We see that what is at stake here is not only the "metaphysical aspects of comedy," but rather the comical aspects of metaphysics, and with that also the comical aspects of all human world-views and philosophies of life, even when they strut themselves in the sublime robes of a "higher wisdom": that is, we have at stake here the comical aspects of myth and religion. (436)

Everywhere that a heavenly realm constructed by man collapses, comedy becomes apparent, and scoffers collect about. But their scoffing is cheap, to be sure, and hardly worth our concern. As long as heaven endures, no one notices the comedy; men remain steadfast and reverential, and look upon it with awe. And just in their awe, they are metaphysically comical objects.

At the end, we might cap this off with the enormous self-deception of man regarding the problem of meaning. The situation is such that a world that was already filled with meaning would be a world unfavorable to meaningfulness for man as a being who bestows meaning; but the meaningless world in which we live is the only world appropriate to man and meaningful for him. And all the while man, blind to that fact since the beginning of history, denies it, and attempts to twist its meaning and make it "better" – that is, make the world precisely unfavorable to meaning. The comedy in this cannot be mistaken. But it approaches the level of tragicomedy.

b) Peripheral phenomena of comedy

At first sight, the question seems strange: are there phenomena at the limits of the comical – of a kind, for example, that we came to discover in the sublime and the charming? It would have to be a question of cases in which the comical, of its own accord, turned about into something opposed to it, thus most likely in the serious, or what one thinks it to be. The question is strange only because we know the comical itself as the product of a turnabout by the sublime. But not all comedy comes for the sublime, as has already become apparent. In the face of that fact, the situation changes.

There are various kinds of peripheral phenomena. We may anticipate one, for it concerns literature, especially, but also indirectly the conduct of the living humorous person, of the jokester, the scoffer, et al. For it lies in the nature of the comical that it resists a broad treatment of its material; it has an innate tendency to limit itself in time.

The reason for this lies in its structure: everything in it forces its way towards a "punch line" that cannot be drawn out to any length, because then the punch line would be guessed at from some other quarter. If the limit is exceeded, the comedy is exhausted also, for one cannot stay with it for any given amount of time. One cannot make the drop have its effect a second time after it is once used.

That is an essential difference from other literature. Of course, there exists the *peripateia*[149] in every drama, in every well-constructed novel, usually even in the great epics, which, however, are not so mindful of it. But everywhere that serious matters are dealt with, the breadth of the material drawn into the narrative and dwelt upon is something positive and usually necessary; it transmits familiarity with a milieu. Only in comedy is the situation otherwise. Neither the preparatory tension nor the slow dissolution of the mood and the aesthetical pleasure it creates can be stretched out further here (437) than is required by the turnabout and its appreciation in the understanding of the audience. Just the slightest violation of this limit – even a felicitous word, if it is one word too many – will have a weakening effect, that is, it will destroy the comedic effect. All violent clinging to comedy that has already been enjoyed dissipates it.

For that reason, comical themes are short. They always maintain something of the anecdotal about them. They cannot fill an entire book, even when they are enigmatic and full of philosophical depth. When the humorist wants to fill a book, he must bring to it ever new comical elements. Since that would produce a monotonous babbling ad infinitum, the writer must concern himself with material of a different kind, about which the comedy may wind itself. That material may be quite earnest, and it must be so for the sake of the contrast (Fritz Reuter). The first phenomenon at the borders of the comical is not only a limitation of the temporal extension, but also the inner thematic possibilities of the comical.

There are other such peripheral phenomena. One that is well known lies in the comedy of invective, especially when, as in life, it carries a marked personal character. Invective, i.e., enjoying attacking others, occurs in every kind of persiflage, every riding roughshod over others that has the form of teasing and mocking. All persiflage has two sides: it is done by an attacker; it can be, for example, very clever, but it is also a challenge to the one attacked – perhaps for a similarly clever defense, perhaps for a good-willed laughing along with his own weaknesses. Both have their limits.

---

149 [Translator's note:] The Aristotelian "turning point" in tragedy.

And these limits are genuine peripheral problems of the comical. For it can come to pass that the laughter of the uninvolved audience suddenly stops, and its attitude changes to disapproval, as when the persiflage has gone over into insult and genuine harm. The intellectually superior victim will not, of course, let the pain be noticed, but instead deflect it in such a way that he brings those who first laughed at him over to his side, and then he can withdraw to a good distance. But not everyone has the proper measure of superiority. And even when a person has it, the pain is still real.

This border phenomenon thus rests upon the fact that comedy has a destructive effect (you "die laughing"). The correct depth of what is drawn into the ridiculous must be considered. If one finds oneself at a great intellectual depth, the small pinpricks become serious insults, the "joke is over," and laughter ceases.

This kind of peripheral phenomenon – the turnabout into offense – plays a broad role in life. This is so less because of the aggressive malice of the man with ready wit, and more because of the temptation that arises from the gift of ready wit and the rousing effect it has on others. The man who teases and jests becomes easily blind to those facts; the power of the jest draws him along and he notices only too late what damage he has done.

This peripheral phenomenon varies in manifold ways, but it rests always upon the same moral defect: the thoughtlessness, the careless play with the weaknesses of others. A species of this phenomenon is the joke that one allows oneself to play with wrongdoing. Depending on what way (438) we interpret the "wrongdoing" in question, the game can turn out badly for the object or for the player: the jester may create unforeseeable damage with his little joke, but he can himself fall into the gunpowder and be blasted in the air. An example of the first is found with Dostoyevsky's Stavrogin [a character in *The Possessed*], who leads the Privy Counselor "by the nose," without intending to cause any great harm.

The derailing of something funny is of a different kind; it is rooted in an excessive heaping of comedy. In such cases we have as yet no question of the phenomenon of the βωμολόχος [buffoon], who draws everything into the domain of jest and thus creates silliness even where all is in earnest. Rather, there is a continuous poking-fun that, without disturbing what is important, at length becomes barren and tedious, because no one can go along forever with mere sharp wit, punch-lines and hilarity; after a while one demands greater sobriety.

Among the various peripheral phenomena of the comical and of humor – for the latter, too, can exceed its limits – this one is surely the strangest. For here amusements that are consciously pursued turn to boredom. It seems as though the real effect of comedy were tied to the Aristotelian μεσότης [mean], such that a purely quantitative Too-much destroys it and lets it turn into its opposite, a Too-little.

Tediousness or boredom is in sharp opposition to comedy as, for example, the sublime or the tragic are contrary to it. For such opposition is entirely negative and contradictory. That conforms quite precisely to our experience: some tragedy in life is entirely compatible with the ridiculous; we know of it in tragicomedy, which often seizes us in life and pulls us in two directions. But boredom is not compatible with it: where boredom takes its place, laughter is dissipated quite differently than when it is dissipated by the approach of seriousness.

Still another border phenomenon is the turnabout of the comical into the banal, insipid, or tasteless. Of course, one may fall into banality from almost any material – for example, it is easy to do so from what is touching or painful – but the change is never as great as with the comical. Why is this so?

For this reason: the comical, when it is consciously apprehended and represented makes a claim to be clever and surprising, or at least entertaining, and when these claims are not met, the result is sobering. For the comical lives entirely from the satisfying of these claims, and nothing is left of it when it does not justify them.

When does the transition to the banal begin? Apparently when not only the intensification of the contrast – the punch line – fails to take place, but also when the contrast itself, which makes up the drop, disappears. In sum, it begins when the contrast turns out to be an inauthentic, artificial one, such that self-resolution is no longer possible at all, indeed when there was no nonsense present at all.

Does anyone doubt that such thing happen? Dilettantism in telling jokes, reciting stories and forced humor, which everywhere dominate (439) social entertainment, abounds everywhere. Think of how a successful joke immediately makes people want to try their hand at telling it – what constantly results in staleness, for the repetition of the same effect is impossible: the drop has been used up.

The same phenomenon can appear in a still more intensified form. Then jokes, comedy, and wit do not simply pass into the banal, but into the foolish and silly. That is, to be sure, no longer a real turnabout, because there was at the start no discernible level in the joke. This happens often when a man entirely without a sense of humor and with no gift for the comical wishes to tell striking jokes but then cannot summon up the slightest material for them. This is true also for children when they want to show how nicely they can do it.

Another peripheral or border phenomenon in this group is the well-known experience of how easily the punch line can be missing from a person's attempts to tell of comical experiences, anecdotes or jokes. He who does not have the peculiar gift needed lacks it entirely, even when he tries hard to imitate a good model.

The teller of tales stands related in these cases to the inventor of the anecdote or to the experience, as the actor stands to the dramatist. He, too, must make his own contribution, that is, poetize. That is not something anyone is good at doing. Only seldom does a man understand this relationship; usually he throws himself into a task of which he is not capable. He "knows" not the whole of the task, and is amazed later on when he has failed to put the punch line across.

How is it that he ruins the punch line, when he himself, drawn along by the comedy, begins to laugh just an instant too early? Why does the genuine professional comic remain serious even in the midst of the most ridiculous comical situations and leave the laughter to the audience?

Because, to begin with, the point of the joke, the punch line, may not be revealed before it has achieved its effect, but must surprise the audience all by itself. That requires the narrator to master his tendency to laugh, but only "up to the punch line," not beyond it. If the comedian remains serious even after the point is made, he must have done so for a different purpose. It might be that by remaining serious he continues to manifest the amazement of one who does not understand even after the moment when the audience has already grasped the point, and in that way he keeps before their minds a bit longer the height from which they have been dropped.

In the same direction we find still another peripheral problem of the comical that has been arrayed, so to speak, behind it. It arises when the comedian, suddenly distracted from the comedy he has in mind, is so shaken with laughter that he can no longer tell his joke. It may happen that he then begins again and again, but never comes beyond the specific point at which the laughter forced his recital to a halt.

What is especially odd is that in such a case the comedy leaps from the material, the joke or the anecdote, to the comedian: he becomes himself the object of comedy, and that in the strict sense of inadvertent comedy. This latter consists obviously in nothing more than the (440) elementary power of laughter, which impacts perforce upon both elements, the story and the teller, a power that in one way does not let a tale get told, and in another way does not let a tale be heard – so that the audience must, in the end, laugh over its incapacity to laugh along.

c) Tragicomedy in life and literature

Related to the border phenomena of comedy, but entirely different from them, is the connection to human fate and the serious, to what is genuinely tragic and tragicomical in human life. The latter should not be understood here as a dubious mixture of forms, as is occasionally produced by weaker poets, but primarily as a unity of the gripping and the ridiculous, as naturally occurs to us in life itself –

just as they infect us all, without our knowledge, and also without anyone sensing the strangeness. This unity poses yet another problem.

This problem concerns the attachment of comedy to quite serious and important types of behavior, actions, entire groups of persons, and the course of their lives. They can also be attached to truly sublime figures and their destinies; that is the reason why it becomes so easy for the jester to "drag the sublime in the dust."

But at this moment we are not concerned with this transition from the sublime to the ridiculous – nor with its reverse – but with an attachment and the mixture of forms, first in life, and then in literature. What is the situation here? Are not life and literature sharply distinct?

That is precisely what is striking here. Once the ancient world created separate forms of literature: the tragedy and the comedy, and, in a smaller format, the ode and the satire. For the most part, the art of literature has stood by these distinctions. In the face of this, the forms not aligned to them, such as the bourgeois drama, had to save a place for itself alongside serious works.

Such distinctions could not be transferred to life itself. Life gallops along counter to such attempts. But that means that life itself is simply not as these schemas would have it. There are no sharp distinctions in life; in it, everything is mixed up in scintillating disorder. Here the comical is really attached to the serious through all the pathways life takes, and it devotedly follows the serious everywhere. The most sublime hero has his all-too-human traits, the wisest of men his foolishness, the morally righteous and the man of disciplined self-control his weaknesses. There is no doubt that these contrasts are comical and challenge our sense of humor, but there is no doubt also that humor makes all great things small, and can even make it vanish. Indeed, the situation is that the danger of being brought low grows with the greatness of the great, the highness of the height, so that one is in the end forced, if one does not wish to abandon the sublime, to protect it from the ridiculous by creating an aesthetical distance from it. (441)

Here we have the true basis of the divisions in art. Art separated what it first found united because it did not know how to unite it.

The attachment of the two is still not a tragicomedy, for tragicomedies do not consist in the amalgamation of tragic and comical traits in man, but in a much more inward interweaving. Specifically, man can, by pure stupidity or other weaknesses that are laughable in themselves (conceit, arrogance, stubbornness, anxiousness) produce consequences whose serious and far-reaching implications stand in no relation to the triviality of his failings. Then his fate is truly tragic, but the consequences of the events remain infected with an irremediable comical element that lies in their disproportionality. Thus here the Aristotelian ἀνώδυνον καὶ οὐκ φθαρτικόν is suspended. That was intended precisely as a protective barrier for tragedy.

Thus we see that in genuine tragicomedy the tragic itself is also comical. And, indeed, it is tragic such that one cannot suspend the other, but both maintain themselves in an irritating identity. Naturally, these are different aspects of the same set of events, but they are not separable from each other. If art tried to separate them cleanly from each other, it would do injustice to both.

That is clearly reflected in literature: material for tragicomedy is rarely found there and it was always considered to be difficult to deal with. But there are examples in the high style: King Lear, who begins with immense stupidity by taking all of his power out of his hands, still allows himself to be led on by hypocritical assurances – the consequences are all unpredictable and genuinely tragic. How could Shakespeare risk so much in such a grand and sweeping play?

The answer may be: he could risk it because in the end life is such, and because he, the poet, could come closer to life than the poet of pure tragedy. Of course, not every poet can do that. He must have sufficient greatness for it, his inner eye must be far-seeing, and at the same time have the unity and power of synthesis, by means of which he can make lucid what appears to be oblique and patchy. But Shakespeare could risk his synthesis because in life ridiculous stupidities having tragic consequences are found everywhere and always. It is impossible to determine whether the Platonic insistence[150] is aimed at achieving this task. But it is surely not by chance that, when his point is met it takes this form.

Moreover, the satisfaction of this requirement takes a double form in Shakespeare, for it also includes the comedy adhering to it that accompanies all seriousness in life. And therefore it has, to a great extent, become accepted in the art of modern literature. The profound comedy of Ulrik Brandel in [Ibsen's] *Rosmersholm* is of this kind – so much so, that it throws significant spotlights on the main characters; similarly, the comedy of the polar opposites Eiferer Relling and Gregers Werle in *The Wild Duck*, or that of Tesman in *Hedda Gabler*. (442) There was a time in which we did not understand such a complexly woven, true-to-life comedy, for we would let nothing distract us from seriousness once we have turned our attention to it. This slowness to understand now belongs to the past, and the demand for an entirely uniform joyous or earnest mood throughout the entire work is now overcome at last.

Three hundred years ago the scenes with Falstaff in *Henry IV* may have led the way to this outcome – entirely without any tragicomical character, but simply as an accompanying comedy: one of a sort, to be sure, that finally came to

---

150 Cf. p. 419 [Chap. 32c. (Plato's) "famous insistence that the tragic poet also be a comical poet."]

dominate the entire great two-part work. Here is concealed the higher form of great poetry. And many kinds of such synthesis may still be possible.

Chapter 39: The Place of the Comical in the Order of Strata

a) The equilibrium of the outer and inner strata

In dealing with the problematic of the comical, it is best to follow the phenomenon for the time being just so far as one can, and only then turn to the systematic study of the basic questions of aesthetics. That procedure is conditioned by the state of the problem, in which many theories are in part in agreement with each other and in part in conflict, while the stock of the relevant phenomena still lack adequate discussion and description. Several of these theories were touched upon above; not much was achieved by those discussions – beyond an account of the goods they have common, in the middle of which stands the Kantian thesis of the nature of the ridiculous. Now it is time to turn again to the basic problem. That can be done in strict analogy to its treatment in connection with the sublime and the charming.

The basic systematic question concerning the comical concerns the strata of the aesthetic object in which it has its proper home. This was the way the question was expressed in the case of the sublime and the charming; in fact, that was true even for the general problematic of the beautiful, which, in the essentials, extended to the relations of stratification and appearance.

Can we now expect that a definite level, at least on the average, will be found for the comical within the series of strata? The sublime was rooted in the inner strata, corresponding to its relative importance; the charming and the values related to it were rooted in the outer strata, as is appropriate for its flighty lightness. What is left for the comical?

At first one might think of the outer strata, even more than in the case of the charming. For a certain lightness is peculiar to comedy, too, a lightness flighty and playful, indeed almost irresponsible. Such things do not easily take root in the deeper strata of an object.

But, on the other hand, one sees that, alongside of light humor there exists also a kind that is profound and even philosophical, and that comedy in general (443) – even the mordant and malicious kind – can sally forth into considerably deeper regions of human life, as it can also seriously wound and destroy.

In that respect, comedy is in no way related to charm, which is always harmless and never forces what is buried out into the light. There is also never the appearance of the alluring that is related to or corresponds to tragicomedy. The alluring is always attached to the surface, close to the senses, and marks itself directly upon them. Even the claim to wittiness is far from it.

One might accordingly expect that comedy would not be tied to the strata of the aesthetic object, but should be rooted at random, according to the ethos it rests upon, and lie sometimes close to the surface and sometimes deeper. To a certain extent, that may well be the case. We see this from the highly diverse nature of humor, the satire most assuredly, and from the comic drama. But the mere diversity of the level of height cannot constitute the nature of the thing. This is true conditionally for the charming, also, which, after all, manifests considerable latitude in its nature. We must therefore look about us here for some additional information.

The integration of the comical into the ordered series of strata of the object ought to be conceived in the following way. The comic can, in conformity to its nature, be tied neither to the inner strata alone nor to the outer strata alone, but only in a relation between the former and the latter. Then the gradient of the contrast, with which the comical deals, is always fundamentally situated between the important and the frivolous, the depths and the surfaces, the weighty and the trivial.

Let us remember that the "drop" was produced from the kind of nonsense that reaches a self-resolution in the comic effect. What is comical is not simply the resolution of any nonsense at all, but only of that kind in which there is pretense to something important but behind which stands something frivolous, so that in the unexpected resolution the former collapses "into nothing."

Now one cannot, of course characterize the outer strata of an object – a work of literature, perhaps – in any way as a "nullity"; and then too not everything in the inner strata can be characterized as "important." But that is not what is intended. Yet the relation might very well be of such a kind that, when something really meaningful and weighty arises, if it does at all, it can spread itself out only among the inner strata, and that similarly a relative nullity can come into its own only in the outer strata. Whatever is close to the surface of a literary work, the movement and gestures of the characters, and in part even the situation and plot, stands quite close to the senses; in it, perception prevails entirely. For that reason, things that have little significance can take hold here. It is precisely the opposite with what is meaningful and important. They can have their place only where there is some latitude for things of importance, that is, where the inner nature of the plot leads us into the attitudes and character of the persons in the work, or where (444) the larger interconnections of life are linked and integrated, which we then experience as the destinies of men.

That is why the "drop" in comedy cannot play a role in just any dimension, but must function as the difference in depth in the series of strata in the aesthetic object. Therefore, in the domain of the comical there is an unambiguous preponderance of individual strata or groups of them: no preponderance of the inner strata exists, as with the sublime, and no preponderance of the outer strata, as in the charming. Rather what dominates here is a certain equilibrium of the groups of strata. Strangely enough, the comical, in this respect, stands closer to beauty in general than does the sublime or the charming.

Of course here the situation is quite different from what, in the fundamental relation of the strata, constitutes the beautiful. For in that case it is the transparency of the stratum that stands in front for the one behind it, the simple and clear appearance-relation, that brings about the beautiful.

In comedy, the relation of the strata to each other is more complicated. For there the audience is first led astray and fooled; this happens when something greater and more important, which therefore would have to belong to a deeper stratum, is merely simulated, just in order to dissolve it into something far more shallow and meaningless, i.e., something in the stratification that is far closer to the foreground.

That means that in the place of the simple transparency in at least one of the outer strata deceitful transparency is introduced: precisely by means of it, the thing that is "greater and more important" is simulated so that for a moment a thing of that order "seems to appear" but does not actually "appear." This half-nonsensical phrase expresses with wonderful clarity the misunderstanding that introduces itself into the lucid beauty of the appearance-relation and then obviously disturbs it.

Of course, it does not remain a disturbance. That alone would not be comical; it would be "mere deception" and quite possibly be ugly. Comedy arises in the removal of deception, when we see through it and recognize it as smoke and mirrors, humbug, a trick that was played on us, so to speak. Then begins the "disintegration to nothing."

We should not find the talk about "seeming appearance" irritating. The expression is no tautology; appearance is far from seeming. The usual appearance in the relation of strata is the proper one: nothing is simulated in it, not even the reality of what appears. In the "seeming of appearance," however, something is simulated, indeed just that which should usually appear, i.e., which should really be present and intended in the deeper stratum. But it is not that at all.

The deception itself depends upon the fact that the transparency is hampered, or blurred, or made difficult in the same way as often happens in life: life shapes its ever new comedy by the pretense to something important and meaningful, while in reality – and in this case, in real reality – a nullity (445) is made to seem great. To see through that pretense is difficult to do with a hasty glance, in life as in an artificially made-up joke, or as in the course of situations in good comedy, and the like. At first there appears, in both life and art, something great, which is then allowed to fall apart into something very small and shallow. All of the humorist's consciously-made comedy is entirely an imitation of the character-istic deceptions that we are subject to in life, whether these be tricks pulled on us – by men who wish to fool us – or imposed by chance, such that we fall victim to them by our own inattention. Here we find the reason why, turning the matter about, the myriad small deceptions in life seem to us to be an intriguing game that is being played with us, whether by some diabolical and malicious being, or by a roguishly grinning divinity who wants to amuse us and himself.

b) Comedy and the true-to-life

From this perspective, it is understandable why comedy in literature is an excel-lent form of expression of the true-to-life. There are so many things in life that are hard to put in words, and impossible to say nicely or to depict. And yet there is a literary necessity of taking hold of these things, of representing them in a penetrat-ing way; for they belong to the whole of life, and their absence would mean being false to what life truly is. What direct representation cannot achieve, indirect representation can, specifically comedy, especially in the mature forms of humor.

What does literature do, in fact, when it takes hold of the picayune and insignificant, the homely, the pitiful, and the miserable? Does it try to beautify them, or change their colors? Does it try to disguise them, to camouflage and conceal them? If it did, it could not bring them before our eyes. No, art proceeds quite otherwise.

All embellishing is untrue to life. Nothing is at a greater distance from art than a conflict with truth. Comedy almost lives from the surprises with which hard, real life assaults us – it lives, if we may, upon "improbabilities," that is, from what to an unsuspecting idealist seems unbelievable, for the improbable is far from always being false.

Here we come immediately upon one of the secrets of comedy. It concerns its connection to the claim to truth in literature. It is precisely comedy, which regularly works with small exaggerations and thus cannot offer a purely faithful picture of real life, that is in a position to show us certain features of human life with amazing objectivity and ruthlessness, without confronting us with an image that affirms what is unbearable, the wretched and the miserable in man. We need not repeat the specific features that are at stake. Here belongs everything about weakness and foolishness that (446) was listed above (Chap. 37b), all the kinds of nonsense the can be imagined. For they all have, when observed in their naked-ness, something in them of our notion of wretchedness and misery.

That is what literature brings into being when its humor takes up the all-too-human: it presents nonsense in the manner in which it would like to conceal itself in life – as good sense, importance, or at least as decent – but comedy does not then leave it tricked out like that, but leaves in such a state as to pull the mask from it, as occasionally occurs in life itself. But here the writer decides how to let the mask fall, such that the effect of the undoing will have the greatest value.

It is easy to see what is achieved in this way: the wretched and the miserable appear indirectly not in the unpleasant drawing-out of details, as full disclosure would demand, but only in their negativity, in making sensible their nullity.

And so the astonishing happens: the nullity, even the wretchedness, rises in the nexus of aesthetic values to a certain level of significance that the nexus of ethical values could never have, and which, in the moral context, would be a world inverted. Here, in contrast, nothing about it is inverted. For its significance is rooted in the fact that the nullity and the nonsense in man is just the folly upon which appears what is genuine and worthy in man. That is what comedy demonstrates in the greatest concrete palpability: in laughter, man lifts himself over nullity and lets it disappear into its own nothingness.

That is possible only because it is a question here of the appearance-relation, because what is low and repugnant has no actuality, thus neither too has the rejection of the repugnant; and the detesting of what is detestable is also no real shrinking away from it. Knowledge of unreality is essential to the entire state of affairs. That means: it is essential that here, too, as in the entire appearance-relation, no reality is simulated. What appears can be taken with amusement and a light heart.

The situation in the dramatic arts is similar: only because onstage intrigue and murder are not felt to be real can the audience have a relaxed attitude while enjoying them. Otherwise, such attitudes would be impossible. And similarly in comedy: only because the disgusting and the nonsensical are unreal can the hearer simply enjoy them. If it were something that we really meet with in life, the demand upon our sensibility would be greater; a person taking a correct moral attitude will at least be reminded by what he sees of its serious aspect. When he is forcefully reminded, comedy passes into tragicomedy. Experience teaches us how ubiquitous the latter is in life.

Beyond its significant function of upholding cheerfulness and a good mood and not allowing man to sink into his everyday misery, comedy is given a special task within literature – and not, as one may think, in "comic" literature, but (447) rather in serious literature. This function concerns the claim of literature to be true to life.

The great forms of literature, especially the novel, but also plays and the minor forms of the short story, have a great need to be true to life. We are sensible of it in nothing less than the requirement for "closeness to life." This requirement cannot always be met by means of direct description, because that would result in an unpleasant or painful dwelling upon the lower things in life, upon wretchedness or upon irritating annoyances. There are poets who, in the end, become unbearable even to hard-boiled readers, because they go too far in the direction of such misery. But since serious writing cannot always stop short before these limits, but must foray into the land of unpleasantness, it is very much in keeping with our current concern to examine how it masters this effort.

Here we find the most splendid means of humor, that is, a comedy that rests upon an ethos that is affirmative and sympathetic. For it is a unique feature of comedy that, corresponding to its material, it deals precisely with the same weaknesses, pettiness, nonsense, stupidity, even the same wretchedness and misery in man and his life, about which we feel a heightened need for being true to life.

All these things can be offered with a touch of the comical without their harshness being thereby diminished in any way. However, the limits to which they can be taken are considerably extended by the comical. Humor takes from unpleasantness all that is bitter and tormenting; at the same time, it elevates us over what it reveals; laughter itself – even when it quietly rings out inwardly – is already an elevation above unpleasantness.

This we see confirmed by very great styles of literature, where writers digging into the depths of humanity are masters of humor. Thus Hamsun (e.g., in *Rosa* [German edition, 1909], the story with a bathtub; and again with all that happens around the title character in *August* [*August Weltumsegler*, 1930]); similarly in Ibsen's dramas (Stockman [*The Enemy of the People*, 1883] Hjalmar [*The Wild Duck*, 1884]). It is not by chance that such things occur in writers who are not at all humorists proper. In their cases, they place weight upon quite different sorts of things, and not seldom upon precisely what is tragic. That causes no problems at all.

c) Implications drawn from the placement in the stratification

Further consequences may be drawn from the place of the comical in the structure of the strata of the object. To what extent our most recent reflections are in themselves such consequences has not yet been adequately discussed. The question can be made clear in the following way.

What was said about the place of the comical in the structure of the strata of the object has proven true. It is not a question here of the absolute depth (the depth of the strata) of the comical – and, since the comical has two components, –

neither of the depth of the simulated meaningfulness, nor of the meaninglessness that is concealed behind it, but exclusively of the (448) difference in depth of the two elements within the series of strata in the object.

With respect to the material, a distance in height corresponds to the difference in depth, whether it is an ontic one, a merely logical one, or a moral one. In the last instance, it is always also a distance of the height of values – and, specifically, not the distance within the value/disvalue dimension, but within the order of relative height of values.

In these differences in height is the play of the "drop" constituting the comical. For it is immediately clear why the drop depends upon the degree of distance alone and not upon the absolute height. We are directly sensible of how the effect of comedy – in the successful telling of a joke, for example – is tied only to the size of the "falling apart into nothing," while the content of the joke can be very different in the gravity of its meaning.

That is the reason why comedy can apply itself to any given contents as a kind of making-visible, without making any assumptions that a certain relative niveau is normal for comedy. Its condition is simply that its content (material) has some place for comedy to gain a footing, regardless of its "height" – in the kind of some nonsense, some weakness, or some folly. For all those things are found on many different vertical levels. The self-torment of the jealous man plays out on a different psychic level than, for example, the fear of scandal in a man in some position of prominence. Genuine humor rules over all ports of entry. We have seen, after all, that humor does not even stop short before the greatest philosophical material.

We see where the consequences derived from the place of the comic in the order of strata lead us. Since significance and depth are only illusory, it follows that when the illusion falls away, its opposite, the nullity, comes in to the light and must "appear." As this is negative, it is subject to dismissal in the form of absurdity. It "falls apart" – compared to the thing of importance that was first simulated (the deeper in the series of strata), and with that it arrives at is rightful place, i.e., at is proper stratum.

The latter is primarily an effect of closure. Until it is reached, the most paradoxical stages are passed through; and, strangely enough, precisely the truth-value of the comic effect depends upon them. That consists in the closeness to reality of the unreal element or – what is the same – in the true-to-life quality of what is purely invented, the product of fantasy.

This relation is erected just upon the ponderousness in what is flighty and non-committal; or, in other words, upon the surprise of earnestness in a mere joke. For this earnestness ambushes us, unexpectedly, just as much as the sudden collapse of the weighty in the comic effect.

In addition to all that, there is also the purely representational value of the comical, the making bearable of the unbearable, or, if we state it simply and bluntly, the winning of charm by that which was entirely without charm and averse to charm. There is no time to be lost here on formulations, and the limits to which one can take paradoxes in the comical may still be debatable. (449) But the principle according to which the difference in depth of the thing of importance and the nullity operate in the comic is throughout the same: the crashing to the ground and the self-resolution of nonsense.

Thus one can also speak here of the "meaningful in the meaningless" The expression is perhaps the most universal. Or of "appearance in disappearance." Both need some explanation. In the first place, comedy is the reverse: as the self-resolution makes the meaningful disappear and, in its place, something entirely meaningless appears, one might rather say that the "meaningless emerges in the meaningful" and the "disappearance remains in appearing."

The relation is just not so simple; at least, it is a double relation. How does it stand with the nonsensical or malformed in the appearance-relation of comedy? Such things in fact disappear in comedy by becoming visible precisely behind the thing thought to be meaningful, and, with that, annuls it: in the process, it dwindles away, because its appearance in its nullity is at the same time its annihilation. Thus it annuls itself by coming into appearance. That means, however, that something else appears instead, so that in its final effect is still once again an "appearance in disappearance." Accordingly, this whole double relation is then the "meaningful" that appears in what is "devoid of meaning."

No doubt words express this too weakly. We can better make the idea come to a head dialectically. We should not consider doing that, however, because artificial conceptual forms can be dangerous. We must also be careful with comparisons. One must therefore limit oneself to descriptions in very imperfect concepts – in concepts that were not at all coined for this relation, and could therefore never correctly apply to it.

In the end, what may be said by means of these concepts is limited, despite diverse expressions of it, to this small outcome: the deeper does not appear in the more shallow, as is otherwise always the case and is the normal relationship in beauty; rather the shallow appears in the deeper. Nullity peers out from behind the meaningful, the ridiculous from behind the sublime: that is the perversion of the appearance-relation. But as it was not the first, so does it not remain the last.

Specifically, the deeper appeared first; it was dissimulated, but since only the surface was given, the deeper could appear only "in" the surface. Of this, of course, the receptive subject knew nothing. But if the first appearance-relation then turns about into the second, and the second (the perverted one) has had its effect, then the disappearance of the more shallow element begins – its redisappearance, after it first showed up in the second relation – yet it no longer disappears behind the deeper element, because this has itself disappeared, but rather disappears behind its own absurdity. Expressed objectively: behind its own presumption that it was the deeper element. (450)

Chapter 40: Reservations and Objections

a) Pleasure taken in the comic and pleasure taken in beauty

The study of the comical is not itself something comical. Whoever wishes to amuse himself with it, will not get his money's worth. So also the study of the sublime was not sublime, that of the charming was not charming. And so is the entire study of the beautiful – not beautiful; no one who wants to deal with beauty itself would undertake aesthetics. But a person concerned with knowledge will undertake studies of beauty, of the sublime, of the charming and the comical. It is the fate of aesthetics to disappoint. For all those who come to its study, come for the sake of beauty, and of the sublime, the charming, and the comic.

In this respect, aesthetics is differently situated from all other philosophical disciplines. Ethics helps the progress of him who struggles after the moral good, its puzzling questions concern in part very serious perplexities in practical life itself; to see clearly is to show the way. Logic protects a thinker from certain dangerous errors in thought; theory of knowledge renders us the limits and conditions of possible knowledge. On the higher levels of knowledge, it has a determining force. Finally, ontology gives a means of entry to those who desire to grasp that which exists; philosophy of history and philosophy of law serve indirectly our knowledge of history and law.

The special status of aesthetics in this respect constitutes one of its difficulties. The peculiarity of its problematic is such that precisely in the domain of comedy this special status appears to us most powerfully. Comedy is in fact that domain of beauty upon which the character of beauty withdraws to its greatest distance – so far, that it often seems questionable whether one may count it as a kind of beauty or not. For there are kinds of beauty that are unquestionably disturbed when comedy appears in them.

Now that is a perverse objection. If there are different kinds of beauty, they may each exclude the others, as the species of a genus exclude each other. And in the case of such objections, one naturally thinks at first of the sublime – or of such cases of beauty that are close to it. One does not have to look far for examples of this; for upon every face that beams with earnest, thoughtful beauty, this is true, and true also for every landscape that opens out to us from a great distance. But even without sublimity, that same effect is valid – charm, too, allure, loveliness – all are disturbed by any aftertaste of comedy.

What, then, does it mean that in comedy the character of the beautiful withdraws the most? For clearly it cannot mean simply a disappearance of beauty. For that, the pleasure we take in comedy is too closely related to the pleasure taken in beauty. (451)

But is this not pleasure of an entirely different kind? What do pleasure taken in the comical and pleasure taken in beauty have in common? This, surely, that both are purely objective, disinterested enjoyments of appearance, without concern for reality.

And what is the difference? People have always pointed to the fact that watching a comedy begins with displeasure: no one can take pleasure in nonsense as such, in folly or weakness. But that is never asserted. Pleasure in the amusement one gets from the comical does not depend on the nonsense, but rather on its unmasking, which is both its resolution and annihilation. The richness of meaning contained in the resolution of the nonsense is without question something positive – even more when the resolution is a consequence of its own nonsensicality – upon which pleasure may take on the form of a lengthy enjoying. We are familiar with this latter in the thorough enjoyment of a good joke, of a humorous twist, a funny picture, or even of an analogy that throws an oblique light upon its object.

The difference in our feeling of pleasure in the comic and in a neutral beauty is thus no larger than it must be for the peculiar kind of a special case. Seen subjectively, the difference is for the most part most likely one of mood, for the ridiculous is simply exhilarating, but in the other realm of beauty there are much more serious matters.

We have therefore no reason to draw a line of separation here. The comical can be integrated quite naturally into the beautiful; it can, as a paradox, easily possess something additional that is "elegant," which then is directly felt as beauty – the art of a humorist of genius – as, on the other hand, the humorous can be tied effortlessly to the charming – resulting in unique creations of higher comedy.

We may still ask about the meaning of the withdrawal of beauty in the comical. To this the results of the previous chapter (39b, c) may respond: the peculiar power of the comical to communicate the distasteful and the low in a fully true-to-life manner, without giving offense or lowering our feelings.

"What" in fact comedy communicates here – seen purely in terms of its material content – is far from being something beautiful. Rather, one may characterize it as ugly. It was already shown why in the end "ugly" does not quite fit the phenomenon: it is a question precisely of the weak and low, the common and the nonsensical in men; of that from which we avert our eyes when we encounter it in life.

Why these weaknesses form the substance of comedy has been shown in detail. Now we must simply draw the further consequence that these material elements constitute what in comedy stands opposed to beauty: just that which "lets the beauty in comedy withdraw."

But is this expressed correctly? Is it really so that in the comical alone the material determines beauty or ugliness, while everywhere else the decisive element is the bestowal of form? – regardless of whether it is either a question of the particular bestowal of form in a single stratum of the work of art, thus in (452) extreme cases of the pure play with form, or of the transparency of the forms in the series of strata?

Naturally that cannot be the settled doctrine. Being beautiful depends, here as everywhere, upon form; and certainly not upon the playful blossoming of form but rather upon its capacity to let some other thing appear. And for that reason, aesthetical pleasure in the comical – that which makes us laugh – is in the end of the same type as the pleasure taken in all other enjoyments of beauty.

The unique feature that characterizes pleasure – just that which makes us laugh – remains entirely within the genus of aesthetical pleasure: it does not limit itself to the content. For the fact that some effect takes place, and that the effect depends upon the simulation of something weighty and then upon the collapse of this heavy weightiness into nothing at all, are elements that all lie within the same appearance-relation. However, they make this relation more complicated; they first make it seem as if it were running counter to itself (perverted appearance), and then again turning about and returning to its natural direction. A peculiar pleasure is tied to this process, a pleasure that has no longer to do with the material, and also does not owe its peculiar nature to it: the enjoyment of comedy.

b) Comedy in painting and music

What has just been said shows that it is worthwhile pursuing whatever reservations may occur to us. There are still others, especially when one considers special cases. Up to now, we have spoken only of the comical in literature and in life, and both quite justifiably, because there we find the real weight of the comical. But it is true that comedy is also found elsewhere. How does it stand, for example, with comedy in caricature? In such a case, we must understand this phenomenon very broadly, and incorporate in our study everything that bears a trace of its character.

Do the above characterizations of the comical apply also to comic illustration? For we are concerned here only with line drawings; color is only a supplementation, almost a softening of comic effect. Perhaps, too, color would make a caricature too realistic. And the effect of that might be unbearable.

Now the question of whether the characterizations rightly apply to caricature asks whether the necessary "contrast" obtains, whether it lies in the correct dimension, whether here something "collapses" that first seemed great and worthy, and even whether we have some nonsense here that annuls itself.

The reservations concern the two last questions. One can, of course, find the contrast just in a clever caricature – but only when one is familiar with the object of the caricature. For this is the worthy personage; the figure distorted in the distortions is the nullity into which he falls. In that way, the correct dimension of the opposition has been secured.

But what about the "collapse"? The drawing knows no "earlier" and "later"; everything is taken in at once. One may nonetheless say (453) that it is so artistically designed that the observer at first recognizes the original in certain of his character-istic features and only then becomes aware of the distortions; these then produce the collapse of the important figure into a nullity. The "nonsense" would then consist in the pretensions of a person who, because of the distortions, has become a puny being, but one who wants to have as much great dignity as the original.

That is not applicable to all cases of caricature. There is also the series in reverse. In this case, we see first the distorted image, and experience it as provocative in its bizarre way; but just then, and despite that, we notice the figure of whom the whole work is supposed to remind us. And it cannot be denied that caricature this way around affects us approximately in the same comic way.

One cannot do otherwise than draw this conclusion from our analysis: the comic effect is indifferent to the order of events in its perception. But is it still possible to retain the "collapse" and the self-resolution of the conflict?

We may respond affirmatively. The "collapse" does not necessarily have to be a temporal one. We saw this above in certain forms of humor, where a simple comparison or an immediately perceived analogy may have in itself the effect of ridiculousness. One can, however, explain this phenomenon in a different way.

Specifically, the "collapse" may very well be experienced and appreciated later on and its comedy enjoyed only then. We are placed before the ruins of the broken idol and we still recognize quite well in the shattered form how great and formidable he must have appeared upon his pedestal.

Or, later on, the familiar picture of the undistorted original leaps before us. Then the contrast is the same as in the reverse series. In a like way, the nonsense is the same, and, a fortiori, its self-resolution, which consists in the disappearance of the false pretense.

A further question concerns the comical in music. It was shown above why pure music is not capable of the comical. How is this consistent with the fact that in program music, comedy can easily find room for itself? There must be at least the possibility of a musical accompaniment that corresponds to the comedy given in the text or on the stage.

We must admit that certain works of music come very close to comedy. Music is capable of brightness and gaiety, likewise of drollery, capriciousness, light-footedness, volatility, and even of frolic and carefree frivolity. From these, is it not just a short step to the comical?

If someone wished on this basis to contend that music itself is a master of comedy, he would nonetheless be taking a false path. He does not notice that he approaches instead special forms of the charming with his "gaiety, drollery, and light-footedness." These special forms were discussed earlier in connection with the charming: they are "brightness, lightness and (454) agreeability," perhaps too the "graceful," but in any case certain forms of the "alluring." But then we have left the domain of comedy and are in a quite different one. Pure music is quite capable of the charming, and even of all its special forms, but they were not in question.

As for program music, there are of course great examples. The best are perhaps to be found in Mozart's operas (the exciting duet [of Susanna and Cherubino in *The Marriage of Figaro*] "Le porte son serrate"), then the scenes with Beckmesser in Wagner, especially the one with Hans Sachs in the second act [of *Die Meistersinger*]; similarly Richard Strauss in *Der Rosenkavalier* (Ochs von Lerchenau); Pfitzner[151] in *Palestrina* (second act) [1917], Humperdinck[152]; perhaps too some excerpts from operettas, but there one must be cautious, because the amusement in the comedy usually runs "along" with the music and scarcely touches it. On the other hand, some good examples can be drawn from collections of *Lieder*.

The question is: what do such examples mean? Do they testify that music that accompanies the comical text or a comical scene is itself comical? Or only that this music, by means of its mood, expresses concretely gaiety and frolic, roguishness and drollery, insofar as it is tied indissolubly to the comedy of the text or the scene?

After a detailed analysis with reference to the examples given, we will have to opt for the latter response. Yet that cannot be established any further; we must simply allow the relevant passages to be run through and then try to decide soberly whether we are suffering under a misapprehension – similarly to when we are victims of a slight of hand: namely, to ascribe to music what really belongs to the comical in comedy. Music fits so wonderfully to all shades of mood that it is almost impossible not to become a victim of the deception.

---

151 [Translator's note:] Hans Pfitzner (1869–1949).
152 [Translator's note:] Engelbert Humperdinck (1854–1921).

Wagner brought about such deception in the most genial way. Yet if one thinks of the Beckmesser passages without the text, without the stage setting, and without the gestures of the comic figures, one will not be quick to conclude that this music is intended to be "comical." One will merely find them strange, and, at some points, even possessing a peculiar beauty.

c) The comical in the domain of individual strata

A more serious objection attacks the whole of all comical works, regardless of whether they belong to works of art or to the comical in life. But the objection is directed primarily to works of art. It asks whether it is really true that the comical rests always upon a "drop" in the strata of an object. This question has not been sufficiently answered in the discussions in Chap. 39a.

There is a phenomenon that appear to conflict with these discussions. Take the case of the comic play or the humorous story. Do they really have only the uniform comedy of the entire plot, which is built up out (455) of many strata and has enough latitude for a drop? Or is not the case rather that a special comedy of external appearances also exists, a comedy of situation and plot, character and behavior, indeed a comedy of destiny?

One cannot dispose of this question by explaining these varieties of the comical as parts of a whole that cannot be resolved into its members. In fact, it can easily be resolved into its parts, so much so that, for example, in the production of a play one or the other of its parts can be executed well or badly.

In *The Twelfth Night*, the external appearance of Malvolio, including his performance of vanity in love, can be magnificently executed, but in contrast, the comedy of the situation (for example, his meeting with the "young woman") can leave us wishing for something better. The same is true for the two in respect of the comedy of character and behavior, and the comedy of destiny (the first in the believability of the entire "person," the second perhaps in the scene with Viola's involuntary swordfight with Sir Christopher [Andrew]).

In precisely this way, each of these elements varies quite freely against the others in a comical story. And, in fact, the special character of the story is to a great extent dependent upon it. Down to the most subtle gradations, the unique nature of a poet can be characterized by means of it (Jean Paul, Sterne[153], Raabe, Reuter ...).

---

153 [Translator's note:] Laurence Sterne (1713–1768).

One may not, therefore, think the relative independence of comedy in the individual strata to be inessential. They demand rather an explanation that gets to the very essence of the case. This can either be rooted in an account of comedy as a whole, in which there is latitude for every kind of drop, or it can concern itself with reflections specific to each individual stratum.

We must quickly note that the last of these prospects is quite doubtful – not because of any conflict with the theory, which could still be false – but because there exist other reasons for not isolating too much the individual comic elements upon a single stratum. Even a spectator's fine sense of the comical warns him against doing so – as though there might still be standing everywhere behind this evident independence a connectedness with something that makes its weight felt there, even if we are not able to trace it out directly.

That is a clue offered by aesthetical feeling itself – one might even say by the feeling of value. The latter would no doubt be too narrow, for it expresses itself more like a sense of structure. Such a thing must not be ignored by the theory; for everything that can be discovered about the foundations of these phenomena depends upon such feelings.

We must therefore inquire further: what, then, do isolatable comic elements within the strata consist in? For example, that of the external bearing, the gestures, the demeanor? Do these comic elements really exist for themselves, even if they have a certain independence from the comical on the strata that follow it?

The external demeanor is comical only when it contrasts vividly with what it is intended to represent. Malvolio contrasts in his external (456) appearance with the personal dignity and importance that he tries to affect. This also expresses itself, to be sure, externally, but it belongs to an entirely different stratum – of the person as much as the "play" – roughly that of the character and of the moral stance taken. The "drop" that makes the comedy would therefore be, exactly as in the whole of the work, – located in the deep regions of the strata.

If that proves true, then the question is decided in favor of the developed theory, that is, it remains true that even the relatively isolatable comic elements on individual strata are not rooted in them alone (although they may appear only in that one), but rather they presuppose other strata and their storehouse of materials.

To elucidate the matter further, one should ask oneself in earnest: is situational comedy (perhaps in a scene) conceivable without the specific form bestowed upon the characters that take part in it? Are there situations among men that are so external that they are not also determined essentially by their peculiar mannerisms, their weaknesses, strengths, fears, and secret hopes? Apparently not. Concrete situations are what they become by the essential features of persons in them, and, taken strictly, the same situation cannot exist among quite different persons. The solution that has been offered should therefore be considered valid.

The question remains: why is it, then, that comedy in individual strata seems to us to be isolatable? But that was the phenomenon with which we began. There is much that can be argued here concerning deceptions, and also concerning presuppositions of which one is unaware – subjective presuppositions in the act, and objective ones in the object. All of that is no longer new, and may be laid to rest here.

But one thing must be said in this connection: in a larger total relation, as that of the appearance emerging from stratum to stratum in an artistically structured work, there are always many peculiar relations. In cases where one cannot tear these relationships from their larger interconnections, they may still appear to us with a certain detachedness and independence. That is what happens everywhere in this context.

And this "appearance" may indeed itself in turn count as entirely objective. It is not wrong to praise the performance of an actor for the one, and to criticize him for the other. For the performance in one and the same role, even in the same scene, is extremely complex and has latitude for many independent variations in which the partial performances are played off against each other. For that reason, each partial performance can be tied to the whole, and can be judged only from the perspective of the whole. (457)

Appendix

Chapter 41: Towards an Ontology of the Aesthetic Object

a) The strata of the aesthetic object and ontic strata

Why art is not imitation was discussed above. Not all art is even representation. There is, however, an inner homogeneity between representational and non-representational art – it extends all the way into ornamental art, in the free play with form, which is not in any way similar to any given forms. And yet all art remains close to what is real. Indeed, if it separates itself from reality, it is untrue to life.

Why does art stay so close to life, to being? Why is this true not only for literature and painting, but also for music and architecture? Because existent things are reflected in all art. All art must lay a claim to the true-to-life. That means it has a tendency to see as we see in life, through the external appearance, concretely, intuitively, in part also veiled and hidden by the appearance. That is even true of music and architecture; with them, the relation is concealed only by the specific matter upon which it bestows form. It is most visible in the representational arts. But how do they represent?

That turned out to be quite clear: they represent by means of the appearance-relation, and this relation is then in turn active in the series of strata; it goes on from stratum to stratum (Cf. Chaps. 11–15). So far the structure of the object remained constant. But there is still another question to be posed: how is it with these strata, how does the aesthetic object come to them? Why is the appearance-relation active precisely in them?

The answer to this question cannot be given via another description of these strata, as has been done here earlier. Nor it is a question of the foundations: how are these strata in the aesthetic object – which after all, repeat themselves in a certain analogous way in the various domains of art – related to the universal ontic strata of the real world?

On the one hand, they remind us specifically of the ontic strata, but on the other hand there are more of them, and the importance does not lie as much upon there being a great distance between the strata, but rather in part upon much shorter leaps. The question is perhaps (458) without importance for aesthetics. But it is of great interest for ontology. For here we have the opportunity to test out the import of the stratification of being.

This must now be stated clearly: at bottom, in the aesthetic object, the same ontic strata exist that make up the constitution of the real world. Briefly and simply, there are four: Thing (sensible) – Life – Soul – World of Spirit; but each one can be broken down further, and broken down in fact very differently in the different arts.

Thus, in painting, for example, the lowest ontic stratum is already broken down into 1) the two-dimensional surface of the picture, with its flecks of color; 2) the three-dimensional spatial field with its apparent space and apparent light; and 3) the appearance of motion in the figures; the apparent animation of the figures begins only with a fourth stratum. In painting, specifically, the outer strata are the most important. Only behind them begin the elements corresponding to the higher ontological strata: that of the psychic realm, of human character, the stage setting, etc.

It is informative to contrast here something quite different, i.e., the art of literature in its larger formats: drama, the epic, and the novel. Here too, we have the same series of strata as in the existing things upon which they are based, but the way they are divided up is different, and their relative importance is differently distributed.

The stratum of sensible objects is represented by nothing more than language (speech, writing); likewise, the stratum upon which animation appears is represented only by that of motion and gesture (apparent or real – by means of the actor –). The psychic stratum lies in character and response; the spiritual stratum can be broadly analyzed as follows: 1) situation and plot, 2) destiny, 3) ideal personality, 4) universal idea. There is a peculiar feature here: a partial stratum of the spiritual is prior even to the psychic (it is a foreground element in relation to the latter). That may lie in the human way of seeing; for the beholder, the situation and action are more immediately apparent than are the elements of character.

It is again different in music. In the external strata, we arrive quickly at the limit to which sounds can be heard together as unities; beyond that limit larger musical unities are superimposed upon each other, and, as such, they are not given to the senses. Yet behind these a further series of strata appears, but of a different kind. Among them the psychic has by far the preponderance; but the stratum of animation is also not lacking there, similarly not that of the spiritual, which again can be analyzed further.

Here in the inner strata, the ontic series of strata is easy to rediscover. In the outer strata, that is not so easy. For the latter, the reason is that form is bestowed upon quite different matter – and without any claim to representation. *Mutatis mutandis,* the same is true for architecture, where heterogeneity is still rather coarse.

The general ontological strata of the world are not everywhere so easily recognizable as in literature, but on the whole they can be identified. The foreground strata are the most vacillating and irregular (459); these stand so strongly under the law of aesthetical matter that the basic ontic law of the strata disappears behind their uniqueness.

One may ask: why, at bottom, must the ontic strata of the real recur in the strata of the work of art? The answer is because the represented objects all contain the same ontic series of strata – expressed more correctly: in so far as they stretch upward into the higher strata, yet retain the lower ones (following the law that the lower strata are the ones that bear, the higher the ones that are borne). In the representational arts, almost every material extends into the human sphere; and since man has all four strata in himself, those must therefore reappear in the representation of the human.

It is therefore very important that an artist does not omit any stratum. If he does, he will immediately become abstract and conceptual, lacking in vividness – like the poet who psychologizes instead of letting his characters speak and act, and in that way reveal themselves. We see, hear, and experience in life the soul and spirit about us in no other way than by the mediation of the psychical-psychic, existential stratum, on which alone we are bound directly by our senses, and, as in life everything else is already given mediately, so too in art. Art takes advantage of these facts. That is the ontic sense of the appearance-relation.

b) Convergence of all great art

Now the general order of things in this context is, in general, that the ontically higher strata lie concealed deeper down in the interior of the work of art and appear only through the transparency of the outer strata. That has an ontic basis: the arts direct themselves towards the senses, but the senses are tied to the physical, and can allow further matters to be grasped only by their mediation. This point of departure cannot be shifted or exchanged. For the fact is that the senses directly communicate nothing that is psychical or living, absolutely nothing but the material world – that which belongs to the broad area of the physical. For that reason, the ontically higher strata must be the aesthetically "deeper" ones. Then, too, nothing can be traded away from this relationship. It is valid, with only slight alterations, for all regions of the arts. And that is also true for human and natural beauty.

But then something quite strange appears. The outer strata, as we have seen, are everywhere different; within the arts, they deviate from each other considerably – the material substances in which the arts work are also of completely different kinds, yet it is through them that the outer strata are determined. One cannot shape the same forms in stone as in tones, in words as in colors.

In comparison, closely related and in many respects almost identical, are the last inner strata; indeed to a certain extent not only just the last ones, for even in the deeper middle strata there begins a convergence. That is not so strange (460) as it may seem. The last inner strata are those having the character of ideas, and the universally human is, after all, what is held in common. What has, however, the nature of an individual idea – the idea of personality – is unusual even in great and profound works of art (we consider here only the representational arts). And when the individual idea is present, it never opposes itself to the universal, but makes it stand out even more prominently by means of the contrast.

But even in the remaining inner strata – those lying more shallow – we see the same tendency toward identity. Human destinies repeat themselves, and they are reencountered in quite different characters; human characters fall entirely under a certain typology, of which we quickly apprise ourselves. These common characteristics, which easily impose themselves upon us, are those that often dominate entirely here, while the others of less importance disappear. This process is different in the inner strata from that in the outer, and it affects the non-representational arts, because in their inner strata the same psychic existence is expressed, and, indeed, in much greater universality.

From this standpoint, it becomes understandable why there exist certain kinship phenomena that pass through the entire domain of artistic creativity. The extraordinary diversity of the arts in the appearances of both a sensible and nearly sensible form has its compliment in the uniformity of their inner contents – and these contents must not be understood merely as raw material, but as fully formed content.

And there we come upon a phenomenon that has often been noticed by aestheticians, but that has never really been explained: namely, the overall kinship among the heterogeneous arts, indeed even quite heterogeneous works of art – if one understands them primarily in their depths, or seeks out works of the great epochs and masters and leaves aside less significant ones.

One can express the matter, very cautiously and in abbreviated fashion, as follows. All art works of slight or even of a more median value diverge immensely and are hardly comparable; but, in contrast, all truly great works of art converge and come close to an impalpable identity.

This process of convergence expresses itself in no other way than this: we experience what is otherwise heterogeneous nonetheless as kindred. Thus the Parthenon and [J.S. Bach's] *Art of the Fugue,* the ceiling of the Sistine Chapel (perhaps in the figures of youths or of the Prophets) and Shakespeare's *Henry IV* (including the figure of Falstaff), Rembrandt's self-portrait in old age (Amsterdam)[154] and the Apollo on the pediment [of the temple of Zeus] at Olympia, Beethoven's fifth or seventh symphony. ...

---

154 [Translator's note:] Perhaps the *Self-Portrait as the Apostle Paul* (1661) in Amsterdam.

No one can say wherein the kinship of what is entirely heterogeneous lies. We can only point to the fact we experience the kinship as such. Specifically: when we experience it in that way. For all of us may not sense it; indeed not all of us can, but only those who penetrate with their eyes to the deepest and most inward domain. (461)

When looked at fleetingly, such monumental works have very little to do with each other, they are inescapably different in kind; one cannot easily find a common genus. One must simply dig very deeply – then surely the kinship will become convincing.

That is not easy to demonstrate. Take Rembrandt's portrait as an old man – an entirely ordinary man – with a somewhat peculiar look in his eyes – it is not easy to go further. But something makes us take notice: the state of being marked by something in the form of destiny, by tragic greatness, stands over the whole, as though the fate of all men were reflected in that face. And then it dawns on us: something of ourselves is reflected there, too.

Or the *Art of the Fugue*. Music can have the deepest transparency, but only when it comes before us bearing the highest standards. That is the miracle of Bach's fugues. Externally, it is the driest music one can imagine, much like a school exercise. Internally it is most moving, most profound in meaning; indeed it is virtually the most inward in its emotional force, and truly metaphysical in its power to lift a man above himself and to seize him and turn him about in his deepest inwardness. It is full of challenges, and is tied to conditions that not many men are capable of meeting. And yet it possesses the greatest directness in the manner of its revelation.

That is characteristic of all great art – of the truly rare ones – which come to be only once in a thousand years. Then, too, not all great art draws such a circle of exclusivity about itself as does the fugue; for that reason, great art is not so salient in all of its domains.

What is the explanation of this peculiar phenomenon? It is now easy to give: in all domains of art, the final inward strata are relatively identical, or at least converge to a high degree, and so too in part the strata located immediately before them. For everywhere in those regions man is in question; however, in the background of man's nature some moral or metaphysical "Something" always lies. Just because great art reaches down into those depths and can allow them to appear after their own manner – and that is done by every truly great work of art –, it must be aimed at a convergence with other art of its kind.

In that way, we receive the impression of close kinship among quite heterogeneous works. The predominance of the last inner strata constitutes the convergence. In fact, upon their background the much more shallow and external series of the outer strata disappears when one at last has penetrated their depths. And that is so despite the variety and peculiarities of the outer strata.

Another matter is connected to this one: this convergence of the greatest in all great art is at the same time a convergence upon the sublime. For the sublime is that kind of beauty in which the inner strata have unconditional predominance.

That is implied by theory. One may compare with respect to this the convergences mentioned above: the Doric temple, Bach's counterpoint, Shakespeare's histories, etc. They are all pure examples of the sublime. And other examples of the sublime that are just as pure are Michelangelo's (462) prophets and youths, Rembrandt's self-portrait in old age, the Olympian Apollo, Beethoven's symphonies.

In all of this, one thing remains quite puzzling. To great art – especially in its masterworks – belongs more than the mere preponderance of the last inner strata: precisely as works of art these creations can be perfect only when they also demonstrate adequately that form has been bestowed upon the outer strata, so that they are able to reveal its profundities with shapes that have clarity and animation.

But how does it happen that in very great works of art we find adequacy of form along with profundity of idea? As though both did not demand very different talents of the artist! One may put the question in this form: why do techniques in execution demanded by the arts and profundity of content (of the idea) go hand in hand in superlatively great artists? ... Why are they widely separated in artists of a lesser order? We have the answer in our feelings: only in imperfect efforts do these two elements become separated; in their perfection, they are not even two distinct gifts, but rather two sides of this same gift.

How does this finally occur? It is simpler than it appears. Consider: the artist does not grasp at all the idea of his work in an abstract intellectual or conceptual way, but rather in an inward vision; this is at the same time a sketch of how form will be bestowed even upon the sensible foreground. And, we must add: great works of art come into existence only where these two aspects of inward contemplation are there from the very beginning, and supplement each other adequately. That happens only rarely; and even in the case of the greatest masters, it does not always occur, but in especially fortunate cases they are brought together as a unity. It is an error to think that such strokes of genius simply have to converge frequently. And we commit this error only because we are careless in our artistic judgment, and hold many things to be great that are far from earning that title.

c) The disappearance of individual strata and leapfrogging

The account given regarding the relation of the objective ontic and the aesthetical strata – that it is at bottom a question of the same stratification, stricter in the former, relaxed and split open in the latter – must not be understood pedantically. Individually the strata cannot be recognized at a first glance: usually several aesthetical strata take the place of a single ontic one. The splitting open of the stratification is what disguises the relation.

In any case, the principle is that here is given the point of intersection between the ontological analysis of general categories and the aesthetical analysis of objects. It would be quite false to divorce the fundamental features of aesthetics from those of ontology; that would also run contrary to the meaning of the theory of categories. This does not extend itself to (463) the real sphere of being alone, but indirectly also to every kind of sphere of appearance.

Here we meet with some oblique questions. One of these asks what happens if an ontic stratum is omitted from a work of art. It is true that, as a whole, the appearance-relation passes from stratum to stratum without any leaps. It does happen, however – first of all in narrations – that the stratum of life – of active movement and the images of persons – can be leapfrogged over, and that in that way the writer brings us directly into the psychic situation. We are encouraged here by the capacity of language to touch even human inwardness directly and, indeed, to do so in a rather conceptual and abstract way. It should of course be understood that in such cases any further transparency fails. At the very last, it will be a bit unclear and, with that, inartistic. This is even clearer in painting. Where the living quality of the figures does not come to appear in a vivid and striking way, the elements in them of deep feeling, character, and morality will also not be clear.

One should not carry these implications too far. It is not as if each stratum for itself must be worked out thematically. It may very well be that at times one of them "disappears" – that is, for the eyes that are peering through it – simply because the transparency of the next stratum in the series predominates, and, as it were, "devours" it. That does not mean that the middle stratum must be "lacking." Rather, it must be present, but it does not appear as an object. In any case, such disappearance has its limits. Beyond those, it has a destructive effect upon the pictorial element of the appearance.

Something similar occurs even in music although it is not directly represented. That is the case wherever the composer wishes to produce directly, as by magic, some effects upon the emotions without allowing them to grow organically out of the structure of the tonal composition. Such music seems shallow and unjustifiably pretentious.

This easily happens, of course, in literature. In such cases, the narrator speaks in concepts rather than in clear, living images. The thought may be expressed very beautifully and may even have a kind of pictorial quality, but it does not grow out of the composition of the material and is instead loosely placed on top of it; thereby the compositional unity is once more in jeopardy.

Very great writers have become victims of this danger. It is a temptation for the highly experienced writer rich with ideas – quite possibly those writers who are highly interested in philosophical matters – to compose in thought rather than in characters and scenes. The greatest example of this is the late Goethe, who was no longer capable of creating tightly organized works, except in a minor literary form, lyric poetry.

This example immediately demonstrates, moreover, that a large dose of intellectual material, when it is weighty and has a unique, tightly constructed form, may still be borne by a work. Thought, for its part can have a pictorial quality (464) even when the picture does not grow out of the total composition. But then, of course, the unity of the greater whole is lost, and the work comes close to being a loose concatenation of thoughts bearing images. That can go so far that one always hears the author lecturing on his opinions – instead of seeing him develop a piece of interconnected life. ...

By far the greatest and most pure art works through our inner vision, and uses words only to awaken the imagination, so that the reader sees the figures come and go, speak and fall silent. That is the natural way of the artist: pure letting-appear. In that respect, literature at bottom is no differently situated from the fine arts. One is more easily deceived by it, however, if one lets oneself be roped in by words, and thereby forget the meaning of poetry. Within certain limits, mere fantasy alone, once it is aroused, is capable of leaping over the empty space left by omitted or only vaguely suggested strata.

Genuinely vivid appearance fails then, to be sure, and concreteness becomes fragile and cracked; yet this does not cause everything to collapse at once. Rather, what is intended to "appear" is now only "guessed at" by means of suggestion, and since such guessing plays a broad role even in the vivid appearance-relation, this requirement does not immediately destroy artistic unity.

Nonetheless, such unity is possible only when, in all the remaining elements, the appearance-relation is intact. That means that on one side and the other of the break in the series of strata the appearance-relation retains the necessary unbroken force of vivid clarity. If not, poetry turns into discussion, and art into the discursive expression of lived experience. And it is well known how easy it is to pass beyond those limits.

What we have before us in such cases is in itself a broader phenomenon of literature. A very flowing borderline is in force here, and there are no clear barriers to speak of that make themselves directly felt. However, a touch of poetry may be found in many scientific presentations, most strongly in the historical, but then too in the philosophical ones.

The last case is seen in all of the greater thinkers. And that could not be otherwise, because, for the philosopher, the conceptualizations already at hand are always insufficient: he must turn to vivid images. Plato and Nietzsche are only extreme cases of this, but at bottom Hegel and Kant have hardly less traces of literary quality. This can go so far that it may put a thinker in danger of playing with fantasy.

But when we ignore even such matters, which obviously lie on the far side of a flowing border, we are faced with a broken appearance-relation even this side of the border. It is "broken" by the breach of transparency, which, properly, should pass through uninterruptedly an intact sequence of the middle strata. (465)

The case is simply that the entire appearance-relation does not fail just because of this. For it is precisely here that the active imaginative capacity leapfrogs over the empty space. We are in any case already too inured by life to such breaches; we are, so to speak, adapted to their appearance. And with utmost ease, the power of supplementation goes to work in our fantasy, which keeps a storehouse of developed forms at the ready.

In certain cases, it takes a special poetic technique to leapfrog artistically over a stratum. The reader is challenged to contribute a powerful synthetic act of fantasy; he experiences the imputation of this capacity to him as a stimulus, and can inwardly grow from it.

d) Two kinds of limits to artistic ability

The question of the limits of artistic ability is connected with these reflections. What do we know of these limits? After reflecting carefully, one must admit: we know very little of them. For the absence of a certain kind of gift or of certain peculiarities of character tells us nothing that we did not know or already understood under the term "talent." It is rather more useful to point to its objective preconditions.

We find that we can say something quite specific if we base ourselves on the perspective of strata: the failure of a created work with reference to the claims that it makes lies always in the relative absence of the real foreground. It never depends upon the lack of a deeper stratum. The breaking off of the series of strata before the last possible stratum is, for art, not an error or a lack; it means only that the art work has entered the domain of a simpler or shallower genre, and thus it renounces greater depth. Such a work can never rise to the level of sublimity, but it can to all levels of the charming, the comic, and the beautiful in general, such as we can see in all simple art, insofar as it has achieved some standing. No doubt, however, the simple forms of art in all areas incline towards the loss of such standing.

Why does it have this tendency? Because the deeper strata are the ones that sternly demand of creativity the achievement of its high tasks. They command insistently a tightness of form, unity, and the appearance-relation, while the outer strata leave greater latitude to the artist and can have an effect just by themselves. Such works cannot achieve the highest levels of beauty – those levels that converge upon the sublime. But that is not to be required of every art (recall what was said in Chap. 18c about shallow and profound art).

While we thus see that the absence of the last inner strata is compatible with having aesthetic value, absence in the foreground and in the outer strata lying near to it is a failure of concreteness, clarity, and animation. One could also say it is an absence of transparency. As a result, the appearance-relation itself comes in danger; it is disturbed and (466) broken. A lack in the outer strata is either something unlovely or a sign that we are not dealing with an aesthetic object at all.

The limits of artistic ability lie, when viewed from this standpoint, in two opposite directions. 1. In becoming shallow – when the inner strata lack weight. In this case, only the deeper effects are lacking, not aesthetical attractiveness; greatness and proximity to the sublime are lacking, but not at all charm, allure, loveliness, magic; not even a carefree innocence. 2. In what is unclear – when form is lacking in the outer strata, or too much of one form is absent. This is the failure of artistry proper, of falling into abstraction or ambition (without capacity). Here lies all botched amateurism, indeed almost all dilettantism (in the bad sense), and, in extreme cases, all kitsch.

What does amateurism consist in? Just in this, that a person cannot express what he has before his mind, but he tries to force the matter with false or inadequate means – especially when he is unaware of what is happening, when he does not notice what damage he does. ...

The essence of art, as of all genuine "ability," consists precisely in the creator reaching after the only correct resource with the certainty of a sleepwalker, and in fact finding the form after which he is searching. He may search for it in an agonizing struggle and experimentation, but in the end, it must be such that when he has once found it, he is also sure of it, that is, he recognizes with intuitive certainty that this is the appropriate form.

Yet we must make still another thing clear. Absolute perfection in the success of what the artist desired may be assumed only in very uncommon cases. No doubt, artistic ability grows in a person along with the greatness of his tasks. But on both sides – that of profundity and that of clarity – his limits remain attached to him. In a practical sense, we deal with the imperfect in art as in all human undertakings – if one may say so, with unachieved tasks.

This insight is important on both sides.

1. A clear consciousness exists in the creative artist that corresponds to this situation: critical knowledge of many of his half-baked efforts and poorly executed works, a consciousness, which often afflicts him, of his not having been able to do better; a vision of the distance between what he has seen into intuitively or of what he has dreamed, and what he has achieved. Overall, one may say: the greater the artist, the stronger the consciousness of failure – if only because his ambitions lie so much higher. And since the greater artist has the greater ability, one may say also: the more marked the ability, the stronger the awareness of inability.

Here also lies the reason why creative people are so often sensitive about criticism at the hands of others: just because he knows better about where he has in fact not been successful, he has a passionate need (467) to be recognized and understood at least in what he is trying to achieve. The alien critic does the opposite: he rejects even what was successful, because he does not see what it was aiming at, and what should really have been achieved by it. Thus he rubs salt on the most painful spot. ...

2. The reverse phenomenon also occurs in observers: an inchoate knowledge of the real impact of the failure, and, as a result, a clairvoyant beholding of what was really desired and sought after. For this process in an observer, the deficiencies in the work are not purely negative (*modi deficientes*), but eminently positive points of departure for his own active artistic powers. These powers do not have to be trained in art, they do not even become creative on their own; it is sufficient that they inwardly activate themselves as after-creativity and let themselves be led by what has been given to the senses, and in that way arrive upon the heights of the original conception of the artist.

One can call this the higher way of enjoying a great work of art. What is lacking in the work is sensed so strongly that it becomes a positive challenge, and the observer, without suspecting how active he has become, enjoys his own activity along with the work. He rises up as a co-creator who perfects the imperfect – in the same way that the actor rises up in a dramatist's masterwork as a co-dramatist.

Chapter 42: On the Historicity of the Arts

a) Historical stability and mutability of great art

How does one recognize "great art"? Idle question! One feels it in the face of its overpowering immediacy – or one does not feel it. In the latter case, if one does not have an organ for it, then one does not need to know, for no knowledge can replace the organ, and such a person is in any case excluded. Yet the question has a meaning, if one understands it objectively – not for the sake of any practical use, but as a question about the external essential signs of "great art." What is assumed here is that as an inner trace of essence, the greater importance must be found in the last inner strata and in the adequate transparency of the outer strata.

One essential outward sign was touched upon in the previous chapter. It consists in the phenomenon of convergence, where, characteristically, the focal point of such convergence lies in the region of the sublime. But this feature is directed at a very delicate artistic sensibility. It would be strange if there were no other features of it that were more tangible.

Of course, there are such. But they lie where one would not expect. The most important of them are found in the domain of the historicity of works of art. What specifically is strange about this is that greater works of art (468) do not descend into history and fade away in time, but rather ascend. This ascending means that they do not only maintain continuously the living objective spirit within themselves, but that they also bear fruit, and permit ever-new interpretations; in this way, they, the works, themselves give to other times things ever different and ever new. Thus they show themselves to be inexhaustible.

Similarly, the great figures of literature ascend: the heroes of the ancient epics, the characters in important novels and dramas, grow larger. The figures of Aeschylus and Sophocles, of Shakespeare and Schiller, exhibit such an ascent. They run through the epochs of history and are brought upon the stage in the attire of ever-new "tastes." It is not at all important whether the dramatist had conceived of them in just those new ways; they have long grown beyond him and the narrowness of his time. What is important is that they always actually present something new, and that they are not exhausted by any given epoch.

We spoke above about how all objectivations that do have their entire detail not in themselves but external to themselves, descend into history. So descend concepts, also, because they are only living so long as they are present to intuitive vision and are fully given with the same intuitive content to every thinking person.

This content, however, does not lie within the concepts, but outside of them, usually in the interconnections of an entire theory (that means literally of a total vision); the latter itself consists in an entire system of concepts, judgments, etc. The single concept receives from such a system of concepts its life, its meaning, and its content; when it is separated from that system it becomes empty of content, and its meaning can no longer be restored. One can reconstruct it only by a return to the system of concepts out of which it grew.

Only what has its entire content in itself can ascend, and that means that it not only has the laws of its form in itself, but also its detail and its inward multiplicity. Only then is it possible that the characters of a literary work can be understood in ever-new ways and thus offer concrete possibilities for interpretation; that a musical composition can undergo ever new interpretations and thereby grow beyond itself; that a painting says new things to new epochs; and a work of architecture speaks to other and different men with a grandeur that is always new.

Again, that is valid only for very great works of art. Only they contain everything in themselves, detail and formal lawfulness. Lesser work cannot stand fast before changes in the historical spirit of an age. Here we have a genuine criterion of "great art." This is of practical importance also. For an individual by himself does not understand through his autonomous sense of values what is surpassingly great.

Here we have touched upon the point at which life and art reveal themselves as close correlatives: namely the historical life of the spirit and the specific, historically conditioned art of an epoch – with (469) the contingent tendencies of its preferences, its tastes, its aims, and its style.

This is, in itself, not strange. Art comes out of life and returns naturally back into life, as does all objectified spirit. It can also not put itself at too great a distance from life, although art seems to resist life and isolate itself. What is strange, however, is that precisely the artistically highest creations turn out to be the most potent in history. Given great art's tendency to self-isolation, we should expect precisely the opposite. And as far as this tendency is concerned, it clearly consists just in the way the individual work of art is set off against the contexts of life.

But that is precisely the great deception: even as observers, we sense upon our own selves the state of separation; the work forces us into its world, to another place and another time, to other events and other life, and, as a result, we think that it has lifted us out of the entire real world and that art itself belongs to an entirely different world. In truth, the work is simply the unique moment, the locus in the context of the real, out of which we have been forced. We remain a part of life, even while enraptured. Otherwise, the claim of the work of art to being true to life would have no sense.

The ascent of great works in the course of time is the unambiguous sign that the rootedness of art in historical life is essential to it, but that, at the same time, it is essential to life. In this great phenomenon, art in fact gives back to life compound interest upon what it received from life. Although, in every epoch of art, only very few works reach this height and everything else sinks into the ash-heap of history, these few great works still suffice to pay back richly the debt of art to historical life.

Something further must be said in this connection: namely that in the historical "ascent" of great masterpieces, the element of imperfection plays an entirely affirmative role. We saw earlier such a turn from the negative to the positive; the one now at hand will cause no further wonderment. But in this case, a different role is at stake.

The imperfection of great works does not consist in an error or an aberration, but rather more in a certain indeterminacy and generality, which challenges the fantasy of the observer, the performer, or the interpreter to supplement it and fulfill it intuitively. Great works of art are static only within certain outlines; in order to take possession of them, one must complete their writing, their painting, and their composition. It is all the same whether one executes that task either in mere seeing, hearing, and reading, or in acting it out, playing it back, etc.

This genuinely active work of the audience is what lifts a work beyond passive appreciation. Naturally, that is only when the audience (470) brings to the work the preconditions of such active appreciation. Furthermore, an entire generation can grow to meet these preconditions, if it stands under the weight of the demands that great works make upon their audience. Under such conditions, it is clear that precisely a certain kind – or perhaps one should say a certain "degree" – of imperfection in a work of art itself works to its advantage: it is not to its disadvantage, but rather to its merit, that there is still something about it that needs to be completed, to be supplemented. That keeps men, keeps whole epochs under its spell. ...

b) The tendency back towards life. Enchainment and inspiration

The function that the arts and aesthetical life in general exert in history depends upon these matters. It is not a question here only of the highest tasks that fall to the lot of surpassingly great art, i.e., of spiritual leadership and direction, of the formation of ideals, the revelation of new concepts of form and the moral education of the epoch. It is a question also of less significant factors, which, as they are omnipresent and attached to creations of a lesser greatness, carry considerable weight. For all objectified spiritual goods tend back towards life. That is a consequence of their attachment to some stable material out of which they are fashioned.

Given this, it is no puzzle why there is the reverse tendency. Recall the members of the threefold relation. Alongside of matter and the bestowal of form is a third thing, the beholding living spirit, whether it appears in the individual, as personal spirit, or in an epoch as objective spirit. This spirit undergoes change, it is always different, and, depending on whether it brings with itself the conditions of a specific kind of beholding or not, the work of art either exists for the objective spirit or it does not. But since any extant objectification at all is there only "for" some person, one can also say: according to the presence or absence of the beholder, the work of art exists or it does not exist at all.

The historical strangeness here is that the existence of works of art has periodic empty spots. There are times that art seems to have disappeared from the very earth and only the "foregrounds" of physicality and reality loiter in museums and libraries, and at other times they are there and vigorously assert their presence – all this according to whether an adequately receptive spirit presents itself or not. Such persons do not come when they are called, yet there is a kind of omnipresence about them – they stand "waiting," so to speak, on the far side of the current spiritual life – and wait for the appearance of a spirit adequate for them; when that appears, they too are there again, resurrected, "reborn."

Now because the living spirit is mutable and, where it strives towards its full maturity, it wins over ever again the organ specific to artistic beholding, there recurs a renaissance of the art of the past. Or, to express the matter in reverse: for that reason, there is always a return of art to life. (471)

Very different effects can be tied to this return. Spiritual goods of the past can fructify, can awaken slumbering powers and encourage autonomous activity, but they can also put the living spirit in chains and, as it were, cripple it. The first case happens in a genuine renaissance, the second where a more youthful and still undeveloped culture is overrun by an older, fully mature one. Thus Roman literature was once overrun by the Greek, thus later the Germanic culture by the late Roman. We see that this occurs not only in the arts; it is true for the entire life of the spirit, and is easier to see in the arts just because its works stand as witnesses to the process in all its phases.

However, both kinds of consequences do not in fact limit themselves to striking upsurges. Rather, there is such enchainment and liberation on a small scale at every time and place. Whenever there is vital activity in one of the arts, it struggles with received forms in order to liberate itself from them; yet at the same time, it goes looking for great models, because it cannot do without the inspiration they give to it.

From this, we are quick to see that the strongest enchainment always emanates from art of slighter value, not from very great art. And when a justifiable reaction begins, when the living spirit defends itself from the danger of such chains and tries to shake them off, it does not as a rule turn away from truly great and surpassing art, but from the huge mass of lesser and mediocre works. For it is not the former but the latter that is burdensome – although the spiritual influence that emanates from the great works has, at bottom, the greater weight.

Why that is so seems at first to be obscure; and one might almost be willing to assume providential powers in the history of spirit, which are kind enough to protect men from incalculable errors. But in truth, the situation is simpler.

The preponderance of this huge mass of works of lesser quality exists, for the most part, only for its own time: in its epoch, great and small talents come to the fore, and it is difficult for a contemporary to distinguish them, for he has to struggle with many innovations, which he, as a layman, cannot follow. No one, even the connoisseur, can judge at first sight where a new trend is leading; he must wait a bit, look carefully, and retrain himself; and, frequently, an entire lifetime is insufficient to deal with it all.

It is otherwise when generations have passed through these developments. These generations have done the work of vetting; the bulk of the lesser works has vanished, one no longer knows of them, and no longer has to grapple with them. ... What remains are the great works that have established themselves. These need not be the greatest works alone; there always remain many works that challenge us to a struggle. But the preponderance of what remains in the spiritual inheritance of an age are still the works that have the power to liberate rather than to enchain. (472)

But if one now asks what is the significance of the fact that it is just the great works of the past that are left to an age, the answer must be: its significance is that these are continuously inspiring; they win us to them and give us direction, but do not enchain us. And they do not "enchain" because they do not tie the work of the appreciating recipient to specific details; they do not bind tightly but rather loosen the bestowing of form in the outer strata. Their effective influence is in general one of depth; and the techniques of an art can very well grow under such tutelage, as under a very high set of standards. But it will not let itself be stifled, as under schoolmasterly rules.

Closely related is the fact that the authority of a work increases considerably with its historical antiquity. We sense this antiquity itself as its venerability, and we mean by that nothing more than the pre-eminent power we accord to its active influence. Very great art has its strongest effect when it has long ago become "historical." Its works and its figures have then become mythical, which, so to speak, creates a world of its own. Even the figure of the creator can rise to the level of myth. With that, of course, both are reconfigured by the living spirit and receive a new face.

c) On life in the Idea[155]

It is a widespread opinion, one almost become legendary, that what enables the artist to create is a "life in the Idea," which also enables the observer to assimilate art properly. Along with these opinions, one always thinks of the relatively rare and great works of art that shake the world, not of the great mass of lesser achievements. One denies of these latter that they were born out of ideas; yet one asserts it of the former. Thus we have two opinions without any orientation at all as to how this "Idea" should be conceived. What is it, really?

There is of course a "life in the Idea" – better, perhaps, to say a creation out of ideas. But it is not what the Idealists take it to be; and it in no wise concerns all art, but only great art. For it is not a question here of the mind's intuitive gaze – neither in the Platonic sense nor in that of the phenomenologists – also not of the grasping *in mente* "the one Idea" in Hegel's sense – which would presuppose an entire metaphysics of spirit – but of something quite different.

This quite different thing is an active-creative, synthetically formal beholding of something that lies over and beyond all real existence. Thus it is a beholding that has nothing more to do with a beholding of existing things, but rather brings into the world, so to speak, non-existent being, i.e., that which never was.

Such beholding is of course not peculiar to artists. The ethical man brings it about, the statesman, who posits great goals for the future, even, on a smaller scale, everyone who works and effects change. However, (473) these agents are then all burdened with realizing what they have beheld, and they must sweat to achieve it.

The artist is not burdened in this way. He realizes nothing at all; he only lets appear, only represents. For that reason he possesses that other kind of freedom that asserts its right to pure possibility without necessity and without a long chain of conditions.

But it is not just that one advantage alone that an artist has over the practical man. He has a quite different talent: he can show, clearly and objectively, what the idea he has grasped looks like. That is his special quality, one that he shares with no one else. The ethical man leads a life in the Idea no less that the artist, likewise the statesman, the practically effective men of all kinds, as far as they survey only what is beyond the given. But none of them can communicate what they have beheld in the Idea, and none can make it concretely visible and palpable, and thereby let it become a determining factor in life. Only the artist can

---

155 [Translator's note:] "Das Leben in der Idee." Phrase used by German idealists, for example by Johann Gottlieb Fichte in *Die Grundzüge des gegenwärtigen Zeitalters.*

do that, because he "lets it appear," living and vital, and therefore convincing – although it remains unreal. Only the artist can do what, according to the faith of believers, otherwise only God can do: reveal.

He does not have life in the idea for himself alone, but certainly the power to reach from this life to the real life of men, to hold before their eyes a light and an image that shows them what they do and what they ought to be. The artist does not do that by uttering, "thou shalt!" but by planting in men's hearts a longing that will not let them go.

Here we meet with the prophetic quality in an artist, with *vates in poeta* [the seer in the poet], with moral leadership in the poet as the bearer of ideas. He does not need to know this himself. He must only be such that the beheld Idea works itself through his creative activity.

The beholding of the Idea passing through the multitude of strata and their variegated contents is the revelation sent forth by the artist. This act is identical to the many-tiered depths of transparency, which now and then is achieved in great artistic works. For it is precisely there that the artist arrives at the last stratum, and what is in that stratum appears in living form on the figures that are beheld there.

Among the variety of levels of the beautiful, it is of course only the highest ones that have such depths of transparency. One ought not to understand that merely in terms of their content. For it is precisely here that the greatest demands are placed upon the forms in the outer strata: these must have the very highest transparency; they must achieve what nothing else in the world can achieve: the becoming visible, for the first time, of what was never in the world at all, and indeed insofar as it is incapable of also being put into words.

Most artists shrink before the greatness of this task. They are, for the most part, no visionaries and bearers of ideas. But it must be said: they usually shrink back even when they possess moral elevation and far-seeing (474) prophetic powers, and thus are bearers of ideas. For success demands something more, that is, the ability to show things, the depths of transparency, and the clarity of what is made to appear. It is no doubt true that the greatest artist knows how to unite these two to an amazingly adequate degree; but there exists much prophetic art that lacks the other side, and thus is unable to present its ideas clearly. In this respect, for example, Nietzsche failed as a poet: he was able to behold and love his new ideal for humanity, but he could not objectify it clearly and give it a concrete shape. And so it remained, despite the great catchphrases that have assembled about it, floating partially in abstractions.

d) The creative power in man

The last observations once again concern the creativity in man. In small things, man is everywhere creative in a practical sense – in all "work," in all activity, in all his planning and his pursuit of ends. But here we are concerned with creativity on a grand scale, with creating for a distant posterity, with great ventures in which man himself is at stake and – can lose the game. In this creative struggle, this bringing of man into being, the revelations of the artist plays their quite determinate and irreplaceable role.

It is important to be clear that this creative function is, in human history, a purely practical – in a broad sense ethical – one, and is not at all identical with that of the artist. The connection between the two is rather one of ends and means; yet the relation is not such that the means are exhausted in the production of the ends; the means remain autonomous, for, after all, they were not conceived and discovered for the purposes of history. In order to clarify this relation, we must return to the general kinds of creativity of which we have knowledge.

We know primarily two kinds of creativity in the world. They are so different that we cannot compare them; and yet they are so similar to one another that philosophy has often attempted to reduce the one to the other. The one is creativity in nature – without consciousness, without aim, a dark impulse, but one driving inexorably upwards within the realm of possible forms. In truth, it is without any "tendency," without will, driven only by the competition among creatures and the cruel process of selection. The other is creativity in man. It is quite the opposite of the first; it is purposive, conscious, willful, and mutable in the choice of its directions and the aims placed before it, but it is very limited, as is the foresight of man; all the while, nature keeps of "producing" without limit.

As far as reduction of one to the other is concerned, the two are close. One simply foists a picture of an enlarged "human" purposiveness upon nature, (475) calls it God, demiurge, or providence, and thus traces the "productivity" of nature back to man. Our picture of the world inevitably becomes anthropomorphic. Or one puts man's consciousness of goals into the processes of nature, and understands man's act as a fragment of the natural process; then the positing of goals becomes secondary, for it is already determined by motives that are rooted in the human essence bestowed upon man by nature. In this case, the peculiar nature of the actions that proceed from human will is nullified, and, with it, the special quality of human nature itself.

We can leave both reductions out of consideration here. One sees just from a cursory glance that they are one-sided; besides, they both contradict two categorial laws, the first one being that of "strength," the second that of "freedom." What is rather more important is that both kinds of creativity are fundamentally distinct, and one cannot be reduced to the other. Man as creator is consciously active, while nature is of course infinitely more powerful and in many ways more "inventive"; but for all that, its own productions stem from a blind drive.

The creativity of man is everywhere active in practical life. In every area of its activity, spirit, utilizing the powers of nature, brings about new syntheses that nature knows not of: the external reworking of things (material) for the realization of its goals, in synthetic chemistry, in technology, in the cultivation and hybridization of plants and animals, in the education and cultivation of its own kind, in the direction of historical processes – as far as he may be capable of it.

Yet the creative power of man does not reach its highest form in the domain of practical life. This higher form is first found where it is no longer a question of the creation of something, but of a mere letting-appear. The aesthetical form of creativity in man is superior to all other forms of production in that it does not need to realize what it creates in beholding.

That is the great, unique freedom of him who sees and produces aesthetically. It is similar to self-propulsion in a vacuum without resistance; and, in fact artistic representation circulates in the domain of "de-actualization." Here we meet perfectly the genuine sense of this word, which denotes the act of distancing ourselves from the real world – the opposite of "realization," which suggests work upon the real world.

But it is especially remarkable that no turning away from real life hereby occurs, that it is much rather the case that from this creativity, hovering in the domain of the unreal, ties of an infinitely subtle nature lead back into the real world and, indeed, precisely into a life on a grand scale, into historical life. (476)

This power is a purely spiritual one, the power to enlighten and to convince in places where no demonstrations and philosophizing ever could convince a man; indeed the power to direct the gaze upon what is to be beheld – in the Platonic image, to execute the act of μεταστροφή [conversion]. For that is decisive. And just for that reason, so much in human life depends upon our living, alongside of all actuality, a "life in the Idea." We can do that, because we possess the power of aesthetical beholding. (477)

Postscript

Nicolai Hartmann wrote the first complete sketch of *Aesthetics* in the summer of 1945 in Babelsberg near Potsdam. He began the manuscript on the 9th of March, and completed it on the 11th of September. This was the time of the destruction of Potsdam, the encirclement and conquest of Berlin, and, in general, of hunger, uncertainty, and confusion. On the other hand, the complete severance form the outside world favored concentrated work. In the midst of this collapse he wrote his pages, day by day.

The completed manuscript served as a basis for his first lecture in Göttingen in winter 1945/46, and was once again worked over for this occasion. In conformity with his lifelong practices in preparing his work, a second manuscript was to be taken up, after an appropriate pause, and this version would then be destined for publication. The first years after the war were nonetheless so filled by the pressure of new tasks and difficulties that the work could not be begun before early 1950; and the summer, too, was burdened by the necessity of reworking a course of intended lectures, as all the lecture manuscripts had been burned.

Nicolai Hartmann was not able to complete the final manuscript of *Aesthetics*. It breaks off with the words, "Ideas in Poetry," the heading on page 196. Accordingly, one third of the work is in the form that the author specifically intended for publication. From page 196 to the end, this edition follows the first manuscript, which, so far that one can compare the two versions, contains only insignificant deviations.

The editor would like to give special thanks to Professor Heinz Heimsoeth for his help in the comparative revisions of the two versions and in preparing the manuscript for publication.

Göttingen, June 1953

Frida Hartmann

Index of Names

Index of Terms

CPSIA information can be obtained
at www.ICGtesting.com
Printed in the USA
BVHW040218080819
555400BV00006B/59/P